Two WPA Outcomes Linked to Each Core Concept

Critical Thinking, Reading, and Writing	Processes
Critical Thinking, Reading, and Writing	Rhetorical Knowledge
Processes	Composing in Electronic Environments
Critical Thinking, Reading, and Writing	Rhetorical Knowledge
Critical Thinking, Reading, and Writing	Rhetorical Knowledge
Rhetorical Knowledge	Knowledge of Conventions
Rhetorical Knowledge	Critical Thinking, Reading, and Writing
Critical Thinking, Reading, and Writing	Processes
Rhetorical Knowledge	Processes
Knowledge of Conventions	Critical Thinking, Reading, and Writing

Writing
Ten Core Concepts

Robert P. Yagelski
University at Albany, State University of New York

CENGAGE
Learning·

Australia • Brazil • Japan • Korea • Mexico • Singapore • Spain • United Kingdom • United States

Writing: Ten Core Concepts,
Robert P. Yagelski

Product Director: Monica Eckman

Senior Product Manager: Margaret Leslie

Senior Content Developer: Leslie Taggart

Content Developer: Margaret Manos

Product Assistant: Kerry DeVito

Media Developer: Janine Tangney

Marketing Brand Manager: Lydia LeStar

Senior Content Project Manager:
Michael Lepera

Art Director: Hannah Wellman

Manufacturing Planner: Betsy Donaghey

Rights Acquisition Specialist: Ann Hoffman

Production Service/ Compositor:
Integra Software Services Pvt. Ltd.

Cover and Text Designer: Bill Reuter

Cover Image: © Jim Barber/Shutterstock.com

For product information and technology assistance, contact us at
Cengage Learning Customer & Sales Support, 1-800-354-9706

For permission to use material from this text or product,
submit all requests online at **www.cengage.com/permissions.**

Further permissions questions can be emailed to
permissionrequest@cengage.com.

Library of Congress Control Number: 2013939717

ISBN-13: 978-0-618-91977-2

ISBN-10: 0-618-91977-5

Cengage Learning
200 First Stamford Place, 4th Floor
Stamford, CT 06902
USA

Cengage Learning is a leading provider of customized learning solutions with office locations around the globe, including Singapore, the United Kingdom, Australia, Mexico, Brazil and Japan. Locate your local office at **international.cengage.com/region.**

Cengage Learning products are represented in Canada by Nelson Education, Ltd.

For your course and learning solutions, visit **www.cengage.com.**

Purchase any of our products at your local college store or at our preferred online store **www.cengagebrain.com.**

Instructors: Please visit **login.cengage.com** and log in to access instructor-specific resources.

Printed in the United States of America
2 3 4 5 6 7 17 16 15 14

Brief Contents

Contents

PART 1 A Guide to Writing Effectively

Chapter 1   Why We Write

Chapter 2   Ten Core Concepts for Effective Writing

Chapter 3 The Ten Core Concepts in Action

Chapter 4   A Student Writer Applies the Core Concepts

PART 2 Writing to Analyze

Chapter 5   Understanding Analytical Writing

Chapter 8   Conducting Rhetorical Analysis

Chapter 9   Analyzing Literary Texts

Chapter 10   Evaluating and Reviewing

PART 3 Writing to Persuade

Chapter 11 Understanding Argument

Chapter 12 Making Academic Arguments

Chapter 13 Making Arguments in Popular Discourse

Chapter 16   Writing Personal Narratives

Chapter 17 Writing Informative Essays

Chapter 18   Digital Storytelling

PART 5 Essential Skills for Contemporary Writers

Chapter 19 Working with Ideas and Information

Chapter 20 Designing Documents

Preface

Writing is a way to understand and participate in the world around us. It is a vehicle for learning, a way to make sense of our experiences and convey what we learn to others. Writing is a powerful means of individual expression and social interaction that has the capacity to change us. As the National Commission on Writing in America's Schools and Colleges put it, "At its best, writing has helped transform the world."

Composition teachers know all this, of course. They understand the power of writing, and they know that writing well is necessary for students to succeed in college and beyond. But instructors also know that a one-semester course is never quite enough to help students develop the sophisticated skills they will need to write effectively in their college classes and in their lives outside school. Research indicates that students need their entire college careers to develop those skills. First-year writing courses can lay the foundation for that process.

To make the most of the composition course, *Writing: Ten Core Concepts* focuses on the most important skills and knowledge that students must develop to be able to write the kind of sophisticated prose expected in college. It teaches the foundational lessons that students need to develop their competence as writers.

A Focus on Important Aspects of Writing

Research underscores what composition instructors well know: most college students tend to have difficulty with a few crucial aspects of writing:

- addressing an audience effectively
- focusing on a main idea and developing it sufficiently
- organizing texts appropriately
- adopting an appropriate register or "voice" in writing
- supporting assertions or arguments
- identifying and using appropriate sources
- revising effectively
- applying the conventions of academic writing.

For the most part, these difficulties apply across disciplines and forms of writing. Significantly, research reveals that most of these problems arise from three main sources:

- students' lack of understanding of the rhetorical nature of writing
- students' inexperience with different rhetorical tasks across the college curriculum
- students' misunderstanding of how to manage the process of writing.

In other words, these problems arise from a basic misunderstanding of the rhetorical and social nature of writing and inexperience with managing the writing process *in the context of varied rhetorical tasks*, especially the kind of writing tasks typical of academic work in college.

Consequently, *Writing: Ten Core Concepts* rests on three central ideas about writing:

- *Writing is a rhetorical act.* Writing is fundamentally an interaction between a writer and reader within a specific social context. In this sense, writing is always a social activity, and effective writing connects writers and readers in complex and powerful ways.
- *Writing is a way to participate in the conversations that shape our lives.* Through writing, writers and their readers collaborate in knowledge-making and share information and opinions about issues that matter to them. Writing enables us to take part in the many ongoing conversations about important matters that affect how we live and how we understand ourselves and the world we inhabit. In the most basic way, writing is a way to *construct* the world by participating in these complex conversations.
- *Writing is a means of inquiry.* Writing is an intellectual activity that can lead to a deeper understanding of ideas, experiences, and information. It is a means of understanding ourselves and the world we share. Writing can engage students in careful, critical thinking about themselves and the world around them. Writing is a unique and powerful vehicle for learning.

These ideas inform both the content and structure of *Writing: Ten Core Concepts*. As students are guided through various writing tasks and learn to manage the process of writing efficiently, they also gain a fuller understanding of the nature of writing as rhetoric, conversation, and inquiry. In this way, *Writing: Ten Core Concepts* can help composition instructors meet a central challenge in working with student writers: helping students develop a sophisticated understanding of writing and gain experience as writers acting on that understanding.

Writing: Ten Core Concepts emphasizes what is essential in writing at the college level and guides students as they apply that knowledge to various writing tasks. It trains students to think rhetorically and helps them manage the fundamental characteristics of effective academic writing. In this regard, the Ten Core Concepts serve as a framework for understanding writing and a practical, step-by-step guide for negotiating the demands of academic writing tasks.

Ten Core Concepts

The Ten Core Concepts distinguish this textbook from other writing guides. Most composition textbooks try to cover every conceivable aspect of writing in college and beyond, presenting far more material than students could ever grasp and retain in a single semester. That approach ultimately waters down the most important lessons that student writers must learn. *Writing: Ten Core Concepts* is different. It emphasizes what students must really learn to become effective writers.

These Core Concepts are not basic skills, nor are they procedures for completing specific kinds of writing tasks. Rather, they are fundamental insights into the nature of writing that students must enact as they complete varied writing tasks. These Core Concepts boil down what has been learned through research and practice into key ideas about what writing is and how effective writing works. For example, Core Concept #4—"a writer must have something to say"—emphasizes the need for a piece of writing to convey a clear main point or idea. Studies indicate that college writing instructors identify the lack of a clear main idea as one of the most common weaknesses in student writing. This concept helps students understand why effective writing in most genres is characterized by a focus on a main idea; it also helps them understand how the different expectations in different academic disciplines can shape a writer's main idea and how that main idea is presented and developed in specific kinds of texts. Most important, it guides students through a process that enables them to identify, refine, and articulate the main idea of any writing project they are working on. In this way, the Core Concepts can deepen students' understanding of key insights about writing at the same time that students practice applying those insights in their own writing.

The Ten Core Concepts are not prescriptive. They are not step-by-step instructions for writing in specific genres. Instead, they are fundamental but flexible guidelines for writing; they serve as a set of heuristics that students can apply to *any* writing task.

The Structure of *Writing: Ten Core Concepts*

Writing: Ten Core Concepts is organized into five parts. Part I introduces students to the Core Concepts. Parts II, III, and IV guide students through the most common forms of three main categories of writing: analysis, argument, and narrative. The focus in these three sections is on helping students understand the uses of various genres *within rhetorical contexts.* Through contemporary examples and engaging exercises, students learn how various forms of writing enable them to address specific audiences and effectively accomplish various rhetorical purposes; moreover, these chapters give students sustained practice in applying the Ten Core Concepts to different kinds of writing and rhetorical situations. Finally, Part V addresses research skills and the conventions of writing. A brief description of each of these main sections follows:

Part 1: A Guide to Writing Effectively. The four chapters in this section introduce students to the essential insights into writing that they must acquire if they are to be able to apply their writing skills effectively in different contexts. In this section, students explore the fundamental ideas about writing described above: writing as rhetoric, as conversation, and as inquiry. Most important, they learn and practice the Ten Core Concepts that form the heart of this textbook. Chapter 2 explains these concepts, using examples to illustrate the lessons as well as exercises to help students understand how to apply the concepts in their own writing. Chapter 3 is an interactive, visual guide students can use to apply the Ten Core Concepts to any piece of writing. Chapter 4 presents a case study of a first-year student writer as she applies the Ten Core Concepts to complete a writing assignment.

Part 2: Writing to Analyze. The six chapters in Part 2 help students acquire competence in the most common forms of analytical writing in college. Chapter 5 introduces important features of analysis. Each of the other chapters explores the purposes and features of a different form of analytical writing and, using the Ten Core Concepts, guides students through an analytical writing project. The chapters also include practice in some of the key intellectual tasks associated with analysis, such as using a theoretical framework, that often challenge students.

Part 3: Writing to Persuade. In this section, students gain an understanding of the principles of effective argumentative writing, and they work through writing projects representing three main kinds of argument. Using the Ten Core Concepts as a guide for their writing, students explore the nature and purposes of argument in various contexts and practice applying the essential elements of argumentation for different rhetorical purposes.

Part 4: Writing to Narrate. The chapters in this section help students learn how to write effective narratives for different rhetorical purposes and also appreciate the important uses of narrative in academic contexts. Like the chapters in Parts II and III, the chapters in this section guide students in applying the Ten Core Concepts so that they produce effective narrative writing that meets the needs of various rhetorical situations.

Part 5: Essential Skills for Contemporary Writers. This section provides students with practical advice about working with source material, conducting research for their various writing projects, and mastering and applying the conventions of written English.

Chapter 19 focuses on essential intellectual skills with which many students struggle in college writing, including summary and synthesis. Chapter 20 guides students in understanding an increasingly important aspect of effective writing today: document design. Chapters 21, 22, and 23 provide an up-to-date guide for finding, evaluating, and using source material in an interconnected world characterized by access to overwhelming bodies of information. Chapters 24 and 25 help students understand and apply the guidelines for citing sources recommended by the MLA and the APA. Finally, Chapter 26 helps students craft effective, engaging prose and avoid errors that can weaken their writing. Rather than trying to reproduce a comprehensive handbook, this chapter focuses on the most common problems in student writing, including the formal errors that research shows are typical of college student writing.

Throughout *Writing: Ten Core Concepts* students encounter varied examples of effective writing in different genres and different media. They see how other writers, including student writers, meet the challenges of contemporary writing in college and beyond, and they are given varied opportunities to practice what they learn, all the while using the Ten Core Concepts as their framework for writing.

Integrated Coverage of Digital Literacy Practices

Writing: Ten Core Concepts focuses on the contemporary student, who lives in an increasingly technological, globalized age. To write well today requires students to manage many different rhetorical tasks using various technologies, including constantly evolving digital media that have become essential tools for communication. Rather than addressing "digital literacy" as a separate skill or topic, *Writing: Ten Core Concepts* incorporates emerging digital technologies and literacy practices into the advice and practice it provides students. Throughout this textbook, students encounter examples and exercises that reflect various uses of communications technologies, and they receive advice for taking advantage of these technologies to meet the needs of the rhetorical situations within which they are writing.

Finally, *Writing: Ten Core Concepts* is informed by the basic idea that practice is essential in developing writing competence. In a sense, this idea is the 11th Core Concept. Only through sustained, guided practice in writing different kinds of texts for various rhetorical situations can students develop the understanding and ability to write effectively for different purposes. Accordingly, *Writing: Ten Core Concepts* relies in part on the repetition of the Ten Core Concepts to give students the practice they need to make these Concepts part of their repertoire as writers.

Acknowledgments

Writing a new textbook can be a daunting undertaking, but it is made less so by the inherently collaborative nature of the work. This book is not mine; rather, it is the result of the sustained efforts of many people, whose ideas, dedication, and hard work helped make this book a reality. It is impossible to thank them enough.

First, I am extremely grateful to Lyn Uhl for identifying this project as an important one and providing the support necessary to realize the vision that informed this project from the beginning. I am also deeply grateful to Margaret Leslie, the senior editor for this project, whose steady guidance helped keep the project on track and who expertly managed its many different components over many years. Without her and her staff, this book would not be.

My sincerest gratitude goes to Margaret Manos and Leslie Taggart, the development editors for this project, whose insight, patience, good humor, and constant support not only were essential in keeping the project moving forward but also made it possible for me to find the wherewithal to finish the work. The quality of this textbook is in so many ways a result of their dedication and their expert advice. I could not have done it without them, and I feel blessed to have had the opportunity to work closely with them on such a complex project.

I also wish to thank Andy Fogle, of Bethlehem High School in Bethlehem, New York, who helped with the research and development of several chapters, and Tony Atkins, of the University of North Carolina at Greensboro, who not only provided invaluable insight about the treatment of technology throughout the book but also helped develop the chapter on document design.

Janelle Adsit, a teaching assistant in the doctoral program at the State University of New York at Albany, graciously opened her writing classroom to me as I refined the manuscript. She and her students offered exceptional insights that shaped the revision of the manuscript and helped make this a more useful textbook. I sincerely appreciate Janelle's generosity, and I am humbled by her students' willingness to share their ideas with me. Very special thanks to Elizabeth Parisi, a student in Janelle's class, who graciously allowed me to use her essay for this textbook. Her writing and her willingness to share her experiences make this a much better book and will benefit many other students whom she will never meet.

My colleagues and friends in the Capital District Writing Project, including Aaron Thiell, Christopher Mazura, Molly Fanning, Alicia Wein, Christine Dawson, and especially Carol Forman-Pemberton, have been my supporters and teachers for many years now. I rely on them much more than they know, and their influence infuses this textbook.

Many thanks also to artist Stefan Saal, who created the striking chapter-opening images for the book. The many experts at Cengage who helped with the design, production, and marketing of this textbook also deserve a special thanks: Hannah Wellman, Michael Lepera, Samantha Ross Miller, Betsy Donaghey, Lydia LeStar, and Erin Parkins.

This textbook greatly benefited from the advice of many insightful reviewers, including several who class-tested chapters with their composition students. These reviewers' comments and suggestions guided development from the beginning: Rebecca Adams, Housatonic Community College; Janelle Adsit, University at Albany, State University of New York; Forrest Anderson, Catawba College; Ellen Arnold, Coastal Carolina University; Carolyn Ayers, Saint Mary's University; Vicki Besaw, College of Menominee Nation; Subrata Bhowmik, Arizona State University; Courtney Brandt, Western Michigan University; Mark Browning, Johnson County Community College; Mary Burkhart, University of Scranton; Jasmine Case, University of Wisconsin-Eau Claire; Maureen Cahill, Tidewater Community College; Paul Cockeram, Harrisburg Area Community College; Cheri Crenshaw, Dixie State University; Karin Evans, College of DuPage; Tyler Farrell, Marquette University; Steve Fox, Indiana University-Purdue University Indianapolis; Michael Franco, Oklahoma City Community College; John Gides, California State University-Northridge; Shauna Gobble, Northampton Community College; Dorie Goldman, Central Arizona College; Betsy Hall, Illinois College; M. Suzanne Harper, Penn State Worthington Scranton; Melvin Clark Heller, South Texas College; Harold Hellwig, Idaho State University; Anne Helms, Alamance Community College; George Horneker, Arkansas State University; Barbara Howard, Central Bible College; Lisa Klotz, University of Alabama; Danielle Koonce, East Carolina University; Lindsay Lewan, Arapahoe Community College; Yingqin Liu, Cameron University; Stephanie Masson, Northwestern State University; James McWard, Johnson County Community College; Robert Mellin, Purdue University-North Central; Benjamin Minor, Arizona State University; Catherine Moran, Bristol Community College; Jessica Nowacki, Marietta College; Pratul Pathak, California University of Pennsylvania; Patrick Quinn, College of Southern Nevada; Alma Ramirez, Mt. San Jacinto College; Susan Roack, Purdue University-Calumet; Bernd Sauermann, Hopkinsville Community College; Patrick Tompkins, John Tyler Community College; Anthony Viola, Marshall University; and Sue Watley, Stephen F. Austin University. Most important, the members of the advisory board for the project provided essential advice in the latter stages of the project, for which I am especially grateful: Lauryn Angel-Cann, Collin College; Anthony Atkins, University of North Carolina-Wilmington; Laura Carroll, Abilene Christian University; Sarah Gottschall, Prince George's Community College; Karen Jackson, North Carolina Central University; and Shevaun Watson, University of Wisconsin-Eau Claire.

Finally, I must acknowledge the support of my family, without whom I could never have completed this work and whose patience with me and confidence in me sustained me through many challenging moments. My parents—Ron and Joan Yagelski—and my siblings—Mary Cooper, Gary Yagelski, and Dianne Yagelski—support me in ways they never really see, and their presence in my life reinforces my belief in myself. My mother-in-law, Charlotte Hafich, never fails to offer encouragement and check in on my progress; I can never thank her enough for her love and support. My sons, Adam and Aaron, who light up my life in ways they can never realize, are always ready to share and debate ideas with me, and I am energized by their pride in what I do; they help me see the world in ways that shape my writing and keep me going. And most of all, Cheryl, my wife of 31 years and the love of my life, is the best partner any writer could ever hope to have. Her love, constant support, and boundless confidence in me are the foundation that make it possible for me to undertake a task as big as this textbook and see it through. I am so deeply blessed to be able to share this work—and my life—with her. She always provides safe harbor.

About the Author

Robert P. Yagelski is Associate Vice Provost and Director of the Program in Writing and Critical Inquiry at the State University of New York at Albany, where he is also associate professor of English education in the Department of Educational Theory and Practice. He directs the Capital District Writing Project, a site of the National Writing Project, and has worked closely with schools to improve writing instruction at all levels of education. He is the author of numerous articles and books on writing and writing instruction. *Writing: Ten Core Concepts* is his fourth textbook.

1950   1970   1990   2010   2030?

Why We Write 1

WRITING IS A POWERFUL MEANS of communicating ideas and information across time and space. It enables us to participate in conversations and events that shape our lives and helps us make sense of the world. In fact, writing can change the world. Consider these examples:

- Adam Smith's economic theories, presented in his 1776 book *The Wealth of Nations*, continue to influence government economic policies today, which in turn affect the lives of almost every person on earth.

- *The Art of War*, believed to have been written in the 6th century B.C.E. by Chinese military strategist Sun Tzu, is still widely read by military leaders, politicians, and business leaders.

- Betty Friedan's *The Feminine Mystique*, published in 1963, is considered by many to have begun the women's rights movement that has reshaped American social, cultural, political, and economic life in the past half century.

- Charles Darwin's *On the Origin of Species*, published in 1859, revolutionized scientific thinking about life on earth and laid the foundation for the modern field of biology.

- *Silent Spring*, by Rachel Carson, which was published in 1962, helped spark the modern environmental movement and influenced the creation of laws to protect wildlife and the environment.

- Al Gore's 2006 book *An Inconvenient Truth* and the film based on it convinced millions of people that global climate change is a grave threat to human life that must be addressed by all nations.

- Messages posted on Facebook and Twitter in 2011 helped provoke protests in Egypt and Tunisia that led to new governments in those nations.

These examples dramatically illustrate the capacity of writing to transform our world.

For many college students, however, writing is mostly a requirement. Most students don't seem to mind writing, but few would choose to write the kinds of essays and reports usually assigned in school. Students consider such assignments necessary, but they don't necessarily enjoy them. For many students, writing in school can be tedious and dull. Maybe you feel the same way.

Yet students write all the time, for all kinds of reasons:

- They send text messages, update their Facebook pages, and tweet to stay in touch with friends, share information, let others know what they think, and keep informed about events or issues that matter to them.

- They respond to their favorite blogs or maintain their own blogs.

- They keep journals or diaries.

- They circulate petitions to support causes on their campus or in their town.

- They rap and participate in poetry slams to express their feelings about important issues in their lives.

- They write essays to gain admission to college or graduate school.

- They create resumes to obtain jobs.

Brian Cahn/ZUMA Press/Corbis

Whether they realize it or not, students regularly use writing to live their lives, to accomplish tasks that they have to or choose to do, and to participate in their communities.

If these kinds of writing don't seem as important as, say, a book like *An Inconvenient Truth* or *Silent Spring*, they should. For if a book can be said to have changed the world, the same is true of tweets and texts and blogs and essays and letters written by ordinary people, including students. A job application letter can change your life. A petition can change a policy on your campus that affects hundreds or thousands of students (see "How Students Changed Their University Through Writing"). An essay can inspire your classmates, change their minds about an issue, or move them to take action. And sometimes ordinary kinds of writing can result in extraordinary changes: In Egypt, in February 2011, tweets, email messages, texts, blog posts, and Facebook entries from ordinary citizens played a key role in the protest movement that led to the resignation of Egypt's president, who had ruled that nation for more than three decades. In other words, writing by ordinary citizens helped change the government of that country—a change that has touched the life of every Egyptian and many people outside Egypt.

During the 2010–2011 academic year, the campus of the Massachusetts Institute of Technology (MIT) was the site of a controversy about the school's dining plan, as explained in the following article. The article, which appeared in February 2011 in *The Tech*, a student newspaper at MIT, includes a great deal of information that only MIT students would be familiar with, but it also tells a compelling story of how the students used writing in various media to express their views and challenge a policy that affected them:

DINING IGNITES CAMPUS CONTROVERSY
Despite loud opposition, new plan still slated to start this fall
By Maggie Lloyd
February 1, 2011

Few topics caused as much tension on campus in 2010 as the ever-changing House Dining Plan, scheduled to go into effect in Fall 2011. In March 2010, the Division of Student Life (DSL) formed the House Dining Advisory Group (HDAG), committed to the creation of a new dining plan with the hope to eliminate the $600,000 deficit from House Dining and to offer more options for student dining.

HDAG consisted of presidents and dining chairs from the five dorms with dining halls (Baker, McCormick, Simmons, Next, and the planned Maseeh Hall), DSL staff, the UA Dining Chair, and other relevant MIT faculty, such as housemasters (including the upcoming Maseeh housemasters).

Throughout the spring, an online Idea Bank collected students' opinions on all-you-care-to-eat (AYCE) service, breakfast offerings, food allergies, and other relevant dining topics, while forums across campus invited students to talk about what they wanted directly to members of HDAG.

On May 19, HDAG released its initial recommendations, introducing AYCE dinner and breakfast to all of the dining dorms seven days a week, including Maseeh Hall, set to open in Fall 2011. Costs for the 10, 12, or 14 meals-per-week options were projected to be $2,900, $3,400, and $3,800 per year, respectively, and the number of meals per week was required to be equally split between breakfast and dinner. Maseeh would also offer lunch Monday through Friday. Freshmen would be required to buy the 14-meal plan, while sophomores would be permitted to choose between 12 and 14 meals, and juniors and seniors would decide between any of the three plans. As with the current House Dining Membership, students in the dining hall dorms would be required to participate in this dining plan.

With the exception of a student protest in Lobby 7 during Campus Preview Weekend, the campus remained relatively quiet in terms of dining discussion as the first semester of 2010 came to a close.

(Continued)

UA survey voices students' concerns; the petitions begin

As the class of 2014 arrived at MIT in the fall, conversations about the new dining plan began again, and concerns about the plan's potential impact on dorm culture and high prices were often mentioned. In the first week of October, the UA distributed a survey to all undergraduate dorms, asking for feedback on several student life topics such as printing, Greek life, shuttles, athletics, and dining, receiving 655 responses. Various comments received in the survey about dining ranged from indifferent—"Dining plan doesn't affect me"—to dissatisfied—"New dining plan is too expensive; too much food, most people don't eat that much"—foreshadowing some of the upcoming tension. As *The Tech* reported on October 12, "out of 222 [survey] respondents who said they lived in a dining dorm, only 98 said they had heard or read specific details about the plan. Of those 98 students, only 8 supported the new dining plan."

The survey results sent a spark through campus, igniting the first of several petitions to be distributed by undergraduates last fall. Next House resident Andres A. Romero '14 initiated a petition against the new dining plan, collecting over 200 signatures, mostly from other students living in Next House. He submitted the petition to the UA, insisting that the petition, which was signed by more than 5 percent of the student population, necessitated an emergency meeting of the UA, according to the UA bylaws.

Within the required 96-hour time limit after a petition submission, on October 13, the UA held its emergency meeting. The UA passed 42 U.A.S E1.1, "Bill to Reform HDAG Dining Proposal and Process in Light of Overwhelming Student Opposition," which called for Chancellor Phillip Clay "to intervene by halting" the approval process for the new dining plan. HDAG representatives claimed they were unable to stop this new plan because the Request for Proposal process, in which a dining vendor would be chosen, had already begun. To stop the process would mean starting over, losing months of work, and rushing to find a new plan in time for implementation in the next academic year.

Changes to HDAG membership

As the noise increased on campus, two of the key students involved in the dining conversations resigned from their positions. On October 26, Paula C. Trepman '13, who represented the UA in HDAG, resigned as UA Dining Chair. In her letter of resignation submitted to the UA, a "very frustrated" Trepman claimed "HDAG has this sense of paternalism and feels that it is their job to regulate and ensure that students eat a normal three meals every day."

Andy Wu '12, who served on HDAG as president of Baker House, followed suit. In a November 29 e-mail to Baker House, Wu stated, "HDAG has regularly dismissed my opinion to the point where I have been unable to contribute to any positive changes for Baker residents."

Student representation, in the form of other dorm presidents and dining chairs, still existed within the HDAG despite these absences.

Fact sheets and petitions fly

In an effort to highlight students' options within the new plan, HDAG released organized fact sheets that covered several topics such as pricing, hours, and other specifics within the new dining plan. These documents, which were released in late October and early November, were available on the House Dining Review website designed specifically for HDAG, *http://studentlife.mit.edu/house-dining-review*.

Throughout November, *The Tech*'s Letters to the Editor and Opinion pages flip-flopped arguments for and against the new plan, starting with a Nov. 9 letter from the administration (Phillip L. Clay PhD '75, Christine Ortiz, Costantino Colombo, and Daniel E. Hastings PhD '80) itself. Then, housemasters from the dining dorms (John M. Essigmann PhD '76, Suzanne Flynn, Steven R. Hall '80, Dava J. Newman PhD '92, and Charles H. Stewart III) chimed in with their support a week later. "Not every student agrees with the final recommendation, but students were involved every step of the way," the administration's letter argued.

"Two of the three plans for Baker, McCormick, Next, and Simmons are in the range of what their residents report spending on meals for the period covered by the new program," they said, adding, "residential life at MIT has never been static."

In the next issue, Tyler Hunt '04 challenged the housemasters' letter, claiming that the administration "must understand that when half of Next House signs a statement of opposition, that it has designed a program that is profoundly unpalatable." DAPER coaches then submitted their support of the plan, right next to Professor Alexander H. Slocum '82's advice for what the plan should be like.

Increasing student concern raised the volume of dining talk, starting with another petition from Next House residents Hannah L. Pelton '12 and Austin D. Brinson '13 on Nov. 8. This document, signed by 63 percent of Next House residents, was submitted to President Susan J. Hockfield, claiming HDAG's proposed dining plan was "wrong for us, wrong for Next House, and wrong for MIT." The petition claimed that the "expensive" plan would encourage Next House residents to move to dorms without dining halls, "making it more difficult to develop long-standing culture."

That same week, one of HDAG's own student representatives started a similar petition at Baker House. Despite supporting HDAG's proposed plan, HDAG representative Cameron S. McAlpine '13 reasoned that as Baker Dining Chair he needed to "accurately represent the opinions of Baker residents."

Then came the largest petition yet. Keone D. Hon '11 started writing blog posts on the popular missed connections site, *http://isawyou.mit.edu*, calling for a more organized student response. On November 17, Hon's *http://sayno.mit.edu* went live,

(*Continued*)

claiming that its perceptions of expense, poor economic sustainability, negative impact on dorms, clubs, and FSILGs, and apparent disregard for student opinion were the main reasons for student dissatisfaction with the new plan. Within 24 hours, the petition had more than 1,400 signatures from undergraduates and others affiliated with MIT, more than all other petitions combined. As of December 2010, 1,570 of the 1,838 signees were undergraduates, 568 of whom were from dining dorms.

From petitions to protests

One day later, roughly 25 students participated in a Baker Dining sit-in, bringing their own food to eat in the dining hall. Two freshmen, Burton Conner resident Michael L. Pappas '14 and East Campus resident Christopher W. Tam '14, organized the protest. Newman, the Baker housemaster, and Senior Assistant Dean of Students for Residential Life Henry J. Humphreys were there to discuss students' concerns, allowing for "civil dialogue," as Pappas described, between students and administration.

As students arrived back on campus after Thanksgiving break on Nov. 29, HDAG released an updated version of the House Dining Plan, introducing a "transition plan" for the classes of 2012 and 2013. This plan would cost $2500 for the year, the cheapest yet offered, allowing those students to choose any 7 meals per week. Students are also able to increase their flexibility in the transition plan by choosing any dining combination of breakfast and dinner "at a modest cost," according to the House Dining Review website. Since news about the new dining plan was available to the Class of 2014 before they came to MIT, DSL said that they must participate in the full-fledged campus dining plan.

On December 3, Hon organized students one more time, this time hosting a protest outside the Media Lab as members of the MIT Corporation walked in for a quarterly meeting. Around 20 students attended to distribute copies of the SayNo petition and to talk briefly to Corporation members attending the meeting. This would be the last organized event concerning dining for 2010, as finals began ten days later. For the first time since October, talk about dining came to a hush.

Although the campus-wide battle of words died down over IAP, only time will tell when the noise will return. As *The Tech* reported this January, MIT Corporation member Harbo P. Jensen '74 said that the members of the Corporation "all agreed that … there is a lot of emotion and energy behind this," acknowledging "it's impossible to make everyone happy." Indeed, the past year has shown that it's the unhappy students who are capable of making the most noise.

Source: Lloyd, Maggie. "Dining Ignites Campus Controversy." *The Tech*, online edition. 1 Feb. 2011. Web. 21 Mar. 2011.

Questions for Discussion

1. What kinds of writing did MIT students use to voice their concerns about the university's dining plan? How did these kinds of writing figure into this controversy?

2. Do you think the students could have accomplished their goals without using writing as they did? Why or why not? What advantages (or disadvantages) do you see in the way students used writing in this situation? What alternatives did the students have?

3. Write a brief essay about a time when you used writing to voice a concern, lodge a complaint, or try to change something. Then, in a group of classmates, share your essays. What similarities and differences do you see in the writing that is described in these essays? What conclusions might you draw from these essays about the role of writing in your lives?

As a college student, you will probably do most of your writing for your classes. This textbook will help you learn to manage college writing assignments effectively. But writing well can also help you live your life in ways that extend far beyond the classroom. So in this chapter—and throughout this textbook—we will examine some of the many different situations in which you might be asked to write.

Understanding Writing

This textbook has another important goal: to help you understand what writing is. One reason so many people struggle with writing is that they don't sufficiently understand the nature of writing. They believe writing is a matter of following arcane rules that are often difficult to remember or grasp. They think writing is a matter of inspiration and creativity, which they believe they lack, or they assume they can't write well because they don't have a large enough vocabulary. These beliefs are based on common misconceptions that can lead to frustration and prevent students from becoming successful writers. Yes, writing well *does* require knowing rules, and having a large vocabulary doesn't hurt. But writing is more than rules or inspiration or vocabulary. Writing should be understood in four important ways:

- Writing is a powerful means of expression and communication.
- Writing is a way to participate in ongoing conversations about ideas, events, and issues that matter in our lives.
- Writing is a unique form of thinking that helps us learn.
- Writing is a way to understand ourselves and the world around us.

For students who come to understand writing in these four ways, learning to write effectively can be a much more satisfying and successful process. Abandoning common misconceptions and appreciating the complexity, power, and joy of writing are the first steps to learning to write well and feeling confident about writing. This textbook will introduce you to the most important ideas—the Core Concepts—that you need to know in order to write well. It is also designed to give you practice in the most common forms of writing for a variety of audiences and purposes—in college, in your community, in the workplace, and in your life in general.

FOCUS   **Think Differently About Your Writing**

What were the most important pieces of writing you have ever done in your life? Under what circumstances did you write them? What form did they take (e.g., were they conventional essays, letters, blog posts, Prezi presentations)? Why were they important? In what ways did they affect your life? What do these pieces of writing suggest about the role of writing in your life? Jot down brief answers to these questions, and consider what your answers reveal about the role of writing in your life.

Writing in College

Let's face it: Students have to write well if they expect to do well in school. Whether it's a lab report in a biology class, a research paper in a sociology course, a proposal in a business class, or a literary analysis essay in an English course, writing effectively means better learning and better grades. In this regard, writing in college serves three main purposes:

- It is a way for you to demonstrate what you know.
- It helps you learn.
- It enables you to join important conversations about the subjects you are studying.

Write to Demonstrate What You Know

Writing is a way for you to show your instructors what you have learned. An essay exam in history, for example, helps your instructor decide whether you have understood a particular concept (say, manifest destiny) or learned about historical events that are part of the course syllabus. Similarly, your economics professor might assign an essay requiring you to analyze a market trend, such as the popularity of SUVs, to determine whether you and your classmates have grasped certain economic principles. For this reason, college students are asked to write many different kinds of assignments: reports, research papers, analytical essays, arguments, synopses, creative writing like poems, personal narratives, reflective essays, digital stories, multimedia presentations, and more.

Think about a recent essay exam or assignment that you wrote for one of your classes. First, describe the writing you did. What was the assignment? What exactly did you write? What do you think was most important about that piece of writing? What did it reveal about what you know about the subject? What do you think it suggests about you as a writer?

When writing essay exams, reports, or research papers for your classes, keep in mind that you are writing to demonstrate what you have learned. Have confidence that your writing reflects what you know. And remember that your writing can also help you identify what you still need to learn.

Write to Learn

Writing an essay exam or a research paper isn't just a way to demonstrate learning; it is also a means of learning in itself. As you will see in the next chapter, writing is a form of intellectual inquiry, and it is essential to student learning, no matter the subject. To write an ethnographic analysis of a culture for an anthropology class, for example, is to learn not only about that culture but also about ethnography as a way of understanding how we live together. It's true that students can learn a great deal by reading, but writing engages the mind in ways that reading does not. Reading about ethnography can help students understand what ethnography is; writing an ethnographic report about a culture enables students to *apply* that understanding, which can lead to a deeper learning of the subject matter.

This idea that writing is learning can be easy to forget when you are trying to meet deadlines and follow detailed guidelines for an assignment. But if you approach your writing assignments as a way to learn about your subject matter, the process of writing can be more satisfying and can lead to more effective essays. And remember that every writing assignment is also an opportunity to learn about writing itself. The more you write, the better you understand the power and joy of writing and the better able you will be to meet the challenges of writing.

And one last point about the power of writing as a way to learn: The more you write, especially when you write as a way to explore your subject matter, the more you learn about *yourself* as a writer and thinker. Knowing your strengths as a writer enables you to take advantage of them; knowing your weaknesses is essential if you are to improve your writing. That understanding will help you become a better writer.

Describe a writing assignment you did for a college or high school class that was especially challenging for you. Explain why you found the assignment challenging. Now consider what you learned by writing the assignment. What did you learn about the subject matter? What did you learn about writing? What surprised you about doing that assignment? What surprises you now as you look back on it? What do you think you learned about yourself as a writer?

If you approach writing assignments as opportunities to discover new information, explore new ideas, and enhance your understanding of your subject, writing can be more satisfying, and you might find you learned more than you think you learned. You might also find that your writing improves.

Write to Join Academic Conversations

Writing is the primary way that experts in all academic disciplines do their work and share their ideas:

- Mathematics professors may work mostly with numbers and formulas, but they also write articles for other mathematicians about current problems in mathematics.

- Historians study ancient artifacts to help them understand past events, and they share their understanding in the articles and books they write for other historians.

- Scientists might spend long hours in their labs, but they test each other's theories by sharing and debating the results of their experiments in articles they write for scientific journals.

- Scholars in all fields regularly share information and debate ideas by posting messages to professional online forums and blogs.

In all these cases, writing is the main vehicle by which scholars discuss the central questions in their fields. They cannot do their work without it.

Writing for a college class, whether it be psychology or business or chemistry, is a way for students to enter these conversations about the ideas, information, and ways of thinking that define academic fields. Part of what students learn when they write in college, then, is how to use writing as a tool for discovering and sharing knowledge in various academic disciplines. In this sense, writing an assignment for a college class is a process of learning to write like a scholar in that academic discipline. When you are asked to write a research paper in a psychology course or a lab report in a biochemistry class, you are learning to do the kind of intellectual work that psychologists or biochemists do. You are learning to participate in the conversations about important topics in those academic fields. And by doing so you are using writing to expand and deepen your knowledge about those fields as well as about the world in general.

FOCUS Think Differently About Your Writing

Take two or more assignments you wrote for different college (or high school) classes. For example, take a literary essay you wrote for an English class, a report you did for a biology class, and a research paper for a history class. Briefly describe the similarities and differences that you notice between them. Look at the writing style you used in each paper, the structure of each paper, and the language you used. What stands out about each paper? In what ways are the papers different or similar? How can you explain the similarities and differences you see in these papers? What do you think the similarities and differences between these papers suggest about the writing you are asked to do in college?

Of course, writing in college also serves another purpose: It gives students genuine practice that helps them become better writers, which can benefit them in their lives outside of school as well.

EXERCISE 1A   Read the three excerpts included here. Each excerpt is taken from an article or book in a different academic subject. The first is from a marketing textbook, the second from an education journal, and the third from a scientific journal. After reading the excerpts, compare them by addressing these questions:

- What do you notice about the writing in these three pieces?

- What do you think are the purposes of the writing in each case?

- Are there similarities or differences in the writing style, language, and structure of these excerpts? What might these similarities and/or differences suggest about writing in different disciplines?

- What does your comparison of these three excerpts suggest about writing in general?

What is Marketing?

What does the term *marketing* mean to you? Many people think it means the same thing as personal selling. Others think marketing is the same as personal selling and advertising. Still others believe marketing has something to do with making products available in stores, arranging displays, and maintaining inventories of products for future sales. Actually, marketing includes all of these activities and more.

Marketing has two facets. First, it is a philosophy, an attitude, a perspective, or a management orientation that stresses customer satisfaction. Second, marketing is activities and processes used to implement this philosophy.

Source: From Lamb, Hair, McDaniel. *Essentials of Marketing.* 7 ed. © 2012 South-Western, a part of Cengage Learning, Inc. Reproduced by permission. Www.cengage.com/permissions.

(Continued)

The American Marketing Association's definition of marketing focuses on the second facet. Marketing is the activity, set of institutions, and processes for creating, communicating, delivering, and exchanging offerings that have value for customers, clients, partners, and society at large.

Marketing involves more than just activities performed by a group of people in a defined area or department. In the often-quoted words of David Packard, cofounder of Hewlett-Packard, "Marketing is too important to be left only to the marketing department." Marketing entails processes that focus on delivering value and benefits to customers, not just selling goods, services, and/or ideas. It uses communication, distribution, and pricing strategies to provide customers and their stakeholders with the goods, services, ideas, values, and benefits they desire when and where they want them. It involves building long-term, mutually rewarding relationships when these benefit all parties concerned. Marketing also entails an understanding that organizations have many connected stakeholder "partners," including employees, suppliers, stockholders, distributors, and society at large.

Source: Lamb, Charles, Joseph Hair, and Carl McDaniel. *Essentials of Marketing*. 7 ed. Kentucky: South-Western, Cengage Learning, 2012. Print.

Brain-Based Teaching Strategies for Improving Students' Memory, Learning, and Test-Taking Success

Decades ago, my high school chemistry teacher slowly released hydrogen sulfide (which produces a smell like rotten eggs) from a hidden container he opened just before we entered his classroom. A few minutes after we took our seats and he began his lecture, a foul odor permeated the classroom. We groaned, laughed, looked around for the offending source. To an outside observer entering our class at that time, we would have appeared unfocused and definitely not learning anything. This demonstration, however, literally led me by the nose to follow my teacher's description of the diffusion of gases through other gases. It is likely that during that class I created two or three pathways to the information about gas diffusion that I processed through my senses and ultimately stored in my long-term memory. Since then, that knowledge has been available for me to retrieve by thinking of an egg or by remembering the emotional responses as the class reacted to the odor permeating the room. Once I make the connection, I am able to recall the scientific facts linked to his demonstration.

Event memories, such as the one that was stored that day in chemistry class, are tied to specific emotionally or physically charged events (strong sensory input) and by the emotional intensity of the events to which they are linked. Because the dramatic event powers its way through the neural pathways of the emotionally preactivated limbic system into memory storage, associated scholastic information gets pulled along with it. Recollection of the academic material occurs when the emotionally significant event comes to mind, unconsciously or consciously. To remember the lesson, students can cue up the dramatic event to which it is linked.

Source: Willis, Judy. "Brain-Based Teaching Strategies for Improving Students' Memory, Learning, and Test-Taking Success." *Childhood Education* 83.5 (2007): 310. *Academic OneFile*. Web. 23 Mar. 2011.

Screening For Depression

Depression is the second most common chronic disorder seen by primary care physicians.[1] On average, 12 percent of patients seen in primary care settings have major depression.[2] The degrees of suffering and disability associated with depression are comparable to those in most chronic medical conditions.[3] Fortunately, early identification and proper treatment significantly decrease the negative impact of depression in most patients.[4] Most patients with depression can be effectively treated with pharmacotherapeutic and psychotherapeutic modalities.[5]

Depression occurs in children, adolescents, adults, and the elderly. It manifests as a combination of feelings of sadness, loneliness, irritability, worthlessness, hopelessness, agitation, and guilt, accompanied by an array of physical symptoms.[6] Recognizing depression in patients in a primary care setting may be particularly challenging because patients, especially men, rarely spontaneously describe emotional difficulties. To the contrary, patients with depression who present to a primary care physician often describe somatic symptoms such as fatigue, sleep problems, pain, loss of interest in sexual activity, or multiple, persistent vague symptoms.[7]

References

1 Wells KB. Caring for depression. Cambridge, Mass.: Harvard University Press, 1996.
2 Spitzer RL, Kroenke K, Linzer M, Hahn SR, Williams JB, deGruy FV 3d, et al. Health-related quality of life in primary care patients with mental disorders. Results from the PRIME-MD 1000Study. *JAMA*. 1995;274:1511–17.
3 Hays RD, Wells KB, Sherbourne CD, Rogers W, Spritzer K. Functioning and well-being outcomes of patients with depression compared with chronic general medical illnesses. *Arch Gen Psychiatry*. 1995;52:11–19.
4 Coulehan JL, Schulberg HC, Block MR, Madonia MJ, Rodriguez E. Treating depressed primary care patients improves their physical, mental, and social functioning. *Arch Intern Med*. 1997;157:1113–20.
5 Elkin I, Shea MT, Watkins JT, Imber SD, Sotsky SM, Collins JF, et al., National Institute of Mental Health treatment of Depression Collaborative Research Program. General effectiveness of treatments. *Arch Gen Psychiatry*. 1989;46:971–82.
6 Diagnostic and statistical manual of mental disorders: DSM-IV-TR. 4th ed, text rev. Washington, D.C.: American Psychiatric Association, 2000.
7 Suh T, Gallo JJ. Symptom profiles of depression among general medical service users compared with specialty mental health service users. *Psychol Med*. 1997;27:1051–63.

Source: Sharp, L. K., and M. S. Lipsky. "Screening for Depression across the Lifespan: A Review of Measures for Use in Primary Care Settings." *American Family Physician* 66.6 (2002): 1001–9. Web.

Writing in the Workplace

In almost any job or career you can think of, you will be expected to use writing in some way to do your work. Consider these anecdotes:

- A few years ago, a student planning to attend law school asked me what she could do now to prepare herself for law school. I called an old friend who is a lawyer to ask what I should tell my student. My friend offered two bits of advice: (1) get good grades, and (2) take as many writing courses as possible. Writing, my friend said, was the most important thing lawyers do.

- A college friend of mine has worked for many years as a management trainer for a large insurance company. Almost every aspect of his job involves some kind of writing: training materials, memos, reports, multimedia presentations, and formal email messages. Effective writing is a central reason he is an effective manager.

- One of my colleagues teaches nursing. His students spend a lot of time as interns in hospitals learning how to take a patient's pulse and blood pressure, obtain blood samples, set up IVs, and administer medication. They also learn to write. Writing accurate and thorough reports, my colleague says, is as important as anything else a nurse does. Communicating with doctors and other nurses is one of the most crucial aspects of a nurse's job, and much of it is done through writing. Without good writing skills, he says, nurses could not care for their patients effectively.

These anecdotes underscore the importance of writing in different work environments and illustrate the different ways that writing enables people to do their jobs well. Professionals already recognize this fact. In one recent study, more than 90% of midcareer professionals reported that the "need to write effectively" is a skill "of great importance" in their everyday work.[1] And because the modern workplace is changing rapidly, you are more likely than ever to be expected to communicate effectively in writing in a number of different media, including traditional print reports, proposals, letters, and memos as well as email, PowerPoint, blogs, wikis, and other online or digital formats. This is the nature of the workplace today, one that already places a great premium on communication and especially on writing—and one that is being reshaped by new media. To succeed in the workplace, you must know how to write well.

---

[1] National Commission on Writing. *The Neglected "R": The Need for a Writing Revolution*. New York: The College Board, 2003. 11. Print.

FOCUS   Think Differently About Your Writing

Examine a piece of your own writing that you finished recently. What do you notice about your writing? What strengths or weaknesses do you see? What might this piece of writing suggest about you as a writer? Now think about how you might present yourself as a writer to a potential employer. What would you say to that employer about your writing? What have you learned about writing that might appeal to an employer? What do you still need to improve upon in order to be ready to write for that employer?

Think of any writing assignment as career training. The better you can write, the more likely you are to succeed in your chosen career. Use your college writing assignments to develop your writing skills in preparation for the writing you will do in your future career. And if you have other kinds of writing experience, such as writing for your school newspaper or developing promotional materials for a student organization, put them on your resume.

EXERCISE 1B   Talk to a few people you know about the writing they do for their jobs. Try to find people who work in different kinds of jobs. For example, maybe you have a relative who is a salesperson, a friend who is a physical therapist, or a neighbor who manages a restaurant. Ask them to describe any writing they do in their jobs and the media they regularly use, such as websites, email, and social media. Ask them about the challenges they face as writers in their workplaces. Also ask them for advice about preparing for workplace writing. Then write a brief report for your classmates in which you share what you learned from this exercise about workplace writing—or about writing in general.

Writing as a Citizen

The idea that citizens must be educated in order for democracy to work is deeply embedded in American culture. It is known as the Jeffersonian ideal, which imagines a free and thriving society based on a productive, educated citizenry. Today, "educated" also means "literate," and it's hard to imagine being an active part of society without writing. In fact, we write to participate in our society in many different ways, from political campaigns to consumer advocacy. Consider these examples:

❯ BECAUSE of a growing budget deficit, your state legislature is considering a tuition increase as well as large cuts in funding for state colleges and universities. Members of your college community, including students, have written letters and emails to legislators urging them to vote against the funding cuts and the tuition hike. Some students have written editorials for the school newspaper expressing opposition to the budget cuts. To organize a rally at the state capitol, students use Twitter, Facebook, email, and blogs, all of which provide information about the rally and background information about the proposed state budget.

❯ A developer has proposed building a giant new retail store near the business district of your town. Some local businesspeople are concerned that businesses on the town's main street will suffer if the new store is built. Residents opposed to the new store have organized a citizens' group and created a Facebook page to advocate for their position. They post information about the proposed store and share opinions about its potential impact on the town. They also write letters to the local newspaper and distribute fliers to local businesses. Other residents, concerned about the town's slow economic growth, have expressed their support for the new store on a blog and in articles and letters they have written for local publications. They also circulate a YouTube video to explain their support for the new store.

❯ THE owners of a major league sports team in your city have threatened to leave the city if a new stadium is not built to replace the aging stadium that the team currently plays in. The team is popular and important to the city, and many residents support the proposal for a new stadium. Other residents oppose the plan on the grounds that it will increase taxes without creating new jobs. These residents form a community organization to publicize their concerns. They use social media to explain what they believe will be the impact of a new stadium. They also write letters to government officials and send press releases to local TV stations.

These scenarios illustrate how we can use writing to participate directly in important discussions, decisions, and events that affect our lives. Writing is a way for individual citizens to express their opinions and share information; it is a way for citizens to take action as members of their communities. Through writing, whether in a traditional print form such as a letter to an editor or in a new kind of forum such as a blog, citizens can shape the ideas, opinions, and actions of others involved in the situation at hand. In all these instances, writing helps transform the world.

FOCUS | **Think Differently About Your Writing**

Have you ever written a letter to a politician or business leader to express your opinion or voice a concern? Have you ever written a response to a blog or tweeted to share your perspective on an issue or controversy? Have you ever written a letter to the editor of a newspaper or magazine or sent an email message in response to an article or editorial? If so, what prompted you to do so? Why did you choose to write in that situation? To what extent do you think your writing made a difference—to you or to anyone else who might have read what you wrote?

A well-written letter, a carefully crafted blog post, or even a provocative tweet can often be more effective than a phone call to express a concern, request an action, or raise awareness about an issue.

EXERCISE 1C   Think about an issue that concerns you. Maybe there is a controversy on your campus or in your town that affects you somehow. (On my campus, for example, the university president canceled a popular student picnic because of concerns about alcohol abuse and vandalism, which led to an outcry among students and some faculty.) Or you might have a special interest in an issue in your state or in the nation, such as standardized testing in schools or the creation of wind farms in rural or wilderness areas. Now consider how you might best make your opinion heard in public discussions about this issue. Could you write a letter to someone in authority who is involved in the situation, such as a politician or business leader? What about a letter or email to the editor of your local newspaper? A blog post? A Facebook page? A brochure or newsletter? Maybe a formal proposal intended for someone in a position of authority? Decide what kind of writing you think would work best in this situation, and explain why. Then write it.

Jesus Keller/Shutterstock.com

Alternatively, if you have ever written out of concern about an issue that was important to you, write a brief essay describing that situation and explaining what you wrote. To what extent did your writing in that situation make a difference to you or others involved?

Writing to Understand Ourselves

A few years ago, my family planned a surprise party to celebrate my father's 70th birthday. Many friends and relatives would attend, and we wanted to do something special to celebrate my father's life. I decided to create a video that would be a kind of documentary about him. (See Chapter 18, "Digital Stories.") With help from my siblings, I spent several months collecting old photographs and memorabilia, gathering facts about my father's childhood and working life, and interviewing friends and relatives about their experiences with him. Using this material, I created a 20-minute video that focused on the important aspects of his life, including his military service and his family. As I composed that video, certain themes began to emerge about my father. I learned a lot about him that I hadn't previously known. More important, I gained a deep appreciation for the impact he had on many other people. Eventually, I screened the video at the surprise party, but composing it gave me a better understanding of my father and the world he grew up in; it also helped me learn about myself and my relationship with him.

My video about my father's life illustrates how writing can help us understand ourselves and the world around us. Here are two other examples:

> A student of mine was a veteran of military service in Iraq during the most intense fighting there between 2004 and 2006. For one assignment, he wrote a graphic and disturbing essay, in which he struggled to understand what he had experienced in Iraq. His essay revealed that he had deeply conflicted feelings about the war because, in the midst of the horror he witnessed, he also developed very special bonds with his fellow soldiers and witnessed profound acts of love and bravery. His essay was one of the most compelling pieces of writing I have ever received from a student—not because it was about war but because it was such a heartfelt effort by the student to understand some very difficult experiences.

> ONE of my students was hired by the university's office for international students to help write a newsletter. She was a good writer who earned good grades, but she found writing for international students much more challenging than she expected. Her supervisor constantly required her to revise his articles. Little by little, however, she began to see that her problems with these articles had little to do with her writing skill but arose from her lack of familiarity with her audience. The more she learned about the international students and their experiences in the United States, the better she appreciated their needs as readers of the newsletter. Her articles improved, and in the process of writing them, she learned a great deal about the international students on our campus and the challenges they face as students in the United States. She also learned something valuable about writing and about herself as a writer—and a person.

1

Writing is a powerful way not only to describe but also to examine, reflect on, and understand our thoughts, feelings, opinions, ideas, actions, and experiences. This capacity of writing is one of the most important reasons we write. In many college classes, you may be asked to write assignments that are designed to help you understand yourself and the world around you in the same way that my student's essay helped him understand his experiences in Iraq. But all of the writing you do in college, whether or not it is directly about your own experiences, presents opportunities for you to learn about yourself.

FOCUS   Think Differently About Your Writing

Think about a time you wrote about an experience or issue that was important to you in some way—in a journal, a letter, a school essay, or on Facebook. Why did you choose to write about that experience? What difference did it make to you to write about the experience? What do you think you learned by writing in that situation?

If you approach every writing assignment as an opportunity to learn not only about your subject but also about yourself, you will find that even the most tedious writing assignment can turn out to be a more rewarding experience.

EXERCISE 1D   Write a brief informal essay about an important experience that helped make you the person you are today. Write the essay for an audience of your classmates, and tell your story in a way that conveys to them why the experience was important to you.

Now reflect on your essay. Did you learn anything—about the experience itself or about yourself—as a result of writing your essay? Did writing about your experience change your view of the experience in any way? What did writing this essay teach you about yourself? What did it teach you about writing?

Ten Core Concepts for Effective Writing

WHEN I FIRST LEARNED to rock climb, an experienced climber gave me some advice: Always climb with your eyes. That may sound strange, since climbing obviously involves moving your body up a cliff, but it actually makes good sense. The key to climbing a vertical rock face is finding the right holds for your hands and feet, which is not always straightforward. To keep moving safely and efficiently up the cliff, climbers have to link together handholds and footholds. So even before starting up the cliff, climbers examine it carefully and identify a possible route that they can follow to the top. Climbers call this process "seeing the line" up a cliff or a mountain. Once on the cliff, they are always looking ahead to the next handhold or foothold. That simple statement—"always climb with your eyes"—turned out to be some of the best advice about climbing I ever received. It was a way to boil down the complicated act of climbing into a single, simple, basic idea.

This chapter does the same thing with writing: It boils down the complex, powerful, wonderful, and sometimes challenging activity of writing into ten essential ideas, or Core Concepts. There's much more to learn about writing than these concepts, just as in climbing you have to learn more than how to "climb with your eyes," and Part II of this textbook goes into much more detail so that you can apply these concepts to various writing tasks. But these concepts are fundamental insights that every writer must learn in order to write effectively. Students who incorporate these insights into their writing process will become better writers, no matter what kind of writing they are doing.

Learning to write effectively also requires developing a certain kind of attitude toward writing. Some climbers talk about "conquering" a mountain, but many climbers reject that way of thinking. For them, the point of climbing is not about defeating a mountain but about respecting it, adapting to it, and experiencing it. That attitude influences their decisions about which routes to follow up a mountain, when to start a climb, when to abandon it. It also affects the meaning of climbing; for them, climbing is about appreciating the experience of being in the mountains and meeting their challenges.

In the same way, the experience of writing can depend a great deal on a writer's attitude toward writing. Students who believe that writing is mostly about following certain rules tend to see writing as a process of learning and applying rules, which can become tedious and diminish the joy of writing. If, on the other hand,

ProfStocker/Shutterstock.com; Dudarev Mikhail/Shutterstock.com you think of writing as a process of discovery, then each writing task can become a way to learn—about your subject, about yourself, and about the world around you. Students who approach writing in this way are open to the possibilities of writing and better able to harness its power. For them, writing isn't primarily about applying rules; it's about understanding and engaging the world and communicating effectively with others.

The ten Core Concepts discussed in this chapter, then, are not rules to learn or directions to follow. They are insights into how to write more effectively. Learning these concepts is a matter of experiencing the variety, complexity, and power of writing so that you can harness that power. Learning to write more effectively is partly a process of learning how to think differently about writing and about yourself as a writer.

This chapter asks you to examine your beliefs about writing and adopt a certain attitude about writing—an attitude that might differ from what you have learned about writing in the past. It encourages you to shift your focus as a writer from remembering and applying rules to exploring your subject, addressing your readers, and accomplishing your rhetorical goals. That shift can change your entire experience as a writer. In learning and applying these Core Concepts, you will, I hope, feel more like a rock climber who is fully engaged in the arduous yet exhilarating act of moving toward a mountain summit.

The Ten Core Concepts for Effective Writing

The ten Core Concepts are based on what research and experience indicate about writing effectively. Each concept is based on a fundamental insight that student writers can learn in order to write well in a variety of situations—in school, in the workplace, and in the community. Understanding these concepts doesn't guarantee that you will always write effectively, but you cannot learn to write effectively without applying these ten essential insights about writing:

1. Writing is a process of discovery and learning.
2. Good writing fits the context.
3. The medium is part of the message.
4. A writer must have something to say.
5. A writer must support claims and assertions.
6. Purpose determines form, style, and organization in writing.
7. Writing is a social activity.
8. Revision is an essential part of writing.
9. There is always a voice in writing, even when there isn't an I.
10. Good writing means more than good grammar.

Core Concept 1 Writing is a process of discovery and learning.

A few years ago, a student in one of my classes decided to write an essay about her relationship with her parents. Writing that essay turned out to be a much more involved—and important— experience than she expected.

In the first draft of her essay, Chelsea, who was 22 years old, described how her relationship with her parents was changing now that she was an adult. Her draft was lighthearted and full of fond memories and funny anecdotes about her parents that revealed how much she enjoyed her new relationship with them. But something was missing from the draft. For one thing, Chelsea mentioned briefly that her parents had recently divorced after more than 20 years of marriage, but she wrote nothing about why they divorced. That seemed strange to Chelsea's classmates, who asked her about the divorce during a workshop of her draft. The more we discussed her draft, the clearer it became that there was a lot more to the story than Chelsea had revealed in her draft.

As Chelsea revised her draft, her essay began to change. It was no longer a lighthearted story about what it was like to have an adult relationship with her parents; it was now a more compli- cated essay that revealed Chelsea's conflicted feelings about what had happened to her parents' marriage and how it affected her (see "Changes" on page 26). There was still humor in the essay, but it was bittersweet, tempered by her realization that her changing relationship with her parents was accompanied by loss as well as gain.

Chelsea's essay became a journey of discovery through which she learned a lot about herself, her parents, and the experience she was describing in her essay. She also learned a valuable les- son about writing. When she began the essay, she thought it would be a simple narrative about her changing relationship with her parents. But the process of writing took her deeper into her experience and the complexities of human relationships. It helped Chelsea gain insight into an important period in her life and, maybe, understand something important about relationships (and life) in general.

Writing her essay also enabled Chelsea to communicate something interesting about rela- tionships to her readers, but what she communicated was knowledge and insight that she gained *through the act of writing*, which enabled her to reflect deeply on her experience. This capacity of writing to help writers learn about and understand something is part of what makes writing so powerful—and so important.

Changes

I didn't know how to handle the fact that my parents were actually two separate people who had ceased to exist as one entity, two people who had other interests and other desires besides just solely being parents. With three grown children they felt that it was their time to move on and become separate people. The combination "Momand-dad" that I had once imagined as this real thing suddenly transformed into a Mom and a Dad who were pursuing their own separate lives and their own interests.

And I had to choose. My brother moved out and found an apartment to hide in, away from the crumbling walls of our family. I was torn—torn between moving out and moving on from the only thing I ever knew, from this Momanddad that was suddenly becoming non-existent. *But we can't leave Dad alone.* And so it was decided that I would live with Mom and my sister would live with Dad. How do you choose? Is who you live with the one you side with, because in that case, it would change everything. Changing. Everything was changing.

—excerpt from "Changes" by Chelsea

As Chelsea discovered, writing is more than a step-by-step procedure for organizing ideas into a specific form, such as a five-paragraph essay, a lab report, or a story. Writing effectively requires understanding that you are on a journey of discovery that enables you to understand something and to convey what you discovered to others. That journey sometimes takes you to places that you didn't expect, and it is rarely a straightforward, linear process from start to finish. If you approach a writing task as such a journey, it won't always be easy, but it can be much more satisfying—not to mention more successful.

The Irish singer-songwriter Conor O'Brien revealed during an interview that his song-writing has been influenced by postmodern poetry. O'Brien says that he developed a deep appreciation for the poetry of John Ashberry in a college English literature course. "I remember having to write an essay about John Ashberry and I absolutely despised his words," O'Brien said. "I thought they were really elitist. But  then by the end of my essay, I actually fell in love with it and I thought the complete opposite about it.... It was very rhythmic and very beautiful."

Joushua Wainwright/Alamy

Any writing task can be a surprising journey that leads to new learning and insight, no matter what your topic is or what kind of assignment you're working on:

- When you write a narrative about an experience, as Chelsea did, you might understand that experience more fully.

- When you write an analysis of someone else's words or ideas, as singer-songwriter Conor O'Brien did (see "Learning by Writing"), you can develop a deeper appreciation for those words or ideas.

- When you write a blog post about a political campaign, you engage the ideas of others who might disagree with you, which can help you examine the basis for disagreement.

- When you write an argument about a problem, you might understand that problem better so that you are able to see solutions that were invisible to you before you began writing.

- When you write a lab report about an experiment you did for a chemistry class, you might gain a better grasp of the experimental process and the specific research question you were examining.

This kind of discovery and learning is possible because writing engages your intellect in a way that goes beyond reading or listening. If you have ever been so immersed in a writing task that the time seems to fly by, then you have experienced this capacity of writing to engage your mind fully.

What This Means for You as a Writer

- **Approach every writing task with curiosity.** Don't assume you already know exactly what you want to say or where your writing will end up, even when you're writing about something you know very well. Don't expect to know at the beginning exactly how everything will turn out in the finished text. Be open to unexpected possibilities as you work through an assignment. Even when your assignment is very specific and has rigid rules to follow (for example, a chemistry lab report with explicit directions for format or a persuasive essay in which you're required to provide exactly three arguments for and against your position), remember that you can't know everything at the start. That's why you're writing in the first place: to learn something new or deepen your understanding of something you thought you knew.

- **Be patient.** To engage in writing as a process of discovery and learning almost always involves working through several drafts as you explore your subject, gather information, develop ideas, consider your audience, learn more about your subject, and refine what you thought you wanted to say. This process can be messy and even frustrating at times, but it can also be illuminating. Forcing this process into a step-by-step procedure will not only make it more difficult (as you probably already know) but also prevent it from becoming a worthwhile journey of discovery. And it will usually result in less effective writing. But if you approach a writing task as a process of discovery and learning, you might be surprised by where your writing can take you.

- **Don't try to make your writing perfect as you work through an assignment.** Early drafts of any assignment are opportunities to explore your subject and learn more about it.

Avoid the impulse to make everything perfect the first time. Rough drafts are just that: drafts. They can be changed and improved. Sometimes you have to allow yourself to write messy drafts, especially in the early stages of an assignment. You can even temporarily ignore rules of usage and style in your early drafts and focus instead on exploring your subject matter and discovering what you want to say in your piece, as Chelsea did. You will go back later to correct errors, tighten up your sentences, develop ideas, or clarify a point. (See Core Concept #10.)

■ **Allow yourself sufficient time to write.** Writing at the last minute forces students to rush the process and undercut the discovery and learning that writing can lead to. It is also stressful and less enjoyable. Allowing sufficient time to move through the process deliberately will result not only in greater learning but also greater enjoyment—and more effective writing.

Practice This Lesson

Keep an informal journal or a private blog as you work on your next piece of writing. Each time you work on your writing, describe in your journal or blog what you did. If you read something and take notes for your writing, describe that. If you make an outline or jot down some ideas for your introduction, describe that. If you get an idea while taking a shower or riding a bus, describe that. If you share a draft with a friend or roommate, describe that. Also record any questions, concerns, or problems that arise as you work on this piece of writing, and explain how you addressed those questions, concerns, or problems. Describe how you feel as you work on the piece. What seems to be going well and what doesn't? Keep a record of *everything* you do and think as you complete the writing task. Once you're finished with the writing task, go back and review your journal or blog. What does it reveal about how you write? What does it suggest about writing in general? What surprises you about your descriptions of what you did to complete your writing task? What do you think you can learn from this journal about writing? About yourself as a writer?

If possible, interview someone who is a professional writer or who writes regularly in his or her work, and ask that person what he or she does when writing. What steps or activities does the person engage in when completing a writing task? How does this person explain what he or she does when writing? After you finish your interview, describe in a paragraph or two what you learned about writing from this writer, and compare what he or she does to what you do.

Core Concept 2 Good writing fits the context.

If writing is a journey of discovery, how do we know when that journey produces writing that is good? The answer is: It depends.

Consider the expression, "Today was a very good day." People say this all the time, but what exactly does it mean? A student who earned a good grade on a test could say it was a good day. Someone receiving a raise at work might consider that a good day, but quitting a job could also make for a good day. Winning the lottery would be a very good day for most people. So would getting married. But getting divorced might also be considered a good day. You get the point: What counts as a good day depends on the person and the circumstances.

The same goes for writing. Students generally believe they know what an instructor means by "good writing," but **what counts as good writing can only be determined by examining the specific context of the writing**.

When it comes to writing, *context* is often understood as the *rhetorical situation*, which traditionally includes the writer, the subject of the writing, and the audience (see "The Rhetorical Situation"). These components determine what constitutes effective writing in a given situation. For example, a lab report that earns an A in a biology class might not qualify as a good report in a pharmaceutical company because the biology instructor and the lab supervisor in a pharmacy might have different expectations for lab reports; moreover, the purpose of the writing differs in each case. Writers have to determine the expectations for each writing situation. They must consider their audience and make decisions about content, form, and style that they believe will most effectively meet the expectations of that audience. Good writing is writing that meets the needs of the rhetorical situation—which often means meeting the specific criteria for an assignment (see "Grades vs. Good Writing").

FOCUS   The Rhetorical Situation

Writer

Subject   Audience

In classical rhetorical theory, the rhetorical situation is represented as a triangle. The metaphor of a triangle illuminates the relationships among the writer, reader, and subject matter in a particular act of writing. The writer and the audience have a specific relationship to the subject matter in the form of their shared knowledge about the subject, their opinions about it, their respective experiences with it, their stake in it, and so on. In addition, the writer has some kind of relationship to the audience, even if he or she doesn't actually know that audience. For example, a historian writing an article for a professional journal assumes that she

(Continued)

is writing as a member of the community of professional historians, with whom she shares certain values, knowledge, and expectations when it comes to the subject of the article and to history in general. To write well requires understanding your audience and its relationship to your subject—and to you—so that you can adapt your writing appropriately to achieve your goals in that rhetorical situation.

The rhetorical situation is an essential concept that helps writers better understand the social nature of writing and thus create more effective texts. Most instructors use the term to highlight the observable elements of the writing situation, especially the intended audience and the writer's purpose in addressing that audience. (In this textbook, I generally use the term in this basic way.) Some theorists, however, have illuminated how other factors can influence writing within a rhetorical situation. These factors might include the writer's identity (including race, gender, ethnicity, and so on), the cultural context of the writing, the historical moment, and the reader's background, among other such factors. These factors can shape not only what and how a writer writes but also how the writer's text is given meaning within the rhetorical situation. (See Chapter 8 for more discussion of the rhetorical situation.)

To write effectively, then, requires assessing the rhetorical situation. Writers should consider four key dimensions of the rhetorical situation to guide their decisions as they complete a writing task:

- Purpose. *Why* you are writing helps determine *what* to write and whether your writing is appropriate and effective in a particular context. A high school guidance counselor might praise your college admissions essay because it is clear and well organized, but can that essay really be considered "good" writing if it does not convince the college admissions officer to admit you to the college? And what if you are rejected by one college but accepted by another? Does that make your essay "good writing" or not? Writing can never really be evaluated without considering the writer's purpose: Are you trying to persuade an admissions officer that you are a good student? Are you attempting to solve a problem by analyzing it carefully? Do you want to share an insight about love by telling the story of a relationship? Good writing accomplishes the writer's goals in a specific rhetorical situation.

- Form or genre. Each rhetorical situation demands a specific form or genre—that is, a specific kind of writing: an argument, a report, a blog post, a multimedia presentation, a poem. And each form is governed by specific criteria regarding structure and style. A lab report will be written in a formal, objective style, whereas a blog post might have a more informal, provocative style. Writers select the appropriate form for the rhetorical situation and adapt their writing to the expectations of that form. Certain forms of writing are appropriate for specific rhetorical situations, and no one style is appropriate for every kind of writing. Understanding and using various forms for different rhetorical situations is essential for effective writing.

- **Audience.** Good writing meets the expectations of the intended audience. That college admissions essay is "good" if it resonates with the college admissions officer who reads it. To write effectively, then, requires identifying your audience, analyzing their expectations, and adapting your text to their expectations for that situation. Sometimes that's a straightforward task: You adopt a formal writing style and avoid irrelevant personal tidbits in a job application letter, assuming that such language and information would be considered inappropriate by the person reviewing job applications. Usually, though, analyzing your audience is more complicated, even when you know the audience. That's because there is always a subjective element to writing. Readers can agree on the general characteristics of good writing but disagree on whether a specific piece of writing is good. For example, they might agree that an editorial is well organized and clearly written—characteristics usually associated with good writing—but disagree about whether that editorial is "good" because one reader finds the writer's style too glib whereas another finds it engaging. Readers react to a piece of writing on the basis of their backgrounds, age, gender, experiences, and personal preferences as well as their reasons for reading that piece. Different audiences might judge the same piece of writing very differently. Writers must understand the challenge of anticipating such differences and adapt their writing as best they can to achieve their purposes with their intended audience.

- **Culture.** The dimensions of context described so far are all shaped by the broader cultural context. *Culture* can be defined as your sense of identity as it relates to your racial and ethnic backgrounds, your religious upbringing (if any), your membership in a particular social class (working class, for example), and the region where you live (for example, central Phoenix versus rural Minnesota or suburban Long Island). Not only does culture shape how readers might react to a text, but it also shapes basic aspects of a rhetorical situation such as the subject matter and language. Consider, for example, how the issue of gender equality might be understood differently by readers from traditional Muslim households as compared to readers with more secular backgrounds. Writers can't be expected to address all the complex nuances of culture that might influence a specific rhetorical situation, but to write effectively requires being sensitive to these nuances and understanding how a factor such as religious background or ethnic identity might shape readers' reactions.

In addition, the rhetorical context for any writing task includes **the medium**, which can significantly affect what and how a writer writes in a given situation (see Core Concept #3).

So the question of whether the writing is "good" is really beside the point. What matters is whether the writer accomplished his or her purposes with a specific audience in a specific rhetorical situation.

Most students understand that producing good writing and getting good grades on writing assignments aren't always the same thing. Usually, instructors have specific criteria for grading student writing based on course goals and their own views about effective writing. Different instructors can have different expectations for writing even in the same course and for the same writing assignments. Getting an A on a specific assignment doesn't necessarily mean that the student is a "good writer"; it means that the student's writing successfully met the criteria for that assignment in the view of the instructor. By the same token, getting a poor grade on an assignment doesn't mean that the student is a poor writer. Students who regularly get good grades in one subject—English, say—are sometimes frustrated when they get lower grades in another—say, psychology. But usually the lower grades mean that the student has not adjusted to the demands of writing in a different subject.

What This Means for You as a Writer

- **Consider your purpose.** What do you hope to accomplish with a specific piece of writing? Answering that question, even in a general way, can guide your writing and make it more likely that your text is effective for your rhetorical situation. For college writing assignments, avoid the temptation to think of your purpose as getting a good grade. Instead, identify your purpose in terms of the assignment and what the instructor expects you to learn or do. If your instructor doesn't provide such information, try to obtain it so that you have a clear idea of the expectations or guidelines to help determine what counts as good writing for that assignment. Have a clear sense of purpose that matches the expectations for the assignment.

- **Consider your audience.** The decisions writers make about matters like content, form, and style should be driven by their sense of what will work best for their intended audience. Even when writing for a general audience (for example, when writing a letter to the editor of a newspaper read by thousands of people with very different backgrounds and expectations), try to identify basic characteristics of your audience (e.g., readers of a regional newspaper are likely to be familiar with a local political controversy or be generally supportive of a local industry) and their likely expectations about a given subject. One of the first things you should always do when you begin a piece of writing is think carefully about your audience.

- **Consider the form of the writing.** Form does matter when it comes to determining whether a piece of writing is effective. The form of your writing will shape your decisions about style, organization, and length as well as the content of a piece. For each writing task, use an appropriate form and identify the standards for organization, style, length, and so on for whatever form of writing you are using.

- **Study good writing.** Although there is no single definition of "good writing," students can learn a lot by paying attention to what others—including their instructors—consider good writing. What counts as good writing in each of your classes? What is different or similar about how different instructors evaluate their students' writing? What is it about a specific piece of writing that certain readers like or dislike? Exploring such questions can lead to insight into what features of writing readers value in different situations.

2

Practice This Lesson

Find a short piece of writing that you think is good. (You might select one of the readings included in this textbook.) Share that piece of writing with two or three friends or classmates, and ask them their opinions of it. What do they like or dislike about the piece of writing? What did they find especially effective or ineffective about it? Ask them to explain their opinions as clearly as they can. Then write a brief reflection on what you learned about "good" writing from this activity. In your essay, compare the reactions of your friends or classmates to the piece of writing you chose, and draw your own conclusions about the role of audience in writing.

Core Concept 3 — The medium is part of the message.

Good writing depends on context, and that context includes the medium—that is, the tools or technology the writer uses and the venue for the writing. Writing a blog entry about a controversial parking policy on your campus will be different from writing an analysis of that parking policy for a business course or a letter of complaint to the campus parking office. Different media place different demands on writers. Effective writing means adjusting to the medium.

Students today are fortunate to be living in an age of astonishing technological developments that open up countless opportunities for writers. Using widely available technologies, students exchange ideas and information in ways that were unimaginable even a few years ago. They can communicate easily and widely through social media. They can use cell phones to send text messages, take and share photos, or download music and videos. They can participate in online discussions with their professors and classmates without leaving home. They can use computers to produce sophisticated documents that only a decade ago would have required a professional printing service. They can easily create multimedia presentations incorporating sound, image, and text.

These technologies are dramatically changing how we communicate and may be changing the very act of writing itself. When I create a website for one of my classes, I write differently than when I create a printed syllabus for the same class, even though most of the content is the same. I organize the website differently, because students will use it differently from the syllabus. I change some of the content, because my students don't access content on the website in the same way they find it on the syllabus. I include images as well as links to other online resources. Even my writing style changes a bit. In short, the medium changes my writing.

Think about creating a Prezi presentation as compared to, say, writing a report for an economics class. The audience and purpose might be the same, but the form and some content will differ. More to the point, the tools for composing are different. Prezi enables you to create documents that include much more than text. All these factors can influence both *what* and *how* writers write. For example, you will probably use less text in a Prezi presentation, which will affect your decisions about the content of your presentation. In addition, you will likely incorporate images and even audio and video clips into your Prezi document but not in your report. You also adjust your writing style: For the report, you will use a formal academic style and probably complex sentences and lengthy paragraphs, whereas the Prezi presentation will require more concise language, bul-

Cameron Whitman/iStockphoto.com

leted lists, and brief titles for most slides. All these differences might seem obvious, but because writers today often have several choices for the medium they will use, they need to be aware of the ways in which the medium shapes what they write and how they use writing to accomplish a specific purpose.

Although most essays, reports, and research papers assigned in college course still require students to write in conventional print formats, increasingly students are asked or choose to write in other media. More and more students are required by their instructors to participate in online discussions about course topics, use multimedia programs to make presentations, and produce videos instead of traditional papers. In each case, the medium can shape the writing task in important ways. The medium can also affect your relationship to your audience (see "Blogging vs. Writing a Newspaper Column"). Part of your task as writer, then, is to understand how different media might affect your writing and to adapt to the medium you're using.

SIDEBAR BLOGGING VS. WRITING A NEWSPAPER COLUMN

Political writer Andrew Sullivan writes a popular blog called *The Daily Dish* as well as a column for the *Sunday Times of London*. Each medium, he says, influences his writing style, choice of subject matter, and interactions with his readers. According to Sullivan, blogging "is instantly public. It transforms this most personal and retrospective of forms into a painfully public and immediate one." It also calls for "a colloquial, unfinished tone." Here's part of how he describes the differences between these two kinds of writing:

> A blogger will air a variety of thoughts or facts on any subject in no particular order other than that dictated by the passing of time. A writer will instead use time, synthesizing these thoughts, ordering them, weighing which points count more than others, seeing how his views evolved in the writing process itself, and responding to an editor's perusal of a draft or two. The result is almost always more measured, more satisfying, and more enduring than a blizzard of [blog] posts.

Source: Sullivan, Andrew. "Why I Blog." *The Atlantic*, 1 Nov. 2008. Web. 24 Apr. 2013.

What This Means for You as a Writer

- **Know the medium.** For most college writing assignments, students use computers to write conventional papers or reports. Such assignments place familiar demands on writers when it comes to organization, style, and so on. Other media, such as blogs, wikis, or Prezi, call for different strategies regarding organization, style, and even content. In many cases, what and how you write may be similar in different media, but not always. Be familiar with the characteristics of the medium in order to use it effectively for the task at hand.

- **Choose an appropriate medium.** If given a choice, consider which medium would enable you to create the most effective document for that rhetorical situation. A Prezi presentation with embedded audio and video clips might be the best choice for an assignment in which your audience will be your classmates. For other writing situations, a blog or even a Facebook page might be more effective, depending upon your message and the audience you hope to reach. Consider the medium carefully as you decide how to complete the writing task at hand in order to achieve your intended purpose with your intended audience.

- **Adjust your writing process to the medium.** All writing tasks require planning, developing ideas, drafting, revising, and editing. But those activities can differ depending upon the medium, so effective writers adjust their writing process accordingly. Obviously, you will organize a research paper for a history course differently than you would a blog entry or video script, but sometimes the differences between one medium and another aren't so obvious. For example, many students make the mistake of writing a PowerPoint or Prezi presentation as if it were a conventional report. As a result, they include too much text in the presentation and fail to take advantage of the capabilities of the medium to engage an audience visually. The outcome can be an ineffective document that may be tedious or difficult for an audience to follow. It is more effective to consider the characteristics of the medium *as you are creating your document*.

Practice This Lesson

Review several text messages or tweets that you recently sent or received. Then write a brief style guide for text messaging and/or tweeting. In your style guide, include what you believe are the main rules for writing text messages or tweets to specific audiences and for specific purposes. Include any advice that you think writers should heed when writing texts or tweets. Also include common abbreviations that writers of text messages use. Consider the different ways that people might use texts and tweets. Now compare your style guide to standard academic writing. What are the main differences and similarities between the two? What might the differences suggest about the role of the medium in writing? (Alternatively, write a brief style guide for another medium, such as Facebook or Prezi.)

Core Concept 4 — A writer must have something to say.

Having a clear, valid main point or idea is an essential element of effective writing—not only in college but also in the workplace and other settings. In most cases, college instructors expect students to have a clearly defined main point or idea that is appropriate for the assignment, no matter what kind of writing the assignment calls for. (Research shows that college instructors identify the lack of a clearly defined main idea as one of the biggest problems they see in their students' writing.) Readers expect writers to have something to say; as a writer, you should oblige them. (See "So What?")

This is not to say that the main point or idea is always simple or easily boiled down to a one-sentence summary. Much college writing is about complex subjects, and students are often required to delve into several ideas or bodies of information in a single assignment. A 20-page research paper for an information science course about how new digital technologies are affecting the music industry will include many complicated points and key ideas. So will a critique of the major arguments about the existence of God for a philosophy course. But even such involved pieces of writing, if they are to be effective, will be focused on a main idea and will convey a clear main point. That critique of major philosophical arguments about the existence of God, for example, might focus on the central point that all those arguments reflect the human desire to understand why we exist or that many philosophers equivocate when it comes to this basic question.

Remember, though, that you when you're beginning a writing assignment, you won't always know exactly what your main point will be. Sometimes the assignment will determine your main idea or point. For example, in an anthropology class you may be asked to write an essay defining *culture* as anthropologists generally understand that concept. In such a case, you will be expected to convey a main point based on what you are learning in the course about how anthropologists understand culture. Sometimes, however, identifying your main point or idea will be more complicated. A student of mine once wrote a research paper about being a vegetarian. She started

out thinking that she would write about the pros and cons of being a vegetarian to show that vegetarianism is not practical for most people. But as wrote, she learned more about the subject and began to shift her focus to the environmental destruction caused by eating meat. In the end, her main point changed; she argued in favor of a vegetarian diet as an ethical response to the environmental destruction caused by the standard American diet. As she explored her subject, she was guided by a sense of her main idea, which evolved as she wrote. Her final paper had a clearly articulated main point but not the one she started with.

FOCUS   So What?

One useful way to help identify and refine your main idea or point in a piece of writing is to ask, So what? Suppose you've written a personal narrative about your first job. So what? Why should readers care about that experience? What's in it for them? What will you say *about* that experience that might matter to others? Answering such questions can help ensure that you are telling your story in a way that conveys a *relevant* main idea or point to your readers. The same applies to just about any kind of writing you will do in college. For an economics class, you might write an analysis of tax cuts as a way to generate jobs. So what? To answer that question requires you to decide whether your analysis is relevant in the field of economics. Why analyze tax cuts now? What makes that topic something that will interest others in the field? Is your main point something that economists would consider relevant and important? Asking this question about your topic also ensures that you are thinking about your audience and connecting your main point or idea to their interests as well.

What This Means for You as a Writer

- **Identify your main idea.** Every kind of writing—even the most formulaic lab report in a biology or chemistry class—should have a main point. However, it is important to distinguish between your *subject* and your main idea or point. The subject of a biology lab report might be osmosis, but the main point might be that osmosis doesn't occur with a certain type of membrane. Similarly, for an American history course, you might write an analysis of the impact of the Civil Rights movement on race relations in the United States. Your subject would be the impact of the Civil Rights movement on race relations, but your main point would be what you have to say *about* that impact on the basis of your analysis—for example, that race relations were changed in specific ways as a result of the Civil Rights movement.

- **Have something relevant to say.** Having something to say is one thing; having something *relevant* to say is another. Whenever you write, you are participating in a conversation (see Core Concept #7), and what counts as relevant or appropriate depends on the nature of that conversation. In college, what counts as relevant usually depends on the academic subject. For example, in an analysis of the social importance of hip hop music for a sociology class, you might conclude that hip hop's popularity reflects discontent among young people of certain social and racial groups. For a paper in a music appreciation class, by contrast, you might argue that certain musical qualities, such as rhythm, account for hip hop's popularity, an argument that might be considered irrelevant in a sociology course. Part of what makes writing effective is not only having something to say but also knowing what is relevant or appropriate to say in a specific context.

- **Make sure that your main idea or point is clear to your readers.** Don't assume that because something is clear to you, it will also be clear to your readers. Sometimes, students can become so deeply immersed in their writing that they lose perspective. They think they have made their points clearly, but their readers may have trouble seeing the main idea. This is especially true when the assignment is complicated and lengthy. So it's important to revise with your audience in mind to make sure your main idea comes through clearly.

- **Don't try to say too much.** A clear main idea is partly a result of what the writer *doesn't* say. Including too many ideas or too much information in a piece of writing can obscure the main point, even if the ideas and information are relevant. Because most college writing assignments address complicated subjects, it can sometimes be a challenge for students to decide what to include in their writing. It's important to decide whether an idea or piece of information is *essential* in an assignment. If not, consider removing it.

Practice This Lesson

Post a draft of an assignment you are working on to your Facebook page or to an online forum for sharing documents, such as GoogleDocs. Ask your friends to summarize the main idea of your paper. Compare their summaries to your own sense of your main idea. Do their summaries match your idea? If not, consider revising your draft so that your main idea is clear to other readers.

Core Concept 5   A writer must support claims and assertions.

"Winters are warmer than they used to be around here."

"Most drivers don't obey speed limits."

"The average person doesn't pay attention to politics."

In casual conversation, we usually don't expect people making statements like these to provide supporting arguments or facts to prove the point. In most college writing, however, appropriate support for claims and assertions is essential.

As we saw in Chapter 1, a central purpose of writing in college is to understand and participate in conversations about the topics and questions that define each academic discipline. To participate in those conversations requires knowing how to make a case for a particular point of view and support conclusions about a relevant topic. In other words, not only must writers have something relevant to say, but they must also be able to back up what they say.

Students sometimes fail to support their ideas or assertions effectively because they are unfamiliar with the expectations for doing so in a specific academic subject. The important point to remember is that *all* academic disciplines have such standards, though different disciplines might have different conventions regarding what counts as appropriate support or evidence for a claim or assertion:

- In an English literature class, you might cite passages from a poem or quote from critical reviews of that poem to support a claim about the work of a particular poet. Your claim would be more or less persuasive depending upon whether readers consider those passages or quotations to be sufficient support for your claim.

- In economics, some kinds of statistical information carry more weight than other kinds when drawing conclusions about economic trends or developments.

- In a biochemistry lab, data from experiments might be the main evidence for conclusions or claims.

In each case, an important element of effective writing is using evidence that is considered appropriate and persuasive by readers familiar with that discipline. The same holds true outside of school, though the standards for supporting your statements tend to be less well defined and less rigorous in most popular writing than in academic or workplace writing.

FOCUS   Supporting a Claim

The need for writers to support their claims or assertions applies to any kind of writing, including newspaper and magazine articles, business proposals, legal documents, government reports, petitions, blogs, and many other kinds of documents. The following examples

(Continued)

are taken from various sources: a government report on higher education, an excerpt from a book on women and careers, and a newspaper column about fair pay for baseball stadium vendors. As you read them, notice how each writer backs up his or her statements, and consider how that support affects your reaction as a reader:

There is a troubling and persistent gap between the college attendance and graduation rates of low-income Americans and their more affluent peers. Similar gaps characterize the college attendance rates—and especially the college completion rates—of the nation's growing population of racial and ethnic minorities. While about one-third of whites have obtained bachelor's degrees by age 25–29, for example, just 18 percent of blacks and 10 percent of Latinos in the same age cohort have earned degrees by that time.

Source: U.S. Department of Education. *A Test of Leadership: Charting the Future of Higher Education.* 2006: 1. Print.

. . . .

When I arrived at college in the fall of 1987, my classmates of both genders seemed equally focused on academics. I don't remember thinking about my future career differently from the male students. I also don't remember any conversations about someday balancing work and children. My friends and I assumed that we would have both. Men and women competed openly and aggressively with one another in classes, activities, and job interviews. Just two generations removed from my grandmother, the playing field seemed to be level.

But more than twenty years after my college generation, the world has not evolved nearly as much as I believed it would. Almost all of my male classmates work in professional settings. Some of my female classmates work full-time or part-time outside the home, and just as many are stay-at-home mothers and volunteers like my mom. This mirrors the national trend. In comparison to their male counterparts, highly trained women are scaling back and dropping out of the workforce in record numbers. In turn, these diverging numbers teach institutions and mentors to invest more in men, who are statistically more likely to stay.

Source: Sandberg, Cheryl. *Lean In: Women, Work, and the Will to Lead.* New York: Knopf, 2013. 14. Print.

. . . .

The Angels are one of the richest and most successful franchises in Major League Baseball—in fact, in all pro sports.

They're valued by Forbes at $554 million (up 6% from a year ago), carry the fourth-largest player payroll in the major leagues, and at this point in the season rank fifth in per-game attendance. As they're very much in the hunt for their division lead, it's quite possible that lucrative post-season games will be added to the schedule.

So why are they trying to nickel-and-dime their stadium ushers, ticket sellers and janitors?...

The Angel Stadium employees are the worst paid among all California ballpark workers in their job classifications, the SEIU says. Here are some comparisons provided by the union, which also represents some of the workers at the other parks:

Angel Stadium ushers (the lowest paid among the affected employees) earn $11.21 an hour. At Dodger Stadium the rate is $12.77, and at the Oakland Coliseum it's $14.03. Janitors in Anaheim receive $11.50 an hour; at Chavez Ravine it's $12.31, in Oakland $17.50 and at the San Francisco Giants' AT&T Park $15.15. Ticket sellers at Angel Stadium get $13.65 an hour, but at the San Diego Padres' Petco Park they get $16.43.

Source: Hiltzik, Michael. "Angel Baseball, Paying the Little Guy Peanuts." *Los Angeles Times,* 7 Aug. 2011. Web. 25 Apr. 2013.

What This Means for You as a Writer

■ **Provide sufficient support.** First and foremost, make sure you have adequately supported your main points, claims, and assertions. Regardless of your subject or the kind of writing you are doing, readers expect you to make a case for what you have to say. Review your drafts to be sure you have provided the necessary support for your ideas.

■ **Provide relevant and appropriate support.** What counts as appropriate and effective support for a claim depends upon the subject, the academic discipline, and the rhetorical situation. The kind of evidence used to support a claim in a history course, for example, won't necessarily work in a psychology course; similarly, readers of newspaper editorials have different expectations for relevant support than, say, economists who read professional journals. As a writer, part of your task is to understand the expectations for evidence and support for the kind of writing you're doing. You should be able to anticipate readers' expectations so that the support you provide for your claims will be persuasive and appropriate for the rhetorical situation.

■ **Evaluate your sources.** Citing relevant sources to support or illustrate a point is a crucial part of effective academic writing, but not all sources are created equal. A self-help blog might not suffice as an appropriate source in an essay about teen depression for a psychology course, whereas a study published in a professional journal would. Having information from a source to support a claim or assertion is not the same as having information from a credible source. Make sure the sources you cite are not only appropriate for the writing task at hand, the course, and the rhetorical situation but also trustworthy. (Chapters 21 and 22 provide detailed discussions of finding and evaluating sources.)

Practice This Lesson

Compare how the authors of the following two passages support their statements or arguments. The first passage is from a report by an economist examining the impact of poverty on educational achievement. The second is an excerpt from an analysis by an economist about how the American public's misconceptions about economics affect their voting habits. First, write a brief summary of each passage, identifying the main assertions or points in each. Then identify the supporting evidence or arguments for each main point. What kinds of evidence or support does each author use? What sources do they use to support their points? Finally, discuss the differences and similarities in how these authors support their points. How might you explain these similarities and differences?

1 The impact of education on earnings and thus on poverty works largely through the labour market, though education can also contribute to productivity in other areas, such as peasant farming (Orazem, Glewwe & Patrinos, 2007: 5). In the labour market, higher wages for more educated people may result from higher productivity, but also perhaps from the fact that education may act as a signal of ability to employers, enabling the better educated to obtain more lucrative jobs. Middle-income countries—which frequently have well developed markets for more educated labour—are particularly likely to see the benefits of education translated into better jobs and higher wages. In Chile, for instance, between one quarter and one third of household income differences can be explained by the level of education of household heads (Ferreira & Litchfield, 1998, p. 32).

Source: van der Berg, Servaas. *Poverty and Education.* UNESCO. Paris: International Institute for Educational Planning, 2008. 3. Print.

2 Consider the case of immigration policy. Economists are vastly more optimistic about its economic effects than the general public. The Survey of Americans and Economists on the Economy asks respondents to say whether "too many immigrants" is a major, minor, or non-reason why the economy is not doing better than it is. 47% of non-economists think it is a major reason; 80% of economists think it is not a reason at all. Economists have many reasons for their contrarian position: they know that specialization and trade enrich Americans and immigrants alike; there is little evidence that immigration noticeably reduces even the wages of low-skilled Americans; and, since immigrants are largely young males, and most government programs support the old, women, and children, immigrants wind up paying more in taxes than they take in benefits.

Given what the average voter thinks about the effects of immigration, it is easy to understand why virtually every survey finds that a solid majority of

Americans wants to reduce immigration, and almost no one wants to increase immigration. Unfortunately for both Americans and potential immigrants, there is ample reason to believe that the average voter is mistaken. If policy were based on the facts, we would be debating how much to increase immigration, rather than trying to "get tough" on immigrants who are already here.

Source: Caplan, Brian. "The Myth of the Rational Voter." *Cato Unbound*, 6 Nov. 2006. Web. 25 Apr. 2013.

Core Concept 6 Purpose determines form, style, and organization in writing.

A resumé is a carefully structured record of the writer's work history and qualifications; a cover letter for a job application is a statement of the writer's suitability for the job. Each document has familiar conventions regarding content, organization, and style, which the reader (usually a person involved in hiring for the job) expects the writer to follow. A resumé shouldn't be organized in the narrative format that might be used for a report on an internship, nor should a cover letter be written in the informal style and tone of a text message or Facebook post.

The conventional forms of a resumé and cover letter serve very specific purposes for both reader and writer. These forms convey relevant information efficiently within the rhetorical situation. They are functional. That's one reason that they have become standard. Writing an effective resumé and cover letter, then, is partly a matter of knowing how to use a well-established *form* to accomplish a specific purpose (to get a job interview) within a specific rhetorical situation (the job application process). The same is true of *any* kind of writing, including academic writing. Every kind of text—a lab report, a research paper, a personal narrative, a blog entry, a proposal, a review—is governed by general expectations regarding form. (See "What Is *Form* in Writing?") A writer must be familiar with these expectations if a text is to be effective.

FOCUS   What Is *Form* in Writing?

You have probably heard teachers refer to *form* when discussing writing assignments, but what exactly is *form*? Generally, *form* refers to the way a piece of writing is organized as well as to any features that determine the shape or structure of the document, such as subheadings or footnotes. *Form* also includes the introductory and concluding sections of a piece of writing. *Form* is often used interchangeably with *genre*—that is, the kind of writing; for example, you might hear an instructor refer to *narrative* as both a form and a genre of writing. (The Merriam-Webster Dictionary defines *genre* as "a category of artistic, musical, or literary composition characterized by a particular style, form, or content.") Often, terms such as *design* and *layout* are used to describe features of documents that include visual elements, such as graphs or photographs; design and layout can therefore be considered part of the *form* of a document. In many kinds of digital texts—including multimedia documents and online media such as web pages—design, layout, and related components can be as important as the text itself. The alignment of the text or the contrast in font sizes and colors can influence how the text is received. (Chapter 20 discusses these elements of document design.)

For most traditional college writing assignments, *form* is generally used in two ways: (1) to refer to the genre, or the kind of writing, expected for that assignment (research paper, narrative, argument, and so on); and (2) to describe the relevant conventions regarding the format, style, and structure of the document for a specific kind of writing.

Notice that *purpose* is implicit in *form*. A writer uses narrative forms to tell a story, a lab report to present the results of an experiment, or an argument to support a particular point of view about a controversial issue. In this sense, it is helpful to think of the form of a piece of writing as a tool to help you achieve your purpose in a specific rhetorical situation.

For many students, however, the problem isn't learning rules or guidelines for specific kinds of writing, such as lab reports or books reports; the problem is that they learn *only* rules and guidelines for specific kinds of texts without understanding the *purposes* of those rules and guidelines and without considering the rhetorical situation—that is, how their intended readers will read that text. As a result, they tend to approach writing as a matter of creating a certain kind of document rather than adopting a specific form that serves a specific purpose for a specific rhetorical situation. Think again about a resumé. An effective resumé requires more than proper format. It must also include appropriate information about the job applicant that is presented in carefully chosen language. An employer reviews a resumé quickly, looking for specific information to determine whether the writer is a suitable candidate for the job. A resumé is designed to present that information clearly and efficiently. Knowing that, the applicant must select and present relevant information strategically so that the qualifications match the requirements of the job. A successful resumé is one in which the writer uses the form to present his or her qualifications effectively to an employer. Form follows function.

The same principle applies to the writing that students commonly do in college. The format of a lab report in chemistry, for example, enables a reader (the course instructor, other students, or perhaps other chemists) to find relevant information about a lab experiment quickly and easily. A literary analysis essay has less rigid guidelines for format, but readers still expect the writer to follow recognizable conventions when presenting an analysis of a poem or novel. The same is true of analytical writing in philosophy or psychology. The specific forms might differ, but in each case, the form serves certain purposes within the academic discipline. Writers in each discipline learn to use the form to achieve their rhetorical purposes.

Many students focus only on *form* (on the rules and guidelines for a specific kind of text) and neglect *function* (the purpose of the text within the rhetorical situation). Good writers learn the rules and guidelines for the forms of writing they do, whether those forms are business letters or lab reports or blog posts, but they also understand the *purposes* of those forms of writing and apply the rules to accomplish their purposes.

What This Means for You as a Writer

■ **Determine the appropriate form for the rhetorical situation.** In many situations, the form will be obvious: a resumé and cover letter for a job application; a lab report for a chemistry class. For most college writing assignments, instructors will specify the form of writing (argument, analysis, review, report, and so on) and provide guidelines for organization, style, length, and so on. When the form of writing isn't clear or specified, assess the rhetorical situation to determine which form would be most appropriate and effective. What is the purpose of the writing? Who is the intended audience? What form of writing would mostly likely reach that audience and communicate your message effectively? Answering these questions will help you decide on the best form of writing for the task at hand. Remember that the form is a rhetorical choice: Select the form that will enable you to accomplish your purpose with your intended audience.

■ **Become familiar with the conventions of the form of writing you are doing.** Writers should follow the conventions of well-established forms (e.g., lab reports) to meet their readers' expectations. But *there are no universal rules governing forms or genres of writing that apply to all situations.* In many instances, writers have a great deal of choice regarding organization, style, length, and similar features of a document. Digital texts such as web pages and social media offer writers great flexibility, and even very specialized forms, such as resumés and cover letters, can appear in many acceptable variations of format, style, and even content. As a writer, your task is to learn the basic expectations for a specific form of writing but to *adjust your style and tone according to the specific rhetorical situation and organize your text accordingly.* In most academic disciplines, there are established conventions for form, style, and so on, but sometimes instructors do not make those conventions clear. If you're not sure about those conventions—for example, how to organize an assignment, whether the style must be formal, and so on—ask your instructor and then draft your assignment accordingly.

■ **Pay attention to organization.** How a document is organized is one of the most important elements of form in writing. It is also one of the most challenging for many students. Studies show that college instructors consider the inability to organize texts appropriately to be one of the biggest problems in their students' writing. So it's important to learn how to organize an essay, report, or digital document appropriately for the specific academic subject. In some cases, the format will be provided. For example, lab reports usually require specific sections in a specific sequence; the same is often true of reviews of assigned readings. Following the guidelines for such assignments will essentially organize the report for you. However, other forms allow for more flexibility in organizing the text. Ask your instructor about the expectations for organizing writing assignments, and if possible, find examples of that form or genre to see how they are organized.

Practice This Lesson

Visit a job search website, such as Monster.com, and read several advertisements for jobs that interest you. Then write a resumé and cover letter for two or three such advertisements. (For this exercise, you might write a "fictional" resumé and cover letter, inventing appropriate job experiences and relevant background information, or you can use your own work experience and background.) Alter your resumé and cover letter for each job. Then consider the differences in your resumés and letters. What changes did you make? What remained the same? Why did you make those changes? Now consider what this exercise might suggest about the conventions for the form and style of resumés and cover letters.

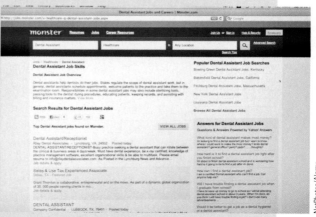

NetPhotos/Alamy

Core Concept 7 | Writing is a social activity.

We tend to think of writing as a solitary activity. The image of the writer working alone in a quiet study is a popular one. But this image is incomplete and even misleading. In fact, **writing is an inherently social act in at least three ways:**

- **First, writers write for an audience.** Unless you are writing an entry in a personal diary that you plan never to share with anyone or a note to remind yourself to take out the trash, your writing is almost always intended to be read by someone else. And as we saw earlier, your audience significantly influences what you write, how you write, and even *whether* you write. Whether the audience is a course instructor, classmates, a friend, an employer reviewing job applications, or a larger audience, writers write with their reader or readers in mind, even if they're not always aware of it. In this sense, writing is always a social transaction between writer and reader, a way to connect writers and readers. In addition, the reason for writing something usually arises from a social situation: a paper assigned in a college class; a problem in your town that prompts you to write a letter to the local newspaper; an essay commemorating an important anniversary; a blog post about a current controversy. Writing happens because our interactions with others give us reasons to write. (See "The Rhetorical Situation" on pages 29–30.)

- **Second, writers often involve others in the process of writing.** Writers regularly receive advice or suggestions from trusted readers as they develop a piece of writing. In class students might share drafts with classmates or comment on their classmates' writing. College instructors offer their students suggestions for improving their drafts. Digital media such as blogs enable writers to receive feedback from their readers; wikis allow writers to collaborate directly. In these ways, the act of writing is social rather than solitary. In fact, in business settings and in many other situations outside of school, collaborative writing is the norm, not the exception.

- **Third, the rules, conventions, and forms of writing are socially constructed.** These rules, conventions, and forms have evolved over time as a result of the way people have used writing to communicate, to share ideas and information, to learn, and to accomplish a variety of other purposes. Familiar forms of writing, such as narratives and business letters and research reports, have developed because people needed these forms in order to accomplish specific purposes in writing. Research reports, for example, help make it easier for scientists to share the results of their experiments and to collaborate in answering important scientific questions. Resumés are efficient forms for conveying information about a job candidate's qualifications. By the same token, certain rules for writing style, such as the rule that you shouldn't use the first person in scientific writing, have evolved to fit the purposes of that kind of writing. Even *what* writers choose to write about is shaped by what others have written. The topics considered relevant in, say, a course on business ethics are determined in large part by what others in that field are saying. So both *what* and *how* we write are shaped by social factors.

This idea about the social nature of writing is important because it undercuts the myth that writing ability is innate or exclusively the result of individual effort. This myth leads many students to believe that they don't have the ability to write or that writing is something that they have to figure out exclusively on their own. Neither belief is true. In fact, many social factors shape an act of writing. Individual skill and experience along with effort and motivation do matter, but many other influences outside a writer's individual control affect writing. In this sense, writing ability is as much a function of how writers respond to specific rhetorical situations, which are inherently social, as it is a result of individual skill. Your effectiveness as a writer depends not only on the effort you put into a writing task but also on the way you fit in and respond to the social situations in which you are completing that task. Learning to respond to those situations effectively begins with understanding the social nature of writing.

What This Means for You as a Writer

- **Place your writing in context.** As we saw earlier (Core Concept #2), all writing takes place in a rhetorical context, which shapes what and how the writer writes. Make it a habit to analyze the rhetorical situation for each writing task you have. Students tend to think of writing assignments as a matter of producing a certain kind of text rather than responding to the rhetorical situation. That kind of thinking can lead to ineffective writing because it tends to focus only on the *what* rather than the *why* of the writing task. Focusing instead on the rhetorical situation can help you adapt successfully to the different kinds of writing tasks you are likely to face as a college student; moreover, emphasizing the *purpose* (that is, the *why*) of your writing rather than focusing only on creating a specific kind of text (the *what*) is more likely to engage you in inquiry and learning about your subject (see Core Concept #1).

- **Remember the larger context.** Even when you write for a college course, you are part of larger conversations about important issues in specific academic fields and in the society at large. For example, an analysis of U.S. involvement in the Vietnam War for a history course can be shaped by current debates about the U.S. military efforts in Afghanistan and Iraq. Broader social, cultural, and historical factors can influence what you write, giving it a sense of immediacy and significance. Being aware of these larger contextual forces can lend a sense of relevance to your writing.

- **Seek the input of others.** Even if you do most of your writing by yourself, at some point it will be helpful to get advice or feedback from others. In your writing course, you may be required to share your writing with classmates or to revise in response to your instructor's feedback. But even if you aren't, you can benefit by asking a trusted friend, classmate, or co-worker to read your work-in-progress and consider their reactions to what you've written. Many online sites enable writers to share drafts and ideas and seek advice about their writing. Listening carefully to what others say about your writing can help you decide how to revise to make your writing more effective. (Much more discussion about getting and using feedback appears later in this textbook.)

- **Write for your readers.** When you're in the midst of creating a document and perhaps struggling with matters such as organization or style, you can easily forget that you are writing for a reader. Reminding yourself that your text is being created for an audience can often help make the task clearer. Instead of focusing on whether a sentence is correct, for example, consider how a reader might respond to it. That shift in perspective can help you keep the purpose of your writing in view and avoid getting bogged down in rules and procedures. The rules and conventions of writing are important, but following rules and conventions doesn't result in good writing if the writing does not effectively address the intended audience and meet the needs of the rhetorical situation (see Core Concept #10).

Practice This Lesson

Take a piece of writing you did recently, and, in a brief paragraph or two, explore the social aspects of that text:

1. Consider the topic. What made you decide to write about that topic? Was your decision influenced in any way by others? Is the topic of interest to others?

2. Think about your audience. What do you know about that audience? What was your purpose in writing to that audience? What kind of reaction did you hope your writing would provoke?

3. Describe any advice or input you received as you completed this piece of writing. Did you share your drafts with anyone? Did you consult an instructor or post a draft on social media?

4. Examine the broader relevance of what you wrote. Does the analysis focus on subjects that concern people other than your classmates in that course? If so, in what ways? What makes the analysis relevant to your life outside that course? What might make it relevant to others?

5. Consider what your experience with this piece of writing suggests about the social nature of writing.

Core Concept 8 — Revision is an essential part of writing.

The famous American writer Ernest Hemingway once told an interviewer that he revised the ending of his novel *A Farewell to Arms* 39 times. The interviewer asked, "Was there some technical problem there? What was it that had stumped you?" Hemingway replied, "Getting the words right."

"Getting the words right" doesn't mean fixing a "technical problem." It means writing and rewriting until the meaning is clear and the message comes through for the reader. Sometimes that requires tinkering with words and phrases, but often it means much larger changes: adding new material, deleting sentences or paragraphs, moving them from one place to another in the draft, or completely rewriting entire passages. Such rewriting is an integral part of the writing process.

Creating an effective text is rarely so simple that a writer can move from beginning to end in a straight line and then go back to "fix" things. Writing is more often a circuitous, recursive process in which the writer stops and starts, goes back, jumps ahead, changes something, adds or deletes something, starts over, and maybe even writes the ending first (as the best-selling novelist John Irving says he does). It is through this process that writers explore their subjects and make meaning for their readers. Rarely does a writer know at the beginning exactly what his or her text will finally look like or what it will say. The text and its meaning emerge from the process of writing, and revising is central to that process.

Inexperienced writers often make the mistake of believing they can get everything right in a single draft, which they can quickly review to correct minor errors. This belief arises from a lack of practice with the various kinds of sophisticated writing required in college. Eventually students learn that writing an effective text can't be squeezed into a single draft. In most college writing assignments (and most other kinds of writing as well), there are simply too many things going on for a writer to attend to all of them at once. For example, if you are struggling to describe a complicated concept in an analytical essay for a political science course, you are probably not going to be thinking much about spelling and punctuation. By the same token, if you are focused on spelling and punctuation, you are probably not thinking in depth about how to explain that concept.

Most experienced writers divide each writing assignment into manageable tasks. When writing rough drafts, they mostly ignore matters like spelling and punctuation, knowing they can address those matters later, and focus instead on larger matters: Is my paper complete? Are the ideas clearly presented? Are there unnecessary passages that can be eliminated? Is the piece well organized? Have I addressed my intended audience appropriately? Does this piece achieve my rhetorical goals? As they revise each draft, they don't just "fix" mistakes; rather, they pay attention to how well they've covered their subject, how effectively they've addressed their audience, and how successfully they've accomplished their purpose. And they "listen" to their draft to see what meaning begins to emerge from it, learning more about their subject as they write and revising accordingly. Only after they have addressed these larger issues do they focus on improving sentences and correcting errors (see "Revising vs. Editing"). Writers who understand revising in this way usually find writing easier—and their writing becomes more effective.

FOCUS   Revising vs. Editing

Inexperienced writers tend to confuse revising with editing. Revising is the process of working with a draft to make sure it explores the subject adequately, addresses the intended audience effectively, and meets the needs of the rhetorical situation. It is not simply correcting spelling or punctuation errors, adjusting capitalization, and eliminating grammar problems. Those activities are *editing*. Editing means making sure that your writing is correct and that you've followed the appropriate rules for form and usage. It is usually the very last step before a piece of writing is finished.

What This Means for You as a Writer

- **Understand revision as a process of discovery and meaning making.** The British writer E. M. Forster reputedly said, "How do I know what I think until I see what I say?" I take that to mean that Forster never began a piece of writing knowing exactly what he was thinking or what he wanted to say. He found out through the process of writing. His statement can serve as advice for all writers. If you believe that writing is simply a matter of putting down on paper what's already in your head, you'll be frustrated and your writing will never feel right. But approaching writing as a process of discovery opens up possibilities, and revising is how writers find and realize those possibilities. It is the process of making the meaning of writing clear—both to the writer and to readers. (In this sense, this Core Concept is an extension of Core Concept #1.)

- **Don't try to do everything at once.** Approach every writing task as a series of smaller tasks, each of which is more manageable than the whole. Write a *first* draft without trying to make it a *final* draft. Once you have a first draft, work on it in stages, focusing on specific issues or problems in each stage. Start with larger issues, such as whether you have developed your main idea sufficiently or supported your main argument adequately, and then revise for organization or structure. Later, revise to make sure your tone is right for your intended audience, and then attend to your word choice and sentence structure to make sure your sentences are clear. Finally, edit for correctness. Working through a draft in this way will make revision easier and more effective.

- **Leave the editing for last.** Focusing on matters like spelling and punctuation while you're writing a first draft will divert your attention away from your subject and make it harder to focus on the meaning you are trying to convey to your readers. The best way to avoid this problem is to ignore minor errors of spelling, punctuation, grammar, and usage until you are just about finished with your text. At that point, after you have worked through your drafts and developed your ideas sufficiently, you can run your spellchecker, look for punctuation mistakes, attend to usage or grammar problems, and make sure that you have followed the basic rules of standard English. Leaving the editing for last will make your writing go more smoothly.

Practice This Lesson

Using a wiki or a site like GoogleDocs, share a draft of your writing with two or three classmates or friends. Be sure to explain the assignment and purpose of your draft. Ask each person to identify the strengths and weaknesses of your draft and suggest at least one revision for each weakness. Then compare the suggestions for revision provided by your classmates or friends. In what ways do their suggestions overlap? Do they disagree about what needs to be changed in your draft? How might their suggestions help you revise so that your text will achieve your rhetorical purpose? Now consider what their various suggestions might indicate about the process of revision. (You can do this exercise without using a wiki or GoogleDocs by simply having your readers comment on the same copy of your draft.)

Core Concept 9

There is always a voice in writing, even when there isn't an I.

When I was in graduate school, I took a course in sociolinguistics. As someone who knew little about sociolinguistics, I found the assigned readings slow and difficult. But one book by a famous anthropologist named Clifford Geertz stood out. Geertz pioneered a research technique called "thick description," by which he would describe in very rich detail the rituals and common beliefs of a culture in order to understand the culture from an insider's perspective. His research profoundly influenced the fields of anthropology and sociolinguistics. What really struck me about Geertz's work, though, was his writing style. Although his work was scholarly, specialized, and theoretical, it was also engaging to read, even for someone who knew little about anthropology and sociolinguistics. When I praised Geertz's writing during a discussion with my professor, he smiled and acknowledged that students often reacted as I did to Geertz. Geertz's writing, he said, was seductive. His comment surprised me because I had never heard anyone describe academic writing as "seductive." (You can judge for yourself: An excerpt from an essay by Geertz appears in "The Voice of a Scholar.")

My professor was really talking about *voice* in writing. Voice is difficult to define, but it has to do with what we "hear" when we read a text, how the writing "sounds." Voice is partly a technical matter of word choice and sentence structure, but it is also a function of the writer's confidence and authority (or lack of it). It is that nebulous quality that makes a piece of writing distinctive. It's what enables a reader to say, "That sounds like Stephen King." Or Clifford Geertz. As I learned in my sociolinguistics course, it isn't only popular writers like Stephen King whose writing can be said to have a distinctive voice. Even the most conventional scientific research report or philosophical treatise can have a distinctive voice. In fact, a strong, distinctive voice is one of the key elements of effective writing.

FOCUS   The Voice of a Scholar

Here are the opening two paragraphs from "Thick Description: Toward an Interpretive Theory of Culture," by Clifford Geertz, one of the most influential essays ever written in the field of anthropology. As you read, consider which features of Geertz's writing contribute to his voice:

> In her book, *Philosophy in a New Key*, Susanne Langer remarks that certain ideas burst upon the intellectual landscape with a tremendous force. They resolve so many fundamental problems at once that they seem also to promise that they will resolve all fundamental problems, clarify all obscure issues. Everyone snaps them up as the open sesame of some new positive science, the conceptual center-point around which

a comprehensive system of analysis can be built. The sudden vogue of such a *grande idée*, crowding out almost everything else for a while, is due, she says, "to the fact that all sensitive and active minds turn at once to exploiting it. We try it in every connection, for every purpose, experiment with possible stretches of its strict meaning, with generalizations and derivatives."

After we have become familiar with the new idea, however, after it has become part of our general stock of theoretical concepts, our expectations are brought more into balance with its actual uses, and its excessive popularity is ended. A few zealots persist in the old key-to-the-universe view of it; but less driven thinkers settle down after a while to the problems the idea has really generated. They try to apply it and extend it where it applies and where it is capable of extension; and they desist where it does not apply or cannot be extended. It becomes, if it was, in truth, a seminal idea in the first place, a permanent and enduring part of our intellectual armory. But it no longer has the grandiose, all-promising scope, the infinite versatility of apparent application, it once had.

Source: Geertz, Clifford. "Thick Description: Toward an Interpretive Theory of Culture." *The Interpretation of Cultures: Selected Essays*. New York: Basic Books, 1973. 3. Print.

Many students believe that academic writing is supposed to be dull and "voice-less." But they're confusing voice with style or tone (see "Voice vs. Tone"). A scientific paper might be written in an objective style, but that doesn't mean it will have no voice. Moreover, college instructors usually expect students' writing to have voice, even when they don't allow students to use the first person in course writing assignments. Being aware that you have a voice in your writing and that voice is an element of effective writing is an important step toward developing your own voice in writing.

FOCUS   Voice vs. Tone

Trying to define voice in writing is like trying to describe the color blue: you can't quite say exactly what it is, but you know it when you see. Still, it's important to be able to talk about voice, because it is a key element of effective writing. It's also important to understand how voice differs from other aspects of writing, especially *tone*. If *voice* is the writer's personality that a reader "hears" in a text, then *tone* might be described as the writer's attitude in a text. The tone of a text might be emotional (angry, enthusiastic, melancholy), measured (such as in an essay in which the author wants to seem reasonable on a controversial topic), or objective or neutral (as in a scientific report). Tone is kind of like your tone of voice when speaking: you can be upset, sad, happy, uncertain, or concerned, and the tone of your voice (how loud or soft it is, how you inflect your speech, how you emphasize certain words—for

(Continued)

example, stretching out *told* in a statement like this: "I *told* you not to go outside in the rain!") reflects that mood. In writing, tone is created through word choice, sentence structure, imagery, and similar devices that convey to a reader the writer's attitude. Voice in writing, by contrast, is like the sound of your spoken voice: deep, high-pitched, nasal. It is the quality that makes your voice distinctly your own, no matter what tone you might take. In some ways, tone and voice overlap, but voice is a more fundamental characteristic of a writer, whereas tone changes depending upon the subject and the writer's feelings about it. Consider how you would describe Clifford Geertz's voice as compared to his tone (see "The Voice of a Scholar").

What This Means for You as a Writer

- **Recognize and develop your own writerly voice.** Part of every writer's challenge is to refine his or her voice and use it effectively. The first step is to recognize that you always have a voice in writing, even in academic writing. Many of the exercises in this textbook will help you develop and strengthen your voice. It takes practice. Listen for the voice in the assigned texts in your classes. Try to get a sense of what makes them distinctive. Listen for your own voice in your writing as well. When revising a draft, pay attention to the "sound" of the writing—not only to make sure your writing is clear and understandable but also to give it the "sound" of confidence and authority. Adjust your style and tone so that they are appropriate for the kind of writing you are doing (for example, avoiding vivid descriptive language in a lab report), but always strive to write with a strong voice. A strong voice is more likely to make your writing effective.

- **Remember that *all* writing has voice.** Although you might have been taught that some kinds of academic writing, such as lab reports or science research papers, should be "objective" and therefore do not have a voice, the truth is that good writing will always have voice. That does not mean you should use "creative" language in every kind of writing you do. It *does* mean that you should follow the appropriate conventions for style and tone and use them as effectively as you can to bring out your own distinctive voice.

- **Don't fake it.** If you are unsure of your main idea or if you are confused about the assignment you are working on, your writerly voice is likely to reflect that. Often when students are unfamiliar with a subject or learning something for the first time, they try to "sound" academic by writing convoluted sentences, using inflated language, or substituting wordy phrases for more common words (for example, using "due to the fact that" instead of "because"). Such strategies usually make the writing less clear and weaken the writer's voice. And it's usually easy for an instructor to see that students are "padding" their writing because they aren't sure they have anything valid to say or they're confused about the assignment or subject (as Calvin does in the comic strip). So one way to have a strong, effective voice is to explore your subject sufficiently (Core Concept #1), do appropriate research if necessary (Core Concept #5), and have a clear sense of your main idea or argument (see Core Concept #4).

Practice This Lesson

Compare the three excerpts below. Each excerpt is the introductory passage from an academic article published in a scholarly journal. How would you describe the voice in each passage? What differences and similarities do you see in the voices of these passages? What specific features of the writing do you think accounts for the voice in each passage (e.g., word choice, sentence structure, use of first or third person, and so on)? Which do you like best? Why? What do you think your reaction to these passages suggests about voice in writing?

1 Writing represents a unique mode of learning—not merely valuable, not merely special, but unique. That will be my contention in this paper. The thesis is straightforward. Writing serves learning uniquely because writing as process-and-product possesses a cluster of attributes that correspond uniquely to certain powerful learning strategies.

Although the notion is clearly debatable, it is scarcely a private belief. Some of the most distinguished contemporary psychologists have at least implied such a role for writing as heuristic. Lev Vygotsky, A. R. Luria, and Jerome Bruner, for example, have all pointed out that higher cognitive functions, such as analysis and synthesis, seem to develop most fully only with the support system of verbal language—particularly, it seems, of written language. Some of their arguments and evidence will be incorporated here.

Here I have a prior purpose: to describe as tellingly as possible *how* writing uniquely corresponds to certain powerful learning strategies. Making such a case for the uniqueness of writing should logically and theoretically involve establishing many contrasts, distinctions between (1) writing and all other verbal languaging processes—listening, reading, and especially talking; (2) writing and all other forms of composing, such as composing a painting, a symphony, a dance, a film, a building; and (3) composing in words and composing in the two other major graphic symbol systems of mathematical equations and scientific formulae. For the purposes of this paper, the task is simpler, since most students

(Continued)

Core Concept 9 There is always a voice in writing, even when there isn't an I **55** are not permitted by most curricula to discover the values of composing, say, in dance, or even in film; and most students are not sophisticated enough to create, to originate formulations, using the highly abstruse symbol system of equations and formulae.

Source: Emig, Janet. "Writing as a Mode of Learning." *College Composition and Communication* 28.2 (1977): 122. Print.

2 Over the past two decades, the presence of computers in schools has increased rapidly. While schools had one computer for every 125 students in 1983, they had one for every 9 students in 1995, one for every 6 students in 1998, and one for every 4.2 students in 2001 (Glennan & Melmed, 1996; Market Data Retrieval, 1999, 2001). Today, some states, such as South Dakota, report a student to computer ratio of 2:1 (Bennett, 2002).

Just as the availability of computers in schools has increased, their use has also increased. A national survey of teachers indicates that in 1998, 50 percent of K–12 teachers had students use word processors, 36 percent had them use CD ROMS, and 29 percent had them use the World Wide Web (Becker, 1999). More recent national data indicates that 75 percent of elementary school-aged students and 85 percent of middle and high school-aged students use a computer in school (U.S. Department of Commerce, 2002). Today, the most common educational use of computers by students is for word processing (Becker, 1999; inTASC, 2003). Given that, it is logical to ask: Do computers have a positive effect on students' writing process and quality of writing they produce?

As is described more fully below, the study presented here employs meta-analytic techniques, commonly used in fields of medicine and economics, to integrate the findings of studies conducted between 1992–2002. This research synthesis allows educators, administrators, policymakers, and others to more fully capitalize on the most recent findings regarding the impact of word processing on students' writing.

Source: Goldberg, Amie, Michael Russell, and Abigail Cook, "The Effect of Computers on Student Writing: A Meta-analysis of Studies from 1992 to 2002." *The Journal of Technology, Learning, and Assessment* 2.1 (2003): 3. Print.

3 Cognitive, or executive, control refers to the ability to coordinate thought and action and direct it toward obtaining goals. It is needed to overcome local considerations, plan and orchestrate complex sequences of behavior, and prioritize goals and sub-goals. Simply stated, you do not need executive control to grab a beer, but you will need it to finish college.

Executive control contrasts with automatic forms of brain processing. Many of our behaviors are direct reactions to our immediate environment that do not tax executive control. If someone throws a baseball toward our face, we reflexively duck out of the way. We have not necessarily willed this behavior; it seems as if our body reacts and then our mind "catches up" and realizes what has happened. Evolution has wired many of these reflexive, automatic processes into our nervous systems. However, others can be acquired through practice because learning mechanisms gradually and thoroughly stamp in highly familiar behaviors.

For example, consider a daily walk to work. If the route is highly familiar and if traffic is light, our mind can wander. Before we know it, we may have gone a considerable distance and negotiated street crossings and turns with little awareness of having done so. In these cases, the control of our behavior occurs in a "bottom-up" fashion: it is determined largely by the nature of the sensory stimuli and their strong associations with certain behavioral responses. In neural terms, they are dependent on the correct sensory conditions triggering activity in well-established neural pathways.

Source: Miller, E. K., and J. D. Wallis. "Executive Function and Higher Order Cognition: Definition and Neural Substrates." *Encyclopedia of Neuroscience*. Vol. 4. 2009. Print.

Core Concept 10 Good writing means more than good grammar.

When I was a brand-new professor of English, I submitted a grant proposal in which I misspelled the name of Christopher Columbus in the very first sentence. (I spelled it "Columbis.") I learned of the error only after one of the members of the review committee told me about it. It was extremely embarrassing, but it wasn't disastrous. My proposal was selected as a finalist for the grant competition. The reviewers obviously saw the error, but they nevertheless selected my proposal. Why? Despite such a blatant error, they considered the proposal good enough to make the first cut in the grant competition. The error didn't mean that the writing was poor.

I sometimes tell this story to illustrate the point that a correct paper isn't necessarily an effective one—or that an incorrect paper isn't necessarily *ineffective*. Following the rules and conventions of standard written English is important, but good writing is much more than good grammar. A perfectly correct essay can also be a perfectly lousy piece of writing if it does not fulfill the expectations of the task and meet the needs of the intended audience. An error-free history paper won't earn a good grade if it does not meet the instructor's guidelines for historical analysis or if it includes erroneous information and unsupported assertions. By the same token, a brilliant historical analysis that also includes numerous misspelled words, punctuation errors, inappropriate word choice, and convoluted sentences is not likely to earn an A+. Those errors will probably distract your instructor and might even suggest that you were unwilling to devote adequate time and attention to the assignment. For better or worse, "grammar," good or bad, makes an impression upon readers, even if it is only one element of effective writing.

As Chapter 26 explains, student writers tend to make the same errors, and for most students, errors of spelling, punctuation, and usage are not a very serious problem. Nevertheless, many students spend too much time worrying about correctness and far too little time attending to larger issues that make writing effective. As this chapter makes clear, effective writing encompasses many things, "good grammar" among them. It is essential that you apply the rules of usage and follow the conventions of written English, because those rules are part of what makes writing effective. However, if you learn the rules and conventions of standard written English but little else about writing, you will most likely not be a very good writer.

What This Means for You as a Writer

- **Learn and apply the appropriate rules for standard written English.** By the time they reach college, most students know most of what they need to know about the rules for correct writing. They may not always be able to explain those rules, but they have learned many of them intuitively. So recognize that you already know a great deal about the rules for correct writing, but also be aware of what you don't know. When you're unsure about a matter of usage or punctuation, consult your instructor, your campus writing center, an online writing resource, or a textbook such as this one.

- **Recognize that few rules apply in every instance.** Many of the rules for correct writing are clear and well established, but some aren't. There is often disagreement among grammarians and writing teachers about specific points of usage and style. As a writer, you have to be aware that such differences occur and that the rhetorical context determines what rules apply. Learn the accepted conventions for the kind of writing you are doing. Remember, too, that these conventions can change from one academic subject to another, so make it a point to become familiar with the conventions for writing in the different courses you take.

- **Always edit your writing for correctness.** Don't be obsessive about minor errors as you're working through early drafts of a piece of writing (see Core Concept #8), but make sure you edit before submitting your work. It usually doesn't take very long to review your finished drafts for minor errors, to reread them for clarity, and to make corrections to words or sentences, and it doesn't take much effort to run the spellchecker on your word processing program. Editing for minor problems and ensuring that you have followed the conventions of standard English should become a regular part of your writing process.

- **Focus on the errors you regularly make.** Identify the mistakes you regularly make, and review the appropriate rule for each one. For example, maybe you often forget to include a comma after an introductory clause (e.g., "When he woke up the next morning, his wallet and keys were missing."). If you're not sure about the rule, talk to your writing instructor or someone at your campus writing center, or review Chapter 26 of this textbook. Studies show that most students tend to make the same kinds of minor errors. If you focus attention on the errors you tend to make, you will learn to look for these errors when you edit your assignments. Eventually, most of those errors will disappear from your writing.

Practice This Lesson

Make a list of the five most common errors of spelling, punctuation, or usage that you tend to make. For each one, consult Chapter 26 to identify the appropriate rule. (You may have to review several past writing assignments to develop this list of common errors.) Use this list when you edit your future writing assignments.

The Ten Core Concepts in Action

3

WRITING GROWS OUT OF A NEED to answer a question, make a decision, or solve a problem. For college students, that need is usually created by course assignments—but not always. Sometimes it grows out of a situation that calls for writing of some kind:

- a problem on your campus that affects you
- a newspaper editorial that you want to respond to
- an event that raises questions for members of your community
- an important anniversary that evokes memories you want to share with others
- a controversial online video that you want to comment on
- a project that you believe might improve your workplace

In each of these examples, circumstances prompt you to create a document intended for a specific audience for a specific purpose. In other words, the need to write grows out of a rhetorical situation (see page 29 in Chapter 2). Sometimes, too, writing grows out of a writer's simple desire to understand something better.

Whatever your motivation for writing, this chapter takes you through the process of creating an effective text for your specific rhetorical situation:

- If your assignment specifies a topic and genre, follow the guidelines your instructor has provided and adjust each of the following steps to fit those guidelines.
- If your assignment doesn't specify a topic or genre and gives you free choice about what to write, develop a project that enables you to answer a question, make a decision, or solve a problem on an issue that interests you; develop your project so that it fits your specific rhetorical situation.

This chapter uses the Ten Core Concepts described in Chapter 2 to help you identify a worthy topic, explore that topic thoroughly, and write an effective document on that topic that is appropriate for your rhetorical situation.

Think of this chapter as a guide rather than a set of rigid instructions for completing a writing project. Parts II, III, and IV of this textbook provide specific guidance for analytical, narrative, and argumentative writing. The chapters in those parts examine different genres in detail; this chapter shows how to put the ten Core Concepts into action. Use this chapter in conjunction with the chapters in Parts II, III, and IV to guide you through the process of effective writing for a specific kind of text.

The ten steps in this chapter correspond to the Ten Core Concepts described in Chapter 2. As you work through this chapter, you might find that you do not need to complete each step or that you need to repeat a step. You might also move through the steps out of sequence. Some steps may take a few moments to complete; others will take much longer. That's OK. Writing is a process of exploration that can lead to insights into complicated issues that matter for you and your readers, and the process will not be exactly the same for every writer or writing task. So use this chapter to learn about your topic and create a project that engages your readers.

Step 1 | Discover and explore a topic.

Begin with a Question

Identify something you are wondering about, something that intrigues or puzzles you, something that calls for a decision or solution.

If your assignment specifies a topic	If your assignment does not specify a topic
Review the guidelines to get a sense of appropriate topics.	Think about problems, issues, or questions that you have been puzzling about.
What intrigues or puzzles you about the subject of this assignment?	Is there a question or issue that you want to address for some reason?
What questions or issues might be appropriate for this assignment?	Are you facing a situation that requires you to understand something better?
Make a list of three or four **questions** that most interest you.	Make a list of three or four **questions** that most interest you.

Explore Your Questions

Write a brief paragraph for each question, explaining why it might be worth exploring for this project. In each paragraph:

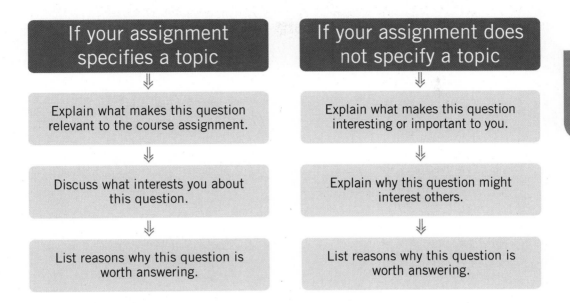

If your assignment specifies a topic
⇓
Explain what makes this question relevant to the course assignment.
⇓
Discuss what interests you about this question.
⇓
List reasons why this question is worth answering.

If your assignment does not specify a topic
⇓
Explain what makes this question interesting or important to you.
⇓
Explain why this question might interest others.
⇓
List reasons why this question is worth answering.

Select a Working Topic

Review your paragraphs and select one of the questions from your list as your working topic for your project. (This question might change as you learn more about your topic, but for now it is the question that will serve as your working topic.)

Identify What You Know About Your Topic

Jot down what you already know about your working topic.

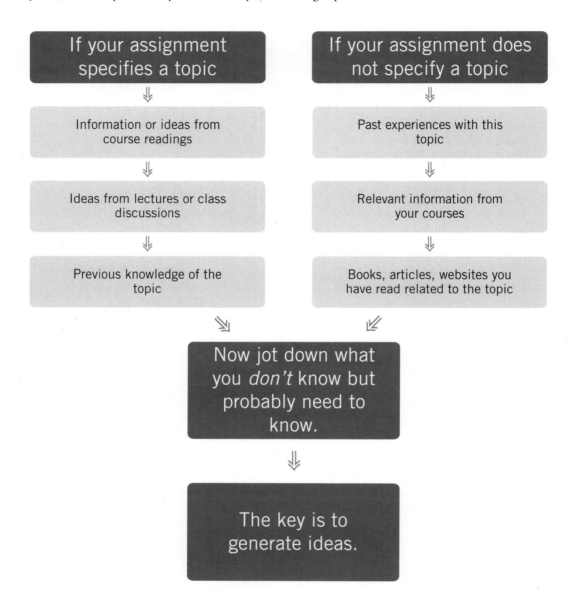

If your assignment specifies a topic	If your assignment does not specify a topic
⇓	⇓
Information or ideas from course readings	Past experiences with this topic
⇓	⇓
Ideas from lectures or class discussions	Relevant information from your courses
⇓	⇓
Previous knowledge of the topic	Books, articles, websites you have read related to the topic

Now jot down what you *don't* know but probably need to know.

⇓

The key is to generate ideas.

Adjust Your Question

Review your notes to determine whether you should amend your question and working topic.

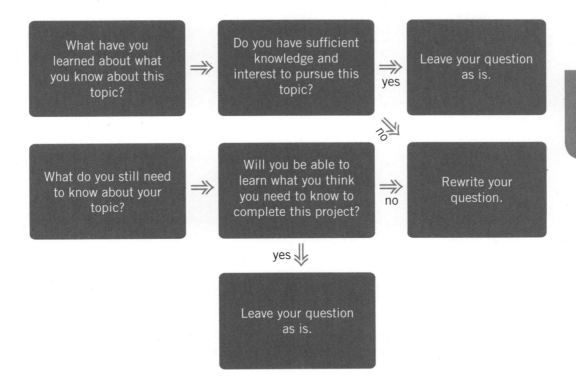

Use Technology to Generate Ideas and Gather Information

Explore your question with digital tools.

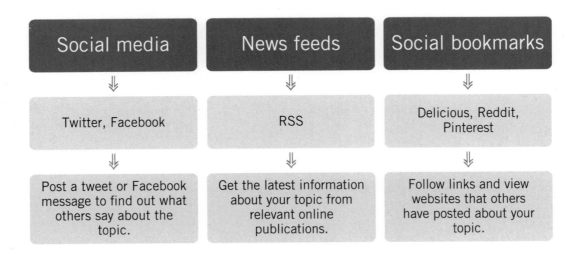

Hearing what others say or think about a topic can help you generate ideas and identify questions you will need to address. These tools provide a fast and easy way to tap into ideas, information, and conversations about your topic.

Write a Discovery Draft

A discovery draft is focused but informal and open-ended writing intended to help you explore your topic. It is not a first or rough draft, nor is it freewriting, in which you just write whatever comes to mind. It is a more purposeful draft to help you generate material you can develop into a complete draft. A discovery draft can be a continuous discussion of your topic, or it can be pieces and fragments, some of which are more developed than others.

Do

Begin writing, using ideas and information you have.

Write as much as you can about your topic.

Make notes about questions to be explored later.

Keep writing until you have nothing more to write about your topic.

Don't

Try to write a finished essay.

Focus on organization or coherence.

Worry about the quality of your writing.

Leave anything out at this stage.

You will eventually use your discovery draft to develop a complete draft of your project, but for now you are exploring your topic and identifying possibilities.

Identify Your Audience

Briefly describe the intended audience for your project.

Describe who you expect or hope will read your project.

If your assignment specifies an audience, describe that audience.	If you have no assignment, identify the audience you would most like to reach.

Be as specific as possible.

If your assignment does not specify an audience, assume that your instructor and/or your classmates are your audience.	If your intended audience is general (e.g., readers of a national newspaper like *USA Today* or people interested in politics), say so. If you are writing for a more specialized audience (e.g., students on your campus, people who snowboard, or video gamers), identify that audience as clearly as you can.

Explore your audience.

Jot down your sense of your instructor's expectations for this assignment. Refer to the assignment guidelines to understand additional audience expectations for the assignment.	Anticipate what your intended audience might know about your topic. Write down what you think they will expect from your project. Consider relevant special circumstances (e.g., video gamers will likely be familiar with online gaming sites).

Consider the Context

Examine how the specific circumstances under which you are writing might influence your project.

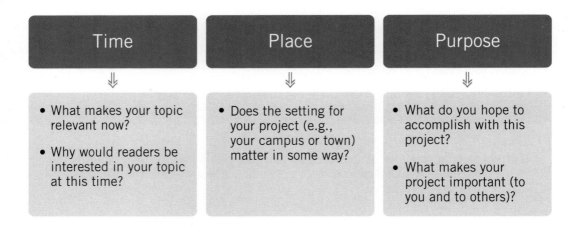

Time

- What makes your topic relevant now?
- Why would readers be interested in your topic at this time?

Place

- Does the setting for your project (e.g., your campus or town) matter in some way?

Purpose

- What do you hope to accomplish with this project?
- What makes your project important (to you and to others)?

Review Your Question

Adjust the question you developed for Step #1 in view of what you have learned about your audience and the context for your project.

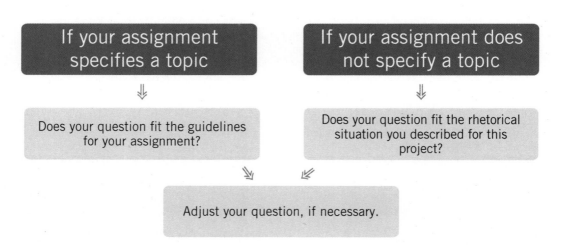

If your assignment specifies a topic

Does your question fit the guidelines for your assignment?

If your assignment does not specify a topic

Does your question fit the rhetorical situation you described for this project?

Adjust your question, if necessary.

Develop Your Discovery Draft

Review your discovery draft in light of what you have learned about your audience and your rhetorical situation.

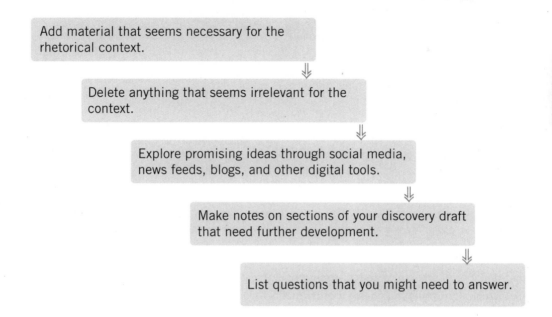

Add material that seems necessary for the rhetorical context.

Delete anything that seems irrelevant for the context.

Explore promising ideas through social media, news feeds, blogs, and other digital tools.

Make notes on sections of your discovery draft that need further development.

List questions that you might need to answer.

Remember that at this point you are still exploring your topic in a way that will make it effective for your audience.

Step 3   Select an appropriate medium.

Most college assignments call for conventional academic essays, which are usually submitted either electronically (as a Word or PDF file) or in hard copy. In such cases, the medium is traditional print text, and you should follow appropriate conventions for standard academic writing. (Assignments that call for conventional writing for non-academic forums, such as newspapers, magazines, or newsletters, might follow slightly different conventions but are still print texts.) However, writers today have access to many different media, including digital and online media.

Select a Medium

Identify a medium that would be appropriate for your rhetorical context.

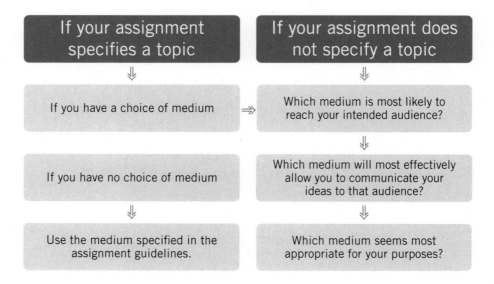

A traditional print text (an essay, report, proposal, research paper) might be the best way to achieve your rhetorical purpose, but consider other media through which you can present your ideas:

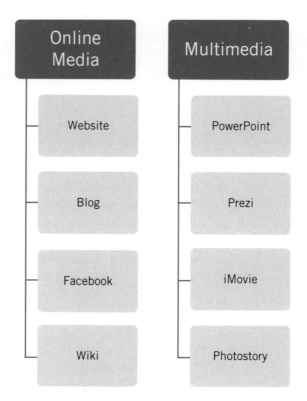

Consider How the Medium Might Shape Your Project

Your choice of medium can significantly affect the way you present your ideas to your audience.

Structure	• Does this medium require you to organize your project in a specific way? • What options for structuring your project does this medium provide?
Length	• Does this medium place any length restrictions on your project? (For example, an essay written to be read aloud on the radio may need to be shorter than a traditional print essay.) • If so, will these restrictions compromise the depth of your exploration of your topic?
Image and sound	• Does this medium enable you to incorporate sound and/or visual elements? • If so, what kinds of images and/or sound are appropriate? • How will you incorporate these elements?
Style	• What are the expectations for writing style in this medium? • Will you have to adopt any specific stylistic conventions for this medium? (For example, blogs usually call for shorter sections, or "chunks," of texts to help readers scroll more easily through the post.)

Return to your Discovery Draft to make notes about how your choice of medium might affect the development of your project.

Step 4   Have something to say.

At this point, you have a topic, but you must determine what you will *say* about that topic. What will be the main point of your project?

Revisit Your Main Question

Reread your Discovery Draft, and then return to the question you developed for Step #1:

If your assignment specifies a topic	**If your assignment does not specify a topic**
How does your main question relate to the subject of the course? (For example, if you are analyzing the causes of high rates of suicide among teens in the U.S. for a psychology class, consider what makes this question relevant in the field of psychology.)	**How does your question relate to larger conversations about your subject?** (For example, a question about whether charter schools help minority students improve their chances of going to college is part of a longstanding debate about education reform in the U.S.)
Consider these questions: • In what ways is your topic important in this academic field? • How will your project contribute to an understanding of this topic? • What will your project say to your readers about this topic?	**Consider these questions:** • Why is your topic important? What makes it relevant now? • Why might your project contribute to ongoing discussions about this issue? • Why would your intended audience find your topic interesting or important?

Write a Guiding Thesis Statement

On the basis of your notes from Step 1, write a brief paragraph explaining your main point and the purpose of your project as you understand it at this point. Include your main question and a brief explanation of why it is important to your intended audience.

This paragraph is your Guiding Thesis Statement, a working summary of the main idea for your project. Your Guiding Thesis Statement may change as you develop your project, but you can use it to guide your work as you explore your topic.

Revise your Guiding Thesis Statement as often as necessary as you gain a clearer sense of the main point of your project.

Review Your Discovery Draft

Use your Guiding Thesis Statement to review your discovery draft:

Identify ideas, issues, or questions that seem important to your main point as described in your Guiding Thesis Statement:
- Which sections of your discovery draft seem especially important to your main point?
- Which sections need more development, given your main point?

Identify gaps in your Discovery Draft:
- Does anything seem to be missing that is relevant to your main point?
- What questions about your topic remain to be addressed?
- What more do you need to know about your topic to address the main point described in your Guiding Thesis Statement?

Consider the Rhetorical Situation:
- Is your main point relevant to your intended audience?
- Does your Discovery Draft present your main point in a way that addresses your intended audience?
- What might be missing from your draft that your audience will expect?

Revise Your Guiding Thesis Statement

On the basis of your review of your Discovery Draft, revise your Guiding Thesis Statement so that it clearly explains the nature and purpose of your project and accounts for audience expectations. You now have a working statement of the main point of your project.

Step 5 Back up what you say.

Most college writing assignments require students to support their claims, assertions, and positions. Even in narrative writing, writers provide support (often in the form of anecdotes or descriptions rather than factual evidence) for the ideas or events they describe. As you develop your project and learn about your topic, be sure to support your main points or claims.

Remember: At this point in the process, you are still exploring your topic, developing your ideas, and gathering information. "Backing up what you say" is as much a process of learning and exploring as it is a matter of identifying evidence or support, so be open to possibilities.

Begin by referring back to your Guiding Thesis Statement to remind yourself of your main question and the main purpose of your project.

Identify Your Main Claims or Assertions

On the basis of your Guiding Thesis Statement, identify and explore the major points you will make in support of your main point.

List your major claims or assertions.

| List any claims or assertions that seem relevant at this stage. | Be as specific as possible, knowing you will adjust your list as you explore your topic. |

⇓

Explore each claim or assertion.

| Write a sentence explaining why each claim is relevant to your main point. | Write a sentence describing what you need to know to support each claim or assertion. |

⇓

Prioritize your list of claims or assertions.

| Which claims or assertions seem most important? | Which claims or assertions might be secondary to other claims or assertions? |

⇓

Identify potential sources.

| What kinds of information or evidence do you need to support your claims or assertions? | Where might you find the information or evidence you need? (See Chapter 21.) |

⇓

Begin exploring each claim.

| Develop your ideas for each major claim or assertion. | Find information or evidence to support each claim or assertion. |

Review Your Discovery Draft

Return to your Discovery Draft and make sure it includes the major claims and assertions you have identified.

Write a Complete Draft

At this point, you should be ready to write a draft of your project. If so, write as complete a draft as you can based on what you have learned so far about your topic and using the information you have gathered for this exercise. Use your Discovery Draft as the basis for your complete draft, or simply refer to your Discovery Draft for ideas to be included in your complete draft.

If you are ready to write a draft

Keep in mind that this is a rough draft.

Make your draft as complete as possible, but don't worry about making it polished.

If you are not ready to write a draft

Write whatever portions of your draft that you feel ready to write.

Continue exploring your topic, and move on to Step 6.

Step 6 | Establish a form and structure for your project.

The form of your project should present your ideas and information clearly and effectively to your intended audience. In deciding on an appropriate form for your project, consider the following aspects.

Genre	• Follow the conventions governing form for the genre (argument, analysis, narrative) in which you are writing. • Parts II, III, and IV of this textbook will guide you in developing a proper form for specific genres.

Medium	• The medium can shape the form and even the content of your project. • Multimedia and online projects will influence how you structure your project.

Rhetorical situation	• The form of a project will be shaped in part by your sense of your intended audience. • The form will also be influenced by your sense of the purpose of your project.

If you have already written your rough draft, use this exercise to determine whether your draft is organized effectively.

Identify the Main Parts of Your Project

Review your rough draft or use your Discovery Draft as well as your notes to make a list of the main sections or components of your project.

Develop an Outline

Use your list to create a basic outline for your project (refer to chapters in Parts II, III, and IV for more detailed guidance on organizing specific kinds of texts).

If you have written a rough draft

Create an outline on the basis of your draft.

Make sure to include the main sections from your list.

If you have not yet written a rough draft

Use your Discovery Draft and your list to develop an outline.

Make your outline as detailed or general as is helpful at this point.

Refine Your Outline

Review your outline to determine whether it effectively meets the needs of your rhetorical situation.

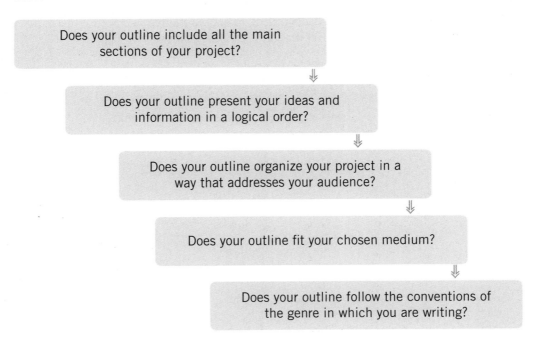

Does your outline include all the main sections of your project?

Does your outline present your ideas and information in a logical order?

Does your outline organize your project in a way that addresses your audience?

Does your outline fit your chosen medium?

Does your outline follow the conventions of the genre in which you are writing?

Write or Revise Your Draft

Using your outline as a guide, write a rough draft of your project or revise the rough draft you have already written to strengthen the structure of your project.

Step 7 Get feedback.

Even writers who work alone are writing in a social context, and their writing is ultimately influenced by others. So it makes sense at this point to involve others in the process to help you determine whether your draft is effective and to identify potential problems to address in your revisions. The goal is to get a sense of whether your project is achieving its purpose with readers and to help you decide which revisions to make.

It helps to have one or more trusted readers—a friend, roommate, co-worker, or classmate—who can respond to your draft. Your course instructor might specify a procedure for sharing your draft with classmates. If so, use that procedure. You can also supplement your instructor's procedure and obtain additional advice for revising your essay.

Use technology to help get the feedback you need.

Post your draft on a blog or Facebook to invite responses.

Use a wiki or GoogleDocs to enable trusted readers to offer reactions and suggestions.

Join a web-based discussion forum that is relevant to your topic to seek comments.

Ask Your Readers to Respond to Your Draft

Use the following sets of questions to guide your readers' responses.

Topic

- Is the topic interesting and relevant?
- Is the purpose of the project clear? Is it worthwhile?
- Is the main point or idea clear? Does the writer have something to say?
- Does the draft sufficiently explore the topic? Is anything missing?
- Are the main claims or assertions adequately supported?

Medium and Form

- Does the medium work for this topic? Does it address the intended audience effectively? Does the writer take advantage of the capabilities of the medium?
- Is the project organized effectively?
- Does the introduction sufficiently introduce the topic and main ideas? Does it draw readers into the project?
- Does the conclusion adequately sum up the project? Does it emphasize the writer's main ideas?

Style

- Is the writing generally clear and readable?
- Are there passages that are confusing or difficult to follow?
- Are there any problems with usage or grammar that impede meaning?
- Does the writer's voice come through clearly and effectively?

In addition, ask your readers to jot down any other questions they have about your draft. **Remember** that the more specific your readers' comments, the more useful they are likely to be, so ask your readers to elaborate on their responses to specific sections of your draft.

Identify Common Themes in Your Readers' Responses

If you had more than one person read your draft, look for similarities in their responses.

If your readers agree that something in your draft is working well →	That part of your draft likely needs little (if any) revision.
If your readers all cite the same problems →	You should probably address those problems in your revisions.

If you had only one reader respond to your draft, pay special attention to that reader's strongest reactions.

Review Disagreements Among Your Readers

Different readers might have different reactions to your project. Such disagreements might indicate sections of your draft that need revision. Consider disagreements among your readers as you decide upon specific revisions.

If your readers disagree about specific aspects of your draft	• Review the readers' comments to understand their disagreements. • Consider each reader's perspective about that part of your draft. • Review that part of your draft carefully, and consider each reader's suggestions for revising it.
If you agree with one reader and disagree with others	• Consider why you agree or disagree. • Review the relevant sections of your draft to see whether your readers' comments might have changed your mind. • If possible, ask readers to explain or clarify their reactions.

On the basis of your review of your readers' responses to your draft, make notes about possible revisions you should make.

Remember that *you* must decide which revisions are best, based on your assessment of the rhetorical situation and your own purposes for your project.

Step 8 Revise.

Revision is part of the process of discovery and learning. It is also a rhetorical process by which you craft your project so that it effectively addresses your intended audience and achieves your rhetorical purposes. As you revise, keep in mind that you will continue to learn about your topic even as you improve your draft.

As you proceed, refer to your notes for Step #7 as well as to your Guiding Thesis Statement to decide on specific revisions.

Focus First on Content

Review your draft to determine whether you have sufficiently developed your ideas and effectively made your main point.

Main idea	• Do you have something to say in this project? • Does your point come through clearly? • Is the relevance of your topic evident?
Focus	• Does your project stay focused on your main idea? • Do you get off track at any point? If so, should you rewrite or eliminate those sections?
Development	• Have you developed your ideas sufficiently? Do any sections of your outline need further development? • Have you presented enough information to support your claims or assertions? • Have you gone into too much detail in any sections? If so, should you condense or eliminate those sections?

Focus Next on Form

Reread your revised draft from beginning to end to determine whether you need to reorganize it or strengthen its form or structure (refer to your outline and your notes from Step #6).

Organization	<ul><li>Have you presented your ideas in a sensible order?</li><li>Should any section be moved so your ideas are more logically presented to your readers?</li><li>Can any sections be combined to make your project tighter?</li></ul>
Transitions	<ul><li>Do you make clear transitions between the main sections of your project?</li><li>Do your transitions help your readers follow your discussion?</li><li>Are any transitions confusing or missing?</li></ul>
Medium	<ul><li>Have you followed the conventions for your medium?</li><li>If you are working in a digital medium, have you structured your project so readers/viewers can follow it easily?</li><li>For multimedia projects, have you placed visual or audio elements effectively?</li></ul>

Consider Your Rhetorical Situation

Review your revised draft to be sure you have addressed your intended audience effectively and fulfilled the needs of your rhetorical situation. Use the questions from Step #2 to guide your review of your draft. Revise your draft to address any issues related to your rhetorical situation.

Revisit Your Introduction and Conclusion

Return to your introduction and conclusion to make sure they effectively introduce and conclude your project in view of your rhetorical situation.

Introduction	• Does your introduction describe your topic clearly? • Does it draw your readers into your project? • Does it provide a compelling reason for your intended audience to read your project? • Does it convey the purpose of your project? • Does it place your topic in proper context?

Conclusion	• Does your conclusion effectively sum up the main idea of your project? • Does it emphasize your main points? • Does it leave your readers with a sense that you have fulfilled the purpose of your project?

At this point, you should have a revised draft that is close to finished. All the main pieces should be in place: a focused, sufficiently developed project that presents your main ideas effectively and clearly to your intended audience; a sound structure; an engaging introduction; and an effective conclusion.

Step 9   Strengthen your voice.

No matter the rhetorical situation, effective writing has a strong voice that reflects the writer's command of his or her subject matter. Your voice will give your readers confidence that your project is worth reading.

Consider Your Rhetorical Context

Review the rhetorical context for your project to gain a better sense of how your voice might meet the expectations of your readers and help you achieve your purpose. Review your draft to identify passages where you might adjust your voice to fit your rhetorical situation.

Are there any specific expectations or restrictions regarding voice, tone, and writing style in this rhetorical context? (For example, a business proposal should not be written in a conversational style.)

Do your voice, tone, and writing style fit the form or genre of your project? (For example, a lab report should have an objective voice and formal writing style.)

Does your draft speak with a voice that fits your rhetorical context? If not, what changes should you make so your voice and writing style fit the rhetorical context?

Consider Whether You Should Use the First Person

Determine whether the use of first person is appropriate for this project:

| If first person is appropriate | Decide whether using the first person will make your project more effective. | If so, revise accordingly. |

| If first person is inappropriate | Review your draft to eliminate any uses of "I." |

Strengthen Your Voice

Reread your draft to "listen to" your voice, and consider the following questions to guide your revisions.

> Does your voice sound authoritative and confident? Does it convey a sense that your project is valid and worthwhile?

> Is your voice consistent throughout your project? If not, where is it weakest? What changes might make it stronger in those sections?

At this stage, assume that your project is complete and appropriately structured and try to ignore those aspects of your project as you review your draft for voice and style.

Step 10 Make it correct.

Edit your draft for clarity and correctness.

| Make your sentences clear. | • Revise sentences that are unclear.
• Eliminate wordiness.
• Restructure sentences that are difficult to follow.
• Refer to Chapter 19 for advice on style. |

| Use sources correctly. | • Integrate source material smoothly into your prose (see Chapter 23).
• Check quotations for accuracy.
• Make sure sources are cited correctly (see Chapters 24 and 25).
• Format your bibliography correctly (if appropriate). |

| Correct errors. | • Correct errors of usage and punctuation.
• Refer to Chapter 26 for guidance in correcting errors. |

A Student Writer Applies the Core Concepts

4

ELIZABETH PARISI was a first-year student at the State University of New York at Albany when she wrote the following essay for her introductory writing course. As a psychology major with a minor in philosophy and as someone who had taken advanced English courses in high school, Elizabeth well understood the importance of writing. When she received an assignment requiring an "analytical argument that will complicate and critique a common conception or construction of literacy, writing, or writers," she didn't have any trouble coming up with an idea for her paper.

Elizabeth Parisi

Step 1   Discover and explore a topic.

Begin with a Question

Elizabeth's essay began with her own experience as a student writer in a state where standardized tests seemed to influence how her high school teachers taught writing. As a high school student, she took honors and Advanced Placement (AP) English courses as well as several elective courses in English because of her interest in writing. But she noticed important differences in those courses. The advanced courses focused on more sophisticated writing skills, especially the ability to analyze a rhetorical situation and write an appropriate piece for a specific audience. By contrast, the elective courses seemed to focus on preparing students to write for the standardized tests required by New York State. She didn't enjoy those courses, but she had assumed that they prepared her for college. Now, as a first-year college student, she wasn't so sure. She wondered:

> *Did the emphasis on preparing students for standardized tests that I endured as a student actually prepare me for college writing?*

She suspected not, but she was interested in learning more. Because these experiences were so recent and important to her and because this topic seemed to fit her assignment so well, Elizabeth felt confident that she could pursue it.

Explore the Question

Elizabeth's instructor, Janelle, asked her students to explore ideas for their essays in a series of short, informal writing exercises that she called "checkpoints." In one such checkpoint, Elizabeth wrote about her concerns regarding the emphasis her high school teachers had placed on correctness in writing. Here's part of what she wrote in that checkpoint:

> When teachers will read text solely to scrutinize proper punctuation and grammar, they will come across errors routinely expected. Students then assume that the teacher doesn't care about what they write because teachers only correct punctuation and grammar. When you think about language, "good writing" is not measured by how well you convey the essence of your message, but rather the number of punctuation errors you have.

Janelle encouraged Elizabeth to explore these ideas further.

Eventually, Janelle asked her students to write an informal proposal describing a potential topic for the assignment. Here's the proposal Elizabeth submitted:

> My topic for my analytical paper is how writing in academic disciplines is too focused on grammatical error and "teaching to the test." I want my readers to know that there is more to writing than punctuation. You have to have a voice in your writing for it to be effective. I would also like to address the fact that teaching according to a test doesn't allow students to learn anything other than how to take the test. I want to be able to show that the Regents Exams are not as successful as they were designed to be. Life does *not* give you tests or hand out specific instructions. You have to learn what works and doesn't work for you. I would like to use research to show the pros and cons of being taught according to a test like the Regents. I predict that research will show that giving kids more than grammatical corrections—like allowing them to have a voice—will make them much better writers.

Even in this brief proposal, Elizabeth was already beginning to delve into her questions about the impact of "teaching to the test." She identified several issues that she might investigate in her paper—including the importance of voice in writing and the pros and cons of preparing students for standardized tests—and she made a prediction about what she would find in researching her question.

Select a Working Topic

Through this process of exploration, Elizabeth quickly identified a working topic: *the impact of standardized tests on high school students' preparation for college-level writing.* This topic is rich with possibilities and presented Elizabeth with several subtopics to investigate, including how writing is taught in schools, the effects of education policies (such as mandated tests), the impact of those policies on students' readiness for college, and the nature of writing ability. Although these issues are related, Elizabeth couldn't cover all of them adequately in a single essay. Eventually she would have to focus on a main idea that she could develop sufficiently in her paper. At this stage of the process, though, she remained open to possibilities and allowed her curiosity about the topic to guide her exploration.

Identify What You Know About Your Topic

Most of what Elizabeth knew about her topic was based on her own experience as a student writer. For example, she knew that "teaching to the test" had become more common in the high school she attended, and she was aware that state and federal education policies (such as the Common Core State Standards) are part of the reason for this new emphasis on standardized tests. She also had taken several different kinds of English courses at her high school, including honors courses and regular-level courses; as a result, she knew that there were differences in how writing was taught in those courses. These experiences were an important starting point for her exploration of her topic. Elizabeth also read some articles about standardized testing and new education policies that place greater emphasis on standardized tests. As soon as she decided on this topic, she began looking for other source material.

Adjust Your Question

On the basis of her preliminary exploration, Elizabeth planned to address the following question:

Does an emphasis on preparing students for standardized tests in high school prepare students adequately for college-level writing?

Use Technology to Generate Ideas and Gather Information

Because Elizabeth's experience as a student writer is common, she could use social media to share her developing ideas with her friends, many of whom might have opinions about the issues she was exploring. Also, the increasing emphasis on standardized testing had become controversial in New York, where Elizabeth attended school, as well as in other states; as a result, many social media sites had been established where students, parents, and educators share their views and, in some cases, discuss strategies for resisting the trend toward more testing. Elizabeth was able to gather information and ideas for her paper by following some of these discussions.

Write a Discovery Draft

Because of her keen interest in her topic and the information she had already gathered, Elizabeth was able to write a Discovery Draft that included some of the key ideas that would become important in her paper. She says, "Once I obtained a substantial amount of information, I began to write a very rough draft, starting with a pretty solid introduction and then using material from the articles I wished to use." Her Discovery Draft was only a partial draft, but it was a good starting point for a complete rough draft. Here's what it looked like:

In New York State, students are required to take a series of Regents Exams in order to graduate from high school, a result of the No Child Left Behind policy enforced by former President George Bush and his administration. However, this approach which attempts to provide students the tools to graduate high school and ultimately be well prepared for their college career may actually be hindering whether students are properly equipped for college. Due to the strict regulations of New York Education Department, teachers must educate students on how to pass the Regents, rather than the essence of what the subject it truly about; it's as if teachers are training students to take a test correctly. The idea that this paper aims to convey is since students are subjected to this style of learning, they are unprepared for college level writing—they lack the skills to create a sophisticated piece or work. Furthermore, students who are enrolled in college level classes while in high school are more equipped to compose an essay more so than students in standard English courses because they touch on topics and abstract concepts that aren't addressed in a typical classroom.

Arthur Goldstein, a teacher from NYS shared his primary encounters with NYS rigid education system. He explains that if a student cannot pass the Regents, then they can't graduate; with this in mind, he has no other choice but to teach students how to take the test to ensure they pass it and receive a diploma. He realizes the faults to this method because students are not obtaining the skills which are needed for them to succeed in their college career. Students are not able to grasp the core concepts of language and are ultimately depriving them of proper instruction. Statistics provided by 2009 graduates in the article *How Many Passed the Regents Tests and Were Deemed College Ready*, strengthened Goldstein's observations even further. The results had determined less than one-third of New York City's class of 2009 graduates met the state's definition of "college ready" in English based on their Regents scores. This reveals that this current teaching method cannot be used on all students; everyone has different writing strengths and weakness, something which the Regents' Exams do not take into account.

Peter Parisi, a high school house principle, will be speaking to me about the opportunity differences of students enrolled in honors English courses as opposed to typical classes. Questions that will be asked are as follows:

1. What are your current views of standardized testing? Do you feel they fulfill the purpose that they are designed for?

2. What are the differences in curriculum of an AP English course compared to a typical English course?

3. Do you feel students who take AP English courses are well prepared for college?

4. Do you feel students who take regular English classes are well prepared for college?

5. What are the advantages/disadvantages of AP level courses?

6. What are the advantages/disadvantages of standard courses?

Notice that writing her Discovery Draft enabled Elizabeth not only to identify key ideas for her paper but also to determine what kinds of information she needed to find. She says, "As I worked on my draft, I acquired the idea of adding a supporting argument about how AP courses influence a student's future in college. To explore this idea further, I set up an interview with a high school principal named Peter Parisi to understand how he feels about New York's current education policies." Writing the Discovery Draft helped Elizabeth discover ideas she had and information she needed for her project.

Notice, too, that Elizabeth did not worry too much about grammar and style in this Discovery Draft. Her primary concern was to get ideas on paper so she could begin her research and develop a more formal draft. In her later drafts, she would focus on correcting errors and making her sentences clearer.

Step 2   Examine the rhetorical context.

Identify Your Audience

From the very start of this assignment, Elizabeth began to think about her audience. The assignment guidelines indicated that students should assume they would be writing for a broader audience of people interested in literacy and writing, which would include students in the class. Elizabeth also knew that many people who might not necessarily have an interest in writing and literacy would still be interested in her topic because standardized testing had become such a controversial issue affecting students in New York and many other states. From the beginning, she imagined that her audience was a broad group of people with some interest in or concern about education policy.

In addition, Elizabeth imagined that she would be writing to officials at the New York State Education Department who set the policies that led to the standardized tests she was required to take as a high school student. She says, "Originally, I thought of my audience mostly as teachers and other interested people, such as students and parents. But then I thought about the policy-makers at the state. I thought that they should read my argument about how tests were affecting the way kids learn to write."

Although Elizabeth's assignment called for an academic paper, she selected a topic that had wide appeal, and she imagined her audience as one that went beyond her class.

Consider the Context

Time: As already noted, Elizabeth's topic was timely because of recent policies that increased the emphasis on standardized testing in high schools. These policies sparked controversies that were heating up at the time Elizabeth was writing.

Place: New York State, where Elizabeth was a high school student, was in the midst of implementing new policies that affected every student in the state. But what was happening in New York was happening in many other states as well. Although Elizabeth was writing about specific policies in New York, she was also addressing issues that were relevant in other states.

Purpose: As she indicated in her proposal, Elizabeth was keenly interested in showing her readers that there is much more to writing than what students learn when preparing for standardized tests. As someone who had already made the transition from high school to college, she hoped to show how educational trends in her state would not necessarily help other students succeed in college.

Review Your Question

In thinking about the rhetorical context, Elizabeth saw no need to make significant adjustments to her question. She felt confident that her topic was relevant to her intended audience. In addition, her instructor indicated in her comments on Elizabeth's proposal that the topic was "appropriate for the rhetorical situation you're writing within."

Develop Your Discovery Draft

Elizabeth now had a clear sense of the rhetorical context. She returned to her Discovery Draft to develop some of her ideas. One of those ideas was to interview a high school principal, which she did. She says, "During this interview I began to realize that the Regents Exams were only part of the problem; there is also the need for family or community support that a child must have in order to be successful. With this new information, I felt ready to start my second draft." She would develop additional ideas for her project as she progressed through subsequent drafts, but for now her examination of her rhetorical situation enabled her to continue exploring her ideas and prepare to write a complete draft.

Step 3 Select an appropriate medium.

Select a Medium

Like most college assignments, Elizabeth's assignment called for a conventional academic essay to be submitted electronically (as a Word or PDF file) or in hard copy, so she did not have to select a medium for her project. However, she knew that she would have to follow the conventions for standard academic writing.

Consider How the Medium Might Shape Your Project

The structure and style of Elizabeth's paper would be shaped by the conventions of academic writing, as you'll see later. As a student who had taken advanced English classes in high school, she was generally familiar with these conventions and kept them in mind as she proceeded with her project.

Step 4 Have something to say.

As you can tell from Elizabeth's proposal, Elizabeth had a sense of her main point from the beginning. In her proposal, she wrote, "I would also like to address the fact that teaching according to a test doesn't allow students to learn anything other than how to take the test. I want to be able to show that the Regents Exams are not as successful as they were designed to be." That's a good start on a main point or claim.

Revisit Your Main Question

Here's Elizabeth's main question from Step #1:

Does an emphasis on preparing students for standardized tests in high school prepare students adequately for college-level writing?

Notice that the first paragraph of her Discovery Draft began to show how her main question fit into larger issues related to education:

> In New York State, students are required to take a series of Regents Exams in order to graduate from high school, a result of the No Child Left Behind policy enforced by former President George Bush and his administration. However, this approach which attempts to provide students the tools to graduate high school and ultimately be well prepared for their college career may actually be hindering whether students are properly equipped for college. Due to the strict regulations of New York Education Department, teachers must educate students on how to pass the Regents, rather than the essence of what the subject it truly about; it's as if teachers are training students to take a test correctly. The idea that this paper aims to convey is since students are subjected to this style of learning, they are unprepared for college level writing—they lack the skills to create a sophisticated piece of work.

Here Elizabeth was beginning to identify what made her topic relevant and why it might matter to her intended audience at that point in time.

Write a Guiding Thesis Statement

Elizabeth could use the first paragraph of her Discovery Draft to develop a Guiding Thesis Statement:

> Education policies have resulted in greater use of standardized tests in schools, which has forced teachers to teach to the test. However, although this approach is intended to provide students with the tools to graduate high school and succeed in college, it may actually leave them unprepared for college-level writing.

Review Your Discovery Draft

After reviewing her Discovery Draft, Elizabeth saw a need to expand her Guiding Thesis Statement to include ideas about the kinds of writing skills she believed students should develop as a result of their high school classes.

Revise Your Guiding Thesis Statement

Here's Elizabeth's revised Guiding Thesis Statement:

> Education policies have resulted in greater use of standardized tests in schools, which has forced teachers to teach to the test. However, although this approach is intended to provide students with the tools to graduate high school and succeed in college, it may actually leave them unprepared for college-level writing. Teaching to the test does not help students develop a strong voice in their writing or learn how to connect with their audience through their writing. High school courses that focus on these skills, such as Advanced Placement English, help students learn to write more sophisticated essays.

This was a statement of the main point she would make in her essay. However, as she conducted research and learned more about her topic, she might have to refine or adjust this statement.

Step 5   Back up what you say.

Almost as soon as she identified her topic for her assignment, Elizabeth began to think about gathering information to support her developing position on the issue of teaching to the test. She says, "I knew I had to do a lot of research because I needed a lot of supporting data to convince my audience." Notice that Elizabeth's research was shaped by her sense of her audience and her rhetorical purpose. As we have seen, Elizabeth had begun her research even before writing her Discovery Draft. She read a few relevant articles and, as a result of writing her Discovery Draft, decided to interview a high school principal to gain a better understanding of some issues relevant to her topic. Now she was ready to engage in a more concerted effort to find relevant information and to explore various perspectives on the issues related to standardized testing and the teaching of writing.

Identify Your Main Claims or Assertions

With her Guiding Thesis Statement, Elizabeth had a good sense of the major claims or assertions she would likely make in her essay, and she could begin looking for information to support those claims and to explore her topic further. Here are the main claims Elizabeth expected to make in her essay:

- State and federal education policies force high school teachers to teach to the test.
- Teaching to the test does not prepare high school students for college-level writing.
- Students who are subjected to a teach-to-the-test approach learn how to write only for standardized tests.
- To write well requires more than being able to use correct grammar; it also means having a voice and connecting with an audience.
- Some high school classes help students develop these skills.

Reviewing this list, Elizabeth realized that she could reorganize the list into two main claims and several supporting claims:

1. Teaching to the test does not prepare high school students for college-level writing.

   a) State and federal education policies force high school teachers to teach to the test.

   b) Students who are subjected to a teach-to-the-test approach learn how to write only for standardized tests.

2. Some high school classes help students develop appropriate skills for college.

   a) To write well requires more than being able to use correct grammar; it also means having a voice and connecting with an audience.

With this list of claims as a guide, Elizabeth used online research tools to find relevant sources. (See Chapter 21 for information about finding sources.) In addition to her interview with a high school principal, Elizabeth found a study of the effect of New York's Regents Exams on student writers; she also found several articles about the controversy surrounding standardized testing.

As she learned more about her topic through her research, she identified other important issues. For example, her interview with the principal helped her realize that some students are so far behind in developing writing skills by the time they enter high school that they would not benefit from courses like Advanced Placement. She also learned about other factors that can affect whether students develop appropriate writing skills. She says, "During this interview, I began to realize that the Regents Exams were only part of the problem; there is also the need for family or community support that a child must have in order to be successful."

Through this process, Elizabeth began to find supporting evidence for each of her claims, but even more importantly, she deepened her understanding of the topic. That understanding would help her develop a more valid argument and a more persuasive paper.

Review Your Discovery Draft

Elizabeth's Discovery Draft already included some of her key claims. As a result of her research, she now had new information to incorporate into that draft. "With all this new information to use in my argument," she says, "I felt ready to start a complete draft."

Write a Complete Draft

Here's the first full draft Elizabeth wrote:

FIRST DRAFT

In New York State, students are required to take a series of Regents Exams in order to graduate from high school, a result of the No Child Left Behind policy enforced by former President George Bush and his administration. However, this approach which attempts to provide students the tools to graduate high school and ultimately

(Continued)

be well prepared for their college career may actually be hindering whether students are properly equipped for college. Due to the strict regulations of New York Education Department, teachers must educate students on how to pass the Regents, instead of the essence of what the subject is truly about; it's as if teachers are training students to take a test correctly. The idea that this paper aims to convey is since students are subjected to this style of learning, they are unprepared for college level writing—they lack the skills to create a sophisticated piece of work. Furthermore, students who are enrolled in college level classes while in high school are able to compose an essay of better quality more frequently than students in normal English courses because they touch on topics and abstract concepts that aren't addressed in a typical classroom.

Arthur Goldstein, a teacher from NYS shared his encounters with the rigid education system. He explains that if a student cannot pass the Regents, then they can't graduate; with this in mind, he has no other choice but to teach students how to take the test to ensure they pass it and receive a diploma. "Regrettably, though the kids worked very hard, writing almost until their hands fell off, the only skill they acquired was passing the English Regents. Because the exam placed more emphasis on communication than structure, I did not stress structure. I knew that when my kids went to college, they would have to take writing tests—tests which would place them in remedial classes." Teachers realize the faults to this method because students are not obtaining the skills which are needed for them to succeed in their college career. Students are not able to grasp the key concepts of language and teachers are ultimately depriving them of proper instruction.

Research has also been conducted in a study called *Talking Back to the Regents*, conducted by Octavia Davis which supports the notion of standardized testing to be severely flawed. In this study, Davis uses her own college students to find out their experience with New York's English Regents examination, and what steps can be put forth to not only to enhance their writing skills, but change their attitude of writing as well. She proposed that her students discussed how they viewed the Regents through open-forum reflective writing in which they would analyze the piece afterward. Only two of the twenty-three students (9%) who participated in the study found that they had a positive outlook of the regent's exam and their writing. (Davis, 364) "I knew it was an easy task but difficult part was taking this seriously. I am telling you if they put anything serious for example current events to 'write to the senator.' I would have been going through with enthusiasm instead of merely looking for the stupid fact that could support my 'stance on vending machines'."(360). Her students emphasized that their responses on the exam resembled what they anticipated would be a passing essay rather than the answer expressing their authentic ideas about the posed question.

Davis's study also demonstrates that this approach to education does not allow the student to be creative or innovative. "Well I started reading and… I remember thinking that going for the band had two sides while going against the band had only one supportive argument.… So I went with the stance that had the most options," said a student in Davis's study (359). Sixty-seven percent of students began their essays with the position that had the most information. More than half of her students assumed that to be successful in terms of the regent's exam they needed to refrain from thinking analytically.(359) This evidence suggests that to obtain a good grade, students feel that they must create an essay which would appeal to the grader, not necessarily an idea which defends the writer's own point of view.

Another objection to the New York State Regents Exams was propose by former assemblymen Steven Sanders, who believed a student's ability should not be determined by a single test. According to the article *Flaws Could Spell Trouble for N.Y. Regents Exams,* "His belief that students entire pre-collegiate careers should not hinge on passing exams… The New York City Democrat suggests that scores on the Regents test should be but one factor among many that local school officials use to decide whether a student should graduate." He recognizes that there is a need for appropriate standards, but to give simply a test which defines their capability to succeed in college does not allow for students to flourish. Every student has different writing abilities, and the regent's generalizes teaching styles rather than adapting to what an individual need to succeed. This reveals that this current teaching method cannot be used on all students; everyone has different writing strengths and weakness, something which the Regents' Exams do not take into account.

I conducted an interview with Peter Parisi, a high school principle, who spoke about the opportunity differences of students enrolled in honors and A.P English courses opposed to typical English classes. Students enrolled in AP courses must obtain an understanding of the curriculum at a faster pace, as well as experience a different level of complexity of assignments. The content in honors and AP classes are more difficult than the Regents, and students must take make it their responsibility to fulfill the requirements of the task. Parisi made note that the more challenging the course curriculum is, the need to obtain the skills to be successful is greater. However, he stresses that prior experience is key to a student's success in writing. "We have juniors in high school reading and writing at a fifth grade level. They would not benefit from taking AP courses because they lack the experience to be learning college-level material. For a student to even consider enrolling in an honors class, they must have the proper level of preparation in the discipline in order to be successful." He views standardized testing as unreliable means of determining if a student is prepared for college level writing, and fails to provide students with the skills and knowledge essential for that discipline. However, students may not be prepared for college for reasons other than Regents Exams.

If students lack the experience to write in a typical English course let alone an AP course, are they destined to fall short of what is expected of them at college? Perhaps if educators examined how elementary students approached reading and writing, they could recognize the problem areas the students face early on rather than at the high school level. Furthermore, a 'home' component can be crucial to whether a child is

(Continued)

successful in the world of academia. A student's level of achievement relies on the support given to them by their family or community; otherwise the child does not see the importance in their education.

Works Cited

Davis, Octavia. "Talking Back to the Regents." *Talking Back to the Regents*. Project Muse, 2012. Web. 4 Mar. 2013.

Goldstein, Arthur. "Students Learn Differently. So Why Test Them All the Same?" *SchoolBook*. WNYC, 2 Feb. 2012. Web. 4 Mar. 2013.

Hoff, David J. "Flaws Could Spell Trouble For N.Y. Regents Exams." *Education Week* 23.10 (2003): 22–27. Education Full Text (H.W. Wilson). Web. 4 Mar. 2013.

Parisi, Peter. Personal interview. 7 Mar. 2013.

Step 6 | Establish a form and structure for your project.

Elizabeth's assignment called for a conventional academic paper, but the guidelines for organizing the paper were vague. Like many college instructors, Elizabeth's instructor did not impose a specific structure but rather left it up to students to decide what kind of structure would work best for their individual projects. Elizabeth found this task challenging. She considered the following:

Genre: She was writing what her instructor called an "analytical argument," so she assumed that the best strategy was to organize her paper according to her main claims, incorporating her analysis into her discussion of each claim. (See Chapter 5 for advice about organizing analytical essays and Chapter 11 for advice about organizing arguments.)

Medium: She would follow the conventions for writing an academic paper, which means that she would present supporting evidence for each claim and cite her sources using MLA style (which her instructor required).

Rhetorical Situation: Elizabeth's primary concern was persuading her audience that her argument about teaching to the test was valid, so she wanted to present her claims in a clear sequence that would make her argument more convincing.

You'll notice that Elizabeth's draft was already generally well organized. She identified her main points and then methodically moved from one main point to the next. Her task now was to decide whether the structure of that draft worked for her rhetorical situation.

Identify the Main Parts of Your Project

As we have seen, Elizabeth began her draft with a clear sense of her main claims. She was making two central claims and several supporting claims. Her list of claims (see Step #5) could serve as a guide to organizing her essay.

Develop an Outline

Normally, Elizabeth does not work from an outline. "It feels restricting when I'm writing a draft," she says. She usually spends a lot of time writing her introduction to make sure she has clearly established her focus and identified the main points she will make. That's what she did in this case. "I started with a pretty solid introduction," she says, which helped her decide how best to organize her draft. With her main claims clearly presented in her introduction, she completed her draft, moving from one main point to the next.

Refine Your Outline

Reviewing her draft, Elizabeth was satisfied with its structure, but she still had questions about whether it was organized effectively. Even after completing her revisions, she says, "I still wonder whether a different way of organizing the paper would make it more convincing for my readers." Notice that Elizabeth's main concern was making sure the structure of her paper fit the needs of her rhetorical situation. Nevertheless, she was unsure about whether she should reorganize her draft at this point.

Write or Revise Your Draft

Although Elizabeth had doubts about the structure of her draft, she did not reorganize it. Instead, she decided to wait to see what her peer reviewers and her instructor would have to say about the paper's structure.

Step 7 Get feedback.

Ask Your Readers to Respond to Your Draft

Elizabeth received feedback on her draft from several classmates as well as from her instructor. The feedback from her classmates was guided by the requirements for the assignment. Her instructor provided students with specific questions to address as they reviewed each other's drafts. But Elizabeth was also eager to see whether her argument was convincing to her peers.

Identify Common Themes in Your Readers' Responses

Elizabeth's classmates generally found her draft to be clear and persuasive. One student praised Elizabeth's use of her own experience to support her claims: "I could relate, because I also took the state tests." The same student also found Elizabeth's evidence to be strong: "Halfway through the analysis I found myself agreeing with your points and examples."

But her classmates also felt that Elizabeth didn't have enough analysis in certain sections of her draft. "My peer editors stressed that I needed to look back at my supporting evidence and elaborate on my views about why the Regents Exams were not a useful tool for students to further their education," she says. This concern would become the focus of her revisions.

Elizabeth's instructor made numerous comments that focused Elizabeth's attention on how to bring her draft into line with the conventions of academic writing, especially the conventions regarding how to support claims:

In New York State, students are required to take a series of Regents Exams in order to graduate from high school, a result of the No Child Left Behind policy enforced by former President George Bush and his administration. However, this approach which attempts to provide students the tools to graduate high school and ultimately be well prepared for their college career may actually be hindering whether students are properly equipped for college. Due to the strict regulations of New York Education Department, teachers must educate students on how to pass the Regents, instead of the essence of what the subject it truly about; it's as if teachers are training students to take a test correctly. The idea that this paper aims to convey is since students are subjected to this style of learning, they are unprepared for college level writing—they lack the skills to create a sophisticated piece or work. Furthermore, students who are enrolled in college level classes while in high school are able to compose an essay of better quality more frequently than students in normal English courses because they touch on topic's and abstract concepts that aren't addressed in a typical classroom.

Your central claim is clearly stated.

Arthur Goldstein, a teacher from NYS shared his encounters with the rigid education system. He explains that if a student cannot pass the Regents, then they can't graduate; with this in mind, he has no other choice but to teach students how to take the test to ensure they pass it and receive a diploma. "Regrettably, though the kids worked very hard, writing almost until their hands fell off, the only skill they acquired was passing the English Regents. Because the exam placed more emphasis on communication than structure, I did not stress structure. I knew that when my kids went to college, they would have to take writing tests—tests which would place them in remedial classes." Teachers realize the faults to this method because students are not obtaining the skills which are needed for them to succeed in their college career. Students are not able to grasp the key concepts of language and teachers are ultimately depriving them of proper instruction.

Don't forget to cite your source. This supports your ethos and gives you credibility.

What's the central point you want to make in this paragraph? A topic sentence can help your readers understand where you're taking them and how each paragraph relates to the larger argument.

Research has also been conducted in a study called *Talking Back to the Regents*, conducted by Octavia Davis which supports the notion of standardized testing to be severely flawed. In this study, Davis uses her own college students to find out their experience with New York's English Regents

This study supports your argument, but you introduce it in a somewhat awkward way that is hard to follow. It might slow down a reader.

examination, and what steps can be put forth to not only to enhance their writing skills, but change their attitude of writing as well. She proposed that her students discussed how they viewed the Regents through open-forum reflective writing in which they would analyze the piece afterward. Only two of the twenty-three students (9%) who participated in the study found that they had a positive outlook of the regent's exam and their writing (Davis, 364). "I knew it was an easy task but difficult part was taking this seriously. I am telling you if they put anything serious for example current events to 'write to the senator.' I would have been going through with enthusiasm instead of merely looking for the stupid fact that could support my 'stance on vending machines'."(360). Her students emphasized that their responses on the exam resembled what they anticipated would be a passing essay rather than the answer expressing their authentic ideas about the posed question.

> You need to introduce this quote to clarify who is saying it. A reader might think that the quote is from Davis rather than from one of the students in her study.

> OK, but what does Davis's study mean? You have presented some relevant findings but you need to interpret them and show how they support your point here.

Davis's study also demonstrates that this approach to education does not allow the student to be creative or innovative. "Well I started reading and … I remember thinking that going for the band had two sides while going against the band had only one supportive argument…. So I went with the stance that had the most options," said a student in Davis's study (359). Sixty-seven percent of students began their essays with the position that had the most information. More than half of her students assumed that to be successful in terms of the Regent's exam they needed to refrain from thinking analytically.(359) This evidence suggests that to obtain a good grade, students feel that they must create an essay which would appeal to the grader, not necessarily an idea which defends the writer's own point of view.

> Nice analytical claim. Your logic is clear in this section. Each sentence follows from the one before it. Use this as a model as you work to improve the coherence of your other paragraphs.

Another objection to the New York State Regents Exams was propose by former assemblymen Steven Sanders, who believed a student's ability should not be determined by a single test. According to the article *Flaws Could Spell Trouble for N.Y. Regents Exams,* "His belief that students entire pre-collegiate careers should not hinge on passing Exams… The New York City Democrat suggests that scores on the Regents test should be but one factor among many that local school officials use to decide whether a student should graduate." He recognizes that there is a need for appropriate standards, but to give simply a test which defines their capability to succeed in college does not allow for students to flourish. Every student has different

> Again, don't forget to cite your sources properly.

writing abilities, and the regent's generalizes teaching styles rather than adapting to what an individual need to succeed. This reveals that this current teaching method cannot be used on all students; everyone has different writing strengths and weakness, something which the Regents' Exams do not take into account.

I conducted an interview with Peter Parisi, a high school principle, who spoke about the opportunity differences of students enrolled in honors and A.P English courses opposed to typical English classes. Students enrolled in AP courses must obtain an understanding of the curriculum at a faster pace, as well as experience a different level of complexity of assignments. The content in honors and AP classes are more difficult than the Regents, and students must take make it their responsibility to fulfill the requirements of the task. Parisi made note that the more challenging the course curriculum is, the need to obtain the skills to be successful is greater. However, he stresses that prior experience is key to a student's success in writing. "We have juniors in high school reading and writing at a fifth grade level. They would not benefit from taking AP courses because they lack the experience to be learning college-level material. For a student to even consider enrolling in an honors class, they must have the proper level of preparation in the discipline in order to be successful." He views standardized testing as unreliable means of determining if a student is prepared for college level writing, and fails to provide students with the skills and knowledge essential for that discipline. However, students may not be prepared for college for reasons other than Regents Exams.

If student's lack the experience to write in a typical English course let alone an AP course, are they destined to fall short of what is expected of them at college? Perhaps if educators examined how elementary students approached reading and writing, they could recognize the problem areas the students face early on rather than at the high school level. Furthermore, a 'home' component can be crucial to whether a child is successful in the world of academia. A student's level of achievement relies on the support given to them by their family or community; otherwise the child does not see the importance in their education.

As a reader, I expected a transition here to help me see the connection between this paragraph and the previous one.

It seems to me that you're advocating for a certain kind of difficulty in writing classes. You don't want a more difficult Regents Exam that's utilizing the same modes; you want an entirely different approach. This might be something to make clearer as you refine your argument.

This point is underdeveloped. I wonder if it can be cut.

You seem to end your essay rather abruptly. Have you considered a more forceful way to sum up your argument and reinforce your main point?

As you'll see, Elizabeth would take many of her instructor's comments into account in revising her draft.

Review Disagreements Among Your Readers

There were no significant disagreements among the students who reviewed Elizabeth's draft, but, she says, the "peer reviews were almost like a wake-up call." They helped her see that she was not allowing her own voice to emerge in her draft. This realization led her to decide to incorporate more of her own experience into her essay—specifically, her experience taking both regular and advanced English classes in high school.

Step 8 Revise.

As she progressed with her project, Elizabeth continued to learn more about her topic and refine her argument. Using her classmates' and instructor's comments as a guide, she worked through several revisions, each time addressing more specific issues to strengthen her essay.

Focus First on Content

Elizabeth focused her revisions initially on two main areas: developing her analysis and incorporating her own experiences to support her claims. She says, "I sought to make a connection between my analysis and my own experiences as a high school student. It was when I wrote about my own familiarity with the Regents-level courses and honors courses that I felt I expressed my views about standardized testing most coherently." To address these issues, Elizabeth added material to support her second main claim about the value of advanced English courses in preparing students for college writing. Here are some of the important changes she made to her draft:

- **She added material to the second paragraph:**

    Draft: Arthur Goldstein, a teacher from NYS shared his encounters with the rigid education system. He explains that if a student cannot pass the Regents, then they can't graduate; with this in mind, he has no other choice but to teach students how to take the test to ensure they pass it and receive a diploma. "Regrettably, though the kids worked very hard, writing almost until their hands fell off, the only skill they acquired was passing the English Regents. Because the exam placed more emphasis on communication than structure, I did not stress structure. I knew that when my kids went to college, they would have to take writing tests—tests which would place them in remedial classes." Teachers realize the faults to this method because students are not obtaining the skills which are needed for them to succeed in their college career. Students are not able to grasp the key concepts of language and teachers are ultimately depriving them of proper instruction.

    Without a good transition from the introductory paragraph, this source material is not introduced in a way that will help a reader understand its relevance.

    The discussion that follows the quote highlights the faults of a test-prep "method" but does not explain why these faults matter.

    Revised version: As a college freshman who endured the Regents Exams in high school, I have begun to realize the different expectations of high school teachers and college professors. College professors tend to focus on the content of an essay and how well the writer conveys his or her message, whereas high school teachers emphasize grammar and correctness so that their students are prepared for the state tests. Many teachers recognize that the skills they teach students are not the ones they should prioritize. Arthur Goldstein, a New York teacher, explains that students who cannot pass the Regents Exams in English can't graduate, so he has no choice but to teach students how to take the test. "Regrettably," he says, "though the kids worked very hard, writing almost until their hands fell off, the only skill they acquired was passing the English Regents... I knew that when my kids went to college, they would have to take writing tests—tests which would almost inevitably label them as ESL students and place them in remedial classes" (Goldstein). Because of this emphasis on test preparation, many students are not able to grasp key concepts of language and develop writing skills needed for college. These skills include the ability to connect to an audience and allow your writerly voice to shine through while conveying your message clearly and effectively. Without these skills, students will have difficulty not only in college English courses but also in other fields of study that require writing.

The three sentences added to the beginning of this paragraph provide a better transition from the introduction and also introduce the source material cited in this passage. Notice, too, that Elizabeth refers to her own experience to begin establishing her credibility as someone who understands these issues.

Elizabeth expanded her discussion of the quoted source material to show readers its importance and connect it to her main point. Notice that she added a new final sentence that points explicitly to the problem she wants to highlight.

■ **She developed an important point in the fourth paragraph:**

Draft: Davis's study also demonstrates that this approach to education does not allow the student to be creative or innovative. "Well I started reading and... I remember thinking that going for the band had two sides while going against the band had only one supportive argument.... So I went with the stance that had the most options," said a student in Davis's study (359). Sixty-seven percent of students began their essays with the position that had the most information. More than half of her students assumed that to be successful in terms of the regent's exam they needed to refrain from thinking analytically.(359) This evidence suggests that to obtain a good grade, students feel that they must create an essay which would appeal to the grader, not necessarily an idea which defends the writer's own point of view.

This paragraph presents evidence for Elizabeth's main point that preparing students for standardized tests does not prepare them for college writing. However, she doesn't show explicitly how this study supports that claim. The final sentence begins to do so, but it doesn't go far enough.

Revised version: Davis's study also demonstrates that a test-prep approach does not allow students to be creative or innovative because they must avoid expressing themselves in their writing if they expect to do well on the exams. Another student who participated in Davis's study explains why he selected one side of an issue for an argumentative essay about a proposed state ban on vending machines in schools: "Well I started reading and... I remember

Adding the *because* clause helps explain the problem more clearly and reinforces the point.

thinking that going for the band [sic] had two sides while going against the band [sic] had only one supportive argument…. So I went with the stance that had the most options" (359). Like this student, 67% of the students in the study began their persuasive essays on the exam with the position that had the most information rather than the position they actually supported. More than half of the students assumed that to be successful on the exam they had to refrain from thinking analytically and simply give the test-scorers what they want (359). This evidence suggests that to obtain a good grade, students feel that they must create an essay which would appeal to the test-scorers and not necessarily write an essay in which they defend their own point of view. A good piece of writing encourages readers to open their mind and may even provoke an audience to view an issue differently. This is not what students learn when they learn to write for standardized tests.

These two new sentences explain why learning to write specifically for standardized tests is not a good way to prepare high school students for college writing.

■ **She added material from her own experience to elaborate on a key point:**

Draft: Moreover, there is a significant difference in students' college performance, depending on if they enrolled in English honors and AP English as opposed to a regent's level course. As a former New York State high school student, I was required to take the Regents Exams in order to graduate high school and register in college. However, if did not enroll in honors classes, I cannot be certain that I would be successful in my current college career. Taking honors English allowed me to learn the curriculum at a college-level pace, with topics including rhetoric and analysis. We were taught to focus more on the context of our writing instead of focusing on grammatical errors. I had also participated in a regent's English course as an elective and found myself 'going through the motions' of writing—not feeling connected to the piece I had created. The guidelines set by the Regents were too structured and did not allow for my voice to be heard in the piece I composed. In my honors English course however, we were taught to develop ideas not according to a critical lens format, but by analyzing a piece of literature and expanding on the topic using our personal views.

This paragraph includes important material from Elizabeth's own experience that exposes the flaws in the test-prep approach. But her discussion of her experience doesn't show clearly that there are alternatives to this approach that work.

Revised version: The flaws in writing instruction that is driven by standardized testing are further illuminated by the differences in college performance between students who take high school English honors or Advanced Placement (AP) courses and students who take standard English courses in high school (which are called "Regents-level" courses in New York state). As a high school student, I was required to take the Regents

This revised sentence serves as a better transition from the previous paragraph and also as a topic sentence that establishes the focus of this paragraph.

Exams to graduate; however, if I had not taken advanced classes, I cannot be certain that I would have been prepared for college. Honors English classes enabled me to learn college-level skills. I learned to focus on the rhetorical context of writing rather than exclusively on avoiding grammatical errors. I also took a Regents-level English course as an elective, in which I found myself just going through the motions with no real investment in my writing.

In order to get a high score on the so-called "Critical Lens" essay, which is a standard part of the English Regents Exam consisting of five paragraphs, each covering various aspects of the topic, the student has to follow a series of steps in each paragraph in order to compose a "good" essay. The most outrageous requirement concerns the development of the essay, which is graded according to "the extent to which ideas are elaborated using specific and relevant evidence from the text." These guidelines don't allow for the writer's own voice to be heard, forcing the student to focus instead on the texts that are supplied for the exam. In my honors English course, however, we were taught to develop ideas not according to a standard format but by analyzing a piece of literature and exploring the topic from our own informed perspective.

> Here Elizabeth explains more clearly the differences between advanced and regular English classes and why those differences are important.

> This new material provides a concrete example of the test-prep approach and further reinforces the problems Elizabeth sees with that approach.

Elizabeth made a number of other revisions (which you can see in her finished version on page 110) to elaborate on important points, reinforce her claims, clarify her arguments, condense unnecessarily lengthy passages, and eliminate unnecessary or confusing passages.

Focus Next on Form

Although Elizabeth was still a little uncertain about the structure of her essay, as she reread her draft and her reviewers' comments, she gained confidence that she presented her claims and evidence in a clear and straightforward way. So she saw no need for reorganizing her draft. However, her instructor had noted several missing or weak transitions, which she addressed in her revisions.

Consider Your Rhetorical Situation

Throughout the revision process, Elizabeth considered changes that would make her argument more persuasive for her intended audience. She says, "I was very mindful of the rhetorical situation. I tried to make the issues understandable for a general audience but I wanted my analysis to be sophisticated and I didn't try to dumb down the issues or the argument. I also reviewed my claims to see if I had adequate and appropriate support for my arguments, keeping in mind the expectations of my audience." In her finished essay, you can see numerous adjustments she made to clarify or strengthen a point, always with her readers in mind.

Here's one example of revisions Elizabeth made to address her specific rhetorical situation. In the third paragraph of her draft, she cited an important study to support her main claim about the problem with test-prep writing instruction. However, this paragraph is not clearly written and doesn't explain the study in a way that helps a reader understand its importance to her claim:

> **Draft:** Research has also been conducted in a study called *Talking Back to the Regents*, conducted by Octavia Davis which supports the notion of standardized testing to be severely flawed. In this study, Davis uses her own college students to find out their experience with New York's English Regents examination, and what steps can be put forth to not only to enhance their writing skills, but change their attitude of writing as well. She proposed that her students discussed how they viewed the Regents through open-forum reflective writing in which they would analyze the piece afterward. Only two of the twenty-three students (9%) who participated in the study found that they had a positive outlook of the regent's exam and their writing (Davis, 364). "I knew it was an easy task but difficult part was taking this seriously. I am telling you if they put anything serious for example current events to 'write to the senator.' I would have been going through with enthusiasm instead of merely looking for the stupid fact that could support my 'stance on vending machines'."(360). Her students emphasized that their responses on the exam resembled what they anticipated would be a passing essay rather than the answer expressing their authentic ideas about the posed question.

In her revised version, Elizabeth explained the study more clearly but did not "dumb it down" for her readers. She used quotations more effectively, and she corrected her citations. This version makes more effective use of the study to support her main claim, which helps make her argument more persuasive to her readers:

> **Revised version:** The faults of a test-prep approach to writing instruction have been documented by researchers. In one study, Octavia Davis asked her own college students to write uncensored, unedited reflections on their experiences with New York's English Regents Examination. Only 9% of the students in the study had a positive outlook on the Regents Exam and on their own writing (Davis 364). One student in her study wrote, "I knew it was an easy task but difficult part was taking this seriously. I am telling you if they put anything serious for example current events to 'write to the senator.' I would have been going through with enthusiasm instead of merely looking for the stupid fact that could support my 'stance on vending machines'" (360). (This quotation is reproduced verbatim from the original study.) It is evident that Davis's students wrote exam responses that they believed would result in a passing essay rather than answering the exam questions with their own ideas about the topic. Davis found that "the exam confined most of my students to scripted situations that compelled them to silence their critical voices" (354). This kind of experience, she writes, teaches students "lessons that are contrary to what we may want to teach in first-year [college] writing" (353).

Revisit Your Introduction and Conclusion

Elizabeth was generally satisfied with her introduction, but she made numerous minor revisions to make her sentences more readable, to state her main ideas more clearly, and to place her argument in the context of ongoing developments in education policy.

Draft: In New York State, students are required to take a series of Regents Exams in order to graduate from high school, a result of the No Child Left Behind policy enforced by former President George Bush and his administration. However, this approach which attempts to provide students the tools to graduate high school and ultimately be well prepared for their college career may actually be hindering whether students are properly equipped for college. Due to the strict regulations of New York Education Department, teachers must educate students on how to pass the Regents, instead of the essence of what the subject it truly about; it's as if teachers are training students to take a test correctly. The idea that this paper aims to convey is since students are subjected to this style of learning, they are unprepared for college level writing—they lack the skills to create a sophisticated piece or work. Furthermore, students who are enrolled in college level classes while in high school are able to compose an essay of better quality more frequently than students in normal English courses because they touch on topics and abstract concepts that aren't addressed in a typical classroom.

> Some readers might be unfamiliar with the Regents Exams, which Elizabeth doesn't explain.

> This reference is somewhat vague.

> Also vague

> Elizabeth's statement of her main points isn't as clear as it could be, and she doesn't reinforce the idea that what's happening in her state is part of a nationwide trend.

Revised version: Like many states, New York requires students to take a series of standardized tests, called Regents Exams, in order to graduate from high school, a result of the No Child Left Behind policy developed by former President George W. Bush and passed by Congress in 2002. This test-based approach to education reform, which continues in President Barack Obama's Race to the Top program, attempts to provide students with the tools to graduate high school and to prepare them for college. However, this approach may actually prevent students from being properly equipped for college. Because of the emphasis now placed on standardized tests, teachers in New York State must focus on teaching students how to pass the Regents Exams rather than helping students truly learn the subject. In this paper, I argue that teaching to the test leaves students unprepared for college-level writing. The current push for "college and career readiness," which is part of the national Common Core State Standards movement, may in fact be pushing students away from college and career success.

> This places New York within a national context.

> Elizabeth more clearly explains the Regents Exams and the connection between New York State policy and national education policy.

> Elizabeth states her main argument more clearly and succinctly.

> This new final sentence reinforces her main argument and explicitly connects it to the larger national context.

These careful revisions made Elizabeth's introduction more effective in establishing the focus of her paper and drawing interested readers into her argument.

Elizabeth's conclusion was a different matter. Her instructor commented that her draft ended too abruptly, and Elizabeth knew the conclusion needed work. "I always have trouble with conclusions," she says. As you can see in her finished essay, she added a concluding paragraph that she believed would reinforce her main ideas.

Elizabeth did not make all these revisions at once. Rather, she worked through several drafts, beginning with the larger issues and eventually focusing on more minor issues until she was satisfied that her essay was adequately developed and her argument well supported.

Step 9 Strengthen your voice.

Elizabeth found that the revisions she made to strengthen her argument also strengthened her voice. As she developed her analysis, she says, "I finally used my own voice and emphasized my opinions." Her confidence in her analysis translated into a more confident voice.

Consider Your Rhetorical Context

As she reviewed her draft, Elizabeth felt that the more confident voice that emerged in her revisions helped make her essay better fit her rhetorical situation. She says, "If you have an argument and you don't show yourself within that argument, it's just words. If you use your own voice and reveal your passion, it's more compelling for your readers." Her goal was to convince her readers not only that her argument was sound but also that her own experience and her passion about the topic gave her credibility as a writer. She accomplished that goal in part by adding material based on her own experience and allowing her own views about that experience to come through more clearly.

Consider Whether You Should Use the First Person

You'll notice that Elizabeth avoided using the first person in her Discovery Draft, but as she moved through subsequent drafts, she incorporated the first person where it felt appropriate, especially when describing her own experiences. She believes that her use of the first person gave her essay a more passionate voice and thus made it more effective in conveying her argument to her readers.

Strengthen Your Voice

The most important revision that Elizabeth made to strengthen her voice was adding material about her own experiences and using the first person strategically. She says, "My early drafts were too factual and straightforward and didn't reflect my passion about this problem." That changed, she believes, as a result of her revisions, which she made with her voice in mind.

Step 10 Make it correct.

Elizabeth's early drafts had numerous minor errors of punctuation, spelling, and usage. She also failed to cite her sources properly. Elizabeth addressed these problems in her final set of revisions. Here are some examples:

- **She introduced quotations more smoothly and succinctly:**

  Draft: Research has also been conducted in a study called *Talking Back to the Regents,* conducted by Octavia Davis which supports the notion of standardized testing to be severely flawed. In this study, Davis uses her own college students to find out their experience with New York's English Regents examination, and what steps can be put forth to not only to enhance their writing skills, but change their attitude of writing as well.

Revised version: The faults of a test-prep approach to writing instruction have been documented by researchers. In one study, Octavia Davis asked her own college students to write uncensored, unedited reflections on their experiences with New York's English Regents Examination.

- **She corrected punctuation errors.** In this example, she inserts a necessary comma before the word *however* and removes an unnecessary comma after *format*:

Draft: In my honors English course however, we were taught to develop ideas not according to a critical lens format, but by analyzing a piece of literature and expanding on the topic using our personal views.

Revised version: In my honors English course, however, we were taught to develop ideas not according to a standard format but by analyzing a piece of literature and exploring the topic from our own informed perspective.

- **She used correct MLA citation format:**

Draft: Only two of the twenty-three students (9%) who participated in the study found that they had a positive outlook of the regent's exam and their writing. (Davis, 364)

Revised version: Only 9% of the students in the study had a positive outlook on the Regents Exam and on their own writing (Davis 364).

Here's Elizabeth's finished essay:

FINAL DRAFT

Are We Trying Too Hard or Not Hard Enough?

Like many states, New York requires students to take a series of standardized tests, called Regents Exams, in order to graduate from high school, a result of the No Child Left Behind policy developed by former President George W. Bush and passed by Congress in 2002. This test-based approach to education reform, which continues in President Barack Obama's Race to the Top program, attempts to provide students with the tools to graduate high school and to prepare them for college. However, this approach may actually prevent students from being properly equipped for college. Because of the emphasis now placed on standardized tests, teachers in New York State must focus on teaching students how to pass the Regents Exams rather than helping students truly learn the subject. In this paper, I argue that teaching to the test leaves students unprepared for college-level writing. The current push for "college and career readiness," which is part of the Common Core State Standards movement, may in fact be pushing students away from college and career success.

As a college freshman who endured the Regents Exams in high school, I have begun to realize the different expectations of high school teachers and college professors. College professors tend to focus on the content of an essay and how well the writer conveys his or her message, whereas high school teachers emphasize grammar and correctness so that their students are prepared for the state tests. Many teachers recognize that the skills they teach students are not the ones they should prioritize. Arthur Goldstein, a New York teacher, explains that students who cannot pass the Regents Exams in English can't graduate, so he has no choice but to teach students how to take the test. "Regrettably," he says, "though the kids worked very hard, writing almost until their hands fell off, the only skill they acquired was passing the English Regents… I knew that when my kids went to college, they would have to take writing tests—tests which would almost inevitably label them as ESL students and place them in remedial classes"(Goldstein). Because of this emphasis on test preparation, many students are not able to grasp key concepts of language and develop writing skills needed for college. These skills include the ability to connect to an audience and allow your writerly voice to shine through while conveying your message clearly and effectively. Without these skills, students will have difficulty not only in college English courses but also in other fields of study that require writing.

The faults of a test-prep approach to writing instruction have been documented by researchers. In one study, Octavia Davis asked her own college students to write uncensored, unedited reflections on their experiences with New York's English Regents Examination. Only 9% of the students in the study had a positive outlook on the Regents Exam and on their own writing (Davis 364). One student in her study wrote, "I knew it was an easy task but difficult part was taking this seriously. I am telling you if they put anything serious for example current events to 'write to the senator.' I would have been going through with enthusiasm instead of merely looking for the stupid fact that could support my 'stance on vending machines'"(360). (This quotation is reproduced verbatim from the original study.) It is evident that Davis's students wrote exam responses that they believed would result in a passing essay rather than answering the exam questions with their own ideas about the topic. Davis found that "the exam confined most of my students to scripted situations that compelled them to silence their critical voices" (354). This kind of experience, she writes, teaches students "lessons that are contrary to what we may want to teach in first-year [college] writing" (353).

Davis's study also demonstrates that a test-prep approach does not allow students to be creative or innovative because they must avoid expressing themselves in their writing if they expect to do well on the exams. Another student who participated in Davis's study explains why he selected one side of an issue for an argumentative essay about a proposed state ban on vending machines in schools: "Well I started reading and… I remember thinking that going for the band [sic] had two sides while going against the band [sic] had only one supportive argument…. So I went with the stance that had the most options" (359). Like this student, 67% of the students in the study began their persuasive essays on the exam with the position that had the most

(Continued)

information rather than the position they actually supported. More than half of the students assumed that to be successful on the exam they had to refrain from thinking analytically and simply give the test-scorers what they want (359). This evidence suggests that to obtain a good grade, students feel that they must create an essay that would appeal to the test-scorers and not necessarily write an essay in which they defend their own point of view. A good piece of writing encourages readers to open their minds and may even provoke an audience to view an issue differently. This is not what students learn when they learn to write for standardized tests.

Steven Sanders, a former New York State Assemblyman, believes that "students' entire pre-collegiate careers should not hinge on passing exams" (Hoff). He suggests that "scores on the Regents test should be but one factor among many that local school officials use to decide whether a student should graduate" (Hoff). Sanders recognizes a need for appropriate standards, but he also understands that using a test to define students' writing ability does not allow students to flourish in college. Every student has different writing abilities, but standardized tests encourage generalized teaching styles rather than instruction adapted to students' individual needs.

The flaws in writing instruction that is driven by standardized testing are further illuminated by the differences in college performance between students who take high school English honors or Advanced Placement (AP) courses and students who take standard English courses in high school (which are called "Regents-level" courses in New York State). As a high school student, I was required to take the Regents Exams to graduate; however, if I had not taken advanced classes, I cannot be certain that I would have been prepared for college. Honors English classes enabled me to learn college-level skills. I learned to focus on the rhetorical context of writing rather than exclusively on avoiding grammatical errors. I also took a Regents-level English course as an elective, in which I found myself just going through the motions with no real investment in my writing. In order to get a high score on the so-called "Critical Lens" essay, which is a standard part of the English Regents Exam consisting of five paragraphs, each covering various aspects of the topic, the student has to follow a series of steps in each paragraph in order to compose a "good" essay. The most outrageous requirement concerns the development of the essay, which is graded according to "the extent to which ideas are elaborated using specific and relevant evidence from the text." These guidelines don't allow for the writer's own voice to be heard, forcing the student to focus instead on the texts that are supplied for the exam. In my honors English course, however, we were taught to develop ideas not according to a standard format but by analyzing a piece of literature and exploring the topic from our own informed perspective.

Peter Parisi, a high school principal in Schenectady, New York, agrees that students enrolled in AP courses must develop an understanding of the curriculum at a faster pace and experience a greater level of complexity in their assignments than students in regular courses. According to Parisi, the more challenging the course curriculum is, the greater need to develop more sophisticated writing skills. He views standardized testing as an unreliable means of determining whether a student is prepared for college-level writing. He also believes that a test-prep approach fails to provide students with the skills and knowledge essential for college writing (Parisi).

There are other reasons besides standardized testing for students' lack of readiness for college-level writing. Some students, for instance, enter high school without the basic skills to succeed even in a typical English course, let alone an AP course. Furthermore, the home environment can be crucial factor in determining whether a child is successful in school. A student's level of achievement relies in part on family and community support. Without such support, a child might not see the importance of their education or develop the ability to further their education.

Standardized tests like the New York State Regents Exams can do more harm than good. Such tests do not guarantee that a student will be successful in college. According to Arthur Goldstein, the exams encourage a curriculum that does not require thoughtful or in-depth knowledge, and studies like Davis's show that students often approach such exams with the idea that they are not writing from their own knowledge and perspective but instead trying to guess how the test-scorer would answer the question. In the end, more standardized testing will not help students prepare for college-level writing. More likely it will mean that more students will struggle as writers.

Works Cited

Davis, Octavia. "Talking Back to the Regents." *Talking Back to the Regents*. Project Muse, 2012. Web. 4 Mar. 2013.

Goldstein, Arthur. "Students Learn Differently. So Why Test Them All the Same?" *Schoolbook*. WNYC, 2 Feb. 2012. Web. 4 Mar. 2013.

Hoff, David J. "Flaws Could Spell Trouble for N.Y. Regents Exams." *Education Week* 23.10 (2003): 22–27. Education Full Text (H.W. Wilson). Web. 4 Mar. 2013.

Parisi, Peter. Telephone interview. 7 Mar. 2013.

The story of Elizabeth's essay illustrates the importance of the Ten Core Concepts in effective college writing and demonstrates how a writer can apply those concepts to create a piece of writing that fits her rhetorical situation. Through this process, Elizabeth learned a lot about her topic—which is part of the reason for writing in college. Although her position about the problems with standardized testing hadn't changed, she now appreciated the complexity of the issues much more than she did before writing her essay. "I have a better understanding of why there is a Regents Exam in New York State," she says. "I understand the need to measure everyone against a single standard." Nevertheless, her view about a test-prep approach to teaching high schoolers to write was strengthened as a result of this assignment. "I feel even stronger now that this approach is bad for students. My position is more informed as a result of the project."

Elizabeth also learned some important lessons about writing. "I learned that writing can be seen as something like a learning process, not necessarily just an assignment to be completed." These insights will help Elizabeth develop into an even more effective college writer.

Understanding Analytical Writing

EACH WEEK on the popular radio show *Car Talk,* listeners call in for help solving problems with their cars. Usually, after listening to a caller's description of the problem—say, the car stalls unexpectedly—the *Car Talk* hosts, Tom and Ray, ask questions: What kind of car is it? How old is it? How many miles are on it? How long has it been stalling? When exactly does it stall? When you're idling at a traffic light? When you first start it up? After you've been driving it for a while? Does it stall in all kinds of weather? Does anyone else drive it? Then Tom and Ray will propose an explanation for the problem. Sometimes they disagree on the reasons for the problem, and each will present his own explanation based on how he has interpreted the information provided by the caller. Their back-and-forth is usually funny, and their efforts to solve their listeners' car troubles are intended to be entertaining. But Tom and Ray don't just make jokes about car problems to keep their audience engaged; they also use analysis to solve problems that matter to their audience. That is, they try to understand how or why something is happening by carefully examining the situation and considering relevant information.

We use analysis every day to make decisions and solve problems. Even something as mundane as deciding which roads to drive home from school or which bus route to take to campus involves analysis. In making such a decision, we consider many factors, such as time, weather, cost, and circumstances like road construction or traffic. More complicated matters—for example, deciding which college to attend or whether to vote for a certain political candidate—might require more sophisticated analysis. But all analysis involves carefully examining an issue, phenomenon, or situation so that you can understand it sufficiently to decide on an appropriate action or draw reasonable conclusions about it. Analysis is an important part of how we live in a complicated world, and it is central to college studies.

Occasions for Analytical Writing

Analytical writing grows out of a writer's need to understand something better. Effective analytical writing communicates clearly to readers who share the writer's interest in the question or problem being analyzed. A main purpose of all analytical writing is to help interested readers better understand the topic at hand. In a sense, then, analytical writing is a kind of collaborative problem solving by which writers and readers explore questions or problems in their quest for answers or solutions. Consider the following scenarios, in which circumstances prompted students to engage in analytical writing:

> AFTER learning in an environmental policy class about the potentially harmful environmental and health impacts of large-scale agriculture, a few students at a college near a large city became concerned about the campus policy to purchase foods from large distributors that transport produce hundreds of miles. When the students approached the food service coordinator about the possibility of buying produce from farms located just outside the city, they were told that such a policy would be too expensive and difficult to implement. The students understood these objections, but they were not convinced that buying food from local farms was not feasible. So they decided to investigate. If such a policy did not save money, would it nevertheless help make the campus "greener"? Would it help the local economy? Would local food be healthier or taste better? Would students be unhappy with changes to the dining hall menus? The students discussed these questions with their instructor and did some research; they also talked to other students about the issue. Their investigation eventually led them to write a letter to their college president to propose a new policy to purchase more locally-produced foods for the campus dining hall. Their letter included an analysis of the advantages and disadvantages of such a policy, including a breakdown of potential costs and a discussion of how other students on the campus felt about such a policy.

> JIM, a student at a large state university, began following a discussion on Facebook about the value of college after a classmate informed his Facebook friends that he was leaving college because he could no longer afford it. Jim's classmate did not think borrowing more money to pay for his final few semesters was a good idea. His comment provoked a debate about whether a college degree is worth the cost. Some students wondered whether their degrees would lead to good-paying jobs, which prompted other students to argue that the purpose of college isn't just to prepare students for careers but to educate them as citizens as well. A few students posted links to articles about the rising costs of college tuition as well as average salaries of college graduates compared with those of workers without degrees. Jim followed the discussion closely because of his own concerns about paying for college. To save money, Jim enrolled in a less-expensive community college for two years before transferring to a four-year university. After he posted a message about his decision, someone asked whether Jim received the same quality of education at the community college as he would have had he enrolled for all four years at the university. Jim wasn't sure. As he followed the discussion, he also read the articles that others had posted, found more information about

the advantages and disadvantages of two-year college degrees, and "pinned" relevant articles on his Pinterest site. Eventually, his investigation helped him understand some benefits and costs of attending a two-year college, which he shared on his Facebook page. One of his friends suggested that Jim write an essay about the issue for his old high school newspaper, which Jim did, using his Facebook post as his starting point.

> AMBER, a part-time college student who serves in the National Guard, took a leave of absence from classes because her unit was deployed to Afghanistan for six months. Part of the unit's mission was to build roads and an irrigation system for farmers in a remote region of Afghanistan. Amber was excited about this mission, which she believed would improve the lives of Afghans and relations between Afghans and Americans. However, during her months there, Amber began to realize that the situation was more complicated than she first believed. Many residents feared reprisals from insurgents if they accepted American help. Others worried that new roads would mean more military vehicle traffic. Also, the new irrigation system didn't reach some of the smaller farmers. Cultural and religious differences between Afghans and Americans exacerbated misunderstandings about these projects. All these problems caused Amber to wonder whether the Americans' humanitarian efforts created more problems than they solved. Amber talked to other soldiers about these concerns. She read articles and online discussions to learn more about the complexities of humanitarian aid in Afghanistan. When she returned to the United States, she continued writing a blog that she began in Afghanistan, focusing on her own analysis of the difficulties faced by American units engaged in humanitarian efforts. Her blog attracted many readers, some who shared her concerns and others who challenged her conclusions.

In each of these situations, complex questions prompted students to investigate further. In each case:

- **the need to understand an important issue** motivated the students to engage in analysis
- **the desire to communicate what they learned** through their analysis with others motivated the students to write up their analysis in some form

All three scenarios illustrate the importance of the rhetorical situation not only in creating a reason for analytical writing but also in shaping the writing itself. The most effective analytical writing addresses the needs of a particular rhetorical situation and communicates to an interested audience what the writer learned as a result of his or her analysis.

Charles C. Mann's award-winning book *1491* examines the state of scientific knowledge about the people who were living in the Americas before Christopher Columbus arrived in 1492. Mann's curiosity about the history of indigenous cultures in North and South America led him to explore a complicated, ongoing controversy about how many people inhabited these continents before Columbus arrived, who they were, and the civilizations they created. His book is an extended analysis of that controversy and how scientists use available bodies of archaeological evidence to understand life in the Americas before 1492. In the preface to his book, Mann explains how he came to his subject:

> My interest in the peoples who walked the Americas before Columbus only snapped into anything resembling focus in the fall of 1992. By chance one Sunday afternoon I came across a display in a college library of the special Columbian quincentenary issue of the *Annals of the Association of American Geographers*. Curious, I picked up the journal, sank into an armchair, and began to read an article by William Denevan, a geographer at the University of Wisconsin. The article opened with the question, "What was the New World like at the time of Columbus?" Yes, I thought, what *was* it like? Who lived here and what could have passed through their minds when European sails first appeared on the horizon? I finished Denevan's article and went on to others and didn't stop reading until the librarian flicked the lights to signify closing time.

EXERCISE 5A EXPLORING OCCASIONS FOR ANALYTICAL WRITING

1. Think about a decision you had to make about an important situation or problem in your life. For example, perhaps you had to decide whether to renew the lease on your apartment or move to a less expensive apartment with new roommates. Or maybe you decided to change your major or take a semester off to volunteer for an organization like Habitat for Humanity. Write a brief essay in which you describe the situation and explain how you came to your decision. Discuss the factors you considered as you arrived at your decision. Did you do any research—for example, by talking to others for advice or by looking for information on the Internet? What information did you gather?

Helga Esteb/Shutterstock.com

How did you use this information? In other words, what did you do to analyze this situation? On the basis of this experience, draw conclusions about how you use analysis in your life.

2. Examine an article or essay in a publication you like to read (online or in print) that analyzes a problem or issue. What led the writer to the topic? What kind of analysis did he or she conduct to understand the question or problem at hand? In what ways does the writer address his or her readers with this analysis? Draw conclusions about how useful the analysis is in this case. What makes it worthwhile? What problems do you see?

3. Think about an issue or problem on your campus that interests you. What do you know about the issue or problem? What do you need to know? Now imagine that you were to write an analysis to address that issue or problem. Who would be your audience? What outcome would you hope for if you were to write such an analysis?

Understanding Analytical Writing in College

Analytical writing is perhaps the most common kind of writing assigned in college classes. The familiar *research paper* is usually an analytical project in which the writer examines an issue or problem and, using appropriate sources, analyzes that issue or problem in a way that is appropriate for that course. For instance, in a psychology course, you might write a paper on how gender affects interpersonal relationships, and part of your task would be to analyze the role of gender in relationships, much as a psychology researcher might do. Your analysis would involve reviewing appropriate sources to understand better how gender plays a role in relationships; it would also involve using psychological concepts or theories to help make sense of interpersonal relationships. Ideally, your paper would demonstrate that you understand those concepts and can apply them to your topic. In this sense, analytical writing is an effective way to learn because, in analyzing a subject like interpersonal relationships, you are likely to think more carefully (and perhaps differently) about that subject and understand it better.

Effective analytical writing in college begins with the desire to understand. Usually, this desire is focused on a complex issue or problem involving a number of different considerations. Analytical writing requires delving into the complexity of a topic by examining available evidence carefully, looking for patterns or trends in that evidence, and drawing reasonable, well-supported conclusions on the basis of the evidence.

In the following sections, we will examine examples of analytical writing to illustrate these three elements of effective analytical writing:

- a desire to understand
- a careful examination of evidence
- well-reasoned conclusions

All three readings focus on the same general subject—education—but the specific topics are different.

A Desire to Understand

This first example is from an essay by a distinguished professor who examines the impact of the increasing competition that American students face as they try to get accepted to college. In this excerpt from the beginning of his essay, Mark C. Taylor notices a problem with his students that leads him to a question, which in turn leads to the beginnings of an analysis of the problem:

> Several years ago I was teaching a course on the philosophical assumptions and cultural impact of massive multi-user online games at Williams College. The students in the course were very intelligent and obviously interested in the topic.
>
> But as the semester progressed, I began to detect a problem with the class. The students were working hard and performing well but there was no energy in our discussions and no passion in the students. They were hesitant to express their ideas and often seemed to be going through the motions. I tried to encourage them to be more venturesome with tactics I had used successfully in the past but nothing worked.
>
> One day I asked them what was or, perhaps better, was not going on. Why were they so cautious and where was their enthusiasm for learning? They seemed relieved to talk about it and their response surprised me. Since pre-kindergarten, they explained, they had been programmed to perform well so they could get to the next level. They had been taught the downside of risk and encouraged to play it safe. What mattered most was getting into a good elementary school, middle school and high school so that they would finally be admitted to a top college. Having succeeded beyond their parents' wildest expectations, they did not know why they were in college and had no idea what to do after graduation.
>
> In today's market-driven economy we constantly hear that choice is the highest good and that competition fuels innovation. But this is not always true. Choice provokes anxiety and competition can quell the imagination and discourage the spirit of experimentation that is necessary for creativity. In a world obsessed with ratings, well-meaning parents all too often train their children to jump through the hoops they think will lead to success.

Source: Taylor, Mark C. "The Perils of Being Perfect." *New York Times* 12 September 2010. Web. 30 April 2013.

Here we see that Taylor's desire to understand something he notices in his class becomes the foundation for his analysis of the students' lack of motivation.

We all have these moments of wondering, driven by a desire to understand something that interests, puzzles, or concerns us:

- Why do more students seem to have trouble with math than with history or English?
- Why is there so much traffic on the roads lately?
- What makes my dog so afraid of thunder but not of loud noises from the street?
- How do social media like Facebook affect the way people date?

Such wondering can lead to a kind of informal analysis: talking with friends, reading relevant newspaper articles, seeking information online. In academic writing, however, such wondering is usually shaped by the academic subject being studied, so that certain questions are considered important or relevant and certain ways of exploring those questions are expected. Psychologists, for example, are interested in certain questions about human behavior (Why are some people shy while others are not? How do children learn concepts? What is depression, and what causes it?), while economists are interested in others (Why do some people buy things they don't need? What factors affect the decisions people make about whether to save or spend money? How does family income influence investment decisions?). In this sense, Taylor's question about his students can be viewed as part of a larger conversation among scholars and policymakers in the field of education, and his analysis of that question will be influenced by what others in his field have said about the topic.

A Careful Examination of the Evidence

The next example also begins with a desire to understand something. Authors Michael McPherson and Morton Shapiro want to know why some Americans are more likely to attend college than others. This question of access to education has been widely studied in the United States, and experts know that several factors, such as family income, affect the ability of different groups of Americans to go to college. Therefore, McPherson and Shapiro can assume that their readers, who are likely to be other education researchers, are familiar with the idea that family income affects access to college. But because this issue is so complicated, they also know that one factor, such as family income, can't entirely explain the problem, so they have to look more closely at the issue. Here's part of their analysis:

> There are certainly significant financing constraints that contribute to differential higher education access. But there are equally important differences in pre-college preparation. Table 5 looks at college enrollment by family income and mathematics test scores. It shows that students scoring in the top third in math are quite likely to go on to college, especially if they come from families above the 25th percentile in income. Even for students in the lowest quartile, the enrollment rate is 82 percent. However, as test score performance declines, enrollment rates plummet. The decrease is especially large for students from lower income backgrounds—for example, the 82 percent rate for those with the highest test scores mentioned above falls to 48 percent when math test scores are in the lowest third. Income clearly plays a role here, but scholastic performance also contributes to explaining college entry.

TABLE 5 Postsecondary enrollment rates of 1992 high school graduates by family income and math test scores				
Math Test Scores	Lowest Income	Second Quartile	Third Quartile	Highest Income
Lowest Third	48	50	64	73
Middle Third	67	75	83	89
Top Third	82	90	95	96

Source for table: Education Pays 2004, pg. 30

Source for excerpt: McPherson, Michael S., and Morton Owen Shapiro. "Opportunity in Higher Education." *Reflections on College Access and Persistence*. Advisory Committee on Student Financial Assistance, 2006. Web. 30 April 2013.

In this excerpt, McPherson and Shapiro carefully review math test scores of high school graduates from different family income levels, looking for patterns in the scores to explain why some students are more likely to attend college than others. But they don't jump to easy conclusions. Although they acknowledge that family income is a key factor, their analysis indicates that even low-income students who have high math scores are likely to attend college. Obviously, the issue is more complicated than just a matter of family income. Most questions worth analyzing are more complicated than they seem at first glance.

Well-Reasoned Conclusions

In this next example, education researchers Linda Darling-Hammond and George Wood examine another complicated education issue: determining which government policies are likely to improve education in the United States. They draw conclusions from test scores and other statistical information about students. Like McPherson and Shapiro, Darling-Hammond and Wood also review test scores and family income, but in this case, they compare U.S. students to students from other nations, using scores from the Programme for International Student Assessment (PISA). Notice how they move from an examination of their data to conclusions about the most effective government policies:

> Of nations participating in PISA, the U.S. is among those where two students of different socio-economic backgrounds have the largest difference in expected scores. On this measure of equity, the U.S. ranked 45th out 55 total countries, right above Brazil and Mexico.[20] On the PISA assessments in reading, math, and science, for example, the distance between the average score for Asian and white students, on the one hand, and Hispanic and Latino students, on the other, is equal to the distance between the United States average and that of the highest scoring countries.
>
> In all these content areas, U.S. students from all groups do least well on the measures of problem-solving. These data suggest, first, that the United States' poor standing is substantially a product of unequal access to the kind of intellectually challenging learning measured on these international assessments. In addition, U.S. students in general, and historically underserved groups in particular, are not getting sufficient access to the problem-solving and critical thinking skills needed to apply this knowledge in a meaningful way.
>
> The reason for these disparities is not a mystery. The United States not only has the highest poverty rates for children among advanced nations with the fewest social supports, it also provides fewer resources for them at school. America is still at risk in large measure because we have failed to ensure access to education and basic family supports for all of our children.

Source: Forum for Education and Democracy. *Democracy at Risk: The Need for a New Federal Policy in Education.* 2008. 30 April 2013.

In the first paragraph of this excerpt, the authors review data that reveal inequities in test performance among U.S. students of different socioeconomic and racial backgrounds. In the second and third paragraphs, they conclude from their analysis that many American students do poorly on international tests because their family income prevents them from having access to high-quality education.

Because most topics for analysis in academic subjects are so complex, writers rarely offer easy answers or simple solutions. Instead, they reach conclusions that are well supported by their analysis of available data—and sometimes they raise new questions.

Doing Analysis

So far we have explored reasons for conducting an analysis, and we have looked at examples of analysis in academic work. But what exactly does it mean to analyze something? This section gives you practice in three important kinds of intellectual tasks that are usually part of the process of analysis:

- using a framework to analyze something
- making reasonable claims on the basis of available data or information
- supporting claims

Using a Framework to Analyze Something

Analysis often involves applying some kind of framework—a theory, a principle, or a set of criteria—to help explain or understand a problem, event, trend, or idea. For example, in psychology a writer might use the theory of behaviorism to explain the actions of children in a school lunchroom. An economist might use the principle of supply and demand to analyze prices of iPhones. For a theater arts class, students might use specific technical criteria to analyze the cinematography of chase scenes in action films.

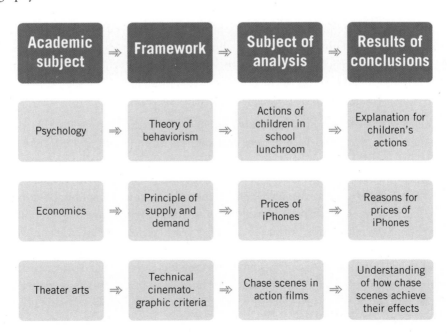

Academic subject	⇒	Framework	⇒	Subject of analysis	⇒	Results of conclusions
Psychology	⇒	Theory of behaviorism	⇒	Actions of children in school lunchroom	⇒	Explanation for children's actions
Economics	⇒	Principle of supply and demand	⇒	Prices of iPhones	⇒	Reasons for prices of iPhones
Theater arts	⇒	Technical cinemato-graphic criteria	⇒	Chase scenes in action films	⇒	Understanding of how chase scenes achieve their effects

The use of a framework helps illuminate what is being analyzed by focusing attention on specific elements, questions, or issues. For example, using technical criteria to analyze chase scenes in action films can help us understand how a director used camera angles, lighting, and editing to provoke certain reactions in viewers.

To be effective, frameworks must be applied appropriately. Students sometimes simply refer to a theory or principle rather than actually use it as a tool for analysis. For example, in this excerpt from an essay about teaching philosophies, the student attempts to apply a theory of teaching (proposed by education scholars Gerald Grant and Christine Murray) to explain the philosophy of a specific teacher:

> Ms. Jones's teaching philosophy stresses the importance of being connected with her students and the community. "When I first started teaching, I didn't understand my students' behavior or home life. I still don't," she said. "The more I learn about my students, the better idea I have of how I can relate to them." Living in the urban community where her school is located has given Ms. Jones certain insights about her students. For example, she is aware that her students are regularly exposed to gangs, drugs, and violence as well as rich cultural traditions. Her first-hand experience with the community has given Ms. Jones an opportunity to learn about her students. "Teachers must be part detective and part researcher, shifting clues children leave, collecting data, testing hypothesis and looking unblinkingly at the way children really are…in order to fill out and make credible the story of their growth and development." (Grant & Murray, 1999, p. 35)

In this case, the student refers to Grant and Murray's theory of effective teaching but does not use it to help readers understand Ms. Jones's teaching philosophy. To *apply* Grant and Murray's theory, the student writer should have used each of the key ideas of that theory (e.g., the teacher as detective and the teacher as researcher) to analyze Ms. Jones's teaching. To be helpful, a theory should be used as a "lens" to enable readers to see more clearly whatever is being analyzed.

Here's an example in which a student writer analyzes a school district to understand why it is so successful. In this excerpt, the writer uses a principle from several studies of the relationship between socioeconomic status and teacher quality in an effort to identify possible reasons for the Ridgefield School District's success. First, the student identifies the principle—that a school district's level of funding influences the quality of teachers it can hire—and then applies that principle to the case of Ridgefield to help explain Ridgefield's success:

> One factor in the success of Ridgefield School District is the affluence of the community. Research shows that minority and poor students are often taught by unlicensed, underqualified teachers, while children in wealthy districts are more likely to have certified, highly capable educators (Haycock and Crawford, 2008). Teachers in the Ridgefield School District are all fully licensed, and competition to gain a teaching position there is fierce. Starting teacher salaries are high. But the district's affluence does not mean that its teachers have cushy jobs. Although teachers at Ridgefield do not face some of the challenges that plague poor urban districts, Ridgefield teachers work hard to insure the rigor of the district's academic programs and they focus on the academic achievement of their students. It is likely that the teachers' hard work improves the students' achievement. In this sense, the district's ability to afford the best teachers probably is a main reason that its students perform so well.

The following passage is an excerpt from a 2011 report titled "Social Media and Gender" from a media consulting company:

> Since the early days of the internet, it's been apparent that women and men tend to behave as differently from one another offline as they do online. The question of social media and gender has grown even more interesting in the age of Web 2.0. According to Huffington Post, a recent study shows that women are more active on social media than are men and that women and men use online channels for different purposes. And when it comes to using social media for networking, men tend to be focused on the end goal, while women tend to value relationship-building along the way.
>
> The study reports that 68% of women participate on social networking sites, mainly to keep in touch with friends and far-flung family members. By contrast, 54% of men are active on social media for this purpose. It must be noted, however, that men are just as active as women on LinkedIn, the professional social networking site, and indeed, LinkedIn dubbed men the "savviest networkers." Statistics are all well and good, but when it comes to motivations for using social networking sites, many variables come into play. Let's not forget that many women excel at multitasking, which means that they might well be forming friendships and building relationships that could also easily fall into the purview of professional networking.
>
> Source: Grindstaff, Thomma Lyn. "Social Media and Gender." Blue Volcano Media, 30 Sept 2011. Web. 30 April 2013.

Using this report as a framework, analyze the way a specific group of people—for example, your family members, students who live in your dormitory, or members of a club to which you belong—use social media. Try to explain their uses of social media in terms of the research on gender that is cited in this article.

Making Reasonable Claims on the Basis of Available Information

Analysis requires examining and interpreting information in a way that leads to reasonable claims or assertions. One of the most common mistakes students make in analysis is going too far in making claims on the basis of available information—that is, making assertions that are not supported by the information at hand. Here's one example of a student making that mistake:

> According to one study, boys tend to associate their academic performance with skills and effort while girls associate it with luck (Grossman and Grossman, 1994). My concern is with the implications of such research. Other studies suggest that American students attribute academic success to ability and intelligence, whereas in other nations, such as Japan, students attribute academic success to effort (Kitayama and Cohen, 2007). Therefore, either there was a paradigm shift in the effort by American boys and girls or the data are false.

In this excerpt, the writer reviews two bodies of research that seem to contradict each other. The student draws two possible conclusions from this apparent contradiction: (1) that there must have been a change (a "paradigm shift") in the way American boys and girls perceive the role of effort in academic success, or (2) that the data are somehow incorrect. Neither conclusion is necessarily supported by the available information. It is possible that the attitudes of American students did change, but we don't know for certain on the basis of the two studies cited. Nor does it follow that the apparent contradiction in the two studies means that the results of the studies were incorrect. In fact, there are many possible explanations for the contradiction between the studies. For example, the studies might have examined very different student populations, or they might have used different methods (surveys, interviews, and so on). In addition, the studies might have treated gender differences differently. Given the information provided in this excerpt, we have no way of knowing whether the two studies were even examining the same thing. (For example, one study might have focused on gender differences in a specific subject area such as math, whereas the other study might have investigated student attitudes in general.)

All these possibilities suggest that the matter is too complex and the available information too limited for the claims the student makes. Given the limited information provided, the student should revise these claims. For example, it is reasonable to claim that student attitudes about the reasons for academic success seem to vary by gender as well as by nation. Such a limited claim is supported by the information provided.

The point is that you should make only those claims that reasonably emerge from your information or that can be clearly supported by your data. Here's an example of a writer doing just that. In this excerpt from a book about diet and health, the author reviews the evidence for the widespread belief that a lack of fiber in one's diet can be a factor in developing diseases of the digestive tract, including colon cancer:

Over the past quarter-century…there has been a steady accumulation of evidence refuting the notion that a fiber-deficient diet causes colon cancer, polyps, or diverticulitis, let alone any other disease of civilization. The pattern is precisely what would be expected of a hypothesis that simply isn't true: the larger and more rigorous the trials set up to test it, the more consistently negative the evidence. Between 1994 and 2000, two observational studies—of forty-seven thousand male health professionals and the eighty-nine thousand women of the Nurses Health Study, both run out of the Harvard School of Public Health—and a half-dozen randomized control trials concluded that fiber consumption is unrelated to the risk of colon cancer, as is, apparently, the consumption of fruits and vegetables. The results of the forty-nine-thousand-women Dietary Modification Trial of Women's Health Initiative, published in 2006, confirmed that increasing the fiber in the diet (by eating more whole

grains, fruits, and vegetables) had no beneficial effect on colon cancer, nor did it prevent heart disease or breast cancer or induce weight loss.

Source: Gary Taubes, *Good Calories, Bad Calories: Challenging the Conventional Wisdom on Diet, Weight Control, and Disease.* Alfred E. Knopf, 2007, pp. 132–133.

The author's purpose is to determine whether a high-fiber diet has specific health benefits, as many health care professionals and researchers have long claimed. Notice that he emphasizes that the best available studies do not support prevailing conclusions about the health benefits of eating fiber; moreover, he limits his claim to what he can reasonably support on the basis of the few available studies, asserting only that the hypothesis about specific health benefits of a high-fiber diet, such as lower rates of colon cancer, is not borne out by these studies. He does not say that eating fiber isn't beneficial; rather, he concludes that eating fiber does not lead to lower colon cancer rates and similar health benefits.

Remember to say only what your information allows you to say. Make sure your claims and assertions are reasonable given the information you have.

EXERCISE 5C MAKING REASONABLE CLAIMS

These charts present data on income and wealth distribution in the United States. For each of the following claims, determine whether the claim can be made on the basis of the data reflected in the charts; if not, revise the claim so that it is supported by the data in the charts:

1. In the past three decades, the rich have become richer while the poor have become poorer.
2. Since 1979, the incomes of the wealthiest Americans have risen more rapidly than those of other Americans.
3. Americans in general have higher incomes today than their parents had.
4. Economic recessions don't significantly affect income growth in the United States.

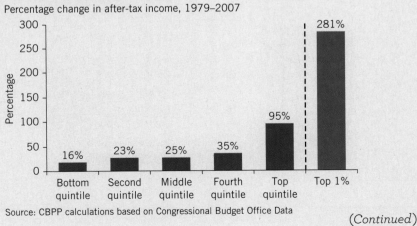

Income gains at the top dwarfed those of low- and middle-income households

Percentage change in after-tax income, 1979–2007

Source: CBPP calculations based on Congressional Budget Office Data

(Continued)

Change in average real after-tax income: 1979–2004

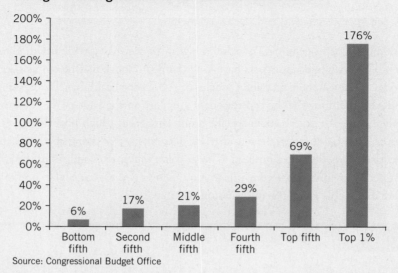

Source: Congressional Budget Office

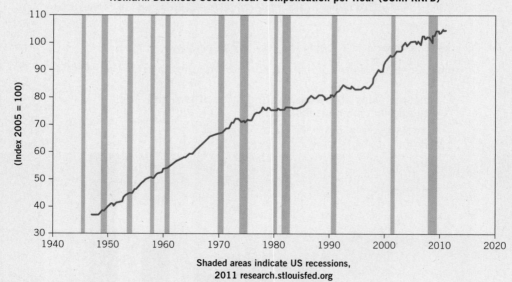

Nonfarm Business Sector: Real Compensation per Hour (COMPRNFB)

Shaded areas indicate US recessions,
2011 research.stlouisfed.org

Source: U.S. Department of Labor: Bureau of Labor Statistics.

Supporting Claims

When it comes to supporting claims in analytical writing, writers must consider two important questions:

- What is "appropriate" support?
- What is "adequate" support?

Both questions require understanding the rhetorical context (see page 29 in Chapter 2), which includes the academic discipline. In other words, what counts as *appropriate* and *adequate* support for a claim will depend on the course assignment, your intended audience, and the purpose of your project; it will also depend on the conventions in the academic discipline within which you're writing. What will be accepted as appropriate and adequate support in a chemistry lab report, for example, will differ from what would be considered appropriate and adequate for a history paper.

FOCUS **What Is a Claim?**

A claim in analytical writing is a statement or assertion you make as a result of your analysis. For example, if you are analyzing the impact of a proposed new football stadium on your campus, you might examine whether the cost of the new facility will affect tuition, increase traffic on campus, complicate parking, or reduce open space that students currently use for various activities. In analyzing the impact of the proposed stadium, you would investigate these possibilities, consulting sources and perhaps examining similar situations on other campuses. Your research might reveal that a new stadium will not likely affect tuition but will reduce open space on campus and probably complicate the parking situation for students. Those would be your claims. In this example, then, you might make three main claims as a result of your analysis: (1) The new stadium will not affect tuition; (2) The stadium will reduce open space on campus; (3) It will likely create parking problems for students on campus.

Consider the following criteria as you decide whether your support for a claim is appropriate and adequate:

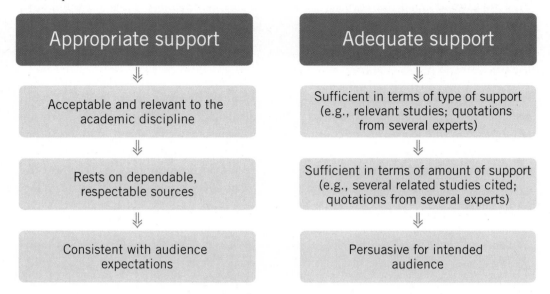

Appropriate support	Adequate support
Acceptable and relevant to the academic discipline	Sufficient in terms of type of support (e.g., relevant studies; quotations from several experts)
Rests on dependable, respectable sources	Sufficient in terms of amount of support (e.g., several related studies cited; quotations from several experts)
Consistent with audience expectations	Persuasive for intended audience

To some extent, the decision about whether support for a claim is appropriate and adequate is subjective. Not all readers will agree that a writer has sufficiently supported a claim, but you can anticipate whether your support is sufficient by considering the expectations your audience is likely to have for your rhetorical situation.

Let's look at a political scientist supporting a claim effectively in a scholarly essay about the value of civility in modern society:

> Because we are all members of the same political community, interacting on grounds of civic equality, we have an obligation to be polite in our everyday interactions with our fellow citizens. In the linguistic analogy developed by the philosopher Michael Oakeshott, civility is a kind of "adverbial" restraint on the civic language we speak with one another. In the same way that one is enjoined to speak politely, modestly or temperately, the adverbial condition of civility modifies and qualifies conduct without specifying its content. We can communicate our wishes or injunctions to fellow citizens—whatever those wishes may be—so long as we agree to subscribe to common conditions on the means we may legitimately use in the pursuit of those self-chosen ends (Oakeshott, 1990, pp. 120–121, 126 and 128; see also Boyd, 2004a). Membership is defined in terms of this common moral relationship and it is this relationship that in turn gives rise to our responsibility to be civil to others.

Source: Boyd, Richard. "The Value of Civility?" *Urban Studies* 43.5 (2006): 864. Print.

The author, Richard Boyd, states his claim in the first sentence of this excerpt. To support his claim, he refers to an analogy by an influential philosopher (Michael Oakeshott). To what extent is Boyd's support *appropriate* and *adequate* for his academic discipline and rhetorical situation?

Appropriate support	Adequate support
Acceptable and relevant to the academic discipline: citing an established philosopher is acceptable in political science	**Type of support:** reference to established scholar is adequate for this rhetorical situation
Dependable, accepted sources: Oakeshott is well known to political scientists	**Amount of support:** generally, citing a well-established scholar would be sufficient in this field
Consistent with audience expectations: readers of the journal would expect references to established scholars	**Persuasive for intended audience:** the prominent scholar cited would likely be persuasive for readers of the journal

This example illustrates the importance of the rhetorical context in supporting claims. Although some readers might disagree, it is likely that most readers in Boyd's discipline (political science) would find his support reasonable.

Deciding what kind of information you need to support a claim and how much support is enough can be confusing. In this excerpt from an essay written for a general writing course, the student provides statistical data to support her claim that the community's economic status is a result of its "low educational achievement." The assignment called for an analysis that would be appropriate for a general audience (for example, readers of the local newspaper):

> One could argue that because of the low educational achievement in this community, the socioeconomic status is relatively low. Thirty-two percent of the adults in the area did not complete secondary education. Twenty-three percent of the population in this district are below poverty level and 35.7% make under $25,000 (the per capita income is $15,272, according to the US Census Bureau, 2000). However, other factors cause this village to struggle economically. First, there are not many high-paying job opportunities. This area's industry primarily consists of manufacturing (17.2%); education, health and social services (19.9%); and recreation and accommodation (16.6%) (U.S. Census Bureau, 2000). There are four main institutions that provide jobs for this community: the Big Mountain Resort, a state prison, the school district, and a regional hospital. A small percentage of the population (3.6%) owns private businesses (U.S. Census Bureau, 2000).

The student provides a great deal of statistical data, but do the figures actually support her claim that the likely cause of the community's economic status is the community's level of educational achievement? For one thing, she provides only one bit of data about educational status (the percentage of residents who did not complete secondary education). For another, although the community's poverty level seems high, we don't know how that level compares with the national average, so it is difficult to place that figure (23%) in perspective. Also, the percentage of specific kinds of jobs (manufacturing, service, and so on) tells us nothing about the number of "high-paying" jobs. In the end, although the writer provides a lot of statistical information, it is not exactly relevant to the claim nor is it sufficient to support that claim:

Appropriate support	Adequate support
Acceptable and relevant to the academic discipline: the kind of support seems acceptable for the rhetorical situation but not relevant to the claim	**Type of support:** statistical information on jobs, income, and education is appropriate, but the specific information is inadequate for the claim
Dependable, accepted sources: Census Bureau is a dependable source	**Amount of support:** too little support that is directly relevant to the claim
Consistent with audience expectations: a general audience would likely expect more relevant information for the specific claim	**Persuasive for intended audience:** although the kind of data is likely persuasive for a general audience, readers might not find the data sufficient to support the claim

EXERCISE 5D   SUPPORTING A CLAIM WITH APPROPRIATE AND ADEQUATE INFORMATION

Use the criteria described in this section to consider what kind of information would be sufficient to support each of the following claims. The basic rhetorical situation is described in parentheses after each claim.

- The economic benefits of a college degree outweigh the costs of tuition. (letter to the editor of the campus newspaper)

- Religion is an important component of American politics. (analytical paper for a political science course)

- Popular films suggest that racist attitudes persist in the United States. (review for a film class)

Features of Analytical Writing

The examples earlier in this chapter illustrate **four main features of effective analytical writing:**

1. **A relevant topic worthy of analysis.** Academic fields are defined by certain bodies of knowledge (the periodic table in chemistry, the nature of human emotion in psychology) and by the kinds of questions or problems that experts in those fields examine (What happens when two substances from the periodic table are combined? Why are some people more likely to suffer from depression than others?). So identifying a worthy topic for analysis requires knowing what kinds of questions are relevant in a specific field and what is known about those questions. The best analytical writing grows out of questions that are genuinely interesting to the writer and relevant to readers. Considering whether your topic might interest other students in your class or other readers familiar with that academic subject is an important step toward determining whether the topic is worthy of analysis.

2. **Complexity.** Rarely are interesting questions or problems as straightforward as they might seem. Good analysis, therefore, is about exploring complexity and trying to understand a question, problem, trend, event, or idea more fully by examining it in depth. Good analytical writing requires a measure of objectivity and even skepticism to avoid oversimplified explanations. It should help readers appreciate and grasp the complexity of a topic.

3. **Sufficient and appropriate evidence and support.** Effective analytical writing involves finding sufficient information about a topic and gathering appropriate evidence to support claims and conclusions. How much information is *sufficient* depends on the topic and the depth of analysis. Similarly, what counts as *appropriate* evidence depends on the subject, the audience, the purpose of the analysis, and the field of study. The right kind of information and evidence can lead to more effective analysis.

4. **Reasonable conclusions.** Because most topics in academic writing are complex, writers must interpret the information they find and draw reasonable conclusions supported by relevant evidence. In good analytical writing, writers resist the temptation to settle on seemingly obvious conclusions. Instead, they examine possibilities and draw conclusions that their readers should find reasonable on the basis of available information and evidence.

All good analytical writing shares these characteristics. Let's look at how one writer employs these features of analysis effectively.

In the following essay, Carolyn Johnson wonders whether boredom is something we should value. Johnson's essay is not an academic essay, but it demonstrates strategies that can be used in any analytical writing.

THE JOY OF BOREDOM
by Carolyn Johnson

1 A decade ago, those monotonous minutes were just a fact of life: time ticking away, as you gazed idly into space, stood in line, or sat in bumper-to-bumper traffic.

2 Boredom's doldrums were unavoidable, yet also a primordial soup for some of life's most quintessentially human moments. Jostled by a stranger's cart in the express checkout line, thoughts of a loved one might come to mind. A long drive home after a frustrating day could force ruminations. A pang of homesickness at the start of a plane ride might put a journey in perspective.

> **A Relevant Topic Worthy of Analysis**
>
> In the **opening paragraphs**, Johnson poses a question that she believes her readers will find worth analyzing: whether boredom is "a good thing." Her question grows out of her observation that people today don't seem to spend their "free" moments as people did before the advent of digital media. That question leads to her analysis, which can be seen as part of a larger conversation about the role of technology in contemporary life.

3 Increasingly, these empty moments are being saturated with productivity, communication, and the digital distractions offered by an ever-expanding array of slick mobile devices. A few years ago, cellphone maker Motorola even began using the word "microboredom" to describe the ever-smaller slices of free time from which new mobile technology offers an escape. "Mobisodes," two-minute-long television episodes of everything from "Lost" to "Prison Break" made for the cellphone screen, are perfectly tailored for the microbored. Cellphone games are often designed to last just minutes—simple, snack-sized diversions like Snake, solitaire, and Tetris. Social networks like Twitter and Facebook turn every mundane moment between activities into a chance to broadcast feelings and thoughts; even if it is just to triple-tap a keypad with the words "I am bored."

4 But are we too busy twirling through the songs on our iPods— while checking e-mail, while changing lanes on the highway—to consider whether we are giving up a good thing? We are most human

> **A Relevant Topic Worthy of Analysis**
>
> In **paragraph 4**, Johnson clearly identifies her topic and focuses her readers' attention on the specific issue that she will analyze.

when we feel dull. Lolling around in a state of restlessness is one of life's greatest luxuries—one not available to creatures that spend all their time pursuing mere survival. To be bored is to stop reacting to the external world, and to explore the internal one. It is in these times of reflection that people often discover something new, whether it is an epiphany about a relationship or a new theory about the way the universe works. Granted, many people emerge from boredom feeling that they have accomplished nothing. But is accomplishment really the point of life? There is a strong argument that boredom—so often parodied as a glassy-eyed drooling state of nothingness—is an essential human emotion that underlies art, literature, philosophy, science, and even love.

Sufficient and Appropriate Evidence and Support

In **paragraph 5** and elsewhere, Johnson uses the opinions of experts to explore and support her main assertion. She is essentially asking the experts, "So what do we know about the value of boredom?"

5 "If you think of boredom as the prelude to creativity, and loneliness as the prelude to engagement of the imagination, then they are good things," said Dr. Edward Hallowell, a Sudbury psychiatrist and author of the book *CrazyBusy*. "They are doorways to something better, as opposed to something to be abhorred and eradicated immediately."

6 Public health officials often bemoan the obesity epidemic, the unintended consequence of a modern lifestyle that allows easy access to calories. Technology seems to offer a similar proposition: a wide array of distractions that offer the boon of connection, but at a cost. Already, mobile technology has shaped the way people interact and communicate. People no longer make plans in the same way; public spaces have

Complexity

In **paragraph 6**, Johnson begins to look more closely at how technology affords people more ways to distract themselves than they had in the past. This kind of close examination is an essential part of effective analytical writing.

become semi-private bubbles of conversation; and things like getting a busy signal or being unreachable seem foreign, even quaint. Today, distraction from monotony is not just merely available; it is almost unavoidable.

7 Perhaps nothing illuminates the speed of social change better than the new fear of disconnection. People driving a car or standing at a bus stop or waiting in a doctor's office by themselves have always had some distractions available to them, from the radio to *National Geographic*. But until the advent of connected devices, they were still, fundamentally, alone in some way.

8 Today, there is a growing fear of the prospect of being untethered in the world without the security blanket of a cellphone. In the timescale of human inventions, the mobile phone is still new, but it is already a crucial part of the trinity of things people fear to forget when they leave the house—keys, wallet, and phone.

9 "There is this hyper-anxiety over feeling lonely or disconnected," said Kathleen Cumiskey, a professor of psychology and women's studies at the College of Staten Island who says her stepdaughter sleeps with her cellphone at arm's length and considers turning the device off unthinkable. "Our society is perpetually anxious, and a way to alleviate the anxiety is to delve into something that's very within our control, pleasurable, and fun.... It feels like it has all the makings of addiction."

10 In a way, the entrepreneurs looking to capitalize on the small moments of spare time that are sprinkled through modern life parallel the pharmaceutical industry. A growing chorus of mental health specialists has begun to question whether normal sadness and social anxiety are being transformed into disorders that people believe need to be cured—by the companies offering elixirs. The tech industry may be doing the same thing with disconnection.

11 Many of the original arguments for having a cellphone—safety, security, emergencies—never figure into the advertisements. Like the commercials that show frowning people transformed into smiling, kitten-cuddling normality, technology companies project a happy world of connection where to intentionally disconnect seems freakish, questionable, undeniably an ailment.

12 Society has accepted connection so well that it takes a step back to see exactly how far things have come. Instead of carrying their entire social universe in a pocket, people used to walk out of their houses and into the world. Today, not picking up the phone for an hour is an act of defiance.

Sufficient and Appropriate Evidence and Support

In **paragraph 9**, Johnson uses a quotation from an expert to support her opening statement in the preceding paragraph. She uses her sources effectively to provide evidence for assertions and to elaborate on a specific point.

A Relevant Topic Worthy of Analysis

Johnson's references in **paragraph 11** to advertisements and commercials support her analysis of how the use of technologies like cell phones has changed. These references also highlight the role of the writer's medium in analytical writing. Johnson originally wrote this essay for the *Boston Globe*, a traditional print publication, so she could only refer to advertisements and commercials or perhaps include images of them in her text. In an online medium such as a blog, however, she could include links to those ads and commercials or embed them in her text.

Reasonable Conclusions

In **paragraph 12**, Johnson interprets what she has learned through her analysis. She concludes that the decision not to use a cell phone for a while is "an act of defiance." In analytical writing, conclusions and interpretations must be supported.

13 Perhaps understandably, boredom has never caught the attention of the psychological world. Emotions like anxiety, fear, or anger have been subjected to a much more thorough examination than merely feeling drab, according to Richard Ralley, a lecturer in psychology at Edge Hill University in England.

14 "What's gone wrong with the psychology of emotion is that the ones that are easy to do are the ones that have been researched: fear, threat, fear, threat, again and again and again," Ralley said. "A lot of other emotions that really make us human—pride, for instance—we kind of avoid."

15 So, Ralley set out to examine boredom more closely, with the idea that the feeling must have a purpose. Just looking around, it was evident that children quell boredom quite naturally, with creativity—even to the point of taking the packaging around a gift and playing with it for hours. But as people get older, anxious parents and cranky children demand more and more specific stimuli, whether it is a video game or a hot new phone.

16 As Ralley studied boredom, it came to make a kind of sense: If people are slogging away at an activity with little reward, they get annoyed and find themselves feeling bored. If something more engaging comes along, they move on. If nothing does, they may be motivated enough to think of something new themselves. The most creative people, he said, are known to have the greatest toleration for long periods of uncertainty and boredom.

17 In one of the most famous scenes in literature, for instance, boredom takes time. Marcel Proust describes his protagonist, Marcel, dunking a madeleine cookie into his teacup.

18 "Dispirited after a dreary day with the prospect of a depressing morrow, I raised to my lips a spoonful of the tea in which I had soaked a morsel of the cake," Proust wrote. "And at once the vicissitudes of life had become indifferent to me, its disasters innocuous, its brevity illusory... I had ceased now to feel mediocre, contingent, mortal."

Sufficient and Appropriate Evidence and Support

In **paragraph 13**, Johnson introduces her readers to another expert (Richard Ralley) to explain the value of boredom. Notice that all Johnson's experts are psychologists or scholars in the field of psychology. But psychology is a large, complicated field, so Johnson has to find psychologists who have expertise specifically in her topic (boredom).

Complexity

In **paragraphs 17 through 19**, Johnson analyzes a scene from Marcel Proust's famous novel *Remembrance of Things Past* to support her point about the role of boredom in fostering creativity. Notice that she quotes an English professor in **paragraph 20** and then a cell-phone user in **paragraph 22**, each of whom is a different kind of "expert" on boredom. Effective analysis involves looking at a question or phenomenon from various perspectives.

5

19 Marcel's senses are recalibrated, his experiences deepened, and the very nature of memory begins to reveal itself. But it is only through the strenuous process of clearing his mind and concentrating that his thoughts begin to unfurl completely, immersing him in memory. Had Marcel been holding a silver clamshell phone in his hand instead of the delicately scalloped cookie, perhaps he could have quieted the boredom with a quick game of cellphone Tetris. And had Proust come of age with an iPhone in his hand and the expectation that his entire world fit in his pocket, he may never have written his grandiose novel.

20 "When we're writing deeply, writing thoughtfully, we are often trying to communicate with ourselves and trying to communicate what ultimately can't be communicated—the greatest mysteries of the world: what is truth; what is beauty; what is being?" said Eric G. Wilson, an English professor at Wake Forest University and author of the new book, *Against Happiness*.

21 Arthur Wright, 55, who works in the travel industry, said that he refuses to carry a cellphone precisely because he has sees the effects every time he ventures out into one of the confession booths our public spaces have become.

22 "You hear these stupid conversations.... You know, it's just 'I'm bored,' and they'll call and chit-chat on the phone," Wright said. "'I'm almost there, I'm turning the corner right now.' What would they do without it? It's like kids who use a calculator in school, and they can't add."

23 Connectivity, of course, has serious advantages. Parents can check in with their kids. Friends separated by hundreds of miles can have a conversation almost as if they were walking side by side. People feel safer.

> ### Complexity
>
> In **paragraph 23**, Johnson acknowledges that the constant connection afforded by new digital technologies can be beneficial. To analyze a topic sufficiently requires considering various sides of the topic, including perspectives with which the writer might disagree. By considering other perspectives, Johnson makes her analysis more thorough.

24 Still, there has been surprisingly little public discussion of the broad sociological and psychological impact the technology will have. Like much change, it has crept up on people and radically changed behavior and expectations in ways few people could have predicted. At one time, the car was a novelty—things like getting gas and driving on good roads were difficult to do. Today, the modern world is built around an automotive infrastructure, and is almost impossible to navigate without one.

> ### Complexity
>
> Writers use rhetorical strategies to help readers understand complicated topics. To help readers understand her point in **paragraph 24** about the potential impact of technology, Johnson compares the development of digital communications technologies to that of the automobile. She uses something familiar to explain an unfamiliar idea.

Examining Causes and Effects

WE ROUTINELY ENCOUNTER situations in our daily lives that raise questions about causes or effects. For example, maybe you've noticed that you seem to have more energy during pick-up basketball games if you've eaten a light lunch. You wonder, Is there a connection between what you eat and how you feel during exercise? So you pay attention to what you eat on days when you play basketball, you ask a friend about her eating habits before exercising, and you look online for information about the impact of diet on exercise. You are trying to determine the effect of your diet on your exercising so that you can decide what and when to eat on the days you work out. Analyzing causes and effects in this way can help us make decisions and solve problems.

In more formal causal analysis, the purpose is usually to identify possible causes or effects in order to understand an event, phenomenon, or trend; to explain a social, economic, or political development; or to develop a solution to a complex problem:

- An economist examines whether a certain federal policy affects how people invest their money.

- A biologist studies the side effects of a new medication.

- A psychologist analyzes the impact of social media on peer-group relationships among teens.

- A political scientist measures the effect of negative ads on the outcome of a political campaign.

Such analyses rarely boil something down to a single cause or effect, but they can help explain a phenomenon, event, trend, development, or outcome. Because of this capacity to illuminate complex matters, causal analysis is essential in academic work.

Occasions for Causal Analysis

In *Born to Run*, a book about the physiology, history, and practice of running, author Christopher McDougall tells his readers that the book began with a single question: "Why does my foot hurt?" As a life-long runner, McDougall was frustrated by chronic running-related injuries and began to investigate why he and most other avid runners suffer so many injuries. His book is an investigation into the causes of injuries among runners and the effects of various approaches to running.

Aspen Photo/Shutterstock.com; Stockbyte/Photos.com

McDougall's inquiry led him to discover the practice of barefoot running, which some studies suggested results in fewer injuries than running with modern running shoes. After examining those studies and the barefoot running movement, he concluded that running with shoes is a primary cause of injury among runners.

Circumstances or an experience can trigger a question that points to causes or effects about something that matters to the writer and to others. McDougal wondered what caused his running injuries, and his analysis was of great interest to the thousands of other runners who shared his worries about injury. In this way, causal analysis can be a means of solving problems. McDougall wanted to avoid injury, but he first had to understand what was causing his injuries. His analysis was driven by his need to understand something; that understanding became the basis for his decisions about how best to run.

The need to answer a question about why something happens can be the best starting point for effective causal analysis. In addition, college writing assignments often provide opportunities to analyze causes or effects:

- A biology lab report might describe an experiment that examines the effects of a specific hormone on the growth pattern of tadpoles.

- For a business class, students might investigate whether low-interest loans to small businesses create jobs in their communities.

- A paper for a psychology class might examine the impact of bullying on self-esteem among teens.

- An assignment in an art history class might ask students to explore the factors that led to the Impressionist movement.

Like McDougall's book about barefoot running, such assignments usually begin with a relevant question about why something happens. The analysis is driven by the writer's curiosity about the causes or effects of something that matters.

Understanding Causal Analysis

Identifying causes and effects demands care to avoid simplistic explanations. In many cases, causes or effects might seem obvious, but often there is greater complexity than meets the eye. For example, many people believe that the widespread use of text messaging has caused students' spelling skills to erode. At first glance, texting does seem to be a reasonable explanation for poor spelling among young people, but a closer look reveals that many other factors—including the schools students attend, the nature of the writing instruction they receive, students' socioeconomic backgrounds, their early experiences with reading and writing—can influence how well (or how poorly) a student spells.

Analyzing causes or effects requires exploring a topic sufficiently in order to determine whether a cause-effect relationship is real. In order to pinpoint texting as a cause of poor spelling, for example, a writer would have to establish, first, that spelling skills have in fact diminished as texting has increased. The writer would also have to find out how widespread texting is among students and how much time most students spend texting as compared to other kinds of writing or reading, making sure that the evidence is trustworthy and convincing. In addition, other possible causes would have to be investigated: for example, the kind of writing instruction students usually receive; how much attention spelling is given in schools; whether students' experiences with reading and writing outside schools have an impact on spelling; and so on. All these factors complicate the picture and make it likely that texting alone does not explain poor spelling in student writing.

To write an effective causal analysis, then, requires examining a topic in depth and thoroughly investigating possible causes and effects. Use **the four main features of effective analytical writing** (described in Chapter 5) to guide your causal analysis:

1. **A relevant topic worthy of analysis.** Establish why it is important and relevant to understand the causes or effects of the event, trend, or phenomenon you are examining:

   - Why would readers want to understand causes or effects when it comes to this topic?

   - What's at stake for them—and for you—in trying to explain causes or effects in this case?

   - What can be gained by identifying causes and effects in this case?

2. **Complexity.** Explore possible explanations and avoid settling for easy or obvious explanations:

   - Are you confident that you have identified the likely causes or effects to explain the phenomenon, trend, or event you are analyzing?

   - Have you ruled out other possible causes or effects?

   - Have you avoided the trap of mistaking correlation for causation? (See "Causation vs. Correlation.")

   - Have you avoided oversimplifying the phenomenon, trend, or event you are analyzing?

3. **Sufficient information and appropriate evidence.** Gather enough information about possible causes or effects to explain the event, trend, or phenomenon you are analyzing and to rule out other possible explanations:

   - Have you investigated possible causes sufficiently to explain the effects you have identified?

   - Have you learned enough about the subject you are studying to rule out other possible causes or effects?

   - Are you confident that your sources are valid and trustworthy and your evidence is adequate to explain the causes and effects you have identified?

4. **Reasonable conclusions.** Present well-reasoned and persuasive conclusions about the causes or effects of the phenomenon, event, or trend you are analyzing:

   - Do your conclusions about causes or effects adequately explain the event, trend, or phenomenon you have analyzed?

   - Do your conclusions present readers with a sound explanation that does not oversimplify the topic?

Perhaps the most common mistake in causal analysis is confusing correlation for causation. For example, some studies show that children who watch a lot of television are more likely to have behavior problems in school. Some people might conclude from such studies that watching too much TV causes children to act out. But in fact the studies did not establish that watching TV for so many hours a day actually causes behavior problems; rather, the studies identified a *correlation* between watching a certain amount of TV and certain kinds of behaviors. The *causes* of those behaviors were not identified. It's possible that the children who watched a lot of TV had other factors in common that might have contributed to their behaviors, such as less adult supervision, fewer opportunities to interact with other children, or even a certain kind of diet. Correlation might *suggest* the causes of something, but it doesn't *prove* them.

EXERCISE 6B | UNDERSTANDING CAUSE AND EFFECT

1. Identify an issue that interests you involving causes or effects. For example, you might be concerned about an increase in the ticket prices of sporting events at your school and wonder why those prices have risen. In a brief paragraph, describe the issue or situation and identify what you believe are the main causes or effects involved. Explain why you believe specific causes or effects are significant in this case. Describe any evidence you might have for your views about those causes and effects.

2. In a group of classmates, share the paragraphs you wrote for question #1. Discuss each person's views about causes and effects in the issue they examined. Do you agree with each person's list of possible causes and effects? Why or why not? As a group, try to identify in each case possible explanations that the writer might have missed. What conclusions about causal analysis might you draw from this exercise?

3. Identify a current controversy that seems to involve disagreements about causes and effects. (For example, the debate about gun control in the United States often focuses on the question of whether stricter gun ownership regulations will reduce gun violence.) Find several articles or editorial essays about the controversy, and examine how the writers discuss causes and effects by addressing the following questions: To what extent do the writers discuss specific causes and effects? Do they oversimplify the issue in identifying specific causes and effects? Do they mistake causation for correlation? In a brief paragraph, describe the controversy and the articles or essays you examined, and draw conclusions about how questions of cause and effect figure into such controversies.

Reading Causal Analysis

This section includes several examples of causal analysis that illustrate the four main characteristics of effective analytical writing:

A relevant topic worthy of analysis	• How does the writer establish this topic as worthy of analysis? • What is the writer's purpose in examining these causes and effects? • Why should readers want to understand the causes and effects examined by the writer?
Complexity	• How thoroughly does the writer explore each possible cause or effect? • Does the writer consider possible alternative explanations for the phenomenon being analyzed? • Do the causes and effects examined reflect the complexity of the topic?
Sufficient information and appropriate analysis	• Has the writer explained the phenomenon sufficiently through his or her causal analysis? • Does the writer present appropriate evidence to support claims and conclusions sufficiently?
Reasonable conclusions	• What conclusions about the phenomenon does the writer reach through this causal analysis? • Do these conclusions grow logically out of the analysis? • Do the conclusions offer a persuasive explanation of the phenomenon?

The United States of Inequality

by Timothy Noah

In this essay, published in 2012 in Slate, *an online magazine of politics and culture, journalist Timothy Noah tries to identify the causes of "the great divergence"—that is, the large difference in the incomes of the very wealthy and the rest of the population in the United States. Noah draws on previous research to identify seven possible causes of income inequality: immigration, technology, political policies, the decline of labor unions, international trade, compensation policies for executives on Wall Street, and education. In the excerpt reprinted here, he reviews three of the most common explanations for income inequality (race, gender, and the decline of the nuclear family) and then focuses on immigration as a possible cause of income inequality. Notice that Noah doesn't settle for obvious answers to his main question, instead thoroughly exploring many possible angles. Ultimately, his analysis does not lead to a single definite cause of income inequality but several likely causes, which can help us better understand this phenomenon and what might be done about it.*

. . . .

Introducing the Great Divergence

In 1915, a statistician at the University of Wisconsin named Willford I. King published *The Wealth and Income of the People of the United States*, the most comprehensive study of its kind to date. The United States was displacing Great Britain as the world's wealthiest nation, but detailed information about its economy was not yet readily available; the federal government wouldn't start collecting such data in any systematic way until the 1930s. One of King's purposes was to reassure the public that all Americans were sharing in the country's newfound wealth.

King was somewhat troubled to find that the richest 1 percent possessed about 15 percent of the nation's income. (A more authoritative subsequent calculation puts the figure slightly higher, at about 18 percent.)[1]

This was the era in which the accumulated wealth of America's richest families—the Rockefellers, the Vanderbilts, the Carnegies—helped prompt creation of the modern income tax, lest disparities in wealth turn the United States into a European-style aristocracy. The socialist movement was at its historic peak, a wave of anarchist bombings was terrorizing the nation's industrialists, and President Woodrow Wilson's attorney general, Alexander Palmer, would soon stage brutal raids on radicals of every stripe. In American history, there has never been a time when class warfare seemed more imminent.

That was when the richest 1 percent accounted for 18 percent of the nation's income. Today, the richest 1 percent account for 24 percent of the nation's income. What caused this to happen? Over the next two weeks, I'll try to answer that question by looking at all potential explanations—race, gender, the computer revolution, immigration, trade, government policies, the decline of labor, compensation policies on Wall Street and in executive suites, and education. Then I'll explain why people who say we don't need to worry about income inequality (there aren't many of them) are wrong.

Income inequality in the United States has not worsened steadily since 1915. It dropped a bit in the late teens, then started climbing again in the 1920s, reaching its peak just before the 1929 crash. The trend then reversed itself. Incomes started to become more equal in the 1930s and then became dramatically more equal in the 1940s.[2] Income distribution remained roughly stable through the postwar economic boom of the 1950s and 1960s. Economic historians Claudia Goldin and Robert Margo have termed this midcentury era the "Great Compression." The deep nostalgia for that period felt by the World War II generation—the era of *Life* magazine and the bowling league—reflects something more than mere sentimentality. Assuming you were white, not of draft age, and Christian, there probably was no better time to belong to America's middle class.

(Continued)

The Great Compression ended in the 1970s. Wages stagnated, inflation raged, and by the decade's end, income inequality had started to rise. Income inequality grew through the 1980s, slackened briefly at the end of the 1990s, and then resumed with a vengeance in the aughts. In his 2007 book *The Conscience of a Liberal*, the Nobel laureate, Princeton economist and *New York Times* columnist Paul Krugman labeled the post-1979 epoch the "Great Divergence."

It's generally understood that we live in a time of growing income inequality, but "the ordinary person is not really aware of how big it is," Krugman told me. During the late 1980s and the late 1990s, the United States experienced two unprecedentedly long periods of sustained economic growth—the "seven fat years" and the "long boom." Yet from 1980 to 2005, *more than* 80 *percent* of total increase in Americans' income went to the top 1 percent. Economic growth was more sluggish in the aughts, but the decade saw productivity increase by about 20 percent. Yet virtually none of the increase translated into wage growth at middle and lower incomes, an outcome that left many economists scratching their heads.

Here is a snapshot of income distribution during the past 100 years:

The Top Ten Percent Income Share, 1947–2008

Great Depression 1929–1941 · Great Compression 1941–1979 · Great Divergence 1979–present

Excluding capital gains
Including capital gains

Income is defined as market income (and excludes government transfers). In 2008, top decile includes all families with annual income above $109,000.

Source: Thomas Piketty and Emmanuel Saez.

Why don't Americans pay more attention to growing income disparity? One reason may be our enduring belief in social mobility. Economic inequality is less troubling if you live in a country where any child, no matter how humble his or her origins, can grow up to be president. In a survey of 27 nations conducted from 1998 to 2001, the country where the highest proportion agreed with the statement "people are rewarded for intelligence and skill" was, of course, the United States (69 percent). But when it comes to *real* as opposed to *imagined* social mobility, surveys find less in the United States than in much of (what we consider) the class-bound Old World. France, Germany, Sweden, Denmark, Spain—not to mention some newer nations like Canada and Australia—are all places where your chances of rising from the bottom are better than they are in the land of Horatio Alger's *Ragged Dick*.

All my life I've heard Latin America described as a failed society (or collection of failed societies) because of its grotesque maldistribution of wealth. Peasants in rags beg for food outside the high walls of opulent villas, and so on. But according to the Central Intelligence Agency (whose patriotism I hesitate to question), income distribution in the United States is more unequal than in Guyana, Nicaragua, and Venezuela, and roughly on par with Uruguay, Argentina, and Ecuador. Income inequality is actually declining in Latin America even as it continues to increase in the United States. Economically speaking, the richest nation on earth is starting to resemble a banana republic. The main difference is that the United States is big enough to maintain geographic distance between the villa-dweller and the beggar. As Ralston Thorpe tells his St. Paul's classmate, the investment banker Sherman McCoy, in Tom Wolfe's 1987 novel *The Bonfire of the Vanities*: "You've got to insulate, insulate, insulate."

In 1915, King wrote, "It is easy to find a man in almost any line of employment who is *twice* as efficient as another employee,"

> but it is very rare to find one who is **ten times** as efficient. It is common, however, to see one man possessing not **ten** times but **a thousand** times the wealth of his neighbor.... Is the middle class doomed to extinction and shall we soon find the handful of plutocrats, the modern barons of wealth, lined up squarely in opposition to the propertyless masses with no buffer between to lessen the chances of open battle? With the middle class gone and the laborer condemned to remain a lifelong wage-earner with no hope of attaining wealth or even a competence in his old age, all the conditions are ripe for a crowning class-conflict equaling in intensity and bitterness anything pictured by the most radical follower of Karl Marx. Is this condition soon coming to pass? [emphasis his]

In the end, King concluded it wasn't. Income distribution in the United States, he found, was more equal than in Prussia, France, and the United Kingdom. King was no socialist. Redistributing income to the poor, he wrote, "would merely mean more rapid multiplication of the lowest and least desirable classes," who remained, "from the reproductive standpoint, on the low point of their four-footed ancestors."

(Continued)

A Malthusian, he believed in population control. Income inequality in the United States could be addressed by limiting immigration (King deplored "low-standard alien invaders") and by discouraging excessive breeding among the poor ("eugenicists are just beginning to impress upon us the absurd folly of breeding great troops of paupers, defectives and criminals to be a burden upon organized society").

Today, incomes in the U.S. are *more* unequal than in Germany, France, and the United Kingdom, not less so. Eugenics (thankfully) has fallen out of fashion, and the immigration debate has become (somewhat) more polite. As for income inequality, it's barely entered the national political debate. Indeed, the evidence from the 2000 and 2004 presidential elections suggests that even mild economic populism was a loser for Democrats. (To sample authentic economic populism, click here.)

But income inequality is a topic of huge importance to American society and therefore a subject of large and growing interest to a host of economists, political scientists, and other wonky types. Except for a few Libertarian outliers (whose views we'll examine later), these experts agree that the country's growing income inequality is deeply worrying. Even Alan Greenspan, the former Federal Reserve Board chairman and onetime Ayn Rand acolyte, has registered concern. "This is not the type of thing which a democratic society—a capitalist democratic society—can really accept without addressing," Greenspan said in 2005. Greenspan's Republican-appointed successor, Ben Bernanke, has also fretted about income inequality.

Yet few of these experts have much idea how to reverse the trend. That's because almost no one can agree about what's causing it. This week and next, I will detail and weigh the strengths and weaknesses of various prominent theories as to what has brought about the income inequality boom of the last three decades. At the same time, I'll try to convey the magnitude of its effects on American life. The Great Divergence may represent the most significant change in American society in your lifetime—and it's not a change for the better. Let's see if we can figure out what got us here.

The Usual Suspects Are Innocent

Most discussion about inequality in the United States focuses on race and gender. That makes sense, because our society has a conspicuous history of treating blacks differently from whites and women differently from men. Black/white and male/female inequality persist to this day. The median annual income for women working full time is 23 percent lower than for their male counterparts. The median annual income for black families is 38 percent lower than for their white counterparts. The extent to which these imbalances involve lingering racism and sexism or more complex matters of sociology and biology is a topic of much anguished and heated debate.

But we need not delve into that debate, because the Great Divergence can't be blamed on either race or gender. To contribute to the growth in income inequality over the past three decades, the income gaps between women and men, and between blacks and whites, would have to have grown. They didn't.

The black/white gap in median family income has stagnated; it's a mere three percentage points smaller today than it was in 1979.[3] This lack of progress is dismaying. So is the apparent trend that, during the current economic downturn, the black/white income gap widened somewhat. But the black/white income gap can't be a contributing factor to the Great Divergence if it hasn't grown over the past three decades. And even if it *had* grown, there would be a limit to how much impact it could have on the national income-inequality trend, because African-Americans constitute only 13 percent of the U.S. population.

Women constitute half the U.S. population, but they can't be causing the Great Divergence because the male-female wage gap has shrunk by nearly half. Thirty years ago the median annual income for women working full-time was not 23 percent less than men's, but 40 percent less.[4] Most of these gains occurred in the 1980s and early 1990s; during the past five years they halted. But there's every reason to believe the male-female income gap will continue to narrow in the future, if only because in the U.S. women are now better educated than men. Ever since the late 1990s female students have outnumbered male students at colleges and universities. The female-male ratio is currently 57 to 43, and the U.S. Department of Education expects that disparity to increase over the next decade.

Far from contributing to the Great Divergence, women have, to a remarkable degree, absented themselves from it. Take a look at this bar graph by David Autor, an MIT labor economist:

The graph demonstrates that during the past three decades, women have outperformed men at all education levels in the workforce. Both men and women have

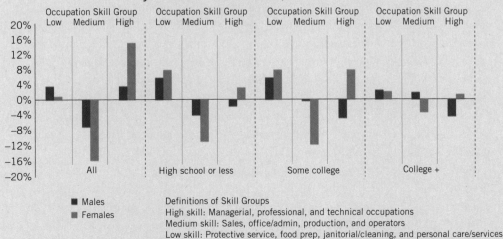

Changes in Occupational Employment Shares
By Education and Sex, 1979–2007

■ Males
■ Females

Definitions of Skill Groups
High skill: Managerial, professional, and technical occupations
Medium skill: Sales, office/admin, production, and operators
Low skill: Protective service, food prep, janitorial/cleaning, and personal care/services

Source: David Autor and Center for American Progress.

(Continued)

(in the aggregate) been moving out of moderately skilled jobs—secretary, retail sales representative, steelworker, etc.—women more rapidly than men. But women have been much more likely than men to shift upward into higher skilled jobs—from information technology engineer and personnel manager on up through various high-paying professions that require graduate degrees (doctor, lawyer, etc.).

These findings suggest that women's relative gains in the workplace are not solely a You've-Come-a-Long-Way-Baby triumph of the feminist movement and individual pluck. They also reflect downward mobility among men. My *Slate* colleague Hanna Rosin, writing in the *Atlantic*, recently looked at these and other data and asked, "What if the modern, postindustrial economy is simply more congenial to women than to men?"

She might have asked the same about the modern, postindustrial family. The declining economic value of men as Ward Cleaver-style breadwinners is a significant reason for the rise in single parenthood, which most of the time means children being raised by an unmarried or divorced mother. The percentage of children living with one parent has doubled since 1970, from 12 percent to more than 26 percent in 2004 (see Table 2). Conservatives often decry this trend, and they rightly point out that children who grow up in single-parent homes are much likelier to be poor. "Single mothers seldom command high wages," confirmed David Ellwood and Christopher Jencks, both of Harvard's Kennedy School of Government, in a 2004 paper. "They also find it unusually difficult to work long hours." But it would be difficult to attribute much of the Great Divergence to single parenthood, because it increased mostly before 1980, when the Great Divergence was just getting under way.[5] By the early 1990s, the growth trend halted altogether, and though it resumed in the aughts the rate of growth was significantly slower.[6]

Also, single parenthood isn't as damaging economically as it was at the start of the Great Divergence. "That's mostly because the percentage of women who are actually working who are single parents went up," Jencks told me. In a January 2008 paper, three Harvard sociologists concluded that the two-thirds rise in income inequality among families with children from 1975 to 2005 could not be attributed to divorce and out-of-wedlock births. "Single parenthood increased inequality," they conceded, "but the income gap was closed by mothers who entered the labor force." One trend canceled the effects of another (at least in the aggregate).

While we're on the topic of single versus two-parent households, perhaps we ought to consider what a "household" is.

Stephen J. Rose is a labor economist at Georgetown best-known for publishing, since the 1970s, successive editions of *Social Stratification in the United States*, a pamphlet and poster much revered by the left that depicts economic inequality in the United States. In his recent book *Rebound*, Rose made an apparent 180-degree turn and argued that worries about rising income inequality and a disappearing middle class were overblown. Rose built his case largely on the notion that the Census Bureau's preferred metric—"median household income"—was misleading.

The trouble, Rose wrote, was that households varied greatly in composition and size. A household might consist of a single young man just starting out on his own or an elderly widow in retirement. Neither would likely enjoy a high income, but that would be a function of mere circumstance (the young man was just beginning his climb up the greasy pole; the retired widow no longer worked at all) and need (neither was likely to be responsible for any children). Another problem, Rose suggested, was that some households were bigger than others. Couples tended to have larger household incomes than single people, but that was because they likely collected two paychecks rather than one. The proportion of Americans living alone had for various reasons increased over time; that needed to be taken into account, too. Correcting for all these factors, Rose calculated that median household income was 30 percent higher than the Census' official figure (about $50,000 in 2007).

That was the good news. The bad news was that even with these new calculations, Rose couldn't deny the existence of a Great Divergence. "Under all circumstances," he wrote, "inequality has risen considerably, and this is a bad thing for America. Those at the bottom of the income ladder have benefited only minimally from the significant gains in overall production over the past three decades."

Back, then, to the drawing board. Conventional liberal and conservative explanations about what ails society can neither explain the Great Divergence nor make it go away.

Stasys Eidiejus/Shutterstock.com

Did Immigration Create the Great Divergence?

In June 1970, when I was 12, my family moved from New York to California. We didn't know it at the time, but our migration came at the tail end of a historic trend that predated California's entry into the union. Starting with the 1849 Gold Rush (which prompted Congress to grant statehood), California had been a place whose population grew mainly because people from other parts of the United States picked up and moved there. In the 1870s, Hoosiers tired of the cold and settled Pasadena. In the 1930s, Okies fled the Dust Bowl and followed Route 66 to the Central Valley. In the 1940s and 1950s, engineers descended on South Bay to create an aerospace industry. My family's migration

(Continued)

came about because television production had been relocating from New York City to Los Angeles for about a decade. (My dad was a TV producer.)

After 1970, people kept coming to California, and new industries continued to sprout there (most notably in Northern California's Silicon Valley). But the engine of population growth ceased to be native-born Americans leaving one part of the United States for another. Instead, California's population grew mainly because foreign-born people moved there. The catalyst was the Immigration and Nationality Act of 1965, which eased up on immigration restrictions generally and on restrictions affecting non-Europeans in particular. Since 1970, the foreign-born share of the U.S. population (legal and illegal) has risen from 4.8 percent to 11 percent. More than half of U.S. immigrants now come from Mexico, Central and South America, and the Caribbean. Although a substantial minority of immigrants are highly skilled, for most immigrants incomes and educational attainment are significantly lower than for the native-born.

Did the post-1965 immigration surge cause the Great Divergence?

The timing is hard to ignore. During the Great Compression, the long and prosperous mid-20th-century idyll when income inequality shrank or held steady, immigration was held in check by quotas first imposed during the 1920s. The Nobel-prizewinning economist Paul Samuelson saw a connection. "By keeping labor supply down," he wrote in his best-selling economics textbook, a restrictive immigration policy "tends to keep wages high." After the 1965 immigration law reopened the spigot, the income trend reversed itself and income inequality grew.

But when economists look at actual labor markets, most find little evidence that immigration harms the economic interests of native-born Americans, and much evidence that it stimulates the economy. Even the 1980 Mariel boatlift, when Fidel Castro sent 125,000 Cubans to Miami—abruptly expanding the city's labor force by 7 percent—had virtually no measurable effect on Miami's wages or unemployment.

George Borjas, an economics professor at Harvard's Kennedy School, rejects this reasoning. Looking at individual cities or regions, he argues, is the wrong way to measure immigration's impact. Immigrants, he observes, are drawn to areas with booming economies. That creates a "spurious positive correlation between immigration and wages," he wrote in a 2003 paper. Immigration *looks* like it is creating opportunity, but what's really happening is that immigrants are moving to places where opportunity is already plentiful. Once a place starts to become saturated with cheap immigrant labor, Borjas wrote, the unskilled American workers who compete with immigrants for jobs no longer move there. (Or if they already live there, they move away to seek better pay.)

Instead of looking at the effects of immigration in isolated labor markets like New York or Los Angeles, Borjas gathered data at the national level and sorted workers according to their skill levels and their experience. He found that from 1980 to 2000, immigration had reduced the average annual income of native-born high-school dropouts ("who roughly correspond to the poorest tenth of the workforce") by 7.4 percent (see Table 3). In a subsequent 2006 study with Harvard economist Lawrence Katz, this one focusing solely on immigration from Mexico, Borjas calculated that from 1980 to 2000, Mexican immigrants reduced annual income for native-born high-school dropouts by 8.2 percent. Illegal immigration has a disproportionate effect on the labor pool for high-school dropouts because the native-born portion of that pool is relatively small. A Congressional Budget Office study released a year after Borjas' study reported that among U.S. workers who lacked a high-school diploma, *nearly half* were immigrants, most of them from Mexico and Central America.

Immigration clearly imposes hardships on the poorest U.S. workers, but its impact on the moderately-skilled middle class—the group whose vanishing job opportunities largely define the Great Divergence—is much smaller. For native-born high-school graduates, Borjas calculated that from 1980 to 2000, immigration drove annual income down 2.1 percent. For native-born workers with "some college," immigration drove annual income down 2.3 percent. Comparable figures for Mexican immigration were 2.2 percent and 2.7 percent. (For *all* workers, annual income went down 3.7 percent due to all immigration and down 3.4 percent due to Mexican immigration.) To put these numbers in perspective (see Figure 1), the difference between the rate at which the middle fifth of the income distribution grew in after-tax income and the rate at which the top fifth of the income distribution grew during this period was 70 percent. The difference between the middle fifth growth rate and the top 1 percent growth rate was 256 *percent*.

Another obstacle to blaming the Great Divergence on immigration is that one of Borjas' findings runs in the wrong direction. From 1980 to 2000, immigration depressed wages for college graduates by 3.6 percent (see Table 3). That's because some of those immigrants were highly skilled. But the Great Divergence sent college graduates' wages *up*, not *down*. To reverse that trend would require importing *a lot* more highly skilled workers. That's the solution favored by Alan Greenspan. In his 2007 book *The Age of Turbulence*, the former Federal Reserve chairman proposed not that we step up patrols along the Rio Grande but that we "allow open migration of skilled workers." The United States has, Greenspan complained, created "a privileged, native-born elite of skilled workers whose incomes are being supported at noncom-petitively high levels by immigration quotas." Eliminating these "would, at the stroke of a pen, reduce much income inequality."

Gary Burtless, an economist at the Brookings Institution in Washington, proposes a different way to think about immigration. Noting that immigrants "accounted for one-third of the U.S. population growth between 1980 and 2007," Burtless argued in a

(Continued)

2009 paper that even if they failed to exert heavy downward pressure on the incomes of most native-born Americans, the roughly 900,000 immigrants who arrive in the United States each year were sufficient in number to skew the national income distribution *by their mere presence*. But while Burtless' methodology was more expansive than Borjas', his calculation of immigration's effect was more modest. Had there been no immigration after 1979, he calculated, average annual wages for all workers "may have risen by an additional 2.3 percent" (compared to Borjas' 3.7 percent).

The conclusion here is as overwhelming as it is unsatisfying. Immigration has probably helped create income inequality. But it isn't the star of the show. "If you were to list the five or six main things" that caused the Great Divergence, Borjas told me, "what I would say is [immigration is] a contributor. Is it the most important contributor? No."[7]

Footnotes

1 Sticklers will note that King was looking at the year 1910, whereas the later calculation, by economists Emmanuel Saez and Thomas Piketty, looks at 1913. The point is that King, who is almost entirely forgotten by today's leading economists, pretty much nailed it.

2 During the 1930s the richest 1 percent's share of the nation's income dropped. Overall, the income-equality trend of the Great Depression was somewhat equivocal. On the one hand, the rich lost income. On the other hand, middle-class incomes stagnated and a high level of unemployment (which peaked at 25 percent) hit those at the bottom of the income scale especially hard. I note all this to emphasize that it is neither necessary nor desirable to achieve equality through economic catastrophe.

3 It is possible to argue that the black/white wage gap grew worse during the past three decades, for instance by factoring in blacks' higher incarceration rate and lower participation in the job market. It has also been shown that, within income groups, blacks enjoyed less upward mobility during this period than whites. But the Great Divergence is a phenomenon that's measured according to family ("household") income, so in examining whether black/white income inequality contributed to it, I'll consider only the 30-year change in black family income relative to white family income. And that change is nonexistent.

4 Some people prefer to compare median *weekly* incomes because women are more likely to take time off over the course of the year, but weekly incomes followed a near-identical trend. Among *part-time* workers, women now enjoy a *higher* median weekly income than men. This is mainly because female part-time workers tend to be older than male part-time workers.

5 By 1980 the proportion of children living with one parent was already 20 percent.

6 The especially worrisome trend of *teenage* births peaked in the early 1990s.

7 A caveat is in order. Economists work from available data, which at the national level is often five to 10 years old. It's possible that immigration is currently having a greater impact on the wages of the native-born than past data indicate. For example, illegal immigrants are currently believed to constitute 20 percent to 36 percent of construction workers in low-skill trades. But a recent survey conducted by the engineering department at the University of Maryland found that in the Washington metropolitan area, illegal immigrants actually constitute 55 percent of construction workers in low-skill trades. Is that finding accurate? If so, does it reflect a local anomaly? A recession blip? Or are the national numbers too low? It could be years before we know. A D.C.-based labor lawyer of my acquaintance, who blogs under the pseudonym of "Sir Charles," recently estimated that in the D.C. metropolitan area the construction industry typically pays undocumented workers about $13 an hour to avoid paying native-born and legal-immigrant workers about $30 an hour. "In the past year," he wrote, "I have negotiated wages cuts of $2, $4, and $12--yes, $12--an hour for various groups with whom I work."

Source: Noah, Timothy. "The United States of Inequality." *Slate*, 14 Sept. 2010. Web. 26 June 2012.

1. How does Noah establish income inequality as a relevant topic for analysis? How do you think his analysis of the possible causes of income inequality contributes to current debates about fiscal policy in the United States?

2. On what basis does Noah evaluate each possible cause of income inequality? How does he reach his conclusions about each possible cause? How persuasive do you find these conclusions? Explain.

3. What does Noah's choice of evidence and sources for his analysis suggest about his intended audience? Do you think you are part of that audience? Why or why not?

Everyone's Gone Nuts: The Exaggerated Threat of Food Allergies

by Meredith Broussard

Many people have questions about the effects of eating certain foods and the causes of food-borne illnesses. In the following piece, writer Meredith Broussard examines the apparent increase in food allergies in the United States. She asks a common question: What causes food allergies? But Broussard's strategy for presenting her analysis is uncommon. Her "essay," which appeared in 2011 as a two-page spread in Harper's *magazine, is actually a series of annotations to a pamphlet from an organization called The Food Allergy and Anaphylaxis Network (FAAN). Each annotation is in effect an analysis of one aspect of the issue of food allergies, with the annotation on the top left serving as the introduction and the one on the lower right as the conclusion. Broussard's essay illustrates the importance of the medium (Core Concept #3) and reminds us that form is driven by the writer's purpose (Core Concept #6).*

. . . .

(Continued)

EVERYONE'S

The exaggerated threat of food

Of little concern to most parents or educators only a generation ago, food allergies are now seen as a childhood epidemic. The American Academy of Pediatrics recently began recommending that peanuts be withheld until a child turns three; hundreds of food-allergy nonprofits and local parents groups have formed; and six states have passed laws requiring food-allergy safety measures in their schools, with similar legislation currently being considered in Congress. Children are even being recruited to help battle this supposed threat, as in this Food Allergy & Anaphylaxis Network (FAAN) brochure, which enjoins young students to "Be a PAL" and protect the lives of their classmates. But the rash of fatal food allergies is mostly myth, a cultural hysteria cooked up with a few key ingredients: fearful parents in an age of increased anxiety, sensationalist news coverage, and a coterie of well-placed advocates whose dubious science has fed the frenzy.

One of the first and most influential of the food-allergy nonprofits, FAAN has successfully passed off as fact its message that food allergies have become more prevalent and dire. Since 2005, more than 400 news stories have used FAAN's estimates that allergic reactions to food send 30,000 Americans to emergency rooms each year and that 150 to 200 ultimately die. The group derived these figures from a 1999 study of a rural Minnesota community, in which 133 people over a five-year period were determined to have suffered anaphylaxis—an allergic reaction that can mean everything from going into shock to developing an itchy mouth. Yet only nine people in the study ever required hospitalization for anaphylaxis from any cause. As for the death estimate, just one person died of anaphylactic shock, prompted not by food allergies but by exercise. The Centers for Disease Control and Prevention, in its most up-to-date figures, recorded only 12 deaths from food allergies in all of 2004. When asked about these statistical discrepancies, FAAN founder and CEO Anne Muñoz-Furlong said focusing on any number misses the point: "One child dying from food allergies is too many."

In 2005, every major American media outlet covered the story of a teenager who died after kissing a boy who earlier in the day had eaten a peanut-butter sandwich. This "kiss of death" confirmed for countless nervous parents their worst fears: food-allergic children were in constant danger—they could "even die!" as FAAN warns here—from any sort of secondhand exposure to certain foods. (In a press release soon after the girl's death, FAAN instructed food-allergic teens to tell "that special someone that you can die.... Don't wait for the first kiss.") But there is simply no evidence that a food allergen can do serious harm if not ingested. Nicholas Pawlowski, an allergist at Children's Hospital of Philadelphia, says he occasionally has to spread peanut butter on a patient's arm to demonstrate to parents that their child will not die from casual contact with a nut. In the case of the peanut-butter kiss, a coroner later ruled, to no fanfare, that the girl had smoked pot soon before the embrace and actually died from an asthma attack.

No one knows exactly why, but more and more kids are becoming allergic to certain foods. Especially peanuts, tree nuts, milk, eggs, soy, wheat, fish, and shellfish.

Sometimes, if they eat even a tiny amount of the food they're allergic to, they can become very ill ... even die!

That's why kids who have food allergies need all of us to help keep them safe. You too can help, and if you do a good job, you could become a PAL™ Hero and receive a special certificate.

Here are some of the ways you can Be a PAL: Protect A Life™

Be a PAL™

A PAL™ Hero is someone whose allergic reaction, or even save a life. Allergy & Anaphylaxis Network (F Heroes with special recognition an might be you!

Just looking out for our friend however, makes us all heroes. Sav forget how to Be a PAL™ ... and P

BE

Prote From F

For more informat The Food Aller 11781 Lee Jackson Hw (800) 929-4

GONE NUTS

llergies, *by Meredith Broussard*

In addition to offering certificates to "PAL Heroes," FAAN presents individuals and businesses with a service award named after Muñoz-Furlong's daughter, a former food-allergic child who, like most people, grew out of her allergies. Anne Muñoz-Furlong says she founded FAAN when her community didn't seem to believe the threat to her child was real. Her organization and others have certainly helped to change the perception of food allergies. (A recent *Newsweek* cover showing a pigtailed girl in a gas mask with a carton of milk in one hand and a peanut-butter sandwich in the other is typical of much recent coverage.) But all we know for certain now is that more parents *think* their children suffer from food allergies. Indeed, even the best allergy tests produce high rates of false positives, and most studies of childhood prevalence interview no one under the age of eighteen. Ken Kochanek, a CDC statistician, says there are far too few recorded incidents of anaphylactic shock triggered by food allergies to draw any sound epidemiological conclusions: "We can't find any hard data that supports the severity."

Hero!

ors help prevent a serious
school and The Food
N) will be honoring PAL
ard certificate. Someday is

ho have food allergies,
is brochure so you won't
ct A Life from food allergies!

PAL

BE A PAL™!
Protect A Life
From Food Allergies

t A Life
d Allergies

about food allergies, contact
& Anaphylaxis Network
uite 160, Fairfax, VA 22033-3309
www.faankids.org

These hugging forms evoke a better world in which we all look out for our food-allergic friends. Such chumminess already exists within the world of food-allergy advocacy. The FAAN children's website was built using a donation from Dey, the distributor of the EpiPen adrenaline injector; Dey and Verus Pharmaceuticals, the maker of EpiPen's chief competitor, sponsor FAAN's major annual fundraising event. (As part of its safety guidelines, FAAN suggests carrying an adrenaline injector at all times and regularly renewing the prescription.) Just about all the leading food allergists also have ties to FAAN or the Food Allergy Initiative (FAI), an organization prone to even more extreme rhetoric. This intimacy helps explain why suspect statistical findings get published. For instance, the coauthors of an oft-cited study on the dangers facing food-allergic children at restaurants were Anne Muñoz-Furlong's husband, who serves as a top FAAN executive, and a FAAN medical-board member whose research is funded in part by FAI. The latter is also an editor at the leading allergy journal where the study appeared; the journal's editor-in-chief is head of FAI's medical board.

There is no question that food allergies are real. Yet instead of creating the healthy, happy children shown here, exaggerating the threat may actually do as much harm as the allergies themselves. The peril is now perceived as so great that psychosomatic reactions to foods and their odors are not uncommon. Recent surveys have also shown that children thought to have food allergies feel more overwhelmed by anxiety, more limited in what they believe they can safely accomplish, than even children with diabetes and rheumatological disease. One study documented how food-allergic youths become terror-stricken when inside places like supermarkets and restaurants, since they know that allergens are nearby. Such psychological distress is exacerbated by parents, who report keeping their children away from birthday parties and sending them to school in "No Nuts" T-shirts. Having been fed a steady diet of fear for more than two decades, we have become, it appears, what we eat. ∎

*Meredith Broussard is a writer
living in Philadelphia.*

Source: Broussard, Meredith. "Everyone's Gone Nuts: The Exaggerated Threat of Food Allergies." *Harper's* Jan. 2008: 64–65. Print.

EXERCISE 6D — EXPLORING CAUSAL ANALYSIS: EVERYONE'S GONE NUTS

1. What conclusions does Broussard reach about the causes of food allergies? Do you find these conclusions surprising? Why or why not? How well do you think her conclusions are supported by her analysis?

2. How effective do you find Broussard's strategy for presenting her analysis? What are the advantages and disadvantages of annotating a pamphlet to analyze it? Do you think her analysis would be more or less effective if it were presented in a conventional essay format? Explain.

3. What kinds of information does Broussard rely on to support her claims? How persuasive do you find her support?

A Blog Is a Little First Amendment Machine

by Jay Rosen

In the following essay, Jay Rosen examines the impact of blogs on modern journalism. In a sense, his essay is a traditional analysis of the effects of a specific trend—in this case, the increasing use of blogs as a journalistic tool. But as you'll see, Rosen's analytical strategy is not traditional. Rosen, an associate professor of journalism at New York University, is a leading voice in a movement called "public journalism," which is devoted to the idea that the press should promote citizenship and democracy. As you read, consider how his advocacy for that movement shapes the purpose of his analysis. Rosen's essay also illustrates how a writer can use form (Core Concept #6) strategically to present a causal analysis. In this regard, it is worth noting that this essay, which was published in 2007 on the Huffington Post, a website about political and cultural affairs, is a slightly revised version of a speech that Rosen gave in 2007 to an audience at a conference of the International Communication Association. Keep that in mind as you read his essay.

. . . .

When in the eighteenth century the press first appeared on the political stage the people on the other end of it were known as the public. Public opinion and the political press arose together. But in the age of the mass media the public got transformed into an audience.

This happened because the mass media were one way, one-to-many, and "read only." When journalism emerged as a profession it reflected these properties of its underlying platform. But now we have the Web, which is two-way (rather than one) many-to-many (rather than one-to-many) and "read-write" rather than "read only."

As it moves toward the Web, journalism will have to adjust to these conditions, but a professionalized press is having trouble with the shift because it still thinks of the people on the other end as an audience—an image very deeply ingrained in professional practice. I'm going to tell you some stories that I think illustrate the disruptive effects that blogging has had, and the democratic potential it represents. But let me say at the outset that, though a blogger myself, I am not a triumphalist about blogging. I do not think that the age of fully democratic media is suddenly upon us because we have this new form. There is a long way to go if we are to make good on its potential.

Now to my five stories, which I offer more as parables, even though they are, of course, true to the facts.

Chris Allbritton: Independent War Correspondent

In March of 2003, Chris Allbritton, a former AP and New York Daily News reporter, became what Wired magazine called "the Web's first independent war correspondent." He did it by asking readers of his blog to send him to Iraq at their expense. Allbritton raised $14,500 from 342 donors on a simple promise: that he would send back from the war original and honest reporting, free of commercial pressures, pack thinking, and patriotic hype.

He needed a plane ticket to Turkey (where he snuck over the border and found the war), a laptop, a Global Positioning Satellite unit, a rented satellite phone, a digital camera, and enough cash to move around, keep fed, and buy his way out of trouble. While some reporters were embedded with the American military, Allbritton sent himself on assignment. No one gave him permission to be in country.

The Internet did the rest. On March 27, his reporting drew 23,000 users to his site, www.back-to-iraq.com. So here you have a journalist collecting his own mini-public, a few thousand people on the Web. They then send him to report on events of interest to the entire world, via a medium that reaches the entire world.

This is journalism without the media. I leave you to contemplate the implications of that. But it was one of the events that caused me to start my own blog.

Trent Lott Speaks; Bloggers Listen

On Dec. 5, 2002, Senator Trent Lott of Mississippi, leader of the Republican party in the Senate and probably the third most powerful person in Washington at the time, spoke at former Senator Strom Thurmond's 100th birthday party on Capitol Hill.

"I want to say this about my state," he said. "When Strom Thurmond ran for president, we voted for him. We're proud of it. And if the rest of the country had followed our lead, we wouldn't have had all these problems over all these years either." He was referring to Thurmond's 1948 third-party campaign for president, which was an explicitly racist campaign. So what was Trent Lott saying in 2002? That a segregationist president would have been good for America in 1948?

(Continued)

There were some reporters present, but they didn't see much significance in it. Except for one young producer from ABC News, Ed O'Keefe, who managed to get a brief story read on the air at 4:30 am, which in turn led to a small item the next day at ABCNews.com. This in turn gave it to the bloggers, who began discussing what Lott had said, and digging into Strom Thurmond's 1948 campaign so as to reveal what his comments really meant.

It turned out that bloggers from the left as well as the right were puzzled and disgusted by Lott's comments, and they continued to discuss them. For three days the story was the talk of the blogosphere while the news cycle moved on to other things. But political reporters were reading the blogs, and by the fourth day they realized…. This was news! The story of what Lott had said re-broke in the major press—five days after it happened—and he began apologizing for it while major political figures reacted. Ten days later he resigned as majority leader; his power was gone.

Here's the part of the story I want you to focus on: the chances of a television producer from CBS or a style reporter from the Washington Post not knowing enough history to see any import in Trent Lott's comments were pretty high. But the chances of the interconnected blogosphere not knowing this background were zero. To this day professional journalists do not understand this fact, even though it was one of the things that helped sink Dan Rather when his badly flawed report on President Bush's National Guard service was attacked (and sunk) by bloggers and their readers

FireDogLake Shines at the Libby Trial

In Boston in 2004, I was part of the first class of bloggers admitted to cover a national political convention. That was where bloggers had their coming out party before the national press. Beyond celebrating that arrival, no one suggested the bloggers had a better product, not even the bloggers.

In January of 2007 there was another first, similar in form: first class of bloggers accredited to cover a big Federal trial. This was the trial of Lewis Libby, Dick Cheney's top aide. A handful of bloggers got passes and joined the courthouse press. One blog, called Firedoglake, put more boots on the ground than the big commercial news operations—six people working in shifts. These writers brought more background, more savvy and more commitment to the case than any of the journalists covering the trial.

Firedoglake got handed a golden opportunity by the reluctance of big news organizations to spend money on the information commons. At the Libby trial, there was no broadcast, no taping allowed. No posted transcript for anyone to consult. Thus the most basic kind of news there is—what was said in court today—was missing.

Converging on Washington, the team from Firedoglake felt they represented people back home who wanted to know everything. And so they decided to live blog the trial. Typing as fast as they could, they produced the only blow-by-blow account of the trial available to the public. They also provided expert interpretation because they knew more about the case than most of those being paid to cover it. In fact journalists covering the trial began to rely on Firedoglake's accounts because it had the most complete coverage.

The expenses were paid by contributions from the blog's readers, giving new meaning to the term "team coverage." I wrote about Firedoglake's achievement because it contradicted everything professional journalists believe about bloggers.

Bloggers do views, not news. They're like a giant op-ed page, but without decorum. Bloggers are parasitic on reporting that originates elsewhere. Bloggers have an ax to grind, so their reports aren't reliable. These ideas are "fixed" points for a lot of journalists. And the example of Firedoglake at the Libby trial disconfirms them all. It was the most basic kind of journalism imaginable. We're there, you're not, let us tell you about it.

TPM Muckraker Gets a Document Dump

On March 20th of this year, the Justice Department released 3,000 pages of documents to the House Judiciary Committee, which was investigating why a group of seven federal prosecutors were fired last year, a scandal that continues to make headlines today. Over at TPM Muckraker.com, an investigative site started by the political blogger Josh Marshall, the guys who work for Marshall were wondering how they were going to sort through those 3,000 pages to see if any clues turned up. And then they realized: "We don't have to. Our readers can help."

The Judiciary Committee had put the document dump online in the form of PDF files. And so Marshall's guys asked readers to pick a PDF and read through the documents. "If you find something interesting (or damning), then tell us about it in the comment thread below," they wrote. Readers finished in a day or two and made some intriguing finds.

The significance is obvious: potentially hundreds or thousands of hands available to work on a single story.

John Markoff Mocks Blogging

In October of 2003 John Markoff, the lead technology reporter for the *New York Times* based here in San Francisco, who by that time had been reporting about the Internet for more than ten years, was interviewed by Online Journalism Review. One of the topics he was asked about was the very subject we are discussing here—the democratic potential of blogging. Markoff was openly dismissive. I want to read to you what he said. And remember, this is the man the *Times* counts on to understand these things.

"It sometimes seems we have a world full of bloggers and that blogging is the future of journalism, or at least that's what the bloggers argue, and to my mind, it's not clear yet whether blogging is anything more than CB radio.

(Continued)

"…Give it five or 10 years and see if any institutions emerge out of it. It's possible that in the end there may be some small subset of people who find a livelihood out of it and that the rest of the people will find that, you know, keeping their diaries online is not the most useful thing to with their time."

When I tell that to people they get very angry with me.… I also like to tell them, when they (ask) when I'm going to start a blog, Oh, I already have a blog, it's www.nytimes.com, don't you read it?"

There's nothing wrong with waiting five years to see if the form develops. In the meantime, Markoff said, I'm (literally) not going to think about it.

By 2003 the press had started to shift social location. Much of it is still based in The Media and will be for some time, but some is in nonprofit hands, and some of the franchise is now in public hands because of the Web, the weblog and other forms of citizen media. Naturally our ideas about it are going to change. The franchise is being enlarged.

The most famous words ever written about freedom of the press are in the U.S. Constitution: "Congress shall make no law…" But the second most famous words come from the critic A. J. Liebling: "freedom of the press belongs to those who own one." Well, freedom of the press still belongs to those who own one, and blogging means practically anyone can own one. That is the Number One reason why blogs—and this discussion—matter.

With blogging, an awkward term, we designate a fairly beautiful thing: the extension to many more people of a free press franchise, the right to publish your thoughts to the world.

Wherever blogging spreads the dramas of free expression follow. A blog, you see, is a little First Amendment machine.

Source: Rosen, Jay. "A Blog Is a Little First Amendment Machine." *Huffington Post* 5 June 2007. Web. 28 June 2012.

EXERCISE 6E   EXPLORING CAUSAL ANALYSIS: A BLOG IS A LITTLE FIRST AMENDMENT MACHINE

1. What are the main effects of blogs on journalism, in Rosen's view? How does he arrive at his conclusions about these effects? What kinds of evidence does he present to support his conclusions?

2. How does Rosen use stories—or what he calls "parables"—in his analysis? What are the benefits and risks of this analytical strategy? Did you find this strategy effective? Why or why not?

3. How does Rosen organize his analysis? In what ways do you think the structure of his essay strengthens his analysis of the effects of blogs on journalism?

Writing Causal Analysis

This section will help you develop a writing project based on causal analysis by taking you through the Ten Core Concepts. Each step described here corresponds to a step described in Chapter 3.

Step 1	Identify a topic for causal analysis.

Begin with a question that interests or puzzles you about why something happens or whether one thing causes another:

- Does the gas- or oil-drilling technique called hydraulic fracturing contaminate groundwater?
- Do higher taxes result in slower economic growth?
- Does illegal sharing of digital music files lead to higher music prices for consumers?

Start with a question provided by your instructor for a course assignment or a question about something that happened in your life, an important trend, or a controversial issue:

Something happening in your life	• Will a proposed new tuition plan at your school mean that some students will not be able to afford college? • Is a new supermarket in your town hurting local businesses?
An important trend	• Do social media affect dating habits among college students? • Are tougher drug laws reducing crime rates?
A controversial issue	• Do charter schools improve graduation rates among poor and minority students? • Does illegal immigration hurt the U.S. economy?

Develop this question using Step #1 in Chapter 3.

Step 2 | Place your topic in rhetorical context.

Your question should be interesting to you but also relevant for your intended audience or your course assignment. Consider your audience or your course assignment guidelines, and address the following questions:

- Why would this question matter to your intended audience? What makes this question important?
- In identifying the causes and effects reflected in this question, what's at stake for your audience? For you?

Using your answers to these questions as a guide, follow the steps for Step #2 in Chapter 3.

Step 3 | Select a medium.

An effective causal analysis can be presented in any medium, although most academic causal analyses will be presented in the form of a conventional paper.

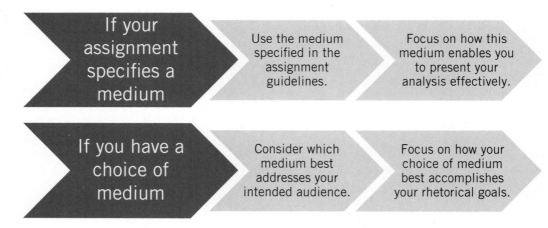

If your assignment specifies a medium → Use the medium specified in the assignment guidelines. → Focus on how this medium enables you to present your analysis effectively.

If you have a choice of medium → Consider which medium best addresses your intended audience. → Focus on how your choice of medium best accomplishes your rhetorical goals.

For example, imagine that you wanted to analyze the causes of bullying to help educate teens about the problem. Your intended audience would include teens, of course, but perhaps parents and school officials as well. In such a case, you might consider several different media that are likely to reach that audience and enable you to present your analysis clearly and provocatively, including a brochure or a video posted on YouTube.

Step #3 in Chapter 3 provides additional advice to help you decide on an appropriate medium for your causal analysis.

Step 4 | Identify your main claim.

In causal analysis, the writer makes a claim about the causes or effects of the event, trend, or development being analyzed.

Question: Will higher sales of hybrid cars reduce greenhouse gas emissions?

Question: Are e-readers making print books obsolete?

⇓

⇓

Analysis: The overall impact of hybrid cars on greenhouse gases is based on several factors and is not yet clear.

Analysis: E-readers are replacing books in some contexts, but print books remain dominant in others.

⇓

⇓

Claim: Hybrid cars might contribute to reducing greenhouse gas emissions, but not enough to make a significant difference without other measures to reduce the use of hydrocarbon fuels.

Claim: E-readers are likely to reduce the demand for print books.

In each of these examples, the writer's task is to develop a causal analysis that supports that claim—or, to state it differently, to present a causal analysis that leads to a main conclusion (claim) about hybrid cars and greenhouse gases or e-readers and print books.

At this point in the development of your project, you probably won't know exactly what your main claim (or claims) will be because you are still investigating your topic and examining various causes and effects. But your main question should suggest possible claims, and you probably have some idea of what you might find as you investigate your topic. So begin there:

- What claim do you expect to make about your main question?
- What do you expect to find as you investigate causes and effects related to your question?
- What are the possible answers to your main question, based on what you know at this point?

Complete Step #4 in Chapter 3 to develop a Guiding Thesis Statement, which is essentially a statement of the main claim(s) you will make in your causal analysis. As you develop your Guiding Thesis Statement, address the following questions:

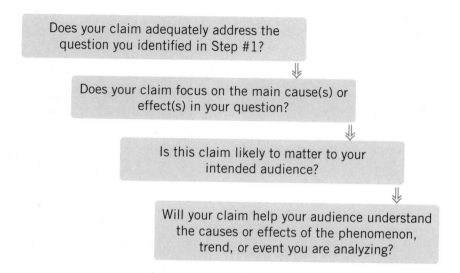

Does your claim adequately address the question you identified in Step #1?

Does your claim focus on the main cause(s) or effect(s) in your question?

Is this claim likely to matter to your intended audience?

Will your claim help your audience understand the causes or effects of the phenomenon, trend, or event you are analyzing?

Step 5 Support your claim(s).

At this point, you should be in the process of researching your topic, and support for your claim or claims will grow out of what you learn by examining the potential causes and effects of whatever you are analyzing.

Let's say you are analyzing the possible effects of a proposed state law based on the idea of "zero tolerance" for bullying. The law would require schools to suspend students who bullied other students. Your main question is:

Do zero tolerance policies reduce bullying?

After investigating the issue, you develop your main claim:

Zero-tolerance policies will probably not significantly reduce bullying in schools.

This claim is based on what you learned through your research about why bullying occurs, who engages in it, and how prevalent it is. You might have found, for example, that students who engage in bullying do so for complicated reasons and are not necessarily discouraged from bullying by rules or punishments. Moreover, zero-tolerance policies have had unintended consequences in schools where they have been adopted; in some cases, students who have had relatively minor disagreements were labeled "bullies" and suspended from school. All of these points provide support for your main claim. Inquiring into causes and effects thus helps you identify specific support for your claim(s).

As you research your topic, look for information that will help you understand the causes and effects you are analyzing and support your claims about those causes and effects. Complete the following exercise:

1. List what you have learned about causes and effects.

   - Bullies were usually bullied themselves.
   - Peer groups can encourage bullying behavior.
   - Bullies usually have low self-esteem.
   - Zero-tolerance policies have had mixed results and unintended consequences.
   - Anti-bullying programs can help reduce bullying.

2. Determine whether each item on your list helps support your main claim(s) eliminate items that don't.

   - *Bullies were usually bullied themselves.* This item seems to support the main claim by showing that the reasons for bullying are complex and have little to do with policies, rules, and punishments.

3. Identify the reasoning, information, and/or source that supports each item on your list.

   - Several psychological studies indicating that low self-esteem seems to lead to bullying.
   - An essay by a school psychologist arguing that zero-tolerance policies may also undermine efforts to help bullies overcome low self-esteem.
   - Report about success of one anti-bullying program.

4. Determine whether your information, reasoning, and sources are sufficient for each item.

   - Is a single essay enough support to make the claim that zero-tolerance policies haven't worked? Is it possible that in this case there was a flaw in the policy itself or that it was not enforced properly? Do you need to find out more about the impact of such policies?

6

Expect to make adjustments in your claims as you learn more about the causes and effects you are examining. If necessary, revise your main claim. That's part of the process of inquiry:

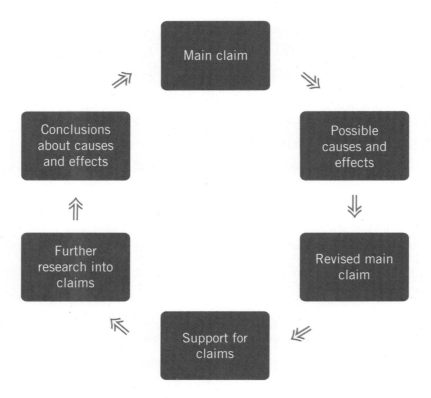

The more thoroughly you explore your topic by examining specific causes and effects and identifying support for your claims, the more likely the next steps in the process will lead to an effective piece of writing.

At this point, you are probably ready to write a complete draft of your project. If not, move to the next step before completing your draft.

Step 6 Organize your causal analysis.

How you organize an analysis of causes and effects depends on what you determine is the most logical and effective way of presenting your topic and your claims to your intended audience. Here we will consider two approaches to organizing a causal analysis:

- according to causes and/or effects
- according to your main claims

Organizing Your Causal Analysis Around Causes and/or Effects

Organize your causal analysis according to the specific causes or effects you have identified through your research. For example, author Timothy Noah organizes his article, "The United States of Inequality" (which is included in this chapter), according to the possible causes of income inequality that he has identified through his research. He presents his analysis of each cause in turn, draws his conclusion about whether each cause can explain the income gap, supports his claim(s) about each possible cause, and then moves on to the next cause. In this way, Noah takes readers systematically through his complex analysis, making it easier for readers to follow his discussion as he moves to his main claims and ultimate conclusions about the causes of income inequality.

You can employ a similar strategy to organize your causal analysis. To do so, follow these steps:

1. List the main causes or effects you have identified through your research. (You can use the list you developed for Step 5 above.)

2. Identify the key points of support or sources for each cause/effect on your list.

3. Arrange the list in the order that makes the most sense. Consider: What order will present your analysis most clearly to your readers? What order seems to be most logical?

4. Identify the main claims you will make on the basis of your analysis of each cause or effect on your list.

5. Use your list to develop an outline for your causal analysis.

For example, let's say you have identified three main causes of bullying:

- Bullies often engage in bullying because they were bullied themselves.
- Peer groups can encourage and reinforce bullying behavior.
- Low self-esteem sometimes prompts children to engage in bullying.

Let's say you have also identified two main effects of zero-tolerance policies:

- Zero-tolerance policies have not significantly reduced bullying behavior.
- These policies have often had serious unintended consequences.

Your analysis of these causes and effects leads to your main claim that zero-tolerance policies should not be implemented in schools; instead, anti-bullying programs, which have been shown to be effective in reducing bullying behavior, should be developed. Your rough outline might look like this:

I. Introduction (why bullying is an important problem to address)

II. Background

    A. The complexity of bullying as a social problem

    B. The development of zero-tolerance policies

III. Causes of Bullying

    A. Bullies being bullied themselves

    B. Peer groups

    C. Low self-esteem

IV. Effects of Zero-Tolerance Policies

    A. Lack of success in reducing bullying

    B. Unintended consequences

V. Main Claims

    A. Zero-tolerance policies should not be implemented in schools

    B. Anti-bullying programs should be developed

VI. Conclusion

Organizing Your Causal Analysis Around Claims

A second option is to organize your project around the main claims you are making about the causes and/or effects you have identified. Returning to the example of bullying, begin with the two main claims that have emerged from your analysis:

- Zero-tolerance policies in schools have not been shown to reduce bullying significantly among teens.

- The most effective approach to reducing bullying seems to be educational programs that help teens understand and respond to bullying.

You can structure your project around these two main claims. Follow these steps:

1. For each main claim, list your supporting claims.

2. Identify your sources for each supporting claim.

3. Arrange the list in the order that makes the most sense. Consider: What order will present your analysis most clearly to your readers? What order seems most logical?

4. Create an outline with each main section of your project devoted to one of your main claims.

Such an outline might look like this:

I. Introduction (why bullying is an important problem to address)

II. Background

    A. The complexity of bullying as a social problem

    B. The development of zero-tolerance policies

III. Main Claims

    A. Zero-tolerance policies should not be implemented in schools

        1. Causes of bullying are complex

        2. Effects of zero-tolerance policies have been mixed

        3. Zero-tolerance policies have had unintended consequences

    B. Anti-bullying programs should be developed

        1. Anti-bullying programs address the root causes of bullying

        2. Anti-bullying programs have been shown to reduce bullying behavior

        3. Anti-bullying programs avoid unintended consequences

VI. Conclusion

These are two common approaches to organizing a causal analysis, but they are not the only options. Refer to your rhetorical situation to guide your decisions about form. Step #6 in Chapter 3 provides additional guidance for organizing your project.

If you have already written a rough draft, revise it according to your outline. If you have not yet written a rough draft, do so, using your outline as a guide.

Step 7 | Get feedback.

Use the following sets of questions to focus the feedback you receive on the main characteristics of analytical writing (a worthy topic, complexity, sufficient support, and reasonable conclusions) and on specific aspects of causal analysis.

Ask your readers to consider addressing these questions:

A relevant topic worthy of analysis	• Is the main point of the analysis clear? • Are the cause(s) or effect(s) of the event, trend, or phenomenon being analyzed clearly identified? • Does the writer provide a rationale for examining causes and effects for this topic?
Complexity	• Is the topic examined sufficiently? Are there important factors or issues that need to be more fully examined? Are alternatives explored? • Does the analysis sufficiently explain the cause(s) and effect(s) the writer has identified?
Appropriate and sufficient support	• Are the main claims supported with strong and appropriate evidence? Is there sufficient support for the causes and effects identified in the analysis? • Are the sources appropriate for this topic and rhetorical situation? • Is there too much evidence or support?
Reasonable conclusions	• Do the writer's conclusions about causes and effects grow logically from the analysis? • Are the conclusions presented clearly and persuasively? • Does the conclusion adequately sum up the analysis and emphasize the main points of the project?

Step #7 in Chapter 3 provides additional guidance for getting helpful feedback on your draft.

Step 8   Revise.

The preceding steps helped you delve more deeply into your topic to expose its complexity. Now you have to manage that complexity—for yourself and for your readers. At this point, then, your primary task is twofold:

- determine what you have learned from your analysis
- sharpen the focus of your project so your analysis makes sense to your intended audience

In analytical writing, revision is largely a matter of refining your analysis and making it understandable to your readers without sacrificing complexity. That process might also mean clarifying for yourself what your analysis reveals and identifying more clearly the implications and importance of your analysis in view of your rhetorical situation.

Address the following questions about your draft as you work through Step #8 in Chapter 3:

A relevant topic worthy of analysis	• Is the purpose of your analysis clear? Should you refine the questions you are trying to answer with your analysis? • Do you have something relevant to say as a result of your analysis? • Are your main claims clearly presented?
Complexity	• Have you answered the question(s) you pose in your project? Have you developed your analysis sufficiently? • Have you explored causes and effects in a way that does not oversimplify your topic? Are there sections of your analysis that need further explanation? • Are any sections of your draft unnecessary?
Appropriate and sufficient support	• Are your main claims supported with sufficient evidence? • Do any sections need more support or stronger evidence? • Can you eliminate any evidence or support without weakening your analysis? • Are your sources appropriate for your topic and rhetorical situation?
Reasonable conclusions	• Do your conclusions address your main question? • Do your conclusions relate clearly to the causes and effects you have analyzed? • Do you present your conclusions clearly and persuasively? • Have you neglected any key issues in your conclusions?

Review your draft with these sets of questions in mind and revise accordingly.

Step 9 | Refine your voice.

The readings in this chapter illustrate some of the different ways that writers can establish their voices in analyses that focus on causes and effects. The advice provided in Step #9 in Chapter 3 will help you construct an effective and appropriate voice for your project. Keep in mind that your voice helps establish your credibility and therefore is a factor in making your causal analysis persuasive to your intended audience. In addition, your voice can be strengthened by your own confidence in your analysis. If you feel confident that you have sufficiently explored the cause(s) and effect(s) of the event or phenomenon you have analyzed, your voice is likely to reflect that confidence and make your project more effective.

Step 10 | Edit.

Complete Step #10 in Chapter 3.

WRITING PROJECTS   CAUSAL ANALYSIS

1. Identify a controversial proposal in your region. For example:

   - Your governor has proposed a new tax cut that has provoked controversy among politicians and voters.
   - Your local government has proposed a ban on skateboarding in public areas such as parks and library parking lots.
   - Your college is considering a proposal for a new general education curriculum that would affect all students.

   Write an analysis of the potential impact of the proposal. Identify an appropriate audience for your analysis (e.g., students on your campus) and a medium that would best reach that audience.

2. If you have made an important decision recently, analyze the effect of that decision in your life. For example, perhaps you decided to attend a two-year college instead of a four-year college. Or you might have joined the U.S. military before attending college. Maybe you chose to move to a new apartment or a different town. For an audience of your classmates, write an essay in which you analyze the factors that led to your decision and the effects of that decision on important aspects of your life. Consider presenting your analysis in a medium other than a conventional essay that might be most effective for your intended audience.

3. In November 2011, campus police at the University of California at Berkeley removed students who were demonstrating on that campus as part of the Occupy Wall Street movement. At one point, the police used pepper spray on some of the demonstrators, and several videos and photos such as this one were widely circulated after the event:

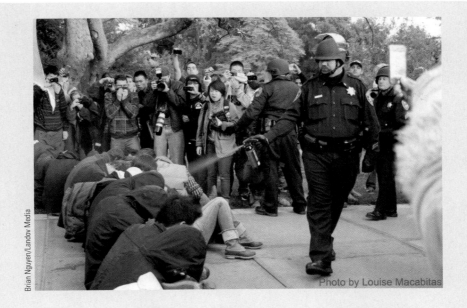

Brian Nguyen/Landov Media

Photo by Louise Macabitas

The images provoked criticism of the Berkeley campus police and administration. James Fallows, a correspondent for the *Atlantic Monthly*, described "the moral power" of that image, and compared it to other iconic images, such as the Chinese protester in Beijing's Tiananmen Square in 1979:

AP Photo/Jeff Widener

Examine the reaction to either of these images (or another image that you believe was important). Then write an essay analyzing the impact of the images.

Comparing and Synthesizing

SOMETIMES, the most effective way to analyze something is by comparing it with something else. Often, we can better understand something that is unfamiliar by comparing it to something we already understand. A mechanic might help you grasp a problem with a car's transmission by comparing it to the gears on a bicycle, which might be more familiar to you. In the same way, a writer can use the familiar to help explain something new by comparing the two. For example, an economist might explain a current development, such as the crash of the U.S. housing market during the so-called Great Recession of 2008, by comparing it to a similar event, such as the Great Depression of the 1930s, which has been studied for many years. Comparing two things can expose insights that might not be evident otherwise. In this way, comparison enables a writer to illuminate a complicated issue.

Comparative analysis is not just a matter of comparing two things, however. In academic analysis, writers often examine several events, trends, developments, or bodies of data in order to understand or explain something adequately. Such analysis usually requires not only comparing but also *synthesizing* ideas or information. *Synthesis is the combining of two or more separate ideas, themes, or elements into a coherent new idea.* The previous example of an economist using comparison to explain a recent economic event illustrates the importance of synthesis in analytical writing. In that case, the writer might compare the recent recession to the Great Depression of the 1930s, but because these events are so complex, the writer will probably also have to examine a number of different perspectives on these two events. The writer will identify common themes or arguments from those different perspectives and bring them together to make a new argument or draw a new conclusion about the current recession. In doing so, the writer synthesizes ideas and information from different sources to help explain the focus of his or her analysis.

In most academic analysis, simply comparing two or more things isn't usually sufficient to complete an analysis that adequately explains a complicated event, development, trend, idea, or problem. Understanding complex matters usually requires bringing together several distinct but related ideas, positions, or perspectives. In this sense, a writer must look for connections as well as contrasts or contradictions in an effort to explain something:

- A historian compares three different explanations for the rise of the women's suffrage movement in the United States in the 1920s and draws on all three explanations to present a new explanation.

- An ecologist examines several contradictory studies of the impact of hydrofracturing, or "fracking," which is a technique for extracting natural gas or oil from underground, to determine whether it is likely to affect drinking water.

- A psychologist reviews a number of studies of the use of social media by college students to draw conclusions about the influence of social media on study habits.

Comparative analysis does not always require synthesis, but very often the two go hand in hand as writers explain complicated subjects. In this chapter, *comparative analysis* is understood to include synthesis unless otherwise noted.

Occasions for Comparing and Synthesizing

We routinely engage in informal comparative analysis, probably without realizing it:

- A customer choosing a new rain jacket from among several different brands compares them to determine which one has the right features, fit, quality, and price.

- A high school student deciding which college to attend compares tuition, financial aid packages, programs, and the quality of campus life at several different schools.

- A voter sees several tweets reflecting different positions on proposed changes in federal tax laws that will affect her own tax bill and then reviews several editorials on the same subject to determine whether to support the changes.

- Students review three studies of the impact of buying local foods as they develop a proposal for their campus food service to support local farmers.

These examples suggest that comparative analysis, like most analytical writing, grows out of a need to understand something better in order to make a decision or solve a problem. In each case, people consider several different perspectives or kinds of information to help them make a decision or determine their positions on issues of importance to them.

Notice, too, that these examples reflect shared concerns. In each case, a number of different people potentially have an interest in the issues or questions that lead to comparison or synthesis. This shared interest connects writers and readers and provides a foundation for effective comparative analysis. The students preparing a proposal to their campus dining service, for example, will synthesize the studies they found not only to explain the impact of using local foods in the dining halls but also to make a more persuasive case to their readers (the dining service administrators and students who use the dining halls). In this sense, comparative analysis is a **rhetorical tool** with which writers can present their ideas more effectively to interested readers.

Dennis K. Johnson/Lonely Planet Images/Getty Images

Comparison and synthesis are essential components of much analytical writing in college, even if the focus of the assignment is not explicitly to compare or synthesize. For example, an assignment for an atmospheric science course might ask students to explain the impact of severe weather on a region's economic productivity. For such an assignment, a student might compare several major hurricanes to illuminate differences and similarities in the economic impact of such storms. The student might then synthesize data from several different analyses to draw conclusions about the overall economic impact of severe weather. In the end, the focus of the student's paper is not a comparison of the hurricanes' economic impact or a synthesis of several economic studies of severe weather, but comparison and synthesis are crucial components of the overall analysis.

Comparison and synthesis can lead to a more in-depth understanding of a topic of importance to a writer and his or her readers. The desire to understand should drive a writer's decisions when comparing or synthesizing ideas or information.

EXERCISE 7A OCCASIONS FOR COMPARATIVE ANALYSIS

1. Think of a recent experience in which you had to make a decision involving two or more distinct options. For example, you might have had to decide which college to attend after being accepted by three different schools. Or you might have purchased a digital tablet from among several different choices. In a brief paragraph, describe this experience and discuss how you made your decision after considering your options. What conclusions might you draw from this experience about the purposes of comparative analysis?

2. Find a newspaper article, essay, blog post, or other kind of text in which several items are compared—for example, an editorial essay comparing two political candidates or a website comparing consumer items such as smartphones. In a brief paragraph, describe the purpose of the comparison and its relevance to a specific audience.

3. Think of an activity you are involved in that requires regular use of specific equipment or services. For example, you might fish, which requires specialized equipment. Or you might cook, which requires certain equipment but also supplies, such as produce or spices. Describe the activity, and identify the equipment or services you need for that activity. Discuss how a comparative analysis of that equipment or service might enhance your involvement in that activity. For example, if you cook, you might examine how a comparison of several sources of produce would help you decide which sources you should use.

Understanding Comparison and Synthesis

The preceding section underscores two important features of analytical writing that involves comparison and synthesis: a reason for comparison and a basis for comparison.

A Reason for Comparison

Comparison for the sake of comparison may be an interesting intellectual exercise—for example, you might compare two breeds of dogs to decide which is more attractive—but such comparisons won't usually help address an issue or solve a problem. Effective comparison or synthesis is based on *purposeful* analysis. Writers should have a compelling reason for comparing or synthesizing two or more things, and readers should share that sense of purpose. For example, a comparison of different breeds of dogs to determine which ones make the best pets for small apartments might appeal to readers considering whether to have a pet. Similarly, dog owners visiting a veterinary clinic might be interested in a pamphlet that synthesizes information about several different kinds of flea and tick protection to help dog owners decide which protection is best for their pets. In such cases, the comparison or synthesis arises from the writer's need to understand or explain something that is important to both the writer and the intended readers:

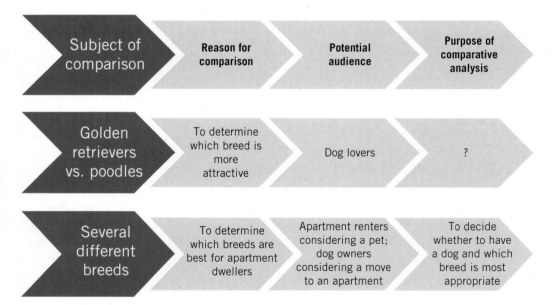

A Basis for Comparison

I once overheard two people debating whether evaluating teachers on the basis of student test scores will actually improve schools. One person argued that if a teacher's students don't meet a certain score on standardized tests, the teacher should be fired. That approach, he argued, works for businesses: employees who don't perform are fired. The other person responded, "You're comparing apples to oranges." You've probably heard that saying—or used it yourself—in

casual conversation. Usually, it is used to dismiss a comparison—or an argument based on a comparison—as invalid or specious.

This common saying actually refers to a fallacy described in formal logic, usually called *false comparison* or *false analogy*. In this example, the first person compares schools and businesses to argue for the use of standardized test scores to evaluate teachers. But as the second person realized, the comparison is problematic in several ways. For one thing, schools and businesses are very different kinds of institutions, so what might work for one won't necessarily work for the other. In addition, the job of a teacher is very different from most jobs in businesses, whose primary purpose is to make money; teachers aren't hired to produce a product for profit but to educate children. Finally, students' test scores might be one kind of information used to evaluate a teacher's effectiveness, but low student test scores don't necessarily mean that the teacher has been ineffective, because there are many factors outside the teacher's control that might have influenced the test scores. Therefore, the first person's implied point—that because businesses fire employees who don't perform, schools can improve by firing teachers whose students don't perform well on tests—is illogical.

This example illustrates that *a valid comparison requires a sound basis for the comparison*. It is possible to compare schools and businesses, but the basis for that comparison must be valid. For example, both schools and businesses are complicated organizations that can benefit from being more efficient. On that basis, we might compare the management policies of a school and a business to determine whether one functions more effectively than the other in managing routine operations, such as payroll, scheduling, and so on. Similarly, we might compare how schools and businesses implement various strategies for wasting less money on expenditures such as supplies or utilities. In such comparisons, the basis for comparison (efficiency) can lead to useful analysis.

Writing effective comparative analysis, then, requires writers to identify compelling reasons and a sound basis for the comparison; moreover, when synthesizing ideas or information, writers must be careful to identify similarities and account for differences or distinctions. Use the **four features of effective analytical writing** (Chapter 5) to guide your comparison and synthesis:

1. **A relevant topic worthy of analysis.** Establish why it is important or relevant to compare the ideas, events, trends, or phenomena you are comparing:

   - Why would readers want to understand similarities or differences among the things you are comparing?

   - What's at stake for them—and for you—in explaining similarities or differences in these things?

   - What are your reasons for comparing or synthesizing in this case?

2. **Complexity.** Explore the ideas, events, trends, or phenomena you are comparing or synthesizing in sufficient depth; avoid superficial comparisons or oversimplified synthesis:

   ■ Have you explored the ideas, events, trends, or phenomena you are comparing sufficiently to explain the similarities or differences among them?

   ■ Have you provided a sound and reasonable basis for comparison on this case?

   ■ Have you synthesized the ideas without oversimplifying them?

3. **Sufficient information and appropriate evidence.** Gather enough information about the ideas, events, trends, or phenomena you are comparing or synthesizing to understand and explain them:

   ■ Are your comparisons based on enough information to make them valid?

   ■ Have you learned enough about the ideas, events, trends, or phenomena you are comparing to explain them sufficiently?

   ■ Do you have sufficient information on which to base your comparisons and synthesize relevant ideas or information about your topic?

   ■ Are you confident that your sources are trustworthy and your evidence is adequate to explain the ideas, events, trends, or phenomena you are comparing?

4. **Reasonable conclusions.** Present reasonable and convincing conclusions on the basis of your comparison or synthesis:

   ■ Do your conclusions grow logically out of your comparisons?

   ■ Have you synthesized different ideas or perspectives in a way that leads your readers to your conclusions?

   ■ Do your conclusions present readers with a sound explanation that does not oversimplify the topic?

EXERCISE 7B   PRACTICING COMPARISON AND SYNTHESIS

1. For each of the following items, identify a **reason** and a **basis** for comparison. Also, describe a specific audience for analysis in each case.

   ■ Compare the views of the candidates in a current political election.

   ■ Compare different brands of smartphones.

   ■ Compare several different programs for weight loss.

   ■ Compare the work of two or more artists (painters, musicians, etc.).

2. Select one of the items in Question #1. Find two or more reviews or essays about those items. In a brief paragraph, synthesize those reviews so that you present to your intended audience (which you identified for Question #1) the main views or criticisms.

Reading Comparative Analysis

The following selections illustrate several different ways in which writers use comparison and synthesis to explore a topic in order to understand it better. As you read, consider how each selection addresses the four main features of analytical writing discussed in Chapter 5:

A relevant topic worthy of analysis	• How does the writer establish the topic as one that is worthy of analysis? • How does the writer establish that the comparison he or she is making is relevant? • What is the purpose of that comparison? Why should readers care about the comparison at this point in time?
Complexity	• What is the basis for comparison? • What claims does the writer make on the basis of the comparison? • How does the comparison reveal the complexity of the topic? • How does the writer avoid oversimplifying the topic through comparison and/or synthesis?
Sufficient information and appropriate analysis	• What kinds of evidence does the writer provide to support his or her claims? • Is the evidence sufficient? Is it appropriate for the rhetorical situation? • Does the comparative analysis sufficiently illuminate the topic?
Reasonable conclusions	• What conclusions does the writer draw from the comparison? • Does the comparison lead logically to these conclusions? • Are the conclusions well reasoned and supported by the writer's analysis? • Are the conclusions persuasive? Are they presented effectively?

War and Football

by Frank Deford

In the following essay, originally broadcast on National Public Radio in 2010, sports columnist Frank Deford uses the common comparison between football and war to help answer a question: Why do Americans seem increasingly uninterested in the ongoing

(Continued)

war in Afghanistan? Comparing the violence in football with other forms of violence, especially modern warfare, leads Deford to some conclusions about why Americans seem so interested in football but less so in war. Deford's essay does not go into the same level of depth in its analysis that is usually expected in most academic essays; moreover, Deford does not use outside sources in the way that is typical of academic writing. But the lack of these features does not mean that his analysis is any less valid than a conventional academic analysis. Deford uses comparison in a way that is appropriate for his intended audience (listeners of National Public Radio) and medium (radio). Despite its brevity and conversational language, his essay explores a complex topic in a way that does not oversimplify it.

....

It's the start of the football season again, just as the war in Iraq officially ends and the one in Afghanistan proceeds. And as always, there's the old cliché that football is a benign substitute for war—ground attack, flanks, bombs, blitz and so forth.

But it is a truth, not a cliché, that our football has gained in popularity in the United States as we've had less success with our wars. It makes me wonder if, ironically, football doesn't provide us more with nostalgia for the way that war used to be, with clear battle maps, focused campaigns, simple battle lines. And, of course, football games have neat conclusions. They're simply won or lost. But our wars are precisely not settled that way anymore. Their goals are vague and imprecise, and they just drag on and on, without resolution.

So, ultimately, given our wistful attention span, war bores us, and since so few of us citizens are asked to actively be engaged in our war, most of us are merely citizen-spectators to it rather than compatriots. And in this television world today, we lose interest in war. Football is better to watch.

Of course, all that aside, the increased popularity of football may be explained by the fact that it has become so much more violent than our other team sports, as indeed we prefer more violence in most all phases of our entertainment today. Mixed martial arts is more violent than traditional boxing. Auto racing is more violent than horse racing, and professional wrestling makes comedy out of brutality. Our movies and television, too, are more violent, and our children grow up devoted to incredibly bloodthirsty videogames. Even our music, that which soothes the savage beast, is more savage today.

Ken Durden/Shutterstock.com

It's been glib to say that violence in America is as traditional as apple pie. I don't think so. The new violence is showbiz. Rather than traditional, it's trendy—a fashionably entertaining part of everyday life, not any by-product of our aggressive heritage. And for all the beautiful excitement of football—the spectacular kickoff returns, the long, perfect touchdown passes—the one constant is the hitting. We very much enjoy watching football players hit one another. That makes the highlight reel.

The NFL has belatedly begun to acknowledge that the potential for damage to athletes' minds and bodies is probably much more the case than we've ever been prepared to admit. It's almost as if we didn't want to recognize that in a sport where hits to the head are so common, concussions are bound to happen. But then, since we no longer pay that much attention to our wars, it's easy to overlook casualties there, as well. Football and war today seem to have that in common, too.

EXERCISE 7C   EXPLORING COMPARATIVE ANALYSIS: WAR AND FOOTBALL

1. What is the purpose of Deford's comparison between football and war? What problem or question is he addressing through this comparison? What does his comparison reveal about American attitudes toward violence?

2. How does Deford support the claims he makes about attitudes toward violence? How does his comparison between war and football lead to those claims?

3. Deford's essay was written to be read on National Public Radio. In what ways does that medium influence his essay? How do you think it shapes his comparison between war and football and his overall analysis?

The Whole Truth

by Julian Baggini

Is lying always wrong? In the following essay, British philosopher Julian Baggini addresses that question by examining what several other philosophers have said about lying and truth in human affairs. Baggini's essay illustrates how a writer can draw on the ideas of others to explore a complicated question, synthesizing the perspectives of other philosophers and ultimately drawing his own conclusions about lying. Notice that the focus of the essay isn't the comparison of various perspectives but the question of whether lying is always wrong. A casual reader might not even realize that Baggini is comparing and synthesizing the ideas of other writers, yet he uses comparison and synthesis to strengthen his analysis without calling attention to the comparisons he is making.

(Continued)

Because Baggini was originally writing for a British audience, some of his references might be unfamiliar to you. For instance, British readers would recognize Lake Buttermere (located in the Lake District, a popular vacation destination in northwest England). Baggini also assumes his readers are familiar with prominent philosophers from the past, such as David Hume and St. Augustine, as well as with recent historical events, such as President Bill Clinton's affair with a White House intern in the 1990s. Consider what these references suggest about Baggini's intended audience: readers of Prospect *magazine, in which this essay first appeared in 2011.*

....

There is nothing more common than inconsistency and confusion over the imperative not to tell a lie. While "liar" is universally a term of opprobrium, almost everyone accepts that the social world would cease turning without a good scattering of white lies, half-truths and evasions.

In his new book *Born Liars: Why We Can't Live Without Deceit* (Quercus), Ian Leslie is the latest writer to try to work out some of what might follow from the simple realisation that lying is not always wrong. As I see it, the key is to recognise that lying is a problem because of what it is not: telling the truth. And if lying is a complex matter that is because truth is too. So once we get to the truth about lying, we're already in a dizzying tangle of ideas. To give one example, I could promise right now to tell the truth, the whole truth and nothing but the truth. The problem is that sometimes telling the truth is not the point, telling the whole truth is impossible, and there may be things other than the truth that matter too. So even if I went on without a single further lie, the promise itself would have been one.

The problem with telling "the truth" starts with the definite article, because there is always more than one way to give a true account or description. If you and I were to each describe the view of Lake Buttermere, for example, our accounts might be different but both contain nothing but true statements. You might coldly describe the topography and list the vegetation while I might paint more of a verbal picture. That is not to say there is more than one truth in some hand-washing, relativistic sense. If you were to start talking about the cluster of high-rise apartment blocks on the southern shore, you wouldn't be describing "what's true for you," you'd be lying or hallucinating.

So while it is not possible to give "the truth" about Lake Buttermere, it is possible to offer any number of accounts that only contain true statements. To do that, however, is not enough to achieve what people want from truth. It is rather a prescription for what we might call "estate agent truth." The art of describing a home for sale or rent is only to say true things, while leaving out the crucial additional information that would put the truth in its ugly context. In other words, no "false statement made with the intention to deceive"—St Augustine's still unbeatable definition of a lie—but plenty of economy with the truth.

This is also the truth of many lawyers, who always instruct their clients to say only true things, but to leave out anything that might incriminate them. This exposes the difference between a truly moral way of thinking and a kind of legalistic surrogate. Legalistic thinking asks only "what am I permitted to do?" whereas truly moral thinking asks "what would be the right thing to do?" As I have argued in my book *Complaint: From Minor Moans to Principled Protest*, moral ways of thinking are increasingly being replaced with legalistic ones. We think more of our entitlements, rights and strict legal obligations and less of what is required to be a good person.

Moral codes that stress the avoidance of telling lies are more legalistic than moral because they ultimately focus on the technical issue of whether a claim is true or false, not on the moral issue of whether one is being appropriately truthful. Not telling lies becomes a virtue in itself when, as the philosopher Bernard Williams argued in *Truth and Truthfulness*, there are two positive virtues of truth, and each is somewhat complex. The first of these he calls accuracy, the second sincerity. People who claim we should never lie not only neglect the second, they also have an impoverished understanding of the first. To say that the truth requires accuracy does not mean simply that everything you say must be 100 per cent correct, but that it must include all the relevant truths. So, for instance, the estate agent may technically be accurate when she describes a property as being 307 metres from the local shop, but it would even more accurate, in Williams's sense, to point out that the direct route is blocked and so it's about half an hour's walk away. Accuracy requires us to say enough to gain an accurate picture; not telling lies only requires us to make sure what we do say is not false.

The second virtue of truth, sincerity, is not required at all by lie-avoiders. Sincerity concerns the earnest desire to say what you truly think and describe what is truly there. That helps explain why one of the most famous "lies" of recent decades is not a lie at all, but objectionable nonetheless: Bill Clinton's famous "I did not have sexual relations with that woman, Miss Lewinsky." As many people have pointed out, to a Southern Baptist, this could indeed be interpreted as being strictly true. "Sexual relations" is, in many parts, a euphemism for coitus, not any other sexual acts between two people. If this is so, then Clinton was accurate only in the legal sense, not in Williams's. Even more clearly, he was not sincerely trying to convey the truth of his situation.

Williams's stress on the virtues of truth is therefore much more valuable than the legalistic stress on the vices of lying. It shows that truthfulness—the whole truth if you like—requires more than just true things being said, while acknowledging that there really is no such thing as "the whole truth" anyway. Full disclosure is never possible. Truthfulness is largely a matter of deciding what it is reasonable to withhold.

Nevertheless, even Williams's account leaves out something else which is very important: the question of whether or not truth always trumps other virtues. "Nothing but the truth" is the wrong maxim if things other than truth matter more. The most

(Continued)

obvious examples are of courtesy and concern for people's feelings, where kindness matters more than revealing the full, naked truth. Even here, however, we need to be careful. There is a risk of second guessing what is best for people or what we think they are able to deal with. Normally, it is better to allow people to make up their own minds on the basis of facts. Withholding truth for someone's own benefit is sometimes justified but often it simply diminishes their autonomy. This is what Kant got right when he claimed that lying violates the dignity of man.

We might sometimes be justified in lying to others for our own dignity too. Bill Clinton lied, for sure. But he only did so only because a zealous prosecutor brought to public light what should probably have remained private. If what you did is nobody else's business, aren't you entitled to lie to preserve your privacy?

Even when it comes to matters that truly belong in the public domain, we should ask ourselves whether we would really prefer politicians to simply speak the truth. Would it really be wise for a prime minister to announce, when a crisis breaks, that no one really knows what's going on yet or has a clue what to do next? Leadership in a crisis may require projecting more calm and control than one really has behind closed doors. More honesty in politics would certainly be a good thing; complete honesty most probably disastrous.

But perhaps the most interesting counter-example to the twin virtues of sincerity and accuracy was proposed by the sociologist Steve Fuller, who has been widely condemned for suggesting that intelligent design theory merits a hearing. Many of Fuller's colleagues know he is a smart guy and can't understand why he persists with this kind of argument. The answer is perhaps to be found in a piece he wrote in the spring 2008 edition of *The Philosopher's Magazine* explaining his modus operandi. The idea that one should always say what one truly believes is narcissistic nonsense, he argued. The role of the intellectual is to say what they think needs saying most at any given time in a debate, not to bear testimony to their deepest convictions. Although this might involve some dissembling, it serves the cause of establishing truth in the long run better than simply saying the truth as you see it. What matters is how what one says helps build and expand the widest, most expansive truth—not whether as a distinct ingredient it is more or less true than another.

I find Fuller's argument very persuasive. Indeed, it fits with my own tendency to want to talk more about the virtues of religion around atheists than with believers, or to question the value of philosophy with philosophers. The quest for truth requires a constant critical edge. In the case of intelligent design, I think Fuller is sharpening the wrong blade, and a dangerous one at that. But the idea that the contemporary consensus needs some shaking from its dogmatic slumber is not such a stupid one, and may justify a suspension of sincerity in the name of furthering debate.

There are, then, numerous reasons why lying is not always wrong, and why telling the truth is not always the main priority. Nevertheless, it is vital to remember that—ultimately—truth matters. You could concoct a hypothetical situation in which we had to choose between lying or creating misery for all humankind, but until and unless we ever come against such scenarios, most of us value truth, even to the detriment of some happiness. That is why we should develop the habit of telling truth, and distaste for lies. Truth should be the default; lying an exception that requires a special justification.

In *Born Liars*, Ian Leslie rightly points out that lying is deeply connected to what makes us human. We may not be the only creatures who have a "theory of mind"—the ability to see the world from the point of view of others—but we are certainly the species in which that capacity is most developed. It is precisely because of this that the possibility of lying emerges. We can lie only because we understand that others can be made to see the world other than as we know it to be.

But theory of mind is also connected to another human capacity: empathy. As Adam Smith and David Hume argued long before modern psychology strengthened their case, our ability to understand how other people feel is what makes morality possible. Emotional insight is what drives the golden rule: simply by imagining what it would be like to suffer a wrongdoing shows us why it is indeed wrong. So it is with being lied to. In that way, our ability to take up the viewpoint of another is both what makes lying possible and gives us a reason not to do it—usually, at least.

EXERCISE 7D   EXPLORING COMPARATIVE ANALYSIS: THE WHOLE TRUTH

1. What is the occasion for Baggini's analysis of lying? What justification does he give to establish the importance of this topic?

2. What, specifically, does Baggini compare in this essay? How is his comparison relevant to his main question? How does his comparison help him answer that question?

3. What answer does Baggini give to his main question about lying? How convincing did you find his answer? Do you think his comparative analysis makes his answer more or less persuasive? Explain.

Taking Science on Faith

by Paul Davies

Sometimes, a writer can make a surprising comparison that leads to new insights about old questions. In the following essay, Paul Davies, a physicist and astrobiologist at Arizona State University, compares science and religion and arrives at the unexpected conclusion that the two are more similar than different. Although he begins with the familiar contrast between science and religion, his comparison leads to a startling position for a scientist. In this sense, his essay provides a compelling example of the power of comparison to help us see familiar things in new ways—and perhaps understand them better. Davies' essay, which was published in the New York Times in 2007, takes up questions that philosophers, theologians, and scientists have been debating for many centuries, and in that sense his subject matter seems timeless. Yet his comparison makes this very old subject seem contemporary.

....

Science, we are repeatedly told, is the most reliable form of knowledge about the world because it is based on testable hypotheses. Religion, by contrast, is based on faith. The term "doubting Thomas" well illustrates the difference. In science, a healthy skepticism is a professional necessity, whereas in religion, having belief without evidence is regarded as a virtue.

The problem with this neat separation into "non-overlapping magisteria," as Stephen Jay Gould described science and religion, is that science has its own faith-based belief system. All science proceeds on the assumption that nature is ordered in a rational and intelligible way. You couldn't be a scientist if you thought the universe was a meaningless jumble of odds and ends haphazardly juxtaposed. When physicists probe to a deeper level of subatomic structure, or astronomers extend the reach of their instruments, they expect to encounter additional elegant mathematical order. And so far this faith has been justified.

The most refined expression of the rational intelligibility of the cosmos is found in the laws of physics, the fundamental rules on which nature runs. The laws of gravitation and electromagnetism, the laws that regulate the world within the atom, the laws of motion—all are expressed as tidy mathematical relationships. But where do these laws come from? And why do they have the form that they do?

When I was a student, the laws of physics were regarded as completely off limits. The job of the scientist, we were told, is to discover the laws and apply them, not inquire into their provenance. The laws were treated as "given"—imprinted on the universe like a maker's mark at the moment of cosmic birth—and fixed forevermore. Therefore, to be a scientist, you had to have faith that the universe is governed by dependable, immutable, absolute, universal, mathematical laws of an unspecified origin. You've got to believe that these laws won't fail, that we won't wake up tomorrow to find heat flowing from cold to hot, or the speed of light changing by the hour.

Over the years I have often asked my physicist colleagues why the laws of physics are what they are. The answers vary from "that's not a scientific question" to "nobody knows." The favorite reply is, "There is no reason they are what they are—they just are." The idea that the laws exist reasonlessly is deeply anti-rational. After all, the very essence of a scientific explanation of some phenomenon is that the world is ordered logically and that there are reasons things are as they are. If one traces these reasons all the way down to the bedrock of reality—the laws of physics—only to find that reason then deserts us, it makes a mockery of science.

Can the mighty edifice of physical order we perceive in the world about us ultimately be rooted in reasonless absurdity? If so, then nature is a fiendishly clever bit of trickery: meaninglessness and absurdity somehow masquerading as ingenious order and rationality.

Although scientists have long had an inclination to shrug aside such questions concerning the source of the laws of physics, the mood has now shifted considerably. Part of the reason is the growing acceptance that the emergence of life in the universe, and hence the existence of observers like ourselves, depends rather sensitively on the form of the laws. If the laws of physics were just any old ragbag of rules, life would almost certainly not exist.

A second reason that the laws of physics have now been brought within the scope of scientific inquiry is the realization that what we long regarded as absolute and universal laws might not be truly fundamental at all, but more like local bylaws. They could vary from place to place on a mega-cosmic scale. A God's-eye view might reveal a vast patchwork quilt of universes, each with its own distinctive set of bylaws. In this "multiverse," life will arise only in those patches with bio-friendly bylaws, so it is no surprise that we find ourselves in a Goldilocks universe—one that is just right for life. We have selected it by our very existence.

The multiverse theory is increasingly popular, but it doesn't so much explain the laws of physics as dodge the whole issue. There has to be a physical mechanism to make all those universes and bestow bylaws on them. This process will require its own laws, or meta-laws. Where do they come from? The problem has simply been shifted up a level from the laws of the universe to the meta-laws of the multiverse.

Clearly, then, both religion and science are founded on faith—namely, on belief in the existence of something outside the universe, like an unexplained God or an unexplained set of physical laws, maybe even a huge ensemble of unseen universes, too. For that reason, both monotheistic religion and orthodox science fail to provide a complete account of physical existence.

(*Continued*)

This shared failing is no surprise, because the very notion of physical law is a theological one in the first place, a fact that makes many scientists squirm. Isaac Newton first got the idea of absolute, universal, perfect, immutable laws from the Christian doctrine that God created the world and ordered it in a rational way. Christians envisage God as upholding the natural order from beyond the universe, while physicists think of their laws as inhabiting an abstract transcendent realm of perfect mathematical relationships.

And just as Christians claim that the world depends utterly on God for its existence, while the converse is not the case, so physicists declare a similar asymmetry: the universe is governed by eternal laws (or meta-laws), but the laws are completely impervious to what happens in the universe.

It seems to me there is no hope of ever explaining why the physical universe is as it is so long as we are fixated on immutable laws or meta-laws that exist reasonlessly or are imposed by divine providence. The alternative is to regard the laws of physics and the universe they govern as part and parcel of a unitary system, and to be incorporated together within a common explanatory scheme.

In other words, the laws should have an explanation from within the universe and not involve appealing to an external agency. The specifics of that explanation are a matter for future research. But until science comes up with a testable theory of the laws of the universe, its claim to be free of faith is manifestly bogus.

EXERCISE 7E   EXPLORING COMPARATIVE ANALYSIS: TAKING SCIENCE ON FAITH

1. Davies focuses his essay on a very old question about the difference between science and religion. What justification does he give for revisiting this question? How compelling do you find his justification?

2. How does Davies organize his comparison between science and religion? How does the structure of his essay build toward his conclusions about science and religion?

3. What assumptions does Davies make about his audience? Cite specific passages from his essay to support your answer. Do you think you are part of Davies' intended audience? Why or why not?

Writing Comparative Analysis

This section will help you develop a writing project involving comparative analysis by applying the Ten Core Concepts described in Chapter 2. Read this section in tandem with Chapter 3; each step described here corresponds to a step described there.

Step 1	Identify a topic for comparative analysis.

Comparative analysis doesn't necessarily begin with comparison; it usually begins because comparison (and synthesis) help the writer answer a question or solve a problem. This question or problem can arise from your own experience, a trend, or an issue of current interest. So start with a question or problem that leads to comparison:

Your own experience	• What are the advantages and disadvantages of attending a two-year college as compared to a four-year college? • Is renting a better financial decision than purchasing a home?
A social or cultural trend	• Why are more young people living together rather than getting married? • Is online dating really a good alternative to traditional dating? • What advantages do digital tablets have over laptops or smartphones?
An issue of current interest	• Is universal health care a better system than the one currently in place in the United States? • Are online classes better than traditional face-to-face classes? • Is solar or wind power a better alternative to fossil fuels?

Develop this question using Step #1 in Chapter 3.

Step 2 | Place your topic in rhetorical context.

The question you developed for Step #1 should point to a comparison of two or more things. For example, you might begin with this question: Is wind or solar power a better alternative to fossil fuels? Obviously, answering such a question requires comparing wind and solar power and fossil fuels. Now consider why such a comparison might matter—not just to you but to others:

Who else might be interested in your question?	• American citizens in general • People interested in environmental issues • Other students in your class • People involved with the energy business
Why would this comparison matter to them?	• Alternatives to fossil fuels is a topic of general interest. • Debates about climate change direct attention to alternative energy. • Many people are concerned about rising energy costs.
What's at stake for them in such a comparison?	• A better understanding of the relevant issues • Concerns about how climate change and rising energy costs might affect various groups of people • A potential change of mind about current controversies

In addressing these questions, you are identifying key elements of your rhetorical context that might shape your comparative analysis. Obviously, if your course assignment specifies an audience and purpose, adhere to the assignment guidelines as you examine the rhetorical context.

Using your answers to these questions as a guide, complete Step #2 in Chapter 3.

Step 3 | Select a medium.

If your course assignment specifies a medium, use that medium. If you have a choice of medium, consider, as always, which medium might best address your intended audience and which might enable you to present your comparative analysis most persuasively.

Depending upon your audience and the purpose of your analysis, a website or perhaps a brochure might be a better way to convey the results of your comparison or synthesis than a traditional paper or essay. For example, if you wanted to participate in a debate in your town about new state policies that would encourage homeowners to use alternative energy sources, you might present your comparative analysis in a brochure, in a video, or on a local social media site so that you might reach your audience most effectively:

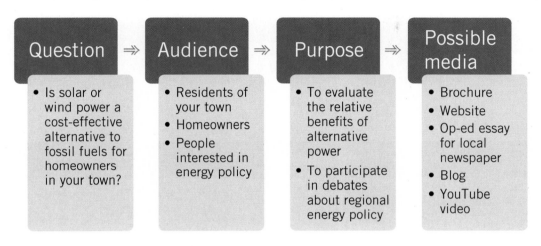

Step #3 in Chapter 3 will help you decide on the most appropriate medium for your comparative analysis.

Step 4   Identify your main claim.

Your comparison of two or more ideas, trends, viewpoints, or products should lead to one or more claims about whatever you're analyzing—claims that address your main question from Step #1. In the example of an analysis of solar and wind power as alternatives to fossil fuels, your comparison might reveal that one is better than the other, so your **main claim** might be that solar is a more cost-effective and practical alternative to fossil fuels than wind power. However, it's possible that your comparative analysis will lead to a more complicated finding. You might have discovered, for example, that solar power is less efficient than wind power, but wind turbines have more serious environmental consequences than solar panels; moreover, you might have learned that solar power is more practical in certain locations, whereas wind power cannot be used at all in neighborhoods where homes are close together. So your analysis does not lead to the conclusion that one is better than the other but that several key factors must be considered in deciding which to use. In that case, your **main claim** might be something like this:

Neither wind nor solar power can feasibly be used on a large scale in all regions of the United States; therefore, both should be used where they are practical.

As this example illustrates, a comparison involving a complicated question might lead to several different claims:

Question

Which is a better alternative to fossil fuels: solar or wind power?

Comparative Analysis

| Cost-effectiveness | Environmental consequences | Geographical considerations |

Possible Claims

| One is better than the other. | No clear choice; each has advantages and disadvantages. |

Because you probably don't yet know what your analysis will reveal, you might not be able to identify your main claim with certainty at this point. Tentatively identify your main claim now, but be open to the possibility that it could change as you learn more through your analysis. Your main purpose at this point is to delve into your comparison and gain a better understanding of your topic so that you can address your question from Step #1.

Follow Step #4 in Chapter 3 to develop a Guiding Thesis Statement, which is a brief statement of the main claim(s) you expect to make in your comparative analysis. In addition, address the following questions:

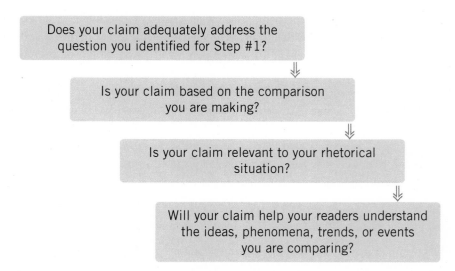

Does your claim adequately address the question you identified for Step #1?

Is your claim based on the comparison you are making?

Is your claim relevant to your rhetorical situation?

Will your claim help your readers understand the ideas, phenomena, trends, or events you are comparing?

Step 5 Support your claim(s).

At this stage, you should be well into your research. As you explore your topic, keep in mind that you are trying to understand what you are comparing so that you can address your main question and meet the needs of your rhetorical situation. Your claims and your support for them will develop through this process of inquiry.

In addition to your main claim, your comparative analysis will likely result in several supporting claims. These claims might change as you explore your topic and find support for each claim.

Let's return to the example of solar power versus wind power. Through your research you should gain a better understanding of some of the considerations related to alternative energy, and as a result you should have developed several supporting claims:

Main claim	• Solar power is a better alternative to fossil fuels than wind power.

Supporting claims	• Solar is less expensive than wind power. • Wind power has significant environmental consequences. • Neither solar nor wind power is feasible in all regions, but solar is more flexible.

These supporting claims essentially build your case for your main claim. But for each of these claims you will need to provide evidence or support. To do so, complete Step #5 in Chapter 3, supplementing it with the following steps:

7

1. List what you have learned through your comparison.	• Solar is generally less expensive than wind power. • Wind power has some significant possible environmental consequences. • Neither solar nor wind is feasible in all geographic locations. • Wind power has a longer history than solar electric power.
2. Determine whether each item on your list helps support your main claim(s); eliminate items that don't.	• Relative costs, environmental impact, and geographical feasibility are relevant to main claim. • History of wind vs. solar power seems irrelevant to main claim.
3. Identify the reasoning, information, and/or source that supports each item on your list.	• Cost analyses by economists of solar and wind power • Articles and essays about the environmental impact of wind power and the controversies surrounding wind projects • Studies of feasibility of solar and wind power for specific regions
4. Determine whether your information, reasoning, and sources are sufficient for each item.	• Do cost analyses compare alternative power to fossil fuels? • Are feasibility studies current and thorough? • Are there other important considerations not addressed by available sources?

As you continue to research your topic, keep the following in mind:

■ **You are not only comparing but also synthesizing ideas or information.** As a result, you might develop claims that don't necessarily grow out of a direct comparison. For example, your comparison of wind and solar power might lead to a claim that neither is clearly preferable to the other in all cases. Your support for this claim will likely be based on synthesizing several different studies or perspectives about different aspects of energy—such as cost, equipment size, weather—rather than just citing studies that show that one is better than the other.

■ **Comparative analysis can lead to unexpected insights that require you to adjust your claims.** For example, you might have learned that many states have special programs to help homeowners pay for solar panels, making solar panels less expensive than wind turbines in those states. That knowledge complicates your claim that solar power is more cost-effective than wind power. As a result, you might have to adjust your claim, as in this example:

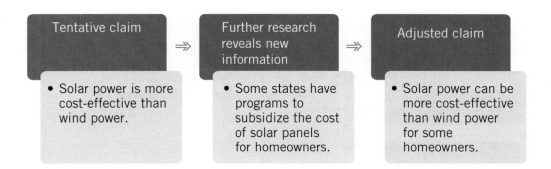

Tentative claim		Further research reveals new information		Adjusted claim
• Solar power is more cost-effective than wind power.	⇒	• Some states have programs to subsidize the cost of solar panels for homeowners.	⇒	• Solar power can be more cost-effective than wind power for some homeowners.

As you continue your inquiry, then, don't hesitate to revise your main claims or adjust your supporting claims.

If you have followed Steps #1 through #5 in Chapter 3, you are probably ready to write a complete draft of your project. Or you can move onto the next step before completing your draft.

Step 6 Organize your comparative analysis.

There are many ways to organize a comparative analysis. Here we will describe two conventional approaches: (1) a point-by-point comparison; and (2) main claims. The first approach works best when you are comparing two things; often, if your research leads to complicated claims, the second approach can work well. Here's how these approaches might work for our example of a comparative analysis of solar versus wind power as alternatives to fossil fuels.

Organizing Your Comparative Analysis According to a Point-by-Point Comparison

In this approach, organize your project according to the criteria or principles that formed the basis for your comparison. Let's say that your research has led to the conclusion that there are three main considerations when it comes to determining whether solar power is preferable to wind power as an alternative to fossil fuels: cost, efficiency, geographical location. You can organize your project by comparing solar and wind power on each of these three considerations:

Basis for comparison	• Feasibility of alternatives to fossil fuels
Cost	• Solar is generally less expensive than wind power. • In states with subsidies, solar is considerably less expensive than wind power. • Both solar and wind remain more expensive than most fossil fuels; however, costs for solar are decreasing.
Efficiency	• Solar panels are less efficient than wind turbines. • Efficiency of both solar and wind power is improving with new technologies.
Geography	• Solar power is most feasible in regions with sunny, dry weather but also useful in most other climates. • Wind turbines are not feasible for homes in urban and many suburban neighborhoods.

A basic outline for this project would look like this:

I. Introduction

II. Background on alternative energy

    A. The need for alternative energy sources

    B. Solar and wind as the best available alternatives to fossil fuels

III. Comparison of solar and wind power as alternatives to fossil fuels

    A. Cost

    B. Efficiency

    C. Geography

IV. Conclusion

To organize your comparative analysis in this way, follow these steps:

1. List the main points of comparison—that is, the criteria or principles on which you based your comparison.

2. Arrange the list in a way that would be effective for your readers: What order will present your analysis most clearly to those readers? What order seems to make the most logical sense?

3. Use this list to adjust the outline you developed for Step #6 in Chapter 3.

Organizing Your Comparative Analysis According to Your Main Claims

You might decide that a point-by-point comparison does not effectively present what you found through your analysis, especially if your comparison revealed a complicated picture or you found yourself synthesizing ideas and information from very different perspectives. In that case, consider organizing your project around your main claims.

Let's imagine that your analysis of solar and wind power led to three main claims: (1) In most cases, solar power is more cost-effective than wind power; (2) the feasibility of solar and wind power depends on several key factors, especially geographical location; and (3) both solar and wind power remain impractical for most homeowners. You might organize your project as follows:

I. Introduction

II. Background on alternative energy

III. Main claim #1: Cost-effectiveness of solar and wind power

IV. Main claim #2: Feasibility of solar and wind power

V. Main claim #3: Practicality of alternative energy

VI. Conclusion

For each main claim, you would include your supporting claims. To organize your project in this way, follow this procedure:

1. **List the main claims you are making as a result of your comparative analysis.**

2. **Identify your support and your sources for each claim.** Organize your main points of support for each claim from most persuasive to least persuasive.

3. **Arrange the list in the order that makes the most sense.** Consider: What order will present your claims most effectively to your readers? What order seems to make the most logical sense?

4. **Create an outline** with each main section of your project devoted to one of your main claims.

Keep these possibilities in mind as you complete Step #6 in Chapter 3 to organize your project.

Step 7   Get feedback.

Follow Step #7 in Chapter 3 to receive useful feedback on your comparative analysis, but have your readers also focus on the main characteristics of analytical writing (as described above in this chapter):

A relevant topic worthy of analysis	• Has the writer explained the reasons for comparison? • Does the writer have something relevant to say? Does he or she show why this comparison matters? • Is the comparison relevant to the rhetorical situation?
Complexity	• Is the comparison thorough? • Has the writer provided a reasonable basis for comparison? • Has the writer compared and/or synthesized key ideas or information without oversimplifying?
Appropriate and sufficient support	• Is the comparison based on sufficient information? • Are the main claims well supported? Do any sections need more support or stronger evidence? • Are the sources appropriate for this topic and rhetorical situation? • Is there too much evidence or support?
Reasonable conclusions	• Do the writer's conclusions grow logically from the comparison? Are the conclusions presented clearly and persuasively? • Does the writer synthesize various perspectives in a way that leads to reasonable conclusions?

Step 8 Revise.

Follow the steps for Step #8 in Chapter 3 to revise your draft. Also use the following questions to guide your revisions:

A relevant topic worthy of analysis	• Does your comparison fit the needs of your assignment or rhetorical situation? • Is the purpose of your analysis clear? Should you refine the questions you are trying to answer with your analysis? • Do you have something relevant to say as a result of your analysis?
Complexity	• Have you answered the question(s) you pose in your project? Have you developed your analysis sufficiently? • Have you explored the things you are comparing in a way that does not oversimplify them? Are there sections of your analysis that need further explanation? • Do you synthesize ideas without oversimplifying them?
Appropriate and sufficient support	• Are your main claims supported with sufficient evidence? • Do any sections need additional or stronger evidence? • Can you eliminate any evidence or support without weakening your analysis? • Are your sources appropriate for your topic and rhetorical situation?
Reasonable conclusions	• Do your conclusions address your main question? Do they grow logically out of your comparison? • Do you present your conclusions clearly and persuasively? • Have you neglected any key issues in your conclusions?

Review your draft with these sets of questions in mind and revise accordingly.

Step 9 Refine your voice.

Sometimes in comparative analysis the writing can become repetitive because the comparison is presented in a way that repeats information about each thing being compared. As you follow the steps for Step #9 in Chapter 3, be alert for passages in your draft that might sound repetitive and revise them accordingly.

Step 10 Edit.

Complete Step #10 in Chapter 3.

1. Identify a current controversy that interests you but about which you have no strong opinion. This controversy could be political (the debate about gun control), cultural (the increasing use of social media), economic (income inequality in the United States), or something else. Identify the main positions or perspectives on that controversy, and write a comparative analysis of them. Be sure to have a clear basis for your comparison of these ideas or perspectives. Draw conclusions about the controversy on the basis of your analysis of the competing positions or perspectives and your own inquiry into the issues.

2. Imagine that you have been asked to be part of a campus committee charged with examining the relative benefits and drawbacks of living on campus as compared to living off campus. Focusing on your own campus and community, write a comparative analysis in which you explore the pros and cons of different student living arrangements. Assume that your campus administration is your primary audience for your report.

3. Identify a technological development that is changing the way we live. For example,

- Social media have influenced many different aspects of our social and political lives.
- Wireless devices such as smartphones have changed how we communicate and conduct our business.
- Online shopping has affected what goods we buy and how we buy them.
- Computers have changed the way we write.

Analyze such a technological development, comparing how we do things now as a result of this development to how we did them in the past. For your project, identify a specific audience and select a medium that would most effectively reach that audience.

Conducting
Rhetorical Analysis

IN MARCH 2008, then-Senator Barack Obama delivered an address that became known as the "More Perfect Union" speech. Obama, who was running for president, gave the speech in the midst of an intensifying controversy surrounding a fiery Christmas sermon delivered by his former pastor, Reverend Jeremiah Wright. As the presidential campaign heated up, videos of Wright's sermon, in which he accused the U.S. government of perpetrating crimes against people of color, deeply offended many Americans and threatened Obama's candidacy, prompting him to write a special speech about race relations. In that speech, which he delivered in Philadelphia, Obama denounced Wright's inflammatory words but also acknowledged Wright's anger about racism as real. To wish that anger away, Obama said, "only serves to widen the chasm of misunderstanding that exists between the races." He called on Americans of all races to acknowledge their shared "history of racial injustice" but also to work together to "move beyond some of our old racial wounds . . . to continue on the path of a more perfect union."

Obama's speech itself ignited a debate that continues today. Many commentators at the time hailed it as brilliant and ground-breaking; critics called it unhelpful and naïve. Today, some experts believe that the speech saved Obama's candidacy and helped him become the first American president of color, while others see it as unsuccessful in achieving Obama's goal of fostering an honest national conversation about race relations. How can we account for these different assessments of Obama's "More Perfect Union" speech? What made it important? What made it appeal to some Americans but not others? How did it contribute to his election as president—if at all?

To answer such questions requires a specialized kind of analysis called *rhetorical analysis*, which explains *how* a text works within a certain set of circumstances. Rhetorical analysis illuminates the impact of a speech, image, video, song, advertisement, or essay by examining the characteristics and strategies that make a text persuasive (or not) within the rhetorical situation. Through rhetorical analysis, we can better understand why the arguments Barack Obama made in his "More Perfect Union" speech resonated with many Americans and explain how elements such as his language and imagery lent persuasive power to his speech. We can also examine the historical and political context to illuminate how his speech might have contributed to his victory in the 2008 presidential election.

Because rhetorical analysis explains how a text affects an audience, it can be a powerful tool, not only for academic assignments but also in our lives as consumers, citizens, and workers.

Occasions for Rhetorical Analysis

If you have ever thought about what makes a particular television commercial so popular, a hit song so catchy, or a movie so engrossing, you have engaged in a kind of rhetorical analysis. For instance, you might have discussed with some friends why you find a certain scene in a popular horror movie so memorable. Examining how camera angles, music, and plot twists make the scene frightening helps you appreciate the director's expertise and better understand film-making in general. Such informal analysis can enhance the aesthetic enjoyment of a movie or song.

But you might also have reason for more formal rhetorical analysis:

> A famous business leader delivers a speech about renewable energy on a university campus. His speech is widely praised, but some students find his main argument questionable. They believe the positive response to his speech is based on his reputation as a pioneer in new technologies rather than on the strength of his argument. After a careful rereading of his speech, which was published in the campus newspaper, one student writes a letter to the editor explaining why the speech was appealing to so many students and pointing out the flaws in the speaker's argument.

> A non-profit organization that collects and distributes food to low-income families has had difficulty recruiting student volunteers. Few students have responded to its fliers to volunteer to help with food distribution for an upcoming holiday. The organization's leaders have appointed a committee to look into recruitment. As part of its work, the committee analyzes recruiting materials for other successful organizations, including U.S. military recruiters, to see what makes them persuasive and how they might be adapted for social media to reach potential student volunteers.

Both these scenarios call for rhetorical analysis. In each case, the analysis, which grows out of the need to understand why a text (a speech or a recruiting flier) seems effective in addressing an audience, becomes a tool for solving a problem, making a decision, or developing a course of action. For example, understanding how military recruitment materials use certain images to appeal to students' sense of adventure can help a non-profit organization design more effective recruitment materials of its own. In this way, rhetorical analysis can help you identify and use appropriate strategies to create persuasive documents of your own.

1. Find an essay, blog post, YouTube video, flier, or letter to an editor about a controversy that interests you. The document might reflect your own views about the issue, or it might be something with which you disagree. Write a paragraph explaining why you do or do not find the document persuasive. Identify specific features, such as the use of language or images, that you believe help explain the document's effect on you.

2. Identify a film or television show that is popular with your friends. Write a paragraph explaining what makes the film or show appealing. Identify specific characteristics, such as the themes or filmmaker's style, that appeal to you and your friends.

3. Think of a time when a document of some kind seemed to have an impact on someone you know. For example, perhaps your parents were persuaded to vote for a political candidate by certain television ads supporting that candidate. Or maybe your roommate decided to buy a certain kind of device, such as a tablet or smartphone, after reading promotional materials about it. In a brief paragraph, describe that situation and examine how an understanding of the persuasiveness of the text might have been useful.

Understanding Rhetorical Analysis

Rhetorical analysis goes beyond describing the features of a text—for example, the writer's style or use of images—to explaining how a text works. You might see a billboard like this one . . .

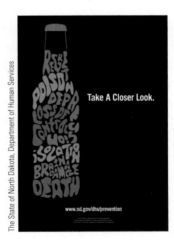

The State of North Dakota, Department of Human Services

. . . and notice the provocative words on the left side of the billboard that form the shape of a beer bottle: *poison, depression, brain damage.* You might also notice the red color of the web address, the stark black background, and the bold white words, "Take a closer look." Describing such features calls attention to *what* is in the text, but it doesn't explain *why* the creators of the billboard included those features or *how* those features might influence a viewer's response. Why use red, for example? What does that color signify? Why make the background black? What effect are the creators of the billboard trying to achieve through these features? Would the effect be different with, say, a yellow or pink background? And who is the intended audience for this billboard? Young people? Casual drinkers? How might the features of the billboard—the beer bottle, the red words, the white command—speak to those audiences?

Such questions point to the rhetorical choices made by the billboard's creators to reach a specific audience. Rhetorical analysis illuminates how a text reflects a rhetorical purpose and whether that text is likely to be persuasive to that audience. In this regard, **rhetorical analysis addresses three main questions**:

- **What** are the main features of the text?
- **How** do those features affect the intended audience?
- **Why** did the writer include those features and craft the text in specific ways?

In rhetorical analysis, you are not evaluating the message itself but how the message is conveyed. *The point of rhetorical analysis is not to agree or disagree with the message but to examine how effectively the message is conveyed to an audience.*

There are a variety of methods for conducting a rhetorical analysis. What follows is a discussion of three main methods, or frameworks, for rhetorical analysis.

Basic Rhetorical Analysis

In its most basic form, rhetorical analysis is a matter of explaining a text in terms of the main elements of the rhetorical triangle: writer, audience, and purpose (see page 29 in Chapter 2). To do so, you must take the following steps.

- **Identify the intended audience.** For whom is the text intended? What is the nature of the intended audience(s)? What characteristics might affect the audience's response to this message? (Would the gender or age of the audience matter?) What are the audience's expectations in this situation? (Is the text part of a special occasion, such as a graduation ceremony, that might shape what the audience expects from the speaker or writer?)

- **Determine the author's purpose.** Why is the author addressing this particular audience? Does he or she have special expertise or authority on the topic? Does he or she have a special connection to the intended audience? What has prompted the author to address this topic at this time?

- **Explain the rhetorical situation.** What are the circumstances surrounding the creation of this text? What specific factors might affect how it is received by an audience? (E.g., Is the topic related to a current controversy? Are there economic or social conditions that might affect how the audience responds to the text?) Does the situation place any constraints on the author or the audience? (Is there a set of conventions that must be followed—as in a commencement address?)

- **Examine the components of the text.** What is the author's message? What strategies are used to convey that message? What features of the text are most important in conveying that message?

- **Evaluate the author's decisions.** How has the author crafted the message to reach the intended audience? How well do the specific features of the text convey the message in this situation? How do those features reflect the author's intentions? How effectively do the strategies communicate the message to the audience? How well has the author accounted for important components of the rhetorical situation?

For example, let's imagine you are analyzing President Abraham Lincoln's famous Gettysburg Address, delivered in November 1863, a few months after that pivotal battle in the American Civil War. Here's the full text of the speech:

Four score and seven years ago our fathers brought forth on this continent a new nation, conceived in liberty, and dedicated to the proposition that all men are created equal.

Now we are engaged in a great civil war, testing whether that nation, or any nation, so conceived and so dedicated, can long endure. We are met on a great battle-field of that war. We have come to dedicate a portion of that field, as a final resting place for those who here gave their lives that that nation might live. It is altogether fitting and proper that we should do this.

But, in a larger sense, we can not dedicate, we can not consecrate, we can not hallow this ground. The brave men, living and dead, who struggled here, have consecrated it, far above our poor power to add or detract. The world will little note, nor long remember what we say here, but it can never forget what they did here. It is for us the living, rather, to be dedicated here to the unfinished work which they who fought here have thus far so nobly advanced. It is rather for us to be here dedicated to the great task remaining before us—that from these honored dead we take increased devotion to that cause for which they gave the last full measure of devotion—that we here highly resolve that these dead shall not have died in vain—that this nation, under God, shall have a new birth of freedom—and that government of the people, by the people, for the people, shall not perish from the earth.

Library of Congress Prints and Photographs Division Washington, D.C. [LC-USZ62-15178]

8

- **Identify the intended audience.** The main goal is to identify (as much as possible) the relevant characteristics of the audience for which the speech was originally composed. Lincoln's immediate audience was the group of 15,000 to 20,000 people gathered for the dedication of the National Cemetery in Gettysburg on November 19, 1863. That audience included other politicians and dignitaries as well as ordinary citizens, but his broader audience was the American people as well as soldiers in the Union army.

- **Determine the writer's purpose.** Lincoln likely had several purposes in giving his speech. He intended not only to honor the soldiers who had given their lives at Gettysburg but also to reassure Americans—and especially the Union soldiers—that their great sacrifices were worthwhile. He hoped to convince them that their cause was worthy and that they must continue fighting despite the costs.

- **Explain the rhetorical situation.** Identify the important features of the rhetorical situation that gave rise to the speech and shaped its impact. Lincoln's address was delivered at a ceremony dedicating the Gettysburg National Cemetery, an important event honoring the thousands who died there. At that point, the Civil War had been going on for two and a half years, with a horrific toll in lives lost and disrupted and no end in sight. Lincoln knew his words would be scrutinized not only by those present for the dedication but also by the nation as a whole. Also, he was not the main speaker at the ceremony, which might have prompted him to give such a short speech.

- **Examine the text.** Analyze how the important elements of Lincoln's speech—including his language and the structure of his speech—convey his message and affect his audience. The brevity of Lincoln's speech suggests that he chose his words carefully. His language is appropriately somber for the occasion, and he honors those who fell at that great battle. The structure of the speech emphasizes the larger cause for which the soldiers who died in that battle fought. He begins with a direct reference to the Declaration of Independence ("all men are created equal") and ends with a now-famous phrase that might be seen as a reference to the U.S. Constitution. His simple but careful word choices underscore sense of the importance of the cause ("nobly advanced"; "great task"). His final statement that the government "shall not perish from the earth" emphasizes both the cost of the war and the importance of the cause.

- **Evaluate the writer's decisions.** Assess the overall rhetorical effectiveness of the speech. Lincoln's speech, now considered one of the greatest orations ever delivered, was widely praised at the time. Its simple but profound words conveyed both a sense of humility and the gravity of the moment and reassured Americans that their suffering was justified because their cause was right. His speech was appropriately solemn for the occasion but also resolute in the face of such great sacrifice.

Basic rhetorical analysis relies on key concepts—writer, audience, purpose, rhetorical situation—to explain how a text works in a given situation. As this example shows, this kind of analysis can be detailed and in-depth, enabling you to focus on elements that seem most important in a specific rhetorical situation.

One helpful approach to analyzing the rhetorical situation was developed by a professor of communications named Lloyd Bitzer. Bitzer argued that understanding the specific rhetorical situation is essential for creating a text that is persuasive in that situation. Bitzer identified three main elements of the rhetorical situation:

Exigence: a situation that creates a need for communication or a problem that calls for persuasion; an urgency created by a situation in which something must change.

Audience: those who have an interest in the problem or situation and can be influenced by the writer or speaker; the audience is somehow involved in the situation such that it can help change that situation.

Constraints: factors that might place limits on the writer, including the time and place, the people involved, and social factors such as race, age, and gender. According to Bitzer, these factors "have the power to constrain decision and action needed to modify the exigence."

These terms are tools for closely examining how a rhetorical situation might shape a text and its impact on an audience. Bitzer uses the example of Abraham Lincoln's Gettysburg Address to illustrate how an effective text fits the rhetorical situation:

- In that situation, the *exigence* was created by the horrible toll of dead and wounded in the Battle of Gettysburg, which was understood to be a crucial victory for the Union but at a terrible price. Lincoln saw a need to comfort the nation and justify the battle.

- His *audience*, the citizens of the Union states, had the power to support or reject his cause. Lincoln's speech spoke directly to their concerns.

- Finally, Lincoln negotiated important *constraints*, including the fact that he was delivering a eulogy for the Union dead. He was also addressing a nation deeply scarred and exhausted by the war. Those factors no doubt shaped his choice of words and even the short length of his speech.

Using Classical Rhetorical Theory for Rhetorical Analysis

In Aristotle's famous definition, rhetoric is the art of identifying the available means of persuasion—in other words, understanding what makes a speech or text persuasive. Because of this focus on understanding persuasion, classical rhetorical theory can be a useful framework for examining how texts work and evaluating their impact on audiences.

Classical theory describes two sets of "proofs" that can be used for persuasion: artistic proofs and inartistic proofs.

Artistic Proofs. These refer to the means of persuasion created by the writer or speaker. There are three kinds of artistic proofs, or "appeals":

Ethical Appeals (Ethos). Appeals based on the character of the writer or speaker, which encompasses the background, expertise, integrity, and status of the writer/speaker; also, appeals based on the character of the subject of a text:

- Who is the author? What is his or her reputation?
- What kind of persona does the author convey? How does he or she relate to the audience?
- What authority does this person have to address the topic? Does he or she have special training, expertise, or experience related to the topic?

Logical Appeals (Logos). Appeals based on reasoning:

- What logical arguments does the author present in support of his or her position?
- Are these arguments well supported and carefully reasoned?

Emotional Appeals (Pathos). Appeals based on emotion:

- How does the writer use emotion in presenting his or her position?
- What emotional response does the writer try to elicit from the audience? (For example, does the writer try to incite anger or evoke sympathy?)

Inartistic Proofs. Existing evidence that a speaker or writer can use to make a text persuasive, such as facts, videos, scientific studies, and witness testimony:

- What evidence does the writer present to support his or her claims?
- How credible is that evidence? Is it appropriate for the topic?
- Is the evidence used appropriately, fairly, and logically?

(See "Making a Persuasive Appeal" and "Appraising and Using Evidence" in Chapter 11 for more information about persuasive appeals and the use of evidence.)

To illustrate how these categories help explain a text's effect on an audience, let's apply a classical framework to a famous speech on women's rights delivered in 1995 by Hillary Clinton. Clinton, who was then the First Lady of the United States, was speaking at the United Nations Fourth World Conference on Women in Beijing. Here is an excerpt from her speech:

> I would like to thank the Secretary General for inviting me to be part of this important United Nations Fourth World Conference on Women. This is truly a celebration, a celebration of the contributions women make in every aspect of life: in the home, on the job, in the community, as mothers, wives, sisters, daughters, learners, workers, citizens, and leaders.
>
> It is also a coming together, much the way women come together every day in every country. We come together in fields

and factories, in village markets and supermarkets, in living rooms and board rooms. Whether it is while playing with our children in the park, or washing clothes in a river, or taking a break at the office water cooler, we come together and talk about our aspirations and concerns. And time and again, our talk turns to our children and our families. However different we may appear, there is far more that unites us than divides us. We share a common future, and we are here to find common ground so that we may help bring new dignity and respect to women and girls all over the world, and in so doing bring new strength and stability to families as well.

By gathering in Beijing, we are focusing world attention on issues that matter most in our lives—the lives of women and their families: access to education, health care, jobs and credit, the chance to enjoy basic legal and human rights and to participate fully in the political life of our countries....

Earlier today, I participated in a World Health Organization forum. In that forum, we talked about ways that government officials, NGOs, and individual citizens are working to address the health problems of women and girls. Tomorrow, I will attend a gathering of the United Nations Development Fund for Women. There, the discussion will focus on local—and highly successful—programs that give hard-working women access to credit so they can improve their own lives and the lives of their families.

What we are learning around the world is that if women are healthy and educated, their families will flourish. If women are free from violence, their families will flourish. If women have a chance to work and earn as full and equal partners in society, their families will flourish. And when families flourish, communities and nations do as well. That is why every woman, every man, every child, every family, and every nation on this planet does have a stake in the discussion that takes place here.

Logical Appeal: This logical argument in favor of supporting women's rights is likely to appeal to conservative members of her audience.

Over the past 25 years, I have worked persistently on issues relating to women, children, and families. Over the past two and a half years, I've had the opportunity to learn more about the challenges facing women in my own country and around the world.

Ethical Appeal: Here and in the following paragraph, Clinton cites her own experience, which gives her credibility as someone who understands women's issues.

I have met new mothers in Indonesia, who come together regularly in their village to discuss nutrition, family planning, and baby care. I have met working parents in Denmark who talk about the comfort they feel in knowing that their children can be cared for in safe and nurturing after-school centers. I have met women in South Africa who helped lead the struggle to end apartheid and are now helping to build a new democracy. I have met with the leading women of my own hemisphere who are working every day to promote literacy and better health care for children in their countries. I have met women in India and Bangladesh who are taking out small loans to buy milk cows, or rickshaws, or thread in order to create a livelihood for themselves and their families. I have met the doctors and nurses in Belarus and Ukraine who are trying to keep children alive in the aftermath of Chernobyl.

> **Emotional Appeal:** These images of caring, hard-working women evoke sympathy and admiration and help persuade the audience that supporting women is a worthwhile cause.

The great challenge of this conference is to give voice to women everywhere whose experiences go unnoticed, whose words go unheard. Women comprise more than half the world's population, 70% of the world's poor, and two-thirds of those who are not taught to read and write. We are the primary caretakers for most of the world's children and elderly. Yet much of the work we do is not valued—not by economists, not by historians, not by popular culture, not by government leaders.

> **Inartistic Proof:** Clinton cites facts to support her claim about the need to address women's issues.

At this very moment, as we sit here, women around the world are giving birth, raising children, cooking meals, washing clothes, cleaning houses, planting crops, working on assembly lines, running companies, and running countries. Women also are dying from diseases that should have been prevented or treated. They are watching their children succumb to malnutrition caused by poverty and economic deprivation. They are being denied the right to go to school by their own fathers and brothers. They are being forced into prostitution, and they are being barred from the bank lending offices and banned from the ballot box.

> **Emotional Appeal:** These images can provoke in the audience a sense that women must be protected from harm.

Those of us who have the opportunity to be here have the responsibility to speak for those who could not. As an American, I want to speak for those women in my own country, women who are raising children on the minimum wage, women who can't afford health care or child care, women whose lives are threatened by violence, including violence in their own homes....

If there is one message that echoes forth from this conference, let it be that human rights are women's rights and women's rights are human rights once and for all. Let us not forget that among those rights are the right to speak freely—and the right to be heard.

Women must enjoy the rights to participate fully in the social and political lives of their countries, if we want freedom and democracy to thrive and endure. It is indefensible that many women in nongovernmental organizations who wished to participate in this conference have not been able to attend—or have been prohibited from fully taking part.

> **Logical Appeal:** Clinton uses deductive reasoning (see "Deductive Reasoning" in Chapter 11) to convince her audience of the need to support women's rights.

Let me be clear. Freedom means the right of people to assemble, organize, and debate openly. It means respecting the views of those who may disagree with the views of their governments. It means not taking citizens away from their loved ones and jailing them, mistreating them, or denying them their freedom or dignity because of the peaceful expression of their ideas and opinions.

In my country, we recently celebrated the 75 th anniversary of Women's Suffrage. It took 150 years after the signing of our Declaration of Independence for women to win the right to vote. It took 72 years of organized struggle, before that happened, on the part of many courageous women and men. It was one of America's most divisive philosophical wars. But it was a bloodless war. Suffrage was achieved without a shot being fired.

> Inartistic Proof: These facts support Clinton's inductive reasoning that securing women's rights is difficult but achievable.

But we have also been reminded, in V-J Day observances last weekend, of the good that comes when men and women join together to combat the forces of tyranny and to build a better world. We have seen peace prevail in most places for a half century. We have avoided another world war. But we have not solved older, deeply rooted problems that continue to diminish the potential of half the world's population.

Now it is the time to act on behalf of women everywhere. If we take bold steps to better the lives of women, we will be taking bold steps to better the lives of children and families too.

Using a classical framework in this way enables you to identify specific persuasive appeals, analyze the writer's choices, and evaluate the potential effect of those choices on a given audience.

FOCUS   More on Ethical Appeals

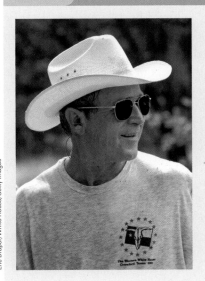

Eric Draper/White House/Getty Images

Ethical appeals are based on the character of the speaker or writer, referred to as *ethos* in rhetorical theory, but the strength of such an appeal can be affected by other factors, including the rhetorical situation, the audience, and the speaker's purpose. To account for the role of such factors in shaping an ethical appeal, we can identify two versions of *ethos*: invented ethos and situated ethos.

Invented ethos refers to a speaker's (or writer's) attempt to construct a particular kind of persona that might be persuasive for a specific rhetorical situation. For example, in U.S. presidential elections candidates often try to present themselves as "regular" citizens to make themselves appear more likeable and appealing to voters, as

(Continued)

in this photograph of then-President George W. Bush, released by the White House in 2002. What message about President Bush does this image convey? How might that message be used to persuade voters to support him or his policies?

Situated ethos is a function of a speaker's reputation or standing in a specific community or context. For example, a physician will have a certain credibility not only in a professional setting, such as a hospital, but also in the community at large because of the social standing of medical doctors. You can use these concepts to lend greater depth to your rhetorical analysis.

Stylistic Analysis

Sometimes, looking closely at figures of speech, diction (word choice), rhythm, and syntax (sentence structure) can illuminate how a writer's language achieves a certain effect on an audience. This kind of analysis is often called *stylistic analysis*.

Here, for example, is an excerpt from the beginning of the famous address that President Franklin Delano Roosevelt gave to Congress on December 8, 1941, a day after the attack on Pearl Harbor by Japanese military forces, an event that drew the United States into World War II. Stylistic analysis enables us to examine Roosevelt's diction and syntax to assess its potential impact on his audience:

> Yesterday, December 7th, 1941—a date which will live in infamy—the United States of America was suddenly and deliberately attacked by naval and air forces of the Empire of Japan.

The seriousness of the situation called for a forceful yet somber speech. Roosevelt accomplishes that goal in part through his syntax and diction. He begins with three short elements separated by commas ("Yesterday, December 7th, 1941") followed by a parenthetical clause that is set off by dashes ("a date which will live in infamy"), creating a slow, somber pace to emphasize the importance of that fateful date. He uses the passive voice to emphasize the phrase *the United States of America* and to ensure that it will appear in the sentence before the phrase *the Empire of Japan*. Consider how different his statement would sound in the active voice: The Empire of Japan attacked the United States of America. The emphasis would shift away from the phrase *the United States of America*. Finally, his diction reinforces the emphasis created by his syntax. Two adverbs (*suddenly* and *deliberately*), for example, highlight the calculated nature of the surprise attack on the United States and reinforce the fact that the United States was the victim.

Stylistic analysis also enables us to examine how writers use various **figures of speech** to create certain effects to achieve their rhetorical purpose. For example, President Roosevelt used *anaphora* (see "Common Figures of Speech for Stylistic Analysis") to underscore the grave threat that the

United States faced from Japan and to highlight the fact that the attack on Pearl Harbor was part of a larger, dangerous pattern:

> Yesterday, the Japanese government also launched an attack against Malaya.
> Last night, Japanese forces attacked Hong Kong.
> Last night, Japanese forces attacked Guam.
> Last night, Japanese forces attacked the Philippine Islands.
> Last night, the Japanese attacked Wake Island.
> And this morning, the Japanese attacked Midway Island.

The repetition of the phrase *last night* at the beginning of four successive sentences highlights the pattern of attack by Japan and creates a sense of doom. Notice, too, that the repetition of sentence structure (an introductory element followed by the subject, verb, and direct object) with the same subject (*the Japanese*) and verb (*attacked*) maintains the emphasis on the perpetrators of the aggression (Japan) and reinforces the belligerence of Japan's actions. This repetitive syntax along with *anaphora* also maintains the strong but somber tone of the speech as well as its plodding rhythm, which helps underscore the seriousness of the occasion and conveys a sense of danger that might encourage Roosevelt's audience to agree that a declaration of war against Japan was not only justified but necessary.

In this way, stylistic analysis illuminates how careful choices about language make a text more likely to accomplish the author's rhetorical goals. At the same time, practicing stylistic analysis can help you become a more sophisticated reader as well as a more successful writer.

FOCUS Common Figures of Speech for Stylistic Analysis

Linguists have identified dozens of figures of speech, but this list includes the most common ones, which can be useful tools in stylistic analysis (and in your own writing):

Alliteration: repetition of the consonant sound at the beginning of a word: "We buy our blankets at Bed, Bath & Beyond."

Anaphora: repetition of the same word or phrase at the beginning of successive phrases, clauses, or sentences: "Never give in to pessimism. Never give in to defeatism. Never give in to nihilism."

Antithesis: juxtaposition of contrasting words, phrases, or ideas for emphasis: "We are here to serve our citizens, not our ambitions."

Epistrophe: repetition of the same word at the end of successive phrases, clauses, or sentences: "government of the people, by the people, for the people, shall not perish from the earth."

Hyperbole: exaggeration used for emphasis: "I received a billion tweets about the election."

(Continued)

8

Irony: using a word or phrase to mean the opposite of its literal meaning or conveying a meaning that is opposite of what appears to be the case: "You'll just *love* waiting in the long line at the post office."

Metaphor: an implied comparison between two seemingly unrelated things: "Life is a journey."

Oxymoron: putting two contradictory terms together: "The senator's affair was an *open secret* around the Capitol."

Personification: assigning human qualities or abilities to inanimate objects or abstractions: "Fear raises its ugly head."

Rhetorical Question: a leading question whose answer is obvious: "Are we going to just give up and let the other team win?"

Simile: a comparison between two fundamentally different things, using "like" or "as": "The brothers were like two peas in a pod."

These three main frameworks for rhetorical analysis can be combined to examine a text in great detail. For example, a stylistic analysis of Hillary Clinton's address about women's rights could enrich a classical analysis of her persuasive appeals.

EXERCISE 8C UNDERSTANDING RHETORICAL ANALYSIS

1. Find an essay, blog post, flier, web page, video, or other document you created in which you present an opinion or point of view. In a brief paragraph, identify what you think are the main features that might make your document persuasive to your intended audience. Explain why you included these features.

2. Using one of the frameworks discussed in this section, analyze the document you selected for Question #1 (or a different document). What did you learn about the effectiveness of the document as a result of your analysis? What changes might you make to the document on the basis of your analysis?

3. Find an essay, speech, blog post, or similar kind of text that presents an opinion on a topic that interests you. Analyze the rhetorical situation, using the concepts of a basic rhetorical analysis.

4. Using the same text you analyzed for Question #3 (or a different text), identify the basic appeals used in the text and evaluate the effectiveness of those appeals for the intended audience.

Analyzing Images

Rhetorical analysis is not limited to written documents. You can also analyze the rhetorical effectiveness of advertisements, websites, videos, photographs, brochures, and similar visual or multimedia texts. In fact, as digital technologies enable us to use images and sound in increasingly sophisticated ways, the ability to understand the rhetorical impact of visual elements—what is sometimes called *visual literacy*—becomes ever more important.

For example, consider this photograph of the Snake River and Grand Teton mountain range in Wyoming made by Ansel Adams:

Such an image dramatically conveys a sense of the majesty of the American landscape in a way that is difficult to do with words alone. Many scholars believe that images like this one influenced the way Americans think about wilderness and helped spark the environmental movement in the 20th century.

Or consider this anti-smoking public service announcement:

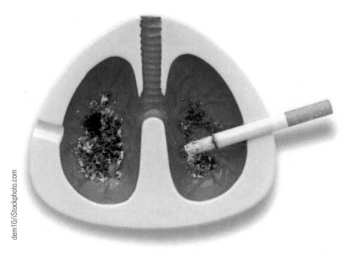

Using familiar items in a surprising way, this image provocatively communicates an anti-smoking message without words.

Finally, consider how combining words and images opens up additional possibilities for conveying a message, as in this advertisement from Amnesty International, a human rights organization:

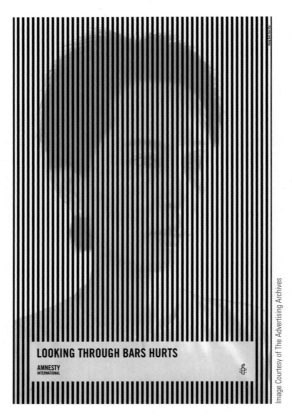

LOOKING THROUGH BARS HURTS

AMNESTY INTERNATIONAL

The ad presents the partially obscured image of Burmese human rights activist Aung San Suu Kyi, a Nobel Peace Prize laureate, who was held under house arrest in her native Burma. The tagline ("Looking through bars hurts") has a double meaning: being imprisoned hurts and so does looking at this ad, in which the vertical bars create an optical effect that is uncomfortable for the viewer.

Visual analysis enables us to examine how texts like this advertisement convey their messages. Like the rhetorical analysis of a written document, visual analysis begins with an examination of the rhetorical situation: author, audience, purpose, and context. You can use the frameworks for rhetorical analysis described earlier in this chapter to analyze images and multimedia documents. For example, a basic rhetorical analysis of the Amnesty International advertisement above would include an examination of the elements described on pages 210–211:

- **Identify the intended audience.** Since Amnesty International (AI) is a global organization, we can assume an international audience for this advertisement. But AI is probably especially interested in reaching two main audiences: (1) the citizens and leadership of Burma, and (2) citizens and leaders in nations, such as the United States and France, that can pressure the Burmese government.

- **Determine the writer's purpose.** Amnesty International's main goal is to achieve the release of Suu Kyi from house arrest. To achieve that purpose, AI hopes to influence international opinion and pressure the Burmese government. This ad is intended to remind its audience of Suu Kyi's plight and evoke sympathy for her.

- **Explain the rhetorical situation.** When she was first arrested, Suu Kyi was a leader of the democratic opposition to Burma's military rulers during the national elections of 1990. In 1991, Suu Kyi was awarded the Nobel Peace Prize while still under arrest, and she remained imprisoned for 15 of the next 23 years (until her release in 2010). Her case became an international cause as nations encouraged the Burmese government to release her and end its suppression of political opposition. While other nations in southeast Asia enjoyed economic development and close ties with western nations, Burma became more isolated, partly because of its refusal to release Suu Kyi. AI's ad campaign during those years can be seen as an effort to keep pressure on Burma by directing worldwide attention on Suu Kyi's case. This ad was published in 2010 just before Suu Kyi was released by the Burmese government.

- **Examine the components of the text.** The ad has three main features: the image of Suu Kyi, the vertical bars, and the phrase "Looking through bars hurts." Together, these three features convey a stark sense of imprisonment and evoke sympathy for the prisoner. Part of the ad's impact rests on the audience's familiarity with Suu Kyi, who is a sympathetic figure for most of the intended audience (citizens and leaders around the world) and a source of concern for part of that audience (the Burmese government). The ad's impact also rests on the vertical bars, which are literally difficult to look at because of the optical effect they create. Finally, the brief phrase explicitly reminds the audience of Suu Kyi's imprisonment and provokes sympathy for her as well as outrage against the Burmese government.

- **Evaluate the writer's decisions.** The simple design of the ad employs visual and textual elements effectively to evoke sympathy for Suu Kyi and communicate its message that her imprisonment is wrong and should be ended. The visual discomfort of looking at the vertical bars symbolizes Suu Kyi's physical discomfort, dramatically reminding the audience of Suu Kyi's situation. Even the likeness of Suu Kyi, with her slightly bowed head, conveys a sense of her situation and contributes to the effort to evoke sympathy in the audience.

You can also use a classical approach (see page 215) to analyze a visual text like this advertisement, focusing on the three kinds of artistic appeals:

Ethical appeal. As a respected human rights organization, Amnesty International has international credibility. As a Nobel laureate, Suu Kyi also has widespread credibility and respect.

Emotional appeal. The image of Suu Kyi partially obscured by vertical bars is clearly intended to evoke sympathy as well as outrage. The tagline strengthens the emotional appeal by calling attention to the physical reality of Suu Kyi's situation. Moreover, the visual effect literally causes discomfort in the viewer, which is likely to enhance the emotional appeal.

Logical appeal. The implicit logic of this ad focuses on the physical discomfort of Suu Kyi, which is highlighted by the visual effect of the vertical bars and the tagline. The reasoning of the ad might be stated as follows: Because incarceration is painful, we should be concerned about the imprisonment of Suu Kyi. The ad also suggests that this imprisonment is morally wrong or illegal. Viewers who recognize the likeness of Suu Kyi will know that she has suffered greatly in promoting human rights for the citizens of her nation. Imprisoning someone with such integrity, the ad suggests, is wrong. Such a logical appeal relies on the cultural meaning of the image of Suu Kyi as a champion of human rights as well as the meaning of the vertical lines (which signify prison bars).

As this example suggests, visual texts use various design features, such as color and layout, to create their effects. Examining these technical components can result in a more sophisticated rhetorical analysis.

FOCUS Principles of Visual Design

Artists and graphic designers create visual texts according to five established principles of composition—balance, proportion, emphasis, contrast, and movement—which can be used to illuminate the effect of specific components of an image. For example, imagine that this photograph is part of a public relations campaign to promote sailing vacations in a certain location. Here's how we might apply these principles to evaluate the rhetorical impact of the photograph:

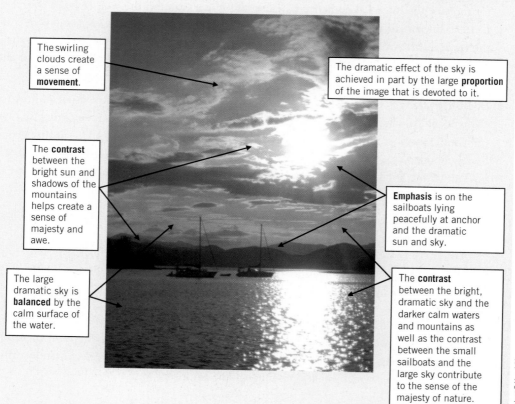

The swirling clouds create a sense of **movement**.

The dramatic effect of the sky is achieved in part by the large **proportion** of the image that is devoted to it.

The **contrast** between the bright sun and shadows of the mountains helps create a sense of majesty and awe.

Emphasis is on the sailboats lying peacefully at anchor and the dramatic sun and sky.

The large dramatic sky is **balanced** by the calm surface of the water.

The **contrast** between the bright, dramatic sky and the darker calm waters and mountains as well as the contrast between the small sailboats and the large sky contribute to the sense of the majesty of nature.

Robert P. Yagelski

1. Using the tools for visual analysis discussed in this chapter, analyze an image that you find compelling.

2. Use the concepts discussed in this section to analyze the effectiveness of this public service announcement:

Zuma Press/ZUMA/CORBIS

3. Analyze a popular television or print advertisement using the concepts discussed in this section. What conclusions can you draw about how the advertisement addressed its intended audience? What conclusions can you draw from your analysis about the impact of visual elements on an audience?

Whether you are analyzing print or visual texts, effective rhetorical analysis involves the careful examination of a text's impact on an audience. Use the **four features of effective analytical writing** (Chapter 5) to guide your rhetorical analysis:

1. **A relevant topic worthy of analysis.** Establish why the text you have selected is important or relevant:

   ■ Why would readers want to understand the effectiveness of the text you are analyzing? What makes the text relevant or important?

   ■ What's at stake for them—and for you—in understanding this text?

   ■ What are your reasons for selecting this text?

2. **Complexity.** Explore the text you are analyzing in sufficient depth:

   ■ Have you examined the main features of the text and their impact on an audience?

   ■ Have you analyzed the rhetorical situation fully? Have you considered the various potential audiences for this text?

3. **Sufficient information and appropriate evidence.** Gather sufficient information to explain the text you are analyzing; apply one or more frameworks to develop sufficient evidence to support your analysis:

   ■ Have you gathered sufficient information about the author and the circumstances surrounding the creation of this text for readers to understand the author's intentions?

   ■ Has the rhetorical situation been sufficiently explained?

   ■ Have analytical framework(s) been used appropriately to provide a sound basis for your evaluation of the text?

   ■ Have appropriate and trustworthy sources been used to support the analysis?

4. **Reasonable conclusions.** Present convincing conclusions on the basis of your rhetorical analysis:

   ■ How do the key concepts and technical terms of your analytical framework(s) help you reach your conclusions?

   ■ Do your conclusions grow logically out of your analysis?

   ■ Do your conclusions present readers with a persuasive explanation of the effectiveness of this text?

Reading Rhetorical Analysis

What follows are three examples of rhetorical analysis, illustrating the four main characteristics of effective analytical writing and the frameworks for rhetorical analysis described in this chapter. Consider these questions as you read:

A relevant topic worthy of analysis	• How does the writer establish that the text is relevant and worthy of analysis? • What is the writer's purpose in analyzing this text?
Complexity	• Has the writer examined the main features of the text? • Has the writer explained the impact of the text on the intended audience?
Sufficient information and appropriate analysis	• What analytical framework has the writer applied to this text? Does this analysis illuminate the effectiveness of the text? • Does the writer support the analysis with appropriate evidence?
Reasonable conclusions	• What conclusions does the writer draw from the analysis? • Does the analysis lead logically to these conclusions? • Are the conclusions persuasive? Are they presented effectively?

Rhetorical Analysis of a National Health Service of England Public Service Announcement

Public service announcements (PSAs) typically provide information intended to promote the public good. Often, PSAs emphasize positive feelings. The famous U.S. Forest Service ad campaign to prevent forest fires, for example, featured the friendly cartoon character of Smokey the Bear, who was meant to appeal to children as much as to adults. Sometimes, however, PSAs are intended to be provocative and even disturbing, such as the anti-smoking PSA from the National Health Service of England analyzed in the

(Continued)

following essay. As you read, notice how the analysis, which appeared on the website writinghood.com in 2009, relies on a traditional classical framework and places the PSA in broader rhetorical context to explain its purpose.

Advertisements often use a variety of techniques to convince viewers of the argument they are presenting. This anti-smoking advertisement by National Health Service (NHS) of England is no exception. It employs pathos and embeds an ethical argument in its visual appeal. It also makes a logical appeal through the text of the ad and its imagery. To under-

The average smoker needs over five thousand cigarettes a year.
Get unhooked. Call 0800 169 0 169 or visit getunhooked.co.uk

stand this advertisement it is also important to consider the point of view, since the advertisement was created by a government program that deals with health care and is funded by the citizens of England.

This National Health Service of England advertisement makes a very strong appeal to pathos, or emotion. The image provokes a strong sense of shock. The young woman, who is understood to be a smoker, is shown with a hook protruding from her mouth, like a fish that has been caught. The NHS intends to shock viewers with this graphic, if metaphoric, depiction of just how addictive smoking can be. The text below the image reinforces the emotional appeal. Like the image, the text is intended to shock the viewer with an alarming statistic—5000 cigarettes per year—that under-scores the addictive nature of smoking. The word choice is deliberate. The ad does not read, "The average smoker smokes five thousand cigarettes in a year"; instead, it states that "the average smoker *needs*" that many cigarettes. Using that term ("needs") reinforces the addictiveness of smoking.

The ethical appeal in this advertisement is made implicitly through the image of the young woman, who is being pulled by a fishing line and hook that is painfully embedded in her lip. This image can evoke sympathy as well as shock, enhancing the emotional appeal, but the NHS is also using the image to suggest that this is what companies that produce and sell cigarettes are doing to their customers. The NHS seems to want viewers to be taken aback and to see just how serious a smoking addiction is and thus to consider what tobacco companies do unethical. The ad is also largely intended to appeal to smokers. Most smokers might not consider their addic-tion serious, but through this ad the NHS seems to be trying to prevent such a compla-cent attitude. The agency wants the smokers themselves to realize just how badly they are "hooked" not only by the cigarettes they are smoking but also by the companies that produce cigarettes.

The advertisement's logical appeal rests on the implicit reasoning that an addiction is painful and therefore bad and should be avoided. Using the image of the "hooked" woman in combination with the fact, which is conveyed by the text, that a smoker "needs" 5000 cigarettes each year, the ad makes a logical argument: Addiction is painful, destructive, and obviously bad for people (an idea conveyed by the image); cigarette smoking is an addiction (a point made by the text); therefore, smoking is bad for people. The logical conclusion to be drawn is that smokers should quit smoking.

Point of view can also help explain the message conveyed by this advertisement. The argument made by the ad reflects the point of view of the National Health Service of England, which is a publicly funded health care system in England. As a publically funded agency, NHS is supported by taxes, which the NHS uses to fund its healthcare services. At first glance it might appear that the NHS ad is being produced for the sole purpose of showing just how devastating a smoking addiction can be, but the ad might reflect a larger purpose. The more people who become sick under the care of the National Health Service, the more tax money the government must provide to the agency. Since smoking can lead to lung cancer and other illnesses such as cardiovascular disease and chronic obstructive pulmonary disease, more smokers means more money that the NHS can expect to spend caring for these patients. So the more people the NHS can prevent or stop from smoking, the more money they will be able to spend on other patients. It seems reasonable to conclude, then, that part of the purpose of the NHS in developing this ad was to reduce the amount of tax revenue that will ultimately be spent on patients with self-inflicted and preventable illnesses.

This advertisement attempts to persuade viewers through strong emotional and ethical appeals, but the larger meaning of the advertisement can be seen by considering the point of view of the ad's creator, National Health Service of England.

Source: "A Great Example of a Rhetorical Analysis." *Writinghood.* Writinghood, 27 Dec. 2009. Web. 25 Apr. 2013.

EXERCISE 8E ANALYZING A PUBLIC SERVICE ANNOUNCEMENT

1. What is the author's purpose in analyzing this public service announcement? Why do you think readers should be interested in such an analysis?

2. What is the context for the public service announcement? How does the author account for that context in explaining the PSA's persuasive appeals?

3. How well do you think this analysis explains the PSA? Do you find the PSA persuasive? Why or why not? What might your response to the PSA suggest about rhetorical analysis?

8

A Rhetorical Analysis of the Declaration of Independence: Persuasive Appeals and Language

by Jim Stover

Jim Stover, an English teacher at the Baylor School in Chattanooga, Tennessee, takes an unusual approach in this analysis of the Declaration of Independence, one of the most famous and important documents ever written. Stover combines a stylistic analysis with a classical approach to examine the arguments forwarded in the Declaration. Instead of a conventional essay, however, Stover presents his analysis in a table format, using different colors to identify and explain the different persuasive appeals and stylistic devices in the document. The substance of Stover's analysis is traditional, but its form is not. Stover produced this analysis for his high school students. As you read, decide whether this format makes his analysis more or less effective for his intended audience.

Color Key

Persuasive appeals

- Green: appeal to ethos (the standing of the writer or speaker).
- Red: appeal to pathos (emotion).
- Blue: appeal to logos (reason): deductive reasoning (navy blue) and inductive reasoning (dark blue).

Language analysis

- Light blue: diction (word choice).
- Orange: syntax (sentence structure).
- Light green: images (figurative language, imagery, and the like).

IN CONGRESS, July 4, 1776.

The unanimous Declaration of the thirteen united States of America,

1 When in the Course of human events, it becomes necessary for one people to dissolve the political bands which have connected them with another, and to assume among the powers of the earth, the separate and equal station to which the Laws of Nature and of Nature's God entitle them, a decent respect to the opinions of mankind requires that they should declare the causes which impel them to the separation.

In the long first sentence of the declaration, the writers set their revolution in the context of human history ("the Course of events"). They also establish their ethical standing—that they are men of good sense, good Zcharacter, and good will—first, by acknowledging that they need to explain to the world the reasons for their actions.

2   We hold these truths to be self-evident, that all men are created equal, that they are endowed by their Creator with certain unalienable Rights, that among these are Life, Liberty and the pursuit of Happiness.— That to secure these rights, Governments are instituted among Men, deriving their just powers from the consent of the governed, — That whenever any Form of Government becomes destructive of these ends, it is the Right of the People to alter or to abolish it, and to institute new Government, laying its foundation on such principles and organizing its powers in such form, as to them shall seem most likely to effect their Safety and Happiness. Prudence, indeed, will dictate that Governments long established should not be changed for light and transient causes; and accordingly all experience hath shewn, that mankind are more disposed to suffer, while evils are sufferable, than to right themselves by abolishing the forms to which they are accustomed. But when a long train of abuses and usurpations, pursuing invariably the same Object evinces a design to reduce them under absolute Despotism, it is their right, it is their duty, to throw off such Government, and to provide new Guards for their future security.—Such has been the patient sufferance of these Colonies; and such is now the necessity which constrains them to alter their former Systems of Government. The history of the present King of Great Britain is a history of repeated injuries and usurpations, all having in direct object the establishment of an absolute Tyranny over these States. To prove this, let Facts be submitted to a candid world.

He has refused his Assent to Laws, the most wholesome and necessary for the public good.
He has forbidden his Governors to pass Laws of immediate and pressing importance, unless suspended in their operation

In the first sentence of the second paragraph, the parallel structure and repetition of *that* enable the writers to enunciate with great clarity their fundamental beliefs, which become the major premise in a deductive argument:

Major premise: the role of government is to protect the rights of the people; when government fails to do so, the people have the right to change it.

Minor premise: the British government has usurped the rights of the colonists.

Conclusion: the colonists have a right to overthrow that government.

The personification of prudence emphasizes how reasonable the writers are. But logic drives them to conclude that they have no choice but to overthrow a tyrannous government. The negative diction about the actions of the British king and his subjects begins in this paragraph —and carries an emotional appeal.

What follows in the body of the document is an inductive proof of the minor premise above: a list of ways in which the British government (and especially the King) has stripped the colonists of their rights.

8

till his Assent should be obtained; and when so suspended, he has utterly neglected to attend to them.

He has refused to pass other Laws for the accommodation of large districts of people, unless those people would relinquish the right of Representation in the Legislature, a right inestimable to them and formidable to tyrants only.

He has called together legislative bodies at places unusual, uncomfortable, and distant from the depository of their public Records, for the sole purpose of fatiguing them into compliance with his measures.

He has dissolved Representative Houses repeatedly, for opposing with manly firmness his invasions on the rights of the people.

He has refused for a long time, after such dissolutions, to cause others to be elected; whereby the Legislative powers, incapable of Annihilation, have returned to the People at large for their exercise; the State remaining in the mean time exposed to all the dangers of invasion from without, and convulsions within.

He has endeavoured to prevent the population of these States; for that purpose obstructing the Laws for Naturalization of Foreigners; refusing to pass others to encourage their migrations hither, and raising the conditions of new Appropriations of Lands.

He has obstructed the Administration of Justice, by refusing his Assent to Laws for establishing Judiciary powers.

He has made Judges dependent on his Will alone, for the tenure of their offices, and the amount and payment of their salaries.

He has erected a multitude of New Offices, and sent hither swarms of Officers to

Through most of the document, the writers appeal to pathos through the words they use in their list of the King's wrongs: check out all the negative words in this section of the document.

The long list of grievances reads like hammer blows because of the parallel structure and anaphora, the vilifying verbs, and the choice of other words that arouse the emotion of the audience.

harrass our people, and eat out their substance.

He has kept among us, in times of peace, Standing Armies without the Consent of our legislatures.

He has affected to render the Military independent of and superior to the Civil power.

He has combined with others to subject us to a jurisdiction foreign to our constitution, and unacknowledged by our laws; giving his Assent to their Acts of pretended Legislation:

For Quartering large bodies of armed troops among us:

For protecting them, by a mock Trial, from punishment for any Murders which they should commit on the Inhabitants of these States:

For cutting off our Trade with all parts of the world:

For imposing Taxes on us without our Consent:

For depriving us in many cases, of the benefits of Trial by Jury:

For transporting us beyond Seas to be tried for pretended offences

For abolishing the free System of English Laws in a neighbouring Province, establishing therein an Arbitrary government, and enlarging its Boundaries so as to render it at once an example and fit instrument for introducing the same absolute rule into these Colonies:

For taking away our Charters, abolishing our most valuable Laws, and altering fundamentally the Forms of our Governments:

For suspending our own Legislatures, and declaring themselves invested with power to legislate for us in all cases whatsoever.

He has abdicated Government here, by declaring us out of his Protection and waging War against us.

He has plundered our seas, ravaged our Coasts, burnt our towns, and destroyed the lives of our people.

He is **at this time transporting large Armies of foreign Mercenaries to compleat the works of** death, desolation and tyranny, **already begun with circumstances of** Cruelty & perfidy scarcely paralleled in the most barbarous ages, and totally unworthy the Head of a civilized nation.

He has constrained **our fellow Citizens taken Captive on the high Seas to bear Arms against their Country, to become the** executioners **of their friends and Brethren, or to fall themselves by their Hands.**

He has excited domestic insurrections **amongst us, and has endeavoured to bring on the inhabitants of our frontiers, the** merciless Indian Savages, whose known rule of warfare, is an undistinguished destruction of all ages, sexes and conditions.

3   In every stage of these Oppressions We have Petitioned for Redress in the most humble terms: Our repeated Petitions have been answered only by repeated injury. A Prince whose character is thus marked by every act which may define a Tyrant, is unfit to be the ruler of a free people.

4   Nor have We been wanting in attentions to our Brittish brethren. We have warned them from time to time of attempts by their legislature to extend an unwarrantable jurisdiction over us. We have reminded them of the circumstances of our emigration and settlement here. We have appealed to their native justice and magnanimity, and we have conjured them by the ties of our common kindred to disavow these usurpations, which, would inevitably

The list climaxes with "He is"—the only phrase other than "He has" in the list. The present tense lends urgency to the need for revolution; otherwise, only "death, desolation, and tyranny" await.

The emotional language reaches a crescendo in the final paragraphs citing the King's actions. He has shown "Cruelty & perfidy scarcely paralleled in the most barbarous ages," and he is "totally unworthy [to be] the Head of a civilized nation."

The two paragraphs following the list of grievances are packed with effective rhetorical devices that only heighten the ethical appeal: the writers are intelligent and eloquent men.

Again, the writers assure the world of their honest efforts to avoid independence. But the King, whose injustices they have just listed, has given them no choice. The colonists have made every appeal, not only to the King, but to "our Brittish brethren." Again—to no avail. They too "have been deaf to the voice of justice and of consanguinity."

interrupt our connections and correspondence. They too have been deaf to the voice of justice and of consanguinity. We must, therefore, acquiesce in the necessity, which denounces our Separation, and hold them, as we hold the rest of mankind, Enemies in War, in Peace Friends.

5   We, therefore, the Representatives of the united States of America, in General Congress, Assembled, appealing to the Supreme Judge of the world for the rectitude of our intentions, do, in the Name, and by Authority of the good People of these Colonies, solemnly publish and declare, That these United Colonies are, and of Right ought to be Free and Independent States; that they are Absolved from all Allegiance to the British Crown, and that all political connection between them and the State of Great Britain, is and ought to be totally dissolved; and that as Free and Independent States, they have full Power to levy War, conclude Peace, contract Alliances, establish Commerce, and to do all other Acts and Things which Independent States may of right do. And for the support of this Declaration, with a firm reliance on the protection of divine Providence, we mutually pledge to each other our Lives, our Fortunes and our sacred Honor.

In the concluding paragraph, the writers (and signers) of the Declaration appeal to God ("the Supreme Judge of the world") and rely "on the protection of divine Providence." God, they argue, is on their side. Furthermore, they are men willing to pledge "our Lives, our Fortunes and our sacred Honor" for the principles enunciated in the declaration.

Like the second paragraph, the concluding paragraph relies on parallel structure and repetition of *that* in declaring the colonies "Free and Independent States." The climax of the last line effective portrays the signers as heroes: men who will risk everything to support the rights of man established by God. Thus the writers of the declaration appeal in a most effective way to ethos (they are reasonable and honorable men), pathos (they have proven emphatically the outrages of the King and Parliament), and logos (they state their beliefs and prove that the King has trampled on their rights).

8

1. Stover does not explicitly provide a reason for his analysis of the Declaration of Independence. What do you think makes his analysis relevant? Do you find it relevant? Why or why not?

2. How effectively do you think Stover uses design and format to present his analysis? Do you think his analysis would be more or less effective in a more traditional essay format? Explain.

3. What can you learn from Stover's analysis? In what ways does his analysis influence your understanding of the Declaration of Independence?

Rhetorical Analysis of National Poetry Month Poster

by Julie Platt

How do you make poetry exciting? That's a question taken up by Julie Platt, author of the following analysis of an advertising campaign for the annual National Poetry Month. As Platt explains in her essay, the special posters issued each year by the Academy of American Poets to celebrate National Poetry Month have become popular, and Platt examines why. She explains how the posters exhibit some of the same components and persuasive strategies used by Hollywood studios to promote their films. In examining the motives of the National Poetry Month organizers, she also places these posters in broader cultural and historical context, reminding us that persuasive strategies are effective only insofar as they address the needs of a specific rhetorical situation. Platt is a poet who blogs for the online publication Inside Higher Ed. *She wrote this analysis in 2009 as part of her doctoral studies at Michigan State University.*

Academy of American Poets

. . . .

In April of each year, America celebrates National Poetry Month. National Poetry Month (henceforth abbreviated as NPM) was created by the Academy of American Poets in

1996. The Academy of American Poets is a non-profit organization created in 1934 to support poets in their lives and careers and to foster the appreciation of poetry in the United States. The Academy of American Poets hands out sought-after awards and prizes, publishes a magazine, and operates a popular website dedicated to its activities.

Each year, a print poster is commissioned to promote NPM. These posters are distributed for free to teachers and to libraries and are requestable online before and after NPM. Some of the "sold-out" posters include the 2006 poster (designed by Number Seventeen, NYC) featuring a Mondrian-esque configuration of text and lines, and the 2005 poster (designed by Chip Kidd) featuring the ghostly-pale image of recluse poet Emily Dickinson's dress against a solid black background.

2006 poster

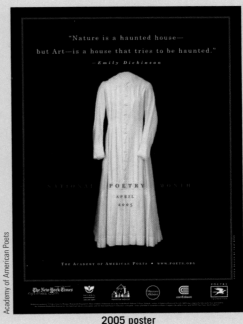

2005 poster

The 2009 official poster for NPM places the viewer in the position of looking through a foggy window or piece of glass. The condensation is thick enough to obscure the image of what is on the other side of the glass; it is amorphous, not definitively a person or animal, neither outside nor inside, neither the natural world nor man-made objects. The colors that come through the glass are misty, silvery shades of green, gray, and purple. The most prominent feature of the 2009 NPM poster image is the text. Written in the condensation by someone's fingertip are the words "Do I dare disturb the universe?" This snippet of text is a line from T. S. Eliot's poem "The Love Song of J. Alfred Prufrock," considered a modern classic and one of the most well-known and frequently-taught poems in the United States. The impact of these

(Continued)

combined visual elements is striking, and renders other text on the poster—such as information about NPM sponsors, or the website address of the Academy of American Poets—relatively inconspicuous.

In an informal discussion I participated in on the Women's Poetry Listserv (WOM-PO) around the time the poster was released, it was revealed that most of the participants found the 2009 NPM poster to be "creepy" but also "eye-catching." Those discussing the poster predicted that it would ultimately be quite successful in promoting NPM. What would be the reason for such success, especially considering poetry's rhetorical position in American culture?

For a number of years, academics, cultural critics, poets, and teachers have claimed that poetry is in crisis because—they claim—its readership is on the decline. It is difficult not to consider this cluster of claims and arguments when thinking about the motives behind the way each NPM campaign is being directed. My argument is that the visual rhetorics of the 2009 NPM poster reveal an attempt to articulate poetry to correlate with particular readings of some aspects of contemporary popular and youth culture in the United States.

The NPM posters, in some ways, are not unlike posters for feature films. Their rhetorical purpose is to encapsulate a larger event using a representative image or collection of images designed to create intrigue and entice the viewer to attend the event. Informational text is usually present on the poster which puts the image in the context of time, place, genre, etc. In recent years, feature film posters trended toward becoming more and more decontextualized, requiring more interpretation by the viewer. Additionally, multiple and/or linked posters are created for the same films, skewing context further.

In these cases, interpretation or the inability to interpret creates intrigue, or desire.

This is the case with two recent posters for popular feature films that bear passing resemblance to the 2009 NPM poster. "Why So Serious?," one of the many posters promoting the 2008 action thriller *The Dark Knight*, was designed to play on the sinister "creepiness" of the film's sociopathic villain, The Joker. The Joker himself is concealed in fog, and his hands, his writing, and his bloody smile are the only things in focus. A second poster, for the 2008 Swedish horror film *Let the Right One In*, similarly conceals an amorphous human subject (the vampire child Eli, the film's female protagonist) from the viewer with a foggy pane of glass, spattered with blood. The subject's hand is clearly revealed as it is pressed against the glass. The title "Let the Right One In" cuts through the fog in printed type. Both posters are eerie, suggesting the imminent violation of the viewer's fragile interiority by a horrific other, and yet also provoking the desire to see the other clearly. The writing in both posters here becomes a kind of voice produced by the other that penetrates the interiority of the viewer. The writing (and in the case of the Joker, the instruments used to create it) penetrates the fog, revealing limited parts of the other the viewer can see unhindered. These posters are intriguing, "creepy," and represent a pop-culture touchstone, a specific kind of horror-movie imagery for the 2009 NPM poster to draw upon to generate interest in its audience.

Poster for *The Dark Knight*   Poster for *Let the Right One In*

So who "dares disturb the universe?" Eliot's poem continues to be a puzzle nearly a century after its publication, but the selected line is one of the most self-contained, and yet highly context-dependent of the entire poem. In conjunction with the visual image of the fog, the anonymous "window-writer" could be "disturbing the universe" by attempting to make legible, orderly words from the chaos of obscurity. The window-writer could also be symbolically rebelling, or "disturbing the universe" by affirming his or her own individual identity through written language. Many popular media use emotional depictions of young men and women writing, crafting, or doing other composing work as plot devices in self-discovery narratives. The invocation of that fascinated/horrified gaze at the unspeaking/unspeakable other, and the move to rhetorically link writing, identity, and a kind of rebelliousness to these images leads to a successful pop- and youth-culture focused campaign for National Poetry Month 2009.

EXERCISE 8G   ANALYZING A POSTER CAMPAIGN

1. How does Platt establish the relevance of her subject? Do you find her subject worthy of analysis? Why or why not?

2. What features of the National Poetry Month posters does Platt emphasize in her analysis? What does she reveal about these features? How effectively do you think she explains these features?

3. What does Platt conclude about the Academy of American Poets' strategy in their poster campaign to promote National Poetry Month? Do you think her analysis supports her conclusions? Why or why not? Do you think the poster campaign is effective? Explain.

Writing Rhetorical Analysis

This section will help you develop a rhetorical analysis using the Ten Core Concepts described in Chapter 3. (Keep in mind that the generic term *text* can refer to a written text such as an essay or speech as well as visual or multimedia texts such a films, advertisements, photographs, or websites.)

Step 1	Identify a topic for rhetorical analysis.

Rhetorical analysis often arises from:

- a **reaction** to a text
- a **question** about a text

For example, you might be moved by a political speech or shocked by a public service announcement. You might wonder why an old film remains popular or a certain book is controversial. Reactions and questions like these can lead to rhetorical analysis, so begin there:

Reactions to a text

- Have you read an essay or seen an ad that provoked a strong emotional response?
- Have you seen or read something that influenced your views about an issue or topic?
- Have you heard or read a speech that aroused your passions about an issue?

Questions about a text

- Is there a film, song, book, or ad whose popularity puzzles or surprises you?
- Does a famous speech, image, or essay seem especially relevant today?
- Does a controversy about a film, ad, photo, speech, or essay interest you?

Make a Brief List of Possible Texts for Rhetorical Analysis

Using these questions, briefly explain what interests you about each text and why each might be worth analyzing. (If you have a course assignment that specifies a text to analyze, skip to "Formulate a Question About the Text.")

Select a Text from Your List That Seems Most Promising or Relevant for a Rhetorical Analysis

Keep your list, though. As you work through the next few steps, you might change your mind and decide to analyze a different text.

Explore your reactions to or questions about the text:

- What is your initial reaction to the text? What interests you about it? Is there a section or aspect of it that appeals to you for some reason?
- What emotions, if any, does it provoke in you?
- What questions does the text raise for you? Why are these questions worth pursuing?
- What might make this text relevant—or provocative or persuasive—to others?

Using these questions to guide you, make notes about your reactions to or questions about this text.

Formulate a Question About the Text

Use your notes from the previous step to develop a general question about the text to guide your examination of it. For example, if you selected a controversial Internet advertisement, you might ask, What makes this ad controversial? Why are so many people so upset about the ad? If you selected a famous text, such as Lincoln's Gettysburg Address, you might wonder about its enduring relevance: Why is this speech still so admired? What makes it resonate with people after so many years?

This question is a starting point for your analysis. You will refine the question as you explore the text and develop your analysis.

Develop this question using Step #1 in Chapter 3.

Step 2 Place your topic in rhetorical context.

An important component of rhetorical analysis is examining the rhetorical context of the text you're analyzing, but your own essay also has a rhetorical context. So it's important to examine what might interest others about the text you have chosen and identify the relevance of your analysis for a potential audience.

Identify an Audience That Might Be Interested in an Analysis of This Text

Your course assignment might specify an audience, such as your classmates, but you might also have a broader, less immediate audience for your analysis. For example, let's say you have decided to analyze Barack Obama's 2008 "More Perfect Union" speech (referred to at the beginning of the chapter). In identifying a potential audience for your analysis, consider these questions:

Who might have a general interest in the text you are analyzing?	• American citizens • Voters
Who might have a more specialized interest in that text?	• Obama's political supporters or opponents • People interested in race relations in the United States
Who might be interested in a rhetorical analysis of this text?	• People interested in politics • Students studying oratory • Students interested in writing or rhetoric

Note that you could address several distinct audiences that share certain interests or characteristics, so it might be useful to think of a **primary audience** and **secondary audiences** for your analysis. In this example, your primary audience might be your classmates and your secondary audiences might include student voters and people interested in politics and political oratory.

Examine the Relevance of the Text for Your Audience

Having a sense of why an audience would be interested in the text you are analyzing can shape your analytical approach. For example, knowing that your readers might be interested in how then-Senator Obama tried to address the divergent concerns of different races in his speech might lead you to focus your analysis on his use of language specifically related to race. Consider these questions:

What makes the text you are analyzing relevant?	• It is an important speech by a presidential candidate. • It addresses a complex issue of enduring relevance in the U.S. • It represents a significant moment in recent history.
Why would an audience care about an analysis of this text?	• It can illuminate the oratorical skills of an important person. • It explains an important effort to address a difficult problem. • It can illuminate what is considered an important factor in the 2008 U.S. presidential election.

Identify Your Purpose in Analyzing This Text

The general purpose of any rhetorical analysis is to explain how the text conveys a message to an intended audience, but your analysis can also have a more specific purpose. For example, political analysts examined Obama's "More Perfect Union" speech for insight into Obama's policies. You might seek to analyze the speech in order to gain insight into the difficulties of talking about race in the United States or to examine the role of race in U.S. presidential politics.

With these considerations in mind, complete Step #2 in Chapter 3.

Step 3   Select a medium.

Although rhetorical analysis essays are often written in conventional print format, other media can be used. For example, analyses of political speeches now routinely appear on blogs and YouTube. Multimedia presentation sites such as Prezi might also be appropriate, depending upon your rhetorical situation.

If the text you are analyzing is a visual text or includes sound or images, it might make sense to select a medium that easily incorporates those elements. For example, an analysis of then-Senator Obama's "More Perfect Union" speech might be more effective if it included video or audio clips from the speech rather than simply quotes from the transcript—especially if you wish to analyze Obama's use of voice, rhythm, and pacing. However, if such a multimedia format is unlikely to reach your intended audience, a more conventional medium might be more appropriate.

8

In selecting a medium for your rhetorical analysis, follow your assignment guidelines (if any), but if you have a choice, consider a medium that will enable you to present your analysis most effectively to your intended audience. Address these questions:

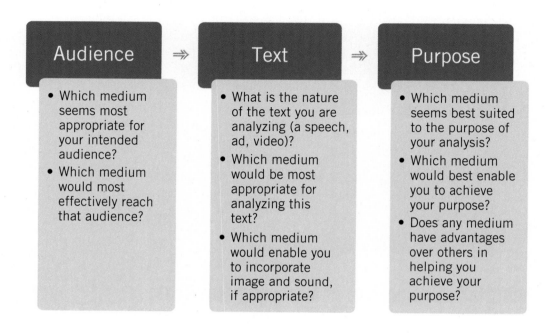

Audience ⇒	Text ⇒	Purpose
• Which medium seems most appropriate for your intended audience? • Which medium would most effectively reach that audience?	• What is the nature of the text you are analyzing (a speech, ad, video)? • Which medium would be most appropriate for analyzing this text? • Which medium would enable you to incorporate image and sound, if appropriate?	• Which medium seems best suited to the purpose of your analysis? • Which medium would best enable you to achieve your purpose? • Does any medium have advantages over others in helping you achieve your purpose?

Step #3 in Chapter 3 provides additional guidance for selecting an appropriate medium for your rhetorical analysis.

Step 4 Identify your main claim and develop your analysis.

In examining the rhetorical effectiveness of the text you are analyzing, you will make one or more main claims about that text. These claims should be related to the purpose of your analysis. For example, if you are analyzing then-Senator Obama's "More Perfect Union" speech to highlight the challenges of talking about race in the United States, your main claim might be that Obama adopted strategies intended to celebrate racial diversity but also to find common ground among Americans of all racial identities. Your task would then be to develop your analysis so it elaborates on and supports that claim.

If you're not yet sure what your main claim will be, use your question from Step #1 to develop a tentative claim for your rhetorical analysis. For example, let's say your question about then-Senator Obama's 2008 speech was this:

How effectively did Obama address concerns about race in this speech?

Your purpose in analyzing this speech is to examine the challenges of talking about race in the United States, so you might state your tentative main claim as follows:

Obama's 2008 "More Perfect Union" speech was a risky effort to meet the difficult challenges of talking about race in the United States.

As you examine the speech, you will develop a more in-depth understanding of the strategies Obama used, the rhetorical situation, and the response to the speech. That inquiry might lead you to refine your claim:

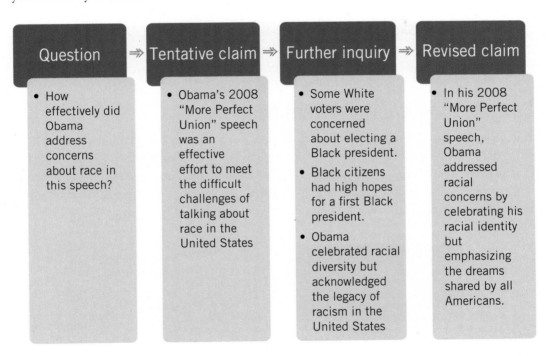

Question ⇒	Tentative claim ⇒	Further inquiry ⇒	Revised claim
• How effectively did Obama address concerns about race in this speech?	• Obama's 2008 "More Perfect Union" speech was an effective effort to meet the difficult challenges of talking about race in the United States	• Some White voters were concerned about electing a Black president. • Black citizens had high hopes for a first Black president. • Obama celebrated racial diversity but acknowledged the legacy of racism in the United States	• In his 2008 "More Perfect Union" speech, Obama addressed racial concerns by celebrating his racial identity but emphasizing the dreams shared by all Americans.

Remember that your claim is tentative. It will guide your inquiry, but as you pursue your analysis, you might need to revise your claim again.

Now, starting with your tentative claim, develop your analysis of the text you have selected by identifying the rhetorical context and by selecting a framework for analysis.

Identify the Rhetorical Context of the Text You Are Analyzing

Examine the circumstances surrounding the creation of this text to identify key factors that can help you understand the text, the strategies used, and its impact.

For example, then-Senator Obama's speech came after the pastor of his church, Jeremiah Wright, made controversial remarks that many Americans interpreted as racist (anti-White), anti-American, and even violent. The intense response to those remarks hurt Obama's presidential campaign. In addition, Obama chose to deliver his speech in Philadelphia, which is known as the "City of Brotherly Love," a decision that seems to reflect his main themes.

Now address the three main questions for rhetorical analysis:

■ **What are the main features of the text?** Identify the key themes, images, language, figures of speech, and other features of the text that seem to make it persuasive (or not). If you are analyzing a visual text, use the tools for visual analysis described in this chapter (see pages 223–228).

■ **How do those features affect the intended audience?** Describe the possible impact of the main features of the text on the intended audience. Identify as best you can how the intended audience(s) might (or did) react to the specific features you have identified.

■ **Why did the writer include those features and craft the text in specific ways?** Explain the reasons that the author might have included specific features. Consider how those features and their potential impact help the author of the text achieve his or her rhetorical purposes.

Select a Framework for Your Analysis

Your analysis so far has considered the main elements of the rhetorical situation. Now choose one (or more) of the frameworks for rhetorical analysis described in this chapter—basic analysis, classical analysis, stylistic analysis (see pages 212–222)—and analyze the text using that framework. (Follow the guidelines for each framework presented in this chapter.) Select your framework with your purpose in mind:

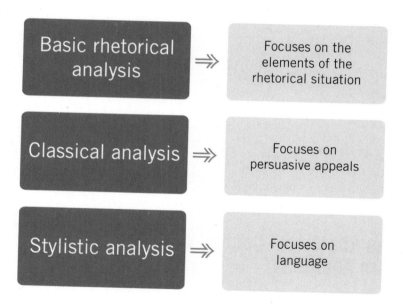

Basic rhetorical analysis	⟹	Focuses on the elements of the rhetorical situation
Classical analysis	⟹	Focuses on persuasive appeals
Stylistic analysis	⟹	Focuses on language

Proceed in this way, adjusting your main claim accordingly. Step #4 in Chapter 3 provides additional guidance for developing your analysis.

Step 5 Support your analysis.

Most of the evidence you use to support your claims and assertions will likely be passages from the text you are analyzing (or features of the images or sound, if the text is a visual or multimedia text). For example, the primary evidence for your claims about the strategies used by then-Senator Obama in his "More Perfect Union" speech will be sections from the speech where those strategies are used. As you develop your analysis for Step #4, you are also gathering evidence to support your analysis. However, you might also find a need to consult outside sources to understand:

- the rhetorical situation
- the background of the author of the text
- the response to the text

In addition, you might use other analyses of the text to support your claims. Let's explore each of these sources of support for your analysis.

Identify Evidence for Your Claims from Your Analysis

As you develop your main claims, identify the specific evidence that supports those claims. The nature of that evidence will depend on the framework for analysis you are using. For example, if you are doing a stylistic analysis, much of your evidence is likely to be figures of speech and other language devices that appear in the text.

Let's imagine you are using a classical framework (see page 215) to analyze then-Senator Obama's "More Perfect Union" speech. Your first step would be to identify the three kinds of appeals (emotional, ethical, and logical) in the speech. For example, here's a passage in which Obama makes an ethical appeal, showing that his own racial identity and family history lend him credibility as someone who understands the complexity of race relations:

> I am the son of a black man from Kenya and a white woman from Kansas. I was raised with the help of a white grandfather who survived a Depression to serve in Patton's Army during World War II and a white grandmother who worked on a bomber assembly line at Fort Leavenworth while he was overseas. I've gone to some of the best schools in America and lived in one of the world's poorest nations. I am married to a black American who carries within her the blood of slaves and slaveowners—an inheritance we pass on to our two precious daughters. I have brothers, sisters, nieces, nephews, uncles and cousins, of every race and every hue, scattered across three continents, and for as long as I live, I will never forget that in no other country on Earth is my story even possible.

If you were making the claim that Obama relies on his own family history to make an ethical appeal and persuade his audience that his argument is valid, you could cite this passage as evidence to support that claim.

You should find evidence to support each main claim in your analysis. For some claims, you might need more than one piece of evidence, especially if the claim is central to the main point of your analysis.

Consult Relevant Outside Sources

Outside sources can strengthen your rhetorical analysis in four ways:

- They can help explain the rhetorical context.
- They provide information about the author.
- They enable you to document reactions to the text.
- They can provide examples of other analyses of the text.

For instance, to learn more about the controversy surrounding the remarks of Obama's pastor, Jeremiah Wright, which were an important part of the rhetorical situation for the speech, you could review newspaper accounts, editorials, and videos of Wright's remarks as well as television news reports about them. Those sources could also provide support for a claim that Obama tried to use the controversy to his advantage.

Similarly, you can use the reaction to the speech to support claims about the impact of specific persuasive strategies used in the speech. For example, you could cite polls taken about the speech, news stories describing public reaction, and editorials written in response to the speech.

Finally, citing other analyses of the text can reinforce your own analysis. For example, if you were making a claim that the power of the speech lies in Obama's effort to speak to both Blacks and Whites, you could bolster your claim by citing a critic such as journalist Roy Peter Clark, who wrote that "Obama's patriotic lexicon is meant to comfort white ears and soothe white fears" (Clark, Roy Peter. "Why It Worked: A Rhetorical Analysis of Obama's Speech on Race" Poynter. org 1 April 2008. Web. 17 Nov. 2012.).

Remember that, in this kind of analysis, there is no "proof" that your claims are true; rather, you are providing evidence so that your analysis persuades your audience. Step #5 in Chapter 3 provides additional guidance for developing support for your analysis.

At this point, you should be ready to write a complete draft of your project. If not, move onto the next step before completing your draft.

Step 6   Organize your rhetorical analysis.

There is no conventional structure for a rhetorical analysis, but you can follow one of two basic patterns for organizing your analysis:

- according to your main claims
- according to an analytical framework

Organizing Your Analysis According to Your Claims

In any rhetorical analysis, you will make claims about the features of the text you are analyzing, the strategies or appeals used in the text, the impact of those features or strategies on the intended audience, and the effectiveness of the text in achieving the rhetorical goals. To develop an outline based on your claims, follow these steps:

1. List your main claims.

Obama's speech was a brave and honest effort to address the challenge of race relations in the U.S.	The effectiveness of Obama's speech rests on his appeals to common ground among the races.	Obama's most effective appeals are ethical and emotional appeals.

2. For each claim, list any supporting claims.

Obama directly addresses the controversy over Rev. Wright to demonstrate his sincerity.	Obama celebrates diversity but emphasizes commonality.	Obama presents himself as an example of racial diversity. He invokes a sense of connection to all Americans.

3. Identify your evidence or support for each claim.

Relevant passages from text; news accounts; editorials about controversy	Relevant passages from the text	Relevant passages from the text; other analyses of the speech

4. Arrange your claims in a logical order that makes sense for your audience.

Begin with the broadest claim (Obama's speech was a brave effort to address race relations) and move to more specific claims (nature of his appeals).

Now use your list to develop an outline:

I. Introduction (the importance of Obama's "More Perfect Union" speech)

II. Background

    A. Historical context of race relations in the United States

    B. Political context for the speech

    C. Controversy over Rev. Wright's remarks

III. Main Claims

    A. Obama's speech was a brave and honest effort to address the challenge of race relations in the United States

        1. Obama directly addresses Rev. Wright controversy

        2. Obama acknowledges the difficulty of race relations in the United States

    B. The effectiveness of the speech rests on Obama's appeal to common ground

        1. Obama celebrates diversity but emphasizes commonality

        2. Obama connects citizens of all racial identities to common American goals and dreams

    C. Main persuasive appeals were ethical and emotional

        1. Ethical appeals

            a) Obama's personal story

            b) Obama's record

        2. Emotional appeals

            a) Obama's personal story

            b) Stories of other Americans

            c) Sense of patriotism

IV. Conclusion

For each main heading and subheading, include the specific evidence you are using to support the claim. Notice that the technical analyses (e.g., the specific kinds of appeals; the rhetorical situation) are woven into the essay where appropriate, so, for example, you might include your analysis of the rhetorical situation in Part II and Part IIIA.

Organizing Your Analysis According to Your Analytical Framework

You can also organize on the basis of the analytical framework you are using: a basic rhetorical analysis (see page 212), a classical framework (see page 215), or a stylistic analysis (see page 220). In this approach, structure your essay around the main concepts associated with each framework. For example, if you are using a basic rhetorical framework, organize your essay using the steps described on page 212. Following those steps, you might produce an outline like this:

  I. Introduction

    (Explain main purpose of your rhetorical analysis.)

  II. Context

    A. Background information about the text being analyzed

    B. Description of original rhetorical context for the text

III. Analysis of Rhetorical Situation

    A. Author's purpose

    B. Examination of audience characteristics and expectations

IV. Analysis of Text

    A. Main features of text

    B. Main persuasive strategies

V. Evaluation of Author's Rhetorical Decisions

    A. Effectiveness of main rhetorical strategies

    B. Impact on intended audience

VI. Conclusion

(Overall assessment of effectiveness of text)

Notice that, in this approach, you would incorporate your main claims into the appropriate sections of your essay. For example, a claim about Obama's use of emotional appeals would likely appear in section IVb, Va, or Vb.

If you are using a classical framework, you might follow a simple outline like this:

I. Introduction

II. Description of Rhetorical Situation

III. Emotional Appeals

IV. Ethical Appeals

V. Logical Appeals

VI. Conclusion

In this case, each main section would contain discussion of:

- the specific appeals of that kind in the text
- the impact of those appeals
- how they advance the speaker's purpose
- evidence to support your claims about each appeal

The order in which you discuss each kind of appeal would depend upon which ones you found to be most important or effective.

More sophisticated analyses that include stylistic or visual analysis would call for more detailed versions of these outlines. Of course, you should always consider the intended audience and the purpose of your rhetorical analysis in deciding how best to organize it.

Follow Step #6 in Chapter 3 for additional guidance.

8

Step 7 Get feedback.

The main purpose for getting feedback on your draft is to determine whether your rhetorical analysis is persuasive to your readers. But you also want to determine whether your evaluation of the text you are analyzing accounts for your readers' reactions to that text.

For example, if you are making a case that then-Senator Obama's "More Perfect Union" speech is effective in addressing the challenges of race relations in the United States, to what extent do your readers share your sense of the effectiveness of the speech? Do one or more of them find the speech unpersuasive? If so, why? By posing such questions, you can use readers of your draft to test your analysis. If they disagree with your conclusions, it's possible that you might need to re-examine them, or maybe you simply haven't made your case effectively. Either way, you can use your readers' reactions to the original text to guide your revisions.

Follow Step #7 in Chapter 3 to obtain useful feedback. In addition, be sure your readers address the four main characteristics of analytical writing:

A relevant topic worthy of analysis	• Has the writer provided persuasive reasons for analyzing the selected text? • Does the writer explain the relevance of the text and the purpose of a rhetorical analysis of it?
Complexity	• Is the analysis thorough? Has the writer explained the text sufficiently? • Has the writer examined the rhetorical situation sufficiently? • Has the writer applied an analytical framework in depth?
Appropriate and sufficient support	• Does the writer support the main claims effectively? • Is the writer's evidence sufficient? Does the writer use outside sources appropriately? • Is there sufficient background information about the text? • Does the writer use technical terms appropriately?
Reasonable conclusions	• Do the writer's conclusions grow logically from the analysis? Are the conclusions presented clearly and persuasively? • Do the conclusions provide a persuasive explanation for the rhetorical effectiveness of the text?

Step 8 Revise.

The advice for Step #8 in Chapter 3 will guide you as you revise your draft. Supplement that advice with the questions listed in Step #7 in this chapter. In addition, make sure your draft addresses the three main questions for rhetorical analysis (see page 212):

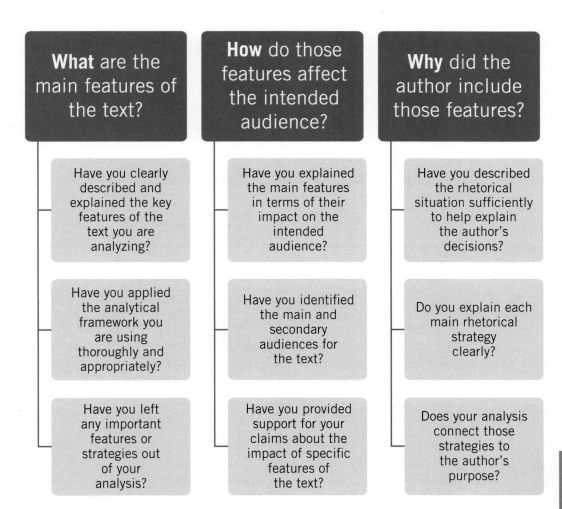

What are the main features of the text?

- Have you clearly described and explained the key features of the text you are analyzing?

- Have you applied the analytical framework you are using thoroughly and appropriately?

- Have you left any important features or strategies out of your analysis?

How do those features affect the intended audience?

- Have you explained the main features in terms of their impact on the intended audience?

- Have you identified the main and secondary audiences for the text?

- Have you provided support for your claims about the impact of specific features of the text?

Why did the author include those features?

- Have you described the rhetorical situation sufficiently to help explain the author's decisions?

- Do you explain each main rhetorical strategy clearly?

- Does your analysis connect those strategies to the author's purpose?

8

Step 9 Refine your voice.

Many essays of rhetorical analysis follow the conventions of traditional academic writing. If your assignment calls for such an essay, make sure your voice is appropriately formal. (See Chapter 19 for advice on developing an academic writing style.) But as the readings in this chapter suggest, the writer's voice can vary widely in rhetorical analyses, depending upon the intended audience and purpose for the analysis as well as the medium. An analysis intended for a blog, for example, is likely to be less formal than one written as a conventional academic essay. Similarly, your voice will likely be less formal in an analysis presented in multimedia format. As you review your draft, decide what kind of voice and style are most appropriate for your own rhetorical context and revise accordingly. In addition, follow Step #9 in Chapter 3.

Step 10 Edit.

Complete Step #10 in Chapter 3.

WRITING PROJECTS   RHETORICAL ANALYSIS

1. Select a classic speech, such as Abraham Lincoln's Gettysburg Address or Martin Luther King, Jr.'s "I Have a Dream" speech, and write a rhetorical analysis of it. Use one of the frameworks described in this chapter for your analysis. Assume your audience to be your classmates or others who might be interested in rhetoric and oratory. (You can easily find lists of famous speeches by searching online.)

2. Alternatively, analyze a contemporary speech you have heard, such as an address given on your campus by a guest speaker or a speech from a current political campaign. (Such speeches are often available on YouTube or news websites.)

3. Do a rhetorical analysis of promotional materials from an organization or agency that is involved in some kind of public advocacy—for example, on public health or environmental issues, social issues such as bullying, or a similar issue that interests you. The document you select for your analysis might be a flier, direct-mail campaign letter, a public service announcement, a website, or an advertisement. For your analysis, conduct research to learn more about the organization and the issue it addresses. Select a framework for analysis that you think is most appropriate for the kind of text you are analyzing—or use a combination of frameworks. On the basis of your analysis, make recommendations to the organization or agency about how they might make their materials more persuasive.

4. Re-create the rhetorical analysis you wrote for Question #1 or #2 in a different medium. For example, convert your analysis for Question #1 into a Prezi presentation or video.

5. Do a rhetorical analysis of your college or university website. On the basis of your analysis, make recommendations for revising the website to make it more appealing to students and other potential audiences.

6. Analyze several different television or Internet advertisements for the same kind of product, identifying which are most effective in addressing their intended audiences. For example, select several ads for different brands of cars or smartphones. On the basis of your analysis, draw conclusions about what rhetorical strategies, especially visual strategies, work best in this kind of advertisement.

8

Analyzing Literary Texts

OUR LIVES ARE FILLED WITH TEXTS: newspaper and magazine articles, books, billboards, Facebook posts, films, brochures. Many of these texts are utilitarian. For example, we read the manual for a DVD player to learn how to program it; we visit Weather.com to find out if rain is predicted. But we use some texts—stories, novels, poems, films, comics, plays—to help make sense of who we are. These texts might entertain and inform us, but they also help us explore important questions about how we live, what we do, and why things are the way they are. Writers analyze these texts to understand what they have to say and how they say it:

- A film critic tries to explain what the controversy surrounding a film like *The Passion of the Christ* reveals about modern attitudes regarding religion and faith.

- A historian examines letters written by George Washington to understand his decisions as the commander of the Continental Army.

- A sociologist analyzes rap music to explain its appeal among specific demographic groups.

Although analyzing texts is a specialized form of analytical writing that is most common in certain academic disciplines, especially English, it occurs in popular culture as well. If you've ever disagreed with someone about what a book, a song, or a film means, you've engaged in a kind of informal textual analysis. Debates about the merits of popular books and films can also involve textual analysis. The 2005 film *Brokeback Mountain*, for example, prompted widespread discussion about social issues like sexuality, tolerance, and moral responsibility in relationships. Some people criticized the film, which depicts a same-sex relationship, for condoning what they believed was immoral behavior. Others saw the film as an honest exploration of the complexities of love. The debates about the film amounted to efforts by viewers to interpret the filmmaker's intentions and draw conclusions about what the film might tell us about matters like changing social mores, romantic relationships, and individual responsibility. In other words, people were analyzing the film to understand it and interpret the significance of its themes.

In academic writing, textual analysis, which is usually called *literary analysis*, is a careful, in-depth examination of a text and the techniques and strategies the author uses to convey ideas and explore themes. Often, this kind of analysis involves the use of theories to help explain a text. For example, a writer might apply the principles of feminist theory to illuminate gender roles or stereotypes in a film like *Brokeback Mountain* (see "Theoretical Frameworks for Literary Analysis" on page 263). In this way, analysis of the text goes beyond a description of what the text might say or mean and leads to a sophisticated interpretation of the text.

If you wrote essays about poems, novels, or short stories for your high school English classes, you have an idea of what literary analysis is. This kind of analytical writing is part of the age-old conversations about the importance and meaning of literary art. In effect, writers analyze works of literature to participate in those conversations and contribute to our collective understanding of literary art and its role in cultural life. For students, literary analysis is a way to engage more deeply with works of literature in order to understand them and explore the ideas they present.

FOCUS   Explication vs. the Search for Hidden Meaning

Students sometimes complain that literary analysis is really a process of finding the "hidden meaning" in a work of literature. Although it's true that literary analysis often leads to conclusions about meanings in a novel or poem that aren't obvious, it is misleading to think in terms of "hidden meanings" when writing essays of literary analysis. Instead, literary critics tend to focus on explication, the process of carefully examining aspects of a literary work as a way to understand that work in greater depth, to see its richness, and to appreciate the complexity of its ideas, techniques, and themes. As a writer of literary analysis, your goal is to explain what you see in a work of literature and to help your readers appreciate that work. You develop an interpretation of the text to illuminate its ideas and techniques for your readers. The meaning isn't "hidden"; instead, you are making meaning by presenting the understanding you have gained through your own careful analysis of the text.

Occasions for Literary Analysis

Literary analysis, like all analysis, arises from a desire to understand something—in this case, a text. It can begin with a question that leads a writer to an interpretation of the text: What does this poem mean? Why does this play end as it does? What does this film suggest about free will? What does this advertisement reveal about contemporary attitudes toward environmental protection? Such questions prompt a writer to look more closely at a text, and, in turn, analyzing the text enables the writer to illuminate it for other readers.

Literary analysis can also arise from controversy or disagreements about what a text means, why it is significant, or even whether it should be read (see "Revising *Huck Finn*"). In such cases, the social and cultural importance of literature becomes evident. As noted earlier, literary texts are a way for people to make sense of human life, so it isn't surprising that disagreements can arise as different readers offer different interpretations of novels, plays, films, and other works of literary art. Such controversies indicate that literary analysis is a way for writers not only to present interpretations of literary texts but also to participate in the broader social and cultural discourse about literature and art.

FOCUS | **Revising *Huck Finn***

In 2011, a publisher named NewSouth Books released a new edition of Mark Twain's classic novel *The Adventures of Huckleberry Finn*. In the new edition, the word *nigger* was replaced with the word *slave*. The publication of this edition ignited great controversy. Some critics charged the publisher with censoring a great American literary work; others hailed the new edition as a way to attract new readers who might otherwise have been offended by its original language. The controversy prompted some writers to re-examine the book and analyze Twain's intentions. Some critics explored the book's meaning in the context of contemporary attitudes about race, which are different from attitudes at the time of the book's original publication in 1884. In a sense, the controversy prompted many writers to ask, What does this novel really mean? Why is it important? Many essays of literary analysis grow out of the need to address such questions.

As a college student, you will most likely write literary analysis for specific course assignments. In such cases, your analysis can be seen as part of an inquiry into the texts you are reading for that course. Your classmates' shared interest in understanding those texts gives your analysis a purpose that extends beyond your own desire to understand a text. And that sense of purpose can energize your analysis.

Even when a course assignment specifies the poem, story, novel, or other text you will analyze, you will still have to develop your own interpretation of the text. That means that no matter how specific an assignment might be, the focus of your analysis will probably arise from your own questions about a text. And because other students in your class are likely to have similar questions about the assigned texts, your analysis is likely to be more effective and more engaging if it focuses on a question or questions about the text that are interesting not only to you but also to your classmates.

EXERCISE 9A | OCCASIONS FOR LITERARY ANALYSIS

1. Think of a thought-provoking film you have seen or a novel you have read. Write a list of three or four questions that the film or novel raised for you.

2. In a group of classmates, identify a recent book, film, television show, song, or similar text that is popular or controversial. Have each person in the group write a few sentences explaining the main theme or point of the text. Then compare what you wrote. What similarities and differences are there in your respective interpretations of the text? What do you think these similarities and differences suggest about the nature of literary interpretation?

(Continued)

9

3. Identify a film, book, or other text that you enjoy and find several reviews of that text. Are there similarities and differences in the interpretations of the text presented in those reviews? Do you agree or disagree with the reviewers' interpretations? Did they change your opinion about the text in any way? If so, how? In a brief paragraph, describe what you learned about the text from these reviews.

Understanding Literary Analysis

Effective literary analysis usually includes **four important features**:

- a thought-provoking interpretation
- evidence to support the interpretation
- careful summary of the text
- appropriate literary concepts and terms

Interpretation

Effective literary analysis engages readers with a thought-provoking interpretation that helps them understand a text, perhaps in a new way. Such analysis might include evaluation, but effective literary analysis is much more than a judgment about whether a text is "good" or whether the writer liked it. There is not much use for readers in a literary analysis whose primary purpose is to tell them whether the writer did or didn't like a play or novel or poem. Instead, readers are interested in whether the writer has insight into what a play means, the way a novel explores a theme, a poet's use of imagery, or the significance of a text.

Evidence

A writer's interpretation should be supported by persuasive evidence and reasoning. It is one thing to say, for example, that Hamlet had a moral responsibility to avenge his father's death, and it is another to build a case for that interpretation by citing passages from the play, referring to other plays by Shakespeare that explore similar themes, and quoting from critics who have analyzed the play. In the end, readers might disagree with the writer's interpretation, but they should feel that the writer has presented a thoughtful, well-supported case for that interpretation.

Summary

Effective literary analysis almost always includes some summary of the whole text or parts of it. Usually, a writer summarizes key passages or scenes to help readers understand the writer's interpretation. Sometimes, students fall into the trap of simply retelling a novel's plot or restating the content of a poem. Such summaries do not advance an interpretation and therefore don't help readers understand the text. Good literary analysis moves beyond summary but uses summary strategically to explain and support the interpretation.

Terminology

In your high school English classes, you probably encountered terms like *imagery, theme, symbol, point of view, setting,* and *motif.* These terms relate to important concepts in literary analysis that help writers explain a text. Many of these terms focus on technique. For example, you might discuss how a poet uses images to create a certain mood in a poem. In the same way that scientific terms help scientists explain the subjects they study, literary terminology helps writers explain sophisticated aspects of a text that might be difficult to explain in common language. *Motif,* for example, describes a specific kind of pattern in a poem, novel, story, or film; a writer can use the term in analyzing a pattern in a poem or story without having to explain the pattern itself. ("The motif of the hero's journey is consistent throughout the *Harry Potter* novels.") Sometimes, writers apply theoretical frameworks in their analysis of a text; such frameworks often include their own specialized concepts and terms (see "Theoretical Frameworks for Literary Analysis"). A writer can use specialized terminology to analyze specific aspects of an author's technique.

FOCUS   **Theoretical Frameworks for Literary Analysis**

Professional literary critics often adhere to certain theoretical perspectives, sometimes called schools of criticism, such as feminism or Marxism, which represent different methods or approaches to studying literary texts. Explaining the many available literary theories is beyond the scope of this textbook, but it is important to be aware that such theories can be useful in textual analysis. Among the most well-established such theories are psychoanalytical theory, reader-response, postcolonial theory, deconstruction, formalism, and structuralism in addition to feminism and Marxism. These various theories can be useful interpretative tools for examining texts in specific ways. Feminist literary theory, for example, which focuses on issues of gender, can illuminate gender roles in a text; using feminist theory, a writer might examine the way male–female relationships are portrayed in a film or play. Similarly, a Marxist critic might explore the role of social class in the plot of a novel. (See "Tolkien: A Marxist Analysis" by John Molyneux on page 270 for an example of a Marxist analysis.) For some assignments, you might be asked to apply a literary theory in analyzing a text. If so, follow your instructor's guidelines in using that theory, keeping in mind that the theory is a tool for developing your interpretation of that text.

Keep these **four features of literary analysis** in mind as you consider the main characteristics of analytical writing:

1. **A relevant topic worthy of analysis.** Identify the question or issue about the text that leads to your interpretation, and explain why that question or issue is important:

   ■ What question or issue does this text raise for you? What specifically are you examining about the text?

- Why is this question or issue important?

- What does your interpretation offer to readers of this text? How might your interpretation relate to other interpretations of this text?

2. **Complexity.** Examine the text in sufficient depth to help readers understand your interpretation:

- Have you explored the text carefully enough so that your interpretation is more than a simple evaluation of the text?

- Does your essay offer readers more than a summary of the text? Have you included summary of the text strategically to help readers understand your interpretation?

- Does your interpretation avoid oversimplifying the text?

- Have you used appropriate terminology to examine the text and present your interpretation?

3. **Sufficient information and appropriate evidence.** Support your interpretation adequately:

- What evidence do you present to support your interpretation?

- Is your evidence sufficient to persuade readers that your interpretation is valid?

- Do you use appropriate terminology in presenting your evidence to support your interpretation?

- Do you summarize relevant passages from the text to help your readers understand your interpretation?

4. **Reasonable conclusions.** Present conclusions that grow reasonably out of your interpretation:

- What conclusions do you draw from your interpretation of this text?

- Does your interpretation of the text lead logically to your conclusions?

- Do your conclusions present readers with a thought-provoking way of understanding the text you have analyzed?

EXERCISE 9B   UNDERSTANDING LITERARY ANALYSIS

1. Identify a film, television show, book, or similar text that is currently popular. Write a brief paragraph describing what you think makes that text popular. Your description might focus on the plot, the characters, the technique, the text's themes or subject matter, or whichever elements of the text seem most noticeable or important to you. On the basis of your description, what conclusions might you draw about what this text means to you and to others?

2. In a group of classmates, share the paragraphs you wrote for Question #1. Have each person in the group defend his or her interpretation of the text. Identify specific kinds of evidence that each person uses to support his or her conclusions about the text. What do you think this exercise suggests about the nature of literary analysis?

3. Using the text you described for Question #1 (or a different text), write a brief summary of the text. In a group of classmates, compare your summaries. What do you notice? What might this exercise suggest about summary? About the role of summary in literary interpretation?

Reading Literary Analysis

The selections in this section include analyses of three very different kinds of texts: a classic short story by a great American writer, a popular series of novels that have become popular films, and graphic novels. Although the authors of these analyses have different purposes and address different kinds of audiences, each essay exhibits the key features of effective literary analysis:

A relevant topic worthy of analysis	• How does the writer establish the text(s) as worthy of analysis? • Why should readers care about this text at this point in time? • What is the context for the literary analysis? What is the writer's purpose in analyzing this text?
Complexity	• What does the analysis reveal about the text? In what ways does it illuminate the text? • What claims about the text does the writer make on the basis of the analysis? Do these claims reflect an analysis of sufficient depth? • Does the analysis enhance our understanding of the text?
Sufficient information and appropriate analysis	• What kinds of evidence does the writer provide to support his or her claims about the text? How persuasive is this evidence? • Does the writer use summary of the text effectively? • Does the writer use appropriate terminology in analyzing the text?
Reasonable conclusions	• What conclusions does the writer draw about the text? • Are the conclusions well reasoned and supported by the analysis? • How convincing is the writer's interpretation of the text?

9

Literary Analysis of "Hills Like White Elephants"

by Diane Andrews Henningfeld

Textual analysis in college courses often focuses on established works of literature. The following essay, which examines a well-known short story by Ernest Hemingway, is a good example of this kind of literary analysis. As the author, Diane Andrews Henningfeld, notes in her essay, Hemingway's story has been extensively studied by scholars and students of literature since its publication in 1927, and debates about the story's meaning continue today. Part of Henningfeld's rationale for choosing to analyze this story is that it has generated so much interest among readers over the years. Using what other critics have said as a starting point, Henningfeld focuses her analysis on an unusual blend of the comic and the tragic that she sees in Hemingway's story. It is a good idea to read "Hills Like White Elephants" before reading Henningfeld's essay, which, like any good literary analysis, might influence your own interpretation.

In 1927, Ernest Hemingway completed and published his collection of short stories, *Men Without Women*. The collection included several important stories, stories that have been closely examined by critics almost since the day of their publication. Among the stories in the collection, however, "Hills Like White Elephants" has become the most widely anthologized and the most frequently taught. The story continues to generate scholarly interest and heated debate among students.

"Hills Like White Elephants" is a very short story. Only about one thousand words, the story itself is comprised almost entirely of dialogue. Although there is a situation, there is no plot; although there are words spoken between the main characters, there is no resolution. The topic of their conversation, an abortion, is never even mentioned by name by either of the characters. In spite of the brevity of the story, and in spite of the absences created by the dialogue, scholars continue to produce pages and pages of critical commentary. Such critical interest at least suggests that the story is a rich, open text, one that invites reader participation in the process of meaning-making.

The story appears deceptively simple. A man and a woman sit at a table at a Spanish railway station, waiting for a train. They engage in a conversation, Hemingway seems to suggest, that has been going on for some time. The reader is dropped in the middle of the conversation without context and must glean what information he or she can from the words the characters say. The setting of the story is contemporary with its writing; that is, although there is no definite mention of the date, it seems to be set sometime during the years after the First World War, but before the Spanish Civil War. In addition, the setting is narrowly limited both in time and space. The story is framed by the narrative announcement in the first paragraph that the "express from Barcelona would come in forty minutes" and by the Spanish woman's announcement near the end of the story, "The train comes in five minutes." Thus, all of the story takes place within the thirty-five minutes. In addition, the characters never leave the train station itself.

There are several important ways that critics have read "Hills Like White Elephants." Some concentrate on the structure of the story, noting the use of dialogue and the placement of the few short descriptive passages. John Hollander, for example, suggests that the story develops the way a film or play might develop and that the short descriptive passages read almost like stage directions. Other critics develop careful and complicated readings of the story based on word level analysis, examining the way that Hemingway uses allusion, simile, imagery, and symbolism. Some of these critics also include an examination of Hemingway's sources, connecting the story to T. S. Eliot's modernist masterpiece, *The Wasteland*. A more recent group of scholars concentrates on the use of gender-marked language in the story, looking closely at the different ways the American and Jig [the main characters in the story] use language to communicate. Still others try to use Hemingway's autobiographical manuscripts and letters to read parts of Hemingway's life into the story. However, the fact that so many critics read this story in so many ways does not mean that the story is flawed; it means, rather, that it is a text that invites participation. As Paul Smith argues, Hemingway does not tell the reader "how the characters arrived at their present condition, or how they will resolve their conflict; we do not need to be told, for the answers are embedded in what we so briefly do see and hear" (15). Although Smith seems to suggest in this statement that the "answers" are there for the reading, it is possible to arrive at a multiplicity of answers, using the same lines of text.

In an early review of the story, Dorothy Parker described the story as "delicate and tragic." Although it is unlikely that Parker meant to suggest that "Hills Like White Elephants" is a tragedy in the classical Greek sense of the word, it is possible to use her statement as an entry point into the story. An examination of both the comic and the tragic elements reveals how these ideas function in the story, and how modernism has transformed the ideas themselves.

To begin, it is important to make clear that the term "comic" here does not imply humor, or laughter. In this discussion, "comedy" does not refer to a television situation comedy that is designed to be funny. Rather, for the purpose of this discussion comedy is a shape that fiction can take. Comedy has its roots in the fertility rituals of spring. It celebrates marriage, sexual union, birth, and the perpetuation of society. Comedy is not always light-hearted, however; it frequently carries with it pain, frustration, and near-catastrophe. The threat of death is always located in the underside of comedy. Ultimately, however, it is the triumph over death that gives comedy its characteristic shape.

(Continued)

Tragedy, on the other hand, has its roots in death and sterility. It announces the end of the line, the end of a family, the end of society. Its characteristic images are winter and wasteland. Modernism, the period of literature generally placed as beginning during World War I, reflects the culture's loss of history, tradition, and certainty in the face of the War's carnage, made possible by human-made technology. Modernism reduces the scope of the tragic in literature, focusing on smaller characters in more limited settings. Unlike the tragedies of the past, they no longer need to be about larger than life characters, trapped by their own tragic flaws. Rather, tragic movement can be seen in the alienation and isolation of contemporary life. Modernist tragedy tends to emphasize ironic detachment and T. S. Eliot's quiet, "not with a bang but a whimper" ending.

Close examination of "Hills Like White Elephants" reveals that Jig and the American are in a moment that teeters on the border between the comic and the tragic. They are at a moment of decision, one that will push them one way or the other. The landscape around them reflects both possible futures. On the one side of the station, the land is fertile and green. The water from the river nourishes new life. This is the comic landscape, the landscape of regeneration. On the other side of the station, the land is bleak and dusty, lacking in sustenance and life. The American, an essentially flawed character, fails to note the dichotomy of the landscape. His vision is limited by his own needs and desires. He lives in the perpetual "now," wanting only momentary pleasure, not lasting growth. The girl's pregnancy, a state that necessarily points toward the future, has upset his equilibrium in the moment. Acknowledging the pregnancy itself forces him to acknowledge the future. Strikingly, he never mentions the word "pregnancy" in the entire story, as if the mere mention of the word will both implicate and complicate his life.

Jig, on the other hand, seems highly aware of the precipice on which she stands. What she wishes for is the comic resolution, one in which the American will marry her, they will return home, and they will establish a family. She will participate in the birth of the next generation, and will focus her attention forward. However, she also realizes that what she wishes for is not likely what she will get. When she stands and walks to the end of the station, she observes the fertile valley of the Ebro in front of her, and she understands the connection between that landscape and the future she desires. As Barry Stampfl argues, "Jig indicates the truth about her relation with the American and about her feelings for her unborn baby by talking about landscapes" (36).

In some ways, this is a choric moment, that is, a moment when a detached observer makes a judgment about the characters and their actions. In this tiny story, Jig must play the part of her own chorus. At this moment, Jig stands outside herself and sees the larger situation. Looking out over the valley she says, "And we could have all this.… And we could have everything and every day we make it more impossible." It is as if she realizes that the comic ending is slipping away from her. She may be about to play a role in a modernist tragedy, a tragedy in which she finds herself, at best, isolated and alone, keenly aware of the absence of life in her womb. At its worst, she may find herself dying in an abortion clinic, surrounded by people who do not speak her language.

Unlike traditional comedies and tragedies, however, "Hills Like White Elephants" does not offer a recognizable resolution. Rather, the end of the story is inconclusive, the possible endings fragmented. For Jig, the longing for the fertile valley is both a longing for an Edenic past and the longing for progeny to carry on into the future. Neither of her choices offers the fulfillment of that longing, and she knows it. The American's glance at their suitcases covered with hotel labels signals his desire to remain in the permanent present, a present without past or future. Again, regardless of their choice, the man's desire will remain unfulfilled.

The story ends, the train still five minutes down the track. Frozen in the space between comic and tragic resolution, the characters remain, Jig and the American, the conversation ended. Although critics, academics, readers, and students may argue about what will "happen next," the truth is that nothing happens to the characters after the story ends. Hemingway leaves his characters as he found them, in the middle of something larger, outside the margins of the story. Jig and the American truly come to represent the lost generation at this moment. Without resolution, each isolated and alienated from the other, they remain in the no man's land of inconclusivity, the possibility of tradition and continuity represented by the fertile valley just outside of their reach.

Works Cited

Hollander, John. "Hemingway's Extraordinary Reality." *Modern Critical Views: Ernest Hemingway*. Ed. Harold Bloom. New York: Chelsea, 1985. 211–216. Print.

Smith, Paul. "Hemingway and the Practical Reader." *New Essays on Hemingway's Short Fiction*. Ed. Paul Smith. Cambridge, UK: Cambridge UP, 1998. 1–18. Print.

Stampfl, Barry. "Similes as Thematic Clues in Three Hemingway Short Stories." *Hemingway Review* 10.2 (1991): 30–38. Print.

Source: *Short Stories for Students*. Detroit: Gale, 2002. *Literature Resources from Gale*. Web. 18 Oct. 2010.

EXERCISE 9C   EXPLORING LITERARY ANALYSIS: LITERARY ANALYSIS OF "HILLS LIKE WHITE ELEPHANTS."

1. How does Henningfeld's analysis relate to what other critics have written about "Hills Like White Elephants"? What do you think Henningfeld adds to the ongoing discussions of this famous short story?

2. What sources does Henningfeld consult in supporting her interpretation of "Hills Like White Elephants"? Does her use of these sources strengthen her analysis? Explain.

3. What did you learn about Hemingway's short story from this analysis? How does Henningfeld's analysis compare to your own interpretation of the story?

Tolkien: A Marxist Analysis

by John Molyneux

The following essay is a good example of a writer using literary theory to illuminate a text (see "Theoretical Frameworks for Literary Analysis" on page 263). In this case, critic John Molyneux examines the immensely popular fantasy novels of J. R. R. Tolkien from a Marxist perspective. As Molyneux notes in his essay, Tolkien's books about the imaginary Middle Earth—including The Hobbit *and* The Lord of the Rings *trilogy—are among the best-selling books of all time, and in recent years they have been made into equally popular films. Such popularity makes a critic like Molyneux take notice. But Molyneux takes an unusual approach to his examination of these works, using Marxism to illuminate what he sees as the conservatism inherent in the fantasy world Tolkien created. You'll notice that Molyneux assumes his readers understand the basic tenets of Marxist theory, which focuses on the means of production and power relations within economic systems, particularly capitalism. One of those tenets is "social relations," which refers to the relations that people necessarily have within a social system that affect their living conditions and even their very survival; another is "production," which generally refers to the forces, institutions, and activities that make up the economic system that is the foundation for society. Even if you are not well versed in Marxist theory or a fan of Tolkien, you can see how Molyneux uses these fundamental concepts from Marxist theory to interpret Tolkien's fantasy world. The excerpt reprinted here is taken from a longer essay that Molyneux posted to his blog in 2011.*

. . . .

The writings of J. R. R. Tolkien might seem a somewhat unusual subject for Marxist analysis, and indeed for me. I usually write about visual art or politics rather than literature and when Marxists write about literature they are more likely to focus on issues of method, or on figures from the canon of high culture—Shakespeare, Dickens, Tolstoy etc.—or modernism—Kafka, Joyce, Beckett—or with avowed radical politics—Gorky, Brecht, O'Casey, Steinbeck etc. Tolkien fits none of these categories. Indeed he is a writer to whom many Marxists would take an instant dislike, who some would decline to read altogether (as not serious literature) or who, if they did like him, they might be slightly shame-faced about, almost as if they had a private taste for James Bond or Mills and Boon, for if Tolkien is not pulp fiction, he is not quite regarded as high culture either. Nevertheless, there already exists a small body of Marxist writing on Tolkien; moreover, there is a serious justification for writing seriously about Tolkien—namely, his exceptional popularity and the need to account for that popularity.

This popularity is truly extraordinary. According to Wikipedia, *The Lord of the Rings*, with 150 million sales world wide, is the second best selling novel of all time (after Dickens' *Tale of Two Cities* with 200 million) and the seventh best selling book of any kind (after The Bible, Mao's Little Red Book, The Qu'ran, the Chinese Dictionary etc.). It has sold more than *The Da Vinci Code* and *The Catcher in the Rye* combined, five times as many as *War and Peace* or *1984* or *To Kill a Mocking Bird* and fifteen times as many as *Catch 22*. *The Hobbit*, with 100 million sales, comes in fourth among novels and twelfth of all books. To this must be added the fact that The *Lord of the Rings: The Return of the King*, with takings of $1,119,110,941, was the third highest grossing film of all time, after *Avatar* and **Titanic**, with *The Lord of the Rings: The Two Towers* only just behind.

Popularity on this scale means that the ideological content of this work is a factor of at least some significance in the consciousness of many millions of people, and thus worthy of analysis. Moreover, this popularity bears with it a conundrum. It is clear that Tolkien's world view is in many respects right wing and reactionary, but if this is the case, how come his work is so popular? Is it despite or because of this reactionary outlook? Or what is the relation between Tolkien's worldview and his audience? Investigating, and hopefully resolving, this puzzle is one of the main aims of this essay. It also throws up a number of interesting points about history, ideology and art.

When I refer to Tolkien's worldview, I mean not his personal political opinions but his outlook as embodied in his novels. Although the personal opinions undoubtedly influenced the outlook of the novels, it is the latter, not the former, that matters. The latter has influenced many, many millions; the former are known only to a tiny minority. Moreover, that worldview is expressed primarily not in the details of the plot of either *The Hobbit* or *The Lord of the Rings* but in the overall vision of Middle Earth as an imagined society.

The Lord of the Rings is not, in my opinion, an allegory. In this I concur with Tolkien who was most insistent on this point in the Forward to the Second Edition (*The Fellowship of the Ring* 8–9) Unlike, say, *Animal Farm*, which is manifestly an allegory for the Russian Revolution and the rise of Stalin, the story of the war of the rings does not correspond to [still less is it an elaborate code for] the First World War, or The Second World War or any other actual historical episode. The real history it most closely resembles is that of the Cold War but we know that it was illuminate any kind of began. The plot of *The Lord of the Rings*, therefore, is largely *sui generis*. The social relations of Middle Earth, however, are not and could not be. It is very easy to imagine futuristic technology—intergalactic spaceships, death stars, transporter beams and the like—and it is relatively easy to imagine strange non-existent creatures—Orcs, Ents, insect people, Cactacae, etc.—but it is close to impossible to invent non-existent social relations and the social relations of Middle Earth are readily recognisable.

The reason the social relations of Middle Earth are so easily recognised is that they are (with one important exception) essentially feudal. We do not live in a feudal society, but feudalism is the social order that immediately preceded capitalism in Europe, and that existed alongside capitalism in many parts of the world until well into the twentieth century. Moreover, there still survive, even in the twenty first century, hangovers of feudalism such as the British monarchy, aristocracy and the House of

(*Continued*)

Lords. In addition, feudal social relations permeate a large part of our classic literature (Shakespeare, Chaucer, *Beowulf*, etc.) of our mythology, (the Arthurian legends, Robin Hood, etc.) and our children's fairy tales (Jack and the Beanstalk, Sleeping Beauty, Snow White, etc.).

According to Marx, social relations correspond to a certain level of development of the forces of production (technology, plus labour, plus science). The productive forces of Middle Earth are resolutely medieval. Not only are they pre-industrial, they are pre-early modern—no steam engines or power driven machinery, no printing, no transport more advanced than the ship and the horse (except eagles in extremis), importantly no guns or cannon (the only explosions or fireworks are courtesy of wizardry or sorcery). Actually, very little attention is paid to production at all. It is clear that Middle Earth is overwhelmingly rural—Minas Tirith in Gondor is the only real city we encounter in the whole epic—and therefore it is more or less assumed that most people are farmers of some sort and not worthy of much mention.

Middle Earth is a world of Kings and Queens, Princes and Princesses, Lords and Ladies. The role of heredity and lineage, of what sociologists call ascribed (as opposed to achieved) status and what in everyday language would be called class, is absolutely overwhelming and completely taken for granted. Almost every single character's social position and part in the story is determined, in the first instance, by their birth. This applies from the very top to the very bottom, in small matters and large. Why, for example, is Sam Gamgee Frodo's servant? It is not age—Merry and Pippin are young but from higher families in the Shire social order—it is class. Aragorn, not Boromir or Faramir, is destined to rule Gondor because he is the heir of Isildur, albeit this was 3000 years ago, and has ancestry stretching even further back to Earendil and the Elven kings of the First Age, whereas they are merely sons of a Steward. True, he has to prove himself and win his throne in many battles but his leadership role is predestined. And Aragorn will love and wed Arwen not Eowyn because she is of matching birth—they are repeating the ancient union of Luthien and Beren. Eowyn, who originally loves Aragorn, instead marries Faramir who is of roughly equivalent standing in the Middle Earth hierarchy.

At first glance the central character of Gandalf may appear not to fit this mold in that his lineage is not spelt out in *The Lord of the Rings*, and that Saruman, not Gandalf, is at first cast as the senior wizard; moreover, wizards do not seem to have a fixed position in the Middle Earth social order (compare the relatively lowly Radagast). But in *The Silmarillion*, the prequel to the saga of the Rings, which provides a creation myth for Middle Earth and tells the history of its First Age, this gap is filled. Gandalf, we are told, was originally Olorin and a Maiar. The Maiar were the servants of the Valar, the Lords of Arda (guardians of creation made in the beginning by Iluvatar, the One) in Valinor, beyond the confines of the world. Gandalf is thus of higher lineage even than Elrond or Galadriel, but, interestingly, matches that of his two great foes, the Balrog in Moria (Balrogs were Maiar perverted by Melkor/Morgoth, the fallen Ainur/

Valar and Great Enemy) and Sauron, Morgoth's emissary, just as Frodo's descent and social status matches that of his nemesis Smeagol/Gollum.

At no point in *The Lord of the Rings* is this hierarchical social structure subject to any form of critique or challenge, either by an individual character or a collective group, or even implicitly by the logic of the narrative. The history of Middle Earth contains no Wat Tylers, John Lilburnes or Tom Paines. On the contrary, acceptance of traditional and inherited authority is invariably a sign of "good" character, resistance to it a sign of siding, or potentially siding, with the enemy. For example, one of the things that marks Faramir as the "good" brother in contrast to Boromir, is his more or less instant recognition and acceptance of Aragorn as his ruler.... Thus from first to last Tolkien's worldview is imbued with a deep seated respect for traditional authority.

To add to this there runs through the whole saga another hallmark of conservatism, namely the belief that things are not what they used to be, that the world is in decline, and that the old days were finer, nobler, more dignified, more heroic than the present. As Elrond puts it when recounting the mustering of the hosts of Gil-galad and Elendil for the assault on Sauron at the end of the Second Age, "I remember well the splendour of their banners... It recalled to me the glory of the Elder Days and the hosts of Beleriand, so many great princes and captains were assembled. And yet not so many, nor so fair [my emphasis], as when Thangorodrim was broken" (*The Fellowship of the Ring* 233).

Finally there is a view of fate, predestination and "the will of the Gods" that is not only pre-modern and pre-enlightenment but reminiscent of Ancient Greece and the plays of Aeschylus and Sophocles. When, at the Council of Elrond, Frodo announces that he will undertake the task of taking the Ring to the Cracks of Doom, Elrond says, "I think this task is appointed for you, Frodo," and indeed the whole episode has been foretold in lines which came to both Faramir and Boromir in dreams....

Similarly, Smeagol/Gollum is fated "to play his part before the end"—an absolutely crucial part as it turns out—and the various acts of mercy that are shown to him by Gandalf, Aragorn, the Elves of Mirkwood, and Frodo himself all facilitate this predetermined destiny. Predictions and prophesies are scattered throughout the story and they always come true. As in Greek tragedy anyone who attempts to frustrate or avoid their fate merely ends up contributing to its inevitable fulfillment. The centrality of this conception of fate, which turns out ultimately to be the will of God, for Tolkien's whole vision is made clear by Iluvatar's response to Melkor's aforementioned original sin of musical innovation.

Then Iluvatar spoke, and he said: "Mighty are the Ainur, and mightiest among them is Melkor; but that he may know, and all the Ainur, that I am Iluvatar, those things that ye have sung, I will show them forth, that ye may see what ye have done. And thou, Melkor, shalt see that no theme may be played that hath not its uttermost

(Continued)

source in me, nor can any alter the music in my despite. For he that attempteth this shall prove but mine instrument in the devising of things more wonderful, which he himself hath not imagined" (*The Silmarillion* 17).

This view of destiny is highly conservative because it both reflects the fact that human beings are not in control of their society or their own lives (in Marxist terms, alienated and dominated by the products of their own labour) and reinforces the idea that that they can never become so.

EXERCISE 9D   EXPLORING LITERARY ANALYSIS: ANALYZING TOLKIEN

1. What justification does Molyneux provide for analyzing Tolkien's novels about Middle Earth? How convincing do you find his justification?

2. What conclusions does Molyneux draw about the worldview that emerges from Tolkien's novels? How does he arrive at those conclusions?

3. Did you find Molyneux's analysis persuasive? Why or why not? Do you think the effectiveness of his analysis depends upon whether you have read Tolkien's works? Does it depend upon your knowledge of Marxist theory? Explain.

Watchmen and the Birth of Respect for the Graphic Novel
by Karl Allen

Writers often use literary analysis to explain a trend or examine the appeal of a specific work or genre. In this essay, Karl Allen explains the genre of graphic novels. At first glance, he seems to be offering an introduction to this increasingly popular kind of text, but his analysis of some of the most popular graphic novels actually leads to an interpretation of Watchmen, *which is among the most influential graphic novels ever published. Allen's essay, which appeared on the website About.com in 2011, was written for a general audience, but his analysis is based on a careful examination of* Watchmen *as well as several other graphic novels in the same way that a literary critic might examine a more traditional work of literature. His essay suggests that effective literary analysis can be used to illuminate any kind of text.*

. . . .

So you want to know more about graphic novels because you've read about Christopher Ware in *The New Yorker*, or you noticed that Alan Moore's labyrinthine *Watchmen* just made *Time Magazine's* 100 best books in the English language list. But you also wish to avoid stores with names like "Forbidden Planet" and "The Dragon's

Den?" You want to know what's good and what's bad. What's hot, what's indie, what's superhero, what's art, what's funny, what's dramatic, or simply what's going to be the next basis for a film? What follows is a highly condensed and thoroughly unfair portrait of a burgeoning genre with the briefest of glimpses at only a few representatives. It's only a start.

Let's look at *Watchmen* first. One of the reasons it's been proclaimed great by such disparate crowds as *Time Magazine* readers and comic book nerds alike is that it manages to spin so much depth into a medium that had been undervalued as a literary resource for so long. In other words, it surprised the hell out of everyone. This is a superhero comic book but Batman it ain't. Released in 1986 and 1987 in individual issues and then collected into a single volume (as is typical of most graphic novels) *Watchmen's* superheroes are going through some existential angst as they reach their forties and they start to feel a little reticent about running around fighting crime in costume. Officially banned from public servitude, costumed superheroes are trying to get on with their lives after having been forbidden to wear their tights and underwear and utility belts. You'll recognize the skeleton of this plot as having been co-opted in various forms since *Watchmen's* release, most notably in films like *Batman Begins*, where the notion of a costumed vigilante is treated in realistic terms, and also in *The Incredibles*.

Where Moore and artist Dave Gibbons take you is much bigger than that, though. *Watchmen* spans the 20th century in a world where Superman was released by DC Comics and instead of spawning an industry it inspired otherwise normal people to create alternate identities for themselves and band together to fight crime. One of their partners in crime-fighting, The Comedian, is murdered at the beginning and as each of the former band of Watchmen reflect on their histories as superheroes we see their influence on world events, from the end of World War II through Vietnam onto the Cuban Missile Crisis and JFK's assassination and up to the book's own bizarre twist of an ending to the century.

Moore and Gibbons opened the door through which the comic book and graphic novel (also referred to occasionally as linear art or novel-length comics) would

(*Continued*)

9

eventually enter the world of respected literature. However, it's doubtful that *Watchmen* would have made *Time*'s list in 1987. A lot has happened since then to pull *Watchmen* back into the forefront of *Time*'s consciousness. Artists working in varying forms of the medium have turned illustration into an art form in its own right and have done much to bridge the gap between literature and visual art.

Charles Burns, who has been doing commercial illustration since the mid-80's (and who has, incidentally, done a cover or two for *Time*), has also been hard at work on a graphic novel about a group of teens in the 1970's who are falling victim to an unexplained disease that changes their physical appearance. His bold and iconic artwork can be spotted on every cover of the literary magazine *The Believer* as portraiture of the different authors interviewed in each issue. Burns was made prominent through his association with Art Spiegelman who himself is best known for the great graphic-novel-to-mainstream-literature jumper *Maus*, about his father's experience in a concentration camp told in the guise of cats and mice.

There's also Daniel Clowes whose book *Ghost World* was turned into a movie a few years ago; James Kochalka who has been publishing his comic journals *American Elf*, several separate titles for both kids and mature; and Adrian Tomine whose *Optic Nerve* series have been collected in various volumes over the years and whose work you might recognize from Weezer album covers and the *2002 Best American Non-Required Reading* anthology—another literary crossover. More recently *Persepolis* and *Persepolis 2* by Marjane Satrapi have been released to critical acclaim—perhaps even more so from the literature world than the graphic novel community.

And then there's Christopher Ware. Oh boy, is there Christopher Ware! With his *Acme Novelty Library* which started in the early nineties, Ware soon became recognized as not merely a comics illustrator but as a supremely talented artist and writer whose work in the full-length *Jimmy Corrigan: Smartest Kid on Earth* placed him on a pedestal in not only the literature world but also in the visual art world, with his work appearing on several best-of-the-year book lists and in the 2002 Whitney Biennial. It's in *Jimmy Corrigan* that the worlds of comic books and novels truly collide. A coinciding history of milquetoast Jimmy meeting the father he never knew and his grandfather's relationship with his father, *Jimmy Corrigan* is (and this isn't said lightly) a work of unparalleled brilliance that ranks high in the annals of melancholy missives along with Thomas Hardy and in the sublime and subtle humor pantheon with Dickens.

Christopher Ware's art is reminiscent of early Bauhaus work in its intricately patterned geometrical structure and yet also contains a parody of the early Disney style character designs as well as a structure influenced by Herriman's early Krazy Kat newspaper dailies. Ware is also responsible for editing what is probably one of the best introductions to comic artists and the graphic novel in the *McSweeneys Quarterly* Issue Number 13 from 2003.

But what does all this have to do with *Watchmen*? It is, after all, a superhero story rooted in very traditional comic book style dialogue and illustration while the aforementioned are anything but. It's hard to say because the history of the graphic novel is being written while this is being read. It is beginning to look like *Watchmen* may get credited for creating a genre—or at least forcing old school denizens of literature to take notice of a form that has been discredited for so long—and still is by many. What is perhaps more important than *Watchmen* itself is *Time*'s placing it on its list of important literature. Certainly other books are better—even other graphic novels. But *Watchmen* is the one that first stood up, the first one that proclaimed a story with emotional depth and historical relevance could be told in words and pictures, and that perhaps, as the old maxim goes, those pictures told more than words ever could.

EXERCISE 9E   EXPLORING LITERARY ANALYSIS: ANALYZING GRAPHIC NOVELS

1. Why does Allen analyze a graphic novel that was published more than 15 years earlier? What justification does he offer for his analysis? Do you think his justification strengthens his analysis in any way? Explain.

2. What is the basis for Allen's claims about the importance of graphic novels? To what extent do you think his analysis of *Watchmen* strengthens his claims?

3. Do you agree with Allen's views about graphic novels? Why or why not? Does his analysis of *Watchmen* influence your view of graphic novels? Explain.

Writing Literary Analysis

Use the Ten Core Concepts described in Chapter 2 to develop an effective analysis of a text. Read this section in tandem with Chapter 3; each step described here corresponds to a step described there.

Step 1   Identify a topic for literary analysis.

A few years ago, a friend told me that Henry David Thoreau's book *Walden*, which was published in 1854, changed his life. When I asked him to explain, he told me that Thoreau's philosophy of simple living deeply influenced the way he thought about his own life. My friend's comment made me wonder why *Walden* seems to resonate with readers today. Such a question is often the starting point for literary analysis. We want to understand what a text means or why it affects us in a certain way. In the same way, your interest in a text can arise from a controversy surrounding a text.

Begin by identifying a text that interests you or others:

<table>
<tr>
<td>Identify a text that interests you.</td>
<td>
• Have you read a novel, story, or play that engaged you for some reason?
• Do you have a favorite poem or song?
• Have you seen a film or television show that you found puzzling or illuminating?
• Does the work of a particular writer, filmmaker, singer, or artist appeal to you?
• Have you encountered a text that seems especially important?
</td>
</tr>
<tr>
<td>Examine a controversy about a text.</td>
<td>
• What makes a novel like The Adventures of Huckleberry Finn controversial? What makes it great?
• Is the depiction of torture in the 2012 film Zero Dark Thirty inaccurate or misleading?
• Why do the Harry Potter novels appeal to so many readers?
• Does the hit TV series Breaking Bad really glorify crime?
</td>
</tr>
</table>

Your course assignment might specify a text or a general topic for your essay. Here are some common examples:

- Choose a short story from the course textbook and develop an interpretation of it.

- Select three novels from the course reading list and discuss how they explore issues of social class.

- Using feminist theory, analyze gender roles in one of the assigned plays.

- Examine a major theme in Walt Whitman's *Leaves of Grass*.

Your assignment provides a starting point for your analysis, but you must still define your specific topic and in some cases decide which text or texts to analyze. The best way to do so is to start with the texts that interest you or the aspects of a text that intrigue you.

Next, formulate a question. Whichever text (or texts) you choose, your analysis should start with a question:

- What does this text mean?

- Why is this text important?

- What does this text say about an important issue or issues?

- How do these texts relate to each other?

- What questions do these texts raise for me?

At this point, your question can be general and open-ended. You will refine it as you explore your topic and develop your interpretation. But your question is the starting point for your inquiry, so it should reflect your interests and your desire to understand the text or texts you will analyze.

Develop this question using Step #1 in Chapter 3.

Step 2   Place your topic in rhetorical context.

Consider what might interest other readers in the text you have chosen and the question you have developed:

If you selected a text that interests you	• Why would this text or these texts be important to other readers? • What might interest other readers about this text? • What does your question (from Step #1) offer readers who might share your interest in this text or these texts?
If you selected a text that is the focus of controversy	• What interests you about this controversy? • What interests you about what others have said about this text? • Are you taking a side in the controversy? Why? • Are you exploring a question that the controversy has raised for you?
If your course assignment specifies a topic	• What might interest your classmates about the question you formulated for Step #1? • How does your question fit the assignment or relate to important course topics? • How will your analysis contribute to your classmates' understanding of the text or texts you will analyze?

Addressing these questions will help you identify a purpose for your analysis and develop an interpretation of the text or texts you are analyzing that will interest other readers.

With these considerations in mind, complete Step #2 in Chapter 3.

Step 3   Select a medium.

Literary analysis is usually written in the form of a conventional academic essay. If you are writing in response to a course assignment, follow your assignment guidelines in developing your essay. However, if your assignment allows you to select media other than a conventional essay for your analysis, consider the medium that will enable you to present your analysis to your audience:

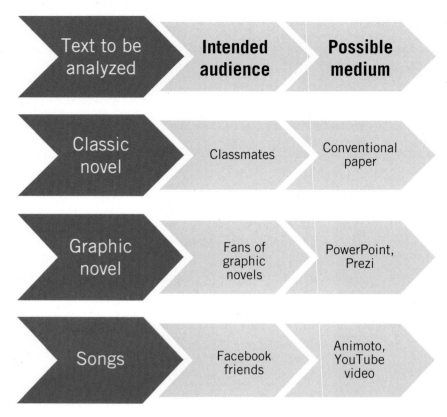

Text to be analyzed	Intended audience	Possible medium
Classic novel	Classmates	Conventional paper
Graphic novel	Fans of graphic novels	PowerPoint, Prezi
Songs	Facebook friends	Animoto, YouTube video

These are just possibilities. The point is to select a medium that will enhance your ability to present a complex literary analysis effectively to your intended audience. A multimedia program such as iMovie or Photostory that enables you to incorporate visual elements, for instance, might work well for an analysis of graphic novels or films. An analysis of poetry might be more effective if you were able to incorporate audio to illustrate how the poet uses sound or rhythm. (Always check with your instructor to see whether your choice of medium is acceptable.)

Follow Step #3 in Chapter 3 to help you decide on the most appropriate medium for your textual analysis.

Step 4 Develop your interpretation and identify your main claim.

What will you say about the text or texts you are analyzing? The answer to that question is essentially your interpretation of the text or texts you are analyzing.

You might already have a good idea of what you want to say about the text(s) you have selected. For example, you might be interested in the debate about a new edition of *The Adventures of Huckleberry Finn* (see "Revising *Huck Finn*" on page 261) and decide to examine the importance of the novel's depiction of race relations for readers today. Perhaps you believe that the novel has an important message about how genuine friendships can transcend racism. That could be the starting point for your **main claim**:

Huck Finn *presents a vision of genuine friendship that transcends race.*

Now your task is to examine the novel to develop your interpretation and refine your main point:

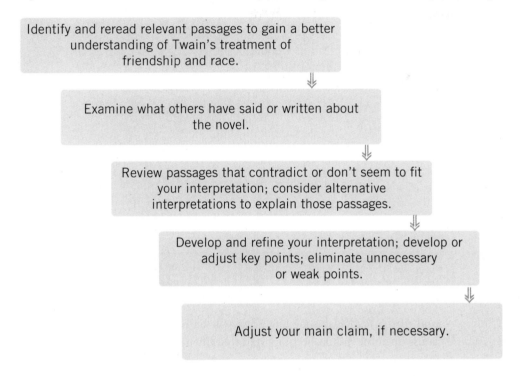

Identify and reread relevant passages to gain a better understanding of Twain's treatment of friendship and race.

Examine what others have said or written about the novel.

Review passages that contradict or don't seem to fit your interpretation; consider alternative interpretations to explain those passages.

Develop and refine your interpretation; develop or adjust key points; eliminate unnecessary or weak points.

Adjust your main claim, if necessary.

If you do not yet have a good sense of what you want to say about the text(s), begin with your question from Step #1. That question might suggest a tentative claim, which you can develop, refine, or change as you explore the novel:

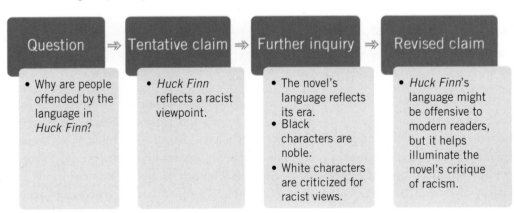

Question ⇒ **Tentative claim** ⇒ **Further inquiry** ⇒ **Revised claim**

- Why are people offended by the language in *Huck Finn*?

- *Huck Finn* reflects a racist viewpoint.

- The novel's language reflects its era.
- Black characters are noble.
- White characters are criticized for racist views.

- *Huck Finn*'s language might be offensive to modern readers, but it helps illuminate the novel's critique of racism.

This step and the next one represent the main inquiry into the text(s) you have chosen to analyze. You might find that your ideas and opinions change as you proceed. Don't expect to know exactly what you will say at the beginning; part of the value of the process is the learning you will do as you examine the text(s) and develop your interpretation.

Your Guiding Thesis Statement, which you develop in Step #4 in Chapter 3, can serve as a summary of your interpretation and your main claim. In addition, consider the following questions as you work on your Guiding Thesis Statement:

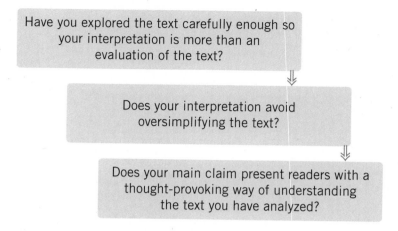

Have you explored the text carefully enough so your interpretation is more than an evaluation of the text?

Does your interpretation avoid oversimplifying the text?

Does your main claim present readers with a thought-provoking way of understanding the text you have analyzed?

Step 5   Support your interpretation.

Your interpretation of the text(s) you are analyzing will be based on several claims about the text(s). Those claims, in turn, should be supported by evidence. The stronger your support for your claims, the more persuasive your interpretation—and the more effective your analysis.

To develop sufficient support for your interpretation, first identify claims you will make about the text. Then identify appropriate support or evidence for those claims. In most literary analysis, support for your claims will take four main forms:

- summaries of relevant passages from the text
- quotations from the text
- quotes from other analyses of the text
- reasoning based on your reading of the text

Let's return to the example of *Huck Finn*. Imagine that in rereading the novel, you found two major scenes that you believe reveal the author's views about race relations. Your interpretation—that Twain saw beyond race to a person's fundamental character—is based on your reading of those scenes. You want to make two claims in support of your interpretation: (1) Twain was actually critiquing the racism he saw in his society by calling attention to its hypocrisy, and (2) the integrity of Twain's characters had nothing to do with race; "good" characters could be Black as well as White, and many White characters were evil or stupid. The two major scenes will become important evidence to support these claims; you might also quote from several essays of literary criticism that generally support your view of the novel:

Claims	
1. Twain critiques racist views of his White contemporaries.	2. The integrity of Twain's characters is not related to race.

⇓

Evidence	
• Summaries of scenes that present the hypocrisy of White characters • Quotations from the text that highlight racism	• Summaries of scenes that show integrity of Black characters and stupidity of Whites • Relevant quotations from critics

Keep in mind that, in most literary analysis, there is no "proof" that a single interpretation is correct; rather, you are providing support for your claims about the text to make your interpretation more persuasive to your readers.

Remember to use appropriate literary concepts and terminology to develop and support your interpretation. Terms like *theme*, *symbol*, and *imagery* can be important tools to help explain your interpretation and support your conclusions about the text(s). For example, to support your claim about Twain's critique of his racist contemporaries, you can use the common description of the raft in *Huck Finn* as a *symbol* of a colorblind refuge from racist society.

Step #5 in Chapter 3 will help you identify sufficient support for your interpretation. At this point, you are probably ready to write a complete draft of your project or move onto the next step before completing your draft.

Step 6   Organize your literary analysis.

Unlike some other kinds of analytical writing that lend themselves to certain ways of organizing the essay, literary analyses rarely follow a straightforward organizational pattern. As the reading selections in this chapter illustrate, writers can take very different approaches to organizing their analyses. Ultimately, a writer must consider the intended audience and the purpose of the literary analysis in deciding how best to organize it. However, most essays of literary analysis will have some version of the following components:

- a rationale for analyzing the text(s)
- the main interpretation of the text
- claims about the text that support the interpretation
- support for the claims
- conclusions about the text on the basis of the interpretation

These five components can be used to develop a basic outline for your literary analysis:

1. **Introduction**: a statement of the focus of your analysis and the main question(s) about the text you are addressing in your analysis.

2. **Rationale**: your reason(s) for analyzing the selected text(s); the purpose of your interpretation.

3. **Summary**: a strategic summary that highlights the important aspects of the text on which the analysis will focus.

4. **Interpretation**: an explanation of your interpretation of the text, including the main claims made about the text.

5. **Support**: your evidence to support your claims about the text.

6. **Conclusion**: the conclusions you draw about the text(s) on the basis of your interpretation.

Using such a basic outline requires you to make decisions about how to organize each main section of your essay. For example, you will still have to decide in which order to present your evidence for each of your claims.

Step 7 — Get feedback.

Step #7 in Chapter 3 guides you through the process of obtaining useful feedback by focusing on the four main characteristics of analytical writing:

A relevant topic worthy of analysis	• Has the writer provided compelling reasons for analyzing the selected texts? • Does the writer have something relevant to say about these texts? Are the writer's claims clearly presented?
Complexity	• Is the analysis of the text(s) thorough? • Has the writer examined the text(s) in sufficient depth? • Does the writer's interpretation do justice to the text(s)?
Appropriate and sufficient support	• Is the writer's interpretation well supported? Do any sections need more support or stronger evidence? • Does the writer use appropriate sources? Are the summaries and quotations accurate and relevant? • Does the writer use literary terms appropriately?
Reasonable conclusions	• Do the writer's conclusions grow logically from the analysis of the text(s)? Are the conclusions presented clearly and persuasively? • Is the interpretation of the text(s) thought-provoking? Does it add something to our understanding of the text(s)?

Step 8 — Revise.

Follow the steps for Step #8 in Chapter 3 to revise your draft. Use the questions listed in Step #7 in this chapter to guide your revisions. Pay particular attention to how you have organized your draft so that your interpretation is presented clearly and logically to your readers.

Step 9   Refine your voice.

Like all analytical writing, literary analysis is more effective if the writer's voice is strong and confident. Students sometimes try to sound academic in their literary analysis essays by relying too heavily on literary terminology or mimicking the writing style of professional literary critics. Such strategies usually weaken an essay. Instead, focus on developing a sound interpretation of the text that you have confidence in and that you explain as clearly as you can to your readers. That confidence will come through in your voice. Keep that in mind as you complete Step #9 in Chapter 3.

Step 10   Edit.

Complete Step #10 in Chapter 3. Pay particular attention to specialized terms, and make sure your quotations from the text are accurate and correctly punctuated.

WRITING PROJECTS   LITERARY ANALYSIS

1. Select a favorite story, novel, poem, film, song, or other literary work, and write an essay for an audience of your classmates in which you offer your interpretation of that work and explain its appeal.

    Alternatively, write an essay for a different audience—for example, readers of your hometown newspaper or your Facebook friends—in which you present your interpretation of your selected literary work and explain why those readers should care about that work.

2. Select two very different literary works—such as a Shakespeare play and several rap songs—that explore similar themes, and write an essay in which you present an analysis of how those themes are developed in each work.

3. Analyze the film version of a novel, and draw conclusions about the director's interpretation of that novel. Present your analysis in a multimedia format for an audience that you think would be interested in it.

4. Rewrite the essay you wrote for Question #1 or Question #2 in a completely different medium. For example, rewrite a conventional essay as a digital story using a program such as Photostory.

5. Using a social medium such as Twitter or Facebook, ask for responses to the essay you created for Question #1. Do the readers who responded agree with your interpretation of the text? Why or why not? What have you learned about the text from their responses to your essay? Now consider what revisions you might make to your essay on the basis of these responses.

Evaluating and Reviewing 10

WE COMMONLY EVALUATE THE FILMS, music, television shows, books, exhibits, and performances that entertain us and maybe even provoke us to think in different ways about important aspects of our lives:

- We tell a friend what we thought of a movie we enjoyed.
- We share opinions about whether a band's new recording is as good as its previous work.
- We recommend a new book we recently finished.
- We debate with family members whether a popular new video game reflects a trend toward more violent games.

No matter how brief, these conversations amount to informal critical evaluations. They are common forms of analysis that help us make sense of works or performances and place them in the context of what others think or say about them.

Perhaps just as often as we share views about films, books, or music, we also evaluate consumer goods: everything from smartphone apps to stereos to cars. With the rapid growth of online reviewing on consumer websites like Yelp.com and social media such as Facebook, more and more people are writing and reading reviews. As a result, reviews have become an ever-more important kind of analysis in our lives as citizens, consumers, and workers.

In academic settings, evaluation usually focuses more directly on the careful analysis of texts and is part of a discipline's inquiry into specific questions, problems, or ideas. For example, a historian might review a new study of the Pilgrims' settlement in New England that challenges prevailing beliefs about the way the new colony was governed. A biochemist might evaluate grant proposals for studies of new blood pressure medications to determine which ones should be funded. Such reviews are a means by which scholars discuss and evaluate each other's work and thus contribute to their field's understanding of important issues, ideas, or developments.

Evaluative writing, then, plays a role in all aspects of our lives: in school, in the workplace, and elsewhere.

Paolo Scarlata/iStockphoto.com; Flas100/Shutterstock.com

Occasions for Evaluating and Reviewing

Writers are often motivated to evaluate something because of their own experience. For example, someone trying to decide where to have dinner might consult reviews of restaurants in a local dining guide or an online review site. Afterward, that same person might write a review of the restaurant to add to what others have said about it. In this way, patrons engage in an ongoing conversation about restaurants and dining. Readers consult reviews to learn from the writer's experience and consider the writer's viewpoint about a topic of common interest. In this sense, writers of reviews and their readers share an implicit sense of purpose. In the case of restaurant reviews, for example, both writers and readers seek information and opinions to help them decide which restaurants to visit. Movie reviews reflect a desire on the part of both writer and reader to evaluate a film, which helps readers determine whether it is worth seeing. Rarely does a writer write a review of something without readers in mind. In this regard, reviews and evaluations serve an explicitly social purpose and highlight the way rhetorical purpose informs a writer's work. As a writer, then, your reasons for writing an evaluation or review are likely to grow out of your sense of something's importance not only to you but also to others.

The same principle applies to evaluations and reviews written in academic settings. Academic journals in all fields contain articles that have been carefully reviewed by other scholars before they are published. In fact, reviewing manuscripts for possible publication is one of the most common kinds of scholarly writing. Many academic journals also regularly publish reviews of books in their fields. These reviews, which sometimes resemble the book reviews in popular publications like the *New York Review of Books* or *ALA Journal*, provide a forum in which scholars evaluate each other's work in their effort to advance their understanding of important topics in their fields. In addition, scholars routinely review proposals that seek grant funding for specific research projects. In these ways, evaluative writing is a crucial component of a scholar's effort to understand important issues, questions, or problems in his or her field.

As a college student, you will be asked to write reviews and evaluations that are in many ways similar to professional scholarly writing. College writing assignments routinely require students to evaluate texts, performances, or exhibits to deepen students' understanding of the concepts or information they are learning and to share insights about the subject matter. The evaluative writing required in such assignments engages students in careful analysis of their topics. For example, in reviewing a research article in sociology, students must apply their knowledge of research methods to evaluate the quality of the study; at the same time, they are learning more about the subject of the study itself. Similarly, students in an English course might be asked to review the film version of a classic novel they have been assigned to read; such reviews require students not only to think carefully about the subject matter of the film but also to apply the literary theories they are learning. In this sense, evaluative writing is not only an opportunity to express an opinion about whether something is effective or worthwhile but also an occasion to build and share knowledge.

1. Think of a favorite film or book. If you were to write a review of it, what would you say about it? To whom would you address the review? What would be its purpose? In other words, what would you want that audience to learn from your review? Now find one or two reviews of the film or book. Compare the purpose of those reviews to your own sense of the purpose of reviewing this film or book. What conclusions might you draw about reviews?

2. Identify a current film you would like to see. Find several reviews of the film. In a brief paragraph, describe what the reviewers have said about the film. What did you learn from these reviews? In what ways might the reviews influence your desire to see the film and your expectations for the film?

3. Have you ever made a decision on the basis of a review? For example, did you decide to purchase a video game or a book after reading a review of it? If so, describe that experience. Explain what you learned from the review and how it influenced your decision. On the basis of this experience, what conclusions would you draw about the nature and purpose of reviews?

Understanding Reviews and Evaluation

As the preceding sections of this chapter suggest, writers write reviews for many different reasons. Ultimately, the rhetorical situation determines what features a review should include and what makes for effective evaluative writing. Despite the great variety of forms that reviews can take, however, reviews share four common features: criteria for evaluation, a summary or description of what is being evaluated, a reason for the review, and something relevant to say.

Criteria for Evaluation

Whatever is being reviewed, the writer must have a set of criteria or standards by which to evaluate the subject of the review. To a great extent, the quality of the review depends on the validity of the criteria used for evaluation and whether readers agree with those criteria (see "What Criteria Should Be Applied?"). In a book review, for example, the reviewer will apply generally accepted criteria appropriate to the genre of the book. For example, reviews of novels will generally evaluate the effectiveness of the plot and the extent to which the novelist explores certain themes. Similarly, movie reviews often include evaluation of technical aspects of a film, such as cinematography and editing. These criteria or standards for evaluation are generally agreed upon and may have been established over many years. Sometimes, reviews are based on specialized criteria. For example, business or research proposals will usually be evaluated according to criteria that reflect the goals or needs of the program in question—say, a program for revitalizing small businesses in a rural region or a grant program to support studies of effective methods of teaching math. In such cases, the criteria reflect the specialized knowledge of the academic field or purpose of the program. But no matter how informal or technical, every review should be based on a standard or set of criteria, whether or not the writer explicitly states it.

A Summary or Description of What Is Being Evaluated

Often, readers will not be intimately familiar with what is being evaluated, so reviewers must include a summary or description of the subject. For example, because movie critics often write reviews of movies before they are released to the general public, their reviews include a summary of the movie's plot so that readers can understand what the critic is evaluating. Similarly, book reviews include plot summaries under the assumption that many (perhaps most) readers will not yet have read the book being reviewed. How much summary or description to include depends on the nature and purpose of the review and what the intended audience can be expected to know about whatever is being reviewed. For example, a review in a campus newspaper of the latest recording by a popular musician would likely not include much background information about the musician because readers will already be familiar with him or her; a release by a new band, however, might include details about the band's musical style and history because many readers will probably know little about the band.

A Reason for the Review

Evaluative writing is part of a broader effort to understand something or contribute to our collective knowledge. A good review should reflect that sense of purpose. Sometimes, the reason for a review is implicit and need not be stated. For example, we expect new movies to be reviewed because of the enormous popularity and cultural importance of film. The same can be said about certain books and musical works. But often a writer will provide a more specific reason for reviewing something. For instance, a reviewer might review several recent books about a controversial topic that has received a great deal of news coverage. A special anniversary—say, of an important historical event—might prompt a writer to review music, books, or exhibits related to that anniversary. The death of a famous actor might be the occasion for a review of films in which that actor starred.

Something Relevant to Say

Even when they pass judgment on something, effective reviews usually have a point to make. For example, a writer reviewing a new book about the Vietnam War might advance a viewpoint about the U.S. involvement in a current war. A review of a fictional film about corruption in politics might make a statement about real-life politics. Although readers often read reviews to see whether the writer did or did not like a film, musical performance, exhibit, or book, the most effective reviews have something more thought provoking to offer. (The readings in this chapter include examples of reviews that make a larger point.) In this sense, a review is an occasion to explore a broader question or issue that goes beyond the subject of the review.

Writers and readers can disagree about the evaluation of something, but reviews are more useful and persuasive when both writer and reader agree on the criteria being used for the evaluation. A novel, for example, will often be evaluated on the basis of its plot, the depth and relevance of its themes, and perhaps the style of writing; by contrast, a work of history will likely be judged on the basis of the quality of its analysis and the clarity of its storytelling. Fans of detective fiction will probably expect a reviewer to evaluate how well the writer of a detective novel builds suspense, but they are less likely to be concerned about whether the novelist's writing style is poetic. Reviewers, therefore, try to apply criteria that readers expect, even when those criteria are never explicitly stated. If the reviewer uses criteria that readers find irrelevant, inappropriate, or even unfair, they are more likely to reject the reviewer's evaluation of the subject. In writing a review, then, examine your rhetorical situation so that the criteria you develop for your review are likely to match your readers' expectations.

These four features will almost always appear in some form in most reviews, but writers must consider their intended audience and the purpose of the review as they decide what to include in a review. Keep that in mind as you consider the four main characteristics of analytical writing:

1. **A relevant topic worthy of analysis.** Identify the reason(s) for reviewing this text, performance, film, exhibit, game, music, or event:

   - What makes this subject appropriate for reviewing?

   - What is the occasion for reviewing this subject?

   - What is the purpose of the review?

   - Why would others be interested in an evaluation of this subject?

2. **Complexity.** Evaluate the subject in sufficient depth:

   - Has the writer examined the subject adequately? Does the review avoid oversimplifying the subject?

   - What criteria are used to evaluate the subject of the review? Are these criteria appropriate for the rhetorical situation?

   - Does the review go beyond a simple judgment about the subject? Does the writer make a point in the review that will interest readers?

3. **Sufficient information and appropriate evidence.** Support your evaluation adequately:

   - Has the writer supported his or her evaluation with appropriate evidence?

   - Does the review include a sufficient summary or description of the subject? Is the summary/description appropriate for the intended audience?

4. **Reasonable conclusions.** Present conclusions that grow reasonably out of your evaluation:

- What conclusions does the writer draw from his or her evaluation of this subject? Does the evaluation lead reasonably to the writer's conclusions?

- Do the conclusions present readers with a thought-provoking way of understanding the subject?

- Does the writer have a larger point to make? Is that point relevant and thought provoking?

EXERCISE 10B   UNDERSTANDING REVIEWS AND EVALUATIVE WRITING

1. Select a favorite book, film, performance, or other subject, and consider what criteria you might use in reviewing that subject. On what basis would you review that subject? What criteria might make sense? What criteria do you think others who would be interested in the subject might expect? Briefly describe these criteria.

2. Compare two or more reviews of a popular book, film, video game, or performance (ideally, one that you enjoyed). Specifically, examine the criteria that each reviewer used in evaluating the subject. Do the reviewers make their criteria explicit? Are those criteria similar across the reviews? If not, what differences in those criteria did you notice? What conclusions might you draw from this exercise about how reviewers select and apply criteria?

3. Using the same reviews you found for Question #2 (or a set of reviews about a different subject), compare the conclusions reached about the subject by the various reviewers. Do the reviewers agree about the subject? If not, what is the basis of their disagreements? Do you agree with any of the reviewers? Explain, citing specific passages from the reviews to support your answer. What conclusions might you draw from this exercise about the nature of reviews?

Reading Reviews

Reviews come in a variety of forms and serve many different purposes for different audiences. The readings in this section reflect that variety. Each reading represents a common form of review: a musical review, a film review, and a book review. And in each case, there is a specific occasion for the review: the death of a popular singer, the release of the last film in an extremely popular series, and the publication of a book about a relevant issue. As you read these selections, notice how each writer crafts his or her review for the rhetorical situation and uses the review to make a larger point that goes beyond an evaluation of the subject. Also consider the four main features of effective analytical writing:

A relevant topic worthy of analysis	• How does the writer establish that the subject is worthy of a review? • What is the context for the review? What is the writer's purpose in reviewing this text, film, performance, etc.?
Complexity	• On what basis does the writer evaluate his or her subject? What criteria does the writer use for evaluation? • Are these criteria appropriate for the subject and rhetorical situation? • In what ways does the review enhance our understanding of the subject?
Sufficient information and appropriate analysis	• What evidence does the writer provide to support his or her evaluation of the subject? How persuasive is this evidence? • Is the summary of the text adequate? Does it help illuminate the subject?
Reasonable conclusions	• What conclusions does the writer draw about the text? • Are the conclusions well reasoned and supported by the evaluation? • Does the review make a larger point? How compelling is this point?

The Imperial Whitney Houston

by Jonathan Bogart

On the weekend of the Grammy Awards in February 2012, news broke that singer Whitney Houston had died at the age of 48. Over the next several days, countless tributes to Houston were broadcast on radio and television and over the Internet, and millions of her fans posted messages about her on social media. Among the many appraisals of her music and career that were published shortly after her death was the following essay by music critic Jonathan Bogart. Bogart's essay, which appeared on the website of the Atlantic Monthly *in February 2012, is a kind of memorial to Houston, in which Bogart acknowledges Houston's remarkable voice that was the source of her widespread popularity. But he also offers a careful appraisal of her work over her entire career, examining*
(Continued)

whether Houston deserved the metaphoric title of "queen" that was so often used to describe her status as a female pop singer and cultural icon. Like most effective music reviews, Bogart's evaluation is based on a set of criteria that are widely used to judge the quality of music, though he never explicitly describes those criteria. As you read, try to identify those criteria and decide whether you agree with Bogart's conclusions about Houston's music. Bogart not only evaluates Houston's music, however; he also explores the qualities of her singing that made her such an important cultural figure. In doing so, he makes a point about the value of music in general.

. . . .

The Queen is dead. Long live the Queen.

Whitney Houston was arguably the most important woman in pop music for 10 years, and for the next 15 years watched the world she had made over in her image slowly unravel in beauty, heartbreak, and eventual squalor.

Between 1985, when "How Will I Know" and "Greatest Love of All" announced a powerful new voice in both dance-pop and balladry, and 1995, when her imperium began to fade into the complacency of soundtracks, the compromise of collaboration, and the indignity of having every new record called a comeback, her only peers were called the King and Queen of Pop—which would have made her also a Queen (or, perhaps, an Empress) if such jockeying for titles weren't beneath her dignity.

To some, her radiance papered over the injustice of American society—a reading borrowed from British punk's attitude towards an actual Queen.

And dignified she was—she even explicitly said so in "Greatest Love of All"—as was fitting of the daughter of gospel, soul, and disco royalty, whose cousin was the eternally poised Dionne Warwick and whose godmother was the ferociously righteous Aretha Franklin. But it was a dignity without hauteur: That smile, both intimately warm and supremely confident, shone out from hundreds of millions of record covers around the globe and mitigated the marble perfection of her voice. She became, if not the

Featureflash/Shutterstock.com

girl next door, then the trusted avatar of our best selves, who embodied her songs of heartbreak, fear, and solitude in widescale productions that erupted into extravagant pirouettes of melody and sleek coruscations of rhythm.

Or so the royalist history goes. There are always revolutionaries in the realm, people who don't believe in the benevolence or utility of the monarchy. The cruelly ironized use of her image and music in Bret Easton Ellis's spiteful satire *American Psycho* came to stand in for an entire subcultural critique of the hyperpolished, precision-engineered music of the '80s mainstream, against which white men who considered themselves disaffected intellectuals raged. In their reading, the bounding, whirling joy of "I Wanna Dance With Somebody (Who Loves Me)" or "So Emotional" falsely papered over the injustice, violence, and destructiveness of American society, and she was a convenient figurehead propping up a corrupt system—a reading borrowed from British punk's attitude towards an actual Queen.

Whitney was not a literal queen, but the theory of monarchy—that while most people are contingent upon the world, there are some people on whom the world is contingent, who define the world, and on whose sufferance the rest of us exist—isn't a bad metaphor for the feelings that Whitney Houston inspired in many of my generation. Whether we were adoring pop-dance royalists (which as often as not meant that we could see ourselves in her; we were women, or black, or queer), or raging indie-punk roundheads (which as often as not meant that our own structures of power were threatened by her metaphorical realm), we understood her as a constant, to be done homage or to be fought against, but always, eternally, there.

Her voice allowed no other understanding. It not only "filled the room" in the ordinary sense of being easily heard—especially when she pushed into her belting range, hard-edged and indomitable—but in the sense that there was no space for anything else; you felt crushed against the walls by the dominating, obliterating power of her voice. This could be ecstasy, or it could be intolerable; not unusually, as in the operatic grandeur of *The Bodyguard* soundtrack, it was both.

She had multiple voices, of course—she was a performer, not a monolith—and it was the elasticity of her voice, which allowed her to make the jump from the just-above-a-whisper longing of the opening a capella verse of "I Will Always Love You" to its cliff-drop, pummeling final chorus, that made her so overwhelming during her decade of dominance. None of her peers or competitors, from Madonna and Janet Jackson to Mariah Carey and Mary J. Blige, had her almost inhuman control, her eerie command of technique and precision. They might outthink, outdance, outcharm, or outemote her, but they could never be as totalitarian as Whitney at her best: Her technique was ruthless and impregnable, cutting off all avenues of escape, bending the listener to her will.

And then, as all monarchs do eventually, she declined. She had achieved the height; she could afford to be retiring for a season. The world shifted under her; and

(Continued)

the multiplicity of voices encouraged by hip-hop assimilated only uneasily into her totalitarian ethos. Her post-*Bodyguard* soundtracks tended to retreat into older soul or gospel forms, and starting with 1998's *My Love Is Your Love*, she sounded less and less indomitable and more and more complaisant, singing duets and riding beats and being remixed, increasingly another functioning part of her productions rather than the still jewel in their active setting. By 2009's *I Look to You*, even the smooth marble voice had grown audibly fissured with age and use; while her technique was still profound, her songs were not, cheerfully going through retro paces rather than setting new benchmarks.

When the news of her death broke Saturday night, in the slow-motion, cascading way news breaks these days—in tweets, emails, wall posts, text messages, unannotated video posts, and hasty, confirming Google searches—the dominant emotion among the music-loving writerly types and pop-besotted humanists who make up my internet social circle seemed to be a horrified disbelief. Not that it was unexpected, exactly, as anyone who'd kept an ear cocked to the gossip industry over the past decade could tell you. But that That Voice could be extinguished seemed an impossibility, a sudden and irretrievable reduction in the scope of the world.

Listening back to her music today, I hear the sadness and pain, loneliness and fear in the lyrics to nearly every song. I hear the heightened-to-tragedy language of romantic convention; like Céline Dion, another overwhelming belter with pain in her past, she did her best work with the tools of melodrama. But I also hear the force with which she beat back the darkness, the shining ebullience that refused to let her, or us, wallow. The world remains unjust, violent, and destructive, but at least there's song.

EXERCISE 10C   EXPLORING REVIEWS: *THE IMPERIAL WHITNEY HOUSTON*

1. How do you think the occasion for this review affects Bogart's evaluation of Houston's music? Do you think Bogart's evaluation is appropriate for the occasion? Why or why not?

2. On the basis of what criteria does Bogart evaluate Houston's music? Do you think these criteria are generally accepted by most fans of pop music? Do you agree with Bogart's assessment of Houston's music? Why or why not?

3. What larger point does Bogart make in this review? Do you find that point valid? Explain.

Harry Potter and the Deathly Hallows, Part II:
The Final Film Is Better Than the Book
by Gazelle Emami

The Harry Potter series of novels by author J. K. Rowling is the best-selling book series of all time. Along with the extremely popular films based on the novels, the series has become a cultural phenomenon since the first novel in the series, Harry Potter and Philosopher's Stone, *was published in 1997. (The book was released a year later in the United States as* Harry Potter and the Sorcerer's Stone.*) The final book in the series,* Harry Potter and the Deathly Hallows, *was published in 2007. Fans anticipated its release, in part because Rowling had indicated that there would be no more books in the series. This final novel, then, would be the climax of Harry Potter's story and would, fans hoped, answer the questions about Harry's fate that had been raised by the previous books. In 2011, the second of two films based on that book was released. Among the many reviews of that film is the following one by writer Gazelle Emami, the culture editor of the* Huffington Post, *an online forum for news, politics, art, and culture, where this review first appeared in 2011. What sets this review apart from most reviews of the* Harry Potter *films is that Emami evaluates both the novel and the film and arrives at a conclusion that many* Harry Potter *fans would likely reject. Readers might disagree with Emami's conclusions, but her review is a good example of an evaluation that delves deeply into its subject.*

. . . .

We pick up right where we left off. Voldemort has broken into Dumbledore's grave and taken the Elder Wand. He lifts it into the air and sparks it like a bolt of lightning, vaguely evoking Harry's scar.

In this final installment of the "Harry Potter" series—10 years after the first film, and 14 years after we first came to know Harry Potter—we find ourselves drawn back to motifs, like Harry's scar, often. The film is spotted with references to moments and characters who have defined it, almost like markers leading us through the final stretch, paying homage to everything that came before. Ollivander reminds us, as he first advised in Book One, that "the wand chooses the wizard," the

Warner Bros/Everett Collection

(Continued)

giant spiders from Book Two still terrify us, and we even get to see Ron screaming like a little girl, just the way he used to before he hit puberty.

All this makes it easy to warm up to this film. But what this series was always about—and what takes up the second half of Book Seven—is beyond these nostalgic draws. It's about losing your innocence, as you literally watch Hogwarts, your childhood school, fall to pieces. In other words, it's always been leading up to the Battle at Hogwarts, where that whole good-vs.-evil problem could be hashed out. When it comes to executing this crucial component, Book Seven falters—to be blunt, this was not J. K. Rowling's best work.

Looking back, its final battle scene is almost a blur. Wands were flying everywhere, spells were being shouted out left and right—it was chaotic, and readers were just trying to get to the end. After all, the most prevalent question rumbling at the time was "Will Harry die?" Clearly, emotions were running high. Reading it was like a race to the finish, more of a desperate need to find out Harry's fate before anyone spilled the beans.

Closure, at that point, meant simply knowing what happened. Now, closure means fully understanding what happened. Seen in this context, "Harry Potter and the Deathly Hallows: Part II" is a triumph of a finale, to both the film series and the entire "Harry Potter" franchise. What was muddled in the book comes into stunning focus with this final installment, and now we can really close the book on "Potter," so to speak.

In part, this is because "Harry Potter and the Deathly Hallows: Part I" absorbed most of the slow portions of the book, especially the trio's extended stay in a tent; but it's also that the sets, the special effects, the storyline and the acting in this movie come together tightly, forming a narrative, emotional, and visual thrill.

The pace is quick from the start, and within 10 minutes, Harry (Daniel Radcliffe) has a plan to find the next Horcrux, which must be destroyed if he is to kill Lord Voldemort. Harry, Ron (Rupert Grint) and Hermione (Emma Watson) set off for Gringotts Bank, which was built in a flight shed for the production and has remarkably convincing faux marble all over its lobby.

Hogwarts is next, and it's here that the movie really takes off. Everything is carefully paced in the battle that unfolds, a point the book did not quite grasp. The film takes a more streamlined approach, communicating the chaos in the background, but tempering it with loud/soft rhythms and visuals that are mind-blowing, in one instance literally (you'll know it when you see it).

It almost goes without saying that Radcliffe, Grint and Watson are at their best here—they're all grown up, and there's no question anymore as to whether they're right for their roles. They are their roles. The mid-sized roles of Luna Lovegood (Evanna Lynch) and Neville Longbottom (Matthew Lewis) are also crucial to the film, and Neville in a few instances shines as the film's star. Draco Malfoy (Tom Felton) is portrayed accurately as an increasingly complicated figure, especially in the Room of Requirement—when it comes down to him killing Harry, it's clear where his heart is.

The older cast, as always, is the backbone of the film. Ralph Fiennes expertly portrays a Voldemort growing more vulnerable, and yet somehow emboldened, with the destruction of every Horcrux, each one hitting him like a spasm as he loses another sliver of his soul—you can see a flicker pass through Fiennes' eyes every time, a sign of his unraveling. Voldemort in this final film is more disturbing than he's ever been, most so when he walks barefoot through the blood of the dead, shoving off attempts to help him, and clinging desperately to his snake, Nagini, who houses one last part of his soul. We don't just see him as an evil villain in this film, but as a sick, deranged madman.

This darkness is countered with that sense of unyielding hope, and strength in the face of adversity, we've also come to associate with "Harry Potter." If there is one line that stands out in the film, it's surely when the brilliant Professor McGonagall (Maggie Smith), who brings to life a platoon of stone soldiers to defend the castle, says, with obvious excitement, "I've always wanted to use that spell." Perfectly timed, and delivered.

Much of the movie feels deeply satisfying in that way. Ron and Hermione always wanted to kiss, and they do; Voldemort (Ralph Fiennes) and Harry always wanted to have a final battle, and they do; and we viewers always wanted to see this series end, and we do. In part you can trace the film's energy by looking at the color return to Voldemort's lips. That's the infusion of life that builds and builds, in Voldemort and in the viewers, until finally it must end.

To be sure, this is not a movie without flaws, and it makes its most notable fumble at the end. The book's saccharine, fan-fiction-y epilogue is included in the film, but instead of using older actors to play Harry, Ginny, Ron and Hermione as adults—19 years later, married with children—the regular actors have been "aged" for the roles. This doesn't work out very well—Hermione looks like a 25-year-old with a 12-year-old child. What has held this series together is a powerful tale of friendship, not a tale of their families from the future. If only it had ended a few minutes earlier, with Harry, Ron and Hermione standing together, having just saved the world. Let's pretend it did.

EXERCISE 10D   EXPLORING REVIEWS: *HARRY POTTER AND THE DEATHLY HALLOWS*

1. What significance does Emami see in this film? To what extent does her review support her views about the *Harry Potter* books?

2. What do you think is the main purpose of this review? Do you think Emami achieves that purpose? Explain.

3. Emami draws the surprising conclusion that the film based on the final novel in the *Harry Potter* series is better than the novel itself. On what basis does she draw that conclusion? Do you think Emami expects her readers to be surprised by her conclusion? Explain. Do find her conclusion persuasive? Why or why not?

Review of *Thirteen Reasons Why* by Jay Asher

by Bryan Gillis

The following essay is an example of a conventional review of a novel. Like most such reviews, this one draws conclusions about the quality of the novel's plot and characterization. In this case, the reviewer, Bryan Gillis, evaluates a novel for adolescent readers called Thirteen Reasons Why *(2007), by Jay Asher. What makes this review noteworthy is that it appeared in 2011 in a journal called* The Journal of Adolescent & Adult Literacy, *which is intended for scholars and other professionals interested in literacy. The purpose of the review goes beyond evaluating the quality of the novel as a work of literary art; Gillis also assesses the appropriateness of the novel for adolescent readers, thus helping his audience (educators, scholars, and other literacy professionals) determine whether the novel might be useful in their work with adolescent students. His review illustrates how audience and purpose can shape a writer's evaluation of a subject. Notice, too, that Gillis also assesses how effectively the novel addresses a relevant but difficult subject: teen suicide. In part, his purpose is to help his readers decide whether the novel might be an appropriate tool for them to use in helping teens understand this challenging subject. Finally, as you read, notice the brevity of this review. Many publications include numerous short reviews, such as this one, so that they can offer their readers reviews of many books rather than only a few longer reviews.*

. . . .

Teen suicide is a hot-button issue. However, unlike abortion, casual sex, or freedom of speech, no one seems to be taking sides on this one. If you poll 100 people, all of them will tell you that they are against teen suicide. If you search teen suicide on the Internet, you will find sites that list reasons and prevention tips. Jay Asher, in his debut novel *Thirteen Reasons Why*, has taken the topic of suicide one step further. What if you really did know the reasons behind a young woman's suicide? What if, before she did it, she left behind audiotapes that explained all of the reasons why she decided to take her own life?

Thirteen Reasons Why tells the story of Clay Jensen, who receives a box in the mail from his now deceased friend, Hannah, containing seven cassette tapes. These seven tapes contain Hannah's voice on 13 recorded sides; one side for each person she wants to receive the tapes and each reason that Hannah perceived had something to do with her choice to commit suicide. Clay is not the first person to receive the tapes, nor will he be the last, and as we listen to the tapes with him, we not only learn about the events that Hannah thinks led to her decision, we learn about Clay, who initially doesn't understand how he could have possibly contributed to Hannah's decision.

The strength of *Thirteen Reasons Why* is the plotting. Readers discover right away that Hannah has already committed suicide. Still, her posthumous narration keeps readers engaged and guessing. The book is impossible to put down, because even though we know Hannah is dead, we want to know why she did it. Character development is also a strength. Asher makes us care about Clay. We want to know how and why he is involved in all of this. Readers won't get the entire picture until they have listened to the last tape. And the picture is quite surprising. No parental abuse stories, no creepy uncles, just a sequence of small incidents that, in Hannah's mind, were not handled properly and led to unmanageable circumstances.

Jay Asher has done a remarkable job of integrating Hannah's voice (via the tapes) with Clay's thoughts, responses, and memories to create an inventive and seamless dual narration. The author pulls no punches, including a descriptive and heart-wrenching (but necessary) hot tub scene that will leave you aching. After I finished reading *Thirteen Reasons Why* (in one sitting), all of those teen suicide websites filled with reasons and preventative measures seem rather ineffectual compared with the experience of reading Asher's story of a girl who felt she was left with no options. His message is clear: Stop being apathetic, pay attention, and, most important, be kind to one another.

Thirteen Reasons Why deals with some very serious subject matter and is probably most suitable for high school students and above.

EXERCISE 10E   EXPLORING REVIEWS: A NOVEL ABOUT TEEN SUICIDE

1. How does Gillis establish the relevance of the novel he has chosen to review? How persuasive do you find his justification? Explain, citing passages from the text to support your answer.

2. Much of this review is devoted to a summary of *Thirteen Reasons Why*. How effective do you find this summary? To what extent do you think Gillis's summary contributes to his evaluation of the novel? Explain.

3. What conclusions does Gillis reach about *Thirteen Reasons Why*? In what sense do his conclusions relate to his audience's concerns and interests? To what extent do you think he achieves his purpose in this review?

Writing Evaluations and Reviews

Use the Ten Core Concepts described in Chapter 2 to develop an effective review of a novel, play, film, exhibit, concert, proposal, video game, or event. Each step described in this section corresponds to a step described in Chapter 3.

Step 1   Identify a topic.

An effective review reflects a writer's interest in something and a desire to share an evaluation of it with others with similar interests:

- Someone passionate about a specific kind of music is likely to have something to say about the work of an accomplished musician who plays that kind of music.

- An avid amateur photographer might be inclined to share an opinion of a well-known photographer's exhibit.

- A new book by a famous author might prompt a strong reaction from a fan of that author.

- A classic movie might provoke a film history buff to think differently about a current trend in film-making.

These examples suggest that evaluations grow out of our engagement with the things that matter to us.

Start with Your Own Interests or Passions

Books	• Have you read a best-selling book that didn't meet your expectations? Or exceeded them? • Have you read a provocative book about an important current issue that you care about? • Is there a book that you think others should know about for some reason?
Music	• Has a favorite musician or band recently released a new recording? • Have you noticed a trend in music that you feel strongly about? • Is there a CD or album that you think is especially noteworthy for some reason?
Film and television	• Have you seen a film that you find especially important, enjoyable, or provocative? • Do you watch a television show that you believe reflects an important social trend? • Do you have an interest in the films of a specific director or actor whose work is noteworthy?

Art	• Have you visited a special exhibit of paintings, photography, or sculpture that is worth attention? • Does the work of a specific artist strike you as especially important for some reason? • Do you have an opinion about a trend you've noticed in photography or painting?

Performance	• Have you seen an especially powerful concert? • Have you attended a play that you believe is unusually good or provocative? • Do you have a favorite musician whose concerts seem different from his or her recordings?

Consumer items	• Do you have an opinion about an item you use for recreation (e.g., skis or snowboards, running shoes)? • Have you noticed an important trend in a specific kind of item (e.g., hybrid cars, smartphones, digital cameras)?

If you are required to review something specific for a course assignment (for example, an assigned book, a research article, a film), try to develop your review in a way that reflects your own interests. For example, an assignment in a criminal justice course might require you to evaluate how several popular television shows portray the criminal justice system. Although such an assignment constrains your choices, you might select specific television shows that you find interesting, which is likely to make the assignment more engaging.

Consider Your Purpose

Once you have identified the subject you intend to review, consider why you are evaluating it: What is the purpose of your review? What do you hope to learn by evaluating this subject? Why is this subject worth reviewing? Identify your purpose as clearly as you can. (Your purpose might be specified by your course assignment.)

Formulate the Purpose of Your Review as a Working Question

Let's return to the example of the criminal justice assignment. The purpose is to determine how selected television shows portray the criminal justice system. Your working question might be, "How accurately do these television shows depict the U.S. criminal justice system?" Here are additional examples:

■ If you are reviewing a book by a favorite author, your question might be, "How does this book compare to this author's previous books in terms of its themes and characters?"

- If you are reviewing several music recordings of a famous symphony, your question might be, "How well do these different performances capture the power of the composition?"

- If you are evaluating proposals for a marketing campaign for a new consumer product, you might ask, "What are the strengths and weaknesses of these proposals in terms of the likelihood that they would market this product effectively?"

Go to Step #1 in Chapter 3 to develop this question.

Step 2   Place your review in rhetorical context.

Identify an Appropriate Audience for Your Review

Who might be interested in your subject? With whom would you like to share your evaluation of this subject? Be as specific as possible. For example, if you are interested in reviewing a performance by a blues musician, you might wish to find an audience of other fans of the blues. (Your assignment might also specify an audience.)

Consider What Might Interest That Audience About the Subject of Your Review

- Why would your intended audience be interested in the book, film, exhibit, performance, event, or item you have chosen to evaluate?

- What makes the subject of your review important to your intended audience?

- What might your review offer your readers?

- What might you have to say about the subject of your review that would be useful or interesting to your readers?

- What larger message do you hope your intended audience will take away from your review?

Addressing these questions will help you clarify the purpose of your review and develop your evaluation in a way that addresses the interests of your readers.

With that in mind, complete Step #2 in Chapter 3.

Step 3   Select a medium.

Most reviews are written in conventional print format, but writers today have many options in selecting a medium that would be appropriate for different kinds of reviews.

If your review is part of a course assignment, follow the assignment guidelines in developing your essay. However, if you have a choice, consider the medium that would be most appropriate for the type of review you are writing and the audience you intend to address:

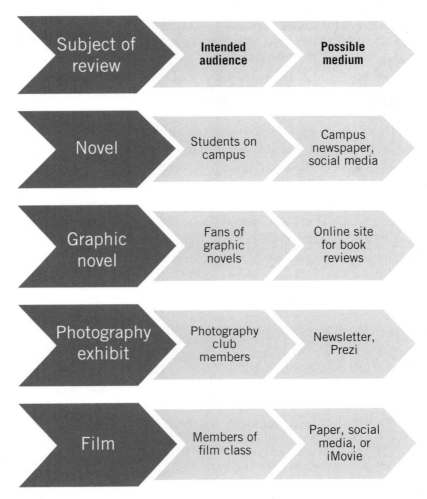

Subject of review	Intended audience	Possible medium
Novel	Students on campus	Campus newspaper, social media
Graphic novel	Fans of graphic novels	Online site for book reviews
Photography exhibit	Photography club members	Newsletter, Prezi
Film	Members of film class	Paper, social media, or iMovie

The medium you select should enable you to present your evaluation effectively to your intended audience but not limit your analysis of the subject. For example, a multimedia program such as iMovie might be a good choice for a film review because it would allow you to incorporate clips from the film. At the same time, an iMovie review might not be appropriate for an audience that typically reads reviews in print or on conventional newspaper websites.

Follow Step #3 in Chapter 3 to help you decide on the most appropriate medium for your textual analysis.

Step 4 Develop the main point of your review.

A review that simply passes judgment on its subject does not offer much for readers. Explaining that you liked an action movie because the chase scenes are exciting, for instance, leaves your readers with only a superficial sense of the film. A good review should provide more.

At this point, you might already have an opinion about the subject of your review (for example, you enjoyed the book you plan to review, you disliked the concert, you were disappointed in the film). The task now is to develop a main point that justifies or supports your opinion about your subject (keeping in mind that your opinion might change as you explore the subject). To do so, consider your rhetorical situation and the purpose(s) of your review.

Imagine that you are writing a review about popular media for an assignment in a communications course. For this assignment, you are to review a popular film, book, or television show that focuses in some way on new communications technologies; the general purpose of the assignment is to examine how modern technology is depicted in popular culture. You've selected the film *The Social Network* (2010), which tells the story of Harvard student Mark Zuckerberg and Facebook, the multi-billion-dollar social media company he created. You chose this film partly because you enjoyed it but also because it tells the story of one of the most important technology developments in recent decades. In addition, although you think the film is provocative, you see problems in the film's portrayal of social media.

Having selected a film for your review, consider what main claim you will make about the film:

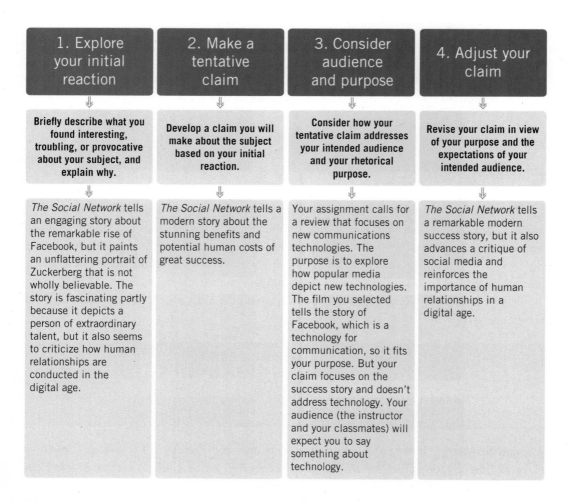

1. Explore your initial reaction	2. Make a tentative claim	3. Consider audience and purpose	4. Adjust your claim
Briefly describe what you found interesting, troubling, or provocative about your subject, and explain why.	Develop a claim you will make about the subject based on your initial reaction.	Consider how your tentative claim addresses your intended audience and your rhetorical purpose.	Revise your claim in view of your purpose and the expectations of your intended audience.
The Social Network tells an engaging story about the remarkable rise of Facebook, but it paints an unflattering portrait of Zuckerberg that is not wholly believable. The story is fascinating partly because it depicts a person of extraordinary talent, but it also seems to criticize how human relationships are conducted in the digital age.	*The Social Network* tells a modern story about the stunning benefits and potential human costs of great success.	Your assignment calls for a review that focuses on new communications technologies. The purpose is to explore how popular media depict new technologies. The film you selected tells the story of Facebook, which is a technology for communication, so it fits your purpose. But your claim focuses on the success story and doesn't address technology. Your audience (the instructor and your classmates) will expect you to say something about technology.	*The Social Network* tells a remarkable modern success story, but it also advances a critique of social media and reinforces the importance of human relationships in a digital age.

Whatever the subject of your review, follow these four steps to develop a tentative claim you will make in your review.

Your claim is the starting point for your Guiding Thesis Statement, which you should develop by completing Step #4 in Chapter 3.

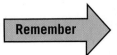 **Remember** Your claim is *tentative*. It can change as you explore the subject of your review and develop your evaluation of it.

Step 5 Support your claim through your evaluation of your subject.

As noted earlier in this chapter, effective evaluation rests on specific criteria. The first step in developing an evaluation that will support your claim, then, is to identify the criteria by which you will evaluate your subject. The second step is to apply those criteria to analyze your subject.

 **Remember** This process is both systematic and exploratory. Although you are analyzing your subject according to certain criteria, you are also learning about it. You might even change your mind about your subject, so be prepared to adjust your claim as you develop your evaluation of your subject.

Identify the Criteria for Evaluating Your Subject

The criteria for evaluating your subject depend upon the nature and purpose of your review and your rhetorical situation. Here are three examples:

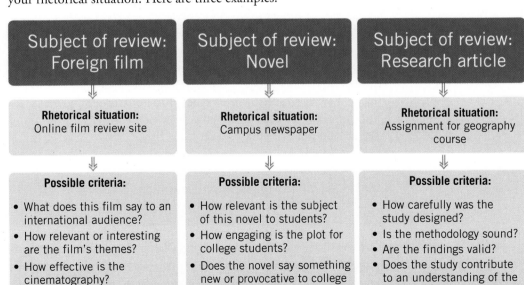

Subject of review: Foreign film	Subject of review: Novel	Subject of review: Research article
Rhetorical situation: Online film review site	**Rhetorical situation:** Campus newspaper	**Rhetorical situation:** Assignment for geography course
Possible criteria: • What does this film say to an international audience? • How relevant or interesting are the film's themes? • How effective is the cinematography?	**Possible criteria:** • How relevant is the subject of this novel to students? • How engaging is the plot for college students? • Does the novel say something new or provocative to college students?	**Possible criteria:** • How carefully was the study designed? • Is the methodology sound? • Are the findings valid? • Does the study contribute to an understanding of the subject?

In these examples, the criteria for evaluating the subject fit the rhetorical situation. If you are reviewing a novel for your campus newspaper, for example, you would consider whether other students at your college would find the subject of the novel relevant and the plot engaging. A review of a research article for a geography course would have more specific and technical criteria, as shown in the example. (See "What Criteria Should Be Applied?" on page 291.) It is also possible that your instructor will expect you to use certain criteria that have been examined in your course.

To determine the criteria that are appropriate for your review:

Consider audience expectations: Which criteria will your readers likely use in evaluating your subject? What standards will they expect you to apply?

⇓

Consider your purpose: Which criteria will help you evaluate your subject effectively in view of the purpose of your review?

⇓

Consider conventions for this kind of review: What kinds of criteria are usually applied in this kind of review? For example, what criteria do film reviewers typically use? What criteria do video gamers tend to use in reviewing video games?

List Your Criteria

Now make a list of the main criteria you will use to evaluate the subject of your review. (You can list these criteria in the form of questions, statements, or simply phrases.) Then complete these steps:

1. Review your list to identify the criteria that seem most appropriate for your rhetorical situation and the purpose of your review.

⇓

2. Eliminate criteria that seem irrelevant or less important.

⇓

3. Revise your list.

Evaluate Your Subject

Now apply your criteria to the subject of your review. Determine how well your subject meets each of your criteria. Continue to explore your subject in order to develop your evaluation fully.

For example:

- If you are examining how effectively a novel develops a specific theme, reread relevant passages where that theme emerges.

- If you are evaluating the methodology of a study described in a research report, reread the sections that describe the methodology and review the sections of your course textbook that discuss research methods.

- If you are evaluating the graphics of a new video game, replay portions of the game to examine the images more closely.

- If you are evaluating a director's technique in a new film, return to specific scenes that illustrate that technique.

Throughout this process, take notes and make necessary adjustments to your main claim.

Develop Your Evaluation

Work your way through your list of criteria, developing your evaluation of the subject for each item on your list. Your goal is to explore your subject as thoroughly as you can so that you not only develop your evaluation adequately but also generate sufficient evidence to support each assertion you make about your subject. For example, if you decide that the novel you are reviewing does not adequately develop one of its main themes, you should identify passages in the novel that support that assessment. Similarly, if you find the cinematography of the film you are reviewing especially effective, identify specific scenes in which the cinematography illustrates your claim.

Once you have explored your subject in this way, you should be ready to write a complete draft of your review. Step #5 in Chapter 3 will help you determine whether to move onto the next step before completing your draft.

Step 6   Organize your review.

There is no standard way to organize a review; however, because most reviews share a few key elements, it is possible to develop a basic outline, adjusting the outline to fit the needs of your rhetorical situation and the medium of your review. (Obviously, some media, such as a multimedia program like iMovie, might require different approaches to organizing your review.)

Most reviews include a statement of the purpose or reason for the review, a summary or description of what is being evaluated, and criteria for evaluating the subject. These three elements can form the basic structure for your review:

I. Introduction: includes a statement of the reason or purpose for the review as well as the occasion for the review.

II. Summary/Description of Subject: a summary of the book, film, play, or television show being reviewed; a description of the exhibit, performance, video game, or consumer item being evaluated.

III. Evaluation: analysis of the subject on the basis of the criteria being used for evaluation.

IV. Conclusion: conclusion(s) about the subject as a result of the evaluation.

Section III, which is the heart of the review, could be organized in a variety of ways depending upon the criteria you are using to evaluate your subject and the expectations for your specific rhetorical situation. For instance, let's return to the example of a review of the film *The Social Network* for a communications course.

Recall that the assignment asks for a review of a popular film, book, or television show that focuses in some way on new communications technologies. Your tentative claim is that *The Social Network* tells a story of remarkable success but also advances a critique of social media and reinforces the importance of human relationships in a digital age. Let's imagine that in developing your evaluation of the film to support that claim, you have identified three main criteria on which to base your evaluation:

■ the effectiveness of the narrative about Mark Zuckerberg and Facebook

■ the validity of the film's critique of technology and social media in particular

■ the development of the film's main themes (especially the theme of the importance of human relationships)

Notice that these criteria do not include anything related to the technical quality of the film, such as cinematography, or the quality of the acting. That's because the purpose of your review is to examine what the film might reveal about technology, not to evaluate the film as an artistic work. Given that purpose, you might order your three criteria from least to most important as follows:

1. the effectiveness of the narrative about Mark Zuckerberg and Facebook

2. the development of the theme about the importance of human relationships

3. the validity of the film's critique of technology and social media in particular

You might organize the third section of your review according to these three criteria. A general outline for your review might look like this:

I. Introduction

   A. Importance of *The Social Network*

   B. Purpose of review

   C. Statement of main claim about the film

II. Summary/Description of Subject

   A. Basic summary of the topic and plot of *The Social Network*

   B. Summary of important relationships depicted in the film

III. Evaluation

   A. Discussion of how well the film tells the story of Zuckerberg's efforts to establish Facebook

B. Evaluation of the film's depiction of key relationships

C. Evaluation of the film's critique of technology

IV. Conclusion

A. Conclusion about the effectiveness of the film's narrative and its depiction of human relationships

B. Conclusions about the film's critique of technology

Notice that your decisions about how to organize a review are driven by a sense of the rhetorical situation. Your review should be structured so that it addresses your audience and achieves your purpose. Step #6 in Chapter 3 provides additional guidance for deciding how to organize your project. If you haven't already completed a draft of your review, you should be ready to do so now.

Step 7   Get feedback.

Follow Step #7 in Chapter 3 to obtain useful feedback on your draft. In addition, ask your readers to consider the four main characteristics of analytical writing in their feedback on your review:

A relevant topic worthy of analysis	• Has the writer provided a sense of the purpose of the review? • Does the writer have something relevant to say about the subject of the review? • Has the writer established a context for reviewing this subject?
Complexity	• Is the evaluation of the subject thorough and substantive? • Does the review go beyond a simple judgment about the quality of the subject? • Does the writer's evaluation do justice to the subject?
Appropriate and sufficient support	• Does the writer summarize or describe the subject adequately for the rhetorical situation? • Are the criteria used for evaluating the subject appropriate? Are they applied effectively? • Does the writer's evaluation sufficiently support the claim(s) made about the subject of the review?
Reasonable conclusions	• Do the writer's conclusions grow logically from the evaluation of the subject? • Are the writer's conclusions persuasive and thought provoking? • Does the writer have a larger point to make?

Step 8   Revise.

Follow Step #8 in Chapter 3 to revise your draft. Use the questions listed in Step #7 in this chapter to guide your revisions.

 **Remember**

Revising is part of the process of exploring your subject and learning about it. As you complete Step #8 in Chapter 3, you might discover that you have to adjust your claim(s) about the subject of your review or delve more deeply into one or more sections of your evaluation.

Step 9   Refine your voice.

Often, reviews are characterized by strong opinions about the subject. The effectiveness of a review therefore depends largely on how well your opinion about the subject you are reviewing is supported by your evaluation. But your voice is also an important component of your review's effectiveness. It should be confident but not overbearing so that you sound authoritative without sounding unfair or overly critical. It is not unusual for reviews to be weakened by a writer's dismissive, arrogant voice or negative tone. Step #9 in Chapter 3 will help you avoid that problem.

Also, the readings in this chapter provide examples of reviews in which the writer's voice contributes to the effectiveness of the review. You might read other reviews of the subject you are evaluating to see how the writer's voice affects the review.

Step 10   Edit.

Complete Step #10 in Chapter 3.

WRITING PROJECTS   REVIEW AND EVALUATION

1. Select a book you have read that you believe is important for some reason. Write a review of that book for a specific audience that would be interested in that book. Alternatively, select a film or television show for your review.

2. Identify a current controversy on your campus or in your region that relates to a larger issue of importance. For example, your campus might be considering allowing its security officers to carry weapons, a measure that has caused controversy at some

colleges in part because it raises questions related to the ongoing controversy over gun control in the United States. Or your state might be considering new restrictions on drilling for natural gas because of environmental concerns. Once you've identified such a controversy, find several books or films related to the issue, and write a review of them. The focus of your review should be on how these books or films might illuminate the controversy on your campus or in your region.

3. Visit several websites related to an activity or issue in which you are interested, and review them for an audience who shares your interest. For example, many websites, such as WebMD and MayoClinic.com, focus on health and medical issues for consumers; there are numerous websites devoted to almost any recreational activity, such as running, hunting, cooking, knitting, and so on. Once you have selected the websites you intend to review, be sure to identify criteria for evaluating those websites that would be appropriate for your intended audience. Present your review as a website or blog post.

4. Identify a recent technological innovation, such as e-readers. Write a review of a recent version of this innovation for an audience who would be interested in it.

5. Many people use websites when planning vacations. Using online resources such as TripAdvisor, investigate a trip you would like to take. Read reviews of the place you wish to visit and plan a three-night/four-day trip that includes travel, sightseeing, meals, hotel/resort stay, and so on. Then write a synthesis of all of the reviews you found about the place you wish to visit.

Understanding
Argument
11

I HAVE A POLICY in my classes allowing students to challenge their grades on any writing assignment. But I tell them that if they believe the grade is unfair, they must explain why and make a case for a higher grade. They must present some kind of evidence or reasoning that the grade they received does not reflect the quality of their writing for that assignment. It is not enough, I tell them, to claim that they should be rewarded for working hard on the assignment. Show me why the essay deserves a higher grade, I tell them. In other words, make a valid and convincing argument.

Even if you have never challenged a grade on an assignment, you probably make informal arguments to support a position, defend an opinion, oppose a plan, or convince someone to do something:

- to explain why a band should be honored by the Rock and Roll Hall of Fame
- to justify a decision to pursue a particular major or attend a specific college
- to express your support for a political candidate
- to convince a roommate to move to a different apartment
- to support your decision to use a certain kind of smartphone

We routinely engage in informal argumentation as we make decisions about important matters, small or large, in our lives.

You have probably also made more formal kinds of arguments that involve specific kinds of writing. In a college application essay, for example, you try to convince the college admissions office that you deserved to be accepted into that school. Or perhaps you have written a letter to the editor of your campus newspaper in favor of a proposed new student center. In such cases, you are making an argument not only to take a stand on an issue (for example, to express support for the proposed student center because it will benefit students and help create a better campus community), but also to achieve a goal or work toward a particular outcome (for example, to help make the proposed student center a reality). Argument, then, is not simply a matter of stating and supporting a position; it is also a way to participate in discussions about important issues, to address complicated situations, and to solve problems. It is a central part of how we live together.

In academic disciplines, argument is an essential means by which ideas are explored and understanding is advanced (see "Argument vs. Persuasion"). Writing effective arguments is an important component of college-level academic work.

Often, we make arguments to try to persuade someone to adopt a point of view, agree to a proposition, or take a course of action. But the goal of argumentation is not necessarily to persuade. Especially in academic contexts, argument is intended to advance understanding. Persuasion, by contrast, does not attempt to engage an audience in a dialogue about an issue; rather, persuasion is an attempt to convince a reader to think or feel a certain way. The distinction is similar to the difference between an advertisement

intended to persuade consumers to purchase a specific product, such as this magazine ad for Cadillac, and one designed to present a point of view on an issue, such as this public service ad for recycling. The Cadillac ad seeks to persuade potential car buyers to purchase a Cadillac. By contrast, the public service ad can be seen as making an argument that recycling is worthwhile because it saves money; if it seeks to persuade viewers to act in a certain way (that is, to recycle), it does so by making a convincing argument that recycling is a good idea.

Occasions for Argument

We engage in argument for four main reasons:

- to solve a problem
- to assert a position
- to inquire into an issue or problem
- to prevail

Arguments to Solve a Problem

In much argumentation, the parties involved address a problem in which they have a shared interest. Let's return, for example, to my course policy of allowing my students to argue for a better grade on a writing assignment. A student's purpose in making such an argument is pretty clear: he or she wants to earn a good grade and demonstrate the ability to write the kind of essay required by the assignment. By the same token, as the instructor, I have an interest in seeing that the student can complete the assignment successfully. I also want the grades I assign to motivate students to develop their writing skills. So our purposes overlap, and we both have a stake in a positive outcome to the argument. Ultimately, "winning" the argument doesn't necessarily help us achieve that outcome. The student's argument, then, is part of an effort to resolve a problem: to assign a fair grade to an essay about which we seem to have different opinions. The argument for a better grade can result in our collaborative effort to reconsider how successfully the essay meets the assignment guidelines. In the process, the argument can be a way to help both of us better understand the essay so that it can be evaluated fairly.

The need to solve a problem is perhaps the most common occasion for making an argument:

- Community residents debate whether to increase property taxes to build a much-needed new school building.
- Members of a student organization decide whether to spend surplus funds on new equipment.
- Parents and school officials debate the best measures for increasing safety at their elementary school.

In each of these examples, the parties argue to solve a problem in which they all have a stake. The purpose of the argument is to achieve the best possible solution.

Arguments to Assert a Position

Some situations call for arguments in which the primary goal is to assert and justify a position:

- in a meeting of a student organization that is considering whether to boycott local stores that sell goods produced in sweatshops
- in a class discussion about legalizing gay marriage
- in a debate about whether to invite a controversial speaker to campus
- in a public forum to discuss whether to arm campus police

In such situations, many voices may be heard. To make an argument that asserts your position effectively can contribute to the discussion of important issues and help you gain credibility as a thoughtful participant. Your argument can also enhance others' understanding of an issue and influence what they think about it.

Arguments to Inquire

In arguments about complex issues, writers often try to discover the best of many possible answers to the question or problem at hand. In such cases, the primary purpose of the argument is to understand the issue better:

- A debate about a new general education requirement enables both supporters and opponents to delve into broader questions about the purposes of a college education.

- In a controversy about whether to publicize the evaluations of teachers in a local school district, participants examine whether such a measure would improve education for the students.

- A proposal to moderate comments posted to a popular social media site leads to a debate about free speech and ethical behavior in online forums.

In such situations, writers make arguments as part of a collaborative inquiry into the issues. In this kind of argument, the writer's position emerges through that inquiry. Through the process of developing an argument, the writer discovers the most reasonable position for himself or herself. Others might reach a different conclusion, because different people can have different but reasonable positions about complex issues. Because the writer isn't trying to win the debate, he or she examines many different viewpoints before arriving at a conclusion. The goal is to understand the issue and make an effective argument to share that understanding with interested others.

Arguments to Prevail

Sometimes, there is a compelling reason for winning an argument, and the writer's primary purpose is to prevail over opposing points of view. Such cases usually involve important and controversial issues that can have a big impact on those involved:

- Students make a strong case against allowing a controversial anti-immigrant organization to demonstrate on campus.

- Members of a law enforcement organization argue against the state's adoption of "stand your ground" self-defense laws, which they believe lead to more gun violence.

- A resident strenuously opposes a town bill restricting gas drilling on the grounds that it will deprive residents of much-needed income.

In such cases, the goal is not only to oppose something but to convince others to oppose it so that it doesn't happen. The writer of an argument in such situations believes strongly that his or her position is right.

Arguments to prevail should be undertaken with a strong sense of ethical responsibility (see "The Ethics of Argument"). Trying to defeat an opponent in an argument for the sake of winning serves little purpose and could have negative consequences for all parties. In some cases, however, the writer might conclude that the issue is such that the ends justify the means and making a forceful argument meant to prevail is not only ethical but also necessary.

FOCUS | **The Ethics of Argument**

Because argument has the power to persuade others to adopt a belief or take an action—often on matters of great importance—writers have a responsibility to engage in argumentation in an honorable manner. An argument should always be informed by a desire to seek truth or find a course of action that is morally justifiable—not to achieve self-serving, questionable, or illicit ends. An example of argument used for immoral purposes is Adolf Hitler's argument that anti-Jewish legislation in Germany in the 1930s was necessary to protect Germany from communism and to protect Jews from further persecution. But argument can be used for dubious purposes in much less dramatic contexts. For example, you might argue in favor of a proposed change in your major because the change will make it easier for you to graduate early, even though you believe that the change will weaken the curriculum and is probably not a good idea for most students. In such a case, you would be making a self-serving argument of questionable ethical merit. To make an ethical argument in such circumstances, you would have to acknowledge your own self-interest. In short, effective argument can be used for honorable or questionable purposes, even in school assignments. Always consider whether the argument you are making is not only sound but also ethical.

These four purposes for argument can overlap, of course. For example, in an argument to prevail, the writer usually asserts a position, and it is often necessary to inquire before you can solve a problem. So an argument can address several purposes at once. But understanding these four main purposes can help you construct arguments that effectively meet the needs of specific rhetorical situations.

EXERCISE 11A | EXPLORING OCCASIONS FOR ARGUMENT

1. Identify an issue or problem that you feel strongly about. It might be a national or international issue (a human rights issue, for example) or a local issue (a controversy on your campus or in your town). Write an informal statement explaining your position on the issue. Now consider three arguments you might make about the issue. Write a brief synopsis of each argument and explain why it matters to you.

2. Find an argument on a topic you care about in a newspaper, a blog post, a magazine article, a pamphlet, something you read in a course, or a YouTube video. Summarize the main argument. Now consider what makes the argument relevant to you and others. In a brief paragraph, describe what you believe was the writer's main purpose in making the argument.

(Continued)

Understanding Argument in College

Argumentation in college is primarily about learning. As a student, you will engage in argumentative writing not only to sharpen your writing and thinking skills but also to understand your subject better. In fact, research indicates that a majority of writing assignments in college require argument of some kind. In some academic disciplines, such as economics and related social sciences, *most* writing involves argumentation, and many common forms of writing in college, such as proposals and lab reports, are actually specialized forms of argumentation.

Because argument is an essential part of the process by which scholars examine, share, debate, and promote ideas, information, and opinions about important topics or developments in their fields, it is a primary vehicle for advancing knowledge. Not surprisingly, then, academic argumentation often takes the form of arguments to inquire. An assignment in a philosophy course, for example, might ask students to take a position on a classic philosophical issue, such as the nature of reality or truth. In such an assignment, the goal isn't to prove a point but to inquire deeply into a complex question that philosophers have debated for centuries. In doing so, students learn what philosophers say about such questions as they develop their own ideas about those questions; at the same time, students learn how to engage in philosophical inquiry and argumentation.

Although the purpose of most academic argumentation is inquiry, arguments in different academic disciplines can have different characteristics. For example, a philosopher relies on logical reasoning to support a proposition about the morality of capital punishment, whereas a criminologist draws on crime statistics to argue that capital punishment does not reduce violent crime. Writing effective academic arguments requires understanding the conventions that govern argumentation in the discipline in which you are writing. Although a philosopher and a criminologist might each make an argument about the same subject (capital punishment), they will make different kinds of claims, use different kinds of evidence, and present their arguments in different ways.

Despite these differences, all effective argumentative writing shares three essential characteristics:

■ a clear main point that is relevant for the academic discipline in which the writer is writing

■ appropriate support for claims

■ shared assumptions or premises as a basis for the main argument

The following examples illustrate these essential characteristics.

In the opening paragraphs of an essay titled "Why We Won't See Any Public Universities Going Private," education scholar John D. Wiley introduces his argument by identifying a relevant problem (reduced state funding for public universities) and a solution that others have proposed (turning public universities into private ones). Wiley then clearly states his main thesis: That solution won't work.

> All around the country the story is the same: States are reducing taxpayer support for public higher education, offsetting those reductions with higher tuition. Using Wisconsin as an example, Table 11.1 illustrates the changes over the last 25 years. In some states, the changes have been even more dramatic; in others, less so. But the trend is essentially universal. Furthermore, the impacts of these changes vary, even within one state. At UW-Madison (the flagship institution of the UW System), for example, state appropriations constituted 43.1 percent and tuition 10.5 percent of our budget in 1975. Today, those numbers are 19.5 and 15.7 percent, respectively. To make matters worse, nearly one-third of our state revenue comes to us with constraints requiring us to return it to the state for specific costs such as our share of the state utility bills, debt service, and mandatory payments to state agencies. Even if we were able to economize or find superior alternatives in any of those areas, we would not be able to reallocate the savings for other purposes. As a result, the state is providing only 13.5 percent of our base operating budget—the budget for hiring faculty and staff, and covering infrastructure and operating costs beyond debt service and utility bills. For the first time in the history of the institution, our students are contributing more to this portion of our operating budget than are the state taxpayers.

TABLE 11.1 The Changing Mix of State Funding and Tuition at the University of Wisconsin (UW) System over the Last 25 Years

	1974–1975	2004–2005
State appropriations for UW System per $1000 of personal income	$12.50	$5.50
State appropriations for UW System as a share of total state spending	11.5%	3.9%
State appropriations for UW System per FTE student (2004 dollars)	$10,600	$7,400
State appropriations for UW System as a percent of UW System budget	49.50%	26%
Tuition as a percent of UW System budget	12%	21%

Viewing these trends, many faculty, alumni, newspaper editors, and even legislators have urged us to consider "going private." By that, they have in mind that we could agree to forego all state support in our base operating budget and rely on increased tuition, coupled with some unspecified amount of additional student financial aid (what they assume to be "the private model" of high tuition and high financial aid) for ongoing operations. These views are often expressed in terms of a comparison: "You're way underpriced at a resident tuition of $6000/year. I'm paying three times that for my daughter's tuition (at a private school), and the education she's getting is certainly not three times better. Even if you simply doubled your tuition, you would still be a bargain, and you would replace nearly all state funds. What's the problem?" Quite aside from political considerations (unwillingness of state to "let go" of prior investments and ongoing oversight), the larger problem is that the "private model," properly understood, simply cannot be scaled up to the extent required. It's a matter of simple arithmetic, and the numbers just don't work!

Source: Wiley, John D. "Why We Won't See Any Public Universities Going Private." *What's Happening to Public Higher Education?* Ed. Ronald G. Ehrenberg. American Council on Education/Praeger, 2006. 327–328. Print.

In setting up his argument, Wiley makes two important moves. First, he places his argument in the context of current debates about the rising cost of college. In doing so, Wiley establishes that his topic is one that his readers (other education scholars as well as policymakers and interested citizens) are likely to find relevant. Second, he supports his claims with evidence that his readers are likely to find appropriate and persuasive. Wiley claims that public support for higher education has diminished dramatically in the past three decades, and he cites statistical evidence to show the reduction in public funding for higher education, using Wisconsin as an example of a national trend.

Wiley's argument is a good example of an academic argument whose main purpose is to inquire into a complex and important issue. The next excerpt is also an argument whose primary purpose is to inquire into a complex educational issue—in this case, whether raising educational standards actually improves student learning. In making their argument, the authors address a well-established problem in education: the challenge of improving learning for all students. Specifically, they examine whether formative assessment—that is, assessment designed to help students learn rather than to measure how much they have learned—can result in higher educational standards for students. Like the previous example, this argument is addressed to an academic audience (education researchers) as well as a wider audience (policymakers, politicians, and the interested public). In this excerpt, which is taken from a longer essay published in a leading education journal called the *Phi Delta Kappan*, the authors introduce their main claims, summarize their argument, and explain the evidence they will present to support their claims:

> We start from the self-evident proposition that teaching and learning must be interactive. Teachers need to know about their pupils' progress and difficulties with learning so that they can adapt their own work to meet pupils' needs—needs that are often unpredictable and that vary from one pupil to another. Teachers can find out what they need to know in a variety of ways, including observation and discussion in the classroom and the reading of pupils' written work....
>
> There is nothing new about any of this. All teachers make assessments in every class they teach. But there are three important questions about this process that we seek to answer:
>
> - Is there evidence that improving formative assessment raises standards?
> - Is there evidence that there is room for improvement?
> - Is there evidence about how to improve formative assessment?
>
> In setting out to answer these questions, we have conducted an extensive survey of the research literature. We have checked through many books and through the past nine years' worth of issues of more than 160 journals, and we have studied earlier reviews of research. This process yielded about 580 articles or chapters to study. We prepared a lengthy review, using material from 250 of these sources, that has been published in a special issue of the journal *Assessment in Education,* together with comments on our work by leading educational experts from Australia, Switzerland, Hong Kong, Lesotho, and the U.S.
>
> The conclusion we have reached from our research review is that the answer to each of the three questions above is clearly yes. In the three main sections below, we outline the nature and force of the evidence that justifies this conclusion. However, because we are presenting a summary here, our text will appear strong on assertions and weak on the details of their justification. We maintain that these assertions are backed by evidence and that this backing is set out in full detail in the lengthy review on which this article is founded.
>
> We believe that the three sections below establish a strong case that governments, their agencies, school authorities, and the teaching profession should study very carefully whether they are seriously interested in raising standards in education. However, we also acknowledge widespread evidence that fundamental change in education can be achieved only slowly—through programs of professional development that build on existing good practice. Thus we do not conclude that formative assessment is yet another "magic bullet" for education. The issues involved are too complex and too closely linked to both the difficulties of classroom practice and the beliefs that drive public policy. In a final section, we confront this complexity and try to sketch out a strategy for acting on our evidence.

Source: Black, Paul, and Dylan Wiliam. "Inside the Black Box: Raising Standards Through Classroom Assessment." *Phi Delta Kappan* 80.1 (1998): 138. Print.

Notice that the authors rest their main argument on the "proposition that teaching and learning must be interactive," a premise that their readers are likely to accept. In effective argumentation, writers must establish clear premises from which to make their arguments, thereby identifying key assumptions or beliefs that they share with their readers as a basis for their argument.

In the following section, we will examine how to construct arguments that have these three essential characteristics to meet the needs of specific rhetorical situations.

EXERCISE 11B   EXPLORING ACADEMIC ARGUMENT

For each of the following excerpts, identify (a) the main point and (b) the evidence or support provided for the author's claims. The first excerpt is taken from an essay about gun control written soon after a gunman seriously wounded U.S. Congresswoman Gabrielle Giffords and killed others attending a political rally in Arizona in 2011. The second is from a report issued by an environmental organization about the growth of the local food movement. How well do you think the authors of the excerpts present and support their claims? Cite specific passages from the excerpts to support your answers.

a). Against the horrific backdrop of the Tucson, Arizona, tragedy, new gun control proposals are on the way. Some of our legislators will be tempted to apply Rahm Emanuel's aphorism, "Never let a good crisis go to waste." For example, Rep. Carolyn McCarthy, D-New York, wants to outlaw magazines with more than 10 rounds—even those already in circulation. She hasn't explained how a ban on previously sold magazines would deter anyone but law-abiding citizens.

Still, the Supreme Court has suggested that sensible gun regulations may be constitutionally permissible. Sensible is not, however, what we have in Washington, Chicago, New York and other cities, where you can probably get a pizza delivery before a response from a 911 call. Police cannot be everywhere.... A regulation must be effective in promoting public safety, when weighed against reliable evidence that past restrictions have not lessened the incidence of gun-related crimes.

Recall that Washington banned handguns for 33 years; during some of those years the city was known as the nation's murder capital. Killers not deterred by laws against murder were not deterred by laws against owning guns. Moreover, anti-gun regulations did not address the deep-rooted causes of violent crime—illegitimacy, drugs, alcohol abuse and dysfunctional schools—much less mental instability.

In 2004, the National Academy of Sciences reviewed 253 journal articles, 99 books and 43 government publications evaluating 80 gun-control measures. Researchers could not identify a single regulation that reduced violent crime, suicide or accidents. A year earlier, the Centers for Disease Control reported on ammunition bans, restrictions on acquisition, waiting periods, registration, licensing, child access prevention and zero tolerance laws. CDC's conclusion: There was no conclusive evidence that the laws reduced gun violence.

So much for the quasi-religious faith that more controls mean fewer murders. There are about 500,000 gun-related crimes annually in the United States. Further, Americans own roughly 250 million guns. Assuming a different gun is used in each of the 500,000 crimes, only 0.2% of guns are involved in crime each year. A ban on firearms would be 99.8% over-inclusive.

Source: Levy, Robert A. "Gun Control Measures Don't Stop Violence." *Cato Institute*. CNN.com. 19 Jan. 2011. Web. 26 Apr. 2013.

b). The system of long-distance food supply has now become the norm in much of the United States and the rest of the world. Apples in Des Moines supermarkets are from China, even though there are apple farmers in Iowa; potatoes in Lima's supermarkets are from the United States, even though Peru boasts more varieties of potato than any other country. Today, our food travels farther than ever before, often thousands of kilometers. The value of international trade in food has tripled since 1961, while the tonnage of food shipped between countries has grown fourfold, during a time when the human population only doubled. (See Figures 1 and 2.)

FIGURE 1

Value of World Agricultural Trade, 1961–2000

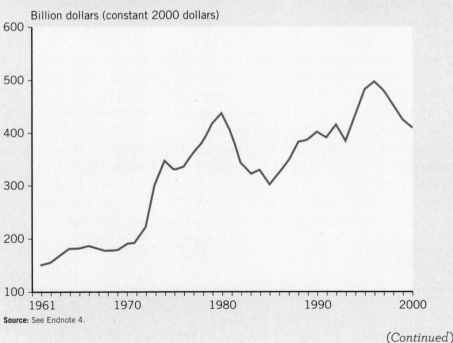

Source: See Endnote 4.

(Continued)

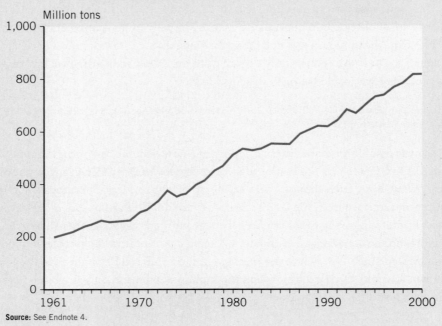

FIGURE 2

Volume of World Agricultural Trade, 1961–2000

Million tons

Source: See Endnote 4.

But, as with many trends that carry serious social and ecological consequences, the long-distance food habit is slowly beginning to weaken, under the
influence of a young, but surging, local foods movement in the Midatlantic and
elsewhere. Politicians and voters in the counties surrounding Washington, D.C.,
have supported aggressive measures to protect farmland using tax credits, conservation easements, and greater emphasis on mass transit. Some of this interest is
inspired by the desire to preserve the beauty of the countryside, but the campaign
to preserve local farmland also rests on the assumption that farmers connected
to a community are likely to farm more responsibly. Accokeek Ecosystem Farm, a
seven-acre certified organic farm located on the Potomac River in southern Maryland, not only produces food for a weekly food subscription service for almost 90
families (and has started a waiting list because demand is so great), but plays a
role in protecting the Chesapeake watershed (farmland holds more water than
sprawling subdivisions) and keeping agrochemicals out of the Bay.

Source: Halweil, Brian. *Home Grown: The Case for Local Food in a Global Market.* World Watch
Institute, 2002. Print.

Making Arguments

To make an effective argument, you must examine the issue sufficiently so that you understand it well, which often requires research. You must also

- develop a main argument that is appropriate for your rhetorical situation
- make an appeal that is likely to be persuasive for your intended audience
- support your claims with appropriate evidence or reasoning
- adopt a format and style appropriate for the rhetorical situation and the medium you are using

Developing a Main Argument

Core Concept #4—a writer must have something to say—is especially true in argument. As you explore your topic and the issues related to it, you must develop a clear main argument. However, your main argument is not the same as your position on an issue.

For example, let's imagine that you and several other residents of your college dormitory are concerned about new security measures that the college is considering because of recent incidents involving intruders in campus dorms. The proposed measures include prohibiting students from having visitors in their dorms except during specified hours. You and your dorm mates have decided to write a letter to the director of residential life urging her not to implement the new security measures. You hope to convince her that the measures would significantly restrict students' social activities without enhancing campus security. Your **topic**, then, is campus security. The **question** is whether the campus needs the proposed measures to improve security. You may be opposed to the proposed security measures, but that isn't your main argument; that's your **position**. You still need to identify the main argument you will make to reflect your position:

Topic
Campus security

Problem or Question
Does the campus need new security measures for dormitories to protect students?

Your Position
Opposed to proposed campus security policies

Your Main Argument
Proposed security measures will restrict students unnecessarily without improving the safety of the dorms.

Your main argument might evolve as you explore your topic and learn more about the issues at hand.

Keep in mind that your main argument is intended to help you achieve a specific goal. In arguing against proposed campus security measures, for example, you not only want to assert a clear position in opposition to the measures, but you also hope to persuade the director of residential life to reconsider those measures and perhaps to make them less restrictive without compromising security. In addition, you hope your argument will win the support of other students who live in the dorms. So the argument must not only state the writer's opposition to the security measures; it must also present a persuasive case that those measures will not achieve the goal of improving security on campus, which is a goal that everyone—the students as well as the residential life director—supports.

EXERCISE 11C   DEVELOPING A MAIN ARGUMENT

1. Identify three issues that you feel strongly about. For each one, write a brief paragraph explaining your position on the issue and describing a main argument that you might make to support that position.

2. Find two or three arguments about the same topic—for example, arguments for or against gun control. Write a brief synopsis for each one that includes a statement of the writer's main argument. Compare the arguments, examining how each writer takes a stance on the issue and develops his or her main argument.

3. Think of two or three changes you would like to see on your campus. Now write a letter to your college president to argue in favor of these changes. Develop a main argument for each change you would like to see.

Considering the Rhetorical Situation

An effective argument must meet the needs of the rhetorical situation. In opposing the proposed security measures for the campus dormitories, for example, you would develop your main argument and supporting claims in a way that takes into account the interests and positions of the intended audience—in this case, the director of residential life and other students on campus. As you develop your argument, then, identify what you know about your audience in that situation by addressing the following questions:

■ **What is your audience likely to know about this topic or situation?** Although you can't know exactly what your audience knows, you can make reasonable assumptions to help you develop an appropriate argument. For example, the residential life director will certainly understand what is involved in keeping campus dorms safe and secure. You wouldn't have to explain to her how the restrictions would work, but she might not fully appreciate what they would mean for students.

■ **What is the audience's interest or stake in the issue?** Your audience might not always have the same level of interest in the issue you're addressing, but identifying why they would be interested can help you identify potentially persuasive points and find common ground. For example, the residential life director obviously has a direct stake in the situation because she is responsible for the campus dorms. Other students also have a stake in a livable, safe campus. Those interests can help you decide how to develop and present your argument so that you address shared concerns and acknowledge common ground.

■ **What does your audience expect?** The residential life director would probably expect a thoughtful letter that acknowledges the importance of safe dorms. She would be less inclined to take your argument seriously if you did not show a reasonable understanding of the situation or if you dismissed her concerns. She would also likely expect a well-written letter that has a respectful tone, even if it makes a strong argument against her position.

Exploring your audience in this way can help you identify claims that are likely to be acceptable to audience members as well as arguments they might reject.

Sometimes, a writer knows that some readers will almost certainly reject a specific argument, especially when the topic is controversial, such as gun control or capital punishment.

Writing about such issues requires care in considering audience, and the writer should assume that some readers will be skeptical. But rather than dismiss the views of a skeptical or even hostile audience, consider their reasons for opposing your viewpoint and try to address their concerns in your argument.

FOCUS   **Do You Have to Win the Argument?**

In theory, an effective argument persuades an audience to accept a proposition, adopt a position, or take a course of action. In reality, an argument can achieve its purpose without necessarily persuading readers to adopt the writer's position, especially when it comes to issues about which people have strong views. For example, imagine that your state legislature is considering a controversial ban on certain kinds of firearms. Citizens support or oppose the ban depending on their opinions about gun control. An argument against the ban is unlikely to change the minds of those who support it, but it might influence the discussion. Because both supporters and opponents agree that lowering crime rates is desirable, an argument that the ban is likely to reduce violent crime would probably interest all parties in the debate. The goal is to contribute to the debate and influence how others think about the issue.

EXERCISE 11D   CONSIDERING THE RHETORICAL SITUATION

1. Take the paragraphs you wrote for Exercise #11C1 and identify an appropriate audience for each argument. Briefly describe that audience and the most important characteristics that might influence the argument you would make for that audience.

2. Find a published argument that you agree with on a topic that matters to you and imagine rewriting it for a different audience. For example, if the argument was published in your campus newspaper, imagine rewriting it for a community website in your hometown. What changes would you have to make to that argument? Why?

3. Imagine writing an argument about a controversial topic for an audience who opposes your position. First, identify a topic that interests you and summarize your position. Next, summarize the opposing position. Finally, identify two or three arguments that might appeal to that audience, trying to find common ground on the issue.

Making a Persuasive Appeal

Even if the main purpose of an argument is not necessarily to persuade readers, writers use persuasive appeals to strengthen an argument. Classical rhetorical theory identifies three modes of persuasion, or kinds of appeals:

- **ethical,** or arguments based on the writer's or speaker's character
- **emotional,** or arguments that appeal to the emotions
- **logical,** or arguments based on reason and evidence

Most academic arguments rely on logical appeals, but even in academic arguments writers often employ all three modes of persuasion in some way.

Ethical Appeals, or Appeals Based on Character. Writers often try to strengthen their arguments by presenting themselves as reliable and trustworthy experts on the topic at hand. For example, in making an argument about a proposed mental health policy, a psychiatrist might emphasize her expertise in working with patients suffering from depression, presenting herself as someone with the appropriate knowledge and experience to understand the issue. Sometimes, a writer will rest an argument on his or her good judgment or integrity, such as when a person presents himself as a nurturing parent in making an argument about child care regulations. In ethical appeals, then, the writer's character, expertise, identity, or experience is a primary reason that the argument is persuasive.

Ethical appeals are common in advertising. Corporations use celebrities to represent them or their products—for example, former basketball star Michael Jordan for Nike shoes (see "Ethical Appeals in Advertising"). The suggestion is that if a world-class athlete endorses this product, it must be good. Ethical appeals are also important in law and politics. Political candidates, for example, present themselves as loving family members or successful in business as a way to make their appeal to voters more persuasive. Conversely, candidates often question their opponents' credibility, suggesting that the opponent cannot be trusted to make the right decisions on important issues.

SIDEBAR ETHICAL APPEALS IN ADVERTISING

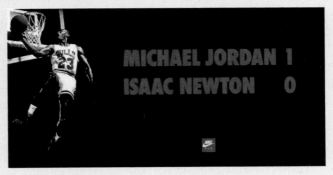

This classic ad for Nike shoes focuses on an image of basketball star Michal Jordan's athletic prowess. What argument does the ad make? How might you describe its ethical appeal?

Courtesy of The Advertising Archives

In the following passage, journalist Barbara Ehrenreich uses her own first-hand experiences to support her argument that life has become more difficult for low-wage American workers. As a college professor, Ehrenreich was an expert on issues related to the working poor, but her best-selling 2001 book *Nickel and Dimed: On (Not) Getting By in America*, in which she described her experiences trying to make a living by working at low-wage jobs, helped establish her as an authority for a larger audience. In this excerpt from a 2011 essay about how the so-called Great Recession of 2008 affected America's poor, Ehrenreich refers to her experiences as a low-wage earner to supplement the statistical evidence she presents:

> At the time I wrote *Nickel and Dimed,* I wasn't sure how many people it directly applied to—only that the official definition of poverty was way off the mark, since it defined an individual earning $7 an hour, as I did on average, as well out of poverty. But three months after the book was published, the Economic Policy Institute in Washington, D.C., issued a report entitled "Hardships in America: The Real Story of Working Families," which found an astounding 29% of American families living in what could be more reasonably defined as poverty, meaning that they earned less than a barebones budget covering housing, child care, health care, food, transportation, and taxes—though not, it should be noted, any entertainment, meals out, cable TV, Internet service, vacations, or holiday gifts. Twenty-nine percent is a minority, but not a reassuringly small one, and other studies in the early 2000s came up with similar figures.
>
> The big question, 10 years later, is whether things have improved or worsened for those in the bottom third of the income distribution, the people who clean hotel rooms, work in warehouses, wash dishes in restaurants, care for the very young and very old, and keep the shelves stocked in our stores. The short answer is that things have gotten much worse, especially since the economic downturn that began in 2008.

Source: Ehrenreich, Barbara. "On Turning Poverty into an American Crime." *Huffington Post.* 9 Aug. 2011. Web. 26 Apr. 2013.

Here Ehrenreich tries to strengthen her argument by invoking her credibility as an authority on the working poor. She provides statistical evidence to support her claim that "things have gotten much worse" for poor Americans in the ten years since her book was published, but she also makes an ethical appeal on the basis of her experience and knowledge about this issue.

Ethical appeals are most effective when they meet the needs of the rhetorical situation, and writers will often present themselves strategically for an intended audience. For example, in making her argument for a general audience—say, readers of a large-circulation newspaper like *USA Today*—Ehrenreich might emphasize her experience in low-wage jobs to establish her credibility, but in an argument published in a scholarly journal, she might rely on her academic credentials. (See "More on Ethical Appeals" in Chapter 8.)

Although ethical appeals usually rest on the *writer's* character, writers sometimes try to strengthen their arguments by relying on someone else's expertise or character. In the following excerpt from an essay about school reform, columnist David Brooks rests part of his argument on the experience and expertise of the director of a charter school called the New American Academy:

> The New American Academy is led by Shimon Waronker, who grew up speaking Spanish in South America, became a U.S. Army intelligence officer, became an increasingly observant Jew, studied at yeshiva, joined the Chabad-Lubavitch movement, became a public schoolteacher and then studied at the New York City Leadership Academy, which Mayor Michael Bloomberg and the former New York Schools chancellor, Joel Klein, founded to train promising school principal candidates.
>
> At first, he had trouble getting a principal's job because people weren't sure how a guy with a beard, kippa and a black suit would do in overwhelmingly minority schools. But he revitalized one of the most violent junior high schools in the South Bronx and with the strong backing of both Klein and Randi Weingarten, the president of the teachers' union, he was able to found his brainchild, The New American Academy.
>
> He has a grand theory to transform American education, which he developed with others at the Harvard School of Education.

Source: Brooks, David. "The Relationship School." *The New York Times*. The New York Times, 23 Mar. 2012. Web. 26 Apr. 2013.

In this case, Brooks argues in favor of a specific approach to school reform in part because it is endorsed by Shimon Waronker, who, Brooks suggests, has the right experience to understand what is needed to make schools work. Brooks establishes Waronker's credibility as an expert whose approach is supported by several prominent people (for example, Joel Klein, the former chancellor of New York City schools), as someone who has studied at Harvard, and as a former intelligence officer in the U.S. Army. In this way, Brooks uses an ethical appeal to support his main argument. Writers can also call someone's credibility into question to help support their argument. For example, in arguing against a proposed school reform endorsed by a politician, a writer might point out that the politician's previous school reform efforts have failed, thus undermining the politician's credibility.

You can use ethical appeals in these same ways. For example, if you are writing an argument about the minimum wage, you might use your own work experience to help support your claims. However, for most academic assignments, you will establish your credibility primarily by demonstrating your command of the issues and knowledge of your topic.

Pathetic Appeals, or Appeals to Emotion. Appealing to readers' emotions is common in argument because it can be so effective. But because emotional appeals can be so powerful, they carry risk as well as potential reward.

No argument is completely devoid of emotional appeal, but some arguments rely on emotions more than others do. Here is part of an essay about the disappearance of migratory songbirds in which the author's primary appeal is emotional:

> Lately I have been sitting with the brooding knowledge that at least 7 million migrating songbirds were killed this spring running the gauntlet of 84,000 American

communication towers that rise as high as 2,000 feet into the sky, braced by invisible guy wires that garrote the birds right out of the air.

This is actually just a fraction of the number of birds killed each year by running a collision course with human activity.

This spring has been more silent than ever. The traditional dawn chorus of birdsong has ebbed to a few lonely little souls, most belonging to non-migratory species like cardinals, bluejays, chickadees and sparrows.

They say that when Europeans first arrived on this continent, the migration of the passenger pigeons would literally darken the sky for minutes on end.

I have never seen a living passenger pigeon, and it seems that my grandchildren will not know what I mean when I talk about the dawn chorus of riotously busy, happy birdsong, any more than they will be able to imagine an apple orchard in full bloom buzzing with the diligent harvest of a million droning bees.

Knowledge like this makes me sick at heart. My rational side is aware that mourning is not productive, but another side of me knows that it is one of the special gifts of us humans to feel grief; to locate particular sadnesses in the larger landscape of suffering; and to use our sadness and anger at injustice as a lightening rod for change.

Other animals and birds feel grief as well, but you won't find the great community of birds gathering together to make plans to topple all the communication towers in North America.

No, the birds will go quietly, one by one, into the endless night of extinction.

Source: Browdy de Hernandez, Jennifer. "Stop the Holocaust of Migrating Birds." *Common Dreams*. Common Dreams. 29 Apr. 2012. Web. 26 Apr. 2013.

In setting up her argument in favor of protecting migratory birds, many of which die in collisions with structures like towers and skyscrapers, Jennifer Browdy de Hernandez relies almost entirely on an emotional appeal. Her choice of language is intended to provoke sympathy and even outrage about the plight of migratory birds: "The traditional dawn chorus of birdsong has ebbed to a few lonely little souls"; the birds "run the gauntlet" of human construction and fly into guy wires that "garrote" them. By inciting readers' emotions with such language, Browdy de Hernandez tries to make readers more sympathetic to her argument. (Even the photograph that accompanies the essay, which depicts a beautiful bird singing its song, can evoke strong sympathies for songbirds.)

Often, emotional appeals are more subtle. In the following excerpt from an essay about the controversial Affordable Care Act that became law in 2010, U.S. Secretary of Health and

Human Services Kathleen Sebelius strategically employs emotional appeals to make her argument more persuasive:

> Two years ago, President Obama signed the Affordable Care Act. The President's health care law gives hard working, middle-class families security, makes Medicare stronger, and puts more money back in seniors' pockets.
>
> Prior to 2011, people on Medicare faced paying for preventive benefits like cancer screenings and cholesterol checks out of their own pockets. Now, these benefits are offered free of charge to beneficiaries.
>
> Over time, the health reform law also closes the gap in prescription drug coverage, known as the "donut hole." This helps seniors like Helen Rayon: "I am a grandmother who is trying to assist a grandson with his education. I take seven different medications. Getting the donut hole closed, that gives me a little more money in my pocket."
>
> In 2010, those who hit the donut hole received a $250 rebate—with almost 4 million seniors and people with disabilities receiving a collective $1 billion. In 2011, people on Medicare automatically received a 50 percent discount on brand-name drugs in the donut hole. Over 3.6 million beneficiaries received more than $2.1 billion in savings—averaging $604 per person last year.

Source: Sebelius, Kathleen. "The Affordable Health Care Act: Strong Benefits to Seniors, Billions in Savings This Year." *The Huffington Post*. TheHuffingtonPost.com, 29 Apr. 2012. Web. 26 Apr. 2013.

Here Sebelius appeals to her readers' sense of fairness by invoking sympathetic images—for example, of "hard working, middle-class families" and "a grandmother who is trying to assist a grandson with his education"—that are likely to make readers more inclined to consider her argument. Notice that Sebelius doesn't rely exclusively on emotional appeals, however; she also cites statistical evidence to support her claims. Her essay illustrates how emotional appeals can be woven effectively into an argument.

Logical Appeals, or Appeals to Reason. Because reason is often assumed to be superior to emotion when it comes to argumentation, rational arguments are often considered more valid than openly emotional ones. Of course, reason can never be completely separated from emotion, so audiences rarely react to logical arguments in a way that is devoid of emotion. Nevertheless, logic is an essential component of argumentation, and even arguments that appeal to emotion or character usually incorporate reasoning. The most common forms of logical reasoning are *inductive reasoning* and *deductive reasoning*. (Patterns of organizing an argument based on inductive or deductive reasoning are reviewed later in this chapter; here the nature of inductive and deductive reasoning is discussed.)

Inductive Reasoning. In induction, a conclusion is drawn from specific evidence. This type of reasoning is common in daily life. For example, you might conclude that bicycles have become more popular among students on your campus because you have noticed more students riding bicycles and several new bicycle racks have been added to the campus. On the basis of this evidence, you might reasonably conclude, or induce, that bicycles have become more popular.

Inductive reasoning is common in academic arguments, in which logical conclusions are reached on the basis of available evidence. The specific kinds of evidence and conventions governing inductive argument might differ from one academic discipline to another, but the basic approach is the same: reasoning from evidence.

Here's an example of a writer using inductive reasoning to make an argument about the value of a college education. In this excerpt from an essay titled "College Is Still Worth It," Mark Yzaguirre presents data about the impact of a college degree on a person's earnings and socioeconomic status:

> Recently, the Pew Charitable Trusts came out with a report that supports what many of us have been saying to critics of higher education: While the system has its problems, by and large those with college degrees are better off than those without them, even during the recent economic turmoil.
>
> The Pew report makes several basic points that should be mentioned anytime someone claims that higher education isn't a good investment:
>
> - Although all 21–24-year-olds experienced declines in employment and wages during the recession, the decline was considerably more severe for those with only high school or associate degrees.
>
> - The comparatively high employment rate of recent college graduates was not driven by a sharp increase in those settling for lesser jobs or lower wages.
>
> - The share of non-working graduates seeking further education did not change markedly during the recession.
>
> - Out-of-work college graduates were able to find jobs during the downturn with more success than their less-educated counterparts.

These aren't trivial observations and they now have even more statistical support than before. The general economic benefits of getting a degree are still pretty clear. That doesn't mean that any college degree plan is a good one and any sensible approach to higher education, whether at the undergraduate or graduate level, should include a clear-eyed analysis of what one is likely to pay to and receive from a given school....

It is simplistic and false to claim that more education always leads to more income or better job opportunities. It is also correct to point out that excessive student loan debt is a terrible burden that may not be justifiable for certain schools or fields of study. But that doesn't mean that it's good advice to tell young people who want to go to college and who are prepared to do so that they shouldn't do so because it's not worth the time or the price. Those with college degrees are still more likely to be employed than those without them and their prospects aren't bleak. While the phrase *caveat emptor* is a necessary one to consider in picking colleges and degree programs, the Great Recession shouldn't claim the idea that higher education is a ticket to a better future as one of its victims.

Source: Yzaguirre, Mark. "College Is Still Worth It." *The Huffington Post*. TheHuffingtonPost.com, 16 Jan. 2013. Web. 26 Apr. 2013.

Yzaguirre concludes that college is worthwhile on the basis of his evidence. He reasons inductively to arrive at that conclusion. Notice, though, that he qualifies his conclusion by saying that "it is simplistic and false to claim that more education always leads to more income or better job opportunities." In other words, the evidence allows him to conclude that, in general, college is worth the cost, but that evidence does *not* allow him to conclude that college is worth the cost for every student. Yzaguirre's care in drawing conclusions that logically follow from his evidence reminds us of one of the challenges of inductive reasoning: identifying evidence that isn't flawed, biased, or limited in some way. If the evidence is problematic, the conclusion will likely be questionable, rendering the argument weak, no matter how careful the reasoning.

Deductive Reasoning. Deductive reasoning begins with a generalization, called a **premise**, and leads to a conclusion that follows logically from that generalization. The premise is the foundation for the argument. Typically, deductive reasoning is effective when the issue involves a basic principle or belief. For example, arguments against capital punishment often rest on the principle that all human life is sacred. That principle becomes the major premise, and the argument is constructed logically from that premise:

> **Major premise:** Taking a human life is immoral.
>
> **Minor premise:** Capital punishment is the willful taking of human life.
>
> **Conclusion:** Capital punishment is immoral.

Evidence can still be cited in support of the argument, but the strength of the argument rests on the main premise and the reasoning that leads to the conclusion.

In the following example, writer Malcolm Gladwell challenges a widespread view of media with a deductive argument. Gladwell questions the claim that social media are the key factor in recent modern uprisings against unpopular governments, such as those that occurred in eastern Europe in 2009 and (after his article was published) in Algeria, Egypt, and Libya during the "Arab Spring" of 2011. To make his argument, Gladwell compares these revolutions to other activist movements,

AP Photo/GENE HERRICK

including the famous "Freedom Summer" protests in Mississippi in 1964, in which three volunteers—Michael Schwerner, James Chaney, and Andrew Goodman—were murdered, many black churches were set on fire, and hundreds of volunteers were beaten, shot at, and arrested. "A quarter of those in the program dropped out," Gladwell notes. "Activism that challenges the status quo—that attacks deeply rooted problems—is not for the faint of heart." What makes people capable of this kind of activism? he asks. He then gets to the basis of his argument, which is his main premise: High-risk activism "is a strong-tie phenomenon." In other words, this kind of activism depends on a strong connection to the movement. Gladwell supports this premise by referring to a study of the Freedom Summer participants indicating that what kept people involved in such a dangerous movement was their "degree of personal connection to the civil-rights movement." Then he works from this premise to argue that current movements that rely on social media are not the same as previous movements like the Freedom Summer:

> The platforms of social media are built around weak ties. Twitter is a way of following (or being followed by) people you may never have met. Facebook is a tool for efficiently managing your acquaintances, for keeping up with the people you would not otherwise be able to stay in touch with. That's why you can have a thousand "friends" on Facebook, as you never could in real life.
>
> This is in many ways a wonderful thing. There is strength in weak ties, as the sociologist Mark Granovetter has observed … But weak ties seldom lead to high-risk activism….
>
> Boycotts and sit-ins and nonviolent confrontations—which were the weapons of choice for the civil-rights movement—are high-risk strategies. They leave little room for conflict and error. The moment even one protester deviates from the script and responds to provocation, the moral legitimacy of the entire protest is compromised. Enthusiasts for social media would no doubt have us believe that King's task in Birmingham would have been made infinitely easier had he been able to communicate with his followers through Facebook, and contented himself with tweets from a Birmingham jail. But networks are messy: think of the ceaseless pattern of correction and revision, amendment and debate, that characterizes Wikipedia. If Martin Luther King, Jr., had tried to do a wiki-boycott in Montgomery, he would have been steamrollered by the white power structure. And of what use would a digital communication tool be in a town where ninety-eight per cent of the black community could be reached every Sunday morning at church? The things that King needed in Birmingham—discipline and strategy—were things that online social media cannot provide.

Source: Gladwell, Malcolm. "Small Change: Why the Revolution Will Not Be Tweeted." *The New Yorker*. The New Yorker, 4 Oct. 2010. Web. 26 Apr. 2013.

Gladwell bases his argument on deductive reasoning:

- He establishes his main premise: that high-risk activism like the Civil Rights Movement in the United States requires strong social ties to succeed.

- He examines the recent activist movements that relied on social media to show that they do not display these strong ties. (This is his minor premise.)

- He concludes that social media cannot be the vehicle for high-risk activism.

Although deductive reasoning can be effective in arguments about issues informed by fundamental values or beliefs, it can also be used effectively in many kinds of arguments, as Gladwell's essay illustrates.

EXERCISE 11E   EXPLORING PERSUASIVE APPEALS

1. Identify an issue about which you might write an argument. In a brief paragraph, summarize the main argument you would make and describe your intended audience. Now describe the appeals (ethical, emotional, or logical) that you think would strengthen your argument for that audience. For example, in an argument supporting anti-smoking laws, you might make an emotional appeal by describing the hardship caused by the death of the parent of young children from lung cancer; you might make a logical appeal on the basis of growing evidence that many serious health problems are linked to smoking.

2. Review the following passages and identify the ethical, emotional, and logical appeals in each.

a). Today introversion and extroversion are two of the most exhaustively researched subjects in personality psychology, arousing the curiosity of hundreds of scientists.

These researchers have made exciting discoveries aided by the latest technology, but they're part of a long and storied tradition. Poets and philosophers have been thinking about introverts and extroverts since the dawn of recorded time. Both personality types appear in the Bible and in the writings of Greek and Roman physicians, and some evolutionary scientists say that the history of these types teaches back even farther than that: the animal kingdom also boasts "introverts" and "extroverts, ... from fruit flies to pumpkinseed fish to rhesus monkeys. As with other complimentary pairings—masculinity and feminity, East and West, liberal and conservative—humanity would be unrecognizable, and vastly diminished, without both personality types.

Take the partnership of Rosa Parks and Martin Luther King, Jr.: a formidable orator refusing to give up his seat on a segregated bus wouldn't have had the same effect as a modest woman who'd clearly prefer to keep silent but for the exigencies of the situation. And Parks didn't have the stuff to thrill a crowd if she'd tried to stand up and announce that she had a dream. But with King's help, she didn't have to.

Yet today we make room for a remarkably narrow range of personality styles. We're told that to be great is to be bold, to be happy is to be sociable. We see ourselves as a nation of extroverts—which means that we've lost sight of who we really are. Depending on which study you consult, one third to one half of Americans are introverts—in other worss, *one out of every two or three people you know.* ... If you're not an introvert yourself, you are surely raising, managing, married to, or coupled with one.

Source: Cain, Susan. *Quiet: The Power of Introverts in a World That Can't Stop Talking.* New York: Crown, 2012. 3–4. Print.

(Continued)

b). Wal-Mart has become the poster child for all that's wrong with American capitalism, because it replaced General Motors as the avatar of the economy. Recall that in the 1950s and the 1960s, GM earned more than any company on earth and was America's largest employer. It paid its workers solidly middle-class wages with generous benefits, totaling around $60,000 a year in today's dollars. Today Wal-Mart, America's largest company by revenue and the nation's largest employer, pays its employees about $17,500 a year on average, or just under $10 an hour, and its fringe benefits are skimpy—no guaranteed pension and few if any health benefits. And Wal-Mart does everything in its power to keep wages and benefits low. Internal memos in 2005 suggested hiring more part-time workers to lower the firm's health care enrollment and imposing wage caps on longer-term employees so they wouldn't be eligible for raises. Also, as I said earlier, Wal-Mart is aggressively anti-union.

Wal-Mart's CEO in 2007 was H. Lee Scott, Jr. Scott was no "Engine Charlie" Wilson, who as GM's top executive in the 1950s saw no difference between the fate of the nation and the fate of his company. Scott has a far less grandiose view of Wal-Mart's role. "Some well-meaning critics believe that Wal-Mart stores today, because of our size, should, in fact, play the role that is believed that General Motors played after World War II. And that is to establish this post-World War middle class that the country is proud of," he opined. "The facts are that retail does not perform that role in this economy." Scott was right. The real problem—not of his making—is that almost nothing performs that role any longer.

The rhetorical debate over Wal-Mart is not nearly as interesting as the debate we might be having in our own heads if we acknowledge what was stake. Millions of us shop at Wal-Mart because we like its low prices. Many of us also own Wal-Mart stock through our pension or mutual funds. Isn't Wal-Mart really being excoriated for our sins? After all, it is not as if Wal-Mart's founder, Sam Walton, and his successors created the world's largest retailer by putting a gun to our heads and forcing us to shop there or to invest any of our retirement savings in the firm.

Source: Reich, Robert. *Supercapitalism: The Transformation of Business, Democracy, and Everyday Life*. New York: Knopf, 2007. 89–90. Print.

Appraising and Using Evidence

No matter what kind of argument you are making, identifying and using appropriate evidence are essential for effective argumentation. Almost anything can be used as evidence: statistics, opinions, observations, theories, personal experience, anecdotes. The challenge is to determine whether a particular kind of evidence is appropriate for a specific claim.

Consider the debate about the state of the U.S. Social Security system. For a number of years, economists, politicians, and financial experts have been debating whether Social Security will run out of money and what, if anything, should be done to prevent that. Experts disagree about the nature of the problem, and participants in the debate routinely cite statistics and factual evidence to support their competing claims. For example, here's an excerpt from a 2012 *USA Today* editorial arguing that Congress should take steps now to avoid a default of the Social Security Trust Fund:

> Self-proclaimed defenders of Social Security maintain that, because of the retirement program's large annual surpluses, it isn't in crisis. That argument is a red herring.
>
> For one thing, those surpluses, also known as the Social Security Trust Fund, have been spent and replaced with IOUs. For another, there aren't any more surpluses. This year, Social Security will collect $507 billion in taxes and pay out $640 billion in benefits. The difference will have to be borrowed, adding to the federal deficit.
>
> Even if you believe that the trust fund is more real than the tooth fairy, the picture is gloomy. This week, the trustees who oversee Social Security reported that if the government makes good on the IOUs by borrowing, taxing or cutting elsewhere, the main trust fund will run out of money in a little more than 20 years. At that point, income from the payroll tax will only be enough to cover 75% of expected benefits. The fund for Social Security's disability program will go bust even sooner, in 2016.

Source: "Editorial: Fix Social Security." *USA Today.* Gannett, 26 Apr. 2012. Web. 26 Apr. 2013.

The authors of this editorial provide what seems to be convincing evidence that Social Security will run out of money in two decades—for example, statistics showing that the Social Security Trust Fund pays out more than it takes in. They rest their argument on a report by the Fund's trustees, who express concern about the possible default of the fund. The question is whether this evidence actually supports the conclusion that the fund will run out of money. The expected deficit for one year, which they refer to in the second paragraph, does not necessarily mean continued deficits over 20 years. In addition, the trustees' prediction in the third paragraph depends upon the accuracy of their assumption about how much money the fund will need to cover benefits, which is a disputed figure.

In a rebuttal to this editorial, Max Richtman, the president and CEO of the National Committee to Preserve Social Security & Medicare, also cites the trustees' report, but he points to figures in that report that lead him to a different conclusion:

- The trust fund solvency date for Social Security has seen fluctuations many times in recent decades, from a depletion date as distant as 2048 in the 1988 report to as soon as 2029 in the 1994 and 1997 reports. This year's report is well within that range.

- Social Security will be able to pay full benefits until the year 2033. After that, there will be sufficient revenue to pay about 75% of benefits.

- There is $2.7 trillion in the Social Security Trust Fund, which is $69 billion more than last year, and it will continue to grow until 2020.

Source: Richtman, Max. "Opposing View: There's No Social Security Crisis." *USA Today.* Gannett, 26 Apr. 2012. Web. 26 Apr. 2013.

Like the authors of the editorial, Richtman cites statistical evidence to support his claim, but he reaches a different conclusion: "There's no Social Security crisis." Who is right?

This example illustrates that the use of evidence in arguments about complicated issues is itself complicated. In this case, the strength of the argument depends not only on the nature of the specific evidence provided but also on how that evidence is interpreted. Each side uses similar kinds of evidence but interprets the evidence differently.

In evaluating an argument, then, we have to appraise the evidence provided.

- **Is the evidence credible?** The evidence should be from a credible source. In the previous example, the source of the figures cited by the authors is a report by the trustees of the Social Security system, which lends those figures credibility. Had the authors cited figures from, say, an economist with little experience in fiscal issues related to Social Security, those figures would carry less weight.

- **Is the evidence appropriate for the argument?** Often, a great deal of evidence is available to support a claim, but the strength of that evidence will depend on how relevant it is to the argument. In this example, the authors could cite a wide variety of economic, financial, and historical statistics or information to support their claims about the fiscal viability of Social Security, but some evidence might be inappropriate for this argument. For example, a statement by a politician who is known to oppose Social Security as an unnecessary government program would be a weak kind of evidence to support the writers' claim that Social Security is running out of money.

- **Is the evidence applied appropriately?** Sometimes, evidence can be strong but used inappropriately. For example, the writers of the *USA Today* editorial note that "Social Security will collect $507 billion in taxes and pay out $640 billion in benefits." They use these figures appropriately to support their claim that such deficits make it more likely that the fund will run out of money. If, however, they cited these figures to argue that Social Security is already running out of money, they would be misusing these figures because a deficit in a single year does not indicate that the fund is bankrupt.

- **Is the evidence interpreted in a reasonable way?** What a piece of evidence means is not always clear, and the same evidence can sometimes be used to support different claims. So writers must often explain what their evidence means. In this example, both Richtman and the editorial authors cite the same figure as evidence to support different claims—the date when the trustees expect Social Security to run out of money (what Richtman refers to as the "solvency date")—but they interpret this piece of evidence differently. The editorial authors assume that the date refers to a specific date when the fund will become insolvent; Richtman interprets the date as an estimate, noting that in the past the trustees have predicted different solvency dates. Part of the strength of each argument, then, rests on whether readers accept the authors' interpretations of the evidence.

- **Is important evidence missing?** Sometimes evidence that seems convincing becomes less so when other evidence is presented. Richtman, for example, notes that the Social Security Trust Fund has "$69 billion more than last year, and it will continue to grow until 2020." The authors of the editorial do not include the fund's growth in their argument, yet this figure seems to be important for estimating whether or when the fund might become insolvent.

It is up to readers to decide whether that "missing" evidence weakens their argument and strengthens Richtman's claim.

Keep in mind that what counts as appropriate and persuasive evidence depends upon context. Personal experience might be acceptable to readers of a popular consumer magazine but not necessarily for a technical report on fuel economy for a government agency. Consider your audience and purpose when determining what kinds of evidence are most appropriate and persuasive for your argument.

EXERCISE 11F   APPRAISING EVIDENCE

1. For each of the following passages, identify the claim(s) and the evidence presented in support of the claim(s). Then evaluate the strength of the evidence using the criteria discussed in this section. Excerpt A is taken from an essay by a political scientist challenging the assumption that voters act rationally when deciding which political candidates to support. Excerpt B is taken from a book by an anthropologist examining what we can learn from traditional societies.

a). Suppose that one scholar maintains that the average voter's belief about X is true, and another denies it. For their debate to make sense, *both* sides have to claim knowledge about (a) what the average voter believes, and (b) which belief is true. How can we get to the bottom of this sort of dispute?

It is fairly easy to figure out what the average voter believes. High-quality surveys abound. The hard thing is figuring out how to "grade" the beliefs of the average voter—to find a yardstick against which his beliefs can be measured.

The most straightforward is to compare voter beliefs to known fact. We can ask voters to tell us the fraction of the federal budget that goes to foreign aid, and compare their average answer to the actual number. Studies that use this approach find that the average voter has some truly bizarre beliefs. The National Survey of Public Knowledge of Welfare Reform and the Federal Budget finds, for example, that 41% of Americans believe that foreign aid is one of the two biggest areas in the federal budget—versus 14% for Social Security. The main drawback of this approach is that many interesting questions are too complex to resolve with an almanac.

Source: Caplan, Bryan. "The Myth of the Rational Voter." *Cato Unbound.* Cato Institute, 6 Nov. 2006. Web. 26 Apr. 2013.

b). Traditional societies are far more diverse in their cultural practices than are modern industrial societies. Within that range of diversity, many cultural norms for modern state societies are far displaced from traditional norms and lie towards the extremes of that traditional range of diversity.

(Continued)

For example, compared to any modern industrial society, some traditional societies treat elderly people much more cruelly, while others offer elderly people much more satisfying lives; modern industrial societies are closer to the former extreme than to the latter. Yet psychologists base most of their generalizations about human nature on studies of our own narrow and atypical slice of human diversity. Among human subjects studied in a sample of papers from the top psychology journals surveyed in the year 2008, 96% were from Westernized industrial countries (North America, Europe, Australia, New Zealand, and Israel), 68% were from the U.S. in particular, and up to 80% were college undergraduates enrolled in psychology courses, i.e., not even typical of their own national societies. That is, as social scientists Joseph Henrich, Steven Heine, and Ara Norenzayan express it, most of our understanding of human psychology is based on subjects who may be described by the acronym WEIRD: from Western, educated, industrialized, rich, and democratic societies. Most subject also appear to be literally weird by the standards of world cultural variation, because they prove to be outliers in many studies of cultural phenomena that have sampled world variation more broadly. Those sampled phenomena include visual perception, fairness, cooperation, punishment, logical reasoning, spatial orientation, analytic versus holistic reasoning, moral reasoning, motivation to conform, making choices, and concept of self. Hence if we wish to generalize about human nature, we need to broaden greatly our study sample from the usual WEIRD subjects (mainly American psychology undergraduates) to the whole range of traditional societies.

Source: Diamond, Jared. *The World Until Yesterday.* New York: Viking, 2012. Print.

2. Identify an argument you might make about an issue that matters to you. In a paragraph, state your main argument and briefly describe the audience you would address. Now list several kinds of evidence to support your argument that would be persuasive for your intended audience. Briefly explain why each kind of evidence would be appropriate for your argument.

Structuring an Argument

The most effective arguments are structured in a way that best meets the needs of the rhetorical situation, and writers generally adopt a format that presents their arguments clearly and persuasively to their intended audience:

- An argument about the influence of social media on peer groups for a communication course would likely be organized systematically around the main claims that can be made on the basis of available research.

- An essay for your campus newspaper in favor of the college's study abroad program might be structured around your own study-abroad experience to make a case for the value of that program.

- A pamphlet supporting the legalization of medical marijuana might present several cases of patients who benefited from medicinal marijuana, with each case illustrating a main point in favor of legalization.

In each of these examples, the writer's decisions about how to structure the argument are shaped by the same basic factors:

- **Audience expectations.** Readers might be less skeptical about supporting the legalization of medicinal marijuana if the argument is presented in the form of the personal stories of patients whose lives were improved by the use of the drug.

- **Conventions governing argument in that rhetorical situation.** Academic arguments, such as a report on social media and peer groups in a communications course, usually follow accepted formats within the academic field. Other kinds of arguments, such as editorial essays for newspapers, tend to be less formally structured.

- **Purpose of the argument.** Structuring an argument around personal experiences and anecdotes, as in an essay arguing for the value of a study abroad program, might make the argument more engaging and persuasive to the intended audience (other students) and therefore be more likely to achieve the purpose of the argument (to assert a position about the issue).

As these examples illustrate, arguments can take many forms; writers should always assess the rhetorical situation carefully to determine how best to structure an argument. However, writers can also use one of four traditional ways of structuring an argument:

- classical arrangement
- Rogerian argument
- inductive reasoning
- deductive reasoning

Classical Arrangement. Classical rhetorical theory defines a standard six-part structure for an argument:

1. **Introduction:** places the main argument in context and explains why it is important or relevant.

2. **Background:** a narrative of events or statement of the facts of the case that sets the stage for the argument.

3. **Proposition:** statement of the writer's position or main argument and an indication of the key points to be made in support of the argument.

4. **Proof:** the core of the argument, in which the writer presents his or her claims and evidence to support the main argument. This section is often arranged so that the strongest claims and evidence are presented first.

5. **Refutation**: consideration of opposing arguments, which can be rebutted or accepted to strengthen the main argument.

6. **Conclusion**: summary of the main points of the argument. Often, the writer will make a final appeal to the audience.

The advantage of this format is that it presents the argument in a clear, straightforward way. Using this format can help writers generate ideas for their argument and ensure that nothing important is left out. Although the format might seem rigid, writers have flexibility in deciding how to organize each main section.

Rogerian Argument. Based on the work of psychologist Carl Rogers, who advocated understanding and listening to resolve conflict, Rogerian argument is generally viewed as a means to negotiate differences and achieve social cooperation. Rogerian argument emphasizes resolution of the issue at hand, so writers make concessions rather than refutations. Like classically arranged arguments, Rogerian arguments have six main sections:

1. **Introduction**: presents the problem to be resolved and raises the possibility of positive outcome.

2. **Summary of opposing views**: opposing views are stated as accurately and neutrally as possible.

3. **Statement of understanding**: the validity of opposing views is acknowledged. Without necessarily conceding that these views are always right, the writer seeks common ground with those who have opposing views.

4. **Statement of position**: presents the writer's position on the issue.

5. **Statement of contexts**: presents situations that illustrate the validity of the writer's position—in effect, providing support for that position to indicate that it can be acceptable even to those with opposing views.

6. **Statement of benefits**: an appeal to the self-interest of those with opposing views who might reconsider as a result of the writer's argument.

   (Adapted from Richard Coe, *Form and Substance.* New York: Wiley, 1981.)

Rogerian argument is most appropriate in situations in which people are deeply divided as a result of different values or perceptions and especially when conflicting parties seek a compromise. For example, an argument in favor of same-sex marriage presented in a Rogerian format would emphasize the common ground shared by those who hold different opinions about the issue. Using a Rogerian approach in such situation, a writer might highlight the desire for strong families, which is shared by those on either side of the debate. In such a case, pointing out the problems with opposing viewpoints is not likely to encourage those who hold such viewpoints to reconsider their position on the issue.

Inductive Reasoning. Arguments based on inductive reasoning present a conclusion drawn from available evidence. When organizing such an argument, follow these guidelines:

- **Demonstrate the relevance of the topic.** The introduction presents the topic and explains why it is relevant to the intended audience.

- **State the main argument and claims clearly.** How clearly and carefully a writer presents his or her main argument can determine how convincing that argument is to the intended audience.

- **Arrange evidence so that it best supports the main conclusion.** Because some kinds of evidence are likely to be more compelling to the audience than others, you should assess how your audience is likely to respond to specific kinds of evidence and arrange that evidence in a way that will make the argument strongest, usually presenting the most compelling evidence first.

- **Interpret and analyze the evidence for the audience.** Although your evidence might be strong, you might have to explain why it is significant. For example, if you use an anecdote about an accident involving a student who parks her car on campus, explain what that anecdote means for your argument against the new campus parking restrictions. (See "Appraising and Using Evidence.")

Because an inductive argument relies on evidence, this approach might be used most effectively when there is strong and abundant evidence to support a main argument or position.

Deductive Reasoning. When constructing an argument on the basis of deductive reasoning, work backward from the main conclusion by following these steps:

- **Identify the conclusion.** Identify the main conclusion you want to reach in your argument. For example, let's say you support the idea of paying college athletes and agree with critics who argue that student athletes are the primary reason for the popularity of college sports and therefore should be compensated for their activities. That's your conclusion.

- **Examine your reasons.** List your main reasons for your position, keeping in mind that some reasons will be more persuasive to an audience than others. For instance, you might believe that the current system of college athletics diminishes the value of the traditional idea of "student athlete." That might be a valid reason for paying student athletes, but it might be less compelling than other reasons, such as the enormous amount of money that colleges and TV networks make from college sports, while most student athletes realize no profit from their efforts. Try to identify all the main reasons for supporting your conclusion.

- **Formulate the premise.** Your premise is the basic principle on which you will base your argument. Ideally, it should be a principle that your audience shares. Let's say your position on paying student athletes rests on your belief that all people should be fairly compensated for their work. That's your premise. It will serve as the foundation for your argument:

  > All people should receive fair compensation for their work. Student athletes are essentially professionals whose efforts result in significant financial benefits for their schools but not for themselves. Therefore, student athletes should be paid for their work.

You can structure your argument accordingly:

1. **Introduction**: State the problem.

2. **Main premise**: Present and explain the main premise on which the argument will be based. Also present the conclusion you will reach.

3. **Reasons**: Present the reasons for supporting the proposition. Address any counter-arguments that can weaken the main argument.

4. **Conclusion**: Restate the main conclusion in light of the evidence presented. Also remind readers of the main premise.

One benefit of structuring an argument in this way is that it encourages you to explore your subject carefully, which could lead to a stronger, more substantive essay.

Features of Argument

Like other common forms of academic writing, argument is a form of inquiry. It is a vehicle for writers to investigate and understand a complex issue or problem and make a claim about that issue or problem to others who have a stake in it.

Effective arguments have five essential features:

1. **A clear main point.** In an effective argument, the writer communicates a clear main point related to his or her position on an issue. As we saw earlier in this chapter, the main argument is not the same as the writer's position on the topic. To state that you support online privacy protection is to take a stance on that issue; to make the case that online privacy should be protected because online communication is a form of constitutionally protected speech is to make an argument in support of that stance.

2. **A relevant purpose.** The purpose of any argument should be relevant to the rhetorical situation. For instance, an argument supporting leash laws to make your campus safer and cleaner would be appropriate for your campus newspaper or a student social media site, the audience for which would likely share your concerns about campus safety. However, the same argument for an assignment in a geography and urban planning course would have to place the issue of leash laws in the context of that field—for example, how land use laws and campus ordinances are intended to create livable public spaces. Even a carefully crafted and well-supported argument is unlikely to be effective if the topic is not relevant to the intended audience.

3. **Appropriate support for claims.** Sufficient and appropriate evidence to support claims is perhaps the most obvious feature of effective argument, but supporting claims with evidence is not always straightforward. For example, statistical data showing that the average global temperature last year was the highest in five years might be true, but such evidence would be insufficient support for an argument that the earth is getting warmer. On the other hand, data showing a rise in global temperatures over several decades would be stronger evidence for a claim that the earth's atmosphere is getting warmer. In some contexts, such as economics, statistical data might carry more weight than expert opinion, whereas in

other contexts, such as art history, the views of respected scholars might be more appropriate support for a claim than statistical evidence.

4. **Complexity.** Effective arguments explore their subjects in sufficient depth to avoid oversimplifying them. For example, it might seem obvious to argue that raising student test scores will improve learning, but a closer look might reveal questions about the reliability of tests or their impact on what students learn. In an effective argument, the writer should acknowledge such questions and address them in a way that reflects the complexity of the issue. Doing so will result in an argument that is stronger and perhaps more valid. It might also foster a deeper understanding of the issue.

5. **A persuasive appeal.** An argument can be based on appeals to reason, emotion, or character, but most arguments employ whatever appeals are appropriate for the rhetorical situation. Moreover, almost all arguments employ logic in some form. Not all reasoning is valid, however. In fact, logical fallacies and flawed reasoning abound in public debates about important issues in politics, education, technology, and culture. (See "Recognizing Logical Fallacies in Popular Arguments" on page 394 in Chapter 13.) An effective argument leads readers logically to the conclusion that the writer supports, based on evidence and sound reasoning, even when the writer is appealing to readers' emotions or invoking character.

The following essay illustrates these features of argumentation. Author and consultant Joe Robinson suggests that Americans work too hard for their own good and argues that they should take more time off from work. His essay was published in the *Washington Post* in 2003, when the U.S. economy was recovering from a downturn brought on by the stock market crash in 2000–2002, which followed a period of rapid growth fueled by the success of technology companies such as Google. So jobs were very much on the minds of his readers. Robinson introduces his argument with an anecdote that underscores his main point: Americans work too much without sufficient vacation time, which is not good either for individual workers or for the U.S. economy. His essay can be seen as an argument to assert a strong position in favor of legalized paid leave for all workers. Although that position might seem counter-intuitive to many of his readers, he explores the issue in a way that might not only persuade some of his readers that more vacation time is a good idea but also contributes to the ongoing conversation about working in contemporary society.

Notice that Robinson appeals to his readers' emotions—for example, by pointing out the personal costs of overworking—but he rests his argument primarily on reason. He builds his case so that it leads logically to his conclusion that American workers should have the benefit of legalized paid leave. His reasoning is deductive. His main premise might be stated this way: People should spend their time in ways that contribute to their well-being. His minor premise is that too much work is not good for individuals or the society and doesn't enhance well-being. His conclusion, then, is that people should not work too much—that is, Americans should have legalized paid leave.

Although Robinson was writing for a general audience, his essay exhibits the same features of effective argumentation in academic settings. It is worth considering whether his argument had more or less appeal a decade later, when the U.S. economy was slowly recovering from the so-called Great Recession of 2008–2010, which many economists consider the worst economic period since the Great Depression of the 1930s. This historical context might affect how readers see the relevance of his argument.

AHH, FREE AT LA—OOPS! TIME'S UP
by Joe Robinson

1   "How do Americans do it?" asked the stunned Australian I met on a remote Fijian shore. He had zinc oxide and a twisted-up look of absolute bafflement on his face. I'd seen that expression before, on German, Swiss and British travelers. It was the kind of amazement that might greet someone who had survived six months at sea in a rowboat.

2   The feat he was referring to is how Americans manage to live with the stingiest vacation allotment in the industrialized world—8.1 days after a year on the job, 10.2 days after three years, according to the Bureau of Labor Statistics. The Aussie, who took every minute of his annual five weeks off—four of them guaranteed by law—just couldn't fathom a ration of only one or two weeks of freedom a year. "I'd have to check myself into the loony bin," he declared.

3   Well, welcome to the cuckoo's nest, mate—otherwise known as the United States. In this country, vacations are not only microscopic, they're shrinking faster than revenues on a corporate restatement. Though it's the height of summer, I'm betting you're not reading this while lolling on the beach. A survey by the Internet travel company Expedia.com has found that Americans will be taking 10 percent less vacation time this year than last—too much work to get away, said respondents. This continues a trend that has seen the average American vacation trip buzzsawed down to a long weekend, according to the travel industry. Some 13 percent of American companies now provide no paid leave, up from 5 percent five years ago, according to the Alexandria-based Society for Human Resource Management.

In Washington state, a whopping 17 percent of workers get no paid leave.

4   Vacations are going the way of real bakeries and drive-in theaters, fast becoming a quaint remnant of those pre-downsized days when so many of us weren't doing the jobs of three people. The result is

unrelieved stress, burnout, absenteeism, rising medical costs, diminished productivity and the loss of time for life and family.

5   In the course of doing my own survey for a book on how we can be productive and have a life at the same time, I've heard all about the vanishing vacation from Americans who say they hardly have a chance to catch their breath or enjoy the fruits of their labor. These are people like Nancy Jones, a nurse in Southern California, who last year put in a vacation request in January to attend her son's wedding in July. "They kept giving me the runaround," she recalled. "They tell you they don't know if you can have the time, because they expect to be busy. It happens all the time." After her manager ignored numerous requests, she wound up having to corner the director of the company, just days before the wedding, to get the time off.

6   An aerospace worker from Seattle sent me an e-mail that sums up the growing dilemma of vacations that are only on paper: "If you try to take a couple of your vacation days, you get told no, so your only recourse is to call in sick … and risk getting management mad and becoming a potential candidate for termination. What happened to families and the reason we go to work to begin with?"

7   As someone raised on summer vacation road trips in my family's intrepid station wagon, I believe that's a question we've lost sight of. After writing about our vacation deficit disorder as a journalist, I decided three years ago to start a grass-roots campaign to lobby for a law mandating a minimum of three weeks of paid leave. Since then, thousands of Americans have signed a supporting petition, and many have volunteered poignant tales from the overworked-place, such

> **Persuasive Appeal**
>
> Robinson makes an ethical appeal in **paragraph 7** by establishing his own credibility as a journalist as well as an American who has experienced the joy of traditional family vacations.

as the 35-year-old victim of a heart attack whose doctor attributed 100 percent of his ailment to unrelieved job stress, or the 50-year-old engineer who was downsized to a job that offered zero paid leave.

8   In the early '90s, Juliet Schor called attention to skyrocketing work weeks and declining

> **Persuasive Appeal**
>
> The anecdotes about workers in **paragraphs 5–8** are likely to generate sympathy among readers, many of whom will identify with the problems these workers face. This is a good example of an emotional appeal that strengthens the main argument. Notice, too, that these anecdotes constitute a different kind of evidence to supplement the statistical data presented earlier and support the claim that too much work can have harmful implications.

free time in her book, "The Overworked American." In the decade since that groundbreaking work appeared, things not only haven't gotten any better—they've gotten worse. We're now logging more hours on the job than we have since the 1920s. Almost 40 percent of us work more than 50 hours a week. And just a couple of weeks ago, before members of the House of Representatives took off on their month-plus vacations, they opted to pile more work onto American employees by approving the White House's rewrite of wage and hour regulations, which would turn anyone who holds a "position of responsibility" into a salaried employee who can be required to work unlimited overtime for no extra pay.

9 Vacations are being downsized by the same forces that brought us soaring work weeks: labor cutbacks, a sense of false urgency created by tech tools, fear and, most of all, guilt. Managers use the climate of job insecurity to stall, cancel and abbreviate paid leave, while piling on guilt. The message, overt or implied, is that it would be a burden on the company to take all your vacation days—or any. Employees get the hint: One out of five employees say they feel guilty taking their vacation, reports Expedia's survey. In a new poll of 700 companies by ComPsych Corp., a Chicago-based employee assistance provider, 56 percent of workers would be postponing vacations until business improved.

10 Guilt works, because we are programmed to believe that only productivity and tasks have value in life, that free time is worthless, though it produces such trifles as family, friends, passions—and actual living. But before the work ethic was hijacked by the overwork ethic, there was a consensus in this country that work was a means, not an end, to more important goals. In 1910, President William Howard Taft proposed a two- to three-*month* vacation for American workers. In 1932, both the Democratic and Republican platforms called for shorter working hours, which averaged 49 a week in the 1920s. The Department of Labor issued a report in 1936 that found the lack of a national law on vacations shameful when 30 other nations had one, and recommended legislation. But it never happened. This was the fork in the road where the United States and Europe, which then had a similar amount of vacation time, parted ways.

11 Europe chose the route of legal, protected vacations, while we went the other—no statutory protection and voluntary paid

> **Complexity**
>
> The historical background that Robinson provides in **paragraphs 9–11** not only helps explain why American workers feel guilty about taking time off from work but also highlights the complexity of this issue. Robinson uses historical facts and comparisons to other nations to show that the issue is not just an economic one but also a social and cultural one.

leave. Now we are the only industrialized nation with no minimum paid-leave law. Europeans get four or five weeks by law and can get another couple of weeks by agreement with employers. The Japanese have two legally mandated weeks, and even the Chinese get three. Our vacations are solely at the discretion of employers. The lack of legal standing is what makes vacations here feel so illegitimate—and us so guilty when we try to take one.

12 Evidence shows that time off is not the enemy of productivity; to the contrary, it's the engine. U.S. companies that have implemented a three-week vacation policy have seen their profits and productivity soar. Profits have doubled at the H Group, a financial services firm in Salem, Ore., since an across-the-board three-week vacation became the rule nine years ago. They have risen 15 percent at Jancoa, a Cincinnati-based janitorial services firm with 468 employees that also went to a three-week policy a few years ago. The owners of both these companies told me they believe the switch in vacation policy is directly responsible for the improvement. Before the change, said the owner of Jancoa, the company had a high employee turnover rate and chronic overtime; after the new vacation policy went into effect, morale went sky-high, and so did productivity, which solved both the turnover and overtime problems. This is not surprising—rested employees perform better than zombies, as fatigue studies have demonstrated since the 1920s. One study showed that if you work seven 50-hour weeks in a row, you'll get no more done than if you worked seven 40-hour weeks in a row. Yet we have made work style—how long, how torturously—more important than how well we do the job.

13 Overwork doesn't just cost employees. The tab paid by business for job stress is $150 billion a year, according to one study. Yet vacations can cure even the worst form of stress—burnout—by re-gathering crashed emotional resources, say researchers. But it takes two weeks for this process to occur, says one study, which is why long weekends aren't vacations. An annual vacation can also cut the risk of heart attack by 30 percent in men and 50 percent in women.

14 Walter Perkins, a finance VP for a large American engineering firm, told me how he became a believer after running a Dutch firm acquired by his employer. He presided over six-week holidays

> **Appropriate Support for Claims**
>
> In **paragraphs 12–14,** Robinson provides statistical data to support his important claim that more vacation time does not decrease productivity. In doing so, he rebuts a main criticism of his position in favor of more time off from work.

for his staff and says he saw no loss of productivity. "The Dutch work just as hard as their American counterparts," Perkins said, "but they have that knowledge that they're going to get that one month or more where they can really recharge the batteries. Guess what? Things don't come to a halt." The stats back him up. Contrary to the American myth, a number of European countries have caught up with the United States in productivity. In fact, Europe had a higher productivity growth rate in 14 of the 19 years between 1981 and 2000, according to the U.S. Federal Reserve Board.

15   I find it strange that the land of the free should be so deficient in vacation time, which is as free as you can get all year. In fact, the word vacation comes from the Latin root *vacatio*, which means "freedom." A vacation is our chance to get out there and discover and travel, to connect with family and friends, to put one over on the survival game. But fear is a specialist in strangling liberty. We're told that, with real vacations, companies would fall apart and the U.S. economy would suddenly turn into Paraguay's.

16   This is why we need a law that will put an end to the bait and switch of vacation time, as well as leave that's being yanked completely. Legalized paid leave also would end the loss of accrued vacation time for downsized workers in their thirties, forties and fifties, who have to start their paid leave banks over again, as if they were at their very first job.

17   I agree that time is money, just not in the way we think it is. Time itself is the truly precious currency, because our supply of it is very limited. We need to pump our fists when we get vacation time and not feel guilty. This was brought home to me while I was on, yes, vacation in the medieval city of Evora, Portugal. There, I visited a bizarre little church whose walls, columns and ceiling are plastered with the femurs, tibias and skulls of hundreds of 16th-century monks and nuns. The Chapel of Bones was designed by a creative sort to aid in the

> **Complexity**
>
> In **paragraph 15** and again in **paragraph 17**, Robinson explores the human side of work and vacation time, taking his argument beyond a simple economic one.

> **A Clear Main Point**
>
> Sometimes, a writer begins an argument by stating the main point up front. Robinson makes his stance in favor of more vacation time clear from the outset, but he states his main argument clearly in his **next-to-last paragraph:** a law is needed to ensure that all workers have sufficient vacation time.

Persuasive Appeal

In his **concluding paragraph,** he reinforces his point by emphasizing the human element, using a persuasive appeal in the form of a personal anecdote to remind readers that life is short. Notice, too, that Robinson brings his readers logically to this point by reasoning that overwork is detrimental to us, which is why we should embrace the idea of using time for important things other than work.

contemplation of mortality. I must admit it provided a very good reality check, particularly the parting words inscribed over the doorway: "We the bones already in here are just waiting for the arrival of yours." Words to remember the next time someone wants to downsize your downtime into a long weekend.

Source: Robinson, Joe. "Ahh, Free at La—Oops! Time's Up." *Washington Post* 27 July 2003: B1. Print.

Questions to Consider:

1. Robinson's essay might be seen as based on deductive reasoning (see the introduction to the essay on page 350). Do you think this was an effective approach to making an argument about this topic? Why or why not? What might have been different about his essay if he had approached it inductively?

2. Using the criteria for appraising evidence described in this chapter (see page 340), evaluate the evidence Robinson uses to support his claims. To what extent does his use of evidence strengthen or weaken his essay?

3. What assumptions do you think Robinson makes about his audience? (Remember that his essay was originally published in *The Washington Post*, a large-circulation newspaper that reaches an international audience.) To what extent do you think his specific persuasive appeals reflect the general nature of that audience? Do you find his appeals persuasive? Explain. What might your answer suggest about the nature of persuasive appeals?

4. In general, how persuasive do you find Robinson's argument? Explain, citing specific passages that you find especially effective or ineffective. On the basis of your response to this question, what revisions would you make to his essay?

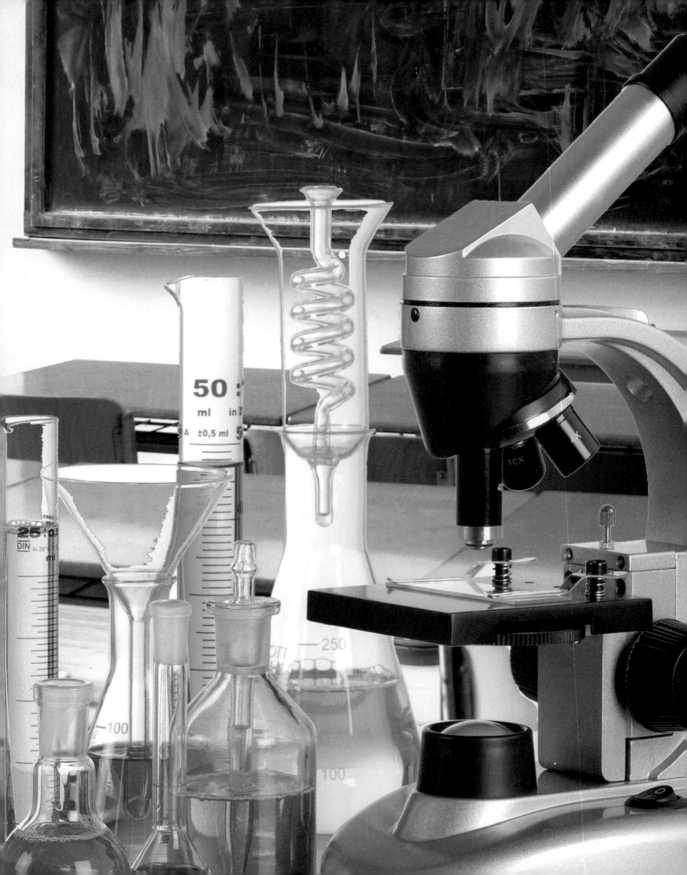

Making Academic Arguments 12

RECENTLY, I was asked to participate in a panel discussion with several faculty members at my university. The panel was part of a colloquium featuring a special talk by a well-known researcher who studies how children learn to write. After finishing his presentation, the researcher answered questions from the panel members, some of whom challenged his stance on the issues he studies. In the ensuing discussion, the panel members and the researcher sometimes took different positions on the questions that were raised. Some audience members participated as well, posing questions for both the panel and for the researcher and offering their own views.

To a casual observer, the colloquium might have seemed like a discussion of intense disagreements among the participants, many of whom presented their views vigorously. In fact, the panel members, the researcher, and the audience were engaged in a common form of academic argumentation. The point of the discussion was not to convince anyone that the researcher or the panel members were right or wrong about the issues that were raised; rather, the point was to explore those issues so that everyone involved might gain a better understanding of them. In some ways, we all had the same goal: to understand writing better so that we could solve the problems we face in trying to teach it effectively. We didn't all agree, but we presented our arguments as a way to advance our collective understanding.

Because the primary purpose of most academic arguments is to inquire into an issue, problem, question, event, or phenomenon, the writer presents a position that reflects his or her effort to understand the topic better. For example, an assignment in an organic chemistry course might ask students to identify an unknown substance. For several weeks, the students conduct lab tests to determine important chemical properties of the substance and analyze the test results on the basis of what they already know about various chemical substances. At the end of the semester, they submit a lab report in which they identify the substance, essentially making an argument using their analyses of their lab tests as evidence to support their conclusions about what the substance is.

In such assignments, students develop arguments by exploring their topics. Trying to "win" the argument in these situations makes little sense. The instructor in the chemistry course, for example, already knows what the substance is; he or she is interested in how the students apply their knowledge of chemistry to arrive at their conclusions. In that regard, their conclusions are perhaps less important than the process by which the students arrive at those conclusions. In such a case, an effective argument is largely a matter of how carefully the writer examines the topic and presents his or her position on the topic. In making the argument, students gain a better understanding of the topic and learn important lessons about the academic field—in this case, organic chemistry.

As this example shows, effective academic arguments are a means to deepen and share learning. That doesn't mean academic arguments are not intense. Sometimes serious disagreements arise as scholars explore important issues and make arguments in which they present provocative or controversial claims. But most academic arguments never rise to such levels of controversy. Instead, arguments are vehicles for inquiry. For students, arguments facilitate learning. Reciting what historians think are the main causes of the Civil War for a history course is one thing; using what historians think to make an effective argument about the main causes of the Civil War is quite another. In making such an argument, you are engaged in genuine inquiry that contributes to your own understanding and perhaps your classmates' as well.

Occasions for Academic Argumentation

There are many formal occasions for arguments whose purpose is to inquire into issues of importance in various academic disciplines or to the campus community. For example, students in a public policy class might debate various government responses to climate change. Faculty members in a foreign languages department might discuss whether to support a proposal to require all students to take two language courses. An ad hoc committee of students and faculty might hold an open forum in which they express their views about free speech in the wake of an incident that has caused racial tensions on campus. In such instances, the participants address important questions and try to solve relevant problems through formal argumentation.

Academic arguments might also take place in less formal ways—for example, classmates working on a project for a philosophy course might defend their differing viewpoints about the usefulness of the assignment, or students in a biology class might debate whether a controversial kind of research should be conducted on their campus. All these examples demonstrate that argument is integral to how students and faculty confront questions or problems that are relevant to their academic work.

Many arguments written for college courses or other academic contexts assume a dual audience, even when the assignment seems to define a specific audience. When writing an argument for a college course, you are implicitly writing for a wider audience that will never read your argument: experts in the academic field you are studying. For example, in a psychology course, you might be asked to write an argument defending a specific viewpoint about the growing use of medication to treat common behavioral disorders, such as attention deficit hyperactivity disorder, in children. Your immediate audience is clear: the course instructor. But you are nevertheless expected to follow the conventions for argument in psychology as if your audience included psychologists. Part of the purpose of such an assignment is to help students understand how knowledge is made in the field and how ideas and information are exchanged and debated by scholars in the field. When writing an academic argument, then, you are playing the role of an expert in an academic field, and therefore you are expected to learn how to make an appropriate argument in that field.

What makes academic arguments different from arguments in other contexts, such as political elections, the opinion pages of newspapers, or popular blogs, is that academic arguments are always assumed to be part of the ongoing effort to advance knowledge and understanding in various fields (See "The Dual Audience for Academic Arguments").

Academic arguments, then, are:

■ occasions for learning

■ opportunities to solve relevant problems

■ invitations to participate in conversations about important issues in academic disciplines

EXERCISE 12A | OCCASIONS FOR ARGUMENT

1. Identify an issue that interests you from one of your courses. Briefly describe the issue and why it interests you. Now identify two or three arguments you might make about that issue.

2. Take one of the arguments you identified for Question #1 and describe how you might make the same argument in a non-academic context—for example, on a social media site or in a letter to the editor of your local newspaper. In what ways might the arguments differ? What might account for those differences?

3. If you have attended a speech, lecture, presentation, or similar event in which a speaker made an argument, describe the situation and the argument that was made. What was the speaker's position? Did you agree or disagree with that position? Why or why not? What do you think you gained by listening to the speaker make his or her argument?

Understanding Academic Argument: A Case Study

Academic argument often addresses complex issues that require students to examine a subject—and their own perspectives about the subject—in depth. Such examination can deepen students' understanding of the subject. Sometimes, that journey of inquiry can be surprising—as some of my own students recently discovered.

The final project in one of the courses I teach requires students, who are studying to become secondary school teachers, to resolve a dilemma involving an important issue in education. Working in small groups, the students are given a scenario that presents the dilemma; each group must propose and defend an appropriate solution to the dilemma. One of the scenarios involves a high school social studies teacher who ignites a controversy by asking his students to examine recent wars in which the United States has been involved, including the Vietnam War and the recent wars in Iraq and Afghanistan. The teacher assigns readings that present various arguments for and against each war and encourages his students to explore some difficult questions about the responsibilities of citizens and their government. The teacher, a military veteran, believes that the primary purpose of social studies is not to teach the facts of history but to prepare students for the challenges of citizenship in a democracy. He claims he does not promote a particular view about the wars studied in his course; instead, he wants to encourage his students to think carefully about what it means to be a citizen in a time of war. Many parents, however, see his teaching methods as anti-American and complain to the school administrators. These parents believe that social studies should not raise questions about American involvement in current wars but instead should promote a sense of patriotism among students. They demand that the teacher stop teaching lessons on the current wars and be formally reprimanded.

The students in my course who were given this scenario found that developing a solution to the controversy turned out to be a much more complicated process than they had expected. They debated vigorously among themselves for several weeks about whether the teacher violated any rules of professional conduct and whether he was protected by his constitutional right to free speech. They argued about what rights the parents had in this situation. Their debates raised many hard questions: Who determines what children should be taught in a social studies class? The school? The teacher? The state? What is the purpose of social studies education? Should students learn to question their government, or should social studies promote patriotism? Is it wrong to criticize the government when American soldiers are fighting and dying in a war? For that matter, what is the purpose of high school education? Who decides what should or should not be taught—and why?

In the end, my students came to an uneasy consensus and developed a solution based on the argument that, although social studies should promote critical inquiry, teachers have a responsibility to leave their own views out of the classroom so that their students are not influenced by the teacher's political beliefs. Here's how my students stated their thesis:

> *The teacher should be allowed to present the material on the Iraq War and other wars, but he should not disclose his personal opinion on this matter to his students.*

To support their position, they presented an argument based on certain principles of education and citizenship. They cited decisions made in similar controversies, and they consulted position papers from professional organizations as well as the state standards for teaching history. In short, they explored their subject in all its complexity to make their case.

Not everyone in the group agreed with the argument made in the final paper, however. Here's what one student wrote in a reflection on the assignment:

> *The final paper is not what I would have come up with on my own, and it isn't necessarily the product I would like it to be. There are parts of me in it, there are some parts I don't like as much, and there are contributions I didn't think of that make it better.*

Still, although the students disagreed about the main argument they presented in their final paper, they all valued the experience of developing that argument. Another member of the group wrote:

> *It is important to note that, although our group did agree on many aspects of our scenario, we never actually reached a unanimous decision regarding the teacher's rights as an educator. While at first this seemed like an obstacle, I found that our differing viewpoints made for an excellent approach to creating a solution. Because we didn't all agree, we were able to consider many different sides of the situation that may have otherwise gone unnoticed.*

For this student, the arguments that group members made in their effort to reach consensus contributed to their own learning. Yet another student was still exploring these questions in her final evaluation:

> *After weeks of preparing and planning, our group was still unable to come up with one definitive answer. We came to a conclusion for the sake of the project, but on an individual level, we never agreed upon a final recommendation (only further pointing to the intricacies of our scenario). Although our group decided that the teacher should not disclose his personal opinion about the Iraq War or other wars, it seems virtually impossible to completely eliminate all judgment, especially when lessons and topics discussed in the classroom are based, to some degree, on the opinion of the teacher.*

TED ALJIBE/Staff/AFP/Getty Images

For these students, argument was the vehicle for an in-depth inquiry into a complex set of questions. Although they were able to reach a consensus for their final paper, that consensus did not necessarily reflect the individual views of the group members. But that wasn't really important because each member gained insight into the complicated issues at hand; each student deepened his or her own understanding as a result of the process of argumentation, regardless of whether he or she agreed with the conclusions presented in the final paper. Moreover, through their research, their debates among themselves, and the development of their argument in their final paper, the group members became part of a much larger conversation about important issues in education.

My students' experience underscores the main purpose of academic argumentation—to inquire into a topic in order to understand it better—and exemplifies the **essential elements of academic arguments**:

- **A clear main point.** Although academic arguments usually address complicated subjects involving social, cultural, political, historical, theoretical, or philosophical questions, writers nevertheless present a clear main point.

- **Appropriate support.** Academic arguments are characterized by specific conventions governing the kind of evidence or support that is considered appropriate and persuasive. Part of the task of writing an effective academic argument is understanding how to follow those conventions and use them to meet the needs of your specific rhetorical situation.

- **Openness to ideas and alternative perspectives.** Arguments are stronger when they reflect the writer's openness to other ideas and viewpoints, which reflects the desire to learn about the subject at hand. Dismissing or ignoring valid positions or claims simply because you disagree with them is likely to weaken your argument. On the other hand, addressing opposing viewpoints might enable you to develop counter-arguments to strengthen your own argument.

- **Complexity.** Because curiosity, a willingness to question, and the desire to understand are hallmarks of academic inquiry, arguments that acknowledge the complexity of a topic are generally more effective than those that oversimplify the topic or reduce it to an either–or proposition. The most effective academic arguments delve deeply into their subjects and expose the complexity of the issues at hand.

- **Relevance.** An effective academic argument addresses issues that others interested in the subject find relevant. Arguments contribute to academic inquiry when they address issues that matter to the academic field.

EXERCISE 12B UNDERSTANDING ACADEMIC ARGUMENT

1. If you have ever written an essay for a class in which you had to make an argument, reflect on what you might have learned by writing that argument. What was the topic? What argument did you make? What do you think you learned about your topic—or about argument in general—by writing that essay? What do you think your experience suggests about argument as a way to learn?

2. The case study presented in this chapter describes a situation in which a group of students collaborated to make an argument about a subject on which they didn't all agree. In a sense, writing their argument together was a process of negotiating differences and solving a problem they all faced, even though they disagreed. Think of a situation in which you or someone you know faced a similar challenge: having to work together with others to solve a problem about which they disagreed. In a few paragraphs, describe that situation and how it was resolved. What role did argument play in that situation?

3. In a group of your classmates, share what you wrote for Question #2. Look for similarities and differences in these experiences. Try to determine what the points of disagreement were in each case. What do you think the experiences described in your essays suggest about solving problems? What might they suggest about argumentation?

Reading Academic Arguments

The readings in this section illustrate the elements of effective academic arguments. As you read, be mindful of the fact that effective arguments in an academic setting are often very specialized yet still relevant to a larger, non-academic audience. Consider these questions:

A clear main point	• What is the main argument? • What is the author's main goal in making this argument?
Appropriate support	• What evidence is presented to support the author's claims? • How persuasive is the author's support for the main argument? • Is the evidence appropriate for the topic and intended audience?
Openness to ideas	• To what extent does the author consider alternative points of view on the topic? • Has the author left out or misrepresented any important considerations that might complicate his or her position?
Complexity	• Has the author explored this topic in sufficient depth? • Does the argument take into account possible complicating factors? • Does the author avoid oversimplifying the issues?
Relevance	• Why is this argument relevant now? • What is the context for this argument? What audience is addressed? • What assumptions does the author make about the audience's interest in this topic?

Crime and Punishment

by Bruce Western

Social scientists, law enforcement professionals, and lawmakers in the United States have long debated the question of how best to reduce crime. Soaring crimes rates in the 1960s and 1970s pushed state and federal governments to adopt "get-tough" policies that increased prison terms for many crimes. As Bruce Western notes in the following essay, this approach resulted in a dramatic increase in prison populations in the United States, which now has the world's highest rate of incarceration. Many politicians and law enforcement experts argue that this high rate of incarceration is the reason for the significant reduction in crime rates in the United States in the past several decades. Western, a professor of government at Harvard University, disagrees. In his essay, which appeared on the Boston Review *website in 2012, he reviews statistical data complicating the view that high rates of incarceration are responsible for reducing crime. Instead, he argues, the United States can—and should—decrease its prison population without weakening the ongoing effort to fight crime. Western's essay is a good example of a strong but measured argument that relies on a careful analysis of evidence to address a complex problem that experts on all sides of the debate hope to solve.*

• •

By the end of the 1990s, policymakers and police were celebrating the great American crime decline. Rates of murder, robbery, and rape had fallen across cities and suburbs, among rich and poor. Less appreciated perhaps is the continuing decline in crime in the 2000s. In every state fewer incidences of serious violence and property crime were reported to police in 2010 than in 2000. The murder rate is now the lowest it has been since the early 1960s.

Research on the 1990s traces the crime drop to better policing; to a subsiding crack trade, which, at its height in the late 1980s, unleashed a wave of murderous violence; and to increasing prison populations. However, some researchers find the apparently large effect of imprisonment controversial. Driven by tough-on-crime policy and intensified drug enforcement, prison populations grew unchecked from the early 1970s until the last decade, but crime rates fluctuated without any clear trend. By the early 2000s incarceration rates had grown to extraordinary levels in poor communities. Whole generations of young, mostly minority and poorly educated men were being locked up, leading to the United States' current status as the world's largest jailer, in both absolute and relative terms.

Prisons may have reduced crime a little in the short run, but at the current scale the negative effects of incarceration are likely to outweigh the positive. Commonplace incarceration among poor young men fuels cynicism about the legal system, destabilizes families, and reduces economic opportunities.

Over the last few years, the rate of prison population growth in the states finally began to slow. (The growth in federal prisons has continued unabated.) As the political salience of crime declined and the cost of prisons ballooned, policymakers and the courts turned to alternatives to incarceration. Twelve states reduced imprisonment in the last decade. These states diverted more drug offenders to probation and community programs, and parolees were less likely to return to the penitentiary. All the states that reduced imprisonment also recorded reductions in crime. For instance, between 2000 and 2010, New York cut imprisonment by about a fifth, and the crime rate fell by about 25 percent.

States that raised their imprisonment rates averaged similar reductions in crime, though the declines show a lot of variation. Where prisons grew by more than 20 percent, crime fell by a little less than the national average. And in some places—such as Maine, Arkansas, and West Virginia—crime barely fell at all.

It seems clear, then, that ever-increasing rates of incarceration are not necessary to reduce crime. Although it's difficult to say precisely how much the growing scale of punishment reduced crime in the 1990s, the crime decline has been sustained even as imprisonment fell in many states through the 2000s.

DON'T THROW AWAY THE KEY

Between 2000 and 2010, the crime rate in the United States dropped by nearly 18.9%. Some observers credit that drop to rising rates of imprisonment. But crime rates in states that reduced incarceration between 2000 and 2010 fell just as much as the rates in states that increased their prison populations.

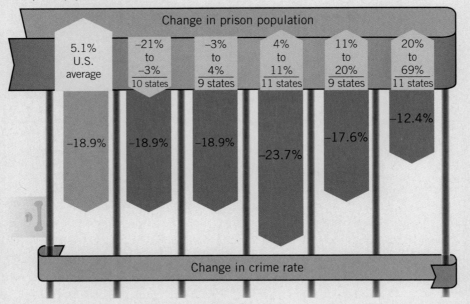

Source: Bureau of Justice Statistics and FBI Uniform Crime Reports, National Imprisonment Data Includes Federal Prisoners. Data Assembled by Catherine Sirois. Harvard University

(Continued)

These data are good news for governors who want to cut prison budgets. But cuts alone may not work. Policymakers should study cases such as New York and New Jersey. These states cut imprisonment while building new strategies for sentencing, parole and after-prison programs.

The era of mass incarceration is not over, but there are signs of reversal. Given the social costs of incarceration—concentrated in poor neighborhoods—these are heartening trends. The last decade shows that public safety can flourish, even as punishment is curtailed.

Source: Western, Bruce. "Crime and Punishment." *Boston Review*. Boston Review, Mar.–Apr. 2012. Web. 30 Apr. 2013.

EXERCISE 12C EXPLORING CRIME AND PUNISHMENT

1. How would you summarize Western's main argument? What makes his argument relevant now? How effectively do you think he establishes the importance of this issue?

2. Western begins his essay by describing a point of view about the relationship between incarceration rates and crime rates that he opposes. Why does he disagree with those who believe higher incarceration rates reduce crime? What kind of appeals (ethical, logical, pathetic) does he use in refuting that opposing viewpoint? (See Chapter 11 for a discussion of persuasive appeals.) Does his discussion of opposing viewpoints and counterarguments strengthen or weaken his own argument? Explain.

3. What evidence does Western provide to support his view that incarceration rates in the United States should be reduced? How well do you think this evidence helps him make his case?

Unpaid Internships Worth More Than Cash

by Jasmine Ako

Internships have long been a rite of passage for many college students, but questions have been raised about the ethics of unpaid internships. Many people believe that unpaid interns gain valuable work experience while still in school, whereas others argue that all work should be fairly compensated, even if it is done by temporary interns. This debate heated up in recent years as the slow economy made it more difficult for college graduates to find jobs. Many students feel pressure to take unpaid internships as a way to make themselves more competitive in a tight job market, but some critics charge employers with taking advantage of this situation and raise questions about the legality of unpaid internships. In the following essay, Jasmine Ako acknowledges these questions, referring in paragraph 10 to a newspaper article about the controversy and in paragraph 5 to the Fair Labor Standards Act. In doing so, Ako places her argument in the context of the ongoing debate about internships. Ako's position in favor of unpaid internships is clear, but she is less interested in prevailing than in contributing to an important conversation that has implications for her, for other college students, and for employers as well. When this essay was published in 2012 in the Daily Trojan, *which is the student newspaper at the University of Southern California, Ako was a senior majoring in business administration at that institution.*

. . . .

It's springtime, which means there's one thing on students' minds: securing a coveted summer internship.

In today's fiercely competitive job market, internship experience has become a necessity for students as opposed to a differentiating advantage. For many students, *unpaid* internships are the only option.

Though the U.S. Bureau of Labor Statistics does not track the number of unpaid internships, a survey conducted by the National Association of Colleges and Employers found that nearly 50 percent of internships held by graduating seniors in 2011 were unpaid.

Unpaid internships can be far from perfect, but they are often a necessary stepping-stone to better opportunities and, ultimately, a job.

To summarize requirements under the Fair Labor Standards Act, unpaid internships must benefit the intern through training, the company cannot derive an immediate advantage from the intern's activities, and the internship should be considered an educational experience.

To make up for the lack of compensation, unpaid interns typically go through the tedious process of registering to receive college credit for their internship, where they end up actually paying to work.

So why are unpaid internships worth it?

Full-time and even paid internship employers typically look for candidates with skill sets obtained through previous work experience. Working for free might seem rough, but if a student has had a blank résumé since high school graduation, chances are that landing a paid summer internship or full-time job would be extremely difficult.

(Continued)

Though they might not provide monetary compensation, unpaid internships provide value in other ways. They offer an inside view of an industry, allow students to grow their professional network, and provide applicable skills that students might not learn in the classroom.

My first internship at a wealth management firm was unpaid and far from glamorous. Though I did spend time making copies and stuffing envelopes, I also made valuable connections within the firm, learned basic financial analysis and research skills, and determined that wealth management wasn't the right career for me.

There are scholarships that provide students who pursue certain kinds of unpaid internships with support. For example, the USC Dream Dollars program awards stipends for students pursuing internships in the government and non-profit fields. Universities and government organizations should look to expand these scholarship opportunities to as many fields as possible, particularly in industries such as entertainment and journalism, where unpaid internships are the norm.

In recent years, the number of illegal internships has risen across the board. According to a 2010 article by *The New York Times*, violations by employers are widespread, but it's hard to crack down when interns are fearful of filing complaints. Though the government should certainly implement more specific, stringent legal requirements to reduce the prevalence of illegal unpaid internships, students can also take their own initiative.

To avoid a potentially miserable unpaid internship experience, students should research the opportunity thoroughly beforehand. Through a simple LinkedIn search, they can contact past interns to get direct feedback on the internship experience. Students should also maintain an open dialogue during the interview process and ask interviewers candid questions about the day-to-day tasks they'll be responsible for during the internship.

Unpaid internships don't have to be characterized by making coffee and becoming a copy slave; there are many out there that provide valuable work experiences. Students should do everything they can to vet the internship beforehand, maximize their experience on the job, and extract as much value as possible out of the internship by establishing connections.

Students should look at unpaid internships as a first step toward paid internship and employment opportunities. With my first internship under my belt, I was able to secure a more competitive, paid internship the following summer by showing my employer I was dedicated, willing to learn and already familiar with the workplace.

Government entities could certainly do better to create more specific compliance standards, and more scholarship opportunities for unpaid interns are definitely needed. But if students do their homework, take initiative on the job and view their internship as a learning opportunity rather than a burden, they'll find that unpaid internships are often a worthy sacrifice.

Source: Ako, Jasmine. "Unpaid Internships Worth More Than Cash." *Daily Trojan* 22 Mar. 2012. Web. 12 June 2012.

EXERCISE 12D — EXPLORING THE DEBATE ABOUT UNPAID INTERNSHIPS

1. Ako uses her own experience as evidence to support her argument in favor of unpaid internships. How effective do you find her use of her own experience as evidence to support her claims? Do you think her evidence is appropriate for her audience? Why or why not?

2. How would you characterize Ako's tone in this essay? Is her tone appropriate for her subject matter? Do you think her tone strengthens or weakens her essay? Explain, citing specific passages from her essay to support your answer.

3. Do you think Ako's argument does justice to the complexity of this issue? Why or why not? To what extent does her effort to address counter-arguments contribute to the effectiveness of her argument?

More Argument, Fewer Standards

by Mike Schmoker and Gerald Graff

Movements to reform American schools have been occurring almost from the very beginning of the modern American school system in the mid-1800s. The latest such movement focuses on the so-called Common Core State Standards, a national effort to establish a set of standards that all American students are expected to meet. By 2012, most states in the United States had adopted these standards, and schools across the nation began revising their curriculums to meet the new standards, which encompass all major school subjects, including writing. Not surprisingly, the Common Core movement sparked controversy and debate among educators, parents, politicians, and scholars. In the following essay, two respected education professionals join the debate. They advance the position that writing instruction in schools should focus on the teaching of argument, framing their own argument explicitly in the context of the new Common Core movement. To make their case, the authors rely in part on logical reasoning (see "Logical Appeals" in Chapter 11), but they also make an ethical appeal on the basis of their own expertise and reputations (see "Ethical Appeals" in Chapter 11). Mike Schmoker is an experienced education consultant who has written widely on educational issues; Gerald Graff is a well-known English professor whose scholarly writing has influenced the ongoing debates about education reform in the United States. Their essay appeared in 2011 in EdWeek, a publication focused on education issues for both an academic and general audience.

. . . .

If we want record numbers of students to succeed in postsecondary studies and careers, an ancient, accessible concept needs to be restored to its rightful place at the

(Continued)

center of schooling: argument. In its various forms, it includes the ability to analyze and assess our facts and evidence, support our solutions, and defend our interpretations and recommendations with clarity and precision in every subject area. Argument is the primary skill essential to our success as citizens, students, and workers.

The new common-core standards, which include the best English/language arts standards to date, fully acknowledge this. They affirm unequivocally that "argument is the soul of an education." But, alas, unless adjustments are made, these new standards documents could drown out and obscure the welcome emphasis they put on argument.

Every K–12 teacher and administrator should know the powerful case for argument. (They currently *do not*.) For decades, the most enlightened educators and academics have put it at the center of education. They implore us to see that argument enlivens learning and is at the heart of inquiry, innovation, and problem-solving. Education researchers like Robert Marzano, George Hillocks, and Deanna Kuhn have demonstrated that in-school opportunities to argue and debate about current issues, literary characters, and the pros and cons of a math solution have an astonishing impact on learning—and test scores. Argument not only makes subject matter more interesting; it also dramatically increases our ability to retain, retrieve, apply, and synthesize knowledge. It works for all students—from lowest- to highest-achieving. Yet many educators never learn this. And they never learn that argument is the unrivaled key to effective reading, writing, and speaking.

Argument, in short, is the essence of thought. So, it is heartening to see that the English/language arts documents of the Common Core State Standards Initiative acknowledge the supreme and "special place" of argument among all other literacy standards. We hope that readers won't overlook the section in the common-core research that asserts that argument is "the soul of an education" with "unique importance in college and careers." One of us—Jerry Graff—was prominently mentioned in this section, for demonstrating that college is fundamentally an "argument culture." To succeed, students can't simply amass information (as important as that is); they must also weigh its value and use it to resolve conflicting opinions, offer solutions, and propose reasonable recommendations. The same could be said for the demands of citizenship and the modern workplace.

"Argument not only makes subject matter more interesting; it dramatically increases our ability to retain, retrieve, apply, and synthesize knowledge."

We are encouraged, then, by the common-core standards, which contain a ringing endorsement of argument as the primary mode for reading, talking, and writing about complex texts. What concerns us is that for all their merits, these standards are still overlong, redundant, and often confusing. Consequently, the most important and powerful standards are at risk of being marginalized—or overlooked entirely.

All standards are not created equal. We believe it is far more critical for teachers to help students to analyze, evaluate, and support their conclusions with evidence than it is for them to spend precious time on puzzling standards like these:

"Compare and contrast the structure of two or more texts and analyze how the differing structure of each text contributes to its meaning and style"; or

"Analyze different points of view of the characters and the audience or reader (e.g., created through the use of dramatic irony) creating such effects as suspense or humor."

We have tested these and similar standards on many teachers. They, like us, have no idea what these mean or how they would teach them. And there are still—despite some reductions from earlier drafts—too many "foundations" standards. Like their lamentable state-level predecessors, these standards would have students learning from long lists of mechanical skills well into the later grades, where they only perpetuate a lower-order, worksheet-driven curriculum at the expense of close, evaluative, and argumentative reading, discussion, and writing.

The overriding lesson from our attempt to create and implement state standards was that clarity is critical and that less is more. To this end, let's make sure that this time around, these new, national standards are seen as true pilot documents, to be learned from, reduced, and clarified as we closely study their implementation by teachers.

In the meantime, let's immediately begin, as the new standards urge us, to give students hundreds of opportunities, every year, to dismantle and defend arguments about increasingly rich, complex texts. From the earliest grades, let's have them argue about the pros and cons of almost anything: literary characters and interpretations, global warming, capitalism vs. socialism, Sarah Palin, or the comparative quality of life in the United States and Canada (based on statistical analysis). Let's ask students to explain their reasoning for which alternative-energy source we should invest in as they read, talk, and write about what they are learning in novels, textbooks, newspapers, and magazines.

As standards and assessments make their necessarily lurching journey from good to (we hope) great, there is no reason to postpone the implementation of the most critical standards, those focused on argument and its corollaries. Tied to a content-rich curriculum, these have unparalleled power to make school interesting—and to prepare students for college, careers, citizenship, or any achievement test that will ever come their way.

Source: Schmoker, Mike, and Gerald Graff. "More Argument, Fewer Standards." *Edweek* 19 Apr. 2011. Web. 7 May 2012.

1. How would you summarize the authors' main argument? What do you think they hope to accomplish by making this argument?

2. Schmoker and Graff address a complicated issue (school reform) that interests a wide range of people, from scholars and policymakers to parents and students. Their essay appeared in a publication intended for both education experts and non-experts. To what extent do you think they succeed in making their argument persuasive for these varied audiences? Explain, citing passages from their essay to support your answer.

3. What support do the authors provide for their position? To what extent do you think the evidence they present would be persuasive for their different audiences? What assumptions do you think the authors make about their readers' knowledge of educational issues?

Writing Academic Arguments

This section provides a framework for developing an academic argument using the Ten Core Concepts. Each step described here corresponds to a step in Chapter 3.

Step 1 Identify a topic for argument.

Begin with a question about a problem or issue that matters to you:

- Should government subsidize student loans to help make college more affordable?
- What, if anything, should be done about climate change?
- Are there situations in which free speech should be restricted?
- Should Americans give up some privacy rights for greater security against terrorism?
- Is rap music more influential than jazz as a cultural phenomenon?

Make a list of four or five such questions.

If your assignment specifies a topic, follow your instructor's guidelines. But you might still need to identify a specific topic. For example, if your instructor asks you to select from a list of approved topics, select four or five topics from that list, turn each one into a question, and proceed with this exercise. Or your assignment might call for an argument about a general subject, such as gender, in which case you can list four or five questions about topics related to gender—for example, should women be allowed to serve in front-line military combat units?

Now **select the one question from your list that is most interesting to you.** Consider the following:

Your interest in the topic	The importance of the topic	Your opinion
Why does this topic interest you? Consider what makes this topic worth exploring. It's best to make an argument about topics in which you have a strong interest.	**Why is this topic important?** Consider whether the topic fits your assignment, is relevant to the academic field for which you are writing, or is important to a larger audience. You don't want to devote time and energy to issues that don't seem important. For example, you might think hunting is fun, but is it worth making an argument about that? On the other hand, an argument about the importance of hunting in protecting wildlife relates to significant debates about conservation, wilderness protection, and the rights of gun owners.	**Do you have an opinion about this topic or a position on the issue?** Consider your feelings or attitude about the topic. What is your stance on this issue? Why do you feel the way you do?
Do you have some special connection to this topic? For example, as a college student, you might have a keen interest in student loan policy; as a mountain climber, you might worry about how climate change is affecting the mountainous regions where you climb.		**Are you unsure?** At this point, it doesn't matter whether you have an opinion or stance. What matters is that the topic is important to you and others who might share your interests or concerns.

Exploring these questions will help you decide whether to pursue the topic. If you decide that the topic you have chosen isn't appropriate, return to your list and select a different question. Once you have a question about which you want to make an argument, develop your question using Step #1 in Chapter 3.

Step 2   Place your topic in rhetorical context.

Effective arguments

- address an intended audience appropriately
- fit the rhetorical context

In academic arguments, the audience is usually assumed to include scholars and students in the academic field in which you are writing (see "The Dual Audience for Academic Arguments" earlier in this chapter), and the context is often assumed to encompass the broader effort to advance understanding in that field. For example, an argument in favor of federally subsidized student loans written for an economics course might be directed primarily at your course instructor and classmates, but it should be made in a way that is appropriate for a wider audience in the field of economics. In other words, the argument should be relevant in the academic field and meet the expectations of readers in the field.

With that in mind, return to your question from Step #1, and consider your audience and the rhetorical context for an argument about your question.

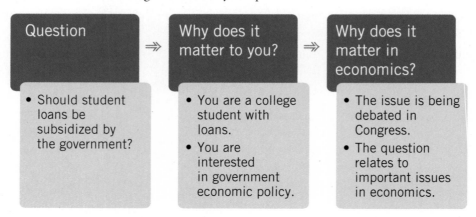

Using this procedure, explore the rhetorical context for your question, keeping notes as you do. Then, using your notes as a guide, complete Step #2 in Chapter 3.

Step 3 Select a medium.

Most academic arguments are presented in the form of a conventional paper, but if you have a choice, consider which medium will enable you to make your argument most effectively.

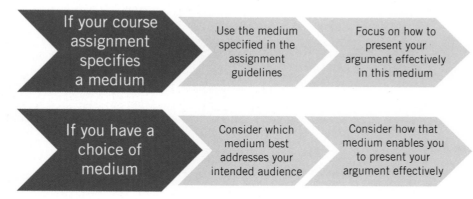

For example, if you are making an argument about whether the federal government should subsidize student loans and you want to reach a wider audience of college students, consider writing your argument for a blog or another social media site that is popular among college students.

Complete Step #3 in Chapter 3 to help you decide on an appropriate medium for your argument.

Step 4 Identify your main argument.

Your argument should grow out of the question you explored in Steps #1 and #2. Remember:

- Your main argument is not the same thing as your position on the issue, though it is related to your position. (See "Developing a Main Argument" in Chapter 11.)

- Your main argument might evolve as you develop it.

You might not know at this point exactly what your argument will be, but as you explore your topic, you will adjust and refine your argument. At this point, the goal is to identify a clear main point as a starting point for developing an effective argument.

First, consider possible arguments you might make about your question. For example, here are some possible arguments to make about the question of whether student loans should be subsidized by the government (let's assume you generally support subsidized student loans, given your own experience trying to pay for college):

- The president should support subsidized student loans for college.

- Student loans should be subsidized by the federal government.

- Subsidized student loans provide clear economic benefits for individual students and society.

In assessing these statements as possible main arguments, consider which one best reflects your own interest. Also consider how each argument fits the rhetorical context. In this example, imagine that you are writing your argument for an introductory economics course:

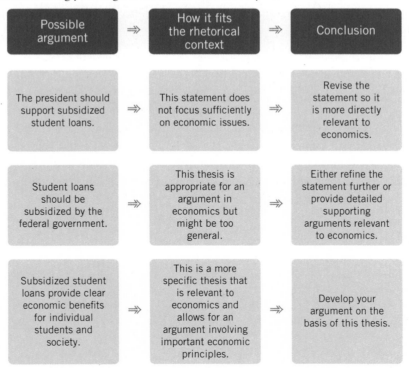

Make a list of a few possible main arguments that grow out of your question, and consider how well they fit your rhetorical situation. On the basis of that analysis, select one statement that will serve as your main argument. By following Step #4 in Chapter 3, you will develop a Guiding Thesis Statement, which is essentially a more refined statement of your main argument.

Step 5 Support your main argument.

As you develop a good sense of your main argument, you will also generate some ideas about your supporting arguments or claims. You have four main tasks at this point:

- identify the supporting arguments or claims you will make in support of your main argument
- begin to identify evidence or reasoning to back up each claim
- identify opposing arguments or complicating factors
- rebut those opposing arguments and address complicating factors

Usually, completing these tasks requires research. As you move through this step, you will learn more about your topic, and, as a result, you might need to refine your argument and adjust your claims. Remember to be open to possibilities as you proceed.

Let's return to the example of an argument in favor of subsidized student loans. Here's your main argument as you have stated it at this point:

> *Subsidized student loans provide clear economic benefits for individual students and society.*

To support that main point, you will need to show how students benefit economically from subsidized loans and demonstrate how society benefits as well. Let's imagine that you have learned that subsidized loans have lower interest rates than regular loans, which means lower costs for students. You suspect that lower interest rates mean fewer loan defaults, which is good not only for students but also for communities and for the banks that make the loans. One drawback to subsidized loans is that ultimately taxpayers pay for any loan defaults, but you believe that this potential drawback is outweighed by fewer defaults. Also, you consider it a benefit to society if more students are able to attend college, even though some people argue that government should not be involved in matters such as loans.

Now you need to develop these supporting arguments and claims and find evidence or develop reasoning to support them; you also need to address opposing arguments. To do so, follow these steps:

State your main argument.

Subsidized student loans provide clear economic benefits for individual students and society.

List your supporting claims.

| Subsidized loans mean more students can attend college. | Lower interest rates mean fewer defaults. | Lower default rates mean a healthier economy. |

Identify possible evidence for each supporting claim.

| Studies showing that such loans encourage more low-income students to attend college | Statistical evidence on student loan defaults | *Statements by respected economists *Data on economic impact of loan defaults |

Identify opposing arguments or complicating factors.

| College isn't necessarily for everyone. | Lower interest rates mean lower profits on loans. | Subsidized loans amount to too much government interference in the loan market. |

Answer opposing arguments and/or complicating factors.

| True, but college should be available to those who want to attend. | Possibly, but that price is worth paying if more students attend college and fewer default on their loans. | Sometimes, strategic government interference is necessary if the potential benefits to society are worthwhile. |

Here are a few things to keep in mind as you develop support for your claims:

■ **Follow the evidence.** Obviously, your evidence should support your claims, but your claims can change as you research your topic and look for evidence. You might find, for instance, that the available evidence does not support a claim. In this example, you might begin with a claim that lower interest rates result in fewer loan defaults, but your research might indicate that the statistical data on this subject are mixed. So you might need to abandon or refine that claim. Don't make claims you can't support, which would result in a weaker (and perhaps unethical) argument. If you find evidence to support your claim, good; if not, adjust your claim.

■ **Explore opposing arguments sufficiently.** Although it isn't always necessary or even possible to identify an opposing argument for each supporting claim, anticipating opposing arguments and identifying potential complicating factors can help you strengthen your argument. In this example, you might not have initially considered the argument that college isn't for everyone, but by identifying that opposing argument, you realize it is an important point to address. In doing so, you explore your topic more fully and make a stronger case for your position.

■ **Remember that not all evidence is appropriate or persuasive.** As you find evidence to support your claims, determine whether that evidence is trustworthy, relevant to your topic, and appropriate for the rhetorical situation (see "Appraising and Using Evidence" in Chapter 11). A quotation from a politician about the value of college might be less persuasive than statistical evidence showing that college graduates enjoy higher employment rates and earn higher salaries than workers without college degrees.

Complete Step #5 in Chapter 3. You should be ready to write a complete draft of your project. Or you can move onto the next step before completing your draft.

Step 6 Organize your argument.

There are four standard ways to organize an argument (see "Structuring an Argument" in Chapter 11). Which one you select will depend upon your rhetorical situation and the nature of the argument you are making.

For example, in making an argument against capital punishment, the kind of argument you make will help determine how best to organize it:

■ An argument against capital punishment based on the belief that all killing is wrong is probably best organized as a **deductive argument** because the argument flows from the basic premise that killing is wrong.

■ An argument that capital punishment should be banned because it does not deter violent crime would likely involve various supporting claims that rest on statistical evidence (such as rates of violent crime in states with and without capital punishment); such an argument might be better organized using **classical arrangement**, which would allow the writer to incorporate the supporting claims more easily.

Keep in mind, too, that many academic disciplines have well-established conventions governing the form arguments take. For example, arguments in philosophy are often based on deductive reasoning. In many social sciences, such as economics or sociology, inductive reasoning is more common because the arguments rely on empirical evidence. So consider whether your argument is subject to expectations for a particular academic field.

To decide how best to organize your argument, take into account the following considerations:

The rhetorical situation	• What structure would present your argument to your intended audience most persuasively? • What expectations will your audience likely have regarding the form of your argument? • How can you organize your essay so your main argument is presented clearly to that audience? • What are the conventions for structuring an argument within the academic discipline in which you are writing?
The nature of your argument	• Does your argument rest on a primary belief or principle (deductive reasoning)? • Does it rely on conclusions drawn from evidence (inductive arrangement)? • Does your argument include a number of complicated supporting claims and kinds of evidence (classical arrangement)? • Is your purpose primarily to solve a problem or negotiate differences (Rogerian arrangement)?

To illustrate, let's return to the previous example of an argument in favor of subsidized loans for college students.

Consider the Rhetorical Situation

For most assignments, you will probably be expected to focus your argument on issues relevant to the academic discipline in which you are writing. For an economics course, for example, your argument should focus on the economic issues related to subsidized loans, such as how default rates might affect the financial well-being of individuals and businesses, the impact of government subsidies on interest rates, and so on. You would be expected to present specific kinds of data to support claims about these factors, so an **inductive argument** (in which you draw your conclusion about subsidized student loans from appropriate evidence) or **classical arrangement** (which would allow you to incorporate many supporting claims and address opposing arguments) would be a good choice for structuring your argument.

Examine the Nature of the Argument

At this point in your project, you have identified several supporting claims for your main argument in favor of subsidized student loans. But you have also identified a fundamental principle on which to rest part of your argument: governments should take certain actions for the common good. In this case, helping students attend college is in the public's interest. So you might consider a **deductive argument** based on that fundamental principle. However, such an approach might make it more difficult to incorporate the supporting claims you have identified; in addition, if you are writing for an economics course or another specialized academic audience in social sciences, a deductive argument might be less appropriate. So **classical arrangement** might be a better option because it would enable you to incorporate your supporting claims and evidence as well as logical reasoning on the basis of a fundamental principle.

Here's a basic outline for an argument in favor of subsidized student loans using classical arrangement:

I. Introduction: explanation of the relevance of the issue of subsidized student loans in economics and to a wider audience.

II. Background:

    A) Discussion of why this problem is important

    B) Brief history of the problem of student loan debt

    C) Explanation of rising college costs

    D) Review of related economic issues

III. Proposition: statement of main argument that government should subsidize student loans because of the potential benefits both to individual students and to society in general.

IV. Proof: presentation of supporting arguments and evidence to support them.

    A) Subsidized loans allow more students to afford college.

    B) Lower interest rates mean fewer student loan defaults, which is better for communities, businesses, and individuals.

    C) Higher college attendance benefits individuals and communities.

    D) Lower default rates help keep the economy healthy, which benefits everyone.

V. Refutation: answers to opposing arguments and complicating factors.

    A) College attendance might not be for everyone, but subsidized loans help make college affordable for those who wish to attend.

    B) Although subsidized loans might mean lower profits for banks, the overall benefit to the economy is worth it.

    C) Although subsidized loans require government involvement in a free market, in this case government involvement results in greater benefit to the society as a whole.

VI. Conclusion: emphasize benefits of college attendance and the need for government assistance in helping students avoid loan debt and defaults.

If you were writing this essay for a different course or rhetorical situation, it might make sense to structure the essay as a deductive argument (see "Deductive Reasoning" in "Structuring an Argument" in Chapter 11). For example, if your essay were intended for a political science course, it might be appropriate to rest your argument on the principle that government should support public education in ways that benefit the society as a whole. In such a case, your essay would likely be more effective if you structured it as a deductive argument.

You can obtain additional guidance for organizing your essay by following Step #6 in Chapter 3.

Step 7   Get feedback.

Feedback on your draft will be more relevant if your readers focus on the following sets of questions related to the features of effective academic argumentation:

A clear main point	• Is your main point clearly stated? • Is the purpose of your argument clear? • Is the focus of your main argument maintained throughout your essay?
Appropriate support	• Do you provide appropriate and persuasive support for each of your supporting claims? • Can any claims be made stronger with additional or different support? • Is your evidence appropriate for your topic and audience?
Openness to ideas	• Do you acknowledge other points of view on this issue? • Do you sufficiently address complicating factors that might weaken your argument? • Do you present opposing arguments fairly?
Complexity	• Does your argument do justice to the complexity of your topic? • Do you explore your topic sufficiently? • Do you avoid oversimplifying the issues?
Relevance	• Do you explain why your topic is relevant for your rhetorical situation? • Does your argument contribute to ongoing discussions of this topic? • Do you address your argument to your intended audience?

Follow Step #7 in Chapter 3 to analyze your feedback and help you decide which revisions to make.

Step 8   Revise.

As you consider the feedback you received for Step #7, you might find that you need to do additional research to identify evidence to support your claims or address opposing arguments or complicating factors. That's OK. Remember that revision is an opportunity to deepen your understanding of your topic and strengthen your argument. It is also a chance to adjust and strengthen your persuasive appeals and make sure that your argument fits your rhetorical situation.

You can divide the task of revising your argument into three steps.

Review Your Draft Using the Questions Listed in Step #7

Make sure you have addressed the key characteristics of academic argument:

- a clear main point
- appropriate support
- openness to other ideas
- complexity
- relevance

As you revise, keep your audience and sense of purpose in mind.

Adjust Your Persuasive Appeals

To make an effective argument, not only must you have appropriate and sufficient support for your claims, but you also must present your case in a way that is likely to be persuasive to your intended audience. That means reviewing your draft to make sure that you have used ethical, emotional, and/or logical appeals effectively (see "Making a Persuasive Appeal" in Chapter 11). As we saw in Chapter 11, the appeals you use in making your argument depend in large part on your rhetorical situation. For example, you probably wouldn't make an exclusively emotional appeal in an argument about subsidized student loans for an economics course. But a carefully made emotional appeal might supplement an argument that is based mostly on a logical appeal.

Review Each Supporting Argument or Claim

Finally, determine whether you have made an appropriate persuasive appeal for each supporting argument or claim. Although you should now have evidence to support each claim, you can strengthen those claims with appropriate persuasive appeals.

Let's review a few claims in our hypothetical argument in favor of subsidized student loans. For each claim, consider the kind of appeal that might be most appropriate:

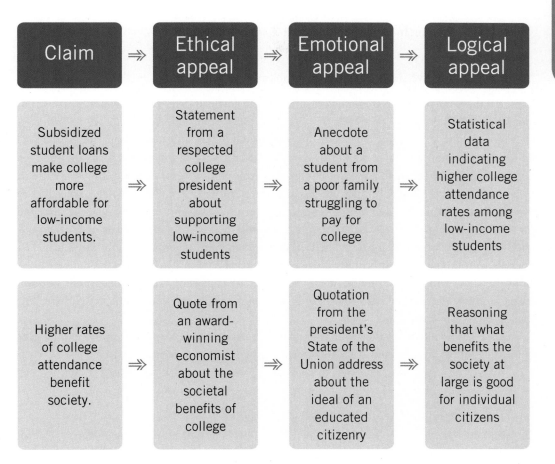

Claim ⟹	Ethical appeal ⟹	Emotional appeal ⟹	Logical appeal
Subsidized student loans make college more affordable for low-income students. ⟹	Statement from a respected college president about supporting low-income students ⟹	Anecdote about a student from a poor family struggling to pay for college ⟹	Statistical data indicating higher college attendance rates among low-income students
Higher rates of college attendance benefit society. ⟹	Quote from an award-winning economist about the societal benefits of college ⟹	Quotation from the president's State of the Union address about the ideal of an educated citizenry ⟹	Reasoning that what benefits the society at large is good for individual citizens

In deciding which evidence to use and how best to present it, consider how each kind of appeal fits your rhetorical situation. Use appeals that will strengthen your argument—but only if they are appropriate for your rhetorical situation.

Follow Step #8 in Chapter 3 to make sure you have addressed all the essential aspects of your essay.

Step 9   Refine your voice.

Voice is part of the means by which you establish credibility, which in turn strengthens your argument. Revise your draft with that in mind.

First, consider your purpose in making this argument, which will help shape your voice. Recall that Chapter 11 describes four main purposes for argument:

- to inquire into an issue
- to assert a position in an important conversation or debate
- to prevail over opponents
- to solve a controversial or complicated problem

Although these purposes can overlap, your primary purpose can determine how best to construct your voice.

For example, let's assume that your purpose in making an argument about subsidized student loans is primarily to understand this complex and important issue—that is, an argument to inquire. You are writing in an academic context (an economics course), so you want your voice to sound knowledgeable and confident but also measured and fair. To construct such a voice means avoiding charged language and writing in a straightforward academic style. By contrast, imagine that you are writing about the same topic in an editorial essay for your campus newspaper and you have recently learned that one of the U.S. Senators in your state opposes subsidized loans. In that case, you might see your primary purpose as asserting a strong position in the public debate about the issue. Your voice in that context should still be confident and knowledgeable, but as a college student who is faced with tuition bills, you might want your voice to be sympathetic and perhaps even provocative.

This example illustrates that your voice should be appropriate for your purpose within your rhetorical context. Review your draft and adjust your voice, if necessary:

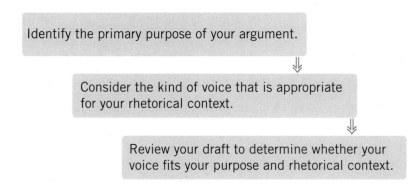

Identify the primary purpose of your argument.

⇓

Consider the kind of voice that is appropriate for your rhetorical context.

⇓

Review your draft to determine whether your voice fits your purpose and rhetorical context.

Make necessary revisions to your draft. Then follow Step #9 in Chapter 3 to refine and strengthen your voice.

Step 10 Edit.

Complete Step #10 in Chapter 3.

1. Identify an issue or controversy you feel strongly about. Ideally, it should be something that matters in your life—for example, a controversy over a proposal to eliminate your major at your college or restrictions on the use of social media for certain kinds of activities on campus. Write an argument in which you take a position on this issue. Write your argument in a way that would be appropriate for both an academic audience and a wider audience. For example, if you wrote about a controversy about eliminating your major at your college, you might intend your argument for readers in an academic field such as education or philosophy as well as for a wider audience interested in educational issues.

2. Rewrite the essay you wrote for Question #1 in a completely different medium. For example, if you wrote an essay for your campus newspaper, rewrite the essay as a multimedia presentation for a different audience or as a letter to a person at the center of the issue.

   Now compare the two arguments. What changes did you make in rewriting your argument for a different medium? In what ways (if any) did you have to adjust important elements of your argument, such as your evidence or your persuasive appeals? What might a comparison of these two arguments suggest about how argument is shaped by rhetorical context and medium?

3. Using the issue you wrote about for Question #1 or another topic, find three or four academic arguments about that issue or topic. In an essay intended for your classmates, summarize the arguments and then analyze them using the five main features of academic argumentation described in this chapter. Be sure to account for the rhetorical situation. On the basis of those features, decide whether the arguments are effective. Draw conclusions about what makes an argument effective.

Making Arguments in Popular Discourse

WHICH ACTOR SHOULD WIN an Academy Award? Who should be the next president? Should colleges pay student athletes? We share opinions and debate matters big and small in every aspect of our lives: in our relationships, as citizens, at work and play. Debating these matters helps us understand issues we care about and consider what others think about them. In this way, everyday argument is part of how we make sense of the world, make decisions, and solve problems.

Expressing an opinion, though, is not necessarily the same as making a persuasive argument. Everyone voices opinions, and, in most cases, such as a friendly debate about whether college football should have a national playoff, a weak or flawed argument has few serious consequences. But sometimes the arguments we engage in can have significant implications for our lives:

- Should a loved one have a recommended but risky surgery?
- Should you borrow money to attend college?
- Should your brother or sister join the military?
- Should you volunteer for a controversial political candidate?

In such cases, a careful argument can often result in a better decision or a workable solution to a problem. It is no accident that in business, politics, and community life, decisions about difficult problems and important issues are made on the basis of extensive discussions in which careful arguments are made:

- After listening to various arguments for and against building a new addition to the local high school, school board members vote on whether to levy a tax increase to pay for the new construction.
- The owners of a small computer software company exchange opinions with their staff about the risks and benefits of purchasing another software company.
- In deciding whether to support a new policy that would give the college access to information about students' online activities, a group of students and faculty listen to each other's positions as they debate how the policy might affect privacy and online security at the college.

In these examples, arguments are presented as part of an effort to address a problem or make a decision. Making good arguments is no guarantee that the outcome will satisfy everyone. In fact, in decisions about important issues that will affect the participants, it is likely that some people will disagree with the outcome. But even they can serve their own interests by making good arguments because the better their argument, the more likely they will influence how others think about the issue.

So arguments matter. Being able to make a sound, reasonable argument—and being able to recognize and refute flawed arguments—can help you better address the questions, problems, and challenges you face as a student, an employee, a consumer, and a citizen.

This chapter examines effective argumentation in popular contexts, such as the mass media, social media, and other public venues in which people present arguments about important issues or problems. We call these arguments "popular" arguments to distinguish them from more formal academic arguments (as described in Chapter 12). Although there is a great deal of overlap between academic argument and the kinds of arguments made in popular contexts, there are important differences that will be examined in this chapter. Understanding these differences can help you make more effective arguments in a variety of rhetorical situations.

Occasions for Popular Argument

On September 17, 2011, several hundred people gathered at a park on Wall Street in New York City to protest the growing income inequality in the United States and what they perceived as the increasing control of the political process by wealthy individuals and corporations. The protesters remained there until November, when police evicted them. By then the protest, which was called Occupy Wall Street, had grown into what became known as the Occupy Movement. In cities throughout the United States and in many other nations, protesters set up camps in parks, squares, and other public places. Their slogan, "We are the 99 percent," focused attention on the gap in wealth between those Americans whose incomes place them in the top 1% of all Americans and everyone else (the 99%).

Not surprisingly, the Occupy Movement was controversial. Not only did it spark debate about income inequality and related issues, but it also influenced political discussions in the United States, including the presidential primaries that took place in 2012, by focusing attention on issues of concern to many Americans. Income inequality became an issue in many national and regional political contests, and candidates debated fundamental questions about government's role in addressing problems such as unemployment and poverty. At the same time, the movement sparked countless arguments in a variety of forms in local newspapers, on blogs and websites, on Facebook, Twitter, and other social media, and in city council and town board meetings throughout the United States (see "Popular Argument via Posters").

The Occupy Movement sparked a proliferation of images, videos, and posters that circulated online. Posters like this one might be seen as engaging in popular argument. One of the arguments made by many Occupy protesters was that political elections in the United States are improperly and undemocratically influenced by the wealthiest 1% of Americans, who spend large sums of money to support their candidates and advance their agendas on political issues, while the rest of the population—referred to as "the 99%"—have little say in the process. Consider how this poster presents that argument.

The Occupy Movement is a dramatic example of how people engage in argument to address complicated issues and problems that affect their lives as citizens, workers, consumers, and community members. But to make an argument in such debates isn't just a matter of voicing an opinion or responding to someone else's opinion; it is also an effort to help answer relevant questions and solve pressing problems. In this sense, argument plays a role in every aspect of our lives, even if we usually engage in argument in less dramatic ways:

- Residents of a neighborhood near a large shopping center use social media to voice support for or opposition to a town plan to build a new intersection near the shopping center to reduce traffic.

- A Peace Corps worker returns to the high school from which she graduated and presents a slideshow to encourage students to consider joining the Peace Corps after they graduate.

- Homeowners write letters to their school district office arguing for or against proposed cuts in the new school budget.

These examples illustrate how prevalent argument can be in our daily lives.

Understanding Argument in Popular Discourse

The informal nature of most popular arguments represents both opportunity and challenge for writers as well as readers. For one thing, the many different forms that popular argument can take—from carefully developed newspaper op-ed essays, to less formal blog posts, to brief messages shared on social media, to fliers and posters—can shape argumentation in different ways. The immediacy and brevity of social media sites, for example, call for different strategies of argumentation than the more fully developed arguments typically seen in traditional media, such as newspaper op-ed pages. Writers have many options for presenting their arguments but often have to adjust their strategies as they move from one rhetorical situation to another. For instance, a writer might be able to present less evidence to support a claim in an online forum as compared to a more formal essay, but an online forum allows a writer to link to other sites on the Internet as a way to provide evidence.

The purposes for popular arguments can also be less clear than for academic arguments (Chapter 12), which generally focus on understanding an issue, or proposals (Chapter 14), which often focus on solving a problem. Although popular arguments serve the four main purposes described in Chapter 11—to inquire, to assert, to prevail, and to negotiate differences and solve problems (see pages 317–319)—often conflicting purposes come into play at the same time. For example, Occupy Wall Street protesters might distribute fliers about the worsening economic inequality in the United States to assert their point of view about that issue. A politician might respond to the protest on his blog by making a vigorous argument intended to undermine the protesters' claims about economic inequality (an argument to prevail). At the same time, the leader of a community group might write a letter to the editor of the local newspaper to make a case for a compromise in the conflict that the protest has provoked (an argument to negotiate differences). And a concerned resident without a political agenda might post a response to a community social media site to make an argument that explores the complex reasons for income inequality in the United States (an argument to inquire). All these parties are involved in the same general discussion about the same general issue, but their goals and perspectives vary, diverging or overlapping in complicated ways and sometimes shifting focus rapidly.

In addition, writers advancing positions in popular venues, such as blogs, newspapers, social media, television talk shows, and similar forums, rarely follow the rules of formal argumentation described in Chapter 11. Important features of argument, such as using credible and appropriate evidence to support claims, can vary dramatically from one rhetorical context to another. Statistical data that might be seen as compelling evidence of income inequality in, say, an economics paper, might have little persuasive power in an argument presented on a social media site; moreover, in many popular contexts, there is little expectation that assertions will be supported with solid evidence of any kind. Similarly, a powerful persuasive appeal in an academic argument might be ineffective in a popular context. For example, the viewpoint of a prominent economist who is a Nobel Prize laureate might be used effectively as an ethical appeal in an academic essay; by contrast, the same appeal might fall flat for a popular audience who associates that same economist with a liberal political perspective because he writes a column for a newspaper known for its liberal slant.

The complexities of popular argumentation can be magnified by online and digital media, which not only provide more venues for argument but also can influence the nature of argumentation in complex ways. As a result, writers and readers must be wary in presenting and evaluating arguments made in popular contexts so that they recognize and avoid common problems in popular argument, which are illustrated in the following example. In 2012, New York City Mayor Michael Bloomberg sparked a nationwide debate when he proposed a ban on so-called "supersized" soft drinks. The proposal would have prohibited restaurants and similar establishments from selling soda and other sugary drinks in containers larger than 16 ounces. The proposal was intended to combat obesity, an increasingly serious public health problem in the United States. Not surprisingly, the proposal provoked a vigorous response from supporters as well as opponents. Jeff Halevy, a fitness instructor, wrote the following essay opposing the ban:

> Last week, New York City mayor Michael Bloomberg unveiled his proposal to ban the sale of sweetened sodas in sizes larger than 16 ounces. While this proposal might intuitively seem like a stride in the right direction—who the heck needs more than 16 ounces of soda at a time anyway!?—I personally couldn't disagree more with the move. For one, the implementation is flawed, with 2-liter-peddling supermarkets and sugar-laden juices escaping the executioner's axe, and I also believe it will be a challenge to stem the actions of a motivated Big Gulp purchaser (two 16-ouncers should do the trick, right?).
>
> But more fundamentally, I disagree with the move on a philosophical basis. We live in the age of corporate social responsibility, whereby we expect corporations to self-regulate themselves in the interest of the environment, consumers, and the world

community. We in fact become outraged when we hear of a corporation that has violated what we believe to be its socially responsible actions; Wall Street, Apple, Nike and BP, to name just a few, have all drawn ire by violating this responsibility. It's easy to vilify corporations that, in their insatiable appetite for profits, have thrown their implicit social contracts out the window. But what about the individual, whose appetite, too, leads him to violate social trust?

I believe America is in a crisis now, not only of corporate or governmental social responsibility, but of *personal social responsibility*; we're uncertain of whether Wall Street or Uncle Sam has our best interest at heart, but just the same we should be looking at our neighbor. Our problem is not simply a matter of sugar, fat and salt; it is a matter of choice, behavior and education. We live in a country where we make sure our children are mathematically educated enough to figure out that two 16-ounce sodas will get them their Big Gulp fix, but where roughly 96 **percent of them are not required to have daily physical education classes in school.** What exactly are we teaching them about behavior and choice?

Set aside what we're teaching young America, let's look at ourselves in the mirror. Most of us know what's healthy and what's not. I have had the privilege of meeting folks all over the country, and getting insight into their daily routines:

John Doe: "What can I do to eat better? I feel like I eat okay but I'm already heavy and continue to gain weight."

Me: "Well, let's start with breakfast—what did you eat?"

John Doe: "I know what you're going to say. I probably shouldn't have had the sausage, egg and cheese on a bagel."

Me: "Bingo. So what could you eat instead?"

John Doe: "I guess I should have oatmeal, and maybe some fruit."

Me: "Well there's a big step in the right direction!"

I cannot tell you how many conversations like this I've had over the years about food and exercise. We know what we're doing to ourselves, and most of us know how to change it. And in situations where additional warnings and information may be warranted, sure, I'm all for it; let's slap a warning label on soda, maybe even a picture of a diabetic amputee's leg—whatever it takes. Education is key.

However, our crisis isn't simply one of education. As I said above, it's one of personal social responsibility. Type 2 diabetes, in which insidious sugar sources like soda play a big role, costs this country in excess of $174 billion each year. Most Type 2 diabetics know that their lifestyles are unhealthy but do not take adequate action to prevent or reverse the disease. And who pays for it? How would we react to a corporation that did the very same? (*Note: This is NOT an attack on diabetics; I am merely illustrating a point.*)

And my point is simply this: Drinking soda, or better stated, our right to drink soda, is actually good for us. Isn't that what makes America great? We're the land of free choice. However, when government takes an arbitrary legislative potshot at the symptom, not the cause, of a problem, how much better off are we? Do we want to be hobbled by government making lifestyle choices for us, or empowered by government teaching and supporting better choices? I for one would much rather see legislation making daily physical education and nutrition classes mandatory for our students, ingraining better lifestyles and choices. And I'd love to see the Big Gulp yanked—not due to legislation, but due rather to poor sales from a healthy, educated consumer.

Source: Halevy, Jeff. "Would A Ban on Supersized Soda Help People Make Healthy Choices?" *Huffington Post*. TheHuffingtonPost.com, 4 June 2012. Web. 30 Apr. 2013.

Halevy leaves no doubt that he opposes the proposal to ban the sale of soft drinks in large containers. He presents several strong arguments against such a ban, including the claim, which he supports with evidence, that American students are not necessarily educated in ways that promote healthy lifestyles. He also rests his main argument on a fundamental principle that individuals, not governments, must bear responsibility for making healthy choices. The question of how to address serious public health problems such as obesity is a complicated and highly charged one, and Halevy contributes to the controversy by pointing out potential problems with the proposal to ban the sale of large containers of soft drinks. But Halevy's argument exhibits three common problems with popular argument:

- **Missing or weak evidence to support claims.** Halevy makes several claims for which he provides no supporting evidence, including the claim that "most Type 2 diabetics know that their lifestyles are unhealthy but do not take adequate action to prevent or reverse the disease." He provides evidence that diabetes is a serious health issue, noting that it costs the United States $174 billion annually, but he doesn't explain the significance of that figure. How does that amount compare to costs associated with other diseases? Nor does he provide evidence that soft drinks are a significant factor in diabetes. It is possible that the consumption of soft drinks contributes to the rise in the incidence of diabetes in the United States, but his assertion that such a link exists does not amount to evidence nor does the figure he presents support such a claim.

- **Flawed reasoning.** Halevy asserts that obesity in the United States is a matter of lifestyle, and he suggests that the problem might be addressed by requiring more physical education for American students. But his implicit claim that requiring physical education will lead to healthy lifestyle choices is flawed. He presents no evidence for the claim; moreover, although it is possible that physical education encourages healthier lifestyles, it does not follow logically that simply requiring students to engage in such activities will necessarily mean that they will make healthy choices in the future. There are too many complicating factors to show that a causal relationship exists between required physical education and a healthy lifestyle. (See "Causation vs. Correlation" on page 145.)

- **Oversimplified or exaggerated assertions.** Halevy oversimplifies the problem in several ways. Notice, for example, how he uses his own experience as a fitness instructor to support his claim that "we know what we're doing to ourselves, and most of us know how

Understanding Argument in Popular Discourse **393**

to change it." His argument is that all we really have to do to combat obesity is "look in the mirror" and start making healthy choices. But the causes of obesity and related health problems are extremely complex, and many factors influence the lifestyle choices people make, including factors over which they have little or no control, such as socio-economic status. It is entirely possible that a person suffering from obesity knows about good nutrition but is unable to make certain healthy choices because of income or other circumstances.

This example illustrates the pitfalls of popular argument. As a writer, take care to recognize when you might be making similar mistakes in constructing your argument; as a reader, be vigilant in evaluating a writer's claims and evidence.

FOCUS | **Recognizing Logical Fallacies in Popular Arguments**

A logical fallacy is a flaw in reasoning. One of the most common fallacies is a *non sequitur* (which is Latin for "it does not follow"), in which a conclusion is reached that does not follow logically from the evidence or premise. For example, you might hear someone say, "Most people believe in God, so he must exist." It might be true that most people believe in God, but that fact does not mean that God exists. This kind of flawed reasoning is common in popular argument, especially in political advertising, where it can often be difficult to identify. For example, during his presidency, Barack Obama was criticized for his approval of the use of remotely

Drone Strikes

Obama, 2009: 51   **Bush, 2001–2009:** 45

controlled flying drones to attack alleged terrorists. In 2012, some advocacy groups distributed posters such as this one to highlight the claim that government has grown dangerously during Obama's presidency. But such an argument is logically flawed. Let's assume that the main argument of this poster can be stated as follows: "Government has become bigger and more dangerous under President Obama." The "evidence" for such a claim is that there have been many more drone strikes in a shorter time period under Obama than under the previous president, George W. Bush. However, the number of drone strikes does not necessarily correlate to the size of government. There are many possible reasons for the increase in drone strikes under President Obama. For example, he might have authorized more drone strikes because he had better information about terrorists than President Bush had. It is also possible that the increase in drone strikes reflects a different military strategy rather than an escalation. In other words, there are many possible conclusions that can be logically drawn from this evidence, but it does not logically support the conclusion that government has become bigger or more dangerous.

Such flawed reasoning can be subtle and difficult to identify—which makes it even more important to evaluate claims and reasoning carefully, both as a writer and a reader of popular arguments.

FOCUS Linking to Evidence Online

Essays such as Halevy's (on pages 391–393) that are published online often include hyperlinks to other websites that contain relevant information or opinions. This strategy, which is common in online writing, enables a writer to refer to evidence without having to incorporate it directly into the text. However, the strategy requires readers to follow the links if they wish to see the evidence and to evaluate the credibility of the websites where the information is located. Whether linked online in this way or presented in traditional footnotes, evidence should always be carefully evaluated (see "Appraising and Using Evidence" in Chapter 11). The ease of access to such an enormous amount and variety of information online sometimes means you have to take additional steps when evaluating sources (see Chapter 22). As a writer, always try to provide relevant, credible support for your claims, which means making sure of the credibility of any websites to which you link in an online essay.

Arguments that avoid these problems are likely to be more successful in achieving the writer's rhetorical purposes. Effective arguments in popular discourse usually have the following four main features:

- **A clear main point.** Because arguments in popular discourse tend to be about complicated subjects, it is important for writers to present a clear main point or position without oversimplifying the issue at hand. Issues worth arguing about can rarely be reduced to simple either–or propositions (e.g., standardized testing is good or bad; all tax increases are harmful or necessary); arguments with a clear main point that reflects the complexity of the issue are more likely to be persuasive (e.g., although standardized tests can provide useful information, schools should not rely on them to evaluate teachers; strategic, carefully designed tax increases can raise necessary revenue without weakening economic growth).

- **A relevant contribution.** By definition, popular arguments focus on current issues that matter to writers and their readers. Effective arguments fit into ongoing debates about those issues, and writers who establish the relevance of their argument are more likely to reach their intended audience. No matter the topic, writers should give their readers a compelling rationale that the topic is important and their position is worth considering.

- **Appropriate but accessible support for claims.** In many venues for popular argument, it is not feasible for writers to present detailed evidence, extensive reasoning, or lengthy discussions to support their claims. So writers must present evidence succinctly and make it accessible to the audience. For example, a writer arguing in favor of a proposed gun control law in a letter to the editor of an online newspaper might have to summarize in a sentence or two the results of a relevant study of similar laws rather than present detailed statistical data from that study. Nevertheless, arguments supported by appropriate and persuasive evidence are more likely to be effective than arguments based on unsupported assertions.

- **A reasonable effort to address opposing viewpoints.** Although ignoring or oversimplifying opposing viewpoints might appeal to readers who already share the writer's perspective, it is unlikely to appeal to readers who might not have strong views about the subject. An argument is usually more effective if the writer acknowledges well-known counter-arguments and recognizes the legitimacy of reasonable or widely held opposing viewpoints. Doing so not only strengthens the writer's argument but also can enhance his or her credibility.

Of course, writers could ignore these features of effective argument if they believe doing so will make their arguments more persuasive for a specific audience. For example, a writer arguing against charter schools for an audience of educators who already oppose charter schools might see no value in acknowledging some of the benefits of charter schools, because he or she knows that the audience is unlikely to be swayed by such a discussion. In such a case, the writer must consider the rhetorical situation and decide whether it is ethical to ignore opposing arguments, even if including those arguments might not make the main argument more appealing to the intended audience. In other words, because writers often make arguments about complicated and highly charged topics, and because they sometimes do so for sympathetic audiences, it can be easy to get away with questionable strategies. Whether it is right to do so is another matter, and every writer must decide whether it is ethical to use certain strategies in making an argument. (See "The Ethics of Argument" on page 319 in Chapter 11.)

1. Find several arguments about the same topic in different media for different audiences. For example, you might find a newsletter, a post on a favorite blog, and an essay in a large-circulation magazine such as *Time* about an issue that interests you. Identify each writer's main argument and the evidence supporting that argument, and evaluate the effectiveness of each argument using the characteristics of effective argument described in this chapter. On the basis of your evaluation, what conclusions can you draw about popular arguments?

2. Evaluate the use of evidence to support claims in each of the following passages. (Each passage is an excerpt from a longer argument.) For each passage, identify the claim(s) and the evidence or reasoning presented to support those claim(s). How strong is the evidence for each claim? How logical is the reasoning? Does the evidence seem credible? How do you know? What conclusions can you draw about the uses of evidence in popular argument?

a). Advocates of small-scale, nonindustrial [farming] alternatives say their choice is at least more natural. Again, this is a dubious claim. Many farmers who raise chickens on pasture use industrial breeds that have been bred to do one thing well: fatten quickly in confinement. As a result, they can suffer painful leg injuries after several weeks of living a "natural" life pecking around a large pasture. Free-range pigs are routinely affixed with nose rings to prevent them from rooting, which is one of their most basic instincts. In essence, what we see as natural doesn't necessarily conform to what is natural from the animals' perspectives.

Source: McWilliams, James E. "The Myth of Sustainable Meat." *The New York Times*. The New York Times, 13 Apr. 2012. Web. 30 Apr. 2013.

b). The literature on fatherhood sends a stark message: All fathers are not equal. Breadwinners married to homemakers earn 30 percent more than those in two-job families and encounter favored treatment at work. One study found that fathers were held to lower performance and commitment standards than were men without children, presumably because respondents assumed that since a father "has a family to support," he will work hard. This study reflects the normative father, a breadwinner with a wife who is responsible for children and home. In contrast, a father who discloses that he has family care responsibilities faces job risks. One study found that men are often penalized for taking family leave, especially by other men. Another found that men with even

(Continued)

a short work absence due to a family conflict were recommended for fewer rewards and had lower performance ratings.

Source: Williams, Joan C. "Let's Rethink Masculinity." *In These Times*. In These Times and the Institute for Public Affairs, 6 Oct. 2010. Web. 30 Apr. 2013.

c). Martin Luther King Jr.'s famous "I Have a Dream" speech continues to inspire a nation. But the Civil Rights Act did not spill forth from the mouth of King; it was the culmination of decades of community struggles, Congressional lobbying and judicial strategy. No speech, no matter how awe-inspiring, could have led a Southern Democrat in 1964, six weeks before his party's nominating convention, in the summer of a presidential election year, to sign the most important piece of civil rights legislation since Reconstruction. That unthinkable political act was made possible by a confluence of factors, including important shifts occurring within the Democratic Party. For example, in the 1958 midterm elections eleven racially liberal Republican senators were replaced by eleven racially liberal Democrats. The election did not alter total Congressional support for civil rights legislation, but it did shift the balance of power on race issues between the parties. For the first time, the party of Lincoln did not have exclusive claim on racial liberalism, and for the first time the Democratic Party's powerful Southern segregationist base was balanced against a progressive Northern force. This shift was just enough, when combined with the visible struggle of disciplined, nonviolent Southern resisters, to give Johnson the courage to act on civil rights.

Source: Harris-Lacewell, Melissa. "What Are Words Worth?" *The Nation*. The Nation, 2 Sept. 2010. Web. 30 Apr. 2013.

3. Find an argument with which you agree about a topic that interests you. In a brief essay, summarize the argument, identifying its main claims, evidence, and persuasive appeals. Explain what you think makes the argument effective. Why do you agree with it? What features of the argument make it persuasive for you? On the basis of your evaluation, draw conclusions about what makes a popular argument persuasive.

Reading Popular Arguments

The following examples illustrate the main features of effective popular arguments. In evaluating these arguments, consider how each writer supports the main argument with the intended audience in mind. Also, look for flawed reasoning (see "Recognizing Logical Fallacies in Popular Arguments" on page 394) and other common problems of popular argument (see pages 395–396):

A clear main point	• What is the main argument? • How clearly does the author present the main point? • What is the author's purpose in making this argument?
A relevant contribution	• Why is the argument relevant now? • What is the context for this argument? What audience is addressed? • To which ongoing discussions or debates does the author seek to contribute? What does this argument add to those discussions or debates?
Appropriate, accessible support	• What evidence is presented to support the author's claims? How strong is this evidence? • Is the evidence appropriate for the topic and intended audience? • Does the author make the evidence accessible and understandable?
Opposing viewpoints	• To what extent does the author consider opposing viewpoints? • Has the author oversimplified or misrepresented opposing viewpoints? • Has the author avoided simple either–or propositions?

13

A Judge's Plea for Pot

by Gustin L. Reichbach

Since President Richard Nixon coined the term the "war on drugs" in the early 1970s, the United States has spent billions of dollars to control illegal drugs. Not surprisingly, this "war" has been controversial, and sometimes the effort to eliminate the terrible effects of drug-related crime has had unintended consequences. One such example is explored in the following argument in support of "medical marijuana" or "medicinal marijuana," which refers to the practice of allowing some patients to use marijuana as part of their medical treatment. Medical marijuana is illegal in most states, and even where it is allowed, notably California, health care workers who supply it can be prosecuted by the federal government. However, unlike many other illegal drugs, marijuana seems to have genuine benefits and few risks for cancer patients like Gustin Reichbach, the author of this essay. His argument in support of medical marijuana is a common one: He states that the issue is humanitarian, not legal; it is a matter of alleviating the suffering of thousands of people who must undergo difficult medical treatments. What makes Reichbach's argument unusual, though, is his identity: He is a judge. His use of marijuana technically makes him a criminal. As you read, consider how Reichbach uses his unusual situation to make his argument, which was published in The New York Times *in 2012, when his home state of New York was considering a bill to decriminalize the medical use of marijuana.*

. . . .

Three and a half years ago, on my 62nd birthday, doctors discovered a mass on my pancreas. It turned out to be Stage 3 pancreatic cancer. I was told I would be dead in four to six months. Today I am in that rare coterie of people who have survived this long with the disease. But I did not foresee that after having dedicated myself for 40 years to a life of the law, including more than two decades as a New York State judge, my quest for ameliorative and palliative care would lead me to marijuana.

My survival has demanded an enormous price, including months of chemotherapy, radiation hell and brutal surgery. For about a year, my cancer disappeared, only to return. About a month ago, I started a new and even more debilitating course of treatment. Every other week, after receiving an IV booster of chemotherapy drugs that takes three hours, I wear a pump that slowly injects more of the drugs over the next 48 hours.

Nausea and pain are constant companions. One struggles to eat enough to stave off the dramatic weight loss that is part of this disease. Eating, one of the great pleasures of life, has now become a daily battle, with each forkful a small victory. Every drug prescribed to treat one problem leads to one or two more drugs to offset its side effects. Pain medication leads to loss of appetite and constipation. Anti-nausea medication raises glucose levels, a serious problem for me with my pancreas so compromised. Sleep, which might bring respite from the miseries of the day, becomes increasingly elusive.

Inhaled marijuana is the only medicine that gives me some relief from nausea, stimulates my appetite, and makes it easier to fall asleep. The oral synthetic substitute, Marinol, prescribed by my doctors, was useless. Rather than watch the agony of my suffering, friends have chosen, at some personal risk, to provide the substance. I find a few puffs of marijuana before dinner gives me ammunition in the battle to eat. A few more puffs at bedtime permits desperately needed sleep.

This is not a law-and-order issue; it is a medical and a human rights issue. Being treated at Memorial Sloan Kettering Cancer Center, I am receiving the absolute gold standard of medical care. But doctors cannot be expected to do what the law prohibits, even when they know it is in the best interests of their patients. When palliative care is understood as a fundamental human and medical right, marijuana for medical use should be beyond controversy.

Sixteen states already permit the legitimate clinical use of marijuana, including our neighbor New Jersey, and Connecticut is on the cusp of becoming No. 17. The New York State Legislature is now debating a bill to recognize marijuana as an effective and legitimate medicinal substance and establish a lawful framework for its use. The Assembly has passed such bills before, but they went nowhere in the State Senate. This year I hope that the outcome will be different. Cancer is a nonpartisan disease, so ubiquitous that it's impossible to imagine that there are legislators whose families have not also been touched by this scourge. It is to help all who have been affected by cancer, and those who will come after, that I now speak.

Given my position as a sitting judge still hearing cases, well-meaning friends question the wisdom of my coming out on this issue. But I recognize that fellow cancer sufferers may be unable, for a host of reasons, to give voice to our plight. It is another heartbreaking aporia in the world of cancer that the one drug that gives relief without deleterious side effects remains classified as a narcotic with no medicinal value.

Because criminalizing an effective medical technique affects the fair administration of justice, I feel obliged to speak out as both a judge and a cancer patient suffering with a fatal disease. I implore the governor and the Legislature of New York, always considered a leader among states, to join the forward and humane thinking of 16 other states and pass the medical marijuana bill this year. Medical science has not yet found a cure, but it is barbaric to deny us access to one substance that has proved to ameliorate our suffering.

Source: Reichbach, Gustin L. "A Judge's Plea for Pot." *The New York Times*. The New York Times, 17 May 2012. Web. 30 Apr. 2013.

1. What are the main kinds of persuasive appeals Reichbach uses in making his argument? (See "Making a Persuasive Appeal" in Chapter 11.) How convincing do you think these appeals would be for the intended audience? Explain. Do you find these appeals effective? Why or why not?

2. What kind of evidence does Reichbach present to support his argument in favor of medical marijuana? How persuasive do you find this evidence? Explain.

3. Reichbach wrote this essay at a time when his home state of New York was considering a law that would permit the use of marijuana for medical reasons. What do you think Reichbach hoped to contribute to the debates about medical marijuana with his essay? Do you think he succeeded? Why or why not?

Senate Wars Episode II: Attack of the Drones

by Victor Lana

In March 2013, Senator Rand Paul of Kentucky engaged in an old-fashioned filibuster, a U.S. Senate strategy whereby a senator speaks continuously to prevent a vote on a bill he or she opposes. Paul's 13-hour filibuster prevented the Senate from voting on the confirmation of President Obama's nominee for Secretary of State, but Paul's real goal was to highlight concerns about the Obama administration's policy governing the use of unmanned aerial vehicles, or drones. Specifically, Paul was objecting to the potential use of drones by the U.S. government to kill American citizens. Paul's filibuster was part of one of the most intense debates in the United States in recent years about the use of drones for various purposes, including killing terrorist suspects and conducting surveillance on citizens. In the following blog post, Victor Lana poses some of the difficult questions that were at the center of this debate, especially questions about whether the government's use of drones violates Americans' constitutional rights. Lana's questions highlight the complicated nature of the issues in this debate, and he acknowledges that there are no easy answers even as he makes it clear that he sides with Senator Rand Paul. His blog post illustrates how popular argument can be an essential part of a nation's effort to address difficult problems. It also illustrates some of the characteristics of popular argument in an online medium, including the informal style that is typical of many blogs and the speed with which arguments are made after relevant events occur. In this case, you will notice references not only to Senator Paul's filibuster but also to some responses to it as well as recent events, including an incident in which the pilot of an airliner saw a drone as he was preparing to land at one of New York City's airports. As you read, be aware of how Lana uses other references, including pop culture references, to help him make his argument. His post appeared on the website Blog Critics *in 2013.*

···

The appearance of Rand Paul (R-Kentucky) on the Senate floor in his marathon filibuster notwithstanding, the subject of Predator Drones is becoming an increasingly hot and debatable topic in Congress, in the media, and on the street corner. We Americans, famous for the "Don't Tread on Me" attitude, have to be a bit wary about this technological marvel that can spy on us or kill us, depending on its mission. Like that old movie slogan tells you, "Be afraid; be very afraid."

Only the other day there were reports that the pilot of an Alitalia flight coming into JFK saw what he believed to be a drone flying over Brooklyn. The NYPD and military said that the pilot was mistaken but, just as pilots who report UFOs seem more credible, I wonder if this is just damage control. New York City Police Commissioner Ray Kelly has spoken about using drones for surveillance in the city in the past, so it makes you think twice, doesn't it?

Whether you see Paul's recent 12+ hours of fili-bluster in the Senate as the second coming of Jimmy Stewart in *Mr. Smith Goes to Washington* or Palpatine from *Revenge of the Sith* (a very bad guy senator in *Star Wars* films), you have to admit that he has stoked the fires of the public concern over drones. What would constitute the right to utilize drones over the continental United States? I would like someone to address that in a clear and expedient way.

For example, would a terrorist action on our soil warrant the use of a drone response? How about another 9/11 type of attack? As we know from the reports we get of drones being used overseas, there always seems to be collateral damage. Yes, you might take out a terrorist commander, but along with him you kill innocent civilians, including children, as well. How can we ever view this as acceptable policy?

If an airplane were heading toward a target over a major city like New York or Washington, how and when would the drone strike? Would not everyone on the ground be in danger? Do you save a landmark like the Empire State Building only to allow thousands of civilians to die on the streets below?

Although there are valid concerns about the use of drones, Senator John McCain (R-Arizona), in full "maverick" mode, took Rand Paul to task for daring to question drone use; however, that makes the argument even more salient. If drones being used overseas are killing innocents, then it can happen here. If someone like McCain is so gung-ho about drone use, it makes me a little worried. Of course, he would like the unmanned aircraft since it keeps our pilots out of harm's way, and he no doubt is thinking of his own days as a pilot and how it led to his capture in Vietnam. I know he was a brave and patriotic guy, but the use of drones worries me because we don't have a trained person in that cockpit. I think that's why there have been mistakes that have

(Continued)

cost lives, innocent ones at that, and how can you ultimately defend that policy or want to extend it in the skies over our homeland?

Also, I can't help but having thoughts about those science fiction films like *Terminator* where the machines turn on us. As of now drones are remote controlled, but I have read about "automated" ones as well. If we are setting up killing machines to function on autopilot, we have to wonder when there will be the inevitable mistake. An unintended missile streaking over Brooklyn from a drone and hitting a neighborhood would be catastrophic.

As always, I like to listen to "talk radio" in the car, and this week the callers were talking drones. Among the usual nuts and "experts" who like to get their few minutes of airtime, some have made valid points. Among them, would law enforcement ever use a drone in a situation like the recent shooting incident at Sandy Hook Elementary School in Connecticut? While some of the opinions were that this was completely insane, a few callers said they felt it would have saved lives if a drone came in and took out the shooter. Of course, the school building and anyone in it would have been decimated, but who cares as long as we get the shooter, right?

I think the specter of drones hovering over our cities and towns has to be alarming to most people. Besides the armed ones, those surveillance babies are scary in their own right. Will we eventually become a completely monitored society? All of us could end up like Winston Smith from *1984*, lost in an Orwellian nightmare where Big Brother loves us and watches over us—24/7/365 for our own "good," of course.

Right now I think we all should question the use of drones anywhere. They are killing machines and machines are indiscriminate, and therein is the problem. Machines don't care or feel or think; they just do. We worry about hurricanes and tornadoes and asteroids from space killing us, but the devastation from one of those drones is just as frightening. Unfortunately, this will not be a natural disaster but a one of our own making.

Now is the time for us to say no to Big Brother and also to the danger posed by armed drones. If they are allowed in the skies over our country, it will change forever the freedom and safety we cherish most, and instead of making us safer they will imperil all those things we hold dear. Rand Paul took a stand, and now it is our turn to do so as well. If not then we better look in the mirror when one day fire rains down from the sky or our every movement is monitored. We will have no one to blame but ourselves.

Source: Lana, Victor. "Senate Wars Episode II: Attack of the Drones." *Blog Critics*, Technorati, Inc., 9 Mar. 2013. Web. 30 Apr. 2013.

EXERCISE 13D — ARGUING ABOUT GOVERNMENT USE OF DRONES

1. How would you summarize Lana's main argument? How does he use opposing viewpoints to help make his argument? What appeals does he use? How effective do you find his argument?

2. What kind of evidence does Lana cite to support his claims? To what extent do you think this evidence strengthens his argument? What do you think Lana's use of evidence suggests about blogs as a forum for popular arguments?

3. How would you describe Lana's style and voice in this blog post? Do you think his voice makes his argument stronger? Explain, citing specific passages from the text to support your answer.

13

American Wind Power

American Wind Energy Association

The brochure reprinted here from a trade organization called the American Wind Energy Association illustrates how popular arguments can be made in alternative formats to advocate for a particular point of view or activity. The authors take advantage of the brochure format to incorporate visual elements into their argument, using color, layout, and other design features to enhance the presentation of their argument (see Chapter 20; also see "Analyzing Images" on page 223 in Chapter 8). The American Wind Energy Association advocates wind power, so the brochure's claim that wind power is good for Americans is no surprise; however, the brochure also makes a case in favor of government policies, especially tax subsidies, that support the development of wind power. Notice that the brochure employs strategies that are commonly used in advertising, including emotional appeals. Being aware of these strategies can help you evaluate the effectiveness of the argument and influence your own reaction to the brochure. Also bear in mind that this brochure was available in 2012 when many Americans were debating the benefits and costs of alternative energy sources at a time of economic hardship; consider how the argument presented in the brochure fits that broader context.

(Continued)

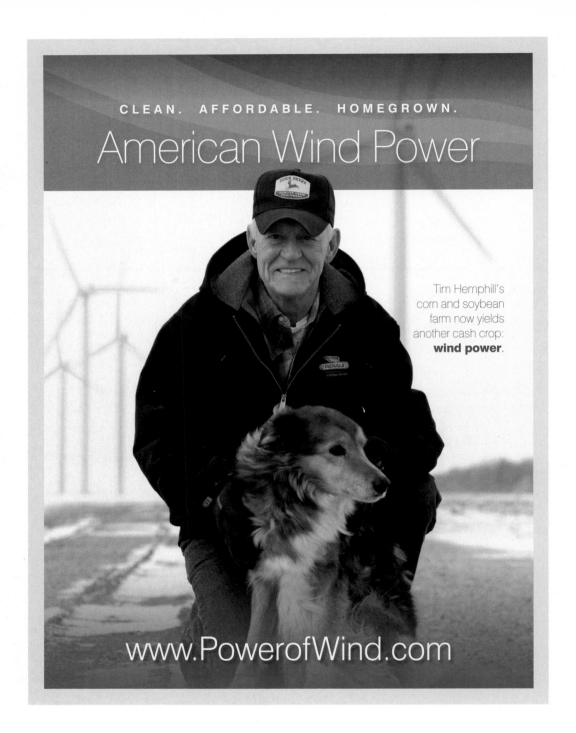

Fifth-generation rancher Shaun Sims has tapped a new revenue stream he can count on: wind power. Evanston, Wyoming

Mike Mayer's tire and oil shop got a big boost in business when developers began work on a local wind farm. Milford, Utah

Thanks to the construction of a nearby wind farm, Judy Cleaves' bed & breakfast gained visibility and visitors. Weston, Maine

Rural economic development fostered by a local wind farm helped build a new hospital, where Nancy Carter works. Milford, Utah

Wind power is good for America

that's why Americans want more of it.

Wind power is good for the rancher who has a new source of steady income that helps preserve a way of life. It's good for the American manufacturer who produces one of the 8,000 components that make up a wind turbine. It's good for the family farmer who can now harvest the natural resource that blows across his land. And wind power is good for the rural school teacher who's been teaching in a trailer, but now educates students in a brand-new school built with revenue generated by way of the local wind farm development.

Wind is cost competitive with all other sources of new electricity. It bolsters America's economy through a supply chain of hundreds of manufacturing plants and over 2,500 companies investing in all stages of American wind power.

Did you know that already, 20 percent of Iowa's electricity comes from wind power? In 2009 alone, the U.S. wind industry installed enough new capacity to power nearly 3 million homes.

An overwhelming majority of Americans – well over 80% of all Republicans, Democrats, and Independents – want more wind power.

When you step back and look at the facts, it becomes clear that wind energy works for America.

To learn more about what wind power can do for America.... and the federal and state policies that will unleash its potential.... please visit www.PowerofWind.com

(Continued)

13

Wind is Affordable

Wind power safeguards our families' checkbooks and creates opportunities for businesses large and small.

Wind is now one of the most cost-effective sources of new electricity generation. That's one reason wind accounts for 35% of all new electricity generating capacity since 2007.

Turbine prices and capital costs have dropped sharply in recent years. More efficient U.S.-based manufacturing is saving on transportation, and technology improvements are making turbines better and more efficient. Because of performance improvements over the years, a turbine with a nameplate capacity seven times larger than a typical turbine in 1990 can produce 15 times more electricity.

And the wind that turns the turbine blades costs nothing, locking in a predictable long-term cost of electricity for 20-30 years and protecting families and businesses from unexpected price spikes.

Alabama Power, a subsidiary of Southern Company, recently purchased its first wind power after the Public Service Commission

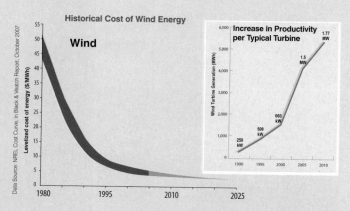

found that the "price of energy from the wind facility is expected to be lower than the cost the Company would incur to produce that energy from its own resource…with the resulting energy savings flowing directly to the Company's customers." [1]

In Colorado, Xcel Energy found that "by displacing natural gas with fixed priced wind energy, the Company has less exposure to potentially volatile natural gas pricing." [2]

Market prices take into account the various incentives that all energy sources receive, and wind energy's is the federal Production Tax Credit. To stay affordable compared with other energy sources and their startup costs – already permanently incentivized over the last 90 years – U.S. wind power depends on Congress extending this single tax incentive.

Wind is Homegrown

Wind energy has been one of the fastest-growing sources of new U.S. manufacturing jobs, even in the depths of the recession. Between 2005 and 2009, a period of relative policy stability never before seen by the industry, wind power grew at a fierce pace. Wind added 35% of all new electricity capacity between 2007 and 2010, neck and neck with natural gas as the top-two new electricity sources.

As a result of this market growth, today over 400 American manufacturing plants build wind components, including all the major turbine components, towers, and blades. Since 2007 over 100 wind energy manufacturing facilities have come online, been announced or expanded. Now over 60% of a U.S.-installed turbine's value is produced right here in America, according to a recent report from the U.S. Department of Energy. A 12-fold increase from just a few years ago. Some turbine manufacturers have already said they plan to make the vast majority of their components in America.

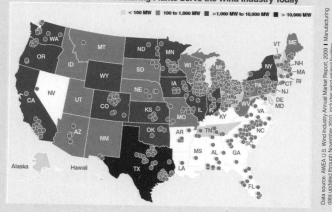

Unlike all too many products now produced overseas, the economics of wind power are such that components are best sourced domestically—that is, near the projects. The trend is expected to continue—if long-term policies are put in place to signal the market stability enjoyed by other energy industries.

[1] Order, Alabama Public Service Commission, Docket 31653, Sept. 9, 2011
[2] Testimony, Public Service Company of Colorado, Sept. 19, 2011.

Wind is Clean and Abundant

The United States boasts the perfect combination of massive electricity demand and a wind resource that is one of the best in the world. The wind power potential to be tapped is nothing short of amazing: 37 trillion kilowatt-hours of electricity annually—equivalent to nearly 10 times the country's existing power needs.[1]

Wind energy is already helping the nation meet America's electricity demand by powering the equivalent of over 9.7 million American homes. Today's wind farms produce enough electricity to power all of Virginia, Oklahoma or Tennessee. In Iowa existing wind projects could produce 20% of the state's electricity. Minnesota, North Dakota, Oregon, Colorado, and Kansas all receive more than 5% of their electricity from wind, and other states are following close behind with ever-growing wind power fleets.

According to the Bush Administration's U.S. Department of Energy report, "20% Wind Energy by 2030: Increasing Wind Energy's Contribution to U.S. Electricity Supply," wind can play a major role in meeting America's increasing demand for electricity, while producing multiple other benefits. Having 20% of the nation's electricity come from wind power is feasible with today's technology, the report found.

Moreover, the report found that installing more wind power would foster rural economic development, job creation, and energy price stability (by sidestepping fossil-fuel price volatility in addition to easing the pressure on natural gas prices). In the decade leading up to the 20% wind power benchmark, the U.S. wind industry could support roughly 500,000 jobs. It could also increase annual payments to rural landowners to more than $600 million in 2030.

Wind provided 35 percent of all new U.S. electricity generation capacity, 2007-10

- Coal
- Petroleum
- Nuclear
- Natural Gas
- Wind
- Other Renewables
- Other

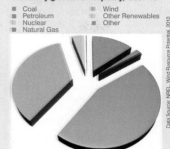

Data Source: NREL, Wind Resource Potential, 2010

Wind is a source of clean energy that has virtually no polluting properties or side effects. Each year, U.S. wind installations will save the nation over 20 billion gallons of water that would otherwise be withdrawn for steam or cooling in conventional power plants.

A Lopsided Playing Field

Some people assume that wind power needs extra help from the government to compete. Since it's relatively new on the scene and boasts so many win-win attributes, are policy incentives really necessary? Only to level the playing field.

Fossil-fuel subsidies are – well, as old as fossil fuels. The Congressional Research Service notes that for more than 90 years, fossil fuel industries have taken subsidies via generous tax breaks. They are seldom debated or even heard of, because they are permanent. Examining the issue during the Bush Administration, the Government Accountability Office concluded that fossil fuels continue to receive nearly five times the tax incentives as renewable energy.[2] American taxpayers have already paid well over $500 billion to fossil fuel industries.[3]

Such strong policy support for old technologies like oil, gas, and coal during the last century succeeded in its goal:

Fossil Fuels Enjoy Permanent Incentives 5x Those of Renewables

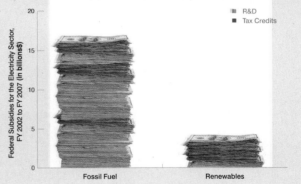

- R&D
- Tax Credits

Federal Subsidies for the Electricity Sector, FY 2002 to FY 2007 (in billions$)

Fossil Fuel   Renewables

Data Source: Government Accountability Office, October 2007

it helped create an abundance of affordable domestic energy, powering strong economic growth. Rising demand, volatile prices and national security concerns have since created a need for a more diverse energy supply.

[1] NREL, Wind Resource Potential, 2010
[2] Federal Electricity Subsidies (Government Accountability Office, October 2007).
[3] An Analysis of Federal Incentives Used to Stimulate Energy Production (U.S. Department of Energy, Pacific Northwest Laboratory Operated by Battelle Memorial Institute, December 1978) and Analysis of Federal Expenditures of Energy Development (Management Information Services, Inc (MISI)., September 2008).

(Continued)

Predictable Policies Improve Investment

It's a wonder there's a U.S. wind industry at all, when you consider the lack of certainty companies have had to confront through the years. First, consider nearly 100 years of policy stability that has provided old techologies with a consistent environment in which to operate, plan, and grow.

Now consider wind power. The federal Production Tax Credit – the primary financial policy for the industry through the years – has been extended mostly in one- and two-year intervals, and even allowed to expire on occasion. The up-and-down nature of the industry is mainly the result of this short-term – and short-sighted – policy environment.

Wind has proven that it's a superior energy source. Why? Because it competes even on this uneven playing field. American wind installed 10,000 megawatts in 2009 – enough to power nearly 3 million homes. In recent years, it has gone head-to-head with natural gas for the leadership position in new power plant installations.

How did American wind power achieve such impressive numbers? Although it still operated with short-term policy,

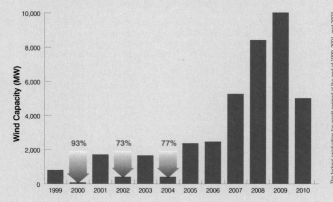

Lack of consistent Market Signals Creates a Boom-Bust Cycle for Wind

The federal production tax credit expired at the end of 1999, 2001, and 2003.

there was a temporary period of stability for the industry. The PTC was extended for several years in a row without being allowed to expire. The frequent eleventh-hour extensions caused the industry some degree of stress as it began to establish a manufacturing base here; nevertheless, through its investments, the industry literally banked on Congress to act on long-term

policy. It's still waiting. One such policy is a national Renewable Electricity Standard, which would set targets for a certain portion of each utility's electricity mix to come from clean, renewable sources. Long-term tax policies, lasting more than just a few years, would also provide consistency and market certainty.

America's Choice

Hands down, the American people support wind energy development. Recent polls consistently show that nearly nine out of ten voters – Republicans, Democrats, and Independents – believe increasing the amount of energy the nation gets from wind is a good idea. That's because wind power doesn't just generate electricity. It powers economic development. It adds a new source of steady income to family farmers' and ranchers' bottom line. It opens the doors of factories previously mothballed. It sends clean, home-grown energy to our homes and businesses, while protecting family budgets and small businesses from volatile price spikes. No wonder Americans want more wind power.

89% of American voters
84% of Republicans | 88% of Independents | 93% of Democrats
believe increasing the amount of energy the nation gets from wind is a good idea

Data Source: March 2010 survey by Neil Newhouse, Public Opinion Strategies, Anna Bennett, Bennett, Petts & Normington

To learn more about these Americans, and more about wind power,

go to **www.powerofwind.com**

AWEA
AMERICAN
WIND ENERGY
ASSOCIATION

1501 M St. NW, Suite 1000 I Washington, DC 20005 I 202.383.2500 phone I www.awea.org

1. How would you state the main argument presented in this brochure? How clearly do you think that argument is presented? Do you think that argument would be more or less effective in a more traditional format, such as an editorial essay? Explain.

2. What kind of evidence is presented in support of the claims made in the brochure? How credible is this evidence? How effectively do you think it is presented? On the basis of the evidence presented, what assumptions do you think are made about the audience for this brochure? Cite specific parts of the brochure to support your answers.

3. What are the main appeals made in this brochure (see "Making Persuasive Appeals" in Chapter 11)? What do you think these appeals suggest about the intended audience for this brochure? Do you find these appeals effective? Why or why not?

Writing Arguments in Popular Contexts

This section provides a framework for developing an academic argument using the Ten Core Concepts described in Chapters 2 and 3. Each step described here corresponds to a step in Chapter 3. You might notice that some of the steps below are similar to the steps described in "Writing Effective Academic Arguments" in Chapter 12. However, there are some important differences between academic arguments and arguments made in popular contexts; those differences are reflected here.

Step 1   Identify a topic for argument.

Begin with a question about a problem or issue that matters to you:

- What limits should be placed on individual freedom in the interest of national security?

- Should marijuana be decriminalized for medical uses?

- How should social media be used in college classrooms?

- What responsibility, if any, do individual citizens have when it comes to addressing problems associated with climate change?

- Should English be the official language of the United States?

- Why should college students be concerned about income inequality in the United States?

Make a list of four or five such questions. If there is a local issue that interests you, such as a current controversy in your town or on your campus, include it on this list.

Now select the question that you would most like to explore. Consider the following:

Your interest in the topic	Its importance	Your opinion

| **Why does this topic interest you?** Consider what makes this topic worth exploring. It's best to make an argument about topics in which you have a strong interest. | **Why is this topic important?** Consider whether the topic fits your assignment or is important to a larger audience. Is the topic part of a current controversy or debate? What might interest others about this topic? Why would your views about this topic be relevant to others? Consider how the topic might fit into ongoing conversations about important issues or problems. | **Do you have an opinion about this topic or a position on the issue?** Consider your feelings or attitude about the topic. What is your stance on this issue? Why do you feel the way you do? |
| **Do you have some special connection to this topic?** For example, as a college student, you might have a keen interest in economic issues that affect the job market, which you will soon enter. Examine whether this topic has special relevance for you. | | **Are you unsure?** At this point, it doesn't matter whether you have an opinion or stance. What matters is that the topic is something you care about or have an interest in pursuing. |

Addressing these questions will help you decide whether to pursue the topic. If you decide that this topic isn't appropriate or doesn't sufficiently interest you to sustain an argument, return to your list and select a different question. Once you have a question about which you want to make an argument, continue to develop your question using Step #1 in Chapter 3.

Step 2   Place your topic in rhetorical context.

Because the contexts for popular arguments are so varied and are sometimes very general, it can be challenging to identify with certainty the specific elements of your rhetorical context.

For example, imagine that the administration of your college has proposed installing security cameras in most public spaces on your campus, including the student center, the open areas outside the main classroom buildings, and the recreation fields where students often play Frisbee or study during good weather. The proposal was prompted by recent violence on other college campuses; however, some students and faculty members at your college object to the plan, citing privacy issues and expressing concern that instead of deterring crime, the cameras will invade students' privacy and be used to monitor student behavior. Some residents of the local community are also interested in the plan because many of them come to the campus for various fine arts and sporting events, meetings, and other activities. Let's imagine that you agree with some of the criticisms of the plan, but you also share the concerns of the college administration about campus security. The main question at this point is:

Should security cameras should be installed in public spaces on the campus?

You are interested in developing an argument that makes a case for a middle ground that might address the concerns of all parties. As you develop that argument, examine your possible audiences:

Possible audience	What is the audience's interest?	How can you reach this audience?
College administration	Must decide whether to install security cameras	• Letter • Campus newspaper or social media site
Students and faculty	Will be directly affected by cameras; have both privacy and security concerns	• Student newspaper • Social media
Community residents	Might sometimes be affected by cameras; care about issues on campus	• Local newspaper • Social media or website
General audience (interested in security and privacy issues)	Will not be directly affected by cameras but care about larger questions of privacy and security	• Regional or national newspaper • Online magazine • Social media sites

This graphic illustrates that the interests of your potential audiences overlap yet differ in some important ways. For example, students and faculty might worry about how their behavior could be affected by the new cameras. By contrast, a general audience (say, readers of a national blog or larger-circulation publication like *USA Today*) would not share that concern but might be very interested in the way your campus administration tries to address the conflict between security and privacy, which is an issue of national debate. It is possible that your argument might be written with all these audiences in mind. Ultimately, your interest in this topic and your audience's interests should overlap, giving your argument greater relevance.

With this in mind, return to your question from Step #1 and explore your audience and the rhetorical context for an argument about your question. Step #2 in Chapter 3 will help you examine your rhetorical context more fully.

Step 3   Select a medium.

In selecting a medium for your argument, consider the advantages and drawbacks of each medium for specific audiences—keeping in mind that popular arguments appear in many different media. For example, using our hypothetical question about the proposal to install security cameras in public spaces on your college campus, compare the advantages and drawbacks of two possible media for the argument: an essay in the campus newspaper and a post on a social media site devoted to campus issues:

Medium: Essay in Campus Newspaper

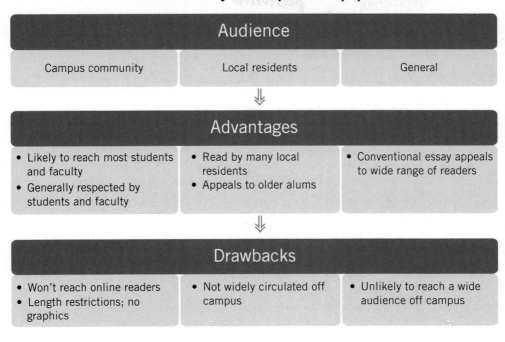

Audience

Campus community	Local residents	General

⇓

Advantages

• Likely to reach most students and faculty • Generally respected by students and faculty	• Read by many local residents • Appeals to older alums	• Conventional essay appeals to wide range of readers

⇓

Drawbacks

• Won't reach online readers • Length restrictions; no graphics	• Not widely circulated off campus	• Unlikely to reach a wide audience off campus

Medium: Post on Social Media Site

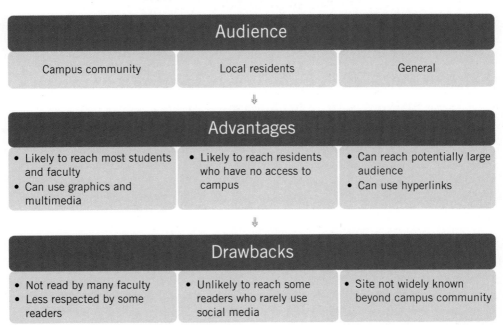

Audience

Campus community	Local residents	General

⇓

Advantages

• Likely to reach most students and faculty • Can use graphics and multimedia	• Likely to reach residents who have no access to campus	• Can reach potentially large audience • Can use hyperlinks

⇓

Drawbacks

• Not read by many faculty • Less respected by some readers	• Unlikely to reach some readers who rarely use social media	• Site not widely known beyond campus community

Return to your main question and identify possible media for your argument. Evaluate each one in terms of its potential advantages and drawbacks for your intended audience, then complete Step #3 in Chapter 3 to help you decide on the most appropriate medium for your argument.

Step 4   Identify your main argument.

The strength of your argument will rest in part on how clearly you can make your main point. Keep in mind:

- Your main point is not necessarily the same thing as your position on the issue, though the two are related (see "Developing a Main Argument" in Chapter 11).

- Your main point might evolve as you develop your argument.

You might not know at this stage exactly what your argument will be, but as you explore your topic, you can adjust and refine your argument. At this stage, the goal is to identify a clear main idea as a starting point for developing your argument.

Let's return to the example of an argument about a proposal to install security cameras on your campus. Imagine that you believe a compromise is necessary to address the legitimate concerns of those who have different positions on the issue, so you don't want to make an argument explicitly for or against the installation of the cameras; rather, you want to develop an argument that captures your support for the proposed cameras and your concern about privacy. You also want to connect your argument to the national debate about the conflict between security and civil liberty. With these goals in mind, develop a working thesis statement. Your working thesis should state as clearly and specifically as possible the main argument you will make. Refine your statement until it captures your main argument:

Thesis: The college should install security cameras in public spaces on campus.

| This statement reflects unequivocal support for the proposed security cameras. | The statement does not reflect your concerns about privacy and civil liberty. |

Adjusted Thesis: Security cameras should be installed in public spaces on campus in ways that do not violate legitimate privacy rights of students, faculty, and others on campus.

| This statement reflects your position about the security cameras more accurately. | The statement still does not capture the larger conflict between security and civil liberties. |

Refined Thesis: Institutions like colleges must carefully consider fundamental principles of civil liberty when taking measures such as installing security cameras in public spaces to protect the safety of students, faculty, and others who use their campuses.

| This statement captures the complexity of the issue and connects it to larger questions about security and civil liberty. | It also retains a focus on the local question about whether to install security cameras on campus. |

Notice that in developing your working thesis statement in this way, you are taking into account your rhetorical context and sense of purpose. In this case, you don't want to make an argument that is relevant only for your campus; you also want to connect the local question to larger issues that might speak to a more general audience. So your main argument should be shaped by your rhetorical situation.

Completing Step #4 in Chapter 3 will help you develop a Guiding Thesis Statement, which is essentially a statement of your main argument.

Step 5 Support your main argument.

At this point, you will develop your main argument by identifying supporting arguments and claims and providing evidence and/or reasoning for each one. Often, completing this task requires research, so keep in mind that as you learn more about your topic, you might need to refine your argument and adjust your claims.

You have three main tasks at this point:

- Identify the claims you will make in support of your main argument.
- Identify evidence or reasoning to back up each claim.
- Address opposing arguments or complicating factors.

As you move through these steps, focus on developing your argument thoroughly. You might identify more claims and evidence than you will ultimately need, but later you can eliminate unnecessary claims or evidence.

Let's return to the example of an argument about security cameras on your campus. Here's your main argument:

Institutions like colleges must carefully consider fundamental principles of civil liberty when taking measures such as installing security cameras in public spaces to protect the safety of students, faculty, and others who use their campuses.

Consider possible claims you might make to support this main argument. First, you could claim that the college's concerns about security are valid, perhaps citing recent violence on other college campuses. You might also claim that security cameras can be an effective tool in preventing or responding to violent crime. In addition, you need to acknowledge the legitimate concerns about privacy and civil liberties. For example, you might cite evidence that security measures have led to violations of privacy rights in some cases. But you also want to show that such violations can be avoided, and you'll need some evidence for such a claim. Ultimately, you want to make the argument that civil liberties cannot be compromised because of security concerns, and that position might require logical reasoning to support. Develop each of these supporting and opposing arguments as follows:

Main Argument

Institutions like colleges must carefully consider fundamental principles civil liberty when taking measures such as installing security cameras in public spaces to protect the safety of students, faculty, and othes who use their campuses.

Supporting Claims

| Colleges have reason to worry about campus security. | Security cameras in public places can be effective in deterring or responding to violent crime. | Security measures can be taken without seriously compromising privacy and civil liberty. |

Possible Evidence or Reasoning to Support Claims

| Recent incidents of violence on other campuses; the campus presents an opportunity for tragic violence | Statistical data showing positive impact of security cameras | Examples of other campuses using cameras with restrictions to protect privacy |

Opposing Arguments or Complicating Factors

| Tragic violence on a few campuses doesn't mean all campuses are at risk; overreaction could be worse than doing nothing. | Security measures have often resulted in the abuse of civil liberties. | Civil liberties are always in danger and must be protected, even if it means accepting some risk of violent crime. |

Answers to Opposing Arguments and/or Complicating Factors

| True, but colleges have a responsibility to prepare for unexpected tragedies. | Yes. That's why restrictions must be placed on the use of security cameras on campus. | Agreed, but protecting civil liberties and enhancing security are not mutually exclusive. |

As you develop supporting arguments and identify evidence to support your claims, keep the following in mind:

- **Present your argument fairly.** Avoid making misleading claims and misrepresenting opposing arguments. Instead, present your own claims and acknowledge opposing claims so that you don't oversimplify the issue. Although exaggerating or misrepresenting opposing viewpoints can win approval from those who might already agree with you, it can also lead to a weaker argument that is less persuasive for readers who might be undecided about the issue.

- **Be judicious in your use of evidence.** Remember that in popular arguments, you might be limited in how much evidence you can provide to support your claims (see "Appropriate but accessible support for claims" on page 396). Be judicious in selecting and presenting your evidence, keeping in mind that you might not be able to cite sources with footnotes or provide lengthy explanations of your evidence. The rule of thumb is to present your evidence succinctly while making sure your readers know that the evidence is credible. For example, in an essay about ocean garbage, Usha Lee McFarling refers to studies to support her claims about the problems with plastic garbage that is dumped in the sea:

  > A study released last month found plastic deep in the water column as well as on the surface, suggesting the ocean holds far more plastic than previously believed. A second study published this month indicates the amount of plastic in the Great Pacific Garbage Patch has increased 100-fold in the last four decades.

McFarling doesn't provide much information about these studies, but she notes that both studies are recent, which suggests that the studies' findings are still relevant. Given that her essay appeared on the opinion pages of a newspaper, she was not able to use footnotes to provide references for the studies. To strengthen the credibility of this evidence, she might have mentioned briefly where the studies were published and whether they are considered sound studies by other scientists. Apparently, she assumes that her readers will trust that she has reviewed the actual studies carefully to establish their credibility.

With these principles in mind, develop your claims and identify appropriate and sufficient evidence to support them. Also identify opposing claims and evidence or reasoning to address them. Step #5 in Chapter 3 will guide you in this task.

You should now be ready to write a complete draft of your project. If not, move onto the next step before completing your draft.

Step 6   Organize your argument.

Popular arguments tend to be more loosely structured than the four traditional ways of organizing an argument described in Chapter 11 (see "Structuring an Argument"). Writers in popular venues usually adjust the structure of their arguments to fit the needs of the rhetorical situation, including the medium and the expectations for form (if any). For example, an editorial essay might loosely follow a classical arrangement (see page 345 in Chapter 11) but eliminate the formal refutation of opposing arguments (which is Part V in classical arrangement). For a brief essay in a traditional format such as a newspaper, with limited space, this structure makes sense. The point is that you can adjust a format such as classical arrangement to suit your needs.

Use the four traditional ways to organize your argument as a guide rather than a rigid format, adjusting the structure of your argument to fit the needs of your rhetorical situation:

The rhetorical situation	• How can you organize your essay to present your argument to your intended audience clearly and persuasively? • What expectations will your audience likely have regarding the form of your argument? • Are you writing within a rhetorical situation that has specific conventions for structuring an argument? • Does the medium restrict the structure of your argument in any way?
The nature of your argument	• Does your argument rest on a primary belief or principle (deductive reasoning)? • Does it rely on conclusions drawn from evidence (inductive arrangement)? • Does your argument include a number of complicated supporting claims and kinds of evidence (classical arrangement)? • Is your purpose primarily to solve a problem or negotiate differences (Rogerian arrangement)?

To illustrate, let's return to the previous example of an argument about the proposed use of security cameras in public spaces on your college campus.

■ **Consider the rhetorical situation.** Imagine that you have decided to present your argument in a blog post on a campus social media site. In many ways, your post would be similar to a traditional newspaper op-ed essay or even an academic essay. It will have to be relatively brief and should be clearly focused on the issue at hand (Should the campus install security cameras?). But your main argument addresses a complicated issue and connects it to the larger question of how to balance security with civil liberties. Given that complexity, using a form of classical arrangement might be a good approach to present your case effectively to a varied audience of students, faculty, and probably community residents. Classical arrangement would allow you to incorporate your several claims about security and civil liberties. On the other hand, because you are presenting what amounts to a solution that could appeal to people with different positions on the issue, Rogerian argument might also make sense.

■ **Examine the nature of the argument.** Classical arrangement can be an effective approach to organizing an argument that includes several complicated claims and different kinds of supporting evidence. But you might consider arranging your post as an inductive argument, in which you are drawing conclusions from available evidence. In this case, the evidence might be the experience of other colleges with security cameras as well as statistical data about how security cameras reduce crime, and your main conclusion is that security measures must be undertaken carefully to avoid violations of civil liberty. An inductive approach will enable you to emphasize your evidence.

On the basis of this analysis, you have three options for organizing your argument: classical arrangement, Rogerian argument, and inductive reasoning. Select one of these approaches (or a different one) and develop a basic outline (see "Structuring an Argument" in Chapter 11). However you decide to organize your argument, the structure should be driven by your sense of how to present your argument most effectively for your rhetorical situation.

Follow these steps to analyze your situation and decide how best to organize your argument. You can get additional guidance for organizing your essay by following Step #6 in Chapter 3.

Step 7 Get feedback.

Ask your readers to focus on two sets of questions about argumentation in popular contexts.

First, focus on the **features of effective argument in popular contexts**:

A clear main point	• Is your main point clearly stated? • Is the purpose of your argument clear? • Is the focus on your main argument maintained throughout your essay?
Appropriate, accessible support	• Do you provide appropriate support for each of your claims? • Can any claims be made stronger with additional or different support? • Is your evidence understandable to your audience?
Relevant contribution	• Do you explain why your argument is relevant for your rhetorical situation? Do you place it in a context that makes sense to your readers? • How does your argument contribute to discussions of your topic?
Opposing arguments	• Do you address opposing arguments? • Do you present opposing arguments fairly and in a way that strengthens your own position? • Do you avoid oversimplifying the issues?

Next, focus on common problems in popular arguments:

Missing or weak evidence	• Do you provide sufficient evidence for each claim you make? • Have you failed to support any claims? • Is the evidence presented for any of your claims weak, misleading, or inappropriate?
Flawed reasoning	• Is your reasoning sound? • Do you fall victim to any logical fallacies? (See "Recognizing Logical Fallacies in Popular Arguments" on p. 394.) • Do your conclusions follow logically from your evidence or claims?
Oversimplified or exaggerated assertions	• Do you oversimplify your topic or your claims? • Does your argument do justice to the complexity of your topic? • Do you make any exaggerated claims or assertions that need to be eliminated or revised on the basis of your evidence?

Follow Step # 7 in Chapter 3 to analyze your feedback and help you decide which revisions to make.

Step 8 Revise.

As you consider the feedback you received for Step #7, you might find that you need to do additional research to identify evidence to support your claims or address opposing arguments or complicating factors. That's OK. Remember, revision is

- an opportunity to deepen your understanding of your topic and strengthen your argument
- a chance to adjust your persuasive appeals and make sure that your argument fits your rhetorical situation

You can divide the task of revising your argument into three steps.

1. **Review your draft using the questions listed in Step #7.** Make sure you have addressed the four key features of effective argument in popular contexts; also, eliminate any of the common problems in popular arguments.

2. **Adjust your persuasive appeals.** Now is the time to review your draft to make sure that you have used ethical, emotional, and/or logical appeals in a way that strengthens your argument (see "Making a Persuasive Appeal" in Chapter 11). For example, the emotional appeal made

by Judge Reichbach in the essay reprinted in this chapter (see pages 400–401) is appropriate in an argument that examines an issue from a deeply personal perspective, as his argument does; however, such an appeal would be less appropriate if his argument focused on the legal complexities of medical marijuana for an audience of lawyers. Review each of your supporting arguments or claims to determine whether you have made an appropriate persuasive appeal for that argument or claim given your rhetorical situation.

Let's return to our hypothetical argument about installing security cameras in public spaces on your campus; consider the appeals that might be appropriate for your main claims:

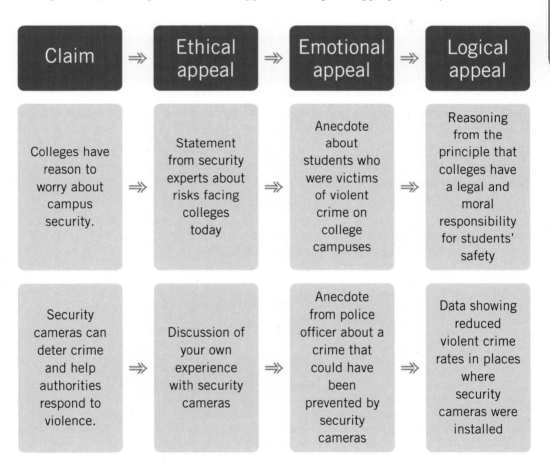

Claim ⇒	Ethical appeal ⇒	Emotional appeal ⇒	Logical appeal
Colleges have reason to worry about campus security. ⇒	Statement from security experts about risks facing colleges today ⇒	Anecdote about students who were victims of violent crime on college campuses ⇒	Reasoning from the principle that colleges have a legal and moral responsibility for students' safety
Security cameras can deter crime and help authorities respond to violence. ⇒	Discussion of your own experience with security cameras ⇒	Anecdote from police officer about a crime that could have been prevented by security cameras ⇒	Data showing reduced violent crime rates in places where security cameras were installed

Notice that different kinds of evidence can be used to make different kinds of appeals. If we assume that all the evidence is valid and credible, then the decision about which evidence to use to support a claim should be a matter of determining which kind of appeal would be most effective for the rhetorical situation.

3. **Finally, follow Step #8 in Chapter 3.** Make sure you have addressed all the essential aspects of your essay in your revisions.

Step 9 Refine your voice.

The reading selections included in this chapter illustrate how varied a writer's voice can be in popular argumentation. For example, compare the heartfelt voice of Gustin Reichbach (page 400) with Victor Lana's more hip voice and somewhat sarcastic tone (page 402), and consider how each voice fits (or does not fit) the topic and rhetorical situation. These examples underscore the point that an argument can be strengthened—or weakened—by the writer's voice. Keep that in mind as you review your draft with a focus on your voice.

Begin by considering your purpose in making your argument, which can shape your voice. For example, let's say your purpose in making your argument about installing security cameras in public spaces on your campus is to negotiate differences among the competing points of view in an effort to find a solution to a difficult problem. You want your readers (students, faculty, and local residents as well as perhaps a wider audience) to consider your solution carefully, even if they disagree with your position. Although you might want your voice to convey your concerns and passion about the issue, especially because as a student you are directly affected by the issue, you also want to sound reasonable and open-minded. Such a voice is likely to win respect among your readers, whatever their position on the issue.

Review your draft and adjust your voice, if necessary:

Identify the primary purpose of your argument.

⇓

Consider the kind of voice that is appropriate for your rhetorical context.

⇓

Review your draft to determine whether your voice fits your purpose and rhetorical context.

Make necessary revisions to your draft. Then follow Step #9 in Chapter 3 to refine and further strengthen your voice.

Step 10   Edit.

Complete Step #10 in Chapter 3.

1. Identify an issue or controversy that you feel strongly about. Write an argument in which you take a position on this issue for an audience of people who have an interest in or connection to the issue.

2. Write an argument in response to an essay on a website or in a publication you regularly read. Write your argument for the same audience for whom the original essay was intended.

3. Rewrite the argument you wrote for Question #1 or Question #2 for a completely different audience or in a different medium. Then compare both arguments. What adjustments did you have to make in revising your argument? What conclusions might you draw about the role of audience and medium in constructing effective arguments in popular contexts?

4. Think of an important experience you had that influenced your life in a significant way. Looking back on that experience, consider what larger issues the experience seems to involve. For example, if you encountered some kind of difficulty in school, you might consider your experience in light of debates about school reform or problems with education. Drawing on your experience, write an argument about an issue related to that experience. Identify an audience for whom your argument would be appropriate.

5. Review the argument you wrote for Question #1, #2, or #4, and identify the persuasive appeals (emotional, ethical, or logical) you used in your argument. Rewrite the argument, using different appeals to make your case. For example, if you relied primarily on an emotional appeal in the original essay, focus on a logical or ethical appeal in your rewrite.

6. Review several recent tweets on a current controversy that interests you. Identify tweets that reflect a position on the issue that you support. Now construct an argument on the basis of one of those tweets. Write your argument for an audience similar to the audience for the original tweet, and adopt a medium that would reach that audience.

Presenting a Proposal 14

A FRIEND ONCE COMPLAINED to me about the writing skills of new employees at his engineering firm. Most are recent graduates from some of the most prestigious engineering schools in the United States, with excellent academic records and relevant work experience but, according to my friend, poor writing skills. Few of them, he says, can write effective proposals, which is an essential skill in his line of work. Without persuasive proposals, his firm could not secure contracts for the large projects that earn them a profit. So my friend spends a lot of time helping new employees learn to write proposals.

Proposals, which are a special kind of argument, are essential in businesses like engineering firms, which compete with other firms for contracts. Proposals are common in many other contexts as well:

- Non-profit organizations write proposals to foundations or government agencies to secure funding for their work.
- Researchers submit proposals to obtain grants to support their research.
- Student leaders submit proposals to college administrators seeking permission to hold special events, such as concerts, on campus.
- Entrepreneurs pitch proposals for new businesses to potential investors.

As these examples illustrate, proposals are a specialized form of argument in which the primary goal is to convince someone to support a project, idea, or plan. Knowing how to write an effective proposal, then, can help you succeed as a student, a citizen, and a professional.

Occasions for Writing Proposals

In a proposal, a writer uses argument not to take a stand or present a point of view but to convince a reader that a specific idea or plan is worthwhile. Proposals take many different forms, and writers in all kinds of situations—business, school, politics, and so on—use them in various ways. Although you might not have experience as a professional writer or businessperson, you have probably written some kind of proposal:

- for an independent study project in a high school or college class
- for a grant or scholarship application to support an activity or study

- to invite a business or foundation to sponsor a school trip or project

- to request permission from your school or church to have a dance or other special event

In such cases, the writer makes an argument that the project, event, trip, or activity is worthy of support.

Notice that these examples all describe very specific rhetorical situations with very specific audiences. For example, a student writing a proposal for an independent study project addresses a teacher, principal, or faculty committee whom the student probably knows. Sometimes, however, a writer might want to make a case for a specific course of action in a more public forum. In such instances, the writer is proposing not a project but a solution to a problem that is of interest to a larger audience. Shortly after the 2008 U.S. presidential election, for example, well-known writer Michael Pollan published an essay in *The New York Times* that was ostensibly addressed to President-elect Barack Obama. In his essay, Pollan proposes several steps that the new president should take to promote local food production. He begins his lengthy essay by explaining why food policy should be a focus of the new president's attention:

> It may surprise you to learn that among the issues that will occupy much of your time in the coming years is one you barely mentioned during the campaign: food.... But with a suddenness that has taken us all by surprise, the era of cheap and abundant food appears to be drawing to a close. What this means is that you, like so many other leaders through history, will find yourself confronting the fact—so easy to overlook these past few years—that the health of a nation's food system is a critical issue of national security. Food is about to demand your attention.

Source: Pollan, Michael. "Farmer in Chief." *New York Times*. The New York Times, 12 Oct. 2008. Web. 30 Apr. 2013.

Pollan goes on to describe the problems with the current system of food production and distribution, and he proposes a solution: to "resolarize" American agriculture. He argues that government policies should create incentives for farmers to give up their reliance on oil-based agriculture and return to more traditional techniques that rely on the sun. The result, according to Pollan, would be a healthy food supply, a healthier environment, and new economic opportunities for farmers.

Pollan's essay amounts to a proposal for a course of action. His proposal is not intended to seek approval or funding for a plan, as in a grant proposal, but to contribute to public discussions about solving a problem that affects a larger audience. This need to solve a problem characterizes proposals:

- A scientist submitting a grant proposal not only seeks funding for research but also hopes to generate new knowledge by answering a specific research question.

- A student proposing a research project for a class not only needs to complete an assignment but also wishes to explore a relevant topic.

- An entrepreneur pitching a business plan not only needs financial support but also wants to innovate in a specific kind of business.

In such cases, proposals are the best way for writers to meet the needs of the rhetorical situation and accomplish their goals.

Sometimes a proposal reflects a stance on an issue and becomes the focus of debate. One such example involves the practice of hydraulic fracturing, or "fracking," a technique to access oil or natural gas that is trapped in certain kinds of underground rock formations. In recent years, fracking has become controversial as energy companies have sought to tap large deposits of natural gas in Wyoming, North Dakota, Ohio, Pennsylvania, and New York. Opponents of fracking claim that it endangers water supplies and causes environmental destruction, leading to serious health problems for humans and wildlife. Proponents argue that fracking can be done safely to develop new energy sources. As new natural gas deposits were being developed, some communities restricted fracking and even banned the practice outright. In 2011, the government of New York was considering such restrictions, and lawmakers debated whether to implement a statewide ban on fracking or allow communities to restrict the practice. This poster reflects the position of those who supported the proposal to ban fracking in the state. It might be considered a succinct version of a more fully developed proposal for such a ban.

14

NEW YORK LEGISLATORS:

Hydraulic fracturing, or "fracking," is a highly dangerous method of drilling for natural gas that threatens our drinking water, health, economy, and environment.

Fracking involves the injection of water, chemicals, and sand underground to release natural gas. Fracking creates risks that are beyond our ability to adequately regulate.

The only safe policy is to ban fracking.

Ban Fracking Now

Protect our water, air, and food. Pass legislation to ban fracking in New York!

Governor Cuomo has proposed opening New York to fracking. Fortunately, bills have been introduced in the State Senate and Assembly to ban fracking (Senate Bill #4220 and Assembly Bill #7218A).

Please contact your State Senator and Assembly member to urge them to co-sponsor legislation to ban fracking:

http://bit.ly/BanFrackingNewYork

There are safer alternatives to natural gas, but there are no alternatives to water!

For more information, visit www.FoodandWaterWatch.org.

To get involved, contact Food & Water Watch at

Food & Water Watch

1. Identify a pressing problem in your community that concerns you. Brainstorm ideas for three different proposals for plans or projects that would address that problem.

2. For each proposal you described in Question #1, identify an appropriate audience. For example, if you described an idea for a research project on the environmental risks of fracking, identify an organization or agency that might support that research.

3. Review the front page of a newspaper or online news source. Find two or three articles that describe problems that interest you for some reason. For each one, describe an idea for a proposal that would address that problem.

4. Have you ever had an idea about how to fix a certain problem or improve something? If so, describe that idea in a brief paragraph. Now consider how you might develop that idea into a formal proposal. What would you propose? To whom would you make your proposal? How would you make a case for your idea?

Understanding Proposals

As a specialized form of argument, proposals have many of the same features that characterize other kinds of arguments, including a clear main idea and support for that idea (see Chapter 11). But because proposals focus on a making a convincing case for a plan to address a specific problem, they have **four main features** that other kinds of arguments typically do not have:

- **A clear statement of the problem.** Because a proposal seeks support for a project or a plan of action, it must provide a statement of the problem that the project or plan of action will try to solve. The writer must clearly identify the problem to be addressed, explain why the problem needs a solution, and show why it should matter to the reader. Whether the proposal is a general one intended for a wide audience or a more specific proposal seeking grant funding, support for an activity, or approval of a proposed project, the writer must convince the intended audience that the problem is significant and worth solving.

- **A description of the proposed project or plan of action.** The main section of most proposals is the description of the plan, project, or idea that is intended to address the problem. Effective proposals present their plans in sufficient detail to give readers a clear sense of what is being proposed. Formal grant or research proposals often follow very specific guidelines for describing the project, including a detailed description of the methods and techniques that the researcher will use in the project, but even in more general proposals, the proposed solution or plan of action should be clearly described.

- **A compelling rationale for the proposed project or plan of action.** The key to a successful proposal is the rationale, which explains why the proposed project or plan of action will solve the problem identified in the proposal. The rationale is the writer's argument for the project or plan. A good proposal not only makes a persuasive case that the problem is an important one but also establishes compelling grounds for supporting the proposed plan of action or project.

- **Appropriate evidence.** Like all effective arguments, proposals should include appropriate and credible evidence for the writer's claims. Usually, in a proposal a writer makes two general kinds of claims: (1) claims about the problem being addressed, and (2) claims about the proposed solution. In both cases, the basic principles governing the use of evidence in argumentation apply (see "Appraising and Using Evidence" on page 340 in Chapter 11). The stronger the evidence, the more convincing the proposal will be.

The following example illustrates these features. This proposal was submitted by George Srour, the founder and director of a non-profit organization called Building Tomorrow (BT), which involves college students in fundraising for educational projects (such as building schools) in poor communities in sub-Saharan Africa. Building Tomorrow was seeking funding from a foundation called Echoing Green to expand its operations in Africa. (Included here are excerpts from the full proposal.)

While interning at the UN World Food Programme in 2004, I spent two months studying the effectiveness of the organization's school feeding program in Uganda. Behind the many faces I encountered were stories of poverty and disease headlined by the personal struggles of 11 and 12 year old children heading their family's households. I spent time in class under tree canopies with just some of the 2 million Ugandan children who have been orphaned by AIDS and learned that an education, while inaccessible for 42 million children in sub-Saharan Africa, is the best assurance of a brighter future for some of the world's most vulnerable children. From this experience grew Building Tomorrow (BT), an NGO encouraging philanthropy among U.S. students by engaging them in fundraising for educational infrastructure projects to benefit orphans and vulnerable children (OVCs) in sub-Saharan Africa. This organization is unique in two ways: • it creates one-to-one partnerships between U.S. colleges and sub-Saharan Africa communities, maximizing both fundraising and the initiative's educational impact on American students • by pursuing an "ownership" model for the African schools being built, it insures that they will be both sustainable and high in quality. BT began as a campaign entitled Christmas in Kampala (CIK) at The College of William & Mary in 2004. The goal of CIK was to raise $10,000 to replace a one room timber structure serving hundreds of OVCs I had visited during my UN internship. In just six weeks, $45,000 was collected to construct a three-story school which opened in April 2006 and currently serves 350 OVCs. From elementary students in the Bronx to seminary students in the Philippines, students around the world

> A compelling rationale: The background about BT helps establish the effectiveness of its approach. Notice, too, the emotional and ethical appeals.

Understanding Proposals **431**

generously offered their support of CIK. BT's vision is to create a scalable model that promises brighter futures by exposing U.S. students to the world of social responsibility and philanthropy while equipping vulnerable children in the Third World with educational opportunities. BT believes that today's youth can be at the forefront of social change through a sustainable program built on solid cross-cultural partnerships.

The AIDS pandemic has single-handedly crippled the infrastructure of sub-Saharan African governments. UNICEF and UNAIDS estimate that 42 million children in this region alone are without access to primary education and the majority of the 15 million children who have been orphaned by AIDS receive no schooling. Uganda is the world's youngest country with over 50% of the population under the age of 15, a percentage that the country's Bureau of Statistics believes will continue to rise. Countries such as Uganda have initiated Universal Primary Education (UPE) programs, guaranteeing a free education to every Ugandan child, however the government simply does not have the means to provide children with even a basic classroom. Officials in the Wakiso District of Uganda, home to future BT schools, estimate that 55% of the district's 600,000 children do not have access to education. Furthermore, due to school, uniform and book fees, the expense of transport and unsafe conditions for young girls traveling long distances, the district's Minister of Education estimates the drop-out rate amongst children enrolled in P1 (1st grade) hit a new record of 80% during the 2005-06 school year. UNESCO estimates that the financial hardships incurred as a result of the HIV/AIDS epidemic will add $950 million to the cost of providing UPE across sub-Saharan Africa by 2015. According to Dr. Peter Piot, the Executive Director of UNAIDS, partnerships encouraging the collaborative efforts of local ministries and development NGOs are what is needed to reach vulnerable populations. By opening doors to new, accessible neighborhood classrooms, BT can help reduce the dropout rate, provide children with the opportunity to receive a valuable education, and be an instrumental partner in building a better tomorrow.

BT believes sustainable social change lies in creating one-to-one relationships that yield social capital as student communities establish and develop long-term connections with the communities they're serving. Most NGOs working in sub-Saharan Africa have turned to mass mailing and internet appeals to increase their donor base. BT sees greater long-term

Problem statement: The writer clearly establishes the seriousness of the problem and the need for the proposed solution.

Appropriate evidence: Here and elsewhere statistical data support the writer's claims.

benefits in cultivating the philanthropic power of younger generations while fostering a culture of social responsibility. This emphasis on grassroots mobilization empowers students to see and believe that they can be at the heart of positive change. Where aid organizations typically hire contractors to design building projects, BT creates opportunities for architecture and engineering students from participating universities to design our schools. Where school children are traditionally referred to clinics for health exams, BT arranges for U.S. medical students to offer basic services at no cost. BT's approach fosters a philanthropic culture among young generations while affording vulnerable children in the Third World life-altering educational opportunities.

BT has developed a new model in funding educational infrastructure development. Working with local officials, BT locates communities where at least 300 OVCs are without access to education. In these areas, BT offers a challenge grant equal to 75% of construction and land acquisition costs (est. $32,000-35,000), with the community providing the remainder through labor, materials and small contributions. An MOU detailing the expectations of all stakeholders is drafted and signed prior to project initiation. By involving all stakeholders, BT ensures long-term sustainability while involving the government in the provision of teachers and operating expenses in accordance with UPE. This differs from the approach NGOs such as World Vision use whereby a school is built on government land and wholly operated by the NGO. By not holding a land title, the NGO could lose control of the building should the land be seized. Furthermore, by shouldering all operational costs, the NGO commits itself for an indefinite amount of time to the financial needs of the school, creating further dependencies that stifle developmental growth. BT believes the community at large is essential in providing an education for the country's youth. Each BT school will be administered by a School Management Committee (SMC), comprised of lay leaders, teachers, parents, government officials and a BT liaison. This body, representing a diverse range of stakeholders in the educations field, allows the school to benefit from the technical expertise and insights of a group of individuals committed to educational excellence.

Description of proposed plan: Here and in the preceding paragraph, the writer explains BT's approach to community action.

14

Source: "Proposal from Building Tomorrow to Echoing Green." *Grant Space*. Foundation Center, n.d. Web. 30 Apr. 2013.

In this proposal, the organization's case for funding rests in part on the seriousness of the problems it seeks to address. Notice how carefully the writer establishes the need for the kind of services provided by Building Tomorrow, citing a variety of statistical information to support the claims made about the extent of the problem and using both emotional and ethical appeals to strengthen his case. Notice, too, the great deal of detailed information both in the statement of the problem and the explanation of how the proposed plan would help solve the problem. The writer makes it clear that he not only understands the problem to be solved but also has significant experience with this kind of work. This is a good example of a writer using effective argumentative strategies to make a strong case for a proposed plan.

Proposals can appear in a great variety of formats. Often, the format is determined by the organization to which the proposal is being submitted, and writers should always follow any guidelines provided by the organization. If no such guidelines are provided, organize your proposal as you would any effective argument, keeping your audience and purpose in mind. Remember, too, that proposals often contain specialized features such as executive summaries and budgets, which are usually described in the proposal guidelines.

FOCUS | Writing an Executive Summary

An executive summary provides an overview of a proposal. Depending on the nature of the proposal and the requirements of the organization for which it is intended, an executive summary can be a few sentences or paragraphs or even as long as a page. The summary should convey the main points of the proposal in a way that draws the reader into the proposal itself. In this sense, the executive summary is more than just a condensed description of the proposal; it is part of the writer's effort to persuade readers that the proposal is worth supporting. Executive summaries should

- provide a brief but clear statement of the problem that the proposal addresses
- highlight the key points of the proposal
- mention points that are likely to be important to the reader
- be as clear, succinct, and engaging as possible

For proposals involving a request for money, a budget is usually required. The specific details of the budget are usually determined by the organization to which the proposal will be submitted, but generally budgets present a breakdown of how the requested funds will be spent. Follow any guidelines for the budget that are set by the organization. For example, if you are applying to a local philanthropic organization for funds to support a class trip, review the organization's website or other materials to determine whether there are specific requirements or restrictions for a budget; use the budget categories identified in those materials (e.g., travel, supplies, stipends). Often, budgets are accompanied by an explanation of these categories (sometimes called a "budget narrative"). For example, if you list a certain sum for travel expenses in your budget, you would include a few sentences explaining the purpose of the travel, the destination, and the specific costs (e.g., airfare, taxi fares, and so on). Your budget should make it easy for your audience to see exactly how you will use the money you are requesting.

14

EXERCISE 14B   UNDERSTANDING PROPOSALS

1. Find an argument about a problem that interests you. The argument can be from a publication such as your campus newspaper, a website, or some other source. Now consider a proposal that might address the problem described in the argument. First, clearly state the problem that your proposal would address. Then, in a brief paragraph, describe a plan or project that would address that problem, explaining why the plan or project would be a good solution to the problem.

2. Identify a problem that interests you from one of your college courses. How would you try to solve that problem? What kind of proposal could you develop for your solution? In a brief paragraph, describe a project you could do that would address that problem. Imagine that the audience for your proposal is the instructor of the course.

3. Write an executive summary for each of the proposals included in the next section ("Reading Proposals"). In a group of classmates, compare your summaries. Identify differences and similarities and draw conclusions about effective summaries.

4. Using your idea from Question #2, consider an alternative medium that would be appropriate for the proposal given your intended audience: a multimedia presentation in a format such as PowerPoint, a video presentation, or another medium. Explain how you would adapt the proposal to that medium.

Reading Proposals

The proposals included in this section reflect a variety of form and purpose. The nature of the proposal (e.g., a grant proposal vs. a proposal in an op-ed essay) and the rhetorical situation will shape its form and content, but all effective proposals include the main features described in the previous section. As you read the following selections, notice the different ways in which these main features are exhibited:

Clear statement of the problem	• What is the problem to be addressed in the proposal? • How effectively is the significance of the problem explained? • Does the writer establish a clear need for a solution?
Description of proposed project or plan	• What solution does the writer propose to address the problem? • How clearly is the proposed plan described? • Is the description persuasive?
Compelling rationale	• What rationale does the writer provide for the proposed solution or plan? • To what extent is the proposed solution or plan appropriate for the problem? • How persuasive is the rationale for the plan or solution?
Appropriate evidence	• What evidence is presented to establish the problem to be addressed? • What evidence is presented to support the proposed solution? • Is the evidence appropriate and sufficient?

University of California Student Investment Proposal

by Fix UC

In 2011, faced with an unprecedented budget crisis brought on by the economic downturn that began in 2008, the University of California system implemented drastic budget cuts and tuition increases. These financial measures, which were the latest and most dramatic of several years of budget reductions, provoked widespread protests by students and faculty. In response to the crisis, students on the editorial board of the Highlander, *the student newspaper at the University of California at Riverside, began discussing a long-term solution to the crisis. Led by editor Chris LoCascio, the students spent nine months developing a formal proposal that they presented to the University of California Board of Regents in 2012. The proposal, which generated a great deal of coverage in the media and was considered seriously by the University system leaders, was a radical one. Under its terms, students who attend UC schools would not have to pay tuition until after they graduated and began earning an income. As you'll see, the proposal addresses many details related to the complexities of college funding and reflects the extensive research that the* Highlander *editorial team did as they refined their plan. Although the proposal was written for the University of California Board of Regents, it was also a public document that became the focus of a larger movement to reform the way students at public universities in California pay for their education. The proposal is available on the website of an advocacy group called Fix UC (www.fixuc.org), which was founded by the students who developed the proposal. As of 2013, the proposal was still a topic of discussion as the University of California leaders continued to try to solve the fiscal crisis. As you read, consider how the student authors of the proposal addressed their primary audience (the Board of Regents) as well as broader audiences interested in the matter of funding higher education.*

....

An education from the University of California offers students an array of skills and opportunities that lead toward both a career and the overall enrichment of one's life. While the latter is an intangible and priceless benefit of graduating from UC, the path it sets individuals on toward a career can be measured by the income one earns from employment. The Student Investment Proposal aims to remedy this discrepancy by allowing students to attend UC with no up-front costs while maximizing revenue for the UC.

The University of California system represents the pinnacle of public higher education. But as it stands, the UC cannot sustain itself through another massive budget cut from the State of California. In order to meet the budget shortfall, students have been asked repeatedly to pay more to attend a UC suffering the loss of resources and faculty members, essentially raising the cost on an education of lessening quality. The UC's dependency on the state leaves it at the will of financial ebbs and flows. Another budget cut like that of 2011 could fatally cripple the University of California.

In order to ensure a promising future, the University of California needs to reevaluate its current revenue system and pursue options that can support it indefinitely while still working to the advantage of students. This proposal outlines a stable and predictable plan toward growth and sustainability for the distant future.

Beyond its practical application as a real long-term solution to the University of California's current revenue system, one of the goals of the UC Student Investment

(Continued)

Proposal is to encourage a shift in thought about the education students receive by attending the university, and their relationship with that university after graduation. Students will begin to think about the value of their education and its significance in the trajectory of their life from graduation to retirement. Therefore, the University of California will invest in the success of its students by providing the up-front costs for attending the university with the expectation that the investment will return once a student graduates and enters a career.

This proposal presents, in detail, a potential solution for the University of California. It is intended for consideration by UC regents as the groundwork for a new long-term funding plan.

Outline

Under the proposed UC Student Investment Plan—Models A and B, graduates of the University of California pay a small percentage of their income, based on 5%, interest free, to the UC upon entering a career after graduation for twenty years of employment. Therefore, undergraduate students pay no fees up-front to the university, and attend school without the financial burden and risk of increased fees.

The current system of prepaid student fees will be dismantled in favor of the new investment plan. The Financial Aid system, including the Blue and Gold Plan, will also cease to exist, its funds being dedicated elsewhere.

Graduates of the University of California, as they begin participation in the new financial contribution program, will have access to extended alumni programs and benefits that help them stay involved with their campus into the future.

The amount of revenue entering the UC compounds annually with an additional graduating class paying into the system. Over time, the UC's annual revenue will exceed that which it currently receives from student tuition.

UC Student Investment Plan—Model B includes all provisions of Model A, but also incorporates caps on minimum and maximum income thresholds for contribution.

Graduates will not begin contributing to the UC until their income exceeds $30,000 annually. A high-income ceiling is also in place, so no income beyond $200,000 annually would be subject to percentage contribution.

Implementation

In order to implement the new UC Student Investment Plan, the UC will change its current Blue and Gold program to incorporate the UC Student Investment Plan. A group of students on the Blue and Gold program whose entire cost of attending is covered by Blue and Gold (UC Return to Aid Funds) will serve as the initial population to enter the plan. These students will attend UC with no up-front costs, just as they would have before the UC Student Investment Plan, but would pay a percentage of their income to the UC upon graduating and entering a career. The revenue the UC would have otherwise not received is then used as capital to put more and more students on the plan, until the entire UC student body is attending with no up-front cost.

Details

Contribution will be enforced by a new department of the United States Internal Revenue Service in charge of collecting contributions from graduates of American universities, beginning with the University of California. This department, in conjunction with the UC, would maintain a database of graduates and arrange the regular contributions of graduates in-state, out-of-state and abroad. Other institutions could then use the infrastructure to implement their own similar funding systems.

Students who transfer into the UC system will pay 1% less of their income.

Students who drop out/transfer out of the system will pay a set amount upon leaving equivalent to the would-be annual tuition rate for their time spent in the system.

Contributions from students who die while attending the UC will be absorbed by UC Student Investment Plan.

Extended alumni benefits for UC graduates paying into the UC will include full career center and employment support. Because the UC will depend on the earnings of its graduates, it is in its best interest to ensure that graduates are in stable, high-paying jobs. The UC will use its tremendous network of graduate and private industry contacts to provide its graduates with job opportunities both upon graduating and afterwards.

Incentives, in the form of decreased percentages of contributions to the UC, will be in place for those who live and work within the state of California after graduation (0.5%), as well as for those who seek careers in the public sector (1%). Individual campuses may also offer incentives to academic and athletic high achievers as a means of recruiting, but with a cap on the amount of students who can receive these incentives per campus.

Out-of-state and international students pay an increase of 1%, with the same incentive option to stay and work in California.

Contribution waivers for emergency situations will be available.

Contribution rate at the time a student enters UC must remain unchanged for that individual's total contribution period. Changes in contribution percentage can only be applied to incoming students.

(Continued)

State of California investment in UC must not fall below 2% of the total state budget at any time. A decrease in state investment cannot go into effect until 10 years after UC Student Investment Plan is initiated, and can only be done in 0.2% annual increments.

Federal and state aid will continue to go directly to students for educational expenses.

The revenue collected from students of each campus will first cover that campus' budget. Additional funds enter a UC savings account, with some of those funds being saved for emergencies, and some being used for investing in bolstered K–12 programs.

Campuses will be encouraged to refrain from giving preferential treatment to departments and majors that lead students to more traditionally lucrative careers.

Campus fees will be covered by graduate contribution percentage. Each new referendum voted on by a student body will be reflected in a small increase in percentage for future incoming classes.

Student on-campus housing will be covered by UC Student Investment Plan, with a 0.65% increase in contribution percentage per year of housing, paid for the first ten years of the twenty year contribution period.

Studying abroad through campus programs will be covered, as long as it is done during the academic year and units taken fulfill full-time student status requirements.

Benefits

To students: No financial burden on parents or students upon entering system and during college. Students will also not incur any debt upon graduation. Students financially contribute to the UC at a time when they are making money, as opposed to when they are not. The annual amount collected by the UC will always be within means, because amount is set on percentage of income earned. The UC's extended alumni benefits will provide graduates with robust employment support.

To UC: Compounded revenue over time, increasing annually with each new class paying into system. Plan puts UC on path towards growth, stability and decreased dependency on fluctuating investment by state of California.

---

source: "UC Student Investment Proposal." *Fix UC*. Fix UC, 28 Mar. 2012. Web. 30 Apr. 2013.

1. What persuasive strategies do the authors of this proposal use to establish the need for their solution to the problem of rising tuition at the University of California campuses? How effective are these strategies?

2. Despite its brevity, this proposal addresses complicated financial problems and procedures. How effectively do you think the authors make the case that their approach will work? Do you think they take the complexity of the problem sufficiently into account in their proposal? Why or why not? Cite passages from the proposal to support your answer.

3. Aside from solving the problem of rising tuition at California's public universities, what purposes do you think the authors of this proposal were trying to achieve? To what extent do you think their proposal achieves those purposes? Explain.

14

Puppies Behind Bars
by Anne Teillon

Grant proposals, like puppies, come in all varieties. Researchers seek grants to support their research, artists to support their art, and, as the following proposal illustrates, nonprofit organizations to support their work. In this proposal, an organization called Puppies Behind Bars seeks funding from a philanthropy called the Planet Dog Foundation for a project titled Paws & Reflect, which uses volunteers and puppies to give homebound elderly people social interaction that they would otherwise not have. As the author of the proposal, Anne Teillon, an official with Puppies Behind Bars, explains, her organization brings puppies into prisons to help terminally ill inmates cope with their diseases. Paws & Reflect is a related program for homebound elderly people who are not incarcerated. As you'll see, this proposal does not include a formal problem statement. Instead, Teillon weaves the problem statement into her description of the work of the Puppies Behind Bars volunteers and the impact of that work on inmates and the homebound elderly. Through that description, Teillon identifies the problems her organization seeks to address. Puppies Behind Bars provides a solution to those problems. This proposal is obviously less formal than the Fix UC proposal (see page 436), but it nevertheless includes the main features of an effective proposal.

(Continued)

January 29, 2007

Ms. Kristen E. Smith
Executive Director
Planet Dog Foundation
322 Fore Street
Portland, Maine 04101

Dear Kristen:

In February 2005, when Puppies Behind Bars (PBB) set out to establish Paws & Reflect, our goal was to promote human interaction in the homebound elderly community by bringing our puppies on socialization visits to their homes. Two years later, this program has transcended even our wildest wishes, filling us with great pride and motivating us to do even more. Planet Dog Foundation was instrumental in allowing PBB to turn our dreams into reality and on behalf of all the staff, seniors, volunteers, puppies, and now inmates who are all deeply affected by this arm of Puppies Behind Bars, I thank you.

We have recently increased the number of seniors who receive visits twice monthly to thirteen which translates into 312 visits per year and hope to increase these numbers to fifteen and 360, respectively, by 2007 year end. One of our newest clients, Helen, is only 59 years old but has been suffering from Multiple Sclerosis for ten years. She has lost most muscular function in her limbs and has speech difficulty. She sits in a wheelchair, with her hands resting on an icepack to soothe the burning sensation that she constantly feels in her fingers. Fully cognizant and in dire need of companionship, Helen currently only interacts with her full-time caretaker who is dynamic and full of life but, only one person. Helen desperately wants a dog but the responsibility that comes along with a four legged friend is too much for her and her aide to handle. Paws & Reflect will be a perfect fit for Helen, who will begin to enjoy a new friendship with her PBB volunteer and the pups that will take part in the socialization visits. Helen, a woman who has lost all of her physical self, will experience companionship, pride in her ability to help socialize a working dog pup and she will have an event to look forward and reflect upon. We are thrilled to be able to offer her a new chapter in her life through Paws & Reflect.

Katie Losey, Director of Volunteers, has been the driving force behind the success of Paws & Reflect. She recruits PBB volunteers, works with elderly services organizations to find seniors interested in participating and coordinates training the volunteers, matching them with their senior partners and organizing weekend visits. Last year 30% of her time was dedicated to running Paws & Reflect and we expect even with increased client participation in 2007, her time should be allocated similarly due to a few changes she will put in place.

One challenge PBB has had to work through is that initially, in order to get the program off its feet, we recruited individuals even if they could not host a dog for the entire weekend and who were solely interested in taking the dog for a couple hour visit to the home of the senior. While we found five fantastic individuals, four of who are still with us two years later, their visits are only made possible by the participation of regular weekend sitters who agree to loan their dog for the senior visit. Initially, we did not foresee how much time would be involved in finding volunteers able to swap a dog for a few hours of their weekend time because of pre-scheduled weekend plans and logistical challenges due to Manhattan's geographic and transit constraints. To alleviate these scheduling dilemmas, we have decided that in the future, we will only recruit Paws & Reflect volunteers who can commit to taking the dog from the Manhattan Shuttle like any regular PBB volunteer and puppysit for the entire weekend. We will of course retain our initial Paws & Reflect volunteers for whom we will continue to find people willing to loan their PBB pup, but overall this will become a deviation from the norm. Katie will remain the sole staff member dedicated to Paws & Reflect and will continue to work to enhance the program and report regularly with PBB's President, Gloria.

As reported at mid-year, Puppies Behind Bars expanded the Paws & Reflect program to include visits at Bedford Hills and Fishkill Correctional Facilities, both of which house terminally ill inmates. The visits are carried out by inmate puppy raisers and their dogs twice weekly and the impact on the dogs, our puppy raisers, the terminally ill and the staff has been incredible. In a *Tell Tails* volunteer newsletter, Carl Rothe, PBB's senior instructor, writes, "It's not just the forlorn inmates in the RMU that are benefiting from the program. The puppy raisers are learning to communicate and work with others who are less fortunate than they. In this environment they are forced to look at and put the patient's needs and desires above their own. Additionally, they see results and progress of short term goals in their dog training. The puppies also benefit as the added socialization and exposure to, and working with, different types of people, helping to better prepare them for their future careers as working dogs."

True to PBB's credo that education is a key component of our work, Carl Rothe developed a course to teach inmates participating in the program how to react to, and interact with, the terminally ill; how to be good listeners; how to detect signs of stress in the people they are visiting as well as in their own dogs; and how to work with medical security staff. Puppy raisers involved in this program come back from their visits beaming with pride – in themselves as well as in their puppies. In the words of Wilfredo, a longtime puppy raiser for PBB, "I really do love going up there to the hospital to visit with the old guys. It makes me feel really good knowing that me and my dog put a smile on their faces."

It is clear that the impact of Paws & Reflect reaches many different populations on a variety of levels. Whether it's an elderly Manhattan resident, a terminally ill inmate, a volunteer or puppy raiser, Paws & Reflect creates common ground enabling people to engage with one another, take pride in their accomplishments and rise above their circumstances.

(Continued)

Planet Dog Foundation's grant of $2,500 accounted for 15% of our Paws & Reflect expenditures in 2006. We were able to secure the remaining financial needs from other foundations and individuals. In all, PBB was able to train potential volunteers, provide over 240 puppy socialization trips to seniors' homes, host a rooftop party to recognize the efforts of the seniors, provide holiday care packages for all homebound individuals, pay for the driver and gasoline to bring the puppies into Manhattan and develop the educational class for inmates interested in making visits to terminally ill patients living out their lives in prison. We expect our costs in 2007 to increase by $2,100 due to a salary increase for the Director of Volunteers (an increase of $1,800 over 2006) and inflated gasoline prices (an increase of $300 over 2006). My hope is that Planet Dog Foundation will raise its funding to $5,000 in 2007 to cover the increased costs of Paws & Reflect. We have already secured a grant from another foundation in the amount of $8,500 to be used for this cause as well.

Gordon T., a 91 year old man who receives visits from PBB volunteer Claudia, summed up his experience with PBB by saying, *"Paws & Reflect gives me an interest that I wouldn't have otherwise and for a man this is very important. The wives are always doing things – chatting, belonging to an organization – but the men are inclined to sit back and wither away. This gives me something to get up and look forward to on Saturday. Not just on Saturday, but the whole week!"* I have enclosed copies of two typed letters and a card that Gordon sent to Katie Losey, our Director of Volunteers, that further demonstrate the impact of Paws & Reflect on Gordon and his genuine, and deeply touching appreciation for his visits. I have also included photographs of Gordon and Claudia at the PBB rooftop party recognizing the seniors' volunteer efforts.

Again, I thank you for your past support. Your financial backing, the voluminous supply of collars, toys and dog beds and your words of encouragement are very much valued and appreciated by every one of us. I have enclosed a current budget for Paws & Reflect and please call me at 212.680.9562 if you would like any further information.

Warm regards,

Annie Teillon
Director of Development

Letter Proposal from Puppies Behind Bars to Planet Dog Foundation. *Grantspace.* N.p. 2013. Web. 17 June 2013.

PUPPIES BEHIND BARS
PAWS & REFLECT Homebound Elderly Visitation Program
2007 Budget
30 visits per month / 360 visits per year

Shuttle Driver Salary*	$936
Gas & Tolls*	$2,067
Insurance on Vans	$390
Director of Volunteer (30% of salary)	**XXXX**
Benefits	$2,970
Supplies for Volunteers (including arts & crafts materials, dog food, toys)	$650
Research, development and production of training materials	$2,000
Senior Recognition Events (3 times per year)	$1,000
Volunteer Training	$2,000
TOTAL	**$28,513**

* 6.5% of transporation costs for Manhattan Shuttle allocated to Paws & Reflect

14

1. What exactly is the nature of the problem that is identified in this proposal? How does Teillon establish that this is a significant problem? Were you convinced by her description? Why or why not?

2. What kind of evidence does Teillon present to establish the problem she proposes to address? How does she support her claim that Puppies Behind Bars can solve that problem? How effective is the evidence she provides? Cite specific passages from her proposal to support your answer.

3. What kinds of persuasive appeals does Teillon use in this proposal? How appropriate are these appeals given her rhetorical situation? How effective did you find these appeals?

Seattle Citywide Skatepark Plan

by Skatepark Advisory Task Force

Over the past decade, skateboarding has emerged as one of the fastest-growing sports in the United States. In response to this trend, many cities and towns have considered creating special parks where skateboarders can enjoy their sport. Often, these parks are created by adding elaborate facilities, such as concrete ramps, to existing public parks; sometimes, abandoned public spaces, such as unused parking lots, are transformed into so-called "skateparks." Although proponents see many benefits to skateparks, including providing young people with safe places to engage in a popular sport, proposals to establish skateparks are often controversial. Opponents worry that they will create problems such as loitering and vandalism. As a result, proposals to create skateparks are sometimes the focus of intense debate, even when the proposals originally grew out of concern about the lack of public spaces for young people to use for popular activities. The following proposal arose from such concerns. In 2006, in response to complaints about young people skateboarding in public places where they might create hazards or safety problems, the City of Seattle appointed a task force to examine the issue. After studying the situation, the task force issued a proposal to create a citywide network of facilities, large and small, where the city's young people could safely skateboard. As you'll see in this excerpt from the full proposal, the task force recognized the need for the city to accommodate the growing popularity of skateboarding and to provide facilities where skateboarding could be enjoyed without creating the problems that led to the creation of the task force in the first place. Since its report was issued in 2007, Seattle has opened seven skateparks and as of 2013 was constructing or planning four others. The task force proposal is an example of how proposals can be part of larger efforts to address problems that affect a wide range of people in a community. It is also a good example of how writers can take advantage of document design to help make their proposal more effective (see Chapter 20). As you read, consider how specific features of the proposal, such as graphics, might have helped make it more persuasive to its original audience, the residents of Seattle and their government.

Arai Jackson Ellison Murakami LLP

CITY OF **SEATTLE**
CITYWIDE **SKATEPARK PLAN**

JANUARY 31, 2007

Skatepark Advisory Task Force

arai jackson ellison murakami LLP
ARCHITECTURE | URBAN DESIGN | INTERIORS

(Continued)

Acknowledgements

Citizens of Seattle

Councilmember David Della, Chair, Parks, Education, Libraries and Labor Committee

Tatsuo Nakata, Chief of Staff to Council member David Della

Task Force members
George Blomberg, Chair

Joe Bell

John Carr

Susanne Friedman, Parks Planner and Project Manager

Jelani Jackson

Matt Johnston

Jeanne Krikawa

Christine Larsen

Joyce Moty

Scott Shinn

Nin Troung

Catherine Anstett, Parks Public Information

Report prepared by Arai Jackson Ellison Murakami.

Credits:
Cover, bottom left photo and boy skating (graphic) photo taken by Mark Tagal.

Arai Jackson Ellison Murakami LLP

SEATTLE PARKS AND RECREATION

Preface

Arai Jackson Ellison Murakami LLP

Why a Plan Now?

More than 10.5 million people skateboard nationwide, making it one of the fastest growing sports in North America. Skateboarding appeals to a wide range of people of all ages and backgrounds and requires specific facilities to appropriately accommodate the sport.

Due to a lack of public places within Seattle to legally skate, many skateboarders practice their sport on public and private property, often competing with other activities. As a means to address this issue, Seattle Parks and Recreation (Parks) adopted a Skateboard Park Policy in 2003, recognizing skateboarding as a healthy, popular recreational activity and a legitimate use to integrate into the parks system.

Several skateparks were sited in the City after the adoption of this policy and one was constructed. However, siting skate facilities proved to be a somewhat controversial process. Therefore, at the urging of skateboard advocates, in February 2006, City Council unanimously approved legislation to develop a comprehensive citywide skatepark plan. (See side bar and Appendix for the full Resolution).

An appointed Skatepark Advisory Task Force (Task Force), comprised of representatives from all areas of the city who have diverse backgrounds, professional expertise and bring both skater and non-skater perspectives to the planning process, worked with Parks and a consultant team during the course of ten months on Seattle's Citywide Skatepark Plan. The Task Force desired a holistic planning process resulting, not only in a network of skate

The Resolution called for Seattle Parks and Recreation, a consultant, and a newly formed Skatepark Advisory Task Force to; "engage the community in a citywide planning process to develop a network of safe and accessible skateparks of various sizes" throughout the City of Seattle.

(Continued)

Preface

facilities, but also in a plan shaped by and reflective of the community as a whole. The Seattle Citywide Skatepark Plan considers a broad range of perspectives and determines the need for skateparks, inventories existing and proposed facilities, identifies skatepark typologies (hierarchy of facilities), creates siting criteria unique to Seattle's dense urban environment, and specifies where and how many public skateparks can best serve Seattle over the next 20 years.

There are a lot of perceptions about skateparks and skateboarders. Some can be tied to the wear and tear the sport can take on the built environment. Some of it is based on stereotypes. Therefore, equally as important as the developing the citywide system, the Task Force sought to learn about and educate others about skate boarding as a sport and skaters as a park user group.

The Task Force learned that when sited appropriately with community involve-ment, skateparks can be successful public spaces that add to the vitality of cities and help to build healthy neighborhoods. The Citywide Skatepark Plan seeks to add skateboarding vibrancy to the City of Seattle.

Seattle Skatepark Advisory Task Force Members

George Blomberg, Chair – Environmental Planner with the Port of Seattle, and Chair, Seattle Planning Commission

Joe Bell – Director of Street Use and Urban Forestry Division, Seattle Department of Transportation

John Carr – PhD candidate at the University of Washington, Chair, Skatepark Advisory Committee

Susanne Friedman – Project Manager, Seattle Parks and Recreation

Jelani Jackson – Active in the Seattle Young People's Project, Powerful Voices, and The Sound Board

Matt Johnston – Producer at PopCap Games, member of the Skatepark Advisory Committee

Jeanne Krikawa – Urban Planner and Architect, former Seattle Planning Commissioner and member of Seattle's Landmarks Board

Christine Larsen – Chair, Friends of Dahl Playfield, involved in Neighborhood Matching Fund projects

Joyce Moty – Involved with Parks projects; sits on the Pro Parks Levy Oversight Committee

Scott Shinn – Computer Programmer, Chair, Parents for Skateparks

Nin Troung – Landscape Architect, Art Director of Manik Skateboards

Arai Jackson Ellison Murakami LLP

Chapter 2: Skaters, Skateboarding & Skateparks

What We Learned

During this planning process a number of different resources were used to gather information (See Appendix: References) about skateboarding, skateparks and skateboarders. The Task Force wanted to know more about the need for skateparks, who participates in the sport, why, and what is the experience of other communities who have skateparks.

THE NEED/DEMAND FOR SKATEPARKS

One way to calculate the demand for skateparks in Seattle is to duplicate the method used by the Portland, Oregon Parks and Recreation department during their citywide skatepark planning process, which is as follows. According to American Sports Data (2005), there are 10.6 million skateboarders nationwide. The U.S. population is 295,734,134 (2005 Census estimate), so we conclude that 3.58% of the population skateboards. Applying that percentage to Seattle's current population of 572,600 (2004 Census estimate), Seattle has about 20,500 skateboarders now, and by the year 2020 there will be upwards of 24,000 based on a projected population of 655,000.

A recent American Sports Data "Superstudy" conducted in the Seattle area estimates that there are 28,000 skateboarders in the City. Out of the thirty-three cities studied, Seattle ranked 6th highest in the number of citizens who skateboard.

According to the State's Interagency Committee for Outdoor Recreation in Washington, skateboarding is the fifth most frequently participated in outdoor activity only behind various forms of walking and jogging, and gardening.

But more important than calculating the exact number of skateboarders living in Seattle, it is important to understand that like all other Seattle Parks and Recreation facilities, such as tennis and basketball courts, soccer and baseball fields, Park's goal is to distribute its facilities equitably throughout the city. Seattle athletes have opportunities within their own neighborhoods to practice these sports: Parks seeks to offer the same opportunity to skateboarders.

Young boy at Seattle Center

"It's hard to get to Burien...something close would be nice. I'm too young to drive, so I have to take the bus or get a ride from a parent to get to a park."
- Citizen comment

14

Arai Jackson Ellison Murakami LLP

(Continued)

Reading Proposals **451**

Chapter 2: Skaters, Skateboarding & Skateparks

Average Age of Participant by Sport	
Skateboarding	14.0
Soccer	17.2
Football	17.9
In-line Skating	19.8
Baseball	20.0
Basketball	23.7
Softball	29.1
Tennis	30.5
Golf	39.0

SKATEBOARDER PROFILE

People of all ages and backgrounds participate in and enjoy skateboarding for recreation and sport. Skateboarders are young and old, male and female. They are engineers, computer programmers, moms, the kid next door, and your neighbor's granddaughters and grandsons.

That said, the average age of skateboarders is 14 years old, which is young compared to other sports (see side bar). This is important to note for several reasons:

- A large number of the skateboarding population is not old enough to drive to a legal and safe place to practice, therefore it becomes even more important to provide opportunities within walking distance or a short bus ride.
- According to the Kaiser Family Foundation, kids devote 6½ hours a day to engaging in media (television, the internet, video games, etc.) as compared to 1½ hours a day spent in physical activity. Access to a skate facility may encourage kids to get outside and be active.

- Limited activities are available to this age group that are not organized and expensive. Skateboarding is a good alternative for those who do want to play on a team, cannot make the team, or cannot afford the costs associated with team sports.
- Since there are limited legal places to skate and social stigmas towards skateboarders, a lot of younger skaters quit the sport before they reach adulthood.

Mother & Daughter

Arai Jackson Ellison Murakami LLP

SEATTLE NEIGHBORHOOD DEMOGRAPHICS

Due the ever-shifting nature of neighborhoods, Parks does not base facility distribution on demographics. However, as a discovery exercise, Parks created a series of maps illustrating where the following age groups live in largest numbers: under 18, 18-34, & 35-44. (See Appendix: Neighborhood Demographics Maps). The southeast and southwest areas of the City have the highest percentages of the under 18 population. The central City and the central-south portion of the north area have the highest percentages of people aged 18-34. The west/northwest area has the largest number of 35-44 year olds.

SKATEPARKS AREN'T JUST ABOUT SKATEBOARDING

Skateboarding promotes physical fitness, self-esteem and discipline. It also provides an opportunity for people to interact in an unstructured activity while learning new skills.

Skateparks provide legitimate, safe, legal places to practice. If they are designed as part of a larger park they will attract a variety of spectators. The mingling of user groups can encourage positive interactions between different users of public space. Visit an area skatepark and you will likely see and hear people of all ages, skaters and non-skaters alike, encouraging the skaters. This interaction can help to break down barriers and build community.

Old Ballard Bowl

Generations of Skaters

"At the Shoreline skatepark a young man said to my seven year old 'Hey little dude, maybe I should get your autograph now because you're going to be famous one day.' Talk about self-esteem boosting. The 'element' at this park was very positive and supportive to the kids. I hope fear of the unknown doesn't take away the opportunity for kids to get exercise and have fun in an appropriate environment." - Citizen comment

Arai Jackson Ellison Murakami LLP

Chapter 2: Skaters, Skateboarding & Skateparks

Parks & Police Departments Spoken To
Burien
Des Moines
Kent
Mill Creek
Renton
Shoreline
Woodinville
Gig Harbor
Puyallup

Surrounding Area Parks & Police Department Perspectives

As part of the planning and educational process, the consultant spoke with nine local municipalities that operate skateparks in order to understand the day-to-day impacts a skatepark may have on a community. (See List of Contacts with Comments in Appendix) Additionally, in 2005, the consultant also spoke with 12 different town and cities in Washington and Oregon (See Appendix: References).

The Parks and Police staff of nine municipalities reported that when skateparks are highly visible, integrated into larger active parks, or next to active roads, minimal or no crime or drug usage is reported. Skateparks that are hidden away from public view and not integrated into a larger park can have more problems. Park and Police agencies stated that location and visibility are the most important aspects of siting a successful skatepark.

Comments from Surrounding Municipalities

"There is a perception that skateboarders are criminals because of the way they look, but Parks and Recreation has not received complaints about increases in crime or drug use at our [two] parks."
– Laurie Flem, Kent Parks and Recreation

"Areas that experience criminal activity could be helped by building a skate facility because bad people don't want to be near kids and their parents."
– Paul Peterson, Kent Police Department

"The skatepark is heavily used and I like to see public money invested in things that get used."
– Bob Crannell, Mill Creek Chief of Police

"There were a lot of the usual fears in the neighborhood about the skatepark, but those fears have not been realized and there are very few complaints about the skatepark. The skatepark in an unequivocal success."
– Scott Thomas, Burien Parks and Recreation

"The community and the police department expected a lot of problems when the park opened, but haven't seen many. There is a basketball court right next to the park and I expected conflict between the two user groups, but it hasn't occurred."
– Cindy Parks, Renton Police Department

Arai Jackson Ellison Murakami LLP

Trash is generated at skateparks, just like at any other heavily used parks facility. If there is a routine maintenance/management plan, litter should not become a problem. Graffiti at skateparks does occur and the faster graffiti is removed, the less frequently it reoccurs. Therefore, it's important to have a graffiti removal plan in place when the facility opens. Only those skateparks sited very close to homes had reports of noise complaints, which are primarily due to due music and yelling, not noise generated by skateboards.

Unanimously, Parks and Police staff reported that their skateparks were good investments. Even the Gig Harbor skatepark, which due to lack of public visibility has experienced more problems than any other skatepark in the area, is supported by the Police Department. A spokesperson from the Police said that the skatepark does have its problems, but it is a positive activity to provide for kids: "You've got to give them something to do or they'll get into trouble." The skatepark was redesigned in October 2006 to increase visibility into the site.

ADDITIONAL INFORMATION ABOUT SKATEPARKS

Liability

Liability for skateparks is just like any other public sports facility – all sports are played "at your own risk." As such, the City of Seattle is not liable for accidents. However, skateboarding isn't as dangerous as most people believe. (See sidebar)

Noise

Noise studies indicate that skateboards produce intermittent noise: noise that occurs occasionally from the 'popping' tails and 'grinding' of the aluminum trucks (a part on skateboards) on the steel coping surfaces (usually around the edges of skateparks). These sounds are not sustained over long periods of time. Studies have shown that sounds emitted from skateparks are diminished completely by other noises such as traffic passing by and planes flying over. Outside urban noises, such as loading docks, automatic dumpsters and power lawn mowers are often much higher that sound made by skateboards.
(See Appendix: Noise Information)

Injuries/100 Participants	
Hockey	2.7
Football	2.2
Baseball	1.8
Basketball	1.6
Bicycling	1.1
Skateboarding	0.7*

- Skateboarders skating for less than a week account for 1/3 of all injuries
- Irregular riding surfaces account for over half the skateboarding injuries due to falls.
- In 2002, the Journal of Trauma concluded in their report that, "Skateboarding is a relatively safe sport."

14

Mill Creek

Renton

(*Continued*)

Chapter 3: The Citywide System

Seattle's System

In order to identify and recommend a range of types and sizes of skate-parks to build, Task Force members studied skateparks in the region, looked at Portland, Oregon's skate-park system and researched types of facilities built throughout the country. Then based on their research and experience the Task Force developed a tiered skate facility system appropriate for Seattle.

TYPES & SIZES

The recommend Seattle skatepark system consists of integrated skateable terrain, a.k.a., Skatedots, smaller neighborhood Skatespots, medium-sized District skate-parks, and one large Regional facility. Please see the next two pages for descrip-tions of each tier.

This system may evolve over time in response to need and new opportunities.

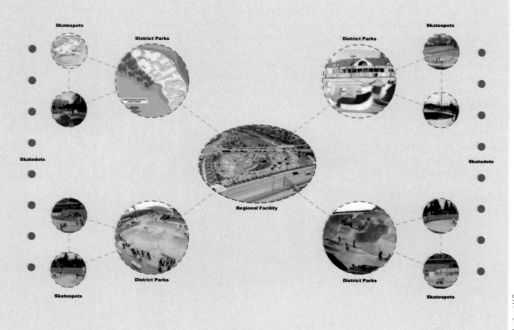

Arai Jackson Ellison Murakami LLP

Chapter 5: Site Recommendations

Site Nominations

In June, a host of citizens and city departments, including Seattle Parks and Recreation, the Seattle Department of Transportation, the Port of Seattle, and the Seattle School District, nominated 130 sites throughout the city for the Task Force to analyze as potential locations for skate facilities (See Appendix: Nominated Sites).

THE EVALUATION PROCESS

During the course of two months, the 130 sites were evaluated in the following manner.

Framework Application

The evaluation team visited each site, applied the Framework of Assumptions, and removed inappropriate sites. For example, sites that did not have enough room for a skate facility were removed from consideration (e.g. Beacon Hill Playfield). Seventy sites were removed during this phase of analysis.

Full Site Analysis

Sites remaining after the Framework application received a full site analysis. First, the team determined the type/size of facility appropriate for the nominated location. Some sites were nominated to be a specific type of skatepark (Skatespot, District, Regional) and some were nominated for general consideration. If the site was nominated for a specific type/size, the team determined whether that size was appropriate. For example, the area around the SDOT Interurban Trail Project at Bitter Lake Reservoir was nominated to be a Regional facility, but was analyzed as a Skatedot based on the area available.

After determining the appropriate type/size of facility, the team completed an evaluation sheet in the field, ranking each criterion on a scale of 1-10 (one being the lowest, ten being the highest). For example, a criterion for a District site is "Are in close proximity to water fountain, trash cans, rest room." If the site had all these amenities the criterion received a score of 10.

Weighting the Criteria

Running parallel to the site visits, weighted scores were developed for each criterion through a Task Force ranking process. Then a score was calculated for each site by applying the weighted criteria. (See Appendix: Alphabetized Individual Site Evaluation Sheets).

Discussed 30 Sites with the Community

The thirty sites scoring in the top 25% were presented to the community at the second series of public meetings. Based on community feedback and the goal to distribute skate facilities equitably, the Task Force eliminated the following sites; Cowen Park, Westcrest Reservoir, Fairmount Playfield and Denny Middle School Athletic Complex.

Evaluated Sites

14

(Continued)

Chapter 6: Costs, Funding Resources & Priorities

Once a Skatepark is Approved for Development - What Next?

Grindline, a company that designs and build skateparks, worked with Parks to develop planning level cost estimates for the different types of facilities outlined in the Citywide Plan. These costs provide a framework for citizens to start fund raising for approved facilities. The Task Force also developed a list of prioritized sites for funding.

PLANNING LEVEL COST ESTIMATES FOR SKATEPARK TYPOLOGIES

Planning level cost estimates are in 2006 dollars, unless otherwise noted. Square footage cost estimates were provided by Grindline and include mobilization, Temporary Erosion Sediment Control, compaction, excavation, formwork, concrete work and finishing. Estimates do not include landscaping, irrigation, benches, etc. (See chart below).

Maintenance and operations costs based on existing and proposed facilities for a District level skatepark, at approximately 20,000 square feet, run in the range of $24,000 annually. These costs estimates are taken from the Lower Woodland Skatepark Project Proposal.

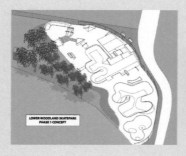

Task Force members visit Lower Woodland site

THE CITYWIDE SYSTEM			
	Size Range	Cost Per Foot	Planning Level Cost Estimates
Skate Dot	Approximately 20 sq. ft., but up to 1,500 sq. ft.	$6.00	Up to $16,000
Skatespot	Up to 10,000 sq.ft. .	Approximately $40.00 per sq.ft.	Up to $640,000
District	Up to 30,000 sq.ft.	Approximately $40.00 per sq.ft.	Up to $2 million
Regional	30,000 sq.ft. or larger	Approximately $45.00 per sq.ft.	$2 million and up

Note: Per square foot construction costs are adjusted to include design, management, sales tax, and other costs to show total development costs.

Arai Jackson Ellison Murakami LLP

14

The Pacific Northwest, despite the rainy climate, is famous for its skate friendliness. Seattle can enhance this reputation by creating a city where skateboarding is embraced and encouraged. This plan is a first step towards that goal.

"I think this is a really awesome and optimistic plan."
- Citizen comment

Arai Jackson Ellison Murakami LLP

1. How do the authors of this proposal describe the problem that their proposal addresses? How effectively do they establish the significance of the problem? To what extent do you think their problem statement addresses their intended audience (residents and government officials of Seattle)?

2. What kinds of evidence do the authors provide to support their claims about the nature of the problem related to the rise of skateboarding as a sport and their proposed solution? To what extent is their evidence appropriate for their specific rhetorical situation?

3. To what extent do you think the design of this document affects its effectiveness as a proposal? Explain, citing specific features of the proposal to support your answer. (Refer to Chapter 20 for information about document design features.)

Writing Proposals

As we have seen, proposals are specialized kinds of arguments. Although they generally follow the principles of effective argumentation described in Chapter 11, they have special characteristics that make them somewhat different from academic arguments (see Chapter 12) and popular arguments (see Chapter 13). This section will guide you in developing an effective proposal. Each step described here corresponds to a step in Chapter 3.

Step 1   Identify a project for your proposal.

Proposals usually begin with a project someone wants to do:

- a scientific study of a particular phenomenon
- a community service initiative that seeks to improve a neighborhood
- a paper or project to fulfill an academic requirement

If you have such a project in mind, write a brief paragraph describing it. This paragraph will serve as a starting point for your proposal.

Sometimes, however, a proposal begins not with a project but with a problem that concerns or interests the writer: homelessness, climate change, the difficulties of making the transition from high school to college. In such cases, the proposal grows out of the writer's desire to address that problem.

If you do not have a specific project in mind:

- make a list of three or four problems or issues that interest you
- formulate a question for each problem
- imagine a project or projects that might address each problem

For example:

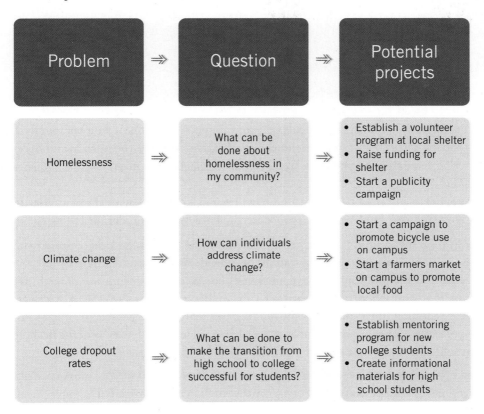

Problem		Question		Potential projects
Homelessness	⟹	What can be done about homelessness in my community?	⟹	• Establish a volunteer program at local shelter • Raise funding for shelter • Start a publicity campaign
Climate change	⟹	How can individuals address climate change?	⟹	• Start a campaign to promote bicycle use on campus • Start a farmers market on campus to promote local food
College dropout rates	⟹	What can be done to make the transition from high school to college successful for students?	⟹	• Establish mentoring program for new college students • Create informational materials for high school students

Notice that the question for each problem is formulated in a way that implies some kind of project. (Framing the question in terms of "how" can help.)

Now, identify the problem that is most interesting or important to you and describe a possible project to address it. Later, in Steps #4 and #5, you will explore the problem more fully.

For example, let's imagine that you are concerned about how difficult it can be for some students to make the transition from high school to college. You know, for example, that a large percentage of college students do not make it to their second year, and you have read in the campus newspaper that the dropout rate at your own college concerns many administrators. Moreover, many of your own friends felt unprepared for college-level work, even if they were successful students in high school. You also know that some advice you received from an older relative who had gone to college helped you avoid some of the struggles your friends were having, and you believe that other students would benefit from the kind of mentoring you enjoyed. So you decide that one possible way to address the problem would be a mentoring program to help new college students adjust to college.

In this way, identify a potential project. Step #1 in Chapter 3 will help you develop your idea for your project more fully.

Step 2   Place your topic in rhetorical context.

Now identify an appropriate audience for your proposal. Depending on the nature of your project, your audience could be very specific (a course instructor, an office on your campus, or a community organization) or broader (students on your campus or residents of your community).

If your proposal is part of a course assignment or a program requirement (such as an honors thesis or capstone research project), follow the assignment guidelines to determine the audience for your proposal.

If your proposal is intended to address a problem beyond a course assignment or a program requirement, you will need to identify an appropriate audience for it. Consider the following:

- **Who would be interested in your project?** Who would support the kind of project you are proposing? Are there specific organizations or individuals who would have an interest in or connection to the problem you have identified? For example, a mentoring program for new students at your school would interest faculty and administrators who work with new students. In addition, there are offices on your campus that provide services for students or have responsibility for supporting students' social and academic activities; officials in those offices would have an interest in such a project.

- **Does your proposed project require permission or approval?** If so, your proposal might best be addressed to the person, office, or agency that must grant approval. For example, if you are proposing to establish a mentoring program for new students on your campus, you will likely need permission from one or more campus offices or officials, such as the person in charge of campus residential life or perhaps the director of academic advising or support services.

- **Do you need assistance to complete your project?** Determine whether you will need an official, office, or service to accomplish the goals for your project. For example, to establish a mentoring program for new students on your campus would likely require work that you could not do by yourself, such as identifying and training current students who can serve as mentors, connecting mentors with new students, securing meeting rooms, and publicizing the program so that new students can take advantage of it. Most likely you would need an office such as student support services to be able to do all these tasks and implement your proposal. In such a case, you would submit your proposal to the person in charge of that office. (Note that that person might be the same person from whom you would need to get permission for your project.)

- **Do you need funding for your project?** If your project cannot be completed without financial support, you will likely have to identify an agency or organization that provides funding for the kind of project you have in mind. For example, a mentoring program for new students would probably require funds to train mentors and publicize the program.

If your proposal is intended for a more general audience, you should identify the best way to reach that audience. For example, let's say you have decided that a mentoring program for new students is a good way to reduce dropout rates at your college but you don't want to be directly involved in such a program. You might write an essay for your campus newspaper or a similar forum in which you propose such a mentoring program.

Once you have identified an appropriate audience for your project, complete Step #2 in Chapter 3 to explore your rhetorical context more fully.

Step 3 Select a medium.

The medium for a proposal is usually a conventional written document. However, as the proposal for a skatepark (see page 446) illustrates, writers often take advantage of document design principles to make their proposals more persuasive (see Chapter 20). Moreover, proposals that are presented in a group or public forum often take the form of a presentation such as PowerPoint. Proposals intended to promote a position on an issue (see "Proposals as Advocacy" on page 429) might be made in a medium that allows for the use of visual elements, but even in such cases, a more conventional written document might also be required. So unless the rhetorical situation for which you are writing your proposal indicates otherwise, it is safe to assume that you should present your proposal as a conventional document. Consult the guidelines for your proposal from the organization, agency, or person to whom you will be submitting the proposal.

The exception is a proposal in the form of an essay intended for a more general audience. If you are writing such a proposal, select a medium that will enable you to reach your intended audience. For example, let's say you've decided to write a proposal for a more general audience about establishing a mentoring program for new college students. You want to argue that such a program would help address the difficulties many students have when making the transition from high school to college and therefore help lower college dropout rates. You hope to reach several distinct but overlapping audiences: students and faculty on your campus as well as other college campuses, high school students and their parents, and perhaps a more general audience of readers interested in education issues. For such a proposal, you would have several possible media to choose from: your campus newspaper, a regional or national newspaper, a flier, or an online forum such as a blog or YouTube video. Compare the advantages and drawbacks of the available media. Let's consider two possible media for your proposal: an essay in a regional newspaper and one posted on a social media site devoted to education issues.

Medium: Essay in Regional Newspaper

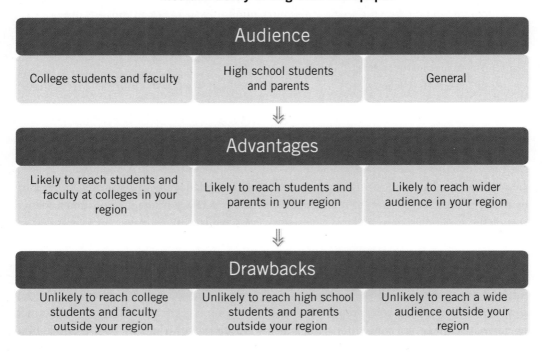

Audience		
College students and faculty	High school students and parents	General

⇊

Advantages		
Likely to reach students and faculty at colleges in your region	Likely to reach students and parents in your region	Likely to reach wider audience in your region

⇊

Drawbacks		
Unlikely to reach college students and faculty outside your region	Unlikely to reach high school students and parents outside your region	Unlikely to reach a wide audience outside your region

Medium: Post on Social Media Site

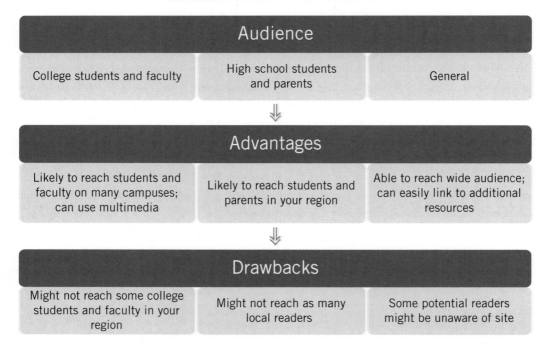

Audience		
College students and faculty	High school students and parents	General

⇊

Advantages		
Likely to reach students and faculty on many campuses; can use multimedia	Likely to reach students and parents in your region	Able to reach wide audience; can easily link to additional resources

⇊

Drawbacks		
Might not reach some college students and faculty in your region	Might not reach as many local readers	Some potential readers might be unaware of site

After identifying and evaluating possible media in these ways, complete Step #3 in Chapter 3 to help you decide on the most appropriate medium for your proposal.

Step 4 Identify your main points.

Most proposals are written to convince a specific audience to approve it, fund it, or support it. In this regard, proposals differ from other kinds of arguments, which usually have a main argument and several supporting arguments but are not intended to seek funding or approval for a proposed plan. In a proposal, by contrast, the writer must identify the problem that will be addressed by the proposed plan and make a persuasive case that the plan can solve the problem. So the task for the proposal writer is twofold:

- to argue that the problem is worth addressing
- to demonstrate that the proposed plan can address the problem effectively

To illustrate, let's return to our hypothetical case of a proposal to establish a mentoring program for new students on your campus. Let's assume that you have decided (after completing Step #2) that your proposal should be submitted to the office of student services. In order for your proposal to be successful, you will have to convince the director of student services that the kinds of difficulties you and other students experience in making the transition from high school to college actually constitute a significant problem that deserves attention. So you need to have a clear sense of the problem and why it matters.

Begin by stating the problem and its significance as clearly as you can:

When they first come to college, many students are unprepared for the social and academic challenges they face, which often leads to low grades or even dropping out of school.

This statement can serve as the thesis of your problem statement. It is your main argument that there is a problem that needs to be solved. (If you need more than one sentence to state the main problem and why it is significant, that's OK. At this point, the goal is to be clear about the main problem your proposal will address. Later, you will elaborate on the problem.)

Now state why your plan can help solve the problem:

Struggling students can benefit from advice and support from a more experienced student who understands the challenges of making the transition to college.

Think of this statement as the thesis of your rationale for your proposed plan. It is your argument in support of your solution to the problem. (Again, you can state this thesis in more than one sentence, but keep in mind that you will develop it more fully in subsequent steps.)

Now you have identified the two main points you will develop in your proposal:

1. why the problem matters
2. why your plan is worth supporting

Follow these steps for your proposal topic, keeping in mind that your two main points might evolve as you continue to develop your proposal. (If you are writing a proposal for a general audience, you still need to identify these two main points.) Step #4 in Chapter 3 provides additional guidance for developing your main points.

Step 5 | Support your main points.

Now that you have identified the two main points you will make in your proposal, you need to develop them more fully by gathering sufficient information and evidence to support them. You also have to develop your plan. At this stage, you have three tasks to complete:

1. **develop your problem statement**, which is your argument in support of your main claim that the problem you have identified should be addressed
2. **develop your plan** to address that problem
3. **develop your rationale**, which is your argument that your plan will address the problem

Return to your two main points from Step #4 and develop your proposal by completing these three tasks:

Develop your problem statement	• What exactly is the problem you want to address? • What evidence is there that this problem exists? • Why is this problem important?
Develop your plan	• What is your plan to address this problem? • What are the components of this plan? What steps or activities does it involve?
Develop your rationale	• Why will your plan succeed in addressing the problem? • What evidence do you have to support your plan as an effective way to address the problem?

To illustrate, let's return to the example of a proposal to establish a mentoring program for new college students. Here's your main argument in your problem statement:

When they first come to college, many students are unprepared for the social and academic challenges they face, which often leads to low grades or even dropping out of school.

Develop Your Problem Statement

First, you'll need to establish that many new students do in fact struggle when they come to college. What does that mean exactly? You might begin with your own experience to illustrate these struggles, which might include adjusting to living with a roommate, meeting the academic standards of college-level studies, and being away from your support system of family and friends. You also have anecdotes from classmates who experienced similar problems. In addition, you might talk to campus officials about the extent of these problems on your campus, and you can search online for data showing the extent of these problems at other colleges. You also need statistics showing the dropout rate in college. In short, research the problem to find support for your main claim.

Develop Your Plan

Once you have made a case that this problem exists and is important, you need to describe in detail the plan you are proposing to solve the problem. You've decided that a mentoring program is a potentially effective way to support new students as they adjust to college. What would such a program involve? The main component is a group of experienced students who have already made the transition to college and succeeded in adjusting academically and socially. These students will need to be trained to mentor new students. The training might include workshops in which staff members from academic support services and the counseling center teach the student mentors about the difficulties of adjusting to college and how to support struggling students. Your plan should also include a way to publicize the program so that new students know it is available to them. You will need a rough schedule for implementing your plan. Will the mentoring take place over a semester? A full year? More than a year? How often will mentors meet with their students? By exploring these questions, you can develop a detailed, concrete description of your plan.

Develop Your Rationale

Finally, you need to make a case for this plan, showing why it will address the problem you've identified. Let's turn to the main point of your rationale:

> *Struggling students can benefit from advice and support from a more experienced student who understands the challenges of making the transition to college.*

How do you know that the kind of mentoring program you're proposing will help struggling new students? Again, you can draw on your own experience, showing that having older relatives who experienced similar difficulties in college helped you overcome those difficulties. You can research similar programs at other colleges to show the impact of such programs. There might also be studies by educational psychologists and other professionals about such programs, which you can find by doing some research. In short, explore possibilities to develop support for your claim that this plan will work.

As you complete these three steps, keep the following points in mind:

- **Use appropriate evidence.** As in any kind of argument, the evidence you present to support your two main points in a proposal should be credible, appropriate for your topic, and persuasive for your intended audience. (See "Appraising and Using Evidence" in Chapter 11.)

- **Keep your audience in mind.** As you develop your arguments and describe your plan, try to anticipate what your intended audience will expect. For example, if you are submitting a proposal for a new mentoring program to the director of student services on your campus, you can assume that he or she will share your concerns about the struggles of new students, so you will want to provide sound evidence that those struggles exist on your campus. You can also assume that the director will be interested in programs that addressed these problems at other colleges, so providing data about such programs will likely strengthen your proposal. As you develop your support for your main points, then, identify the evidence and information that will most likely resonate with your audience.

- **Include an executive summary and budget, if necessary.** Depending upon the nature of your proposal and the audience for whom you are writing it, you might need to include an executive summary and budget. Follow any guidelines provided by your intended audience in developing these components of your proposal. Remember that they are part of your effort to persuade your audience that your proposal is worth supporting. (See "Writing an Executive Summary" and "Proposing a Budget" on pages 434 and 435.)

Step #5 in Chapter 3 provides additional guidance to help you develop support for your main points and your description of your proposed plan. You should now be ready to write a complete draft of your proposal. If not, move onto the next step before completing your draft.

Step 6 Organize your proposal.

Few proposals follow the four traditional ways of organizing an argument described in Chapter 11 (see "Structuring an Argument" on page 344). Most proposals are organized according to the guidelines of the organization, agency, or person to whom the proposal is addressed. So the first step in deciding how to organize your proposal is to consult such guidelines. For example, if you are writing a grant proposal, it is likely that the foundation you are applying to expects you to follow a specific format.

If you do not have such guidelines, you can use a general format the includes the main components of a proposal:

I. Introduction: Briefly introduce the problem and describe the plan you are proposing. Your introduction should not only engage your readers but also lay the foundation for your main arguments in Parts II and IV.

II. Problem Statement: Describe the problem you will address, demonstrating its significance and providing evidence for your claims. Organize this section so that your strongest claims and evidence come first.

III. Description of Your Plan: Provide a detailed description of your plan to address the problem. Include a statement of the goals of the plan.

IV. Rationale: Explain how your plan will address the problem described in Part II, providing evidence to support your claims about your plan and its expected impact.

If you are including a budget, place it after the rationale. An executive summary (if you include one) should be placed before your introduction.

Your proposal should be organized in a way that will present your plan as clearly and effectively as possible to your intended audience. Remember that your goal is to convince them that your proposal is worth supporting. To achieve that goal, you want to make it easy for your audience to understand the problem you are addressing and the plan you are proposing. Step #6 in Chapter 3 provides additional guidance for organizing your proposal.

Step 7   Get feedback.

Ask your readers to focus on the main features of effective proposals as they review your draft:

Clear statement of the problem	• Have you clearly defined the problem you are addressing in your proposal? • Do you explain the significance of this problem? • Do you establish a need for a solution or plan of action?
Description of proposed project or plan	• Have you described your plan clearly and in sufficient detail? • Does your description explain how the plan will work? • Is anything missing from this description? Can anything be eliminated?
Compelling rationale	• Do you explain why your proposed plan can succeed in addressing the problem? • Does you show how your plan is appropriate for the problem? • Does your rationale address the concerns of your intended audience?
Appropriate evidence	• Do you provide evidence to support your claims about the problem you have identified? • Do you provide evidence to support your rationale for your proposed plan? • Is this evidence sufficient? Is it persuasive?

Step #7 in Chapter 3 will help you analyze your feedback and decide which revisions to make.

Step 8   Revise.

As you consider the feedback you received for Step #7, remember that revision is an opportunity to develop your proposal more fully and adjust it to fit your rhetorical situation. You are still developing and strengthening your proposal.

Revising your proposal draft can be divided into three steps.

Review Your Draft Using the Questions Listed in Step #7

As you do, make sure the main components (problem statement, description of proposed plan, and rationale) are strong.

Adjust Your Persuasive Appeals

Like any argument, a proposal can be strengthened with appropriate persuasive appeals (see "Making a Persuasive Appeal" in Chapter 11). At this point, review your draft to determine whether you have made appropriate appeals:

- **Consider your rhetorical situation.** In some proposals, certain kinds of appeals might be inappropriate. For example, a researcher submitting a grant proposal to fund a study of the impact of road construction on traffic patterns would not likely include emotional appeals to support his claims about the importance of his study. Similarly, if you are proposing a lab experiment for a course project, you would probably not use emotional appeals to support your assertions about the appropriateness of your experimental methods. By contrast, the proposal from Puppies Behind Bars (see page 441) includes emotional appeals to help convince the reader that the program is worthwhile.

- **Review your problem statement and rationale.** Determine whether the persuasive appeals you have made are appropriate for the problem you are addressing. Consider additional appeals that would likely be effective for your rhetorical situation. For example, here are some possible appeals you might make in support of your two main points in a proposal for a mentoring program for new college students:

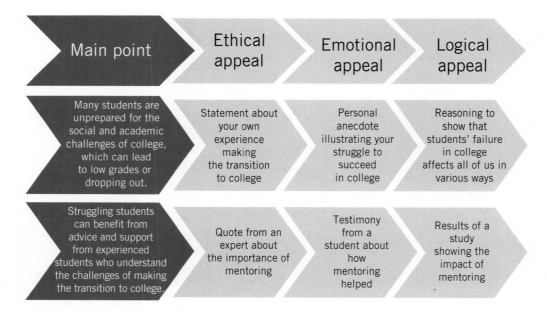

Assuming that all the evidence is valid and credible, you should decide which kind of appeal would be most effective for the rhetorical situation.

Follow Step #8 in Chapter 3

Make sure you have addressed all the essential aspects of your proposal in your revisions.

Step 9 Refine your voice.

As in all arguments, the writer's voice in a proposal should be appropriate for the rhetorical situation. Many proposals, especially for grants and research projects, call for a measured, objective, authoritative voice, as demonstrated in the proposal for a skatepark (page 446). In other cases, such as the Puppies Behind Bars proposal (page 441), a less formal, more personal voice can be effective.

First, review your rhetorical situation, and consider the kind of voice your intended audience might expect.

Then review your draft and adjust your voice, if necessary.

Step #9 in Chapter 3 will help you refine and strengthen your voice.

Step 10 Edit.

Complete Step #10 in Chapter 3.

WRITING PROJECTS   PROPOSAL WRITING

1. Identify a problem that interests or concerns you. What is the nature of the problem? Why does it interest you? Consider what might be done about the problem. Then develop a proposal that addresses the problem. Write your proposal for an audience that has an interest in that problem. For example, if the problem involves safety in youth sports, you might write your proposal to the community organization that sponsors youth sports in your community or to a local foundation interested in youth issues.

2. Rewrite the proposal you wrote for Question #1 as an essay for a general audience. Identify a specific publication or forum for which your essay would be appropriate.

3. Find an argument on a website or in a print publication about a problem that matters to you. Using that argument as a starting point, develop a proposal that would address the problem described in that argument.

4. Think of a problem that somehow figured into your own life. Drawing on your own experience, develop a proposal that describes a plan to address that problem. Identify an appropriate audience for your proposal.

Understanding Narrative Writing

READ THE OPENING PARAGRAPHS of Chapters 2, 8, and 12 in this textbook, and you'll notice that they all begin the same way: with a story. That's no accident. Stories are an important way to convey information, explore ideas, and make sense of our experiences. We use them every day in many different ways:

- A classmate tells you a story about an experience with a professor who teaches a course you're thinking about taking.
- A patient tells a doctor the story of how he was injured.
- A business manager uses anecdotes in a report to her boss to explain the company's struggles to develop a new market for its products.
- A politician describes an event from her childhood to show voters that she understands their concerns.
- A relative tells you about a trip he took to another country.

Historians use narrative to organize and analyze the past to help us understand who we are and how we got here. Scientists use narrative to explain the natural world (see "Narrative in Science"). Most religious texts are narratives—for example, the parables in the Christian Bible, Zen koans, and the creation myths of Native American peoples.

Stories help us make sense of complicated events or phenomena. They give shape to our experiences. They turn the abstract (the pain of loss, for example) into the concrete (a story about losing a beloved relative). Through stories we impose order on the chaos of life. In fact, some scholars believe that narrative is as fundamental to human life as language itself. The influential scholar Jerome Bruner has written, "We seem to have no other way of describing 'lived time' save in the form of a narrative" (Bruner, Jerome. "Life as Narrative." *Social Research* 54.1 (1987): 11-32. Print.).

Pikoso.kz/Shutterstock.com

Although we tend to think of science as providing an objective description of the natural world, much of the writing scientists do has elements of narrative. In his revolutionary *On the Origin of Species*, published in 1859, which laid the foundation for the modern field of biology, Charles Darwin uses narrative techniques to help readers understand scientific principles and to tell part of the story of how his theories emerged from his famous expedition to the Galapagos Islands off the western coast of South America:

> When on board H.M.S. 'Beagle,' as naturalist, I was much struck with certain facts in the distribution of the inhabitants of South America, and in the geological relations of the present to the past inhabitants of that continent. These facts seemed to me to throw some light on the origin of species—that mystery of mysteries, as it has been called by one of our greatest philosophers. On my return home, it occurred to me, in 1837, that something might perhaps be made out on this question by patiently accumulating and reflecting on all sorts of facts which could possibly have any bearing on it. After five years' work I allowed myself to speculate on the subject, and drew up some short notes; these I enlarged in 1844 into a sketch of the conclusions, which then seemed to me probable: from that period to the present day I have steadily pursued the same object. I hope that I may be excused for entering on these personal details, as I give them to show that I have not been hasty in coming to a decision.

Narrative, then, might be understood as a tool by which we grasp reality. It is a way for novelists, memoirists, biographers, and journalists as well as scientists, philosophers, businesspeople—indeed, writers in *any* field—to explore and communicate ideas and do their work.

In general, we use the term *fiction* to refer to stories that a writer makes up, whereas *nonfiction* is assumed to be an account of something that happened. Fictional stories are not assumed to be accurate accounts of whatever the writer is describing but creations of the writer's imagination, even when the stories are based on real events. We know, for example, that the writer Herman Melville was a sailor on whaling ships, but we don't assume that his novel *Moby Dick* is an account of his actual experiences on those ships. Rather, it is a story he made up, based on his own sailing experiences and on a real event that he did not witness. So we call it fiction. By contrast, *The Wreck of the Whaleship Essex* by Owen Chase (1821) is a first-hand account of the sinking of a ship by a whale. Chase was a sailor on that ship, and he tells the story of what happened as he experienced it. His book is considered nonfiction. Although writers of both fictional and nonfictional narratives use similar techniques for storytelling, this textbook focuses on nonfiction narrative.

Occasions for Narrative

One of my first professional writing assignments was a magazine article about rural health care. I was still in college and excited to have an opportunity to write something for which I would be paid. After several months of researching medical issues, interviewing doctors, and writing the article, I proudly sent my manuscript to the editor, thinking I was finished. All I had to do now was wait for the article to be published and cash the check I would receive from the magazine. A few weeks later, however, instead of a check, I received a long, detailed message from the editor in which he described the many revisions he expected me to make. He explained that my article needed to be better adapted for readers of his magazine, and he included many suggestions for improving the piece, including deleting some of my favorite sections and adding new material that would require additional research. To say that his message surprised me would be an understatement. I was deflated. It was like getting a bad grade on a course assignment. I had expected that writing the article would be similar to what usually happened when I wrote essays for my college classes: I would work hard, submit the essay, receive a grade (or a check), and move on. But now I began to realize that writing effectively was much more involved than that. The editor's comments were not like a teacher's grade; instead, they were part of a collaborative effort to create an effective article for the readers of that magazine. Eventually, I got over my disappointment, carefully reviewed the editor's suggestions, and set to work revising the article. Some months later, it was finally published, and I did receive my check. And I had to admit that the published article was much better than the one I originally submitted.

I have told this story many times—usually to my students. I tell it for several reasons: to illustrate the importance of revision and the collaborative nature of writing; to demonstrate the importance of experience in learning to write; to emphasize the role of audience. And right now I am telling the story again for another purpose: to make a point about the uses of narrative.

We use narrative for various purposes in many different contexts:

- You tell a close friend about the challenges of caring for a relative with a debilitating illness.

- A roommate tells you the story of how a longstanding relationship ended.

- A soldier returning from Afghanistan describes his experience in battle there.

- A mountain climber tells other climbers about what happened when she tried to climb an especially challenging mountain.

- An employee describes to her boss a difficult encounter with a customer.

In each of these examples, narrative helps both storyteller and listener make sense of what happened. And each of these situations might lead to narrative writing:

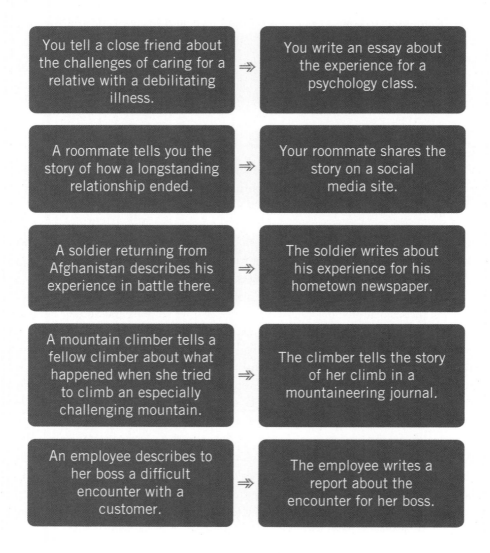

You tell a close friend about the challenges of caring for a relative with a debilitating illness. ⟹ You write an essay about the experience for a psychology class.

A roommate tells you the story of how a longstanding relationship ended. ⟹ Your roommate shares the story on a social media site.

A soldier returning from Afghanistan describes his experience in battle there. ⟹ The soldier writes about his experience for his hometown newspaper.

A mountain climber tells a fellow climber about what happened when she tried to climb an especially challenging mountain. ⟹ The climber tells the story of her climb in a mountaineering journal.

An employee describes to her boss a difficult encounter with a customer. ⟹ The employee writes a report about the encounter for her boss.

In such instances, narrative enables the writer to explore a complex and perhaps difficult experience and convey its significance to a reader. In writing a story, a writer not only describes what happened but also can examine *why* it happened and, perhaps more important, what it means. Writing about the challenges of caring for a sick relative, for example, can illuminate the importance of relationships in dealing with illness or reveal the joys of caregiving even when the experience is painful. Similarly, an employee's report describing a difficult encounter with a customer can help the company understand problems it might be having in customer relations. Writing about my experience with my rural health care article helps me continue to learn from the experience and convey what I've learned to you.

You have probably used narrative to find and share meaning in similar ways many times: in messages to your friends or relatives, in a college admissions essay, in writing you have done for a class. Narrative, then, is a tool for living. The better you can tell a story in a piece of writing, the more useful narrative can be in all aspects of your life.

EXERCISE 15A   EXPLORING OCCASIONS FOR NARRATIVE

1. Think about the last time you told someone a story. What was the context? Why did you tell the story? What do you think you accomplished by telling the story? Write a few paragraphs describing this situation and explaining why you told your story. Now, in a group of classmates, share what you wrote. Try to identify commonalities in the reasons that you and your classmates told your stories. What do you think your respective experiences suggest about the uses of narrative in our lives?

2. Is there a story about an experience you had that you have told many times? If so, think about what makes that story important—to you and to others. Why do you tell that story over and over? To whom do you tell it? Do you tell it simply to entertain friends or relatives? Or does the story have greater significance to you?

3. Look over the front page of a newspaper or visit an online news source. Identify two or more reports that interest you. For each topic you identify, think of an experience you had that somehow relates to that topic. Now consider how you would tell the story of that experience to someone if you happened to have a conversation about that topic. What would you tell that person about your experience? Why?

15

Understanding Narrative Writing in College

- In an economics class, students are given statistical data about populations in the United States, including percentages of various racial and ethnic groups, in different regions and during different time periods. The data also include employment figures, educational attainment statistics, and income levels. From this information students are asked to construct the "story" of a particular group in the United States during a specific time period.

- In an introductory geology course, students write a memo to a specific audience (such as a government office or a town engineer) in which they explain current techniques for measuring seismic activity and determining the probability of an earthquake in a specific location. The memo includes a specific example of one town's experience in using these techniques to predict the possibility of earthquake.

- An assignment in a psychology course requires students to write an essay about an experience in which their gender somehow played an important role. The stories are then used to examine how attitudes about gender can shape social relationships.

Martin Shields/Alamy

- Students in a zoology class make several field trips to a river near their campus, each time recording their observations of wildlife species that inhabit the river. In their final report for the class, the students describe the behaviors of the wildlife they observed, narrating what they saw the animals doing over time.

As these examples suggest, narrative writing is not only prevalent in college courses but also an important form of knowledge-making in academic disciplines. Narrative serves many different purposes and takes a variety of forms in different academic disciplines. The memo for the geology class, for instance, includes an example that tells the story of a place where earthquake prediction techniques were used; the zoology reports include passages that tell the story of what the students observed. To be an effective writer in college—and elsewhere—you need to be able to tell stories in ways that meet the needs of your rhetorical situation.

Before looking more closely at narrative writing in college, we need to distinguish between common forms of storytelling and the kinds of narrative writing reflected in the examples above:

- **Conventional narrative.** In conventional narratives, writers tell stories about something that happened—to themselves or to others—as a way to make sense of the experience and convey the meaning of the experience to an audience. Conventional narratives have the familiar features we traditionally associate with stories: a plot, characters, and descriptive writing; they often include dialogue. Memoirs, personal essays, and biographies are all forms of conventional narrative. Most novels and short stories are also conventional narratives. So are most movies, television dramas, and comedies.

- **Embedded or academic narrative.** Narrative is often used within another kind of text—for example, an analysis or an argument. In this "embedded" kind of narrative, writers tell a story to illustrate a relevant point, illuminate an idea, or support an argument. For example, in an argument against decriminalizing marijuana, a writer might include the story of a person whose life was made difficult by his use of that drug. In such a case, the writer's primary purpose is not to tell an entertaining story that explores an experience but to use the story to make a point—for example, that using marijuana is risky.

Although you are likely to write some conventional narratives in college, most narrative writing in college courses tends to be embedded narrative, which is the focus of this chapter. (Conventional narratives are examined in Chapter 16.) The differences between these two categories have to do mostly with purpose. Conventional and embedded narratives share basic features, as we will see below, but in an embedded narrative, the writer's main purpose is not to tell an entertaining story but rather to make a specific point. In either case, an effective narrative should engage readers and draw them into the story, even when that story is embedded in another kind of text.

Narrative writing in college generally exhibits four key features:

- **A clear, narrow focus.** In academic writing, narratives tend to be narrowly focused on the event, experience, or phenomenon that the author is writing about to make a point. Unlike many conventional narratives, stories in academic writing usually do not include subplots that can make a narrative long and complex. In most cases, narrative in academic writing serves a very specific purpose, which is generally achieved through maintaining a narrow focus.

- **Brevity.** Most narratives included in academic texts tend to be brief. Often they take the form of anecdotes that are rarely longer than a few paragraphs. Even when they are longer, they are usually briefer than conventional narratives, which often try to bring readers deeply into the imaginative world of the story.

- **A basic structure.** Academic writers tend to tell stories in a straightforward way. Rather than using complex plots or manipulating chronological time, they structure their narratives to help readers follow the story and easily grasp the point of the story.

- **Succinct, purposeful description.** Whereas conventional narratives often include detailed, vivid descriptions of scenes or events, most narratives in academic contexts rely on succinct descriptions to convey a scene or point efficiently. Descriptions are used in a way that keeps the focus on the point and does not call attention to the writer's language.

Let's look at some examples that illustrate these features. In this passage from the introduction to a study of Pueblo Indian schools, ethnographer Alan Peshkin begins his book-length study by highlighting what he calls the "dual-world existence" of Native American peoples, which is a major theme of his study. He uses a brief narrative to make his point:

> Disconcerted by the images of his people often held by non-Indians, Mateo Romero, a young Pueblo painter and Dartmouth College graduate, tried to set the record straight: "People think of Native American Indians in these noble, savage stereotypes. In reality, they're just human beings like everybody else. Being "like everybody else," however, is belied by the reality of lives shaped by these many objects of loss, but also by the recurrent mention by Pueblos of their dual-world existence and the resulting complications.
>
> In 1990, for example, Pueblo mother Bonnie Candelaria enrolled her daughter in a public school located outside San Felipe reservation, where she lived. Tribal authorities protested her decision to remove her child from the local reservation school and, thereby, from the influence of her tribe. Candelaria argued for her child's need "to learn to adapt to the world out there, rather than the world in here." It is debatable whether tribal authority established under the circumstances of tribal sovereignty as a nation-within-the-nation, extends to parental decisions about where reservation

members send their children to school. That tribal authorities can even consider it a possibility indicates the magnitude of the issue of if and how children are to be socialized for Indian culture and community. Sam Montoya, Pueblo Indian and Bureau of Indian Affairs official, placed this issue in the perspective of the dual-world challenges and opportunities that confront his people:

> Some people are waking up and saying we have to be more aggressive about protecting our way of life. We have existed here for hundreds of years … There is an awareness now that, yes, there is a challenge to these values. I'm not trying to say that any tribe is trying to shut out the outside world. They're trying to strike a balance between what they feel is unique … and the new opportunities provided by the other world. [quoted in Barringer 1990:B9]

Many Americans have grown up informed by and living to varying extents in two worlds. As generations pass, the distinctiveness of their subgroup culture diminishes, sometimes to the vanishing point. Indian cultures are decidedly different. In no other American group is there a Sam Montoya who can speak as he did after 500 years of culture contact between Indians and non-Indians.

Source: Peshkin, Alan. *Places of Memory*. Mahwah: Erlbaum, 1997. Print.

Notice that Peshkin doesn't tell the whole story of Bonnie Candelaria's efforts to find the right school for her daughter; rather, he tells just enough to illustrate his point about the challenges faced by Pueblo people as they navigate their "dual" existence. His narrative is not only brief but also narrowly focused so that his point is clear. (Brevity and a narrow focus are often evident in the kind of visual storytelling that is common in advertising. See "Telling a Story Visually.") Still, the story is engaging and likely to evoke emotion in a reader, even if it is not meant to entertain.

To appreciate how effectively this single image can tell a story, try writing the story you see in this ad.

In the same way, television commercials often tell a story, sometimes in as little as fifteen seconds. In this ad for Volkswagen cars, called "Young Darth Vader" (2012), a child dressed as the *Star Wars* character Darth Vader seems to use "the force" to control the new car in his family's driveway. In the one-minute ad, we eventually learn that the child's father is controlling the car remotely, which highlights Volkswagen's new technology:

AP Photo/Volkswagen of America

Scholars also use narrative to explain *how* they conducted their research. Here's Peshkin again:

An American institution: it is Friday night. Indian High School's basketball team is playing a home game. Students, usually long gone for the weekend to their reservation homes, spill out of the school's several male and female dormitory buildings. They merge with the procession of cars and pickup trucks heading toward parking lots next to the gym. The gym is packed. Students, teachers, parents, and relatives mill about in the gym lobby, greeting friends, buying food and drink, anxious to return to their seats before the national anthem is sung. Then the game begins.

I have watched high school teams play basketball since my own student days. Never before had I seen a team play like Indian High School's varsity squad. They were quick, athletic, and relatively short—shorter than their opponents, who came from a non-Indian school in their non-public school athletic league. The home team won the game, but it was how they played the game that fascinated me: a full-court press, their basic strategy, literally overwhelmed their opponents. Indian High School players swarmed at both ends of the court. Sometimes I'd count the players on the floor, in disbelief that a legal five were able to do such damage. The result was one fine game in an overall winning season.

Many months later, I began my year-long contact with Indian High School and observed students at work in their classrooms. Regrettably, I saw no academic counterpart to this stellar athletic performance. Indian students take to and excel in the non-academic aspects of their school life. They acknowledge that they can and ought to achieve more academic success; they are disappointed that they do not.

About 1 month into my observations of Indian High School students in their classrooms, I decided that my initial fascination with the dual-world character of the students' lives—the one, their traditional, tribal, Indian, reservation world, the other, the mainstream American, dominant Anglo, non-Indian world—would be oriented to exploring why these students reacted as they did in their classrooms. From their school's many documents, I knew it had accepted as one of its main purposes helping students "to make fulfilling life choices." *Life choices* cover much ground. The choice of most interest to me—doing well in and with schooling—did not appear to be fulfilled.

Source: Peshkin, Alan. *Places of Memory*. Mahwah: Erlbaum, 1997. Print.

In this excerpt, Peshkin explains his perspective as a researcher studying the Pueblo community. You can recognize some familiar features of conventional narrative, especially the vivid but purposeful description of the basketball game, which helps readers imagine the scene he witnessed. But the description does not distract readers from his main point about the dual existence of Pueblo students. Like the previous excerpt, this one is brief and tightly focused. Peshkin doesn't get carried away by the story but uses the story effectively to convey an important idea in his research.

In some academic writing, narrative is used more extensively to explore an idea or make a point. For example, the following essay, written by a professor of English education for a professional journal, tells the story of the author's experience with a specific student. Notice that the author uses features of conventional narrative, including plot and dialogue:

A number of years ago, I was a middle school teacher. One morning I was standing outside my classroom as my first-hour group assembled when one of my students approached me in tears.

"Mr. Goodson," she sobbed, "I think my neighbor skinned his dog."

As she stood there crying, and I stood there looking at her, it occurred to me at that moment that I really had no clue how to handle this situation. I knew there were interpersonal and cultural and ethical and perhaps even legal issues unfolding in front of me, but I didn't even know what they were, much less what I, as a teacher, was obligated to do. But as a crowd of curious middle-schoolers gathered around us, I knew I had to do something. I decided to start with the obvious question.

"What makes you think your neighbor skinned his dog?" I asked.

"Because it's hanging from his clothesline," she wailed.

Her answer didn't help my state of mind all that much. For a moment I wondered whether it was the neighbor's *dog's skin* or the neighbor's *skinned dog* hanging from the clothesline, but I decided it probably didn't matter. (Except, of course, to the dog.) The real problem at the moment was my student, still standing there, crying, waiting for me to resolve this matter. I decided on a bold course of action.

"Have you told your mother about this?" I asked.

She shook her head no. "I saw it on my way to school," she said.

"Why don't you go down to the office and call your mother?" I suggested, and I was more than a little grateful when she nodded and turned away, leaving me to curse those idiot education professors who didn't prepare me for this encounter.

A few minutes after she left to call her mother, she came back to my classroom. She wasn't upset anymore. In fact she bounced to her seat and started whispering and giggling with her friends. I drifted through the room and back to her seat.

"Is everything all right?" I asked, now thoroughly puzzled by her dramatic change in mood.

She seemed confused, as if she didn't know what I was talking about.

"Your neighbor's dog," I reminded her.

"Oh, yeah," she said. "It was just a coyote."

"Great," I said. And I suppose it probably was. (Except, of course, for the coyote.)

Years passed. Today I'm an "idiot education professor," trying to figure out a way to teach young people things they can only really learn from experience and writing about the curious magic of literacy and its teaching.

But I've reflected considerably on the skinned-dog matter over the years, to the point that the skinned dog has become, for me, a darkly comic metaphor for the uncertainty that is the beauty and the challenge of teaching. You see, I was just minding my own business that morning, standing in the hallway, waiting for classes to start. I've long since forgotten what I had planned for that day, but I'm sure it was something that seemed important at the time. I had probably prepared my lessons according to the Madeline Hunter Model, which was popular in those days, and I imagine I had something cute planned to launch the first hour.

The skinned dog changed everything that day. The skinned dog forced me to step out of my abstract plans and deal with students in a world that doesn't respond to even the most carefully worded behavioral objective, a world where students are human beings and not the idealized student construct we have in mind when we produce the standards documents, curriculum guides, and lesson plans. The ideal student of the standards document comes to school like one of the McGuffey's Reader "scholars" of a long ago era: well-scrubbed and eager for the learning we have designed. But real students sometimes live in neighborhoods where anything can happen. Despite our best efforts to take the mystery out of teaching and learning and to standardize the process, we will never standardize or eliminate the skinned dog. No matter how many years I teach, I know that each time I open the classroom door, the skinned dog might well be waiting on the other side, ready to force me to confront a situation I have not planned for and could not have planned for because schools and students are, by nature, nonstandard.

We live and work in a time when we have tried to preordain crisp and neat learning outcomes for all of us. We have studied teaching and learning. We have invested lots of money in writing standards and spelling out benchmarks for students from kindergarten all the way through high school, and we have created the same sorts of expectations

15

for teachers, from their preservice years through their completion of National Board certification. And it is good to spell out our goals and to rigorously investigate our practice and to measure ourselves and our students against ideals, but the certainty of our current approaches neglects the stark image of the skinned dog, reminding us that the art of teaching, like the art of writing, lies as much in how we respond to the irregular as in how we plan to create regularity. The skinned dog teaches a few simple-but-powerful rules about teaching.

Truisms of the Skinned Dog

We never know what to expect.

We've never seen it all.

In every interesting situation, we never really know what to do.

We should always proceed with caution.

We should always proceed.

And if we apply the truisms of the skinned dog to our contemporary educational reform effort, we come to understand how our efforts to raise standards for all students in an effort to narrow the gap between the top and the bottom don't take into consideration the unpredictable quirkiness that is part of the teacher's and learner's daily diet. The skinned dog helps us understand that students at the bottom of the achievement gap are there because of complicated social, economic, and cultural reasons and a forceful application of the upper-middle-class system of rewards and consequences will not likely have the desired effect.

When a student confronts a skinned dog on her way to school, the last thing she needs from the school is the opportunity to sit in class and move through a carefully scripted lesson pointed toward a high-stakes test. She needs an opportunity to tell her story. She needs a little help in understanding and interpreting her world, and she depends on us for that help. The fundamental flaw of our contemporary model for school reform is this: It begins with what we want students to know not with the students themselves. It is nice (perhaps even essential) for us to know and agree upon what we want students to know and be able to do, but we will never be successful with this as our starting point. We can only improve schools and schooling by taking the students and their worlds and their cultures as our starting point. We have to work from the students toward the standards. We cannot simply work through the standards. In short, we have to account for the skinned dog.

Source: Todd Goodson, "Teaching in the Time of Dogs." *The Quarterly* 26.3 (2004). Web. 21 July 2012.

In this example, the author, Todd Goodson, devotes about half of his essay to the story of his student and the skinned dog, focusing the rest of the essay on the lessons he learned from that experience. Notice that he tells the story much as any good storyteller might, using dialogue to give readers a sense of being there, creating tension to keep readers engaged, and following a basic plot to convey what happened. The drama created by the plot propels readers to the second half of the essay, in which Goodson explores the implications of his experience. But despite his use of features of conventional narrative, the purpose of his narrative is to make a point about education reform for his audience of professional educators.

EXERCISE 15B   EXPLORING NARRATIVE WRITING IN COLLEGE

1. For each course you are enrolled in (or courses you have taken in the past), think of an experience you had that is relevant to the course subject. For example, if you are taking an economics course, you might think about your experience in securing a college loan. Now consider how you might tell this story in a way that is appropriate for and relevant to that academic discipline.

2. Find an example of narrative writing in a textbook for a college or high school course you have taken. In a brief paragraph, describe the features of that narrative. How does the writer tell the story? What do you notice about the story and how it is used? Can you draw any conclusions from this example about narrative writing in that academic discipline?

3. If you have written a narrative essay for any of your college (or high school) courses, analyze the rhetorical purpose of that essay. In a brief paragraph, describe the assignment. What was the goal of your narrative? Who was your intended audience? What expectations did that audience have for your narrative? Draw conclusions about narrative writing in an academic context.

Telling Stories

Writing effective narrative is largely a matter of learning some basic techniques that enable you to take advantage of your natural ability to tell a story. This section offers advice about using narrative techniques to meet the needs of your rhetorical situation. In most academic writing, that means writing **embedded narrative** (see page 478); however, you will likely have occasion to write **conventional narratives** as well. The techniques described here will help you write both kinds of narrative.

Maintaining Focus

Because stories often have so many different components—people, events, scenes, background—it can be easy to get off track. As we saw in the previous section, however, effective narratives, especially in academic writing, keep to the point. The trick is to determine not what is relevant but what is *necessary* to your point.

The following two essays were written in response to the same assignment for an education class. Students were asked to tell the story of an experience that influenced them as a writer or reader.

They were writing their stories for their classmates, all of whom were studying to be teachers. One student, Carrie, wrote about several unpleasant experiences she had as a young student:

> When I was in third grade I was supposedly so lucky to have been placed with my third grade teacher. I don't remember my teacher's name and barely remember what she looks like. She was young with a high pitched voice. She developed a writing lab in order to continue improving our newly developed reading and writing skills. Each week was a different piece of writing; we would develop drafts which would continue to evolve through the course. During these writing labs, we were designated to meet with our teacher once a week to work one-on-one with her. One day my teacher told me, "You are just not a good writer." I don't remember the assignment or the rest of the conversation during that meeting; all I remember is that statement. I was embarrassed by my teacher in class and cried in front of my peers. The worst part was that I believed her.
>
> Teachers make lasting impressions upon their students. As students, we don't remember every irregular verb in Spanish or memorize every area formula we were taught in math, but we do remember the teachers that taught those classes. We remember how the teacher made us feel, whether that feeling was pleasant or quite the opposite. Most often for students, negative experiences involved with learning have more of an effect than positive ones. The teacher can make a difference in the development of skill sets in an area of study; positive reinforcement can lead to motivation and success, whereas negative feedback can lead to resentment and disinterest in a subject. Even after this experience, I do not believe that I was completely shut off to reading and writing. I still really enjoyed reading and I learned a lot from the process of reading. Even as a third grader I understood the importance of literacy and being a literate person. However, writing did become less important. I did not want to be critiqued or humiliated. Thus my fear of writing began.
>
> Before entering high school, eighth grade teachers recommend classes that fit a student's ability in a particular subject. I was recommended for honors history, science, and Italian. Honors English was the only accelerated class that I wasn't enrolled in. I went to my English teacher and asked her to recommend me. My teacher responded, "Why would you want to take honors? You're a terrible writer." She dismissed my question. Once again, I don't remember my teacher's name, I don't remember what she looked like, and I don't remember the rest of the conversation. I do remember her tone, what she said, and the way she made me feel. The worst part of this particular conversation was that I believed her.
>
> I didn't like writing then and I still don't like writing because I don't think I'm good at it. As a result, I avoid writing. Instead of taking an English elective I take an extra science class. If projects allow for alternative approaches other than writing a paper, I would always opt out of the paper, eliminating the messy and overwhelming process of writing. Avoiding the practice of writing may explain the writer that I am today; I am unconfident in my writing. I feel that my thought process on paper is unorganized and hard to follow. Generally, people like to do things that they are good at. I think I can even go as far as to conclude that my uncomfortable feelings towards writing led me to choose my major. I chose science and mathematics because it involves reading

and critical thinking to prove my knowledge rather than proving it through a piece of writing. I was never given encouragement to succeed in the process of writing as I was in other subject areas, and it's this fact that brought me to love chemistry.

Over the course of my development as a literate person I have grown as a student. I used to write to complete assignments (the night before they were due), caring little about the quality of writing I had produced but instead concentrating on minor details. For instance, I would concentrate on whether the paper was long enough or whether my commas were correct instead of focusing on the more important questions that I ask myself now: Did I answer the question? Is this really what I want to say? How will my readers interpret this? I am still not confident in my writing; however, the attitude with which I approach writing and the process of writing is different. I know that I can create a quality piece of writing if I work at it. I have realized that writing is a process of revision, rewriting, and then revising.

Being literate is essential to being successful. Reading and writing differ from most skill sets; both are used in all disciplines of study. We see these skills in all professions. A scientist writes to share their research, politicians write to pass bills, and mathematicians read to understand and problem solve. Literacy in my life has been primarily through schooling. I understand that literacy in my life will turn into an everyday skill as a form of communication and expression. I will continue to work on developing as a professional teacher, improving my abilities and encouraging my students to do the same. My experiences also shaped my role and views as a teacher; constructive feedback is a lot more meaningful than negative criticism. As I evolve as a student, I see more importance in literacy. Overall, negative feedback I received about my skills in literacy as a young student has shaped a negative outlook on my ability to express myself in a written form. But I hope to instill and inspire my students to embrace and take an interest in literacy.

In this essay, Carrie tells a disheartening story of how her early experiences with a few teachers shaped her self-image as a writer and affected her decisions about her college major many years later. That's the focus of her story. Notice, though, that, in her final two paragraphs, the focus shifts away from the story of her development as a writer and toward a discussion of the implications of her experience for her career as a teacher. Those final paragraphs are not irrelevant to her story, but they are probably unnecessary to convey her main point about the damage a teacher can do to a student's confidence as a writer. In fact, the focus of her story would probably be clearer if she eliminated those final two paragraphs.

Here's another essay written for the same assignment. In this case, the student, Nate, tells a story about coming to understand himself as a young man in part as a result of an experience he had with his grandfather; through that experience he learns something important not only about himself and his family but also about literacy:

I was never the one to be open about my feelings or personal life to others. However, this doesn't mean I never had feelings about life choices or events in my life. Despite growing up in a developed country and coming from a liberal family, I still felt it my duty to be strong for my family. My mother was born in Haiti, and my grandfather is particularly traditional about the gender role of men in the family. When I was born, my parents and I lived in my grandparents' house for about five years while my mom worked and my dad went back to college. As the oldest of two, I was seen by my grandfather as the man of the family, the one who must carry the proverbial torch when he passes.

My grandfather has always been quite fond of literature in general. Often I would catch him reading books on technology, our Haitian heritage, and even the manuals that come with electronic devices these days. As I grew up I never really read for enjoyment or fun. Instead, reading seemed like a chore or something I had to do. When I went to my grandparents' house, there was always some pseudo-philosophical discussion going on about life. I would always leave with some old world saying or an idea my grandfather would plant in my head. For my grandfather, getting me to think about the world in a different way was always his focus. This is why, according to my grandfather, it was less than ideal that I did not enjoy reading.

He tried different strategies to get me to read by quizzing me about what I was supposed to read. At one point my grandfather even paid me for each book I read. My grandfather would coerce me to carry around a pocket notebook to write down words I did not understand while reading in order to revisit them and build my vocabulary. However, in the off chance I actually did read, I would never share what I thought about that topic. It was engrained in my mind that I should not discuss my feelings with my family because I needed to be the foundation.

One day, much like any other day at my grandparents', I was speaking to my grandfather and actually started to discuss how I felt about a particular reading. I had read *The Black Jacobins,* which is a history of the Haitian Revolution. We discussed life back in Haiti and my ancestors, and out of nowhere my grandfather started talking about his father. My grandfather was young when his father died and was essentially forced to become the father figure in the household. As he cried, my grandfather detailed his struggle to get his siblings to focus on school and create a better life. It was the first time I had ever seen my grandfather cry, and to this day I am the only one in my family to ever see him cry.

I left the house confused as to what I just witnessed. There was a long period of time before I had another real conversation with my grandfather, and we never really discussed what actually happened to this day. However, as time passed I started to realize that it is okay to have emotions and not to be ashamed of my feelings. Gradually, I was able to become more personal with my writing in school and for myself. I started to write more music because music has been a large part of my life. It is particularly interesting to see my earlier musical endeavors because of how crude they were and how devoid of any feeling they really were.

It was quite a new experience to feel comfortable with my own emotions. I was always the type to think deeply about a topic that I was interested in. Now I was able to allow my thoughts to flow freely without restriction. In a sense, it was like my brain was full and instead of using the knowledge constructively, I just constantly allowed it to overflow. I had a clear mind and I flourished academically. Clubs started to look more enticing to join, and I was able to take an active role (often a leadership role) in many academic avenues.

Eventually I started having more in depth conversations with my grandfather about news, my life, academics, etc. I had countless conversations, debates, and lectures from my grandfather and they were so much more personal than ever before. He was able to cry on several occasions since then (although I can count them all on one hand), and I can remember each and every one of them.

It is in the reading and writing of people that we gain emotional understanding of others and ourselves. For my grandfather, literacy was a way to connect with me on a deeper level, a level that may have otherwise been hidden because of the strong and dominant male mentality. With his help I learned that literacy is much more than reading and writing; it is an emotional tether to others.

At first glance, Nate's story has much in common with Carrie's. Both writers tell about early experiences that shaped them as readers and writers and as human beings. Notice, however, that Nate's essay doesn't lose focus as he moves from his anecdote about the first time he saw his grandfather cry (paragraph 4) to his transformation as someone in touch with his own emotions. Whereas Carrie's essay drifts to a discussion of what her early experiences mean for her future career, Nate returns in his final paragraphs to his relationship with his grandfather and how it has influenced his understanding of reading and writing, thus reinforcing the main point of his essay. Moreover, he discusses each subtopic in terms of this main idea about literacy and relationships. For example, in paragraph 5, he describes his interest in music, but he does so in reference to his point about how his experience with his grandfather affected him as a person (rather than, say, in terms of his musical abilities or the power of music as a form of expression—both of which would be perfectly valid but not really relevant to his main idea). In this way, he maintains his focus on his main point, even though he covers a lot of ground in describing his relationship with his grandfather and his own development as a person.

Maintaining focus in a narrative, then, is a matter of:

- carefully selecting what to include and exclude
- presenting material in terms of the story's main point

You can use this approach in your own narrative writing:

> 1. State as clearly as you can the main point or idea you want to convey with your story.

> 2. Review each section of your story (anecdotes, background information, etc.), and consider whether it is necessary to help convey your main point.

> 3. For each main section you decide to include, consider how it contributes to the main point or idea of your story.

For example, imagine you are writing a college admissions essay about your experience in a musical production in high school. You want to convey to the admissions people that you have learned to work hard to overcome challenges in your life. In this case, you had to switch your role in the play just a few days before the first show because the student playing the lead role became ill. The director asked you to take that lead role, which you had only a few days to learn. Let's imagine, too, that the student who became ill was a close friend of yours with whom you had competed for the lead role. In fact, that competition led to an argument with your friend. Now you are taking your friend's part in the play.

So you have several important events or scenes to consider including in your essay: the auditions, your argument with your friend, being asked to take the lead role, and working diligently to prepare for the lead role in a very short time. What should you include?

First, state the main point of your story as best you can:

Overcoming unexpected challenges often requires one to be dedicated, work hard, and believe in oneself.

Now consider each main event or scene in terms of the two principles described above:

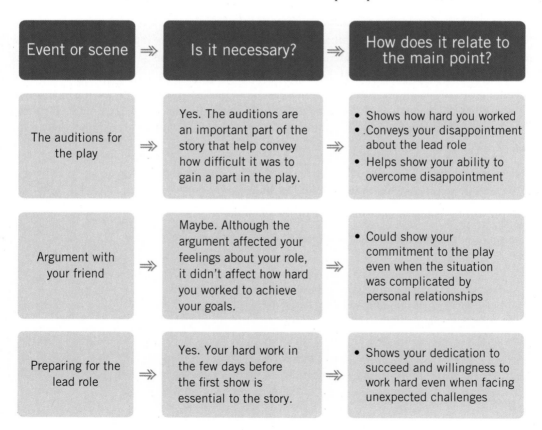

Event or scene ⇒	Is it necessary? ⇒	How does it relate to the main point?
The auditions for the play ⇒	Yes. The auditions are an important part of the story that help convey how difficult it was to gain a part in the play. ⇒	• Shows how hard you worked • Conveys your disappointment about the lead role • Helps show your ability to overcome disappointment
Argument with your friend ⇒	Maybe. Although the argument affected your feelings about your role, it didn't affect how hard you worked to achieve your goals. ⇒	• Could show your commitment to the play even when the situation was complicated by personal relationships
Preparing for the lead role ⇒	Yes. Your hard work in the few days before the first show is essential to the story. ⇒	• Shows your dedication to succeed and willingness to work hard even when facing unexpected challenges

Such an analysis will help you decide not only what to include but also how to keep it focused on the main point of your story. Following these steps will help you maintain the focus of your narrative, even when (like Nate's) it tells a multilayered story.

1. In a few paragraphs, tell the story of an important experience you had. (Don't try to write a polished version of your story; just tell the story as clearly as possible.) Now review what you wrote to see whether you have included anything that isn't necessary. Using the technique described in this section, identify any passages that can be eliminated without losing important information.

2. Find a few stories posted by your Facebook friends or on another social media site you frequent. Use the technique described in this section to analyze whether the story is effectively focused. Identify revisions you might make to sharpen the story's focus.

Structuring a Narrative

The most common way to structure a narrative is chronologically, in which the story is told from beginning to end without significant interruption. In a chronologically structured narrative, the writer tells the story in a way that mimics the passage of time, taking the reader back to the point in time when the story begins and working forward to the point when it ends. However, writers use several other well-established strategies for manipulating time in a narrative to create tension, heighten drama, and emphasize specific events or moments in the story:

■ **Slowing the story down.** Even the most strictly chronological narrative cannot include everything that happened in a story, nor can it tell a story in real time. So writers pass quickly over less important parts of their stories and focus on the more significant moments or events. For example, in writing an essay about your experience on a soccer team that overcame long odds to win an unlikely championship, you might include only a few sentences about early-season matches but devote several paragraphs to a match that was a turning point in the season.

■ **Flashbacks.** One of the most common narrative techniques is the flashback, in which the writer interrupts the story to return to something that happened earlier in time. Usually, flashbacks provide important background information or context. For example, in your hypothetical essay about your championship soccer season, you might interrupt the story to include an anecdote about an injury you suffered several years earlier that affected your play

Bob Thomas/iStockphoto.com

15

during your championship season. In "flashing back" to that earlier moment, you provide readers with important information that helps explain the situation in the "present" moment of the story.

- **_In medias res._** *In medias res*, which is Latin for "in the middle of things," is a common technique for creating tension or drama and drawing readers into the story. In this technique, the writer begins the story at a point just before the climactic moment but stops the story before reaching that moment to return to a point earlier in time, telling the story from that point to the end. For example, you might begin the story of your soccer season with the championship match, describing the hard-fought contest to give your reader a sense of that dramatic moment but not yet telling the outcome of the match. Instead, you stop short of describing that outcome and return to the beginning of the season, when your team was facing difficulties that made it unlikely for them to win a championship. From that point, you tell the story up to the climactic moment during the championship match and then move to the conclusion.

- **Fractured narrative.** Sometimes a writer tells a story by moving back and forth in time. In this way, a writer highlights important moments but does not narrate those moments in chronological sequence. Instead, the writer might begin the story at some point in the middle, jump ahead to a point near the end, jump back to an earlier moment, and then back to an even earlier moment before returning to the present. An example of this approach is Jon Krakauer's *Into the Wild*, which tells the story of a young man named Chris McCandless who went alone into the Alaskan wilderness to try to live off the land. Krakauer moves back and forth between McCandless's childhood, adolescence, and adulthood as well as events that occurred after McCandless dies.

Using such techniques to manipulate time can sometimes distract readers from the main purpose of the narrative, which is why they are rarely used in academic writing. If you use these techniques, do so strategically to help bring out the main point of your narrative.

EXERCISE 15D   STRUCTURING A NARRATIVE

1. In a few paragraphs, tell the story of something important that happened to you. Tell your story in chronological order.

2. Restructure the story you wrote for Question #1 using one of the techniques described in this section.

3. Compare the two versions of the story you wrote for Questions #1 and #2. Evaluate each version. Which version do you think tells the story more effectively? Why? What conclusions might you draw from this exercise about narrative structure?

Writing Purposeful Description

Effective description in narrative writing should convey a vivid sense of the place, person, thing, or event being described, but also serve a purpose in the narrative. For example, let's return to Alan Peshkin's brief description of a high school basketball game:

> An American institution: it is Friday night. Indian High School's basketball team is playing a home game. Students, usually long gone for the weekend to their reservation homes, spill out of the school's several male and female dormitory buildings. They merge with the procession of cars and pickup trucks heading toward parking lots next to the gym. The gym is packed. Students, teachers, parents, and relatives mill about in the gym lobby, greeting friends, buying food and drink, anxious to return to their seats before the national anthem is sung. Then the game begins.

This paragraph vividly conveys the scene in the gym and the feeling of anticipation that Peshkin sensed as fans awaited the start of the game. His passage exhibits **two key features of effective description:**

- **Appropriate details.** Peshkin includes just enough detail for the reader to get a clear sense of what is being described. He succinctly describes the scene without going into great detail about the gym or the people. He doesn't describe the gym itself (the color of the walls or the kind of floor), leaving it to the reader to imagine a typical high school gym, nor does he provide details about the people he observed there. Adding such details is unnecessary because the focus of his description is on the sense of anticipation as the crowd gathers for the game. In fact, adding such details might distract readers and blur his focus.

- **Careful word choice.** Describing a scene vividly requires selecting words judiciously and avoiding "over-writing" the scene with unnecessary language, especially adjectives and adverbs. Careful word choice is the key to vivid description. For example, Peshkin writes that the students "spill out of the school's several male and female dormitory buildings," using the verb *spill* efficiently to convey an image of many students moving in a crowd from their dorms to the gym. Similarly, he writes that "they merge with the procession of cars and pickup trucks heading toward parking lots next to the gym." Again, he uses a verb (*merge*) to convey the sense of movement. The noun *procession* creates an image of a line of cars and trucks moving slowly, bumper to bumper, into the parking lot. Notice that he uses no adjectives or adverbs to create these images; rather, he carefully selects verbs and nouns that efficiently convey the scene and help readers imagine it. Adding details or descriptive language to this passage might actually make it less vivid, as in this version (the added words are in boldface):

> Students, usually long gone for the weekend to their **distant** reservation homes, **excitedly exit** the school's several male and female dormitory buildings. They merge with the **slow** procession of **modest** cars and **well-worn** pickup trucks **crawling** toward **soon-to-be full** parking lots next to the **old** gym.

Almost all the added words here are adjectives (*slow, modest*) or adverbs (*excitedly*) that at first glance seem to bring concrete details to the description. But do they make the scene more vivid? More important, does that additional language help achieve Peshkin's purpose in describing this scene? Probably not. In this case, as is so often true in descriptive writing, less is more.

In describing something in your narrative writing, then, **follow these simple guidelines:**

- include only as much detail as you need
- use appropriate details
- choose words that efficiently convey an image or scene
- avoid elaborate or "flowery" language

EXERCISE 15E   DESCRIBING A SCENE VIVIDLY

1. In a brief paragraph, describe a scene. It can be a place you frequent (such as a coffee shop or bus stop), an event (a basketball game, a parade), or some place that interests you for some reason. Describe the scene as clearly and vividly as you can. Now review your description. What details did you include? Why did you include them? Are they necessary? If so, why? Is anything missing from your description?

2. Rewrite the description you wrote for Question #1 so that it is only half as long. Now examine what you removed from the original description. Is the description more or less vivid now? Explain. What conclusions might you draw about descriptive writing from this exercise?

3. Working with a group of three or four classmates, select a place (as in Question #1) and write a description of it. Everyone in your group should describe the same place. Now compare your descriptions. What similarities and differences can you identify in your descriptions? What might this exercise suggest about descriptive writing?

Showing and Telling

Writing instructors sometimes tell student writers, "Show, don't tell." That can be good advice, but what does it mean exactly?

In general, *showing* in narrative writing means conveying an idea or occurrence through description rather than explanation:

Telling: She was afraid of what he might say.

Showing: Her heart quickened, and she felt the knot in her stomach tighten as she waited for him to speak the words she desperately didn't want to hear.

Telling:	The house was run down.
Showing:	The torn screen on the front door flapped in the breeze. Paint peeled from the windowsills. The porch steps, which looked like they hadn't been swept for months, creaked underfoot, and the porch sagged. A visible layer of grime covered the siding.

As these examples suggest, *showing* generally involves the use of details to convey the scene or action. In much narrative writing in academic settings, such *showing* is unnecessary, though it can sometimes be effective—as in Alan Peshkin's description of the high school basketball game. In such cases, adding details can make a passage more vivid—and often longer. But whether the added details improve the narrative is another matter. You have to decide whether *showing* in a passage is appropriate for your rhetorical situation.

When writing descriptive passages that are intended to *show* an action, scene, or event, **follow these two guidelines:**

■ **Assess your rhetorical situation.** If you include description, be sure you describe the scene or event in a way that is appropriate for your rhetorical situation. For example, if you are writing a narrative for a psychology class about an experience with a school counselor, you might need to describe a meeting in which the counselor became frustrated and angry. Does that situation call for you to *show* the counselor's frustration by describing his face and mannerisms? If the purpose of the narrative is to examine the experience in terms of important concepts in counseling psychology, maybe not. For such a purpose, it might be sufficient just to state that the counselor became angry. By contrast, if you were writing about the same experience for a composition class, your purpose would likely be different, and you might want to describe the scene in a way that *shows* the counselor's anger in order to emphasize it.

■ **Don't overdo it.** In academic writing, narratives tend to be succinct and focused, so writers should use *showing* carefully. But even in conventional narrative, students often try too hard to *show* and end up describing scenes or events with too much detail that can distract readers. To avoid that problem, carefully review any passages in which you are trying to *show* something and analyze whether the passage is necessary and whether you can condense it without weakening your description.

15

EXERCISE 15F   SHOWING AND TELLING

1. Write two or three statements about how you feel. For example, "I'm tired." "I am anxious about my upcoming interview." Then rewrite each statement in a way that *shows* the feeling expressed in that statement.

2. Select one of the statements you wrote for Question #1, and share it with two or three classmates. Ask them what feeling the statement shows. If they do not interpret the statement as you expected, revise it to try to convey the feeling more effectively.

Features of Narrative

Effective narrative writing in academic settings has **four important features:**

1. **A clear, narrow focus.** Unlike conventional narratives, stories in academic writing usually do not include long, complex plots and many have no plot at all. Narrative in academic writing generally serves a very specific purpose, and stories are told in a way that achieves that purpose.

2. **Brevity.** Narratives written in academic contexts are usually briefer and more narrowly focused than conventional narratives, and they generally do not attempt to create the world of the story or the experience in the way many conventional narratives do. Depending upon the rhetorical situation and subject matter, narratives in academic writing will vary a great deal in length and style, but the general rule of thumb is to keep them short.

3. **A basic structure.** Narratives in academic writing usually follow a basic, chronological structure and rarely exhibit the more complex structures of many conventional narratives. Academic writers structure their narratives to help readers easily grasp the point of the story.

4. **Succinct, purposeful description.** Description in narratives in academic contexts is usually intended to convey a point quickly and clearly. Academic writers use language efficiently and rarely rely on elaborate diction in describing a person, scene, event, or thing.

The following essay by feminist scholar bell hooks exhibits these features of effective narrative writing (bell hooks, which is a pen name, is deliberately not capitalized). A distinguished scholar who has taught at numerous universities and written 30 books, hooks is well known not only for her provocative ideas about the role of race, gender, and social class in education, but also for her unusual writing style, which does not always follow academic convention. As she does in this essay, hooks often uses her own experiences as subject matter for her analyses of how race, gender, and class shape our identities and influence how we engage in academic work. In this essay, originally published in 1989, hooks tells part of the story of the impact of her pursuit of an academic career on her family relationships and her understanding of the power of social class as a part of her identity. Her focus, however, is not so much on the story of her academic career as on her analysis of the complicated role of social class identity in higher education and academic culture. Her story thus becomes the vehicle for her analysis. Although hooks's subject matter is complex and her analysis sophisticated, she doesn't use conventional footnotes and she writes in a much less formal style than is common in scholarly writing.

The essay reproduced here is a slightly shortened version of the essay published in hooks's book *Talking Back: Thinking Feminist, Thinking Black.* As you read, pay attention to how hooks uses her story to pursue her provocative analysis. Consider as well the following aspects of her essay:

■ **A clear, narrow focus.** Although this is a complex essay that examines several challenging issues, hooks never loses her focus on her main topic: social class in education. She explores a number of points related to that main topic, and her own story encompasses her experiences in higher education as well as her relationships with her family. Nevertheless, the focus of her story remains clear throughout.

- **Brevity.** This is not a short essay, but the narrative sections are brief and tightly focused. In these sections, hooks tells us a great deal about herself, her family, and her experiences, but she doesn't go into detail about her upbringing or her life as an academic. Instead, she tells just enough of her story to make her points.

- **A basic structure.** hooks follows a loose chronological order in telling her story, using flashback as a way to fill in important details and connect her present situation with her past experiences. The structure of her essay is sophisticated yet straightforward. It enables her to make her points accessible and allows readers to follow her story without getting lost in details.

- **Succinct, purposeful description.** This essay includes several descriptive passages, each of which is short and focused on a specific point. The descriptions convey a sense of the scene or event (e.g., walking along the streets of New Haven) without losing focus on the point being made.

KEEPING CLOSE TO HOME: CLASS AND EDUCATION
by bell hooks

1 We are both awake in the almost dark of 5 a.m. Everyone else is sound asleep. Mama asks the usual questions. Telling me to look around, make sure I have everything, scolding me because I am uncertain about the actual time the bus arrives. By 5:30 we are waiting outside the closed station. Alone together, we have a chance to really talk. Mama begins. Angry with her children, especially the ones who whisper behind her back, she says bitterly, "Your childhood could not have been that bad. You were fed and clothed. You did not have to do without—that's more than a lot of folks have and I just can't stand the way y'all go on." The hurt in her voice saddens me. I have always wanted to protect mama from hurt, to ease her burdens. Now I am part of what troubles. Confronting me, she says accusingly, "It's not just the other children. You talk too much about the past. You don't just listen." And I do talk. Worse, I write about it.

2 Mama has always come to each of her children seeking different responses. With me she expresses the disappointment, hurt, and anger of betrayal: anger that her children are so critical, that we can't even have the sense to like the presents she sends. She says, "From now on there will be no presents. I'll just stick some money in a little envelope the way the rest of you do. Nobody wants criticism. Everybody can criticize me but I am supposed to say nothing." When I try to talk, my voice sounds like a twelve year old. When I try to talk, she speaks louder, interrupting me, even though she has said repeatedly, "Explain it to me, this talk

about the past." I struggle to return to my thirty-five year old self so that she will know by the sound of my voice that we are two women talking together. It is only when I state firmly in my very adult voice, "Mama, you are not listening," that she becomes quiet. She waits. Now that I have her attention, I fear that my explanations will be lame, inadequate. "Mama," I begin, "people usually go to therapy because they feel hurt inside, because they have pain that will not stop, like a wound that continually breaks open, that does not heal. And often these hurts, that pain has to do with things that have happened in the past, sometimes in childhood, often in childhood, or things that we believe happened." She wants to know, "What hurts, what hurts are you talking about?" "Mom, I can't answer that. I can't speak for all of us, the hurts are different for everybody. But the point is you try to make the hurt better, to heal it, by understanding how it came to be. And I know you feel mad when we say something happened or hurt that you don't remember being that way, but the past isn't like that, we don't have the same memory of it. We remember things differently. You know that. And sometimes folk feel hurt about stuff and you just don't know or didn't realize it, and they need to talk about it. Surely you understand the need to talk about it."

Source: From hooks, bell. *Talking Back: Thinking Feminist, Thinking Black*. Boston: South End, 1989. Print.

3   Our conversation is interrupted by the sight of my uncle walking across the park toward us. We stop to watch him. He is on his way to work dressed in a familiar blue suit. They look alike, these two who rarely discuss the past. This interruption makes me think about life in a small town. You always see someone you know. Interruptions, intrusions are part of daily life. Privacy is difficult to maintain. We leave our private space in the car to greet him. After the hug and kiss he has given me every year since I was born, they talk about the day's funerals. In the distance the bus

approaches. He walks away knowing that they will see each other later. Just before I board the bus I turn, staring into my mother's face. I am momentarily back in time, seeing myself eighteen years ago, at this same bus stop, staring into my mother's face, continually turning back, waving farewell as I returned to college—that experience which first took me away from our town, from family. Departing was as painful then as it is now. Each movement away makes return harder. Each separation intensifies distance, both physical and emotional.

4   To a southern black girl from a working-class background who had never been on a city bus, who had never stepped on an escalator, who had never travelled by plane, leaving the comfortable confines of a small town Kentucky life to attend Stanford University was not just frightening; it was utterly painful. My parents had not been delighted that I had been accepted and adamantly opposed my going so far from home. At the time, I did not see their opposition as an expression of their fear that they would lose me forever. Like many working-class folks, they feared what college education might do to their children's minds even as they unenthusiastically acknowledged its importance. They did not understand why I could not attend a college nearby, an all-black college. To them, any college would do. I would graduate, become a school teacher, make a decent living and a good marriage. And even though they reluctantly and skeptically supported my educational endeavors, they also subjected them to constant harsh and bitter critique. It is difficult for me to talk about my parents and their impact on me because they have always felt wary, ambivalent, mistrusting of my intellectual aspirations even as they have been caring and supportive. I want to speak about these contradictions because sorting through them, seeking resolution and reconciliation has been important to me both as it affects my development as a writer, my effort to be fully self-realized, and my longing to remain close to the family and community that provided the groundwork for much of my thinking, writing, and being.

> **A Clear, Narrow Focus**
>
> In **paragraph 4,** hooks explains the purpose of telling her story about her relationship with her mother. As she continues her narrative, she keeps her focus on exploring the relationship between social class and education.

5   Studying at Stanford, I began to think seriously about class differences. To be materially underprivileged at a university where most folks (with the exception of workers) are materially privileged provokes such thought. Class differences were boundaries no one wanted to face or

talk about. It was easier to downplay them, to act as though we were all from privileged backgrounds, to work around them, to confront them privately in the solitude of one's room, or to pretend that just being chosen to study at such an institution meant that those of us who did not come from privilege were already in transition toward privilege. To not long for such transition marked one as rebellious, as unlikely to succeed. It was a kind of treason not to believe that it was better to be identified with the world of material privilege than with the world of the working class, the poor. No wonder our working-class parents from poor backgrounds feared our entry into such a world, intuiting perhaps that we might learn to be ashamed of where we had come from, that we might never return home, or come back only to lord it over them.

> ### A Basic Structure
>
> In **paragraph 5,** hooks moves from the present moment she described in the first four paragraphs to a time in her past when she attended college. Notice that from this point in the essay to the end she will move more or less chronologically from past to present. The structure of her essay might be seen as a version of *in medias res* (see page 492). Structuring her essay in this way allows her to introduce her themes in an engaging and slightly dramatic way.

6   Though I hung with students who were supposedly radical and chic, we did not discuss class. I talked to no one about the sources of my shame, how it hurt me to witness the contempt shown the brown-skinned Filipina maids who cleaned our rooms, or later my concern about the $100 a month I paid for a room off-campus which was more than half of what my parents paid for rent. I talked to no one about my efforts to save money, to send a little something home. Yet these class realities separated me from fellow students. We were moving in different directions. I did not intend to forget my class background or alter my class allegiance. And even though I received an education designed to provide me with a bourgeois sensibility, passive acquiescence was not my only option. I knew that I could resist. I could rebel. I could shape the direction and focus of the various forms of knowledge available to me. Even though I sometimes envied and longed for greater material advantages (particularly at vacation times when I would be one of few if any students remaining in the dormitory because there was no money for travel), I did not share the sensibility and values of my peers. That was important—class was not just about money; it was about values which showed and determined behavior. While I often needed more money, I never needed a new set of beliefs and values. For example, I was profoundly shocked and disturbed when peers would talk about their parents without respect, or would

even say that they hated their parents. This was especially troubling to me when it seemed that these parents were caring and concerned. It was often explained to me that such hatred was "healthy and normal." To my white, middle-class California roommate, I explained the way we were taught to value our parents and their care, to understand that they were not obligated to give us care. She would always shake her head, laughing all the while, and say, "Missy, you will learn that it's different here, that we think differently." She was right. Soon, I lived alone, like the one Mormon student who kept to himself as he made a concentrated effort to remain true to his religious beliefs and values. Later in graduate school I found that classmates believed "lower class" people had no beliefs and values. I was silent in such discussions, disgusted by their ignorance.

7   Carol Stack's anthropological study, *All Our Kin,* was one of the first books I read which confirmed my experiential understanding that within black culture (especially among the working class and poor, particularly in southern states), a value system emerged that was counter-hegemonic, that challenged notions of individualism and private property so important to the maintenance of white-supremacist, capitalist patriarchy. Black folk created in marginal spaces a world of community and collectivity where resources were shared. In the preface to *Feminist Theory: from margin to center,* I talked about how the point of difference, this marginality can be the space for the formation of an oppositional worldview. That worldview must be articulated, named if it is to provide a sustained blueprint for change. Unfortunately, there has existed no consistent framework for such naming. Consequently both the experience of this difference and documentation of it (when it occurs) gradually loses presence and meaning.

8   Much of what Stack documented about the "culture of poverty," for example, would not describe interactions among most black poor today irrespective of geographical setting. Since the black people she described did not acknowledge (if they recognized it in theoretical terms) the oppositional value of their world view, apparently seeing it more as a survival strategy determined less by conscious efforts to oppose oppressive race and class biases than by

A Clear, Narrow Focus

In **paragraphs 6–8,** hooks offers an analysis of social class, using theoretical concepts from another scholar, Carol Stack. Notice how hooks uses her story of her experiences in higher education as a vehicle for her analysis. She writes about her own experience not only to understand it but also to illustrate important concepts about social class and education.

circumstance, they did not attempt to establish a framework to transmit their beliefs and values from generation to generation. When circumstances changed, values altered. Efforts to assimilate the values and beliefs of privileged white people, presented through media like television, undermine and destroy potential structures of opposition.

9   Increasingly, young black people are encouraged by the dominant culture (and by those black people who internalize the values of this hegemony) to believe that assimilation is the only possible way to survive, to succeed. Without the framework of an organized civil rights or black resistance struggle, individual and collective efforts at black liberation that focus on the primacy of self-definition and self-determination often go unrecognized. It is crucial that those among us who resist and rebel, who survive and succeed, speak openly and honestly about our lives and the nature of our personal struggles, the means by which we resolve and reconcile contradictions. This is no easy task. Within the educational institutions where we learn to develop and strengthen our writing and analytical skills, we also learn to think, write, and talk in a manner that shifts attention away from personal experience. Yet if we are to reach our people and all people, if we are to remain connected (especially those of us whose familial backgrounds are poor and working-class), we must understand that the telling of one's personal story provides a meaningful example, a way for folks to identify and connect.

10   Combining personal with critical analysis and theoretical perspectives can engage listeners who might otherwise feel estranged, alienated. To speak simply with language that is accessible to as many folks as possible is also important. Speaking about one's personal experience or speaking with simple language is often considered by academics and/ or intellectuals (irrespective of their political inclinations) to be a sign of intellectual weakness or even anti-intellectualism. Lately, when I speak, I do not stand in place—reading my paper, making little or no eye contact with audiences but instead make eye contact, talk extemporaneously, digress, and address the audience directly. I have been told that people assume I am not prepared, that I am anti-intellectual, unprofessional (a concept that has everything to do with class as it determines actions and behavior), or that I am reinforcing the stereotype of black people as non-theoretical and gutsy.

11   Such criticism was raised recently by fellow feminist scholars after a talk I gave at Northwestern University at a conference on "Gender, Culture, Politics" to an audience that was mainly students and academics.

I deliberately chose to speak in a very basic way, thinking especially about the few community folks who had come to hear me. Weeks later, KumKum Sangari, a fellow participant who shared with me what was said when I was no longer present, and I engaged in quite rigorous critical dialogue about the way my presentation had been perceived primarily by privileged white female academics. She was concerned that I not mask my knowledge of theory, that I not appear anti-intellectual. Her critique compelled me to articulate concerns that I am often silent about with colleagues. I spoke about class allegiance and revolutionary commitments, explaining that it was disturbing to me that intellectual radicals who speak about transforming society, ending the domination of race, sex, class, cannot break with behavior patterns that reinforce and perpetuate domination, or continue to use as their sole reference point how we might be or are perceived by those who dominate, whether or not we gain their acceptance and approval.

> **Brevity**
>
> In **paragraph 11,** hooks shares an anecdote about an experience she had at an academic conference. She tells this story in a single paragraph, keeping her focus on her main point about the disconnection between academic culture and working-class people.

12 This is a primary contradiction which raises the issue of whether or not the academic setting is a place where one can be truly radical or subversive. Concurrently, the use of a language and style of presentation that alienates most folks who are not also academically trained reinforces the notion that the academic world is separate from real life, that everyday world where we constantly adjust our language and behavior to meet diverse needs. The academic setting is separate only when we work to make it so. It is a false dichotomy which suggests that academics and/or intellectuals can only speak to one another, that we cannot hope to speak with the masses. What is true is that we make choices, that we choose our audiences, that we choose voices to hear and voices to silence. If I do not speak in a language that can be understood, then there is little chance for dialogue. This issue of language and behavior is a central contradiction all radical intellectuals, particularly those who are members of oppressed groups, must continually confront and work to resolve. One of the clear and present dangers that exists when we move outside our class of origin, our collective ethnic experience, and enter hierarchical institutions which daily reinforce domination by race, sex, and class, is that we gradually assume a mindset similar to those who dominate and oppress, that we lose critical consciousness because

15

it is not reinforced or affirmed by the environment. We must be ever vigilant. It is important that we know who we are speaking to, who we most want to hear us, who we most long to move, motivate, and touch with our words.

13   When I first came to New Haven to teach at Yale, I was truly surprised by the marked class divisions between black folks—students and professors—who identify with Yale and those black folks who work at Yale or in surrounding communities. Style of dress and self-presentation are most often the central markers of one's position. I soon learned that the black folks who spoke on the street were likely to be part of the black community and those who carefully shifted their glance were likely to be associated with Yale. Walking with a black female colleague one day, I spoke to practically every black person in sight (a gesture which reflects my upbringing), an action which disturbed my companion. Since I addressed black folk who were clearly not associated with Yale, she wanted to know whether or not I knew them. That was funny to me. "Of course not," I answered. Yet when I thought about it seriously, I realized that in a deep way, I knew them for they, and not my companion or most of my colleagues at Yale, resemble my family. Later that year, in a black women's support group I started for undergraduates, students from poor backgrounds spoke about the shame they sometimes feel when faced with the reality of their connection to working-class and poor black people. One student confessed that her father is a street person, addicted to drugs, someone who begs from passersby. She, like other Yale students, turns away from street people often, sometimes showing anger or contempt; she hasn't wanted anyone to know that she was related to this kind of person. She struggles with this, wanting to find a way to acknowledge and affirm this reality, to claim this connection. The group asked me and one another what we do to remain connected, to honor the bonds we have with working class and poor people even as our class experience alters.

> **Brevity**
>
> Here again in **paragraph 13,** hooks shares anecdotes about her experiences related to attitudes among academics about social class. In these brief narratives, she continues to explore her main theme yet she keeps her story narrowly focused.

14   Maintaining connections with family and community across class boundaries demands more than just summary recall of where one's roots are, where one comes from. It requires knowing, naming, and being ever mindful of those aspects of one's past that have enabled and do enable

one's self-development in the present, that sustain and support, that enrich. One must also honestly confront barriers that do exist, aspects of that past that do diminish. My parents' ambivalence about my love for reading led to intense conflict. They (especially my mother) would work to ensure that I had access to books, but would threaten to burn the books or throw them away if I did not conform to other expectations. Or they would insist that reading too much would drive me insane. Their ambivalence nurtured in me a like uncertainty about the value and significance of intellectual endeavor which took years for me to unlearn. While this aspect of our class reality was one that wounded and diminished, their vigilant insistence that being smart did not make me a "better" or "superior" person (which often got on my nerves because I think I wanted to have that sense that it did indeed set me apart, make me better) made a profound impression. From them I learned to value and respect various skills and talents folk might have, not just to value people who read books and talk about ideas. They and my grandparents might say about somebody, "Now he don't read nor write a lick, but he can tell a story," or as my grandmother would say, "call out the hell in words."

15 Empty romanticization of poor or working-class backgrounds undermines the possibility of true connection. Such connection is based on understanding difference in experience and perspective and working to mediate and negotiate these terrains. Language is a crucial issue for folk whose movement outside the boundaries of poor and working-class backgrounds changes the nature and direction of their speech. Coming to Stanford with my own version of a Kentucky accent, which I think of always as a strong sound quite different from Tennessee or Georgia speech, I learned to speak differently while maintaining the speech of my region, the sound of my family and community. This was of course much easier to keep up when I returned home to stay often. In recent years, I have endeavored to use various speaking styles in the classroom as a teacher and find it disconcerts those who feel that the use of a particular patois excludes them as listeners, even if there is translation into the usual, acceptable mode of speech. Learning to listen to different voices, hearing different speech challenges the notion that we must all assimilate—share a single, similar talk—in educational institutions. Language reflects the culture from which we emerge. To deny ourselves daily use of speech patterns that are common and familiar, that embody the unique and distinctive aspect of our self is one of the ways we become estranged and alienated from our past. It is important for us to

have as many languages on hand as we can know or learn. It is important for those of us who are black, who speak in particular patois as well as standard English to express ourselves in both ways.

16   Since I left home and entered college, I am often asked, usually by white people, if my sisters and brothers are also high achievers. At the root of this question is the longing for reinforcement of the belief in "the exception" which enables race, sex, and class biases to remain intact. I am careful to separate what it means to be exceptional from a notion of "the exception."

17   Frequently I hear smart black folks, from poor and working-class backgrounds, stressing their frustration that at times family and community do not recognize that they are exceptional. Absence of positive affirmation clearly diminishes the longing to excel in academic endeavors. Yet it is important to distinguish between the absence of basic positive affirmation and the longing for continued reinforcement that we are special. Usually liberal white folks will willingly offer continual reinforcement of us as exceptions—as special. This can be both patronizing and very seductive. Since we often work in situations where we are isolated from other black folks, we can easily begin to feel that encouragement from white people is the primary or only source of support and recognition. Given the internalization of racism, it is easy to view this support as more validating and legitimizing than similar support from black people. Still, nothing takes the place of being valued and appreciated by one's own, by one's family and community. We share a mutual and reciprocal responsibility for affirming one another's successes. Sometimes we have to talk to our folks about the fact that we need their ongoing support and affirmation, that it is unique and special to us. In some cases we may never receive desired recognition and acknowledgement of specific achievements from kin. Rather than seeing this as a basis for estrangement, for severing connection, it is useful to explore other sources of nourishment and support.

18   I do not know that my mother's mother ever acknowledged my college education except to ask me once, "How can you live so far away from your people?" Yet she gave me sources of affirmation and nourishment, sharing the legacy of her quilt-making, of family history, of her incredible way with words. Recently, when our father retired after more than thirty years of work as a janitor, I wanted to pay tribute to this experience, to identify links between his work and my own as writer and teacher. Reflecting on our family past, I recalled ways he had been an impressive example of diligence and hard work, approaching tasks with a seriousness of concentration

I work to mirror and develop, with a discipline I struggle to maintain. Sharing these thoughts with him keeps us connected, nurtures our respect for each other, maintaining a space, however large or small, where we can talk.

A Clear, Narrow Focus

In **paragraph 18,** hooks returns to telling about her relationship with her family, picking up where she left off earlier in her essay. In returning to her story about her relationship with her family, she reminds us of the purpose of that story.

19   Open, honest communication is the most important way we maintain relationships with kin and community as our class experience and backgrounds change. It is as vital as the sharing of resources. Often financial assistance is given in circumstances where there is no meaningful contact. However helpful, this can also be an expression of estrangement and alienation. Communication between black folks from various experiences of material privilege was much easier when we were all in segregated communities sharing common experiences in relation to social institutions. Without this grounding, we must work to maintain ties, connection. We must assume greater responsibility for making and maintaining contact, connections that can shape our intellectual visions and inform our radical commitments.

20   The most powerful resource any of us can have as we study and teach in university settings is full understanding and appreciation of the richness, beauty, and primacy of our familial and community backgrounds. Maintaining awareness of class differences, nurturing ties with the poor and working-class people who are our most intimate kin, our comrades in struggle, transforms and enriches our intellectual experience. Education as the practice of freedom becomes not a force which fragments or separates, but one that brings us closer, expanding our definitions of home and community.

Questions to Consider:

1. What do you notice most about hooks's story of her own experiences? What do you take away from her story? To what extent do you think her story makes her analysis of the role of social class in education easier to understand? Explain.

2. In what ways do you think hooks's analysis would be different if she did not include her own story? Would it be more or less effective, in your view? Explain.

3. Do you agree or disagree with hooks's conclusions about the role of social class, race, and gender in education? Why or why not? To what extent do you think hooks's story affects your reaction to her analysis? Explain, citing specific passages from her essay to support your answer.

Writing Personal Narratives

16

I ONCE ATTENDED a memorial service at which the eulogy was delivered by the grandson of the man who had died. Writing and delivering that eulogy was not an easy thing for the grandson to do, having just lost his beloved grandfather, whom he had known for all of his 29 years. But the grandson wanted to honor his grandfather. In his eulogy, he chose to tell the story of a day when he was much younger, about ten years old, and was helping his grandfather with some minor plumbing repairs in the basement of his grandfather's home. On the surface, it wasn't much of a story. The grandson told the grieving audience how his grandfather had carefully worked on the plumbing over many years. On the particular day that was the focus of his story, he listened as his grandfather explained in detail which pipes went where, the specialized tools he used, and the many problems he had solved over the years. The grandfather took great pride in the work he had done to this seemingly mundane and unglamorous part of his home, and that was the point of the grandson's story: His grandfather cared deeply about doing small chores that no one really noticed but that made his family's life a little easier. Nearly 20 years after that day in the basement, the grandson could still vividly remember his grandfather's pride in his work and his dedication to doing even a very minor job right. And the story he told in his eulogy allowed his audience to share in that long-ago moment.

When we write about our experience, we give it meaning. The grandson's story was a way for him to understand an important moment in his life. In this regard, personal narratives aren't simply stories about what happened to us; they are part of our effort to understand ourselves and our world and share that understanding with others. Writing an effective personal narrative, then, is not a matter of just reporting on something that happened; it is a process of getting at some truth or insight about what happened.

Writing about experience can be challenging, illuminating, and deeply satisfying—both for writers and readers. Learning to write effective personal narratives can help you not only improve as a writer but also appreciate and use the power of writing as a tool for understanding and learning.

Occasions for Personal Narrative

Some rhetorical situations call for personal narrative: to honor an accomplishment, mark an anniversary, or celebrate a life. A politician giving a speech on Memorial Day might tell the story of a particular American soldier as a way to honor all soldiers and their sacrifices for their country. A minister's sermon at a wedding service might include a story of the newlywed couple's devotion to one another. If you wrote an essay as part of your college application, you might have told the story of an experience to make a point about something important that you learned or to illustrate important personal qualities you possess. In such cases, stories not only convey something relevant about the writer's experience but also often make a larger point about what that experience means.

Sometimes, writers write about their experiences as a way to enter ongoing conversations about important issues. In the following essay, *Los Angeles Times* columnist Gregory Rodriguez tells part of the story of his own life as a Californian of Mexican ancestry to make a point about immigration in the United States. The occasion for Rodriguez's essay was the release of a report showing that immigration to the United States from Mexico, which had been increasing for decades, had diminished. This change in immigration patterns has various implications, which Rodriguez explores in his essay. Notice that Rodriguez doesn't tell the story of a specific experience; rather, he writes more generally about his experience as a Hispanic in California from his childhood to the present, connecting his experiences to the changing demographics of his state:

> The news that Mexican immigration to the United States has come to a virtual halt has me thinking about all the ways that will change things. It will affect politics, culture, labor and the nation's racial climate. And it will also change how we see each other and ourselves as Americans and as Californians, me included.
>
> I'm one of those mythical native Californians you might have read about. I was born near the corner of Sunset and Vermont in Hollywood. My father was born in L.A. and baptized, as was I, at La Placita Church downtown. My mom was born in northern San Diego County and baptized at the San Antonio de Pala mission there. My paternal great-grandfather arrived in the U.S.—Arizona—from Mexico in 1893. My family has been American so long that sometimes I think I should wear one of those buckled Pilgrim hats.
>
> And yet, despite my rootedness in Southern California, migration has had an inordinate effect on my life, especially my intellectual and professional life. I've always been something of a tour guide, interpreter and even a booster for my regional homeland. As a young Dodgers fan I always resented that half the stadium would root for the Chicago Cubs. I pronounced the glories of L.A. to my friends whose parents longed for the hometowns—New York, Milwaukee, Saigon—they left behind. (And then there's my love life. I once realized that most of the women whose lives have collided with mine were from families—Korean, Japanese, Vietnamese, German, Mexican—that arrived here because of migration's big catalyst: wars we fought or labor shortages caused by those wars.)
>
> As a kid, of course, some still saw my ethnicity and skin color as signs of my being an outsider. In third grade I was called the "N-word." By the 11th, the haters had wised up and switched to more "accurate" ethnic slurs. There were also incidents outside school, and what they all had in common was that they were committed by white kids who had

fewer choices than I did. Their words stung, but they didn't keep me from being elected class president. As a suburban upper-middle-class kid from an educated family, I pretty much felt I could be what I wanted to be, and I chose to be an Angeleno.

Back then, although I was sometimes rudely reminded that I was supposedly lesser than white folk, my identity as an American, a Mexican American and a local was secure and expansive. Sure, in college more than a few people just figured I was from the barrio. But my ethnicity wasn't automatically assumed to determine all my cultural tastes or political stances.

But that began to change as Mexican immigration reached historic numbers. In 1970, 84% of adult Latinos in L.A. County were U.S.-born, and the majority of them were the grandchildren of immigrants. Twenty years later, that number had been turned upside down: two-thirds of adult Latinos here were foreign-born. Suddenly, like many latter-generation Mexican Americans, I had to grapple with immigration and what it meant for me, my city, my country.

Businesses of all sorts, including newspapers, started looking for educated English-dominant Latinos to interpret the newly transformed marketplace. Once again I found myself in the position of interpreter, not as the prideful insider I'd been growing up but as an observer of a cultural shift.

It was impossible not to be swept up in the debate over immigration, legal and illegal. Though immigrant-bashers always insisted their beef was with illegal immigrants, long-established Mexican Americans were not immune from their invective. A combination of demographic change and a polarized debate had imposed the specter of foreignness— even illegality—on all of us.

And stereotyping didn't come just from your racist yahoos. A few years ago, the organizer of a Los Angeles Times-sponsored event asked me to sit on a panel discussing democracy in Latin America. Although I had written a weekly column for the paper for six years, she didn't seem to get that the focus of my writing, my expertise, has always been U.S. society.

There are worse assumptions, to be sure. But in my career, I've had to contend with my apparent foreignness over and over. You'd be shocked to know how many smart people presume to know what I like or think based on my last name, or ascribe beliefs to me based on my ethnicity. And then there are the people who insist on speaking to me in pidgin Spanish.

Now comes the end of the largest wave of immigration from a single nation in U.S. history. It carries all sorts of benefits.

Mexico can start rebuilding a civil society that's been hemorrhaging productive people for far too long. California, where migration from other states is all but over as well, now has an emerging homegrown majority population that has a demonstrably intense attachment to its state. After a generation of massive global migration, it's high time for all of us to settle in and make ourselves at home.

This time, I think I'll interpret it for myself. As an Angeleno, same as I ever was.

Source: Rodriguez, Gregory. "Immigration and the New Old Me." *Los Angeles Times*. Los Angeles Times, 14 May, 2012. Web. 2 May 2013.

Rodriguez's story is a way to understand a large demographic shift that affects millions of people through the lens of one person's experience. In a sense, the story of his experience as one Californian is a particular version of the larger story of race and immigration in California. The essayist E. B. White once advised writers, "Don't write about man. Write about *a* man." In this regard, personal narrative can be a way to tell a specific story that is part of a much bigger story. Rodriguez tells his story as one person in order to say something about what it means to be Hispanic in California today. In doing so, he begins to get at a larger truth about human beings and their racial identities.

Rodriguez's essay demonstrates how personal narrative can be a way for writers to find common ground with their readers. In writing about our particular experience, we identify common human concerns, hopes, fears, and joys. Sometimes, however, writers tell stories out of a need to make sense of an experience that puzzles, provokes, surprises, or troubles them. The motivation for writing the story isn't to make a point but to try to understand the experience. By telling the story of the experience, a writer can figure out what it means. Often, such personal narratives begin with a problem situation or a conflict that creates the need to understand: a teen struggling to deal with her parents' divorce; a son reconciling with his estranged father as a result of the father's terminal illness; an athlete trying to decide whether to continue competing after a serious injury; a grandson confronting the loss of his grandfather. In such situations, the writer might simply begin writing the story without really knowing what it means or whether it has a larger point. Something about the situation compels the writer to find a way, through the writing, to understand what happened. Usually, the writing leads to understanding—and often to a point that readers find compelling as well.

Personal narrative, then, emerges from a writer's need to:

- make sense of an experience
- connect that experience to others' experiences

College will provide various opportunities for you to write about your own experience or someone else's. But, ultimately, the personal narratives you write should reflect your desire to understand your own experience—and perhaps discover something about human life as well.

EXERCISE 16A EXPLORING OCCASIONS FOR PERSONAL NARRATIVE

1. Think about an experience you had that was important to you for some reason. What made the experience important? What impact did it have on you or others? What did you learn from it? Now consider whether others might be interested in that experience. What might make your experience relevant to others? What could others learn from it? Write a brief paragraph describing the experience and explaining its significance to you and to others.

2. Using the experience you wrote about for Question #1 (or another experience), identify an audience to whom you might tell the story of that experience. If you were to write a personal narrative about that experience for that audience, what would be the motivation for telling your story? What would you want to convey to others about your experience?

3. Review a newspaper or online news source, and identify three or four articles on topics that interest you. For each article, think about an experience you had that somehow relates to the topic of the article. Now consider how you might tell the story of that experience. In what ways might your story enrich or complicate the issues addressed in the article?

Understanding Personal Narrative

Personal narratives need not be about a momentous event. Any experience can be important enough to write about. What makes a personal narrative effective is how well the writer tells the story so that the significance of the experience is conveyed to the audience. Effective personal narratives usually have four key characteristics:

- **A focus on an experience that is important for some reason.** Stories matter to us because our experiences matter. Sometimes, an experience is significant for obvious reasons: losing a loved one, surviving a natural disaster, overcoming a great challenge such as military combat or a serious illness, winning an important athletic victory such as an Olympic gold medal. But more often writers focus their personal narratives on common experiences that reflect the happenings of our daily lives. What makes the experience appropriate for a personal narrative is that the experience matters to the writer.

- **Relevance.** Effective personal narratives focus on experiences that are not only significant to the writer but also relevant to readers. We might be interested in someone's story about a common kind of experience—say, learning to cook a new recipe or taking an important test in school or at a job—because we have such experiences ourselves. But even when telling the story of an unusual or unique experience, the writer must find a way to make that experience compelling and relevant to readers who might never experience something similar. The story of surviving a terrible automobile accident, for example, engages us because we know it might happen to us, and the writer can make it feel relevant to us even though something like that has never happened to most of us.

- **A compelling interpretation.** An effective personal narrative is not a simple recounting of an experience; it is the writer's interpretation of that experience. Through the narrative, the writer conveys a sense of the meaning of the experience to readers, and the effectiveness of the narrative rests in part on how compelling or valid the readers find the writer's interpretation. A narrative that describes a bad car accident might interest us to some degree, but a story about how the writer learned something about the fragility of human life by surviving a bad accident would probably be more compelling. What the writer makes of the experience helps determine how effective the story will be.

- **Engaging storytelling.** *How* writers tell stories can matter as much as *what* the stories are about. Writers use various techniques to tell stories in ways that keep readers interested and convey the meaning of the experience. (See "Four Elements of Effective Storytelling.")

Although writers use many different storytelling techniques, most effective narratives have four main elements in addition to the four key characteristics described in this chapter:

1. **Plot.** The sequence of events that make up a story. A plot consists of what happened in a story. It is the basic framework within which other elements of the story must fit. It keeps the story moving from start to finish.

2. **Characterization.** The creation and development of characters in a story. Characterization is the process by which writers bring characters alive for readers. It encompasses description of the characters and their actions, dialogue, and impact on other characters.

3. **Sensory appeals and figurative language.** The uses of language to convey a scene or action. Writers choose words and structure sentences strategically to describe sights, sounds, feelings, and action. They also use figures of speech to enhance descriptions and convey ideas (see "Figures of Speech" in Chapter 8; see also "Telling Stories Effectively" in Chapter 15).

4. **Setting.** Where and when a story takes place. Setting is often used to refer to the specific physical location of a story, but it also encompasses time and culture.

In-depth discussion of these elements is beyond the scope of this textbook, but a basic awareness of them can help you write more effective narratives.

These key features are evident in the following excerpt from a personal narrative about losing a beloved pet. The writer, Doree Shafrir, tells the story of dealing with her aging, increasingly ill dog, Lee. In the opening paragraphs, she tells how she first discovered that Lee was ill; then she provides some background about Lee's place in her life before continuing the story:

> I was in a rush that morning and so our walk was shorter than usual. As I brought Lee back inside our building and fed her and put water in her bowl and put her pills between two slices of salami, I told myself that her dog walker was coming in the afternoon and, in any case, the day before we had gone to Fort Greene Park and I had let her off her leash and she had scampered around.
>
> It was the beginning of November and when I got home that night, it was dark and getting cold and I was tired, and I had to take Lee out for another walk. She ran up to me and barked as I came through the door, but then, when I went to get her leash, all of a sudden she couldn't get up at all....
>
> In the eight years I had her, Lee was my only constant: I lived in seven apartments in two cities; I am on my fourth job, not counting internships and freelance work; I went to two graduate programs, one of which I finished, one of which I didn't; I dated a bunch of guys, some for a while; I made and lost friends. And knowing I had to take care of her meant I couldn't do certain things that people do in their 20s, like take spontaneous trips or stay out until dawn.

Atlantagreg/iStockphoto.com

Even though I knew on a rational level that she wouldn't always be there, I sort of assumed that she would be. I couldn't picture a world of mine in which she wasn't.

The first thing I did when it seemed like Lee couldn't get up was try to make her get up. Maybe, I thought, she just needed a little help. She was almost 14, after all, and she had had arthritis for the last three years. Lately her feet had been dragging on her walks, and sometimes she would collapse on the sidewalk, or fall as she went up or down the four steps leading into our building. But she had always managed to make it back up, and so I assumed this time would be no different: I put her collar and leash on and tried lifting her hind legs while simultaneously pulling up her front half with her leash. She just stared at me. She didn't seem aware that her back half wasn't working.

Source: Shafrir, Doree. "My Dog Days Are Over." *Opinionator. New York Times*, 23 Mar. 2011. Web. 2 May 2013.

The experience Shafrir describes in this essay is a common one for a pet owner, and it obviously mattered to Shafrir because her dog had become such a central part of her life. Her narrative is effective in part because we can sense how important the experience was to her. But she also tells her story in a way that makes it relevant even to readers who are not pet owners. As she continues telling about trying to figure out what was wrong with Lee and how to care for her, Shafrir also explores the meaning of the experience:

> Watching a dog age comes with its own set of daily, incremental choices and changes. Her tan spots have mostly faded; she is grizzled and gray, and her eyes have the same film over them that I remember seeing in my great-grandmother's eyes when I was a child. One day she can get up on the bed; the next day she falls, whimpering, when she tries to leap onto it, and no amount of coaxing can get her to try again. One day she stops barking when I turn the key in the lock and that is when I realize she's losing her hearing, and at the park, when I'm not directly in front of her, she seems panicked and lost and I know she can't see as well as she used to. She can't make it up three, then two, then one flight of stairs.
>
> Lee getting old reminds me of my own mortality; in her I see what it is to become elderly, to not be able to do the things you used to be able to do, to have things happen slowly, seemingly forever, and then very and irrevocably quickly. And for this I am irrationally and deeply jealous of people whose dogs die suddenly and young, because although they feel a different kind of pain, this is something they never have to face.

Here Shafrir begins to get at why this experience matters to her—that is, her interpretation of the experience. Her story conveys the pain of losing a beloved pet, but it also explores larger questions about being human, including the realization of our own mortality. Ultimately, her story is about loss, which is a fundamental part of human life. That's what makes this story about someone losing her pet relevant to readers. Shafrir tells the story of something that happened specifically to her, but it is the story of a kind of experience that everyone has.

Shafrir also tells her story in a way that helps keep readers engaged, using elements of effective storytelling (see "Four Elements of Effective Storytelling"). She creates a **plot** that takes her readers through the terrible night when she had to take Lee to the animal hospital and she chronicles the painful decision she had to make:

> The first thing I did when it seemed like Lee couldn't get up was try to make her get up. Maybe, I thought, she just needed a little help. She was almost 14, after all, and she had had arthritis for the last three years. Lately her feet had been dragging on her walks, and sometimes she would collapse on the sidewalk, or fall as she went up or down the four steps leading into our building. But she had always managed to make it back up, and so I assumed this time would be no different: I put her collar and leash on and tried lifting her hind legs while simultaneously pulling up her front half with her leash. She just stared at me. She didn't seem aware that her back half wasn't working.
>
> I didn't know what to do, so I called Sam. We had broken up over the summer—I'd moved out of the Carroll Gardens apartment we shared and back to Fort Greene—and we were friendly, but distant. He hadn't seen Lee since the breakup, but a few weeks before I had run into him at a party and promised him that if it looked like things were getting bad he could see her one last time. I wasn't sure if things were in fact getting that bad but I knew I wanted him there.

In this excerpt and the next one, you can also see how Shafrir uses **characterization** to convey a sense of her friend Sam as well as her dog. She uses **sensory appeals** and **figurative language** to describe events and convey a sense of the connection between her and her dog:

> Lee was everyone's favorite dog in part because she didn't make it easy for you to like her. She was stubborn and needy and scared of almost everything: kids, loud noises, basketballs and footballs, dancing—any sudden movement, really—and cats. She wouldn't fetch. She barked, loudly, when people were having sex. When friends came over she would insist on being petted and if they stopped she would nudge them with her head, sometimes so hard that people who were holding glasses of wine spilled it on themselves.

Finally, she conveys a **setting** for important moments in the story:

> It was the beginning of November and when I got home that night, it was dark and getting cold and I was tired, and I had to take Lee out for another walk.
>
> Lee almost never slept in my bedroom—she would usually either sleep in the living room or in the bathroom—and especially since she stopped being able to walk, getting around the apartment meant she had to drag herself. But when I woke up in the morning she was lying on the floor next to my bed.

Shafrir's essay illustrates how writers use specific storytelling techniques to help readers imagine the events being described and to provoke certain responses in their readers. It also demonstrates that personal narratives share the characteristics of all effective narrative writing described in Chapter 15:

■ **Clear focus.** Notice that Shafrir keeps her focus on her final days with her aging pet. Usually, the experiences we write about in personal narratives are multifaceted, and Shafrir's experience is no exception. In such cases, it can be challenging to avoid going off on tangents or telling unnecessary anecdotes, but in effective personal narratives, writers stick to the story.

■ **Careful structure.** Effective narratives are structured to bring the story alive for readers and maintain focus on the main story. Shafrir uses a basic chronological format, incorporating flashbacks to convey important background information. Such a structure helps her maintain focus and keep readers engaged.

■ **Vivid, purposeful description.** Effective personal narratives usually include descriptions of scenes, people, or events to help the reader imagine them. Notice that Shafrir's descriptions convey a vivid sense of how her dog looks and acts, but just as important, the descriptions support her interpretation of the experience.

FOCUS | **Literacy Narratives**

One form of personal narrative that has become increasingly popular in recent years is literacy narrative. A literacy narrative tells the story of a writer's experience with reading and writing. For example, a writer might tell the story of being placed in a special reading class in elementary school; in telling such a story, the writer might examine the impact of that experience on his or her school performance, attitudes about literacy, or self-esteem. Sometimes, a literacy narrative tells the broader story of the writer's development as a reader or writer over time as a way to explore the factors that shaped him or her as a literate person. Usually, when literacy narratives are assigned in college courses, the purpose is to examine the role of literacy in our lives and gain insight into the nature of literacy as a social practice.

Like other personal narratives, literacy narratives are based on the writer's experience. What makes a literacy narrative distinctive is that it focuses specifically on a writer's experiences with literacy. Nevertheless, an effective literacy narrative has the same features of effective personal narratives described in this chapter, and writers of literacy narratives use the same techniques described in this chapter and in Chapter 15.

16

EXERCISE 16B | UNDERSTANDING PERSONAL NARRATIVE

1. Find a personal narrative (maybe one assigned in a class or one you read in a newspaper, magazine, or blog) and analyze it in terms of the four main characteristics of effective personal narrative explained in this section. On the basis of your analysis, draw conclusions about the effectiveness of the narrative.

(Continued)

2. Read the three essays included in the next section of this chapter. Which of them most appeals to you? In a brief paragraph, explain why. What features of the essay engage you? Does the subject matter interest you for some reason? On the basis of this analysis, draw conclusions about effective personal narratives.

3. In a group of classmates, share the paragraphs you wrote for Question #2. Compare your choices and the reasons for them. What conclusions might you draw from this exercise about personal narrative? What conclusions can you draw about the role of audience in effective personal narratives?

Reading Personal Narrative

The three reading selections in this section illustrate the variety of form, style, voice, and perspective in personal narratives. Although each writer tells the story of a particular experience for a specific purpose, all three writers share their stories as a way to explore some aspect of being human. As you read these essays, be aware of the differences in the way these writers tell their stories, and identify similarities in the way these writers find meaning in their experiences. Also address these questions:

An experience that matters	• What makes the experience described in the essay significant? • Why does the writer tell the story of this experience?
Relevance	• In what ways might the experience described in this narrative be relevant to the intended audience? • What makes the experience important to others?
A compelling interpretation	• What meaning does the writer find in the experience or event described in the narrative? • To what extent does the writer's interpretation enhance the story?
Engaging storytelling	• How effectively does the writer tell his or her story? • What storytelling techniques does the writer use? • How well does the writer use these techniques?

Hot Mint Tea in July

by Marissa Dearing

In many ways, student writer Marissa Dearing's story of her study-abroad experience is a typical one. Marissa quickly overcomes her fears about living in an unfamiliar place and learns how to fit in with her host family. She sharpens her language skills and gains an understanding of Moroccan culture, and she finds that teens in Morocco are similar in many ways to American teens: they have fun together, they listen to music, they use social media, they make new friends. But Dearing also develops a deep love for aspects of Moroccan culture that are very different from her life as an American teen. In these differences, Dearing finds insight—not only into Moroccan culture but also into herself.

As you'll see, Dearing tells her story in a conventional way. She organizes it in a basic chronological format, and she shares anecdotes to illustrate specific aspects of her experience, even using some dialogue to help her readers gain a better sense of what it was like for her to be there. And despite her sense that Morocco is an exotic place for an American teen, the real subject of her essay—experiencing a different culture—is not exotic. In this regard, her story is likely to appeal to a variety of readers. It is a good example of a story about a relatively common experience in which a writer finds greater meaning. Dearing's essay appeared in The Best Teen Writing of 2009.

....

"*Peen?*" Sara asks.

"*Qareeb min al-burtuqal.*"

Near the orange, I tell her, because I can't remember the plural for "orange." We are meeting our friends, and the fruitstands are the designated meeting spot. Sara nods and smiles instead of correcting me and leads me by the hand through a sea of brilliantly colored kaftans: oranges, pinks, teals, and reds. Clutching my purse and her hand, I stammer "*smebli*" and "*sembili*" (the masculine and feminine forms of "excuse me") in every direction as we squeeze through the tangle of clothing, children, motorcycles, and taxis. We stop in front of a row of ten cobalt-blue carts piled high with oranges, identical except for the man standing behind each. My sunglasses slide slowly down my nose as we wait for our friends to arrive, and I can feel the back of my neck starting to burn. The chanting beat of a song blares from a nearby stereo, mingling with the calls of dinner specials, jewelry prices, "*Allah ak bar,*" and "*Hello, American princess.*"

I let my hair down, having forgotten my sunblock.

This past summer I went to Morocco to study Arabic and explore Moroccan culture as one of a group of 20 American students. The immersion program, hosted by Legacy International and funded in part by the U.S. State Department, involved intensive Arabic instruction and home stays with Moroccan families in Marrakesh and Rabat. There were side trips to Zagora, the Sahara Desert, Essaouira, Fez, and Casablanca, as

(Continued)

well as guest speakers, intercultural dialogues with Moroccan students, and community service opportunities. When I heard about the program, I was entranced by the idea of spending the summer in an exotic location, immersed in a language I had come to love. I knew I had to apply.

My excitement was mixed with concern that my language skills would be tested far more than they had been in my twice-weekly Arabic lessons. For two years, I had studied homemade flash cards, pored over Modern Standard Arabic grammar, and listened to Arabic dialogues on my computer. I had come a long way since my initial fascination with Arabic culture. Still, would I really be able to communicate with my host family? I redoubled my efforts to absorb as much as possible before the trip. As I packed and exchanged emails with other student participants, I couldn't help thinking: Will I like my host family? Will they like me? Will we connect?

But from the start, I knew that six weeks would not be nearly enough. In Marrakesh, my host family embraced me with open arms and stuffed me with food. Their home was small, but beautifully exotic. I loved the room where we shared our meals, a room bordered by couches covered in rich fabrics. We watched movies together, sometimes in French and sometimes in Arabic. I looked on as my host mother wrapped her scarf over her hair, color-coordinating her scarf-pin and heels.

In addition to my host sister Sara, I met brothers, uncles, aunts, grandparents, and cousins on weekend visits to nearby towns and cities. Over the abundant feasts these visits invariably entailed, I spoke in my still-shaky Moroccan dialect, and marveled when the relatives seemed to understand me.

At first, my host mother drove me to school, afraid that I would be "stolen" if I rode alone in a taxi. (She reminded me of my mother at home.) Later, I would navigate taxis with ease. We attended school everyday except Sunday. There, we studied not only Modern Standard Arabic, but also the less formal Moroccan spoken dialect, called *darija*—a mix of French, formal Arabic, and modifications (usually contractions) of formal Arabic. Our teacher was very animated; he moved around the classroom, gesturing and calling on us, encouraging us to speak. Although the pace was much quicker than it had been at home, the atmosphere was relaxed and the students eager.

When I had studied Spanish, I was hesitant to speak until I was sure I could do it very well. But having class every day and being able to practice my Arabic with people around me made a tremendous difference. I strained to hear and understand all the conversations around me, and tried out the language every opportunity I got. It was nerve-wracking, exhausting, and exhilarating.

I spent endless hours at the *Djemaa el Fna,* the famous open-air market in Marrakesh, where bargaining is an art form. In many ways, it was my language laboratory. Initially, Sara did all the negotiating, but soon after my arrival, I dove in. Some of my most meaningful conversations were with merchants and shopkeepers, debating politics and global health. I remember one shopkeeper telling me that language makes a world culture, and that America is a place where every culture can flourish.

One thing we could always talk about was food. I think I daily ate my bodyweight in Moroccan bread, which is dense, delicious, and plentiful. Breakfast went on forever; dinner sometimes began at midnight. The tagines—beef, chicken, lamb, all slow-cooked—were ubiquitous. In Rabat, we ate without utensils, sopping up the rich sauces with bread.

On Fridays—holy days for Muslims—we had couscous with nuts, chickpeas, and sweet onions. Occasionally, there were sizzling chunks of chicken or beef mixed in. Feeling adventurous, I ate snails for the first time. They were a cumin-and-saffron paradise. I discovered dates, *harira*—a traditional Moroccan soup—and *bastilla*, made with squab and a great deal of brown sugar. I devoured almond-filled pastries and caramel flans and fell in love with mint tea, the national beverage. I loved feeling the steam of the still-boiling tea on my face as I inhaled the mint. I bought a set of tea glasses for home.

I immersed myself in the rhythm of daily life in Morocco. Time is not as fixed there as it is at home, and I savored the slower pace. I discovered haunting *Gnawan* music (a mix of Arabic, Berber, and African influences) and danced onstage at a concert alongside musicians wearing hats with tassels that whirled in circles. I was enthralled by the music of Umm Kulthum, an Egyptian singer famous throughout the Arab world.

At school, we listened to a talk given by an *imam* (the religious, social, and political leader of a community) and learned about the Muslim faith. I bought a Koran. I watched street vendors spiral dirty hands with intricate calligraphy, and took a calligraphy lesson (far more difficult than it looks). Everywhere, I waded through traffic, having learned to make eye contact with the drivers, to wave and smile.

Mai Chen/Alamy

I dressed more conservatively than at home, although there was a great deal of variety in dress in the larger cities. We saw *burkas* and skin-tight jeans walking side by side. I bought one of the lovely embroidered blouses I had seen the girls in Marrakesh wearing. On a trip to the Sahara Desert, I donned a *jellaba*, a long flowing shirt that stretched down to my ankles. Sitting on a camel for the two-hour ride to the dunes, I enjoyed the added protection of a turban.

Led by our Moroccan teachers and guides, we explored the diverse Moroccan landscape, crossing the Atlas Mountains and visiting beautiful cities and villages: the colorful, palm tree-dotted city of Marrakesh, the humid city of Rabat, the blue-and-white fishing village of Essaouira, the cultural and spiritual jewel that is Fez, and the soft, reddish dunes of the Sahara, which burned during the day and felt like cool iron filings at night. We slept on those dunes, blanketed only by the still-warm desert air. I watched the sun rise

(Continued)

from behind an enormous dune and admired colors my camera could never, ever capture. I took hundreds of photos every day and still felt like I missed a million opportunities.

We tutored Moroccan students who were eager to learn English, painted blackboards at a school in Essaouira, and visited children in an orphanage in Marrakesh. I had brought pencils, stickers, and little toy cars from the States, and gave them to the children. They clamored for the goodies. I noticed a little boy smiling shyly at me, and I drew a smiley face on his hand and gave him my pen. Afterward, he was beaming. I spoke to the kids with the darija that I knew, but mostly we communicated with hand gestures and smiles. We talked at length with Moroccan high-school students, exchanging Facebook and e-mail information. We made friends.

My experiences in Morocco will stay with me for a lifetime. I miss hearing that my eyes are beautiful while wearing reflective sunglasses, and having my conversations leavened with "thanks be to God" and "to your health." Answering blind panhandlers with "May God make it easy for you." Forgetting the English words for things. Waking up covered in sweat and not looking frantically for a fan. Feeling overwhelmed and excited and ashamed and grateful all at once by the constant and excessive hospitality. Saying "Thank you" more often than blinking, and meaning it.

Source: Dearing, Marissa. "Hot Mint Tea." *The Best Teen Writing of 2009*. ED. Virginia Lee Pfaehler. Ner York: Alliance for Young Artists and Writers, 2009. 184–188. Print.

EXERCISE 16C   EXPLORING ANOTHER CULTURE

1. What significance does Dearing find in her experience? What makes her study-abroad experience, which thousands of other exchange students have had, compelling?

2. How would you summarize the main theme or point of Dearing's story? What ideas do you think she tries to convey to her readers?

3. Assess Dearing's use of storytelling strategies, including plot, description, setting, and characterization. How effectively does she use these strategies to tell her story? Cite specific passages from her essay to support your answer.

Hunting Deer with My Flintlock

by Seamus McGraw

In Pennsylvania, where writer Seamus McGraw lives, hunting is so deeply entrenched in the local culture that many school districts still cancel school on the first day of deer-hunting season, which is traditionally the Monday after Thanksgiving. Despite this long tradition in Pennsylvania and elsewhere in the United States, however, hunting remains controversial. Some critics argue that hunting exclusively for the thrill of the hunt or to kill "trophy" animals is unethical and violates the traditional purpose of hunting for food. Such critics point out that many hunters never consume the game they kill. Proponents point to the tradition of hunting and the important role hunters play in conservation efforts. This controversy has been shaped in recent years by debates about sustainable food production and the movement to support local food sources. For some hunters, including McGraw, hunting is a more ethical way to obtain food than simply buying meat that was processed hundreds of miles away out of sight of the consumer. In this essay, McGraw tells the graphic story of a particular hunt to highlight the idea that, although killing is not the goal of hunting, it is inevitable. In telling his story, McGraw addresses larger ethical issues related to the responsibilities that all of us, hunters and non-hunters alike, have for the food we consume. In this sense, McGraw's essay illustrates how writers can use personal narrative to join ongoing conversations about important issues. McGraw uses his experience to make a point—and he does so in a rather dramatic way. This essay was published in The New York Times *in 2011.*

She took me by surprise. Though I had been stalking her through the dense undergrowth for about 40 minutes, I had lost sight of her as the afternoon light began to fade. It was getting late and I was about ready to call it a day when, just as I hit the crest of a shadowy depression in the mountainside, I caught a glimpse of her, a beautiful doe, the matriarch of a small clan that foraged behind her.

She saw me, too.

She stepped out from behind a shagbark. Even in the spreading dusk I could see her eyes as she glared at me. She stomped out a warning on the rocky ground.

I had to admire her guts. I dropped to one knee, fumbled in my pocket for my old brass powder charger, freshened the powder in my frizzen, and pulled back the hammer on my .50-caliber flintlock. I took a deep breath and then I drew a bead on her.

An instant that felt like an hour passed before I squeezed the trigger. The hammer fell, the powder in the frizzen flashed, startling me even though I was prepared for it, and a heartbeat later, the whole world exploded with the thunder of 90 grains of black powder erupting in fire and blinding acrid smoke from the barrel of my gun, sending a lead minié ball rocketing toward the doe at a lethal 1,400 feet per second.

(Continued)

In the smoke and the confusion I couldn't tell if I had hit her. And then I saw that I had. The impact of the bullet had knocked her to the ground, and as the rest of the herd high-tailed it over the ridge, she struggled to stand, staggered a few yards and then collapsed again. I had hoped for a clean kill. But I had failed. I knew what had happened—I had flinched when the powder in the pan went off. Instead of hitting her in the heart or lungs, which would have killed her instantly, I had mortally wounded her. Now I would have to finish the job.

I hate to kill.

I know that must sound like an odd confession coming from an avid deer hunter, a guy who, like thousands of others in my home state of Pennsylvania, spends the better part of the year looking forward to those few short weeks in October and November, and especially to the special flintlock season that begins the day after Christmas, when I can load up my rifle and get lost in the mountains behind my home all alone. But I suspect that if you could wade through their boot-top-deep braggadocio and really talk to hunters, many of them would tell you the same thing.

For me, and I suspect for many others like me, the art of hunting is far more profound than taking trophies. It's about taking responsibility. For my needs. For my family. For the delicate environmental balance of this wounded but recovering part of the country. There is something sobering about hunting for your food. Meat tastes different, more precious, when you've not only watched it die, but killed it yourself. There is no seasoning in the world that can compare with moral ambiguity.

Biologists estimate there are now 1.6 million deer in Pennsylvania's woods, far more than when white men first set foot there. I took up deer hunting a decade ago when I realized that this staggeringly large population was decimating many of our forests, forests that after hundreds of years of clear-cutting were at last poised to recover. With no predators to speak of—the wolves were wiped out centuries ago and the last mountain lion in the state was killed more than 70 years ago—the responsibility for trying to restore a part of that balance fell to me. And to all the other hunters.

Maybe it's because I grew up in a family that always did things the hard way, or maybe it's because I'm basically a Luddite, but when I took up hunting, I eschewed all the technological gadgets designed to give modern hunters an extra edge over their prey. I like to believe that there's something primitive and existential about the art of hunting, and that somehow, stripping the act of hunting to its basics makes it purer.

I wanted a weapon that required more of me, one that demanded all the skill and all the planning that I could muster, a weapon that gave me just one chance to get it right. I made the decision to hunt only with the most basic firearm there is, a muzzle-loading black-powder rifle, fired by a piece of flint striking cold steel. I often tell my more conservative friends that I carry the gun the Second Amendment explicitly guarantees me the right to carry.

There are hundreds of us in the state. Some are history buffs, guys who believe in the sanctity of some imagined past. Some, like me, are purists. In late December we wander into the woods, usually alone, with our antique weapons and our obsolete notions of what a hunt should be.

But those antique weapons also carry with them an antique sense of responsibility. To kill with a flintlock, you must get close. And because these ancient guns are notoriously balky and inaccurate, there is a very good chance that you'll miss your target altogether or, worse, that you'll simply wound the creature and in so doing, inflict greater suffering than is necessary. And so you take every precaution to make sure that your one shot is clean, that it kills quickly and mercifully. And still, sometimes you fail, just as I did that late afternoon in midwinter when I flinched as my gun went off.

I followed the blood trail a few yards and found her. She was still alive. I could see her breath. It was ragged. She looked at me. I loaded my gun, charged the frizzen, and pulled the trigger. There was a flash in the pan—that is where the expression comes from—and then nothing. I tried again. Still nothing.

The sun was sinking behind the ridge. I didn't have the time or the tools with me to fix the gun—I had carelessly left them behind—and so I laid my rifle down on the ground, pulled my knife from its sheath, wrapped my arms around the wounded and frightened doe, and … I hate to kill.

But if I'm going to profit by death, and to some degree we all do—even those who find the very act of eating flesh to be offensive still benefit from the restorative act of responsible hunting in the nation's wild places—then I believe I also have an obligation to do it in the most honest way possible. It has to cost me something. And it does. I would not be so presumptuous as to suggest that the obligation extends beyond me. But speaking only for myself, it is compelling. It's a debt I owe the place I've chosen to live. And it's why, if you're looking for me on the day after Christmas, you'll find me in the woods of Northeastern Pennsylvania with a flintlock rifle in my hand, and a few gnawing regrets in my heart.

Source: McGraw, Seamus. "Hunting Deer with My Flintlock." *New York Times*. The New York Times, 25 Dec. 25. Web. 2 May 2013.

16

EXERCISE 16D   EXPLORING THE ETHICS OF HUNTING

1. A majority of Americans do not hunt. How does McGraw make his story relevant to his readers, even those who do not hunt?

2. What do you think is McGraw's main point in telling the story of a particular hunting experience? How effectively does he conveys that point?

3. What storytelling strategies does McGraw use to tell his story? To what extent do you think these strategies make his narrative effective? Explain, citing specific passages from his essay to support your answer.

Red Boat, Blue Sky

by Edmund Jones

At first glance, this essay tells a typical tale of youthful bravado in which a teenage boy takes an unnecessary risk and has a rather exciting, if brief, adventure. Edmund Jones looks back on a frightening but thrilling moment from his earliest days as a sailor—a foolish act on a small sailboat that could have had disastrous consequences. Although the story seems to be one that would appeal only to a specialized audience (sailors—or perhaps readers interested in sailing), it is also a coming-of-age story about an important moment in a boy's transition to adulthood. Jones's essay was published in Sail *magazine in 2009, which means that he originally wrote it for an audience of other sailors who would understand the technical details of his brief but potentially dangerous sail. (His intended readers would know, for example, that "sheets" refers to the ropes used to control the sails.) As you read, consider what makes his story interesting—and relevant—to a broader audience, including readers who have no interest in or experience with sailing.*

. . . .

Summers in South Carolina could be unbearable before air conditioning became commonplace. That's why my family spent most of each summer at our lake cottage, and why I spent hours on, or in, the water.

One August morning the heat struck the cottage the instant the sun rose above the trees across our cove. A cool breeze ruffled off the lake, and I wanted to sail before it got too hot. My parents were asleep, so I slipped into the kitchen and had a quick bowl of cornflakes—a state-of-the-art breakfast in 1948. I carried the cotton sail for my boat, an 8-foot pram named *Red Boat,* to the dock.

Modern parents would be aghast. Where's the sunscreen? And the life jacket? And wasn't I going to tell anyone where I would be? At age 13 I was innocent of any such concerns. Wooden boats don't sink, I thought, so why worry?

Daily thunderstorms were routine on Lake Murray. While rigging the boat, I looked at the sky. A few popcorn-like cumulus clouds were forming already. As I pushed the boat across the sand, a water moccasin emerged from under the dinghy and wriggled toward the shallows.

Lake Murray is a large lake, shaped like a maple leaf, some 30 miles long. The lake itself had been created in the middle of the Depression to provide hydroelectric power, and there were few houses on its shores. The lake was empty as I glided though a light chop. I cleared the point and entered open water. The far shore was only 4 miles distant and my plan was to reach across the lake and back before the weather turned bad.

The light breeze was steady as *Red Boat's* bow wave made a happy chuckling sound. I sat crosswise on the floorboards, my back against the starboard side, feet propped up on the port gunwale. The sail was blinding white against the deep blue sky, and my only worry was those clouds.

On the far shore a meadow was a favorite camping spot for my family. I hoped to take a peek at it and then skeedadle. As I neared the shore, though, I could see the clouds growing like genies out of bottles. The closest one, just upwind, was the biggest, and it boiled rapidly upward. It looked like it was going to be a monster storm, and I hastily tacked and headed for home. But I'd gone too far—there was no way I could outrun it.

The cloud covered the sun and the warm breeze suddenly turned chilly. I looked back upwind and saw, beneath the jet-black underside of the cloud, a line of whitecaps heading toward me. Uh oh, here It comes. I had about three miles to go, but it looked like forever. Then a bolt of lightning lit the dark water followed immediately by a sharp crack. I shivered, knowing how close It had struck. And my mast was sticking up like a lightning rod.

As the whitecaps approached, I uncleated the mainsheet, getting ready to ease it quickly. Then, with a roar, the first gust was on me as I let it run all the way out, the manila line scorching my bare hand. The mainsail flogged as the boat heeled, the lee side dipping a few gallons before I got my weight onto the windward gunwale. A hard rain came with the wind, stinging my bare back like needles. I wished I'd worn a jacket.

I tried sheeting in just a touch and was thrilled as my ungainly little tub suddenly accelerated, almost hydroplaning on a broad reach. With a mixture of terror and excitement, I pumped the sheet as the gusts blasted through, luffing in the puffs and then trimming just enough to keep us racing toward home. It was a wild ride. My arm ached and my bare hand blistered as I worked the sheet. Despite my best efforts, I continually shipped water over the leeside. As I neared our cove, the boat was wallowing in the waves, but still moving fast. Curtains of rain made it hard to see the entrance.

Another lightning strike, even closer, made me instinctively sheet in more, trying to eke out as much speed as possible. At last I blew past the point and was in our cove, riding the half-submerged boat like a cowboy. I felt triumphant as the beach neared, yanking up the centerboard and pulling off the rudder as *Red Boat* ground onto the sand. I lowered the sail, turned the boat on its side to dump the water, and dragged it to safety.

Wearily, and still shivering, I stumbled up the walk and onto our screen porch. I wondered if I would be in trouble with my parents for doing something so foolhardy. My father sat there, drinking coffee. He tossed me a beach towel and said, "Dry off before you go in. Don't drip in the house."

I wrapped the towel around me and asked, "Did you see me sail in?"

"Yep. Looked like a real fun ride."

(Continued)

16

He didn't act like he'd been worried.

Then I noticed the binoculars. They usually sat on the mantle, but today they were on the table beside him.

"Want some coffee?" he asked.

I was surprised, but pleased. I'd never drunk it before—it's not for kids, my mother would tell me.

"Sure, I'll take a cup."

"Cream and sugar?"

I stood tall, like a young Masai warrior after killing his first lion. "Nope, just black."

Source: Jones, Edmund. "Red Boat, Blue Sky." *Sail* July 2009: 37. Print.

EXERCISE 16E   EXPLORING A MOMENT OF YOUTHFUL BRAVADO

1. How would you describe the lesson Jones learned from his experience? How does he convey that lesson through his story? What other lessons might he have taken from his experience? How might he have told his story differently to convey those other lessons?

2. How would you describe Jones's voice in this narrative? Do you think his voice helps make his story more or less effective? Explain, citing specific passages from the essay to support your answer.

3. Jones originally wrote this essay for an audience of other sailors. Evaluate his essay's effectiveness for a wider audience that would include readers who are not sailors. Do you think his essay is relevant to readers who do not share his interest in sailing? Why or why not?

Writing Personal Narrative

This section will help you tell your story effectively in a personal narrative. Read this section together with Chapter 3. Each step described here corresponds with a step in Chapter 3.

Step 1 Identify a topic for your personal narrative.

Any experience that matters to you can be the basis for a personal narrative, but there are **two basic sources for topics for a personal narrative:**

- an **experience** that was significant to you in some way
- an **issue** of interest to you that somehow connects to your own experience

Explore each source for a possible topic for your essay.

Make a List of Experiences That Were Important in Your Life

A milestone	• Graduating from high school • Earning a black belt in karate • Becoming old enough to vote
An accomplishment	• Winning a championship in soccer or debate • Earning academic honors • Learning to swim
A challenge	• Dealing with a serious illness • Moving away from home • Surviving basic training in the military
A mistake	• Violating a rule or law • Cheating • Misjudging someone *(Continued)*

An activity	• Gaming • Hunting • Running
A transition	• Going to college • Moving abroad • Joining the military
A decision	• Whether to take or quit a job • Getting engaged • Sharing a difficult secret

Make a List of Issues That Interest You and Connect with Your Own Experience

A controversy	• **Gun control:** You might be involved in an effort to oppose arming your campus police force; a relative might have law enforcement experience; you might be a hunter.
An activity	• **Gaming:** You might be an avid gamer who is concerned about efforts to restrict the distribution of violent video games; you might have won a gaming competition.
Advocacy	• **Privacy:** You might have concerns about how your private data are being used online without your knowledge or permission; you might have been the victim of identity theft.
A trend	• **Social media:** You might be involved in an interesting project with social media; you might have had an unusual experience with social media.

List three or four such issues. For each item on the list, identify a relevant experience and describe it in a few sentences. For example, you might be interested in the national debate about health care insurance because you have a relative whose illness placed your family at great financial risk. On your list, you would briefly describe that experience:

Issue: health care reform

Experience: My brother was diagnosed with a serious illness; his medical care nearly resulted in my parents declaring bankruptcy. The illness created great difficulties for the family.

Identify the Experience That You Would Most Like to Write About

Review your two lists, and select an experience that most interests you and that you would most like to explore in a personal narrative. Keep in mind that the experience you choose has to matter to you. If it doesn't matter to you, it is unlikely to matter to your readers.

Step #1 in Chapter 3 will help you further develop your topic.

Step 2 Place your topic in rhetorical context.

One of the key features of effective personal narrative is that the writer's story has to be relevant to readers in some way, even though the experience is the writer's alone. At this point, your task is twofold:

- identify an audience for your narrative
- determine why that audience would be interested in your experience

Let's say you have a younger brother who became seriously ill with a rare disorder, and you have decided to write about that experience. It was an extremely challenging time for you and your family that deeply affected your views about yourself, your family, and issues such as medical care. Consider the following:

Who might be interested in my experience?	• People who have experienced serious illness • People with concerns about health care • Young people who have experienced serious illness in their families • Parents who have had a child with a serious illness
Why would they be interested in my experience?	• Anyone can experience serious illness in his or her family. • Your experience might speak to readers' concerns about caring for family members and dealing with health care issues. • Your story might illuminate how to confront these challenges.

In this example, your potential audience would be quite broad, since everyone has to deal with illness at some point and everyone has family or friends they might have to care for. More specifically, your experience might interest people who have followed the debates about health care and medical insurance. Your story would potentially connect to all these readers in a variety of ways.

Explore your topic using these two questions to identify a potential audience and the relevance of your experience to that audience. Then complete Step #2 in Chapter 3 to explore your rhetorical context more fully.

Step 3 Select a medium.

Today writers have a variety of options for choosing a medium for their stories:

- conventional print essays
- online media, including blogs and social media sites
- multimedia programs such as PowerPoint, PhotoStory, and iMovie
- multimedia sites such as Flickr, Prezi, and Animoto
- video sites such as YouTube and Go!Animate

To decide on a medium for your personal narrative, consider these questions:

Will a conventional print essay enable you to tell your story effectively?	
Yes: Write a conventional print essay.	**Maybe not:** Consider a different format.

Will incorporating images and sound enable you to tell your story more effectively?	
Not necessarily: Write a conventional print essay.	**Yes:** Consider a multimedia format.

Will a multimedia version of your story more likely reach your intended audience?	
Not necessarily: Write a conventional print essay.	**Possibly:** Consider a different format.

Keep in mind that a conventional print essay can easily be shared via social media (posted on a blog or Facebook page). If you decide to tell your story in a multimedia or video version, Chapter 18 ("Telling Digital Stories") offers advice to guide you through the process. But you should still complete the remaining steps in this chapter to construct an effective personal narrative, no matter the medium.

Step #3 in Chapter 3 provides additional guidance to help you decide on the most appropriate medium for your argument.

Step 4 Identify the main point of your narrative.

Your narrative tells the story of an experience, but what is the point of that story? You are telling your story for a reason, and you should be clear about your purpose. Otherwise, you run the risk of telling a story that might be engaging but does not say anything of substance to your readers. Your task now is to develop a clear idea of the main point you want to make by telling the story of your experience.

Begin by stating as clearly as you can the idea, insight, lesson, or point you want your readers to take away from your story. Try to capture this main point in a sentence or two. For example, let's return to the hypothetical story about your younger brother's illness. That trying experience helped you gain insight into yourself, your family, and the challenges of caring for someone you love who is seriously ill. It also taught you some hard lessons about the health care system. You would like to share these insights with readers, so you might state the main point of your essay as follows:

Caring for a very sick family member can bring out the best in us, even as it forces us to face some of our worst fears about ourselves and our own mortality.

This statement can serve as your Guiding Thesis Statement, which can help you keep your story focused.

However, trying to boil down an experience as complex as caring for a seriously ill family member into a sentence or two can be tricky. You don't want to oversimplify the experience; rather, you want your story to capture the richness of your experience while remaining focused. So remain open to possibilities. A key reason for writing about your experience is to understand it better. It is possible that you aren't sure at this point what your experience means or what central ideas you will convey to your readers. That's OK. Working through the process of writing about your experience will help you make sense of it.

In writing about a family member's illness, for example, you might find that you begin to remember your embarrassment about your own fears during that period of your life. Maybe you feel that you didn't quite live up to expectations as your family struggled with the challenge of such an illness. So it's possible that your story is not so much about the difficulties of caring for a sick family member as about the lessons you learned about yourself by facing hardship. If so, explore that possibility. As you develop your draft, be alert to such possibilities, even if they seem to deviate from your guiding thesis statement. The more you explore your experience, the more you will learn about it. That learning might lead you to change the main point of your story.

As you clarify your main point and develop a Guiding Thesis Statement, you will gain a better understanding of your experience and a clearer idea of how you want to tell your story. Complete Step #4 in Chapter 3 to develop your Guiding Thesis Statement further.

Step 5 Support your main point.

We don't usually think about "supporting" the main point of a personal narrative in the same way that we support claims in an argument or assertions in an analysis; however, effective narratives include descriptions of events, background information, and explanations of important ideas or occurrences that help the reader understand the writer's experience and its significance. In other words, everything you include in your personal narrative should somehow contribute to telling your story effectively and conveying your main point to your audience.

If you have followed the first four steps here and the corresponding steps in Chapter 3, you should have either a Discovery Draft (see page 66) or notes and other material for your draft. The task now is to make sure you have the necessary material to tell your story effectively.

Begin by considering what should be included in your narrative. Review your discovery draft, notes, and other materials to determine whether you have included the essential information, scenes, events, and moments to convey your experience sufficiently to your readers. Address these questions:

- **What specific events or moments must be included for a reader to understand what happened?** For example, in your hypothetical essay about your brother's illness, you will probably need to include the moment when you learned of the diagnosis. Maybe there was also a time when a parent or other family member felt despair about the situation. You would likely include key scenes in the hospital or with specific doctors or other health care workers. Maybe you had an important conversation with your brother about what was happening. With your Guiding Thesis Statement in mind, make note of important and relevant scenes, events, and related material in this way. The goal is to identify anything about your experience that is essential for readers to know.

- **What background information will readers need to understand the experience described in the story?** For example, you will probably include information about your brother and your relationship with him. You might also need to provide information about where you live, your parents' financial circumstances, and so on. Consider anything that isn't part of the main story but is essential for readers to know in order to understand your experience.

At this stage, more is better, so if you're not sure about something, include it. You can eliminate when you revise if you determine it isn't necessary.

You should now be ready to write a complete draft of your personal narrative. If not, move to the next step. But first complete Step #5 in Chapter 3, which provides additional advice to help you develop your narrative.

Step 6 Organize your narrative.

How you structure your narrative will help determine not only how engaging readers will find your story but also how effectively you convey your main point.

In most personal narratives, the writer tells the story more or less chronologically. But as the examples in this chapter indicate, you have several options for structuring your narrative. Review the techniques for structuring a narrative described in Chapter 15 (pages 491–492). Your decision about how to structure your narrative should be based on the following:

- how to convey your experience vividly and completely to your readers
- how to incorporate background and related information

To develop a structure for your narrative, follow this procedure:

Begin with a Basic Chronological Structure

Tell your story more or less in order from beginning to end. Tell it as completely as you can. Remember that this is a draft. You can eliminate unnecessary material and reorganize the story during revision.

Start Your Narrative as Close to the End of the Story as Feasible

For example, in your hypothetical essay about your brother's illness, you could begin the story years before his diagnosis—when he was previously injured in a fall, for instance—but doing so might make your story too long. Alternatively, you might begin with the diagnosis and tell the story from that point, filling in necessary background where appropriate.

Incorporate Essential Background Information

Even in a basic chronological story, you must find a way to incorporate background information. That usually means interrupting the story to explain something, fill in important facts, or include an important anecdote that occurred before the "present" story. There are several techniques for doing so: flashbacks, *in medias res*, and fractured narratives (see page 491 in Chapter 15). Decide at which point in your narrative your readers will need specific background information or other material related to your main story, then use one of these techniques to work that information into the narrative. For example, in your essay about your brother's illness, you might include a scene in which you received the doctor's evaluation that your brother's condition could worsen. At that point, you might interrupt the narrative to explain relevant medical facts so that your readers understand the gravity of the situation. Alternatively, you might want to convey how difficult you found it to face your own fears at that point in the story, so you might include a flashback to an earlier time when your brother was healthy, using that scene to show how close you and your brother were and what might be lost as a result of his illness.

Emphasize Important Scenes and Passages

Your narrative should focus on the most important moments or events in the experience you are writing about. Develop the passages about those events or moments so that they come through clearly and vividly. Devote less time to less important events or information. For example, you probably wouldn't need two or three paragraphs to describe the boredom of waiting in the hospital while your brother was undergoing tests. However, you might devote several paragraphs to the few moments when your family learned about the seriousness of your brother's condition.

Make Sure Your Introduction and Conclusion Establish and Reinforce the Focus of Your Narrative

Your introduction not only draws your reader into your story but also establishes its focus as well as your tone and voice. Similarly, your conclusion should reinforce your main point and highlight an idea, image, or feeling that you want your readers to take away from your narrative.

One of the most common mistakes student writers make in personal narratives is using what I call "life, the universe, and everything" beginnings. In other words, students start their narratives not with the story but with a kind of introductory statement that explains the significance of the subject of the story. For example, here are the opening two paragraphs of a student literacy narrative (see "Literacy Narratives" on page 517):

> Today, literacy is essential for success. It is an ability that opens doors beyond school. We all have to create resumes and cover letters, no matter our future occupation. I did not always believe in the importance of reading and writing, but that changed drastically during my high school career.
>
> Before sophomore year of high school, I had never considered how beneficial reading and writing could be, not only for school, but for my development as a person. Going into 10th grade, I had never read an entire book. Up until that point, I had been able to get by on my ability to "do school." To "do school" is being able to follow directions and work within the teacher's instructions. It requires little creative thinking and even less actual ability because it is like following a recipe. I had been considered a good writer by my teachers. They also labeled me a determined student, which was false. In truth, I was lazy, and laziness became second nature because "doing school" was much easier than actually doing the work. Instead of truly reading, I was taking shortcuts just to complete the assignments. That all was about to change however.

Notice that this student delays the start of the story with an explanation of the importance of literacy. The opening paragraph sums up a main theme of the story and perhaps helps establish its focus, but it doesn't do much to draw readers into the narrative. This introduction would be more effective if the first paragraph was eliminated and the essay began with the second paragraph.

Remember that your introduction is your opportunity to bring your readers into your narrative and encourage them to keep reading. Often, the best way to accomplish these goals is simply to begin your story rather than introduce it with an explanation.

16

You can use these five steps to develop an outline. If you have already completed a draft, use these steps to determine whether you should adjust the structure so that your story is told more effectively.

Step #6 in Chapter 3 provides additional guidance for structuring your essay.

Step 7 Get feedback.

The most useful feedback on your draft is likely to come from readers who attend to the key features of effective narrative:

A story that matters	• What is the significance of the experience? • Does the narrative bring out the significance of the experience? • Does the story make a point? Is that point clear?
A relevant story	• What makes your experience important to others? • Is the story told in a way that makes its relevance evident?
Interpretation	• What meaning do you find in your experience? • Does the meaning of your experience come through in your narrative?
Engaging storytelling	• Is the story effectively structured so the experience is conveyed clearly? • Do your descriptions help make your story vivid and contribute to your main point? • Have you used appropriate storytelling techniques?

Step #7 in Chapter 3 will help you analyze your feedback and decide which revisions to make.

Step 8 Revise.

There are three main issues to address in revising a personal narrative draft:

- telling an engaging story
- making sure the story conveys the main point or themes
- maintaining a clear focus

To address these issues, follow these four steps.

Reread Your Draft

Read from start to finish without stopping. Focus your attention on how effectively you tell your story. Address these questions:

- Does the story keep your interest from start to finish? Are there sections that seem slow or tedious? Are there sections that seem too long or detailed?

- Does the story make sense? Are the key events and essential background information included? Is anything missing?

Review Your Draft Using the Questions from Step #7

Focus on the first three sets of questions. Return to your Guiding Thesis Statement from Step #4:

- Does your story convey the ideas in that statement?

- Does each main section of your narrative contribute to those ideas?

- Does your conclusion reinforce your main point?

Evaluate How Well Your Draft Maintains Its Focus

Determine whether your story conveys your main ideas and does not wander into irrelevant material. Follow the advice from Chapter 15 (see "Maintaining a Clear Focus"):

State the main point or idea you want to convey with your story.

Review each section of your story (scenes, anecdotes, background information, etc.), and consider whether it is necessary to help convey your main point. If not, consider condensing or eliminating it.

For each main section you decide to include, consider *how* it contributes to the main point or idea of your story.

For example, let's imagine that in the draft of your hypothetical essay about your brother's illness, you have included several important moments from that your experience. Consider each one in terms of how it contributes to your main point:

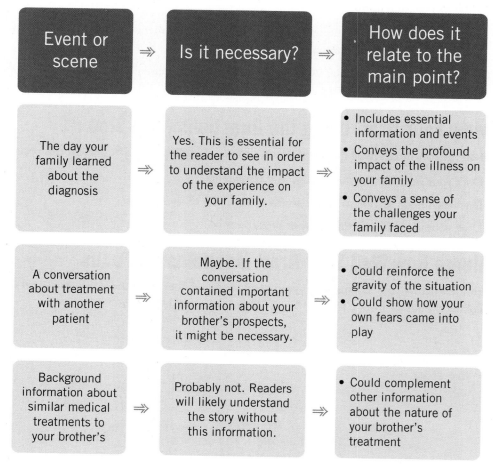

Event or scene	⇒	Is it necessary?	⇒	How does it relate to the main point?
The day your family learned about the diagnosis	⇒	Yes. This is essential for the reader to see in order to understand the impact of the experience on your family.	⇒	• Includes essential information and events • Conveys the profound impact of the illness on your family • Conveys a sense of the challenges your family faced
A conversation about treatment with another patient	⇒	Maybe. If the conversation contained important information about your brother's prospects, it might be necessary.	⇒	• Could reinforce the gravity of the situation • Could show how your own fears came into play
Background information about similar medical treatments to your brother's	⇒	Probably not. Readers will likely understand the story without this information.	⇒	• Could complement other information about the nature of your brother's treatment

Review Your Introduction and Conclusion

Make sure your introduction establishes the focus of the essay and draws readers into the story (see "Introducing Your Story" on page 537). Determine whether you conclude your story in a way that reinforces your main themes.

Follow Step #8 in Chapter 3 to make sure you have addressed all the main aspects of your essay in your revisions.

Step 9   Refine your voice.

Although voice is important in any kind of writing, personal narrative often relies on the extent to which the writer's voice engages readers. The examples in this chapter reveal different ways a writer's voice can come through in a personal narrative. As you revise, listen carefully to your own voice to determine how well it contributes to the effectiveness of your narrative. Make sure your voice "sounds" right for the story you are telling and the point you want to make:

- Does your voice fit the story you are telling?
- Is it consistent? If not, in which passages does your voice get weak or change?

Step #9 in Chapter 3 provides additional advice for refining your voice.

Step 10 Edit.

Complete Step #10 in Chapter 3.

WRITING PROJECTS | PERSONAL NARRATIVE

1. Identify an experience in your life that you believe has shaped you into the person you are today. In an essay, tell the story of that experience in a way that conveys the importance of your experience so that readers understand how it affected you.

2. Identify a general issue of interest to you that is also the subject of ongoing controversy—for example, gender roles, race relations, privacy, free speech, bullying. Write an essay about an experience you had that relates to that issue. For example, you might be concerned about bullying among adolescents. Your essay might tell the story of a time when you were confronted with bullying. Write your essay in a way that addresses a general audience who might share your concerns about the issue. Use your story to make a point about that issue.

3. Write an essay for an audience of your classmates about a time when you were faced with a difficult decision. Tell your story in a way that conveys what you learned from the experience.

4. Rewrite the essay you wrote for Question #3 for a different audience. Consider using a different medium to reach that audience. For example, if you wrote a conventional essay, consider using a blog or other social medium to reach a broader audience.

5. Adapt the story you wrote for Question #1, #2, or #3 for a different medium. For example, if you wrote a conventional essay, consider a multimedia format, such as Prezi.

6. Using the experience you wrote about for Question #1, #2, or #3, tell the story of that experience in two or three tweets. Now compare your "tweeted" story to the original. What are the main differences aside from length? What conclusions about effective storytelling can you draw from this exercise?

16

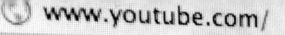
www.youtube.com/

You Tube

Videos | Music | Shows | Movies | Trailers

All Categories   Categories ⌄

Introducing: Teaching Channel
Teaching Channel showcases innovative and effective
teaching practices in America's sch...

Most Viewed Today

Writing Informative Essays

17

LOOK AROUND YOUR HOME, and you will probably find more informative writing than any other kind of writing:

- instruction manuals for your DVD player and smartphone
- cookbooks
- brochures from a local museum and government agency
- newspapers
- magazines

Go online, and you'll find digital versions of all these kinds of texts—and more: instructional videos on YouTube, Prezi presentations, and other multimedia texts that convey information. Indeed, it is difficult to imagine going through a typical day without encountering a piece of informative writing or referring to some kind of informative writing in order to complete a task.

Some scholars believe that writing, as a technology for language, emerged from the need to convey information across space and time—for example, as a way to record the buying and selling of grain between two people so that information about the transaction is available to them or to others at a later date or in another location. Referring to writing systems that developed in pre-Columbian America, Elizabeth Hill Boone has noted that writing "keeps and conveys knowledge, or to put it another way, ... presents ideas" (Elizabeth Hill Boone and Walter D. Mignolo, eds., *Writing Without Words*, p. 3). In other words, informative writing is as old as writing itself.

Informative writing takes many different forms, but all informative writing has one essential characteristic: Its primary purpose is to convey information or ideas as clearly and effectively as possible. An instructional manual for a DVD player should help the reader understand how the equipment should be operated and what to do if it doesn't work properly. A flier from a health care agency provides information to help readers understand, identify, avoid, and perhaps treat a specific illness. In this sense, informative writing is often decidedly practical and even utilitarian.

Although informative writing is usually distinguished from narrative, it can be understood as telling a story, albeit without the storytelling conventions of most narratives, such as plot or setting. A lab report, for example, is a way to tell the story of a lab experiment. A public service flier might convey information in a way that tells a kind of story of a problem. As we will see in this chapter, though, informative writing often includes narrative as a way to convey information or illustrate a point.

As a college student, you will be asked to compose various kinds of informative texts: research papers, lab reports, explanatory essays, fliers, multimedia presentations. To be able to create documents that convey information and ideas efficiently and effectively for various audiences, then, is an essential skill for successful college writers. It is also a necessary skill in the workplace and other aspects of your life. This chapter will help you develop that skill.

Occasions for Informative Writing

Not long ago, I took my car, which was more than seven years old, for inspection. The mechanic told me that the tires needed to be replaced. So I went online to gather information about tires: what to look for in a tire, what to avoid, how much I would have to spend, what safety issues to consider. Among the websites I visited were several that sold tires exclusively. In addition to a great deal of information about tires, these sites had forums where customers posted comments about tires they had bought. The comments often included detailed information about how the tires were used (e.g., mostly on highways or city streets, on sedans or sports cars, in snowy weather) and how they performed. Although these customers were writing in an informal context (an online discussion forum), many of their comments were actually sophisticated, if brief, informative essays that conveyed a lot of technical information. In addition, the test reports on these websites were carefully written informative essays describing how the tests were conducted and explaining the results for each tire that was tested. All this writing helped me make a decision about which tires would be best for my aging car.

My experience choosing tires underscores how often we turn to informative writing in our lives as consumers, citizens, and workers to share information, make decisions, and solve problems. You have probably had opportunities to write various kinds of informative texts, both formal and informal, that serve various purposes, from formal informative essays such as lab reports for a chemistry class to a how-to video about caring for a bicycle that you post on YouTube. Often, such informative texts are narrowly focused and serve very specific purposes. You might, for example, create a video about specific bicycle maintenance techniques for members of your campus bicycle club who ride on certain kinds of trails or roads. The purpose is to provide useful information for a specific audience who uses that information for a specific purpose.

At the same time, informative writing is about inquiry as much as it is about conveying information. When you write an informative text, you engage in a sophisticated process of discovery and learning, even if your rhetorical purpose is straightforward and utilitarian. You have likely had this experience in your own informative writing:

- Writing a research paper about the uses of social media for political activism can help you understand social media and shape your views about activism.

- Writing a report about your volunteer activities for a scholarship application might reveal something about you as a community member that you had not previously realized about yourself.

- Developing a multimedia presentation about a campus organization you belong to can help you better appreciate the challenges facing that organization.

In each of these examples, the primary purpose of the informative text is to convey information to a specific audience, but the process of composing the text is more than just selecting, organizing, and presenting information for that audience. It is also a process of inquiry that can lead to sophisticated learning—about your subject, about your audience, about the world around you, and about yourself. In this sense, informative writing is as sophisticated as any other kind of writing you do. It is an important tool for living.

EXERCISE 17A   EXPLORING OCCASIONS FOR INFORMATIVE WRITING

1. Make a list of four or five activities or subjects about which you are knowledgeable or have experience. For example, you might play a musical instrument, compete in gaming competitions, work on a cattle ranch, or volunteer at a local retirement home. For each item on your list, imagine an informative document you might create for an audience who does not have your level of knowledge or experience with that topic. For example, if you volunteer at a retirement home, you might create a Prezi to explain what such volunteer work entails and the challenges and rewards of such work. If you work on a cattle ranch, you might write an essay for a general audience explaining the process of raising cattle.

2. Make a brief list of topics about which you are interested but have limited knowledge. Select one item from that list, and find one or more informative texts about that topic. For example, you might be interested in learning about tea: where it grows, how it is cultivated, its different varieties, its history. Search online to find articles, websites, videos, or other documents that explain some aspect of that topic. Now evaluate those documents. Which were most helpful? Why? As a reader, what did you look for in the documents? On the basis of this exercise, what conclusions might you draw about informative writing? About how informative texts are used?

3. Think of a situation in which you had to explain a technical or specialized subject to someone who knew little about that subject. For example, maybe a friend asked you for help transferring a number from one phone to another. Or maybe you helped a teammate learn to do a proper header with a soccer ball. In a brief paragraph, describe how you explained the topic to the other person. How did you decide what information to share? What were the challenges of explaining the topic in that situation? Consider what conclusions you might draw from that experience about informative writing.

Understanding Informative Writing

As the examples throughout this chapter suggest, informative writing is a broad category. Sometimes referred to as expository writing, it encompasses many different genres and forms. As noted earlier, informative writing is included in this section of this textbook devoted to narrative writing because it is a form of writing that tells a story about a topic, although not necessarily in the conventional sense of a story. Nevertheless, many kinds of informative writing include elements of conventional narratives, including the use of first person, description, and even action. **Effective informative writing has two main characteristics:**

- **Clear, engaging exposition.** In effective informative texts, technical information and complicated concepts are presented in ways that make them accessible to readers who might not be expert in the subject matter. The writer attempts to keep readers engaged, even when the subject matter is dense and challenging, and to explain complex material clearly and in ways that interest readers. (See "Presenting Information Visually" on page 551.)

- **A clear sense of purpose.** Informative writing is meant to inform, and the most effective informative texts convey information with a specific sense of purpose. Even when writers share their own experiences or present detailed technical explanations, their sense of their main purpose remains clear.

The following examples illustrate these characteristics. In this excerpt from an article about his effort to restore his lost hearing, science writer Michael Chorost informs readers about the latest developments in hearing aid technology and cutting-edge medical procedures for hearing-impaired patients. Chorost uses the story of his own experience as a way to organize his article and present to his readers what he has learned about treatment for hearing problems. As a music lover, Chorost is especially fond of the classical composition *Bolero* by the composer Maurice Ravel. He begins his essay by telling the story of the moment when he lost his hearing altogether; this passage appears a few paragraphs into his article:

> And then, on July 7, 2001, at 10:30 am, I lost my ability to hear *Bolero*—and everything else. While I was waiting to pick up a rental car in Reno, I suddenly thought the battery in my hearing aid had died. I replaced it. No luck. I switched hearing aids. Nothing.
>
> I got into my rental car and drove to the nearest emergency room. For reasons that are still unknown, my only functioning ear had suffered "sudden-onset deafness." I was reeling, trying to navigate in a world where the volume had been turned down to zero.
>
> But there was a solution, a surgeon at Stanford Hospital told me a week later, speaking slowly so I could read his lips. I could have a computer surgically installed in my skull. A cochlear implant, as it is known, would trigger my auditory nerves with 16 electrodes that snaked inside my inner ear. It seemed drastic, and the $50,000 price tag was a dozen times more expensive than a high-end hearing aid. I went home and cried. Then I said yes.

Source: Chorost, Michael. "My Bionic Quest for *Bolero*." *Wired* Nov. 2005. Web. 5 June 2012.

Notice that Chorost provides information about the special medical procedure called cochlear implants by telling the story of his own experience. In other words, he is telling his own story primarily to inform readers about state-of-the-art medical treatments for hearing loss. As he continues with his story, he provides increasingly detailed information about hearing loss treatments and the challenges facing patients, like him, who have these treatments. In this passage, for example, he provides historical background to help explain the medical procedure he underwent:

> For centuries, the best available hearing aid was a horn, or ear trumpet, which people held to their ears to funnel in sound. In 1952, the first electronic hearing aid was developed. It worked by blasting amplified sound into a damaged ear. However, it (and the more advanced models that followed) could help only if the user had some residual hearing ability, just as glasses can help only those who still have some vision. Cochlear implants, on the other hand, bypass most of the ear's natural hearing mechanisms. The device's electrodes directly stimulate nerve endings in the ear, which transmit sound information to the brain. Since the surgery can eliminate any remaining hearing, implants are approved for use only in people who can't be helped by hearing aids. The first modern cochlear implants went on the market in Australia in 1982, and by 2004 approximately 82,500 people worldwide had been fitted with one.

This passage looks more like what we might typically think of as expository writing, and it underscores Chorost's primary purpose of informing readers about hearing loss technologies. Notice that this information seems more important in the context of his own situation as someone who lost his hearing. In that sense, telling his own story helps readers better appreciate the information and "see" what it is like for a patient to have this treatment, as in this passage:

> When technicians activated my cochlear implant in October 2001, they gave me a pager-sized processor that decoded sound and sent it to a headpiece that clung magnetically to the implant underneath my skin. The headpiece contained a radio transmitter, which sent the processor's data to the implant at roughly 1 megabit per second. Sixteen electrodes curled up inside my cochlea strobed on and off to stimulate my auditory nerves. The processor's software gave me eight channels of auditory resolution, each representing a frequency range. The more channels the software delivers, the better the user can distinguish between sounds of different pitches.

Chorost's use of the story of his own experience helps make his article more engaging and accessible to readers. Using his own experience to describe technical procedures helps make complex, abstract scientific concepts and medical treatments more concrete and therefore easier for readers to imagine and understand. Notice that although Chorost's article includes a great deal of information about his own experience, his focus remains squarely on the issue at hand: hearing loss technology. No doubt Chorost's experience with his hearing loss treatments included many other moments or events that he might have included in this article, but he selected only the experiences and information that are directly relevant to his main focus on hearing loss technology and treatment.

Here is an example of a more conventional kind of informative writing that exhibits these same features. In this extended excerpt from an article about the global water crisis, author Sandra

Postel begins with an anecdote to introduce the scale and complexity of the problem and then provides background information before moving to her main discussion:

In June 1991, after a leisurely lunch in the fashionable Washington, D.C., neighborhood of Dupont Circle, Alexei Yablokov, then a Soviet parliamentarian, told me something shocking. Some years back he had had a map hanging on his office wall depicting Soviet central Asia without the vast Aral Sea. Cartographers had drawn it in the 1960s, when the Aral was still the world's fourth-largest inland body of water.

I felt for a moment like a cold war spy to whom a critical secret had just been revealed. The Aral Sea, as I knew well, was drying up. The existence of such a map implied that its ongoing destruction was no accident. Moscow's central planners had decided to sacrifice the sea, judging that the two rivers feeding it could be put to more valuable use irrigating cotton in the central Asian desert. Such a planned elimination of an ecosystem nearly the size of Ireland was surely one of humanity's more arrogant acts.

Four years later, when I traveled to the Aral Sea region, the Soviet Union was no more; the central Asian republics were now independent. But the legacy of Moscow's policies lived on: thirty-five years of siphoning the region's rivers had decreased the Aral's volume by nearly two-thirds and its surface area by half. I stood on what had once been a seaside bluff outside the former port town of Muynak, but I could see no water. The sea was twenty-five miles away. A graveyard of ships lay before me, rotting and rusting in the dried-up seabed. Sixty thousand fishing jobs had vanished, and thousands of people had left the area. Many of those who remained suffered from a variety of cancers, respiratory ailments and other diseases. Winds ripping across the desert were lifting tens of millions of tons of a toxic salt-dust chemical residue from the exposed seabed each year and dumping it on surrounding croplands and villages. Dust storms and polluted rivers made it hazardous to breathe the air and drink the water.

The tragedy of the Aral Sea is by no means unique. Around the world countless rivers, lakes and wetlands are succumbing to dams, river diversions, rampant pollution and other pressures. Collectively they underscore what is rapidly emerging as one of the greatest challenges facing humanity in the decades to come: how to satisfy the thirst of a world population pushing nine billion by the year 2050, while protecting the health of the aquatic environment that sustains all terrestrial life.

The problem, though daunting, is not insurmountable. A number of technologies and management practices are available that could substantially reduce the amount of water used by agriculture, industry and households. But

Eye Ubiquitous/Glow Images

the sad reality is that the rules and policies that drive water-related decisions have not adequately promoted them. We have the ability to provide both people and ecosystems with the water they need for good health, but those goals need to be elevated on the political agenda.

Observed from space, our planet seems wealthy in water beyond measure. Yet most of the earth's vast blueness is ocean, far too salty to drink or to irrigate most crops. Only about 2.5 percent of all the water on earth is freshwater, and two-thirds of that is locked away in glaciers and ice caps. A minuscule share of the world's water—less than one-hundredth of 1 percent—is both drinkable and renewed each year through rainfall and other precipitation. And though that freshwater supply is renewable, it is also finite. The quantity available today is the same that was available when civilizations first arose thousands of years ago, and so the amount of water that should be allotted to each person has declined steadily with time. It has dropped by 58 percent since 1950, as the population climbed from 2.5 billion to six billion, and will fall an additional 33 percent within fifty years if our numbers reach 8.9 billion, the middle of the projected range.

Source: Postel, Sandra. "Troubled Waters." *The Sciences.* Mar./Apr. 2000: 16–24. Print.

In this excerpt, Postel provides a great deal of information about the dire situation with the Aral Sea and about the global water crisis in general. Despite the complexity of her topic, all the information she presents, including the anecdote at the beginning, is directly relevant to her topic. In addition, note how carefully she organizes her discussion. After beginning with her anecdote about the Aral Sea, she includes relevant background information and then discusses several key points about the growing water crisis. In informative writing, a writer often works with a lot of material—as Postel does here—and must find a way to organize the text so that the material is presented logically to readers.

Postel's article also demonstrates the importance of clear explanations in informative writing. Often, writers must discuss unfamiliar or technical information or concepts in ways that readers can grasp. Here, for example, a writer explains a complex problem with the way "views" are calculated on YouTube:

YouTube junkies are probably familiar with a mysterious glitch in the video platform's view-count system; a new video will show up all over the web, clearly going viral, but the view count is stuck at 301. Why 301 (or sometimes 302, or another number in the low 300s)? YouTube's trends manager, Kevin Allocca, says it's one of the most common questions he gets. Brady Haran, who produces the numberphile channel on YouTube, enlisted Ted Hamilton, a YouTube analytics project manager, to explain this puzzling phenomenon.

The answer, it turns out, hinges on the rather existential question of what constitutes a "real" view. Up until the arbitrary number of 301, a view is a view. It doesn't matter where it came from, or at least, YouTube won't bother to check. After 300, YouTube decides it *does* matter, and a new counting system takes over, analyzing the views to make sure they're "real." What counts as a view? Hamilton explains:

Well, that's actually a bit of a YouTube secret. A view should be a video playback that was requested by an actual user who got what they were intending to get and had a good user experience. We think of views as a currency and therefore we have to make a significant effort to eliminate counterfeit views, if you will.

While YouTube processes the data, "a statistical verification process," Hamilton says, the view count just plateaus at 301 (or thereabouts). This process can take as long as a day, according to Haran. What is YouTube filtering out? Views from bots, or views accumulated as the result of a "misleading" thumbnail (a sexy bikini babe on a video containing no sexy bikini babes, for example). If people watch a video for only a few seconds, YouTube takes this as an indication that these are not "legitimate" views and filters them accordingly.

The most interesting takeaway from this video is the glimpse into how YouTube values views, considering them a "currency" worth protecting. Videos are monetized based on views, so YouTube would appear to benefit from more views, from any source, yet artificially inflated view counts could actually devalue the "currency." YouTube's statistical verification process seems to be a measure to prevent inflation, and make sure a million views continues to be worth something. Haran promises to upload more video from his extensive interview with Hamilton soon, so stay tuned to his YouTube channel.

Source: von Baldegg, Kasia Cieplak-Mayr. "Only 301 Views? Why That YouTube Video Is Actually Going Viral." *TheAtlantic.com*, 25 June 2012. Web. 17 Aug. 2012.

As in Postel's article, this writer uses straightforward language to explain a technical problem. Although the writer does use some jargon (such as "bot"), it is jargon that most readers are likely to recognize. To explain highly specialized subject matter to readers who are not specialists, writers rely on careful word choice, clear sentence structure, coherent paragraphs, and well-organized passages.

The examples in this section demonstrate that most effective informative writing also exhibits the main characteristics of all narrative writing described in Chapter 16:

- **Clear focus.** Informative texts tend to be tightly focused, no matter how complex the subject matter. Even when they present a lot of information to readers, effective informative texts maintain a focus on the main point.

- **Careful structure.** Well-organized texts present information and ideas systematically and logically so that they are accessible to readers. Writers organize informative texts to maintain a clear focus and keep readers engaged. In some ways, organizing an informative essay can be more challenging than organizing other kinds of essays because there is no conventional structure for writers to follow—as there is in narratives (see "Structuring a Narrative" in Chapter 16) or arguments (see "Structuring an Argument" in Chapter 12).

- **Vivid, purposeful description.** Informative texts often include vivid description that helps convey important and complex information effectively to readers. Notice, for example, Chorost's careful description of his experience with his hearing-loss treatment or Postel's description of the Aral Sea. In each case, the descriptions help the writers accomplish their purpose in informing readers about their subjects.

Often, the most effective way to present information, especially statistical information, is in visual form. Digital technologies make doing so easier than ever. Using graphs, charts, and similar visual elements not only enables a writer to include a lot of information efficiently in a text but also can make information easier for readers to understand. (See also Chapter 21, "Designing Documents.")

Here's an example of a writer who takes advantage of visual components to present statistical information about how Americans spend their time—in this case, on a blog. Consider whether this text would be more or less effective if the writer had not used graphics and had simply discussed the statistical data in textual form.

People over the age of 75 watch twice as much television as teenagers. On any given day, women are 30 percent more likely to do chores than men. The typical college student spends about an hour sleeping for every 25 minutes he spends studying.

Those are just three of the facts you can harvest from the Bureau of Labor Statistics' latest American Time Use Survey, which uses polling data to illustrate a day in the life for Americans by age, gender, and education. Here are ... charts with ... more observations:

Americans spend about eight times as many hours working as we do eating and drinking.

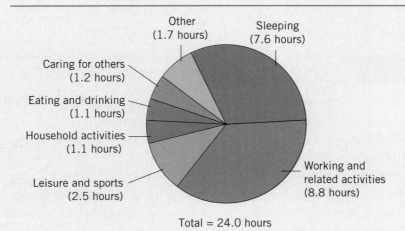

Time use on an average work day for employed persons ages 25 to 54 with children

Other (1.7 hours)
Sleeping (7.6 hours)
Caring for others (1.2 hours)
Eating and drinking (1.1 hours)
Household activities (1.1 hours)
Leisure and sports (2.5 hours)
Working and related activities (8.8 hours)

Total = 24.0 hours

NOTE: Data include employed persons on days they worked, ages 25 to 54, who lived in households with children under 18. Data include non-holiday weekdays and are annual averages for 2011. Data include related travel for each activity.

SOURCE: Bureau of Labor Statistics, American Time Use Survey

(Continued)

Compared to the average American over 15, college students spend 40% more time engaged in leisure/sports and 10% more time sleeping.

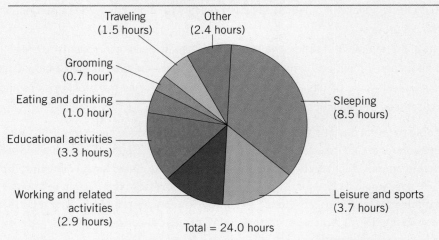

Time use on an average weekday for full-time university and college students

Traveling (1.5 hours)
Other (2.4 hours)
Grooming (0.7 hour)
Eating and drinking (1.0 hour)
Educational activities (3.3 hours)
Working and related activities (2.9 hours)
Sleeping (8.5 hours)
Leisure and sports (3.7 hours)

Total = 24.0 hours

NOTE: Data include individuals, ages 15 to 49, who were enrolled full time at a university or college. Data include non-holiday weekdays and are averages for 2007–11.

SOURCE: Bureau of Labor Statistics, American Time Use Survey

Source: Thompson, Derek. "Your Day in a Chart: 10 Cool Facts About How Americans Spend Our Time." *The Atlantic.com*, 25 June 2012. Web. 1 July 2012.

EXERCISE 17B   UNDERSTANDING INFORMATIVE WRITING

1. Find an article, book, website, video, or other text that explains a topic of interest to you. For example, if you own a pet, find something about caring for that kind of pet. Evaluate how effectively that text explains the topic. What features of that text do you find helpful? What sections are confusing or unclear? On the basis of your evaluation, draw conclusions about what makes an informative text effective.

2. Using the Internet, find two or three texts (articles, websites, and so on) that explain how to do something you have never done. For example, if you have never cooked an omelet, find texts that explain how to do so. Compare the texts you have found. Which one is most helpful in explaining the topic? What makes that text better than the others? What conclusions might you draw about informative writing on the basis of this comparison?

3. Using the texts you found for Question #2, compare how the writers organized the information. Why do you think each writer organized his or her text in that way? What do you find effective—or not—about the way each writer organized the text? What conclusions can you draw about structuring an informative text?

Reading Informative Writing

Informative writing can vary tremendously in terms of format, style, and structure. The readings in this section reflect that variety. They also exhibit the features of effective informative writing. As you read these selections, compare the ways in which the authors convey information and help readers understand the subject matter. Be mindful of the audience each writer seems to be addressing and how the writer adjusts explanations to help make the material more accessible to that audience. Also consider these questions:

Clear, engaging explanations	• What main information and ideas does the author present? • How effectively does he or she explain technical or complex information?
Purpose	• What is the author's purpose in presenting this topic? • Is that purpose clear? • How does the author convey his or her sense of purpose?
Focus	• What is the main focus of the text? • How does the author maintain that focus? • How well does he or she incorporate relevant ideas and information without losing focus?
Organization	• How does the author organize the text? • How well does the structure of the text help maintain the author's focus and keep readers engaged?
Description	• How effectively does the author describe important scenes, events, or processes? • How do these descriptions help convey important ideas or information?

17

A U.S. Crew's Urgent Flight into the Afghan Desert

by C. J. Chivers

Most news reporting can be considered informative writing, and often reporters rely on traditional storytelling techniques to convey information about important events or developments. In this article about a medical evacuation in Afghanistan, reporter C. J. Chivers not only tells the compelling story of one dramatic case but also informs his readers about the work of American military medical units in a combat zone. Chivers's article reads like a conventional narrative of an exciting and risky medical rescue, but as you'll see, his story subtly but effectively conveys a great deal of information about what American medical units do, the risks they face, and how they accomplish their mission. The article, which illustrates the four elements of effective storytelling described in Chapter 16 (see page 514), demonstrates how narrative can be used effectively to inform. As you read, notice how Chivers structures his article to keep readers engaged and also to provide important information about the case he is describing and the expertise of the medical personnel (see "Structuring a Narrative" in Chapter 16). This article appeared in The New York Times *in 2010, when the United States was still engaged in significant military operations in Afghanistan.*

FORWARD OPERATING BASE WILSON, Afghanistan—Beneath the blanket, the veiled Afghan woman slid her feet along the stretcher toward her hips, causing her knees to rise. She was in labor, with contractions two minutes apart, seeking a comfortable position in a military helicopter as it rushed over the desert below. Her baby was in a breech position, lodged in the birth canal.

The woman's face could not be seen. The crew did not know her name, nor that of her husband, who was sitting nearby. The soldiers knew this: She had been in labor almost nine hours, and the intensity with which she clutched Specialist Charles J. Williams, a flight medic, suggested worry and pain.

"She's clamping on my hand like she's about to tear it off," the specialist said into his helmet's microphone.

"Oh, she's in pain," answered Sgt. Patrick E. Schultz, the senior flight medic. He looked at a monitor showing her vital signs. "How much longer?"

From the cockpit, Capt. Amy L. Bauer, an Army pilot, replied: "Seven minutes."

For an American Black Hawk crew and an Afghan woman in a life-threatening labor, a fast and roaring flight this month was a tour of separate worlds and of both the promise and the difficulties when these worlds meet. The poverty and absence of medical services in Kandahar Province are nearly total, especially away from the agricultural zone and highway running along the Arghandab River. A woman in the arid outskirts who faced a dangerous delivery that local midwifery could not resolve usually had few choices beyond a bumpy ride over a rocky track and the hope of reaching the city of Kandahar before she and her baby died.

Since last summer, there has been another possibility. American helicopters and medical evacuation crews have been positioned in small outposts along the river, deployed beside NATO and Afghan soldiers fighting the Taliban. The helicopters have been assigned away from the airfield at Kandahar to reduce flight times for wounded troops to reach modern trauma care. But a patient is a patient. Afghans with ordinary but often grave conditions—victims of heart attacks, accidents or advanced illnesses—often seek help, too.

Each case poses a question. Should the medevac crews pick up and ferry civilians, and risk not having a helicopter available for a soldier struck by a bullet or blasted by a bomb?

A Dangerous Labor

On Dec. 11, the mission assignment came to a tent at Forward Operating Base Wilson, where a detachment from the 101st Combat Aviation Brigade waited for its next call. It was just past 1:25 p.m. No nearby American or Afghan units had suffered a casualty. The flight to pick up the woman was approved. The pilots and crew ran across the gravel-covered landing zone toward two helicopters—a medevac aircraft without heavy weapons and an escort craft with two door gunners at machine guns. That morning Sergeant Schultz, 31, had told the crew that he had had a strange dream. In it, they had delivered a baby in the air. Now, Sergeant Schultz appeared on the landing zone, sprinting. He had been in the shower tent. Shaving cream streaked his face.

"Schultz!" Specialist Williams, 21, shouted. "It's you! That dream!"

The sergeant stepped inside as the rotors began to turn and the noise rose. Soon the aircraft were lifting away. The patient was about 30 miles away, in the desert south of Khakrez, near a Special Forces and Afghan compound. Word from the Special Forces was relayed through a command post in Kandahar: the woman had been in labor since before dawn, and she would be accompanied on the flight by her husband.

Sergeant Schultz issued instructions, wondering how to balance medical and cultural demands. An examination by two young Western men, he said, might be impossible, especially since nobody aboard the aircraft could speak Pashto, the dominant language of southern Afghanistan, and he did not expect the patient to speak English. He worried that treating the woman would offend her husband and cause the family shame. The woman or her husband might even resist.

Barring a surprise, the sergeant said, doctors in Kandahar would help her complete the delivery. "We're not touching her unless it is an emergency," he said. Unless

(Continued)

She arrived in the back of a pick-up truck, accompanied by her husband, at a Special Forces and Afghan outpost in Kandahar Province where the medevac picked her up.

her condition worsened, he said, all they would risk doing was to start an IV and get her vital signs. He glanced to the back. Specialist Williams was flipping through an Emergency Medical Services field guide. He was on pages 43 and 44, reading the section on childbirth. "Most births are normal," it read. "Reassure mom and dad." The next heading read: "Breech." Here the letters were printed in red. "Rapid transport—patient may need emergency C-section."

Sergeant Schultz seemed to read his mind. "Hey," he said. "Ever do an emergency Caesarian?"

"Nope," Specialist Williams said.

"Me, neither," Sergeant Schultz said.

The desert seemed to roll past underneath.

A Veiled Patient

At 1:45 p.m., the helicopter landed at a small landing zone beside the outpost. A bearded American soldier, wearing blue jeans, stood beside the entrance, talking into a hand-held radio. There was no patient. Wait, he said.

Another soldier pulled up on an all-terrain vehicle. He said the woman was not far back. A pickup truck arrived. The woman, completely covered and veiled, was on a stretcher in the truck. A physician's assistant working with the Special Forces passed the patient's information to Sergeant Schultz: the woman had been in labor since 5 a.m.; only the child's arm could be felt in an exam. The soldiers quickly loaded the woman and her husband onto the aircraft. The Black Hawk took off for Kandahar.

Specialist Williams gestured to the woman's husband to get permission to lift her veil and put on an oxygen mask. Sergeant Schultz started an IV on her left arm. The patient, Sergeant Schultz said, was stable. The helicopter flew through a mountain pass. The irrigated steppe of the river valley opened up below. In the distance was Kandahar.

At 2:07 p.m., the helicopter settled onto a landing pad beside the Afghan National Army's hospital. The medics escorted the woman inside, where they met briefly with a team of American doctors who assist the Afghan staff. Sergeant Schultz returned to the Black Hawk and briefed Captain Bauer, after the helicopter took off. "I had a good talk with the doctor," he said. "He was like, 'I have no pediatrician and no OB-GYN.'"

"What capabilities do they have?" Captain Bauer asked.

"None," Sergeant Schultz said.

Had they flown for nothing?

The Primary Task

On medevac crews, each flight medic is different. Some are curious about their patients' conditions later. Others do not want to know. The trauma caseload in wartime is high, and many wounds are gruesome and devastating. Some medics focus narrowly, understandably, on the first job: preventing death.

The work of the flight medics stops near the hospital doors, where the patients are rushed on by others to further care. Inside military hospitals, the wounded are evaluated and stabilized. Then they often are wheeled to surgery, and soon—to free beds for the next patients that the war can produce at any time—they are transferred, often to Europe and a journey home.

In this case, the woman had not died in the Black Hawk. Her condition had not worsened. Once she entered the hospital, she was in the crew's past. But how did she and her baby fare? Curiosity prevailed.

Back on the forward operating base, Sergeant Schultz said he did not expect the woman or the child to live. Three days later, a check at the Afghan military hospital found no answer. Upon arrival, the military said, the Afghan woman had refused treatment and asked to be transferred to Mirwais Hospital, the hospital co-run by Afghans and the International Committee of the Red Cross, in Kandahar. With the same speed that she had entered the military medical system, she had vanished from it.

(Continued)

Registration records at Mirwais seemed to tell much of the rest. Late in the day of the medevac crew's flight, the records showed, a man named Karimullah Jan had arrived with his wife, Bibi-Shakira, who needed a surgical delivery. A Caesarian was performed at about 6 p.m. It was successful. Her baby, a boy, was healthy. After three more nights of recovering, Bibi-Shakira and her family left the hospital, passing beneath dusty skies busy with military helicopters, back to the desert near Khakrez.

Source: Chivers, C. J. "A U.S. Crew's Urgent Flight into the Afghan Desert." *New York Times.* 19 Dec. 2010. Web. 2 June 2013.

EXERCISE 17C TELLING THE STORY OF AMERICAN MILITARY MEDICS

1. How would you describe the main purpose of this article? How effectively does the author accomplish that purpose? Explain.

2. What information about American military medical units is conveyed through the story of this one evacuation? How effectively do you think the story of that case informs readers about the work of medical units in Afghanistan?

3. What technique for structuring a narrative does the author use (see "Structuring a Narrative" in Chapter 16)? To what extent does this technique help keep readers engaged? Did you find it effective? Why or why not?

Gamification: How Competition Is Reinventing Business, Marketing, and Everyday Life

by Jennifer Van Grove

In the following article from a popular online social media site, Jennifer Van Grove explains how gamification—the application of gaming design concepts to non-gaming activities or contexts—is being used by businesses, social scientists, and others to address problems or enhance certain processes. As Van Grove notes in her article, gamification is being used in a variety of ways to influence even the most routine everyday activities. She also notes that although the term gamification *has only recently come into widespread use, the idea of applying gaming concepts to non-gaming contexts has been around for a while. Van Grove's article, which appeared on* Mashable.com *in 2011, was written for a general audience with an interest in technology, but in many ways her article is similar to the kinds of reports college students are often asked to write. In this kind of informative writing, the writer examines a trend, phenomenon, or development about which readers might be aware but have limited knowledge. The writer's goal is to inform the audience about the topic, going into sufficient depth to give readers a general understanding of it. As you'll see, Van Grove explains gamification in general and then looks more closely at specific ways in which the trend is affecting different aspects of contemporary life, including business and social relations. Pay attention to how she organizes her article to take readers on a kind of "tour" of the gamification trend.*

. . . .

Can life, and all the menial or routine tasks that come with it, be transformed through game mechanics into an engaging, social and fun recreational activity? Such is the idea behind the emerging trend of "gamification."

Gamification is most often defined as the use of gameplay mechanics for non-game applications. The term also suggests the process of using game thinking to solve problems and engage audiences.

The word "gamification," much like the phrase "social media" a few years back, is being lobbed around in technology circles as the next frontier in web and mobile. Just as nearly every application, website, brand and marketer now employs social media in some capacity, so too will these entities gravitate toward game mechanics in the years ahead.

A recent Gartner report from April of this year suggests as much. Analysts predict that by 2015, more than 50% of organizations will gamify their innovation processes.

"By 2014, a gamified service for consumer goods marketing and customer retention will become as important as Facebook, eBay or Amazon, and more than 70% of Global 2000 organizations will have at least one gamified application," the Gartner report concludes.

Here we take a deeper look at the term, the trend, the mechanics and the real world implications.

An Intro to the Gamification Trend

Gamification, as a concept, is far from a new idea.

"Companies have been using games in non-game context for a long time," says Gabe Zichermann, the author of *Game-Based Marketing* and the CEO of Gamification. co. Zichermann cites the military, Hollywood and the hospitality sector—think airline frequent flier programs and hotel loyalty clubs—as three key industries utilizing game mechanics prior to the "coming out party" of gamification in 2010.

"What's changed over the past couple of years is the confluence of a few different factors," he says. Zichermann, like many others, specifically points to the success of startups such as Foursquare and Zynga as instrumental in embedding the idea into techie consciousness.

(Continued)

The second, and perhaps more significant factor, says Zichermann, is that once long-standing marketing techniques are now failing. "They're failing because people today are seeking more reward and more engagement from experiences than ever before," he explains. "The younger generation—the millennial generation and younger—is more game-attuned than previous generations."

Today's youth mandates a more engaging experience, he argues. "Gamification is required to bring those things into balance, and to make things engaging enough so people will pay attention to them and stay focused on them for a longer period of time."

The gamification trend is particularly hot in today's world because, should we follow this line of thinking, younger entrepreneurs are building applications and services for younger audiences who demand these features.

SCVNGR founder Seth Priebatsch agrees. "It feels like the next natural evolution of human-technological interaction to me," he says. "As we complete the social layer, we'll begin construction in earnest on the game layer."

The Mechanics

The five most commonly used game mechanics, as identified by Zichermann, are as follows:

- **Points:** Points are everywhere, and they're often used in non-game apps as a way to denote achievement. Points also measure the user's achievements in relation to others and work to keep the user motivated for the next reward or level. They can even double as action-related currency. Health Month, for instance, uses points in an interesting fashion. The site asks users to set up weekly health-related goals and stick to them for an entire month. Each person starts with 10 "life points" and the goal is to end the month with at least 1 life point. The player loses a point every time he breaks a rule, but friends can help the player "heal" and earn back points.

- **Badges:** While badges have their origins in the physical world, Foursquare popularized the digital variety with its oh-so-clever set of real-life merit badges that range from easy (Newbie badges are awarded to users on their first checkin) to nearly-impossible to unlock (it takes 10 movie theater checkins to earn the Zoetrope badge).

- **Levels:** Zynga uses levels to make the seemingly mundane task of tending to crops all the more enticing, and LevelUp encourages mobile users to level up and get better discounts for becoming more loyal patrons.

- **Leaderboards:** Leaderboards rank users and work to motivate and encourage them to become players. Foursquare started with city-centric leaderboards, but now places the emphasis on ranking users against their friends. Earn a few points for a checkin, and Foursquare will show you which of your friends you've flown by on the leaderboard.

- **Challenges:** These range from the simple to complex and often involve communal activity or group play. Priebatsch gamified his South by Southwest Interactive keynote with a group challenge that required all attendees to work together in rows. A proffered $10,000 donation to the National Wildlife Foundation was used to sweeten the deal.

Game Design & Plug-and-Play Gamification Platforms

"At the start of any new market … you need to have these catalyzing technology platforms," Zichermann says.

He's speaking, of course, of gamification platform providers such as Bunchball, Badgeville and BigDoor. Businesses can use these platforms to add plug-and-play game mechanics to their websites and applications.

The platforms, in Zichermann's eyes, bring a scalable technology solution to market that makes it easier for companies to participate in the gamification trend, and it allows them build and deploy products faster.

Priebatsch, however, is a bit uncertain of these platform providers. "This sub-set of the trend has always confused me a little bit," he says. "I see a real difference between utilizing game mechanics to improve a core experience from the ground up, and what I call 'bolt-on gamification,' where you basically just tack a badge on to something and call it a day. That doesn't really work in my opinion."

The two do agree on the significance of game and product design. "[Platforms] don't obviate the need for good design," Zichermann says.

Game and product design, as Zichermann sees it, is an important science. Design, he argues, needs to be centered around the customer's needs and wants and should determine the mechanics that companies use.

Nike+, says Zichermann, is an example of a brand properly merging design with mechanics, mostly because Nike is always iterating on the product, he says. "Gamification isn't like doing an ad campaign—it requires ongoing maintenance."

Recycle rewards company RecycleBank is getting it right on the design front as well, he says. "They've had tremendous success by designing really compelling and interesting gamified systems that people can interact with to recycle more," he says. "They know their audience really well."

Gamification & Real World Problems

Email overload, fitness phobia, diet and medication apathy. These are all real world problems and challenges that game mechanics can address.

Simple applications such as The Email Game and Health Month are meant to be stimulating and enjoyable tools to help people complete tasks they would otherwise dread.

(Continued)

17

"The game mechanics that I use are all about helping people feel less guilty about failure, since we've found that this is one of the primary obstacles to following through on a diet or fitness plan," explains Health Month creator Buster Benson.

"Games are one area of life where failure isn't taken personally. In games, failure is expected, and there's always a way to play again," he says. "Games help us appreciate the story of our failures and successes as an entertaining narrative rather than as a story about how you just aren't good enough for this or that."

Health Month users have been most responsive to the notion of being "healed" by friends when they lose their points. "By far, the most popular game mechanic is being able to 'heal' other players when they fall off the wagon," he says. "Social forgiveness and camaraderie are fairly untapped game mechanics, and yet really powerful."

One radical example of gamification in real life is changing the way people drive in Sweden. Kevin Richardson came up with a genius idea to get drivers to slow down: The Speed Camera Lottery.

"One troubling observation is the obscene amount of energy that goes to the one bad driver who speeds. Police, courts, fines, traffic school, points (the *bad* kind), increased insurance, and on and on," Richardson writes of the speed camera conundrum. "And where is the reward for people doing the *right* thing? What happened to that? Obeying the law is a pretty lonely endeavor."

Eventually, Richardson's thoughts materialized into an idea and he submitted the following to Volkswagen's Fun Theory contest: "Can we get more people to obey the speed limit by making it fun to do? The idea here is capture on camera the people who keep to the speed limit. They would have their photos taken and registration numbers recorded and entered into a lottery. Winners would receive cash prizes and be notified by post. Better still, the winning pot would come from the people who were caught speeding."

Richardson's Speed Camera Lottery idea won the 2009/2010 challenge, and the idea has since been tested by the Swedish National Society for Road Safety in Stockholm. The result: A 22% reduction in driver speed in the first week after implementation.

"That's game thinking at its purist form," says Zichermann. "It gives people direction about what they should be doing in small, incremental positive ways." One has to wonder, can anything be gamified? "Everything can be made more engaging and more fun by using game techniques," Zichermann argues.

Take cancer, a potentially awkward thing to gamify. "I don't presume to think that we can make having cancer into a purely fun experience," he says. "But, we have data to show that when we give cancer patients gamified experiences to help them manage their drug prescriptions and manage chemotherapy, they improve their emotional state and also their adherence to their protocol."

"You cannot gamify *anything*," Priebatsch says, taking a slightly different position. "Game mechanics can fix lots of problems and do lots of great things, but they are not a good fit for everything. Just like social is super powerful, but not a great fit for everything … everything has limitations and the beauty of both of these mega-trends is that they're a great fit for more situations than not."

EXERCISE 17D   REPORTING ON GAMIFICATION

1. How effectively do you think Van Grove explains gamification and its applications? How well do her explanations convey the trend toward the uses of gamification in various walks of life? Explain, citing specific passages from the article to support your answer.

2. What makes this topic relevant to readers today? How does Van Grove establish the relevance of the topic? To what extent does her effort to establish the relevance of the topic also reveal her purpose in explaining gamification?

3. Van Grove does not rely on anecdotes or stories about her own experience to inform her readers about gamification. What storytelling techniques does she use? (See Chapters 15 and 16 for explanations of storytelling techniques.) Does her use of these techniques make her article more or less effective? Explain.

What Honeybees Can Teach Us About Gang-Related Violence
by Emily Badger

One of the biggest challenges in informative writing is explaining a complicated idea or concept to readers who have little or no expertise in the subject. The following selection is an example of a writer meeting such a challenge. In this blog post from 2012 on The Atlantic.com, Emily Badger explains how a sophisticated mathematical model that anthropologists use to explain the behavior of social organisms such as bees can also be used to predict gang violence. As is often typical of blogs, Badger's writing is relatively informal, and her voice is almost personal, despite the sophisticated nature of her subject matter. But her post is an example of a very common form of informative writing in which a writer reports on a study or development from a technical field for an audience of readers who are not experts in that field. In that sense, her task is similar to one that college students often face: writing about a specialized subject in a field in which they themselves are newcomers. For example, if you have to write a report about a psychological personality test for an introductory psychology course, you are essentially doing what Badger has

(Continued)

*done: learning about a concept as a novice and writing about it in a way that will make
sense to other novices.*

*Because she is not an expert in theoretical ecology or mathematical modeling,
Badger relies on experts to explain the use of a specific kind of model to explain gang
behavior. Notice that she quotes liberally from experts to explain the concepts and how
they are used. She also includes graphics that help readers appreciate how mathematical
modeling can enable researchers to "see" territorialism in animal species. Throughout
her blog post, she keeps her language simple and her use of technical jargon minimal.
She explains difficult concepts in relatively simple language. As you read, consider how
effectively her explanations help you understand the concepts she is discussing.*

....

There is a mathematical model in the field of theoretical ecology that describes how
honeybees and chimpanzees and lions divide up space. In the grand competition for
limited resources—i.e., dinner—bee colonies and prides of lions will generally create
non-overlapping territories. Boundaries form between one group and the next, as the
least bit of competition arises between them, and invariably that boundary sits smack
in the middle between the beehives (or lion dens) on either side of it.

All of this sounds a little too simplistic to describe human behavior. As humans,
we'd like to think that we rationalize our actions, that we fit them into more complex
worldviews than a honeybee could ever contemplate (example: I believe in the importance of small businesses, therefore I shop at the local mom-and-pop corner store). But
P. Jeffrey Brantingham, a professor of anthropology at UCLA, believes that human
behavior is often far more predictable than we think. And as it turns out, those same
spatial Lotka-Volterra competition equations that explain honeybee behavior appear to
explain some territorial human behavior, too: specifically, that of rival urban gangs.

"Organisms all tend to have an anchor point for their activities, and gangs are no
different."

Oftentimes, the way we use space is driven by the physical constraints of that
space. When you need a gallon of milk, you don't drive to the grocery store five miles
across town. You head for the nearest one, regardless of whether if it's a Food Lion or
a Whole Foods. Social scientists, Brantingham says, tend to look at human behavior
from the top-down, examining how people feel and think about such a situation. But in
reaching instead for mathematical models, he and his colleagues look at human behavior (and particularly crime) from the bottom-up, examining the basic ways in which
our behavior is constrained by physical space.

"If that's something that constrains humans, that's also something that constrains
many other organisms," he says. "We're no different than hyenas or lions, or honeybees
for that matter."

Honeybees and hyenas stake out territory over a pretty obvious scarce resource:
food. But why might gangs do the same? Brantingham and colleagues Martin B. Short,

George E. Tita and Shannon E. Reid suggest in a paper published online this week in the journal *Criminology* that they're motivated by a similar limited resource: reputation.

"Ultimately, what's being competed for is your good name, or street credibility, your street rep," says Brantingham, who was the lead author of the paper. "If people recognize you as the toughest person around, then that has all sorts of benefits." (And, of course, more tangible benefits accrue from reputation, too.)

The authors used this mathematical model to identify the territories of 13 street gangs that operate in the Hollenbeck Policing Division of Los Angeles. (Random trivia: not all gangs are territorial by nature. Los Angeles and Chicago have predominantly territorial gangs; the gangs of Vancouver, British Columbia, on the other hand aren't particularly spatial.) The researchers identified anchor points of activity for each gang, relying on prior research: the home of a senior gang member, say, a street corner, or a neighborhood park.

"All people are like this," Brantingham says. "You have focal points around your house, or your community center. Honeybees have their hive. Hyenas have their den. And lion prides have their den. Organisms all tend to have an anchor point for their activities, and gangs are no different."

Using these anchor points, the mathematical model drew territorial boundaries between each gang. This is what the development of such territories looks like over time, starting from small densities of initial gang activity:

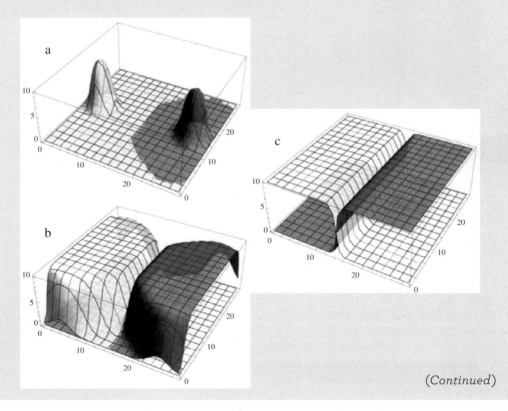

(Continued)

A mathematical equation obviously can't take into account the level of detail sociologists can collect on the ground, interviewing gang and community members, documenting graffiti and crime locations. But this theoretical model turned out to predict with pretty remarkable accuracy actual gang violence in Los Angeles. This model suggests most violence would occur not deep into gang territory, but on the contentious borders between gangs. The researchers overlaid actual crime data on top of their model—covering 563 violent crimes, between 1999 and 2002, involving these 13 gangs—and that's exactly what they saw.

Violent crime in this part of Los Angeles clustered along the theoretical boundaries between gangs produced by the same math equation that tells us how rival honeybees divvy up space. As a practical matter, this suggests police officers might want to focus their resources on these seams between gang territories.

This research also gives us a few other compelling clues about how gangs interact and what causes violence among them. The Lotka-Volterra equation suggests that, all things being equal, gangs will divide up space equally (and that may not mean along neat street boundaries). This process occurs when gangs experience more competitive animosity toward outsiders (other gangs) than among themselves. But, importantly, it takes very little competition to create these territories in the first place, or even to maintain them.

"Every time there's a gang-on-gang shooting, everybody talks about how there's an 'all-out gang war,'" Brantingham says. "But no, the numbers don't seem to suggest that."

Source: Badger, Emily. "What Honeybees Can Teach Us About Gang-Related Crime." *The Atlantic.* The Atlantic Monthly Group, 26 June 2012. Web. 2 June 2013.

EXERCISE 17E   EXPLAINING A THEORETICAL MODEL

1. How would you describe the focus of this blog post? Is it on theoretical modeling? Is it on explaining gang behavior? How does the author establish this focus? How well does she maintain it?

2. How clear did you find Badger's explanations of mathematical modeling and its uses in addressing gang violence? What makes her explanations effective—or not—in your view?

3. Badger includes some graphics in her post. How helpful did you find these graphics in explaining the concepts Badger is discussing? Would additional graphics have made Badger's explanations clearer? Why or why not?

Although much informative writing might appear to be objective and not intended to persuade a reader, even the most seemingly straightforward informative writing reflects the writer's perspective and can thus convey a stance on the subject matter. The very choice of subject matter reflects a writer's perspective. For example, a writer's decision to write a report about the growth of alternative energy sources, such as wind farms, reflects that writer's view that alternative energy is an important topic and that there might be a need for alternative sources of energy. Moreover, although a writer might seek to inform an audience about a topic in a neutral or objective way, the writer's stance will inevitably be reflected in the way the writer chooses to present information, which information to include or exclude, and what tone to adopt. For example, Jennifer Van Grove's explanation of gamification presents it in a relatively positive way. Even though she is ostensibly explaining a process, how she presents information and her tone reflect her belief that the process is worthwhile. You can imagine a different writer with a less positive view of gaming describing the process in a very different way, even though the information would be the same.

Similarly, a writer might compose a report about a controversial topic such as the use of hydraulic fracturing (or "fracking") to obtain natural gas without mentioning the fact that the procedure is controversial. Another writer might write a report on the same topic that includes a discussion of the controversial aspects of the topic. Both reports might seem neutral because both writers explain the process and do not take an overt position on the issue, yet the reports reflect each writer's viewpoint about the issue. The first writer might be generally supportive of fracking and therefore not mention the controversy; the second writer, by contrast, might feel suspicious of fracking and thus include information about the controversy. In each case, the writer is making an ethical decision about how to present information to readers.

As a writer, you must decide whether information you present conveys an accurate and fair representation of the topic, regardless of your own views about the topic.

Writing Informative Essays

The advice in this section will guide you through the process of developing a piece of informative writing. Read this section together with Chapter 3. Each step described here corresponds with a step in Chapter 3.

Step 1 Identify a topic.

Informative writing grows out of a desire to share information with others about a topic of interest to you. Often, we are asked to report on a topic that is assigned to us (such as in a class or at work). Sometimes, however, informative writing emerges from our own curiosity or experience. So begin by identifying:

- issues or topics of interest to you about which you would like to know more
- activities or topics about which you are knowledgeable or have direct experience

<table>
<tr><td>

Topics you are curious about

</td><td>

Activities or subjects you have experience with

</td></tr>
<tr><td>

- A current trend (e.g., social media)
- A controversy (e.g., individual liberty vs. national security)
- An important development (e.g., alternative energy)
- A concern (e.g., bullying)
- An activity that's new to you (e.g., dancing)
- A local issue (e.g., a new charter school)

</td><td>

- A hobby (e.g., painting or gardening)
- An experience that raised questions for you (e.g., an unfamiliar medical condition that someone you know developed)
- A topic you have expertise with (e.g., woodworking, politics, baseball)
- An important decision that others might share (e.g., going to college)

</td></tr>
</table>

Make a Brief List of Possible Topics in Each Category

For each item, jot down a few sentences about the topic: What do you know about it? What interests you about it? What do you want to know or share with others about it?

Select the Topic That Seems Most Promising to You

Remember that the topic you choose should be one that engages you for some reason: You're curious about it, you're passionate about it, it is important in your life in some way. Your genuine engagement with the topic is likely to result in a piece of writing that is also engaging for your readers.

Step #1 in Chapter 3 will help you further develop your topic.

Step 2 | Place your topic in rhetorical context.

Who will have an interest or stake in your topic? That is the primary question to address as you begin exploring your topic. At this point your task is twofold:

- identify an audience for your informative text
- consider your purpose in informing that audience about your topic

In some cases, your topic might appeal to a wide audience. For example, an informative essay about the problem of bullying would likely interest readers of many different age groups, those who work with young people, and parents, among others. By contrast, some topics will interest a more specialized audience. For example, a report on developments in psychotherapy techniques for a counseling psychology course would likely be written for an audience with an understanding of counseling psychology. Remember, your topic must have relevance for your intended audience. Considering that relevance will help you write an informative text that engages your audience and effectively conveys information about your topic.

Imagine, for example, that you recently became involved in an effort on your campus to create a community garden. Let's say that the college has designated some land to be used for the garden, which will be open to both students and local residents. As a result of your involvement, you have begun to learn about a national movement to identify and grow rare varieties of common vegetables such as tomatoes. Although you have been gardening for a number of years, you have never heard of so-called "heirloom" vegetables. Some of the people who use the community garden, for instance, have planted several different varieties of heirloom tomatoes that vary dramatically in color and size and have different flavors compared to the tomatoes you are familiar with. Obtaining seeds for these varieties, however, is difficult, and you have learned that not only gardeners but also scientists are interested in this movement as a way to preserve biodiversity. You decide you'd like to learn more about this movement and create an informative text to share what you learn with others. Consider the following:

Who might be interested in this topic?	• Gardeners • People involved with community projects • Readers interested in science and issues related to biodiversity • Students in certain science courses, such as botany or agricultural economics • Readers interested in issues of sustainability and food
Why would they be interested in this topic?	• Gardeners might want information about obtaining and growing hierloom plants • People interested in science might be curious about the scientific aspects of hierloom movement • Readers concerned about sustainability might see the movement as part of broader social and environmental developments

In considering your potential audience and their interest in your topic, you can see several possibilities for thinking about the purpose of your project:

■ to convey practical information for gardeners and others interested in gardening

■ to examine the movement in terms of broader developments related to sustainability and biodiversity

■ to explore technical matters related to raising rare varieties of vegetables

As you develop your project, your sense of purpose will shape the information you decide to include and how to present it to your intended audience.

With this in mind, explore your topic using these two questions to identify a potential audience and determine the relevance of your topic to that audience.

Now complete Step #2 in Chapter 3 to explore your rhetorical context more fully.

Step 3 Select a medium.

Which medium is best for your informative project depends upon your audience and your purpose.

Let's return to the example of an informative project about heirloom plants. Consider your audience and purpose in deciding which medium might be most appropriate for such a project:

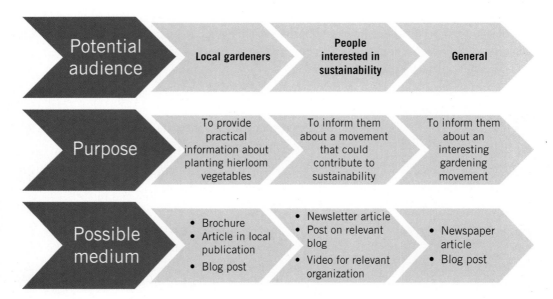

Potential audience	Local gardeners	People interested in sustainability	General
Purpose	To provide practical information about planting hierloom vegetables	To inform them about a movement that could contribute to sustainability	To inform them about an interesting gardening movement
Possible medium	• Brochure • Article in local publication • Blog post	• Newsletter article • Post on relevant blog • Video for relevant organization	• Newspaper article • Blog post

In evaluating the possible media for each audience, consider the capabilities of each medium. For example, a brochure enables you to use graphics, color, and other design features. By contrast, a conventional newspaper article would allow you to go into greater depth about your topic, which might be an advantage if you want to reach an audience of readers interested in sustainability issues. (If you are working on a specific course assignment, you should follow the guidelines for the assignment and select an approved medium.)

Step #3 in Chapter 3 provides additional guidance to help you decide on the most appropriate medium for your informative project.

Step 4 — Identify the main point of your informative project.

In one sense, the point of any informative writing is to inform readers about a subject. But *why* should readers be informed about the subject? Your subject might interest you for some reason, but why would it interest readers? In other words, what makes this subject relevant to others? You need to answer these questions to determine the main point of your informative project.

Begin by returning to the purpose of your project. If you have followed Steps 1–3, you have already identified a purpose for your project. In our hypothetical example, we identified several possible purposes for an informative piece about growing heirloom vegetables, depending upon the intended audience. Let's imagine that you have decided to direct your project to an audience with a general interest in issues of sustainability and biodiversity. For Step #3, you expressed the purpose of your project as follows:

> *to inform readers about an important movement that could contribute to sustainability*

You can recast that statement of purpose into your **Guiding Thesis Statement**:

> *Raising heirloom crops is a growing movement that holds promise for efforts to increase sustainability and preserve biodiversity.*

This statement captures your sense of purpose and expresses the main point you will make in your informative piece. In effect, you will be informing readers about the heirloom plant movement as a promising part of the larger effort to promote sustainable lifestyles.

Keep in mind that your Guiding Thesis Statement might change as you learn more about your topic and sharpen the focus of your piece. For example, you might learn that the heirloom plant movement is driven mostly by private citizens interested in gardening and by a few small farmers. If so, you would adjust your Guiding Thesis Statement to reflect that shift in the focus of your piece.

Complete Step #4 in Chapter 3 to develop your Guiding Thesis Statement further.

17

Step 5 — Support your main point.

Now that you have a good idea of the main point of your project, you can begin to explore your topic and gather sufficient information to inform your readers about that topic. Doing so involves three main tasks:

- identify what you already know about your topic
- gather additional information about your topic
- eliminate unnecessary information

Identify What You Already Know

Review your discovery draft, notes, and other materials to collect the information and ideas you already have, including your own experiences with your topic. Include everything that seems potentially useful or relevant.

Gather Additional Information

Review the materials you have generated so far to determine what additional information you need. At this point, you might have to do some research, especially if your topic is unfamiliar to you. Use appropriate resources, including online resources, people who might be knowledgeable about your topic, and printed materials you have access to (such as newspapers, books, fliers, and so on). However, rather than just looking for anything at all related to your topic, your research will be more efficient (and probably more effective) if you have an idea of what kind of information you need. So it's important to identify gaps in what you know or have already learned.

For example, let's say you have gathered the following information about your topic:

- how to raise certain types of heirloom plants
- the history of the modern movement to discover and preserve heirloom varieties of common vegetables (such as tomatoes)
- the challenges of finding heirloom varieties
- the benefits of raising heirloom vegetables

What else might your readers need to know about your topic? Given that your main point involves connecting the heirloom plant movement to the larger movement for sustainability and preserving biodiversity, you probably need some information about how raising heirloom plants contributes to a sustainable lifestyle and how it might address concerns about biodiversity. The more you research your topic, the easier it will be to identify issues or information that you should include in your project.

Review your materials in this way, keeping your main point and purpose in mind. If you identify gaps in the materials you have, look for appropriate information to fill those gaps. (Chapters 22 and 23 will guide you in identifying and evaluating source material.)

Eliminate Unnecessary Material

Review your materials to determine whether any information you've collected can be eliminated without weakening your project. Keep in mind that some information might seem relevant but not be necessary. For example, through your research you might have learned about a person who has amassed an unusually large collection of heirloom tomato seeds and has become a supplier for gardeners seeking heirloom varieties. Although this information is interesting and relevant to your project, it probably isn't essential for readers to know in order to understand the heirloom movement and its potential role in fostering biodiversity.

Complete these three steps to develop your project and gather sufficient information to support your main point. You should now be ready to write a complete draft of your informative project. (If not, move to Step #6.) Step #5 in Chapter 3 provides additional advice to help you develop your project.

Step 6 — Organize your informative project.

Clear organization is one of the hallmarks of effective informative writing, but unlike some other forms of writing (such as argument), there are no well-established formats for organizing an informative text. Your main consideration is how to present information so that readers understand your topic. Follow these five steps.

Begin with Your Main Point

Return to your **Guiding Thesis Statement** (from Step #4), and adjust your main point, if necessary, on the basis of what you have learned about your topic as you completed the first five steps. Ultimately, the way you organize your project should help readers grasp your main point.

Determine Which Information or Ideas Are Most Important for Supporting Your Main Point

Review the materials you developed for Step #5 (or review your rough draft), and identify the pieces of information and ideas that are essential for readers to know in order to understand your topic. Organize the information or ideas in order of descending importance, starting with the most important and moving to the least important.

Identify Supporting Information or Ideas

Decide whether the supporting material should be placed *after* the essential material or incorporated into the essential material. Decide on the basis of your sense of which approach would make the information easiest for readers to understand.

Incorporate Essential Background Information

You have probably gathered background information that will have to be worked into your discussion. For example, in your hypothetical project about the heirloom plant movement, you might have relevant scientific information explaining biodiversity. Although that information isn't directly related to the heirloom plant movement, it is essential background so that readers understand how this movement can affect biodiversity. Decide where to fit this information into your project so that it is easy for readers to understand and doesn't interrupt the overall flow of your draft.

Make Sure Your Introduction and Conclusion Establish and Reinforce the Focus of Your Project

Your introduction should introduce readers to your topic and convey a sense of your main point. Your conclusion should reinforce that main point. Also keep in mind that you want to present that information in a way that will engage your readers and draw them into your piece.

Use these steps to develop an outline. (If you have already completed a draft, you can use these steps to review it and determine whether you should reorganize your project.) Keep in mind that this outline is a guide and might need to be adjusted to reflect your sense of how best to convey your information to your audience.

Step #6 in Chapter 3 provides additional guidance for organizing your project.

Step 7   Get feedback.

Ask your readers to focus on **the key features of effective informative writing:**

Clear, engaging explanations	• Does your draft present sufficient information and ideas about the topic? • Is technical and complex information explained clearly? • Do the explanations engage your readers?
Purpose	• Is the main purpose of the text clear? • Does the text convey a sense of purpose so readers understand the relevance of the topic?
Focus	• Is the text clearly focused? Is the focus maintained throughout the text? • Are relevant ideas and information incorporated without weakening the focus?
Organization	• Is the draft well organized so it presents information clearly to readers? Is anything missing or out of place? • Does the structure of the text help maintain the author's focus and keep readers engaged?
Description	• How effectively does the author describe important scenes, events, or processes? • Do these descriptions help convey important ideas or information?

Step #7 in Chapter 3 will help you analyze your feedback and decide which revisions to make.

Step 8   Revise.

The most important consideration in revising your draft is making sure you have covered your topic sufficiently and conveyed information clearly so that your intended audience understands your topic and grasps your main point. Before revising, then, return briefly to Step #2 to remind yourself of your rhetorical context. Then follow these four steps.

Review Your Draft Using the Questions from Step #7

It is a good idea to return to your **Guiding Thesis Statement** from Step #4 and make sure your project conveys your main point.

Evaluate How Clearly Your Draft Conveys Information and Explains Your Topic

Clarity is a key feature of informative writing. Try to read your draft from the perspective of someone who doesn't have a background in this topic. Keep these questions in mind:

- Have you conveyed ideas and information in a way that such a reader will understand?
- Are there any technical or complicated passages that might be difficult for readers unfamiliar with this topic to understand? If so, how can you make those sections more accessible?
- Is anything missing that is essential for readers to know about your topic?
- Have you included information that isn't essential and might blur the focus of your project, making it harder for readers to understand? If so, can you eliminate those sections without eliminating important information?

Review the Structure of Your Project

Re-examine the way you have organized your project to make sure you present information in a clear fashion and effective order.

Follow Step #8 in Chapter 3

Make sure you have addressed all the main aspects of your essay in your revisions.

Step 9   Refine your voice.

Your voice in your informative project will depend a great deal on your rhetorical situation (see Step #2). In informative writing, the most appropriate voice is often a measured, authoritative voice that doesn't call attention to itself. This is especially true if you are writing in the third person. However, if your project incorporates your own experiences and employs the first person, your voice might be somewhat less formal and more conversational (such as in the excerpts from the article by Michael Chorost beginning on page 546).

To help determine whether your voice is appropriate for your project, follow these steps.

Return to Your Guiding Thesis Statement

Remind yourself of your main point. Consider whether your voice in your revised draft seems appropriate for a project with this main point.

Return to Your Rhetorical Context

Briefly revisit Step #2 to remind yourself of your audience and purpose. Will your voice likely engage your intended audience and help you achieve your rhetorical purpose? For example, in your hypothetical project about the heirloom plant movement, you have decided to address an audience interested in issues of sustainability and biodiversity. Such an audience is likely to see your topic as a serious one and will probably be put off by a voice that is very light and conversational. On the other hand, if you are writing an essay intended to inform a general audience about an interesting gardening movement, your readers are likely to expect your voice not to be overly serious and formal.

Follow these steps to help determine whether your voice "sounds" right for your subject matter, audience, and purpose. Step #9 in Chapter 3 will also help you refine your voice.

Step 10 Edit.

Complete Step #10 in Chapter 3.

WRITING PROJECTS   INFORMATIVE WRITING

1. Think of something you know how to do well that involves specialized knowledge or a skill that most people are unlikely to have. It could be an athletic activity, a hobby, or something similar. Develop an informative project that explains that process. Identify an appropriate audience, and select a medium that is likely to reach that audience. For example, you might create a brochure about protecting your computer from hacking or viruses for private computer users.

2. Think of an experience you had that led to a new understanding or insights. For example, maybe you witnessed an accident and learned something surprising about how emergency medical services work. Or you might have taken a trip and encountered unexpected problems that you could have avoided. Develop an informative project on a topic related to that experience. For example, if you witnessed an accident that

made you wonder about how emergency medical services are organized and funded in the United States, you might develop a report about emergency medical services. Incorporate your own experience into your project.

3. Identify a general issue of interest to you. It could be an ongoing controversy, a subject of current interest, or something that you have always been curious about. Explore that issue. On the basis of what you learn about it, develop an informative project. Identify an audience that might share your interest in the topic.

4. Rewrite the project you did for Question #1, #2, or #3 in a completely different medium. For example, if you wrote a conventional print report for Question #1, develop a multimedia or video version of that report.

Digital Storytelling

DIGITAL STORYTELLING IS A POWERFUL NEW WAY for writers to connect with readers. Using digital media, writers can incorporate sound, images, video, and special effects into their narratives to engage readers in ways that are not possible in conventional print media. Digital stories enable writers to participate in an increasingly multimedia world.

What is a digital story? For our purposes, *digital story* refers to narratives presented in a digital format that includes multimedia components such as photographs, video clips, and sound in addition to text. It is important to note that digital stories are not simple videos. Although digital stories might include video clips, the video clips are one component of the whole presentation into which the writer carefully integrates those clips with other images (such as still photographs), music, sound effects, and voice-over narration. Videos, by contrast, are usually composed entirely of video footage accompanied by sound. This distinction is important because the process of composing a digital story is not the same as making a video.

Composing a digital story encourages a writer to explore an experience in ways that can enrich storytelling. The digital format requires writers to think about elements that are not available in print formats—such as video clips, music, and other kinds of sound and graphics—and consider how these elements can be used to convey the writer's experience or ideas. Video and sound can make a story more engaging for a reader, but just as important, such elements change the way a writer composes a story. In addition to considering how matters like word choice and organization might influence a reader's response to a story, writers must consider the potential impact of images, colors, music, and similar elements on an audience. In digital media, images and sound become powerful rhetorical tools with which writers can meet the needs of a rhetorical situation, and writers must compose their stories with these elements in mind. They must go beyond words and anticipate how these other components can help make their stories more compelling for an audience. The process of creating a digital story, then, is not a simple matter of converting a written story into a digital format; it is a different process by which the writer explores his or her experience with different tools.

This is not to say that digital stories are better (or worse) than stories told in conventional print formats; both digital stories and conventional print narratives convey an experience to an audience. However, digital storytelling offers writers new opportunities for sharing their experiences and presents them with new challenges as well.

As someone living in this rapidly evolving digital age, you have probably used various media to tell a story:

- a Prezi presentation about a field trip you took for a biology course
- a video of a trip you took to a city you had never visited before
- a PowerPoint presentation about a community service project you participated in
- a blog post with photos and embedded video clips about your experience as an exchange student

These various media enable you to connect with readers in different ways to convey your story. Digital storytelling is likely to continue to grow in popularity and importance as new and ever-more sophisticated technologies become increasingly available to writers. This chapter will help you develop a better understanding of digital storytelling so that you can take advantage of its capabilities to meet your rhetorical needs.

Occasions for Digital Storytelling

Not long ago I was browsing an online discussion forum devoted to sailing and came across a heated discussion about a video someone had posted to the forum. The video, which was about 30 minutes long, had been created by a young sailor in his mid-20s. It told the story of his experiences sailing an old sailboat with two friends. The narrator and his friends (two women about his age) found the boat deteriorating in a marina in south Florida. After working for several months to scrape together enough money, they bought the boat and then spent several more months repairing it to make it seaworthy. For the next year, the three friends lived aboard the boat and sailed along the southeastern coast of the United States and throughout the Caribbean, stopping here and there to earn extra money for supplies and to make additional repairs to the boat. The video told the story of their adventures. Through video clips, still photographs, and voice-over narration, the writer created a story about sailing through all kinds of weather to new places and making do with very little money and without the sophisticated technology that mariners rely on today. Part of the point of the story was that if you seek adventure, you don't need much more than the desire for new experiences and the willingness to make do with what you have. It was an engaging story expertly told in a digital format.

The video sparked an intense response from some members of the discussion forum where it had been posted. Many of the participants in that discussion were older, having retired after long careers and now enjoying their later years by sailing. Some of these people objected to what they considered the irresponsible behavior of the three young people in the video, who knew how to sail but had limited experience sailing in coastal waters, which can be dangerous. Other participants defended the young sailors, admiring their adventurous spirit, resourcefulness, and problem-solving ability. They envied these young sailors the courage to follow their dreams in a little sailboat. The online discussion, which spanned a few weeks, wasn't really about sailing but about how to live. Participants shared their views about responsibility, happiness, and even the purpose of human life. They also shared their own stories—not only about sailing experiences but also about careers, families, dreams, and regrets. In many ways, the discussion was as compelling as the video itself.

That video revealed the power of digital media to tell a story. It was a well-crafted story that included carefully edited video footage, compelling still photographs, and an engaging voice-over narration. The story was engrossing not only because of the adventures it depicted and the narrator's provocative views about living but also because of the skillful use of imagery and sound. The intense debate in the online discussion forum suggests that the video deeply affected its audience. I don't know whether the young man who made that digital story followed the debate, but it seems clear from how carefully he composed his digital story that he felt a need to share it with other people interested in following a dream.

Of course, you don't have to have an adventure to tell a compelling digital story. Like any narrative about our own experiences (see Chapter 16), a digital story can be about any experience, no matter how mundane or common it might seem:

- A student creates a digital story for a criminal justice class about a family member's experience with the juvenile court system.
- A YouTube video tells the story of a family's vacation at a famous national park.
- The website of a community organization includes digital stories about the experiences of elderly residents of a historic neighborhood that is being renovated.
- Veteran teachers create digital stories about their professional lives to share with new teachers at the beginning of their careers.
- A college student creates a digital story about coming to college to help new students adjust to life in a college dorm.

In these examples, writers use digital media to tell stories about experiences that matter to them and to others. Given the growth of digital media in recent years, digital stories can sometimes make it easier for writers to find an audience for their stories. For example, potential viewers might be more inclined to watch a digital story posted to an organization's website than to read the organization's newsletter because the digital story can be accessed and viewed so quickly and easily online.

In many cases, telling a story in a conventional print format might still be preferable, despite the advantages of digital storytelling. For instance, in Chapter 16, we used the example of a narrative about the experience of dealing with a family member who is diagnosed with a serious illness. Such a story can certainly be told in digital format, but it is a story that is also quite involved and multilayered, encompassing the person's health, sophisticated medical treatments, health insurance concerns, financial pressures, difficult decisions, and the impact of the experience on other family members. As a writer, you might decide that a conventional print story enables you to explore these many aspects of the story more fully than a digital story might allow, especially if you did not have relevant video footage or still photographs from that period of your life. In such a case, telling the story in digital format might not be a viable option. On the other hand, you might decide that the multimedia capabilities of a digital story enable you to tell your story in a different but equally compelling way.

Telling a story in digital format, then, is partly a matter of taking advantage of the media and materials available to you as a writer and deciding whether the format fits your rhetorical situation. Any experience that is important enough to share with others can be told in digital format if you have the necessary components, such as relevant video clips or photographs, to convey your story sufficiently to an audience. And in some situations, a digital format might be the best choice. For example, a student who belongs to a campus organization for business majors might create a digital story about her experience as an intern with a company that makes virtual reality software. Her digital story, which is intended for the organization's website, might include video footage showing her testing the software as well as graphics illustrating important elements of the software. In such a case, the availability of video, sound, and other multimedia elements would enable the writer to convey her experience in ways that would be difficult or impossible in a conventional print format. For example, she can show video footage of the virtual reality test she experienced that might be challenging to describe in words.

Deciding whether to tell your story in digital format is partly a technical matter (Do you have relevant images? Do you have access to the right equipment?), but like any effective narrative, an effective digital story is one that meets the needs of a specific rhetorical situation. You can be a more versatile writer by learning how to craft digital stories and by taking advantage of digital media to achieve your rhetorical goals.

EXERCISE 18A   OCCASIONS FOR DIGITAL STORYTELLING

1. Think of a recent experience you had that might best be conveyed to an audience as a digital story. What might you include in a digital story about that experience? What images or sound would be appropriate in telling that story? What advantages or disadvantages do you see in telling the story of that experience in digital form?

2. Find one or two digital stories online. (A simple search for "digital stories" or "digital storytelling" should yield many links to sites where you can find digital stories.) After viewing the stories, imagine a print version of each story. In what ways might a print version of that same story be more effective? In what ways might it be less effective?

3. If you have ever submitted a college essay or some other kind of application essay (such as for admission to a special sports or music workshop), consider how you might have converted that essay into a digital story. Would you have changed the story in any way? What advantages or disadvantages would a digital story have in such a case as compared to a conventional print essay?

Understanding Digital Stories

At first glance, digital stories can seem straightforward: a narrator reading a story as images appear on the screen and music plays in the background. In fact, part of the appeal of many digital stories is that they can tell a story in simple terms with images, sound, and voice-over narration. But even the simplest digital story is actually a sophisticated combination of image, sound, and text that results from a writer's many careful decisions about what to include in the story and *how* to present it visually and aurally.

The following digital story illustrates the complexity of the decision-making that writers engage in as they design digital stories. "Good Will" tells the story of a daughter's decision about what to do with the many sweaters her mother has knitted over the years. On the surface, this four-minute video focuses on a few moments in the life of the narrator, Christi Clancy, as she drives to a homeless shelter to donate the sweaters. While on her way, she thinks about the sweaters and about her mother, whose impressive skill at knitting reflects her other qualities as a person. In the process of telling the story of her drive to the homeless shelter and her decision about whether to donate the sweaters, Clancy delves into her mother's sometimes difficult life and gains insight into her mother—and herself.

Here are the first few frames of Clancy's digital story along with the text of the voice-over narration. Keep in mind that each image appears on screen for several seconds to coincide with the narration. Also, some frames zoom in or out to highlight specific components of an image, and there is often a transition between images (for example, one image fades into another). All these design features contribute to the viewer's experience and enhance the story being told but cannot easily be represented on the pages of this textbook.

1.

good will

Christi Clancy

[soft background music]

Narrator: I took some of the sweaters my mom made to the homeless shelter.

2.

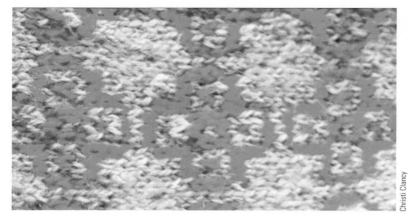

Christi Clancy

Narrator: I only wanted to take the ones that were too big, too itchy, too boxy, and too old.

3.

Christi Clancy

Narrator: I have so many sweaters that if you poked a hole in my house, yarn would burst out.

4.

Christi Clancy

Narrator: My mom doesn't just knit for me but for everyone else in our family. Last year alone she made 24 sweaters. Lately, all those sweaters have become a problem.

In these opening frames, Clancy sets up her story by telling us that she is on her way to the homeless shelter. She introduces her mother, provides a little background information, and, at the end of the fourth frame, introduces tension into her story: "Lately, all those sweaters have become a problem." Notice that this information is conveyed efficiently through the brief text of the voice-over narration. At the same time, the images enable viewers to see the sweaters without Clancy having to describe them (as she would have had to do in a conventional print narrative). In addition, the photograph in the third frame allows viewers to see what her mother and family look like. In these ways, Clancy carefully combines simple images with brief text to convey information and establish the focus of her story. In effective digital storytelling, the writer uses images and sound together with text to convey ideas and information, not to decorate the story.

In the next frame, Clancy begins to delve into her mother's character and explore her main themes of responsibility, resilience, and perseverance:

5.

Christi Clancy

Narrator: When I asked my mom why she knits so much, she said that unlike most things in life, a sweater has a beginning, middle, and end. As someone who had to start her life over again, I'm not surprised by her answer. She's incredibly practical, paying herself a quarter for every load of laundry she does. We used to call her "Smart Pat" because her approach to conflict is just to get over things and move on.

Here Clancy combines two still photographs to create an unusual image that represents the role of knitting in her mother's life and reinforces one of the story's main themes: resilience. This frame demonstrates how a writer can use simple still photographs to achieve a specific effect, convey information, and introduce or reinforce ideas.

In the next three frames (#6, #7, and #8), Clancy reveals that she herself does not knit, showing images of sweaters as well as photos of her and her mother and telling the viewer, "I tried a few times, but I get frustrated sometimes when I hit a snag." In this way, she establishes a contrast between herself and her mother, using knitting as a metaphor. Then in frame #9 she introduces a central part of her story: her family's difficulty with her father, who suffered from addiction and mental illness:

9.

Narrator: She's a problem-solver, but my dad was one problem she couldn't fix. He was handsome and charming—and a manic-depressive alcoholic.

10.

Narrator: Once he threw her down the basement stairs. Another time he told her to hide his gun because he was afraid he would use it.

11.

Narrator: She put my sisters and me in a plane in the middle of the night after that. She finished her masters degree in speech pathology, and we started over in Milwaukee.

Notice that Clancy uses a single photograph in these frames, zooming in on specific components of the photograph as her narration tells the story of how her mother left her father and started a new life in another city. These frames illustrate **an important feature of effective digital storytelling: design features enhance the story without distracting from the ideas or themes.** In this case, Clancy zooms in on an image to emphasize the information she is conveying through her voice-over narration. The zooming doesn't merely catch the viewer's attention or make the image "snappy"; it contributes to the storytelling.

As this digital story illustrates, simple images can contain a great deal of information and introduce complex ideas if they are used carefully in conjunction with the narrative text. For example, notice how Clancy uses very basic photos in the next three frames to fill in more information and begin to reveal her own feelings about her mother's ability to care for her family:

12.

Narrator: She didn't make much money, sometimes not even enough for lunch.

13.

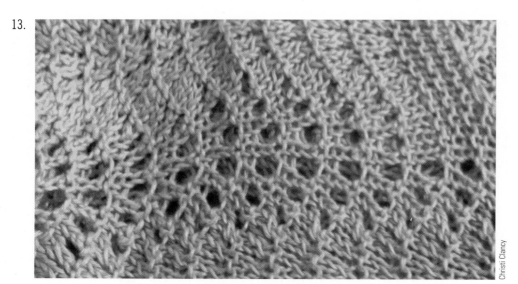

Narrator: But she could send me to school in a gorgeous hand-knit sweater that people would always compliment.

14.

Narrator: I loved the steady clicking sound of her knitting needles and the competent tap of her heels on the linoleum floor of the hospital when I visited her at work.

Clancy returns to images of the sweaters her mother made. She uses these images not only to show readers the quality of her mother's knitting but also to explore her themes and to keep her narrative clearly focused. Note also that in the 14th frame she includes a close-up photograph of her mother as a young woman. This photo not only provides readers with an accurate depiction of what her mother looked like at that time in her life, but it also shows her mother as happy and confident. This frame is another example of how a simple image can convey complex information and reinforce important themes in the story.

Clancy's repeated use of photos of her mother's sweaters also helps move the story along by reminding us that she still has to decide what to do with all the extra sweaters. At the same time, as she displays more and more photos of those sweaters, she reinforces their importance to her as symbols of her mother's qualities and her own sense of identity as her mother's daughter. Using this same strategy of repeatedly showing images of the sweaters, Clancy continues her story, informing her audience that her mother is now retired and works part-time in a yarn store, still knitting and helping others learn to knit. Then Clancy returns to the problem at the center of her story: what to do with all those sweaters. Notice that she uses a photo of a sweater in the frame that depicts the moment of decision (frame #17):

16.

Narrator: I wonder if she knew we'd struggle with what to do with the sweaters she's given us.

17.

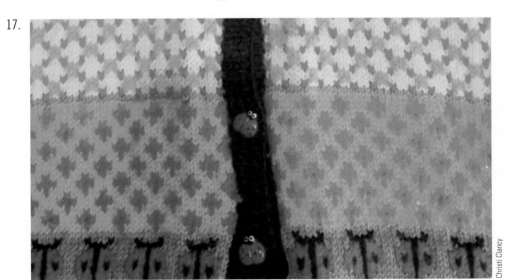

Narrator: Did she anticipate that we would experience a moment just like the one I was having in my car, trying to decide whether or not to let them go to strangers?

18.

Christi Clancy

Narrator: I thought of a dream I once had of my dad, who died homeless on the streets of Denver when he was only 51.

Here again Clancy relies on images of her mother's sweaters to highlight the difficulty of her decision. The narration informs viewers of Clancy's struggle, while the images remind them of the beauty of the sweaters, which brings Clancy's difficult decision to the forefront: How could she part with such beautiful sweaters that were so expertly and lovingly crafted by her mother? That struggle intensifies when she remembers a dream she had of her father:

19.

Christi Clancy

Narrator: He came back to visit me. He was wearing a sweater my mom knit for him, but it had come unraveled.

20.

Narrator: He was dragging strings of yarn behind him that stretched back as far as I could see.

21.

Narrator: I couldn't donate them.

22.

Narrator: Every single stitch is a captured moment from her life, every sweater as much a part of her as her tissue. Knitting is her language.

23.

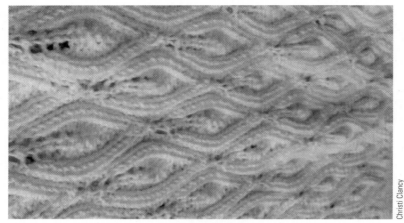

Christi Clancy

Narrator: I drove back home, but even now, months later, the sweaters are still in the trunk of my car. Maybe for her the sweaters have a beginning, middle, and end, but she goes on and on.

24.

Christi Clancy

Once again Clancy uses images to communicate ideas and reinforce themes. When she makes her decision (frame #21), she shows a photo of a sweater. In frame #22, she superimposes an image of her mother on that same sweater, reinforcing a main theme of her story and reminding us why she could not part with those sweaters. These are all very simple images, but Clancy uses them to convey complex ideas.

Clancy's story demonstrates perhaps the most important feature of effective digital storytelling—and indeed of *all* narratives: It must tell a story that matters to the writer and be relevant to the intended audience. Clancy doesn't simply describe a difficult decision she had to make about whether to donate prized family possessions; rather, she tells the story of that decision in a way that explores complex themes of love and loyalty. Her story examines how a simple item such as a sweater can acquire significance beyond its practical purpose. In that regard, her story explores fundamental themes that her audience can relate to, whether or not they are interested in knitting.

Note, too, that the text of Clancy's narrative is spare, almost poetic. It conveys only what is essential to the story and works in conjunction with the images to provide necessary information for viewers to understand the story. Digital storytelling enables writers to use images and sound to communicate ideas and therefore to say more with less prose. As a result, writing the text of a digital story means choosing words carefully so that they complement the images rather than repeat information conveyed by the images.

Effective digital stories:

- **Tell stories that matter.** Like all effective narratives, digital stories relate experiences that matter to the writer and are relevant to viewers. A story that has little significance for an audience is unlikely to be any more compelling if told with images or sound. What matters most in a digital story is what matters most in any good narrative: It must tell a compelling story that connects with readers and conveys a relevant idea or point.

- **Use images, sound, and other multimedia elements to convey ideas and information.** The multimedia components of a digital story are more than illustration or decoration; they are essential elements that communicate information, convey ideas, and reinforce themes. Simply adding images or sound doesn't necessarily improve a narrative. Images, sound, and special effects must contribute to the story in some way; moreover, they should engage the audience without distracting from the point of the story.

- **Employ design elements to enhance the story.** Design elements such as transitions, zooming, color, and sound effects can be used to communicate ideas and reinforce themes in a story. For example, a writer can make a gradual transition between two still photographs to suggest a connection between the images; music can contribute to a certain mood that is appropriate for the story. In these ways, design elements help the writer tell a story and reinforce the writer's themes.

EXERCISE 18B   EXPLORING DIGITAL STORIES

1. Think of an experience you might want to share in a digital story. Write a brief paragraph describing one important moment or scene in that experience. Now imagine that brief description as one or more frames of a digital story. What images would you use? How would you revise your paragraph so that it is an appropriate narration to accompany those images? What sound would you include? On the basis of this exercise, what conclusions can you draw about the similarities and differences between digital stories and conventional print narratives?

2. Rewrite Christi Clancy's digital story "Good Will" as a conventional print narrative, using as much of her narration as possible and adding whatever new text you believe is necessary to tell her story effectively. Now compare the original digital story to your print version of it. What do you notice in comparing these two versions? Which do you think is more effective in conveying her experience? Why? What does this exercise tell you about writing digital stories?

(Continued)

18

3. Select two of the digital stories included in this chapter (see "Reading Digital Stories"), and compare how the authors use the capabilities of digital media to tell their stories. Analyze each author's use of images and sound. Evaluate the voice-over narration. On the basis of your comparison, what conclusions can you draw about composing effective digital stories?

Managing the Technical Components of a Digital Story

The primary difference between a conventional print narrative and a digital story is technology. A writer telling a story in conventional print format generally does not have to consider matters of document design, such as layout, color, or graphics (except when using a medium such as a website or brochure that allows for such features); as a result, the writer can concentrate on the text. Telling a story in digital format, by contrast, requires a writer to think carefully about design, especially the use of images and sound. As the example in the preceding section of this chapter indicates, these features significantly affect the quality of the narrative and the reader's experience. As a writer, then, you must manage these **technical components** when telling your story in digital format:

- a storyboard
- images
- sound
- narration
- transitions

Creating a Storyboard

When composing a digital story, the writer creates a kind of script, usually called a **storyboard**, which is an outline of the digital story that includes information about images, sound, and design elements. A storyboard allows you to map out the story and to organize the multimedia elements. It enables you to "see" your entire digital story before you begin creating it with the appropriate software (see "Software for Digital Storytelling").

Although you can find software programs for creating storyboards, you can also use a word processing program to create a basic storyboard. To do so, simply create an outline with each main heading corresponding to a frame in your digital story. Each frame should include the following information:

- image (photo or video clip)
- audio (background music, sound effects)

- design (color, subtitles, special effects such as zooming)
- narration (the text of the story)

Let's imagine that you are creating a digital story about a study-abroad experience in Brazil. A basic storyboard for the first few frames would look like this:

I. Frame #1

- Image: photo of you and your host family
- Audio: Brazilian salsa music
- Design: Title in standard font at bottom of frame
- Narration: "I thought I knew something about Brazil (pause) until I spent three months there as a high school senior."

II. Frame #2

- Image: panoramic photo of the city where you stayed
- Audio: Brazilian salsa music
- Design: pan across the photo
- Narration: "This is the Brazil I thought I knew: a sunny, busy place full of life and color."

III. Frame #3

- Image: split photo of shimmering beach and crowded barrio
- Audio: Brazilian salsa music
- Design: zoom in and out of each photo
- Narration: "This is the Brazil I discovered: a land of contrast, of joy and hope alongside despair; a land of possibility."

A storyboard should contain this kind of information for each slide or frame in your digital story. You can also create your storyboard as a table to help you visualize your story:

I. Frame #1	II. Frame #2	III. Frame #3
• Image: photo of you and your host family • Audio: Brazilian salsa music • Design: title in standard font at bottom of frame • Narration: "I thought I knew something about Brazil (pause) until I spent three months there as a high school senior."	• Image: panoramic photo of city where you stayed • Audio: Brazilian salsa music • Design: pan across photo • Narration: "This is the Brazil I thought I knew: a sunny, busy place full of life and color."	• Image: split photo of shimmering beach and crowded barrio • Audio: Brazilian salsa music • Design: zoom in and out of each photo • Narration: "This is the Brazil I discovered: a land of contrast, of joy and hope alongside despair; a land of possibility."

18

Creating a storyboard is an integral part of the composing process. Many writers find it easiest to write their story as a complete text and then create a storyboard, revising the text of the story as they include the narration for each frame. Some writers prefer to compose the story as they develop the storyboard, considering appropriate images and sound as they write the narration. There is no right way. Do what works for you as a writer. The important point is that a storyboard enables you to develop your story as a multimedia presentation and helps you coordinate images, sound, design, and text.

FOCUS Software for Digital Storytelling

Several different software programs and online sites can be used to create digital stories. One of the most widely used programs is *Photo Story*, which is available online for free. *Photo Story* is easy to use and enables writers to incorporate still photographs and music into their digital stories. (Some versions of *Photo Story* cannot accommodate video, however.) *PowerPoint* can also be used for digital storytelling. It includes a wide variety of special effects and allows the user to embed video and audio clips into a presentation.

Most personal computers have operating systems that include video software that can also be used for making digital stories. Microsoft Windows usually includes a program called *Moviemaker*. Apple computers have a similar program called *iMovie*. Both these programs are sophisticated tools that can be used to create digital stories, enabling writers to incorporate video clips as well as still images and sound; they also include many special effects and design features.

Increasingly, writers are using online resources to create their digital stories. *Flickr*, a social media site for distributing images, is one such resource. Podcasting, in which digital audio recordings are combined with photos or video clips, can also be used for creating digital stories.

If you have never created a digital story, it is probably best to use a basic program, such as *Photo Story*, that is easy to learn. As you gain more experience with digital storytelling, you might find a need for more sophisticated digital tools. Your course instructor might provide resources for creating digital stories. You can also check with your college library.

Using Images

Video clips, photographs, and other kinds of images are powerful tools for telling a story. They can communicate information, convey ideas, reinforce themes, emphasize a point, and evoke a feeling in an audience. Selecting and using images is one of the most important components of composing an effective digital story.

Many technical aspects of images are beyond the scope of this textbook, such as the composition of an image, image quality, camera angles, and so forth. You can find resources about these topics online. (Also, see "Analyzing Images" in Chapter 8 and "Working with Images" in Chapter 20.) For our purposes, the most important considerations are what an image communicates to a viewer and how it contributes to your digital story. In selecting and using images, keep the following questions in mind:

- **What does this image communicate?** Some images provide information in a straightforward way. For instance, in our hypothetical example of a digital story about a study-abroad experience in Brazil, a photo of the host family enables viewers to see what the family members looked like; similarly, a video clip of the neighborhood where you stayed provides information to help viewers understand your experience there.

  Images can also communicate ideas and introduce or reinforce themes in more subtle ways. For example, in Christi Clancy's digital story earlier in this chapter, the photos of the sweaters not only enable viewers to appreciate her mother's knitting skill but also convey important ideas about Clancy's relationship with her mother.

- **How does this image contribute to the story?** An image should advance the story in some way, so consider the specific information or idea you want to convey or reinforce with a particular image. For example, a story about my grandparents might include an anecdote about a time they visited a religious shrine that was important to them. I might use this photo, taken in front of a fountain at the shrine:

Robert P. Yagelski Family Photo

This photograph shows a specific location mentioned in my narration, but it also suggests the affection and warmth my grandparents felt for one another. Selecting this photo enables me to show viewers the place referred to in the narration and at the same time reinforce an important idea about my grandparents' relationship. By contrast, a common vacation photo, in which my grandparents were posing for the camera, might provide information about the location but would not necessarily convey anything important about their relationship. When selecting images for a digital story, then, consider not only the information you want the image to convey but also whether the image enables you to introduce or reinforce important themes.

- **Is this image necessary?** Effective digital stories include only the elements that are essential to the story. If an image does not contribute to the story in some way, consider removing or replacing it. Avoid including images just because they are compelling unless they also move your story forward or enhance it in some way.

These same principles apply to *any* image: still photographs, video clips, sketches, cartoons, or paintings. Remember that you are telling your story by combining images with other media. Any image you use should contribute something important to your story. Also keep in mind that you can't always simply copy images from online sites and use them in your story. You must respect copyright laws.

FOCUS **Intellectual Property Considerations**

Using images and music in a digital story can raise questions about copyright. If you created the images or sounds yourself, in general you own the right to use them in a digital story. However, if you obtained an image, video, or audio clip online or from some other source, it might be subject to copyright restrictions and you might be unable to use it in your digital story. If you wish to include images or audio made by someone else, you should determine whether you are allowed to use them or whether you need to obtain permission to do so.

In general, the fair use clause of U.S. copyright law allows students to use most images or music that belong to someone else as long as the image or music is used exclusively for a course assignment and will not be distributed to larger audiences or for profit. If you plan to post your digital story to a public website, you might not be protected by the fair use clause and should probably obtain permission to use any images, videos, or audio clips that belong to someone else. Often, copyright information is included on the websites or in the print materials where you found images or audio. Check there first. You can also usually find good advice about copyright and intellectual property issues on the website of your campus library. If you're not sure about whether you need permission to use an image, video, or audio clip, check with your course instructor or a librarian.

Also, if you plan to use in your digital story an image you made of someone else (for example, a photo or video clip showing some friends), you should obtain their permission.

Incorporating Sound

Most digital stories include background music that accompanies the voice-over narration. In effective digital stories, music helps establish an appropriate mood for the story, reinforces the writer's tone, reflects themes the story explores, enhances the image in some way, and evokes a certain feeling in viewers (joy, melancholy, excitement). In many digital stories, the same music plays throughout; in some stories, the music changes to signal a shift in the story or reinforce an important moment in the narrative. In these ways, the sound you select can help convey your experience more vividly to your audience.

Digital stories can also include sound effects. For example, a story about an experience at a beach might include the sound of crashing waves in the background. Often, such sound effects can be used to emphasize an important moment in the story and make the story more vivid. But in selecting sound effects, be careful that they do not distract viewers and take away from the narration or the images.

When considering sound for your digital story, address these questions:

- **What mood do you want to convey?** Music is a powerful way to evoke feelings and set a mood. Consider the main point of your story and the nature of the experience you are sharing. If you decide to include background music, select music that fits your story and will help convey the appropriate mood to your audience. For example, a heartfelt and somber story, such as the one by Christi Clancy included earlier in this chapter, calls for soft, perhaps slightly melancholy music.

- **How can sound be used to convey relevant information or ideas?** In addition to setting a mood for your story, music or sound effects can also communicate information and ideas or supplement the images and text to highlight an important theme. For example, a story about your experience with a hip hop band might include clips of specific songs that were significant to you or your band members. Similarly, the lyrics of a song might reinforce an important idea in a story; for example, a segment about a difficult break-up in a long-term relationship might include a clip from a love song with lyrics that highlight the difficulty of the experience.

Narrating a Digital Story

Effective voice-over narration is more than a matter of reading the text of your story. The narration must work in conjunction with images and sound to tell your story, explore your themes, and communicate your main points. In this regard, writing a digital story is different from writing a conventional print version of your story. Moreover, how you narrate your story will have an impact on your audience. In addition to your choice of words, your tone, pacing, and inflection can significantly affect the quality of your digital story and influence your audience's reaction to it. In narrating a digital story, then, keep these two main considerations in mind:

- **The text of a digital story works with the images and sound to present the subject matter.** The narration does not tell the whole story. Instead, the narration relies on images and sound to convey information and reinforce important themes. Writers don't try to include everything in the narration; they tell what is necessary, using images and sound where appropriate to communicate information and ideas. For example, there's no need to describe what someone looks like if you are including a photo of that person. Similarly, rather than describe an event or action, let a video clip or photograph show it. Use the narration to provide background information, ideas, and impressions that can't be conveyed through images

18

or sound. The main thing to keep in mind is to include in the text only what you need. (To get a better sense of the difference between writing the narrative for a digital story and writing a conventional print narrative, complete Question #2 in Exercise 18B on page 593.)

- **The narration reflects an interpretation of the story.** Voice-over narration gives you the opportunity to use the tone of voice, inflection, and pace in a way that fits your subject matter and reinforces important moments or ideas in your story. In this sense, your voice-over narration reflects your *interpretation* of your story, allowing you to highlight important moments in the text, pause for emphasis, slow down or quicken your pace to match the action you are referring to, and evoke a certain emotion or mood with your tone of voice. As you prepare to record the voice-over narration for your digital story, consider these questions:

  - What tone of voice is most appropriate for the subject matter of your story? What mood do you want to convey?

  - What points in the narrative require emphasis? At such points, should you pause, change your tone, or inflect the words in some way (e.g., saying a word with a rising tone that indicates surprise or shock)?

  - What pace of your narration feels appropriate for your subject matter? Should you slow down or speed up?

Making Transitions

Most software programs for digital storytelling allow for various kinds of transitions from one slide or screen to the next (see "Software for Digital Storytelling"). For example, you can dissolve one image into the next one, fade to black and then have the next image fade slowly into view, or cut abruptly from one image to the next. You can also use more dynamic transitions in which images rotate, wipe from left to right or top to bottom across the screen, or dissolve into specific patterns. It can be fun to experiment with transitions in this way, but transitions and other special effects can be distracting to viewers if they are overused or inappropriate for the subject matter. Like other components of effective digital storytelling, transitions should be used to reinforce ideas, emphasize a point, reinforce a mood, and help convey the story clearly to the audience.

When selecting transitions in your digital story, anticipate how each transition will help your audience appreciate your experience. Transitions should be engaging but not distracting. Ultimately, the goal is to take advantage of the technical capabilities of the software program you are using, not to show them off. In general, changing the style of transition too often can detract from your digital story. In this case, the rule of thumb often is less is more.

Reading Digital Stories

The three stories included in this section illustrate the different ways in which writers can take advantage of the capabilities of digital media to convey their experiences to an audience. Two of these digital stories are personal narratives in which the writers explore important experiences. Such personal stories are common in digital storytelling, and these selections will help you understand why. In the third selection, the writer tells the stories of others, using digital media in a way that is typical of documentary filmmaking. All three of these digital stories exhibit the features of effective storytelling. As you read, pay attention to how each writer uses images and other multimedia components in combination with the narration to tell the story in a way that explores important themes. Consider these questions:

A story that matters	• What is the main point of the story? • What is the significance of the experience the author shares in the story? • What makes the story relevant to the intended audience? • What themes does the author explore in the story?
Images and sound	• What kinds of images are included? • How do these images contribute to the story? • How is sound incorporated into the story? How does sound enhance or detract from the main point of the story? • How effectively does the voice-over narration convey the experience?
Design	• What design features does the author use? • To what extent do these design features contribute to the story and help convey the main themes? • In what ways do these design features enhance or detract from your experience viewing the story?

Mountain of Stories

by Nazbah Tom

In this selection, college student Nazbah Tom tells the story of coming out to her parents. Tom's sexual orientation creates an obstacle between her and her family that she must find a way to overcome, but her decision to come out to them also reveals the power of love and teaches her an important lesson about acceptance. In this sense, her story explores themes that go beyond the challenges of confronting difference, whether that difference involves sexual identity or something else. Tom's story also explores other elements of identity. She is Navajo, and she draws on that sense of identity to help her accept other aspects of her identity. As you'll see, she incorporates into her story images of Mount Hesperus, a sacred place in Navajo culture, and even as she identifies herself as different from her family, their common identity as Navajo binds them together. In this regard, Tom learns something deeply important about her cultural heritage and her connection to her ancestral homeland.

(Continued)

In technical terms, Tom's story is relatively simple but exhibits expert use of multimedia components to make her story vivid and bring her themes into relief for her audience. You'll notice, too, that her narrative is spare, and she relies on carefully selected photographs to do much of the storytelling, especially in the final frames. Nazbah Tom's digital story was published on the website of the Center for Digital Storytelling in 2012.

[traditional Native American music plays softly in the background]

Narrator: As I write my coming out letter to my mother, I look out from the wonder of my dorm room and see Mount Hesperus. I ask the mountain for strength to send this story. I send the letter.

Harry Walker/AlaskaStock/Glow Images, Inc.

Narrator: Three months go by without a word from my mother.

Nazbah Tom

Narrator: An elder tells me, "Give your mother the same amount of time you gave yourself to accept who you are." . . .

Source: Tom, Nazbah. "Mountain of Stories." Online video. *Center for Digital Storytelling. YouTube.*
YouTube, 14 June 2012. Web. 25 Sept. 2012.

1. What elements of conventional narrative does Tom use in telling her story digitally? To what extent do these elements help make her story more (or less) effective? (In answering this question, refer to the discussions of the elements of effective storytelling in Chapters 15 and 16.)

2. What important information about Tom and her family is communicated through the images in this story? How effective did you find Tom's selection of images? Explain, citing specific sections of the story to support your answer.

3. What do you think Tom's use of music contributes to this story? What important themes does the music reinforce?

Mother to Son, Father to Daughter

by Molly Fanning

The experiences that matter most to us are often difficult to understand. In this digital story, educator Molly Fanning confronts one such experience: her father's decision to leave his wife and children. Fanning explores her identity as a member of a close-knit family and especially her complicated relationship with her father. She also explores her sense of connection to her grandmother, her father's mother. Her story examines the impact of her father's decision to leave his wife and seven children when Fanning was just a girl, but the focus is on her own struggle to reconcile her complex feelings about him. Like Nazbah Tom in her digital story, Fanning relies on carefully selected still photographs to convey her experience. Her story is a good example of how a writer can use images to enhance a story and communicate ideas and information, even when those images are little more than typical family photographs. Fanning created her story in 2008 as part of her work as a teacher and an educational consultant.

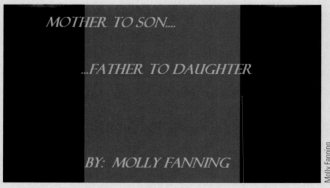

MOTHER TO SON....

...FATHER TO DAUGHTER

BY: MOLLY FANNING

Molly Fanning

[soft background music]

Narrator: Growing up, I have always been told that I take after my grandmother.

Source: Fanning, Molly. "Mother to Son, Father to Daughter." MP3. 2009.

1. What do you think is the main point of Fanning's story? What makes her story of her relationship with her father relevant to others who might not know her?

2. How does Fanning use conventional family photographs to help tell her story? What information or ideas does she convey through these photographs? How effectively does she use images to tell her story and convey her themes? Explain, citing specific images from her story in your answer.

3. How effectively does Fanning use design features, such as zooming and transitions? What do these features contribute to her story?

Common Ground

by Scott Strazzante

In this digital story, Scott Strazzante examines the impact of suburban sprawl on one family farm in Illinois, which is sold and then demolished to make room for a suburban housing development. Strazzante's story focuses on the experiences of two families, one of them the farmers who lost their farm, the other a young family who realizes their dream of owning their own home. Through these stories, Strazzante reveals the complexity of land development and the ways in which one person's loss is another's gain. His story invites viewers to confront difficult questions about how best to use the land.

"Common Ground" displays the full range of multimedia capabilities available to writers of digital stories. Strazzante uses photographs, subtitles, and music as well as video clips to tell the interconnected stories of these two families. His digital story is characterized by lengthy segments in which there is no voice-over narration. Notice, too, that Strazzante himself does not narrate this story. Instead, he uses the recorded voices of the two families to tell their stories and share their feelings about their situations. "Common Ground" was published by MediaStorm in 2008.

[piano music]

Scott Strazzante

Scott Strazzante

Scott Strazzante

18

Voice of Jean Cagwin: We're watching all the buildings going down.

Voice of Jean Cagwin: The house was the last thing to go down. Didn't take long.

Voice of Jean Cagwin: It was quite an emotional thing for Harold, because he lived there all his life.

Voice of Jean Cagwin: But we knew it was time.

Source: Strazzante, Scott. "Common Ground." Video. *MediaStorm*. Mediastorm, 29, July 2008. Web. 14 Sept. 2012.

18

1. This story focuses on two families. How would you summarize the main point of the story? How effectively does the story of these two families convey this point? Explain, citing specific sections of the story to support your answer.

2. This digital story contains lengthy segments without voice-over narration. During these segments, the viewer sees a series of still photographs and hears spare music—either a solo piano or guitar playing a stark melody. How does the juxtaposition of photographs during these segments highlight the main themes of the story? How effective do you find these segments?

3. The author of this story does not narrate it. Instead, he uses the voices of the people whose experiences he is sharing to tell their stories. Why do you think the author chose to take this approach? Do you find this approach effective in conveying these stories? Why or why not? Would the story be more or less effective if the author narrated it instead? Explain.

Creating Digital Stories

This section will guide you through the process of creating a digital story. Read this section together with Chapter 3. Each step described here corresponds with a step in Chapter 3. As you work through this section, keep in mind that the principles of effective narrative described in Chapter 15 apply to digital stories. Also, if your digital story is a personal narrative, review the advice on Chapter 16; if your digital story is an informative narrative, review Chapter 17.

Step 1   Identify a topic.

Like any effective narrative, a digital story tells a story that matters. Your story should be important to you but also relevant to your audience. To identify a topic for your digital story, consider:

- an **experience** that was significant to you in some way
- an **issue** that connects to your experience in some way
- an **activity** or **subject** about which you are knowledgeable or have direct experience

Explore each of these categories:

A significant experience

- A milestone (e.g., graduating from high school, getting married)
- An accomplishment (e.g., winning a scholarship, earning academic honors, running in a marathon)
- A difficult challenge (e.g., moving away from home, losing a loved one, completing basic training in the military)
- A mistake (e.g., violating a rule or a law, cheating, misjudging someone)
- An activity (e.g., singing, hunting, rock climbing, running, rapping, gaming)
- A transition or turning point (e.g., going to college, moving abroad, joining the military, coming of age)
- A decision (e.g., whether to take or quit a job, choosing a college, whether to tell someone a difficult truth)

An issue that interests you

- A controversy (e.g., gun control: you might be involved in an effort to oppose arming your campus police force; a relative might have law enforcement experience; you might be a hunter)
- An activity (e.g., gaming: you might be an avid gamer who is concerned about efforts to restrict the distribution of some violent video games; you might have won a gaming competition)
- Advocacy (e.g., privacy: you might have concerns about how your private data are being used online without your knowledge or permission; you might have been the victim of identity theft)
- A trend (e.g., social media: you might be interested in the growth of a specific kind of social media that you regularly use; you might have had an unusual experience using social media)

Something you know about

- A hobby (e.g., playing drums, photography, gardening)
- A challenge that others have faced (e.g., divorce, losing a job)
- An experience that raised questions for you (e.g., an unfamiliar medical condition that someone you know developed, a cheating scandal at your school)
- A topic you have expertise in (e.g., politics, sports, skateboarding)
- An important decision that others might share (e.g., going to college, joining the Peace Corps)

■ **Make a brief list of possible topics in each category.** For each item, jot down a few sentences about the topic, describing the nature of your experience, what you already know about the topic, and what interests you about it. For example, if you had an enlightening experience on a church-sponsored trip, briefly describe the trip and what made it important to you. If you are a photographer, perhaps you had a specific experience in which photography helped you gain insight into yourself or someone else.

- **Select the topic that seems most promising to you.** Review your lists and select the experience that you would most like to share in a digital story. Remember that your digital story is likely to be more engaging for an audience if it tells a story that has significance for you.

Step #1 in Chapter 3 will help you further develop your topic.

Step 2 | Place your topic in rhetorical context.

Many digital stories have wide appeal and are not necessarily intended for a specific audience. A story about struggling with one's identity, such as Nazbah Tom's, is likely to interest many people. At the same time, a story that focuses on a more specialized topic—such as competing in a motocross championship—might best be directed at a more specialized audience that shares an interest in that topic. Whatever the case, it is important to have a sense of an audience for your digital story and why your story might interest that audience. So at this point your task is twofold:

- identify a potential audience for your digital story
- consider why your story would interest that audience

Let's imagine that you want to tell a story about learning how to play banjo from your grandfather. From a young age, you spent many hours with him as he helped you learn the intricacies of the instrument and perfect your technique as a banjo player. Eventually you developed into a capable musician, and in your grandfather's later years, you played with him at several public events, such as county fairs. During that time, you learned some things about your grandfather and your family's history that you had not known before. In the process, you came to understand your grandfather—and yourself—more deeply. So your story not only involves the challenge of learning to play banjo but also explores your relationship with your family and your own sense of identity. Now consider who might be interested in your story.

Who might be interested in this topic?	• Banjo players • Musicians • People interested in music • Readers interested in matters of family history • Anyone interested in stories of coming of age
Why would they be interested in this topic?	• Musicians might be curious about how you learned to play and the role of the banjo in your life. • Your story has general appeal because of its focus on family history and personal identity.

Such a topic has broad appeal and would likely interest a potentially wide audience, including people who are not musicians. Notice that what is potentially engaging for an audience are the themes you might explore through your story. In other words, what makes the experience important to you—not only developing expertise as a musician but also gaining a deeper appreciation for your grandfather and yourself—is what will make it relevant for your audience. In this sense, the point of your story—not necessarily the specific subject matter—is what really matters.

With this in mind, explore your topic using these two questions to identify a potential audience and the themes that might engage that audience. Then complete Step #2 in Chapter 3 to explore your rhetorical context more fully.

Step 3 Select a medium.

You have already selected the medium for your story, but you should consider how your finished digital story will reach your intended audience. If you are completing a course assignment, your instructor will likely have a way for you to submit and distribute your digital story. If so, follow those instructions. However, if you have no such guidelines, consider the possible forums for distributing your digital story:

- **YouTube.** This site is perhaps the most common vehicle by which people distribute videos, including digital stories. Many organizations now have their own YouTube channels (e.g., the Center for Digital Storytelling), and depending upon the nature of your story, one of those channels might be an appropriate venue for your story.

- **Social media.** Many people post videos and other multimedia files on Facebook, Flickr, and similar social media sites. You might consider distributing your digital story on such a site, either through your own page or by posting it to the page of an appropriate organization. For example, our hypothetical story about learning to play the banjo might be posted to the social media site of a relevant organization such as the American Roots Music Association.

- **Organization websites.** Many organizations include member forums for posting comments, stories, and multimedia files. Consider whether an organization focused on issues or subjects related to the topic of your story might be a good place to post it.

Although you have already selected the medium for your project, Step #3 in Chapter 3 will provide additional help as you consider an appropriate venue for your digital story.

Step 4 Identify the main point of your digital story.

What do you want your digital story to say to your audience? That's the question you have to address at this point.

Begin by stating as clearly as you can the main ideas you want your audience to take away from your story. Try to capture these ideas in a brief paragraph. For example, in our hypothetical story about learning to play banjo from your grandfather, you might explore several themes involving relationships, family, and identity; you are also telling a story about meeting a challenge and dedicating yourself to developing a skill—that is, about perseverance and commitment. You might articulate these main ideas as follows:

This is a story about the importance of a precious family relationship in shaping my sense of identity and teaching me important lessons about dedication and persistence in meeting challenges, whether those challenges have to do with learning a skill such as playing the banjo or overcoming difficulties in life. It is also a story about confronting some unpleasant realities about my own family but ultimately coming to appreciate the importance of my family, especially my grandfather, in my life.

This statement can serve as your Guiding Thesis Statement and help you keep your story focused. However, be careful to avoid oversimplifying your experience by trying to boil it down into a brief statement. Part of the purpose of narrative is to explore the complexity of an experience and make sense of it. The meaning of your story should reflect the richness of your experience and complexity of the themes you are exploring by telling your story. So keep these caveats in mind:

- **Your Guiding Thesis Statement should guide but not restrict you.** A Guiding Thesis Statement expresses the main ideas of your story, but you are still exploring your experience. Remain open to possibilities, keeping in mind that you are composing a digital narrative in part to understand your experience better. In writing about learning banjo from your grandfather, for example, you might discover feelings about your relationship that you weren't entirely aware of. You might remember parts of the experience that were important but not entirely positive. Exploring those aspects of the experience might shape your perspective and thus affect the meaning you convey to your audience. In short, your main ideas could change as you develop your story. Be alert to such possibilities, even if they take you in a different direction from the one reflected in your Guiding Thesis Statement.

- **Your Guiding Thesis Statement might change.** The more you explore your topic, the more you will learn about it, which might lead you to change the main point of your story. If so, adjust your Guiding Thesis Statement accordingly. Revise it as often as you need to as you are exploring your experience and developing your story.

Following this advice will help you develop a clearer idea of the main ideas you want to convey through your story. Step #4 in Chapter 3 provides additional help for developing your Guiding Thesis Statement.

Step 5 Support your main point.

Although we don't usually think about "supporting" the main point of a personal narrative in the same way that we support claims in an argument, in an analysis, or in an informative essay, effective narratives include descriptions of events, background information, and explanations of important ideas or occurrences that help the audience understand the story. Everything you include in your digital story—images and sound as well as text—should somehow contribute to telling your story effectively and conveying your main ideas to your audience. The task now is to make sure you have explored your experience sufficiently to develop the material you need to tell your story effectively. Doing so involves three main steps:

- identify what should be included in your digital story
- gather additional information
- develop multimedia components

Identify What Should Be Included in Your Digital Story

Review your discovery draft (see Chapter 3), notes, and other materials to determine whether you have included the essential information, scenes, events, and moments to convey your experience sufficiently to your readers. Address these questions:

- **What specific events or moments must be included for a reader to understand what happened?** For example, in your hypothetical essay about learning to play banjo from your grandfather, you will likely include information about him, his banjo playing, and your own experience learning to play. You will also want to include relevant background information about your family as well as about your relationship with your grandfather. You might have experienced a particular challenge in developing the skill of banjo playing, or perhaps a specific event, such as a divorce or illness, affected your relationship in some way. Using your Guiding Thesis Statement to remind you of the main ideas you want to explore in your story, make note of any important and relevant scenes, events, and related information. The goal is to identify anything about your experience that is essential for readers to know.

- **What background information will readers need to understand the experience described in the story?** What else will your readers need to know that isn't directly a part of the experience you are describing? For example, will you need to explain anything about the banjo or the skill of playing it that is necessary for readers to understand your story? Consider anything that is essential for readers to know in order to understand the experience you are sharing.

At this stage, more is better, so if you're not sure about something, include it. Don't worry if your story seems to be getting too long. You can eliminate unnecessary material when you revise.

Gather Additional Information

Review your materials to determine whether you need additional information. Depending upon your topic, you might have to do some research. For example, in your hypothetical essay about learning to play the banjo, you might want to look into the history of the instrument because that was something your grandfather emphasized in learning to play. Or you might have to find out more about your grandfather's life—for example, what he did for a living as a young adult, how he learned to play banjo, and so on. Use appropriate resources to gather necessary information. (Chapters 21 and 22 provide advice for identifying and evaluating source material.)

Develop Multimedia Components

By now you have probably identified some photographs, videos, or related materials that are relevant to your story. You might also have music or other sound effects in mind. At this point, you should focus on finding the images and sound to help you tell the story of your experience. In many cases, that might mean looking through old family photo albums, searching computer files for digital images, or reviewing videos you or others might have made. You can also search online for images you might need. (See "Intellectual Property Considerations.") Some computer programs for digital storytelling include archives of images and sounds that you can use for your story. You might decide to make new photos, videos, or sound recordings for your digital story. The goal is to gather still and video images as well as music or sound clips that will enable you to tell your story effectively.

Again, more is better. If you find several photos of your grandfather as a young man, for example, but you only need one, keep all of them until you decide which one works best in your story. Try to find images for each of the main events, moments, or aspects of your experience that you identified in Step #1.

You should be now ready to complete a draft of the text of your digital story. If so, write a draft of your story in textual form. You will use this draft as the basis for your storyboard in Step #6. Write as complete a draft as possible, following these guidelines:

- **Tell the whole story.** Include in your draft everything that is relevant. Incorporate all the material you have developed for this step. If something feels unnecessary, leave it out, but if you're not sure, keep it for now.

- **Don't worry about length.** You can condense and eliminate unnecessary materials during Step #8.

- **Write the story, not the voice-over narration.** The story draft is not necessarily the same thing as the voice-over narration. Eventually, you can use your draft as the basis for the narration, but for now, just tell your story as completely as you can.

- **Don't focus yet on images and sound.** As you write your draft, consider places for appropriate images or sound, but don't focus on those components yet. Rather, focus on telling your story completely and clearly. You will incorporate images and sound in the next step. At the same time, if an image seems especially important at a particular point in your draft, make a note about it at that point in the draft.

Step #5 in Chapter 3 provides additional advice to help you develop your project. Some writers prefer to "draft" their digital stories as a storyboard rather than writing a text of the story. If that approach works better for you, move to Step #6 before writing a draft of your story.

Step 6 Organize your digital story.

Organizing your digital story involves two main steps:

- organizing the narrative itself
- developing a storyboard

Here we will concentrate on developing a storyboard. For guidance in organizing your story, see "Organizing Your Narrative" in Chapter 15. (If your digital story does not focus on a specific personal experience but is an informative narrative, see "Organizing Your Informative Project" in Chapter 17.)

Most digital stories tend to be organized chronologically. All three digital stories in the previous section of this chapter, for example, are organized chronologically, though "Common Ground" does not always follow a strict chronological order. However, you can tell your story in any order that you think will make it engaging and accessible for your audience. If you have already written a draft of your story, review the draft to make sure you have organized your story in a way that conveys your experience clearly. (Step #6 in Chapter 3 can help you do so.)

Once you have decided how to organize your narrative, develop a storyboard. As noted earlier in this chapter, a storyboard is a kind of outline of your digital story that includes information about images, sound, special effects, and the voice-over narration (see pages 594–596):

- **If you have already written a draft of your story,** use your draft as the basis for an outline of your digital story.

- **If you have not written a draft of your story,** develop a detailed outline of your story.

Then follow this process to create a storyboard:

Create an outline		Convert outline to single frames		Add images, sound, and narration
• Make a detailed outline of your story. • Include each important scene, moment, or event. • Include background information.	⇒	• Create a single frame for each heading and subheading in your outline.	⇒	• For each frame, include an image. • Indicate background sound (for entire story or individual frames). • Write voice-over narration for each frame.

Once you have mapped out your digital story in a completed storyboard, you can add special effects: zooming, transitions, subtitles, colors.

For example, here's what the process might look like in our hypothetical digital story about learning to play banjo from your grandfather. Remember that your story explores themes of family identity, relationships, and important life lessons as well as developing the skill of playing a banjo.

The first few headings of your detailed outline might include the following:

I. Introduction

    A. Anecdote about playing banjo with your grandfather at a local fair

    B. Statement of the importance of your relationship with your grandfather

    C. Hint that learning to play banjo with your grandfather included difficult life lessons

II. Background About You and Your Family

    A. Basic information about your immediate family

        1. Family members

        2. Where you live

        3. Information about you

    B. Background information about your grandfather

        1. Biographical information about him (when and where he was born, where he lived, his working life)

        2. Information about his banjo playing

III. Learning to Play Banjo

    A. How you began learning banjo from your grandfather

    B. Difficulties learning to play

        1. Anecdote about wanting to quit

        2. Anecdote about learning difficult scales

Here's what the first headings in Part I of the outline might look like as frames:

Frame #1: Anecdote about playing banjo with your grandfather at a local fair

Frame #2: Statement of the importance of your relationship with your grandfather

Frame #3: Hint that learning to play banjo with your grandfather included difficult life lessons

Continue in this fashion until you have a separate frame for each subheading.

Using your word processing program or digital storytelling software, add information about images, sound, and the voice-over narration for each frame:

Frame #1	Frame #2	Frame #3
Image: photo of you and your grandfather playing banjo at a fair Audio: banjo music (maybe a song you both liked) Narration: "A few years ago, I had the great joy of playing banjo with my grandfather in front of family, friends, and neighbors at a county fair. It was one of the last times we would play together, and it was a long journey to get there."	Image: earlier photo of your grandfather showing you how to play a banjo Audio: slower banjo music Narration: "My grandfather taught me to play banjo when I was just seven years old. He taught me how to master the instrument, how to work hard to perfect my technique. He gave me the gift of his love for the banjo."	Image: same as frame #2 Audio: same as frame #2 Narration: "But I learned a lot more than how to play the banjo from my grandfather. I learned many important life lessons. And not all of them were happy ones."

Proceed in this way to the end of your story. Once you have mapped out the story, add special effects to complete the storyboard. For example, for frame #3 in this example, you might zoom in your grandfather's face to emphasize the point in the narration that you learned a lot of lessons from your grandfather.

As you develop your storyboard, you will likely discover a need to add or eliminate material and make adjustments so that your narration works together with the images and sound to tell your story. Don't hesitate to make such adjustments. It's part of the process of developing and refining your digital story. However, at this point, don't worry too much about length. You will revise your digital story in Step #8, at which point you can condense it if necessary. Step #6 in Chapter 3 provides additional guidance for organizing your project.

Once you have completed your storyboard, you can begin creating your digital story using the software you have selected (see "Software for Digital Storytelling").

18

Step 7   Get feedback.

Show your digital story to a few trusted friends or classmates for their feedback. Ask them to focus on the key features of effective digital storytelling:

A story that matters	• How effectively does your digital story convey the experience you are telling about? • Does the story communicate a main idea or point that is relevant to your audience? Does it sufficiently explore your main themes? • Is the story complete? Is it too long or too short?
Images and sound	• How do the images you've selected contribute to the story? Are they sufficient? Are there too many? • Does the sound enhance or detract from the main point of this story? • How effectively does the narration combine with the images to tell your story?
Design	• To what extent do the design features you've incorporated contribute to the story? Are they effective? • In what ways do these design features enhance or detract from your experience of this story? • Should any special effects be added or eliminated to enhance the quality of the story?

Step #7 in Chapter 3 provides advice for analyzing your feedback and deciding on possible changes to make to your digital story.

Step 8   Revise.

Revising your digital story draft involves addressing **two main concerns:**

Narrative	How well have you told your story?	Review your narrative.
Technical	How effectively have you used multimedia?	Evaluate your use of images, sound, and effects.

Narrative: Review Your Story Using the First Set of Questions from Step #7

- How effectively does your story convey the experience you are telling about?
- Does the story convey a main idea or point that is relevant to your audience?
- Does the story sufficiently explore important themes?
- Is the story complete? Is it too long or too short?
- Is the story well organized? Are the frames in the proper order to tell the story clearly?

In addition, address the following considerations:

- **Review the feedback** you received to determine whether any sections of the story are confusing, incomplete, or unnecessary.
- **Make sure every frame contributes** important information or ideas.
- **Evaluate your opening frames** to make sure they engage your audience and introduce your story effectively.
- **Review your final frame** to see whether it reinforces your main ideas and leaves an impression on your audience.

Technical: Review Your Story Using the Second and Third Set of Questions in Step #7

- **Images:** Do the photographs, video, and other images you've selected contribute to the story? Do they effectively convey the information, ideas, and feelings you intend? Are there unnecessary images that should be eliminated? Can any images be replaced with more effective ones?
- **Sound:** Does the background music enhance the story and reinforce important information, ideas, or emotions? Does it establish an appropriate mood for your story? Do the sound effects fit the story and help move it along?
- **Narration:** How effectively does the voice-over narration combine with the images to tell your story? Is the narration too wordy or too sparse? Is it clear? Is the tone of the narrator's voice appropriate for the story in each frame?
- **Design:** Are the transitions effective? Do they distract the viewer? If you have used subtitles, are they clear? Are they necessary? If you haven't, do you need them in any frames? Do any background colors or patterns you've used enhance the story?

Review each frame using these questions.

Step #8 in Chapter 3 provides additional guidance for revising your digital story.

Step 9   Refine your voice.

"Voice" can refer to two separate but related aspects of a digital story:

- the voice of the narrative itself (as explained in Chapter 2; see page 52)
- the tone of the voice-over narration

Unlike voice in a conventional print narrative, which is conveyed exclusively through the words of the narrative, voice in a digital story is a combination of the narrative text, the images, and the sound as well as the tone of the voice-over narration. For example, the voice in Nazbah Tom's digital story included in this chapter (page 601) is created not only by the words of her narrative text but also by the photos she selected of Mount Hesperus, her family, and her partner. Scott Strazzante's digital story (page 606) has no voice-over narration. Instead, it includes the voices of the two families whose stories he tells as well as the piano and guitar music that plays while photographs are displayed. In that case, the music he selects helps establish the "voice" of the digital story.

To help determine whether your voice is appropriate for your project, consider these questions:

Text	• Does the text of your voice-over narration fit your story? • Are your word choices appropriate for the subject of each frame? • Does the text "sound" right for the experience you are conveying?
Images	• Do the photographs, video clips, or other images help convey the right tone for your story? • Are the images consistent in contributing to the voice of your digital story? • Are any images out of place?
Sound	• Does the background music help create an appropriate mood for your story? • Are the sound effects consistent with the voice you want to create? • Is the tone of the voice-over narration appropriate?
Design	• Do the specials effects (zooming, transition, etc.) help create an appropriate voice for your story? • Are the background colors and patterns consistent with the voice?

Complete Step #9 in Chapter 3 for additional guidance in refining your voice.

Step 10 Edit.

Complete Step #10 in Chapter 3.

WRITING PROJECTS   DIGITAL STORIES

1. Identify an experience you have had that has shaped you into the person you are today. Create a digital story in which you share that experience.

2. Take a personal narrative or an informative essay you have written and turn it into a digital story.

3. Identify a general issue of interest to you. It could be an ongoing controversy, a subject of current interest, or something that you have always been curious about. Create a digital story in which you explore that issue. Incorporate any experiences you have had that are relevant to your topic.

4. Create a digital story about an important person in your life. If possible, focus your story on a particular aspect or event involving that person (as Christi Clancy does in her digital story about her mother, which appears in this chapter).

Working with Ideas and Information 19

BY THE TIME they enter college, most students have developed the ability to write grammatically correct sentences, use proper punctuation, form verb tenses appropriately, spell correctly, and so on. Of course, *all* students, even the most successful writers, make mistakes and sometimes have trouble remembering certain rules of formal writing (such as when to use a semi-colon rather than a comma). But for the vast majority of students, learning to write effectively in college is not about learning these "basics." For most students, the main challenge is learning to write effectively in an appropriate academic style and conveying complex ideas and information clearly in the kind of authoritative voice that college instructors expect—in other words, learning to write like a scholar. And that means learning some strategies and skills that are essential for effective academic writing.

This chapter will help you learn essential stylistic strategies and develop key skills necessary to write the kind of prose expected in academic settings. These strategies and skills, which will enable you to convey complex ideas clearly without oversimplifying the subject matter, correspond to the Ten Core Concepts described in Chapter 2. For example, in most academic writing, supporting claims or assertions (Core Concept #5) requires *summarizing* the ideas or arguments of others, *quoting* from other texts, and *citing* appropriate sources. If you can't do these tasks well, your writing is likely to be less effective, no matter how compelling your point or how sound your ideas. Summarizing accurately and strategically, quoting appropriately, and citing sources properly not only enable you to convey your ideas clearly to your audience but also contribute to a strong, authoritative voice and help establish your credibility as a writer.

These skills and strategies are integral to the process of discovery and learning that academic writing should be (see Core Concept #1):

- developing an academic writing style
- writing effective paragraphs
- summarizing and paraphrasing
- synthesizing
- framing
- introducing
- making transitions

The more effectively you apply these skills, the more you are likely to learn from your writing—and the better your writing is likely to be.

Developing an Academic Writing Style

A few years ago, my son, who was a first-year college student at the time, complained to me about a comment a professor had written on his paper in a political science class. The assignment required students to use a certain theory to analyze a recent political event. My son was keenly interested in the topic, had read the assigned readings carefully, and understood the theory, but he had very little experience writing about such specialized topics. He tried his best to write prose that sounded like the scholarly articles he had been assigned to read. In other words, he tried to write like a scholar of political science. He worked hard on the paper and was confident that his analysis was sound. His professor agreed but nevertheless criticized the paper, calling it a parody of bad academic writing. In the professor's view, there was nothing wrong with the analysis my son had written; the problem was with *how* it had been written.

In trying to write like a scholar, my son was using unfamiliar language in a style he had not yet mastered. The professor's comment that the paper sounded like a parody of bad academic writing was unfortunate, but in a sense it was accurate. My son had not yet developed the skills a writer needs to write in an appropriate academic style about such a sophisticated topic. So it was inevitable that he would make some mistakes. After all, like just about every new college student, he was on unfamiliar terrain. Although he knew the material, he didn't have the tools to write about that material effectively in appropriate academic style.

Learning to Write Like a Scholar

My son was like a novice skier trying to descend an expert slope for the first time: the novice knows how to ski, but his skills are not developed enough to tackle the more challenging slopes. So, although he can descend an easy slope with smooth, controlled turns, on the expert slope his turns are sloppy, he loses control now and again, and he looks like a complete beginner. My son was venturing onto the expert slopes of a challenging kind of academic analytical writing without the experience and skill to negotiate that slope smoothly; as a result, his prose was full of sloppy turns and slightly out-of-control sentences.

This story underscores three important lessons for effective academic writing:

- *How* **you write affects** *what* **you write.** To complete most academic writing tasks success-fully requires more than having something relevant to say (Core Concept #4); it also requires saying it well. In academic writing, that means adopting an appropriate style and presenting your ideas in a way that meets the expectations of an academic audience. Academic audiences expect writers to know how to summarize relevant information and other points of view, to quote properly from appropriate sources, to synthesize ideas clearly, to write coherent paragraphs about complicated subject matter, and to place their arguments or analyses in the context of the larger academic subject within which they are writing.

- **Good writing isn't necessarily always good writing.** Core Concept #2 ("Good writing fits the context") reminds us that what counts as good writing always depends upon the rhetorical situation. In college-level academic writing, students must learn to fit into the ongoing conversations about the subjects that are the focus of the academic disciplines they are studying. Sociologists examine how human societies function. Anthropologists explore culture. Biologists describe the living world. Scholars and researchers in every field engage in continuous conversations about specialized topics by reporting the results of their studies, proposing hypotheses, debating conclusions, and raising questions. This is the nature of academic discourse, and students must eventually learn to write in ways that enable them to become part of that discourse. Good academic writing is writing that fits into the relevant academic conversation.

- **Practice might make perfect, but it also means making mistakes.** My son was trying to write like a scholar without yet having mastered the skills of scholarly writing. So he made mistakes. His professor did not recognize that those mistakes were actually a sign of growth. My son was stretching just beyond his ability as a writer, and ultimately he learned from those mistakes, in the process gaining valuable experience and insight into academic writing. Like the novice skier trying to ski down the expert slope, my son was advancing his skills by challenging himself to go beyond his present level of ability. Through practice, he eventually acquired those skills and was able to write effective academic prose—but not without first making mistakes. Just like that skier, when you try to do something that is beyond your skill level, you'll stumble and fall, but by practicing you will eventually master the necessary skills and avoid those early mistakes. You'll make it down the expert slope smoothly. So expect some stumbling as you develop the specialized skills described in this chapter. If you struggle, it doesn't mean you're a "bad" writer; it just means you haven't yet developed the specialized skills needed to write effective academic prose.

Keep these lessons in mind as you work on your writing assignments. These lessons will help you keep your mistakes in perspective, understand and build on your strengths, and identify aspects of your writing that need improvement.

Principles of Academic Inquiry

The conventions of academic writing reflect the fact that writing is central to academic inquiry. Developing an effective academic writing style is partly a matter of learning to use language in a way that reflects the basic principles of academic inquiry.

- **Qualify your statements.** Academic writers must back up what they say (Core Concept #5). Often, that means avoiding unsupported generalizations and qualifying your statements. For example, in casual conversation or informal writing, it's acceptable to say something like this:

  > Drivers just don't pay attention to speed limits.

  In academic writing, which values accuracy and validity, such statements usually need to be qualified, depending on the rhetorical context:

19

Drivers *often* seem to ignore speed limits.

Many drivers ignore speed limits.

Studies show that *most* drivers *sometimes* exceed speed limits.

The italicized words in these examples make the statements more "true." If you can't support a statement with evidence, then qualify it so that it is valid.

- **Be specific.** Academic audiences value specificity, and good writers avoid vagueness. Here's an example of a vague statement from a student essay:

In order for education to work, things need to change.

Such a statement seems reasonable enough, but it doesn't quite hold up under scrutiny. What does it mean to say that education must "work"? What "things" must change? And what kinds of "changes" are necessary? Often, vague terms like *things* are a sign that a statement itself might be vague. Even if this statement appears in a longer paragraph explaining those "things" and "changes," such a statement is weak by the common standards of academic writing. We might revise it as follows:

If schools are to solve the problems that prevent students from obtaining a sound education, several reforms should be implemented.

Notice that in this statement the writer avoids vague terms and tries to be more specific about what it means for schools to "work." Specificity isn't always possible or even desirable, but often vagueness can weaken your writing. (By the way, you'll notice that the revised sentence employs the passive voice, which many teachers discourage. See "Active vs. Passive Voice" on page 630.)

These examples illustrate that strong academic writing is partly a result of careful word choice, which should reflect your effort to make valid, accurate, and clear statements.

- **Give credit.** Giving credit in academic writing is not just a matter of citing sources properly (which is discussed in Chapters 23–25); it is also a matter of using appropriate language to signal to readers that you are using source material or referring to someone else's ideas. For example, here's a student referring to a source in a paper about education reform:

The article states that money spent on schools can do little to improve educational outcomes.

Technically, there is nothing wrong with this sentence, but it is an awkward way of introducing information or referring to material taken from a source. For one thing, it isn't the article but the author who makes a statement. That might seem to be a minor point, but minor revisions can make this sentence stronger by bringing it into line with the conventions of academic writing:

The author claims that money spent on schools can do little to improve educational outcomes.

According to this author, money spent on schools can do little to improve educational outcomes.

These versions make it clear that the assertion being made is attributed to the author, not to the writer of this sentence.

In general, unless the assertion is yours, credit the author or source for the assertion. Because academic writing is essentially a matter of participating in ongoing conversations, crediting a source for a statement not only indicates to a reader who deserves credit for the statement but also helps place your own writing in the context of the larger academic conversation in which you are participating. It shows that you are part of that conversation.

■ **Use specialized terminology judiciously.** A common complaint about academic writing is that it is full of jargon. The complaint assumes that jargon is bad; however, when used properly, jargon—or specialized terminology—is not only useful but essential. All academic fields have specialized terminology that refers to important ideas and concepts within those fields. In education, for example, *pedagogy* refers to a teacher's instructional approach and the beliefs about teaching, learning, and knowing that inform that approach. It would be difficult to convey that concept efficiently and clearly without that term. Equivalent terms using common language, such as *instructional approach* or *teaching technique*, don't quite capture the complexity of the concept. In such a case, *pedagogy* is an efficient term that conveys important ideas to readers and reflects the writer's familiarity with the field. The challenge for student writers is to become familiar enough with such terminology so that it becomes a tool for effective writing.

In the following passage, for example, the writer discusses the increasing socio-economic inequality in higher education:

> At the same time that family income has become more predictive of children's academic achievement, so has educational attainment become more predictive of adults' earnings. The combination of these trends creates a feedback mechanism that may decrease intergenerational mobility. As children from higher socio-economic strata achieve greater academic success, and those who succeed academically are more likely to have higher incomes, higher education contributes to an even more unequal and economically polarized society.

This passage contains terms that are widely used in academic discussions about poverty, education, and education reform: for example, *academic achievement* and *intergenerational mobility*. These terms have specialized meaning in fields like sociology, education, political science, and public policy and therefore can be useful for writers in those fields. Not only do these terms convey important ideas efficiently to a reader, but they also signal that the writer is knowledgeable about the subject. At the same time, such terminology can make a passage dense and difficult to follow. Some careful revisions (which are highlighted) to reduce wordiness can make the passage clearer without eliminating necessary terms:

> At the same time that family income has become more predictive of children's academic achievement, so has educational attainment become more predictive of adults' earnings. The combination of these trends could decrease intergenerational mobility. As the children of the rich do better in school, and those who do better in school are more likely to become rich, we risk producing an even more unequal and economically polarized society. (Adapted from Edsall, Thomas. "The Reproduction of Privilege." *New York Times* 12 Mar. 2012. Web. 27 July 2012.)

19

In this revised version, some jargon (e.g., *higher socio-economic strata, greater academic success*) is replaced with more common language (*rich, do better in school*), but key terms (*academic achievement* and *intergenerational mobility*) are preserved. Replacing those key terms with common language would result in a lengthy passage that might not be clearer. For example, *intergenerational mobility* refers to the process by which children do better economically than their parents; in other words, children attain a higher socio-economic status than their parents. Explaining that idea in a sentence or two would unnecessarily lengthen the passage. If this passage were intended for a general audience, then it might be necessary to define the term or replace it entirely; for an academic audience, however, the term enables the writer to keep the passage shorter while at the same time making an important point.

The rule of thumb is to use language that communicates your ideas clearly to your intended audience:

- Use appropriate terminology to communicate specialized ideas, but make sure you understand the terminology.

- Replace confusing terms or unnecessary jargon with common words if you can do so without undermining your point or changing the meaning of the passage.

Following these guidelines will help you write prose that is both clear and sophisticated.

FOCUS **Active vs. Passive Voice**

It is a common dictum to avoid the passive voice and use active voice in writing. The prevailing belief is that using the active voice strengthens your prose, whereas the passive voice weakens your writing by making it unnecessarily wordy and vague. Like most such "rules," this one is misleading. Remember Core Concept #2: "Good writing fits the context." Although it might be true that in many contexts the active voice makes for better writing, the passive voice is not only acceptable but also essential in academic writing. In some cases, the passive voice is actually preferable because it can change the focus of a statement to emphasize a point or idea. To illustrate, let's return to the example on page 628:

> If schools are to solve the problems that prevent students from obtaining a sound education, several reforms should be implemented.

The main point of this sentence is that school reform is needed. Notice that in the main clause (*several reforms should be implemented*), which is in the passive voice, the emphasis is on *reforms* (which is the subject of the clause). Revising the sentence to place the main clause in the active voice changes that emphasis. Here's how that sentence might look in the active voice:

> If schools are to solve the problems that prevent students from obtaining a sound education, they should implement several reforms.

Is this version clearer, more succinct, or more valid than the original sentence? Not necessarily. Notice that in the revised version the subject of the main clause is now *they* (presumably referring back to *schools*), which shifts the emphasis of the statement. But who exactly is "they"? School reform involves a lot of different people and institutions: teachers, administrators, school districts, government agencies, consultants, voters, politicians. Does "they" refer to all of these? Some of these? It isn't clear. In this regard, the passive voice enables the writer to keep the emphasis on the need for school reform—which is the main point of the sentence—not on *who* will accomplish the reform—which is an important and related topic but not the issue here. So the use of passive voice in this example does not weaken the writing but allows the writer to maintain the appropriate focus. If the writer's focus happened to be on a specific entity responsible for education reform, the active voice might be more appropriate. For example, let's assume that the writer was discussing reforms that only elected politicians could enact. In that case, the subject would be clear and the active voice more appropriate:

> If schools are to solve the problems that prevent students from obtaining a sound education, elected officials should undertake several reforms.

The passive voice should be used judiciously. Overuse or inappropriate use of the passive voice can weaken your writing. Usually, active voice results in more concise prose, but as this example illustrates, writers can use the passive voice as an important tool for emphasis and clarity.

EXERCISE 19A   PRACTICING ACADEMIC STYLE

Using the advice for academic writing style in this section, revise the following statements so that they are clearer and appropriately supported or qualified. For each item, imagine an appropriate rhetorical context and indicate how that context would shape your revisions. (For example, you might imagine the first statement in an argument supporting gun control for a criminal justice course.)

- We need better gun laws to make our communities safer. Otherwise, we'll just have more and more violence.

- Poverty-stricken Americans of low socio-economic status will be adversely affected by legislative actions that facilitate the attainment of citizenship by undocumented residents.

- Smartphones are convenient, but they are making everyone dumber because people rely on them rather than on their own minds.

19

Writing Paragraphs

By the time they enter college, most students have had many hours of instruction in writing correct sentences and paragraphs. Yet new college students often struggle to write effective paragraphs that convey complex ideas clearly and coherently. Part of the problem is that the subject matter in college writing is often new and challenging, and students have to learn how to write clearly about unfamiliar ideas, concepts, and information. But students can also improve their writing by learning how to create more effective paragraphs, no matter what subject they are writing about.

Effective paragraphs in academic writing have three key characteristics. They are:

- **Well developed.** A paragraph should cover its topic sufficiently. Often, that means elaborating on key points, ideas, or facts and including examples. Under-developed paragraphs tend to be superficial and suggest that the writer has not explored the topic in sufficient depth.

- **Coherent.** Coherence refers to the extent to which the paragraph retains a focus on a main idea or point. In a coherent paragraph, all the sentences relate clearly to one another and communicate ideas or information relevant to the main point. Usually, but not always, a strong paragraph also has a clear topic sentence that states the main point and establishes the focus of the paragraph.

- **Cohesive.** Cohesion means that the statements, ideas, and information in a paragraph are explicitly linked together. To a great extent, cohesion is a function of the use of specific words and phrases that indicate to a reader that statements are connected: *similarly, by contrast, also, therefore, on the other hand, moreover, in addition,* and so on. Writers also achieve cohesion by repeating key words or phrases.

Writing Well-Developed Paragraphs

The key to writing a well-developed paragraph is making sure the topic of the paragraph is sufficiently explained or examined and the main point adequately supported. When necessary, elaborating on a point and illustrating it with examples also contribute to paragraph development. Here's an example of an under-developed paragraph from an essay about the relationship between poverty and educational achievement:

> The culture of poverty is defined by Paul Gorski as "the idea that poor people share more or less monolithic and predictable beliefs, values and behavior" (32). This is not true. Later studies show that a culture of poverty does not exist. This belief was constructed from data collected in the early 1960s showing that certain behaviors, such as increased violence and failure to foresee or plan for the future, were common among poor people. The original study portrayed stereotypes of poor students, not a culture of poverty.

In this paragraph the student tries to explain the idea of "the culture of poverty," relying on a source for information about the origins of that idea and how it has been interpreted. The author of that source, Paul Gorski, argues that the idea of a culture of poverty is actually a misunderstanding of a particular study of poverty; he cites subsequent studies that invalidate the whole idea of a culture of poverty. In this paragraph, the student attempts to communicate Gorski's position. However, although the student defines the term *culture of poverty*, the problems associated with that idea are not sufficiently explained. The student states simply that the idea "is not true" and that studies show it "does not exist," but the lack of explanation makes it difficult for readers to understand the problems with the original study and how the data were interpreted. In short, the paragraph does not communicate this complicated information well.

In situations like this one, in which the writer is trying to convey complex ideas and information in a single paragraph, the solution is to elaborate on key ideas. In this case, the student must provide more information about the origins of the idea of the culture of poverty, how it was misinterpreted, and how it was invalidated:

> The culture of poverty, according to Paul Gorski, is "the idea that poor people share more or less monolithic and predictable beliefs, values and behavior" (32). The idea emerged from a 1961 book by Oscar Lewis that reported on ethnographic studies of several small poor Mexican communities. Lewis's data indicated that those communities shared fifty attributes, such as frequent violence and a failure to plan for the future. From this small sample, he concluded that all poor communities share these attributes, which reflect a culture of poverty. The idea that "people in poverty share a persistent and observable 'culture'" (32–33) became popular among scholars trying to understand poverty. However, numerous later studies revealed great differences among poor communities and called the very idea of a culture of poverty into question. According to Gorski, these subsequent studies make it clear that "there is no such thing as a culture of poverty" (33). Gorski concludes that "the culture of poverty concept is constructed from a collection of smaller stereotypes which, however false, seem to have crept into mainstream thinking as unquestioned fact" (33).

In this developed version, the writer elaborates on specific points, such as how Lewis arrived at the idea of a culture of poverty and how the idea was subsequently challenged. The writer also uses quotations from the source text to provide additional information about this topic, which makes it much easier for a reader to grasp the main idea and supporting points.

Longer is not always better, of course, but when you are writing about complex ideas in academic contexts, under-developed paragraphs can result in superficial and sometimes confusing prose.

Achieving Coherence

In effective academic writing, paragraphs are not only sufficiently developed but also clearly focused and organized. In a coherent paragraph:

- The writer is in control of the subject matter and takes the reader deliberately from beginning to end.
- All the sentences contain relevant information.
- The discussion follows a clear and logical progression.

Often there is a topic sentence, but even without one, the main point of the paragraph is clear.

Students sometimes lose control of a paragraph when they are writing about complicated, abstract, or unfamiliar ideas and aren't sure what information to include and how to organize that information. In the following example, a student tries to explain what he believes is a basic principle of social life: competition. However, he struggles to make the main point of the paragraph clear and to present his ideas about competition in an orderly way:

> Our society is based on competition. It is natural for all of us to compete. Probably cheating is caused by our desire to succeed in competition. The first place we experience competition is at home when we cry to be held by our parents. We compete with their busy schedules to get their attention. Our next major competition is school, where we are all compared with other students. Until this time we only know that the time we spend with our parents is limited but if we exert ourselves we get what we want. Being compared with other students is when we first realize that we compete for others' time and compliments. As children we only know that we need get someone's attention to achieve what we need. We find that most competition is based upon being recognized.

Although this paragraph has a general focus, the main idea seems to shift. The opening sentence suggests that the paragraph is about the central role competition plays in human society, but the final sentence suggests a somewhat narrower point: that competition arises from the need to be recognized. In addition, the third sentence is irrelevant to the main point about competition, and the paragraph isn't well organized.

To address these problems, the first task is to identify the main point of the paragraph. Stating that point in a topic sentence can help, but the topic sentence does not have to be at the beginning of the paragraph. Let's assume that the writer wants to make the point that competition arises from the human need to be recognized. That can serve as a topic sentence. We want to keep the focus of the paragraph on that main point. We also want to order the sentences so that the reader can follow the discussion easily from one supporting point to the next. Here's a revised version:

> Our society is based on competition, and it is natural for all of us to compete. But why? Competition, it seems, arises from a basic human need to be recognized. We first experience competition very early in our lives when we cry to be held by our parents, actually competing with their busy schedules for their attention. For the first years of our lives, we learn that the time we spend with our parents is precious but limited, so we exert ourselves to get the attention we need. Our next major competition occurs in school, where we are compared with other students. We are still seeking the time and attention of others, but now we realize that we must compete with other students to be recognized. Every stage of our lives is characterized by different versions of this competition to fulfill our basic need for attention and recognition.

In this version, much of the original language is retained, but the focus on the main idea has been sharpened by adding a clear topic sentence (*Competition, it seems, arises from a basic human need to be recognized.*), eliminating unnecessary material (the sentence about cheating), rewriting some sentences so that they relate more clearly to the topic sentence, and reorganizing the paragraph. The paragraph is now more coherent, which makes its main point more evident to the reader.

Coherence can be difficult to achieve, but following these three steps can help make your paragraphs more coherent and effective:

1. State the main point of the paragraph in a sentence (topic sentence).	⇒	2. Make sure every sentence in the paragraph relates to the main point.	⇒	3. Order the sentences to make it easy for a reader to follow the discussion of the main point.

Achieving Cohesion

Cohesion refers to the extent to which statements, ideas, and information in a paragraph are related and explicitly connected to one another. In concrete terms, cohesion is a measure of how well the individual sentences in a paragraph are linked together so that the reader can see the relationship between the ideas or information in one sentence and those in another sentence. If a writer does not make those relationships clear, the paragraph becomes harder for a reader to follow. Even a coherent paragraph (that is, one in which all the sentences relate clearly to the main topic of the paragraph) can lack cohesion. Fortunately, cohesion can usually be achieved in two main ways:

- by the strategic use of certain "linking" words and phrases (e.g., *also, similarly, by contrast, in addition, then, therefore,* etc.)
- by the repetition of key words and phrases

Here's a paragraph that is coherent but not cohesive. Like the example in the section on developing a paragraph (page 632), this example also addresses the idea of "the culture of poverty" and draws on the same source. In this case, the paragraph retains its focus on the main topic, which is Paul Gorski's explanation of the concept of the culture of poverty, but the paragraphs lacks cohesion that would help a reader follow the writer's discussion more easily:

> In "The Myth of the 'Culture of Poverty'" (2008), Paul Gorski examines the concept of the "culture of poverty" and how it relates to education. Numerous case studies and academic articles as well as first-hand experience are discussed. Research shows that the culture of poverty doesn't exist. Many teachers have a preconceived notion that a culture of poverty is responsible for creating unmotivated students and uninvolved parents. He goes into great detail about the bias of educators, which leads them to promote a "culture of classism" that results in an unequal education for those living in poverty. Gorski suggests several ways that teachers can better address the needs of poverty-stricken students and avoid the problems associated with bias in education.

19

Compare this paragraph with the following one, which has been revised to make it more cohesive. The key revisions are highlighted. Yellow highlighting indicates the repetition of key words or phrases; blue highlighting indicates a linking word or phrase.

> In "The Myth of the "Culture of Poverty" (2008), Paul Gorski examines the concept of the "culture of poverty" and how it relates to education. Gorski draws upon numerous case studies and academic articles as well as the first-hand experience of a classroom teacher to explain the origins and interpretations of this concept. In addition, he cites research to show that the culture of poverty doesn't exist. Gorski points out that many teachers have a preconceived notion that this "culture of poverty" is responsible for creating unmotivated students and uninvolved parents (2). He carefully examines this bias, which, he argues, leads educators to promote a "culture of classism" that results in an unequal education for those living in poverty (3). Gorski also suggests several ways that teachers can better address the needs of poverty stricken students and avoid this "culture of classism" and its damaging effects on poor children.

Notice how simple linking words (e.g., *also, this*) and careful repetition of key phrases (e.g., *"culture of poverty"*) create connections among the sentences and enable the reader to follow the discussion more easily. Students sometimes mistakenly believe that repeating words and phrases is a mark of poor writing, but, as this example illustrates, strategic repetition actually makes the passage more cohesive and therefore strengthens the writing.

EXERCISE 19B WRITING EFFECTIVE PARAGRAPHS

Using the advice in this section, revise the following paragraph to make it more coherent and cohesive. Also, revise the sentences so that they reflect a more effective academic prose style:

> Religion is a man-made device that has allowed people to find a meaning in life. Whether it is monotheism or polytheism, or whether it is mixes of various beliefs regarding a creator, idols, or an overall power, people revert to some form of belief for solace. Spiritualism, which is not the same as religious faith, is on the rise. Studies routinely show that Americans are much more religious than most other nations. As religions grow, cultural aspects come into play, and it is the spiritual and physical actions that tend to dictate societal and personal beliefs. Some people want to hold onto traditional values. Many traditional values and actions have faded in religions, especially in mainstream, secular society. Judaism, among other religions, has become secularized, except for some sects. The same is true of many Christian denominations.

Summarizing and Paraphrasing

Summarizing and paraphrasing are among the most important skills in academic writing. It is a rare writing task that does not include some summary or paraphrase:

- In an argument about capital punishment, the writer summarizes the main positions for and against capital punishment before defending a position on the issue.

- A chemistry lab report about campus air quality includes summaries of previous analyses of air quality.

- An analysis of housing density in a neighborhood near campus for a sociology class includes a paraphrase of a seminal study about the relationship between housing density and key socio-economic and demographic factors.

- In a literary analysis essay for an English literature course, a student summarizes the plots of several plays by Shakespeare and paraphrases a critic's evaluation of them.

These examples underscore not only how common but also how useful summary and paraphrase can be in academic writing. They also indicate that, although students often need to summarize other texts, they might also need to summarize an argument, perspective, or theory that arises from multiple sources.

Usually, *summary* is distinguished from *paraphrase* (see "Summarizing vs. Paraphrasing"); in practice, however, the distinction is not always clear—or useful. For our purposes, distinguishing between summary and paraphrase is less important than understanding how to represent information and ideas from a source text accurately and how to credit the source appropriately. Accordingly, the advice in this section generally applies to both summarizing and paraphrasing.

FOCUS | **Summarizing vs. Paraphrasing**

Students are often confused by the difference between a summary and a paraphrase. That's understandable, because summary and paraphrase are very similar and textbooks as well as online resources often contribute to the confusion.

Paraphrase. The Merriam-Webster Dictionary defines *paraphrase* as "a restatement of a text, passage, or work giving the meaning in another form." A paraphrase expresses the ideas or information from a source text in your own words. Usually, a writer paraphrases when the information and/or meaning of a source text is important but the original wording of that text is not. Sometimes writers paraphrase when the source text is specialized and difficult to understand. (When it is important to convey the original wording to readers, the writer should *quote* from the source text. See "Quoting from Sources" on page 743 in Chapter 23.)

(Continued)

19

Summary. *Summary*, by contrast, is a condensed version of a source text that conveys only the main ideas or information from that text in the writer's own words. Writers summarize when they need to convey

- a key idea from a source text

- a point of view expressed in a source text

- the results of an analysis reported in a source text

- an argument made in a source text

The main difference between a summary and a paraphrase is that a summary boils a source down into a brief passage (a sentence, a few sentences, or a paragraph), whereas a paraphrase restates the source text. Both use the writer's own words, but the purpose of each is slightly different. In a summary, the writer conveys the main point or idea of a source text; in a paraphrase, the writer restates the source text to convey the information or ideas of that source text.

Although summarizing seems to be a straightforward task, students encounter **two main problems when summarizing:**

- inaccurately representing the main point, idea, or information from the source text

- using too much of the original language from the source

For example, here's a passage from an article in which a law professor offers an analysis of the so-called "war on poverty" initiated by President Lyndon Johnson in the 1960s:

> The commitment and symbolism of the "war on poverty"—and the energy and enthusiasm of those who fought it—were vital. For a brief period, the idea of conducting a war on poverty captured the nation's imagination. The phrase is surely one of the most evocative in our history. Yet the war's specific components were a tiny fraction even of the Great Society programs enacted between 1964 and 1968 during the administration of Lyndon Johnson, let alone those enacted during the New Deal and those added since, many during the presidency of Richard Nixon. And, even considering all these, we never fought an allout war on poverty.

> Source: Edelman, Peter. "The War on Poverty and Subsequent Federal Programs: What Worked, What Didn't Work, and Why? Lessons for Future Programs." *Clearinghouse Review Journal of Poverty Law and Policy* (May–June 2006): 8. Web.

The following summary misses the main point of the source text:

> According to Edelman, the war on poverty captured the nation's imagination.

The source text does state that the war on poverty captured the nation's imagination, but the author goes on to argue that the United States "never fought an allout war on poverty." The main point of the passage is that, despite the popularity of the idea of a war on poverty, the federal efforts intended to alleviate poverty were a small part of total government social programs. This summary, although accurate to an extent, misrepresents the point of the source passage. Here's a summary that better represents the point of the source text:

> Edelman argues that although the idea of a "war on poverty" captured the country's imagination, programs focused on addressing poverty never amounted to more than a small part of President Lyndon Johnson's Great Society programs and the social programs of other administrations both before and after Johnson's.

Notice that this summary represents the source passage *as a whole* rather than focusing on one part of it.

It's possible that a brief summary like this would be insufficient, depending upon the nature of the writing assignment and rhetorical situation. For example, you might be writing an argument in response to the source text, in which case you would probably need to include a more complete representation of that source. In such a case, you would probably need to paraphrase the source passage. Here's a paraphrase that illustrates the very common problem of using too much of the original language of the source text (the passages that are taken from the source text are highlighted in yellow):

> The commitment and symbolism of the "war on poverty" were important. For a short time, the idea of a war on poverty captured the nation's imagination. But the specific components of the war were a tiny fraction of government programs enacted during the administration of Lyndon Johnson, not to mention those enacted before then and those added since. Even considering all these programs, an allout war on poverty was never really fought.

In this example, not only are too many words and phrases taken verbatim from the source text, but much of the sentence structure is also reproduced in the paraphrase. A more acceptable paraphrase transforms the source passage into the writer's own words while preserving the original meaning of the source text:

> According to Edelman, the idea of a "war on poverty" was important for its symbolism as well as for the national commitment it reflected. But although this idea resonated with Americans for a time, the programs intended specifically to fight poverty were never more than a small part of total government social programs, whether those programs were part of Lyndon Johnson's Great Society, the earlier New Deal, or initiatives undertaken by Richard Nixon and subsequent presidents. As a result, Edelman states, a total war on poverty was never really fought.

This paraphrase borrows only essential phrases from the source text (such as "war on poverty") and restructures the passage so that the diction and syntax are the writer's own.

19

When summarizing or paraphrasing, follow these guidelines:

- **Accurately represent the main idea or point of the source text.** This is not simply a matter of including important information or ideas in your summary or paraphrase but also making sure that you convey the original author's intent or meaning.

- **Use your own language.** In many cases, using your own language means finding appropriate synonyms for words in the source text, but it also means writing your own sentences rather than using the sentence structure of the source text.

- **Place quotation marks around important words or phrases from the source text.** If you reproduce key words or phrases from the source text, place them in quotation marks to indicate that the language is taken from the source text. In the example above, the phrase *war on poverty* is placed in quotation marks not only because it is taken from the source text verbatim but also because it has become a phrase associated with a specific set of programs and period in history. (See "Quoting from Sources" on page 743 in Chapter 23 for advice about how to quote appropriately from a source text.)

- **Cite the source.** Whether you are summarizing, paraphrasing, or quoting directly from a source text, you must cite that source properly to indicate to your readers that you are taking ideas or information from another text. (See Chapters 24 and 25 for information about citing sources.)

EXERCISE 19C   PRACTICING SUMMARY AND PARAPHRASE

1. Write a summary and a paraphrase of the following passage:

Individualism-collectivism is perhaps the broadest and most widely used dimension of cultural variability for cultural comparison (Gudykunst and Ting-Toomey, 1988). Hofstede (1980) describes individualism-collectivism as the relationship between the individual and the collectivity that prevails in a given society. In individualistic cultures, individuals tend to prefer individualistic relationships to others and to subordinate ingroup goals to their personal goals. In collectivistic cultures, on the other hand, individuals are more likely to have interdependent relationships to their ingroups and to subordinate their personal goals to their ingroup goals. Individualistic cultures are associated with emphases on independence, achievement, freedom, high levels of competition, and pleasure. Collectivistic cultures are associated with emphases on interdependence, harmony, family security, social hierarchies, cooperation, and low levels of competition.

Source: Han, Sang-Pil, and Sharon Shavitt. "Persuasion and Culture: Advertising Appeals in Individualistic and Collectivistic Societies." *Journal of Experimental Social Psychology* 30 (1994): 327–28. Print.

2. Revise the summary below so that it more accurately reflects the original passage:

Original passage: Prior to the official acceptance of the low-fat-is-good-health dogma, clinical investigators, predominantly British, had proposed another hypothesis for the cause of heart disease, diabetes, colorectal and breast cancer, tooth decay, and a half-dozen or so other chronic diseases, including obesity. The hypothesis was based on decades of eyewitness testimony from missionary and colonial physicians and two consistent observations: that these "diseases of civilization" were rare to nonexistent among isolated populations that lived traditional lifestyles and ate traditional diets, and that these diseases appeared in these populations only after they were exposed to Western foods—in particular, sugar, flour, white rice, and maybe beer. These are known technically as *refined* carbohydrates, which are those carbohydrate-containing foods—usually sugars and starches—that have been machine-processed to make them more easily digestible.

Source: Taubes, Gary. *Good Calories, Bad Calories.* New York: Knopf, 2007. Print.

Summary: Another hypothesis was proposed based on decades of eyewitness testimony from physicians and the observations that these "diseases of civilization" didn't occur in isolated populations until they were exposed to Western diets of refined carbohydrates. Refined carbohydrates include sugar, flour, white rice, and maybe beer.

Synthesizing

In much academic writing, writers must do more than consult sources for relevant information. They must also bring together information or ideas from a variety of sources and synthesize the material into a coherent discussion that is relevant to the task at hand. Not only is synthesizing material from several sources an essential task in most academic writing, but it also lends depth to the writing. Consider this passage from *The Young and the Digital*, an analysis of the role of media in the lives of young people today:

In years past, social scientists expressed serious apprehension about the media content, especially violent and sexual imagery, that's exposed to young children and teenagers. And though violent and sexual themes in media continues to be a serious topic of debate, a growing amount of attention is shifting to the proliferation of screens in homes and in young people's lives. There is rising anxiety about the sheer amount of time children and teens spend with media and technology. According to a 2006 study conducted by the Kaiser Family Foundation, kids spend between six and eight-and-a-half hours a day with media. Today, playtime for many young children

usually involves time with a screen. As they observe their parents' connection to mobile phones, BlackBerrys, laptops, and other electronic gadgets, many young children mimic those behaviors. We often hear, and for good reason, that young people are leading the migration to digital. But in many homes across America, parents are unwittingly teaching their kids to be digital. In the midst of the marketing and selling of the digital lifestyle, the American Academy of Pediatrics recommends that children's daily screen time be limited to one to two hours.

Source: Watkins, S. Craig. *The Young and the Digital*. Boston: Beacon, 2009. Print.

In this passage, author S. Craig Watkins draws on several sources to make his main point about the increasing amount of time young people spend using digital media. Notice that Watkins cites two specific sources (a study by the Kaiser Family Foundation and a recommendation from the American Academy of Pediatrics), but the first few sentences of the paragraph provide an overview of an important development (the shift in attention from questionable media content to the amount of time children spend with media) that Watkins likely gleaned from several additional sources. In other words, Watkins is synthesizing ideas and information not only from the two sources he cites but also from other sources that he consulted while researching his topic. As this example suggests, synthesis can be extremely useful when a writer is working with complex subject matter and many different sources.

Effective writers follow three basic guidelines when synthesizing ideas and information.

- Keep larger goals in mind
- Identify a main point
- Use only source material that you need

Keep Larger Goals in Mind

When working with several different sources, especially in a longer project on a complicated topic, it can be easy to lose track of your reasons for consulting the specific sources you found. As you review sources and identify relevant information or ideas, remind yourself of the main goal of your project and identify how the section you are working on fits into that main goal. For example, the passage above from Watkins' book *The Young and the Digital* is taken from a chapter titled "The Very Well Connected: Friending, Bonding, and Community in the Digital Age," in which Watkins examines the increasingly central role digital media play in the social lives of young people. The passage above focuses on the increasing amount of time young people devote to digital media, a point that supports Watkins' analysis that digital media have become one of the most significant factors in how young people manage their social lives. Notice that in synthesizing material from his sources to make his point about the time young people devote to digital media, Watkins also connects that point to his larger point about the social impact of digital media.

Identify a Main Point

Source material is often varied and complicated, and when synthesizing this material, you must identify what is relevant to the task at hand. In effect, you are managing information from different sources that might seem unrelated and connecting them to make a point. That task is easier if you keep focused on a main point. Here's an example in which a writer synthesizes information from several very different sources to make a point about the longstanding debates about vegetarianism:

> Debates about the efficacy of vegetarianism follow us from cradle to wheelchair. In 1998 child-care expert Dr. Benjamin Spock, who became a vegetarian late in life, stoked a stir by recommending that children over the age of 2 be raised as vegans, rejecting even milk and eggs. The American Dietetic Association says it is possible to raise kids as vegans but cautions that special care must be taken with nursing infants (who don't develop properly without the nutrients in mother's milk or fortified formula). Other researchers warn that infants breast-fed by vegans have lower levels of vitamin B12 and DHA (an omega-3 fatty acid), important to vision and growth.

Source: Corliss, Richard. "Should We All Be Vegetarians?" *Time* 2002: 48+. Print.

In this passage, the author draws on at least three separate sets of sources: (1) material about the 1988 controversy surrounding Dr. Benjamin Spock's recommendations about feeding young children a vegetarian diet; (2) the American Dietary Association's recommendations; and (3) nutritional studies of infants who were breast-fed by vegans. Although these difference sources all relate to the topic of the impact of vegetarianism on children, they each have a different focus. The author brings them together to make a single main point, which is stated in the first sentence of

19

the paragraph. The information from each source is clearly related to that main point. As a result, the author makes it easy for a reader to make sense of the information from these different sources.

Use Only the Source Material You Need

When working with multiple sources, you might find a great deal of relevant material that is interesting and seemingly important, but don't overwhelm your reader by trying to synthesize information from too many sources at once. In the examples in this section, the authors select information from their sources carefully and use only what they need to make their points. It is likely that in each case the author had much more information than he used. Part of your task when working with sources is to evaluate the information you have gathered and select the material that helps you achieve your rhetorical goals. Synthesis can be a powerful tool in academic writing, but if you try to squeeze too much information from too many different sources into a passage, it is likely that your prose will be less clear and your discussion more difficult for your readers to follow.

EXERCISE 19D   PRACTICING SYNTHESIZING

Write a brief paragraph in which you synthesize the following information about the job market for college graduates:

> A Bachelor's degree is one of the best weapons a job seeker can wield in the fight for employment and earnings. And staying on campus to earn a graduate degree provides safe shelter from the immediate economic storm, and will pay off with greater employability and earnings once the graduate enters the labor market. Unemployment for students with new Bachelor's degrees is an unacceptable 8.9 percent, but it's a catastrophic 22.9 percent for job seekers with a recent high school diploma— and an almost unthinkable 31.5 percent for recent high school dropouts.

Source: Anthony, Carnevale, et al. *Hard Times: College Majors, Unemployment, and Earnings*. Publication. Georgetown University Center on Education and the Work Force, 2013. Web. 21 May 2013.

> More than half of all recent graduates are unemployed or in jobs that do not require a degree, and the amount of student-loan debt carried by households has more than quintupled since 1999. These graduates were told that a diploma was all they needed to succeed, but it won't even get them out of the spare bedroom at Mom and Dad's. For many, the most tangible result of their four years is the loan payments, which now average hundreds of dollars a month on loan balances in the tens of thousands.

zimmytws/Shutterstock.com

Source: McArdle, Megan. "Is College a Lousy Investment?" *The Daily Beast*. Newsweek/Daily Beast, 9 Sept. 2012. Web. 17 June 2013.

[In 2011] about 1.5 million, or 53.6 percent, of bachelor's degree-holders under the age of 25 last year were jobless or underemployed, the highest share in at least 11 years. In 2000, the share was at a low of 41 percent, before the dot-com bust erased job gains for college graduates in the telecommunications and IT fields.

Source: Associated Press. "Half of Recent College Grads Underemployed or Jobless, Analysis Says." *Cleveland.com*. Cleveland Live LLC, 23 Apr. 2012. Web. 17 June 2013.

Underemployment also tends to be temporary for college graduates. Even after the recession hit, Pew found that annually, about 27 percent of BA's stuck in high-school level jobs transitioned to college-level employment… Unemployment for college graduates is higher than normal. Underemployment is more prevalent, though it's less severe than college critics portray, and perhaps no worse than during the Reagan days.

Source: Weissmann, Jordan. "How Bad Is the Job Market for College Grads? Your Definitive Guide." *The Atlantic*. The Atlantic Monthly Group, 4 Apr. 2013. Web. 17 June 2013.

19

Framing

You might have heard an instructor comment about "framing" an argument, analysis, or discussion:

> Be sure to frame your argument clearly.

> Frame your analysis of the new health care law in terms of the ongoing debates about the role of government in citizens' lives.

> Try to frame your discussion in a way that makes it relevant for your readers.

In these statements, "framing" means placing your project in a context that gives it relevance or significance for your audience. It is a technique for putting into practice Core Concept #2: "Good writing fits the context." All writing must fit into a specific rhetorical situation that includes an intended audience and a context for communicating with that audience. It is part of a writer's task to show his or her audience why the topic at hand is important and meaningful and how the writer will approach it. "Framing" is a term used to describe a technique for doing that.

For example, in the following passage, the authors, three biologists, frame their argument about "eusociality" in terms of an ongoing debate in their field:

> For most of the past half century, much of sociobiological theory has focused on the phenomenon called eusociality, where adult members are divided into reproductive and (partially) non-reproductive castes and the latter care for the young. How can genetically prescribed selfless behaviour arise by natural selection, which is seemingly its antithesis? This problem has vexed biologists since Darwin, who in *The Origin of Species* declared the paradox—in particular displayed by ants—to be the most important challenge to his theory. The solution offered by the master naturalist was to regard the sterile worker caste as a "well-flavoured vegetable," and the queen as the plant that produced it. Thus, he said, the whole colony is the unit of selection.
>
> Modern students of collateral altruism have followed Darwin in continuing to focus on ants, honeybees and other eusocial insects, because the colonies of most of their species are divided unambiguously into different castes. Moreover, eusociality is not a marginal phenomenon in the living world. The biomass of ants alone composes more than half that of all insects and exceeds that of all terrestrial nonhuman vertebrates combined. Humans, which can be loosely characterized as eusocial, are dominant among the land vertebrates. The "superorganisms" emerging from eusociality are often bizarre in their constitution, and represent a distinct level of biological organization.

Source: Nowak, Martin A., Corina E. Tarnita, and Edward O. Wilson. "The Evolution of Eusociality." *Nature* 466.26 (2010): 1057. Print.

In this passage, the authors place their specific argument in the context of a problem that evolutionary biologists have long confronted in their efforts to test Darwin's theories. In this way, the authors show how their argument is relevant to biologists by connecting it to a recognized problem in the field.

Here's another example, this one from a scholarly article reporting on a study of college students' use of digital media. In this passage, the author cites evidence of the increasingly important role that social media play in the lives of young Americans:

> According to the Pew Internet and American Life Project, as of August 2011, 83% of 18–29 year-olds used a social network site (Madden, 2012). Their interactions on these sites were also purposeful, as Pew reports that this age group is that most concerned with online identity management: 71% of them have changed the privacy settings on the sites they use (Lenhart, Purcell, Smith, & Zickuhr, 2010). Living a "literate life in the information age" (Selfe & Hawisher, 2004) increasingly means learning to navigate these spaces, managing one's identity and online data, and considering complex issues of privacy and representation. Using ethnographic case study data, this article examines how one undergraduate student integrated his use of social network sites into his everyday literacy practices to represent his identity. I approached this case study with three research questions: 1) How does this writer integrate social network sites into his everyday literacy practices? 2) How does this writer use those literacy practices to represent his identity for multiple audience groups on social network sites? 3) How does this writer negotiate site interfaces to represent his identity and communicate with others?

Source: Buck, Amber. "Examining Digital Literacy Practices on Social Network Sites." *Research in the Teaching of English* 47.1 (2012): 10. Print.

Here the author frames her own case study of a college student in terms of larger social and technological developments in contemporary society. She cites other research to establish the importance of social media and place her study in the context of these important developments.

Both these examples illustrate how authors use framing not only to introduce readers to the subject matter but also to identify why their arguments or analyses are relevant. By framing their discussions, these authors explicitly connect their arguments or analyses to larger debates or conversations that matter to their readers and show how their own arguments or analyses fit into those conversations.

Framing typically happens in the introduction to a piece, but a writer might see a need to frame a segment of a piece of writing, especially in a longer piece that might contain several sections. For instance, in an analysis of the economic impact of a proposed tax on gasoline, the writer might include a section presenting a specific kind of cost-benefit analysis using a new economic model. In such a case, the writer might frame that section in the context of, say, an ongoing debate about whether certain kinds of taxes hurt the average consumer or benefit the economy as a whole.

When framing an argument, analysis, or discussion, use these questions to guide you:

- What makes your argument, analysis, or discussion relevant to your intended audience? Why would your audience be interested in this topic?

- To which larger debates, conversations, or arguments is your topic related? How might you connect your topic to those larger debates, conversations, or arguments?

- What makes your topic important or relevant now? How can you show your readers that your topic is important and timely?

These questions can make it easier for you to frame your discussion in a way that makes it relevant for your readers and enables them to place it in a larger context.

1. Imagine an argument you might make about a current issue that interests you. Using the bulleted list of questions on page 647, describe briefly how you would frame this argument. In your answer, identify your intended audience and a purpose for your argument.

2. Using your answer for Question #1, reframe your argument for a different audience.

3. In a brief paragraph, describe how the authors of the following passage frame their research in this introduction to their series of studies about "Millennials" (that is, people born between 1981 and 2000):

Generations, like people, have personalities. Their collective identities typically begin to reveal themselves when their oldest members move into their teens and twenties and begin to act upon their values, attitudes and worldviews. America's newest generation, the Millennials, is in the middle of this coming-of-age phase of its life cycle. Its oldest members are approaching age 30; its youngest are approaching adolescence. Who are they? How are they different from—and similar to—their parents? How is their moment in history shaping them? And how might they, in turn, reshape America in the decades ahead? The Pew Research Center will try to answer these questions through a yearlong series of original reports that explore the behaviors, values and opinions of today's teens and twenty-somethings.

Source: Keeter, Scott, and Paul Taylor. "The Millennials." *Pew Research Center*. Pew Research Center, 10 Dec. 2009. Web. 17 June 2013.

Introductions

An introduction is a kind of roadmap to your paper: it tells your readers where you plan to go and why. In most forms of academic writing, the introduction not only presents the topic of the paper but also conveys a sense of why the topic is relevant and what the writer will say about it.

Below are four examples, each illustrating a common approach to introductions. The first three examples are from student essays: one from a paper written for an economics course, the second from a course on the history of modern China, and the third from an introductory psychology course. The fourth example is from an article by Deborah Tannen, a professor of linguistics at Georgetown University. Notice that, regardless of the approach, each introduction clearly establishes the focus of the paper and conveys a sense of the writer's main idea. Notice, too, how each introduction establishes the tone and style of the paper.

Getting Right to the Point

One of the most common mistakes students make when introducing an essay is saying too much. Often, the most effective introductions are those that get right to the point and move the reader quickly into the main body of the paper. Here's an example:

> ### The Legalization of Prostitution
>
> Prostitution is the "contractual barter of sex favors, usually sexual intercourse, for monetary considerations without any emotional attachment between the partners" (Grauerhold & Koralewski, 1991). Whenever this topic is mentioned, people usually shy away from it, because they are thinking of the actions involved in this profession. The purpose of this paper, however, is not to talk about these services, but to discuss the social, economic and legal issues behind prostitution.
>
> Source: "Comments on an Economic Analysis Paper." *WAC Student Resources.* Coe Writing Center, 2001. Web. 17 June 2013.

This brief introduction quickly establishes the focus and main purpose of the paper. It also places the topic in the context of general perceptions of prostitution and clarifies that the writer will be examining that topic from a different angle. This is a good example of a writer efficiently introducing a topic. As this writer demonstrates, sometimes the best approach is the one that uses the fewest words.

Focusing on Context

This next example, from a history paper about the impact of Mao Zedong on modern China, illustrates how an academic writer can use techniques from narrative writing to introduce a topic and at the same time establish a context for the topic. This introduction begins with a brief description of the birthplace of Mao Zedong as a way to dramatize the main point of the paper that Mao "remains the central, dominant figure in Chinese political culture today." The second paragraph provides background information so that the reader can better appreciate Mao's significance to modern China, while the third paragraph establishes the focus of the paper, which examines Mao's enduring legacy in contemporary China.

19

Mao More Than Ever

Shaoshan is a small village found in a valley of the Hunan province, where, a little over a century ago, Mao Zedong was born. The first thing heard in Shaoshan is the music, and the music is inescapable. Suspended from posts towering over Mao's childhood home are loudspeakers from which the same tune is emitted over and over, a hit of the Cultural Revolution titled "We Love You, Mao."

The Chinese people were faced with an incredibly difficult situation in 1976 following the death of Mao Zedong. What was China to do now that the man whom millions accepted as the leader of their country's rebirth to greatness has passed away? China was in mourning within moments of the announcement. Although Mao rarely had been seen in public during the five years preceding his death, he was nevertheless the only leader that China had known since the Communist armies swept triumphantly into Peking and proclaimed the People's Republic twenty-seven years earlier. He was not only the originator of China's socialist revolution but its guide, its teacher, and its prophet.

Common sense foretold of the impossibility of erasing Communism and replacing Chairman Mao. He departed the world with his succession and China's future uncertain. With his death, historians and reporters around the world offered predictions of what was to become of China. They saw an instant end to Maoist theory. Through careful examination of Chinese life both under and after Mao, it is clear that the critics of 1976 were naïve in their prophecies and that Mao Zedong still remains the central, dominant figure in Chinese political culture today.

Source: "Comments on a Research Paper." *WAC Student Resources*. Coe Writing Center, 2001. Web. 17 June 2013.

In this example, the writer establishes the context by "telling the story" of Mao's enduring influence on China. This approach is common in the humanities (history, literature, and so on).

Using a Reference Point

Another common approach to introductions in academic writing is to use an established idea, point of view, development, text, or study as a reference point for the topic of the paper. In this example from a paper written for a psychology course, the writers begin by referring to a study of the anxiety people experience while waiting in hospital waiting rooms:

Sitting Comfort: The Impact of Different Chairs on Anxiety

Kutash and Northrop (2007) studied the comfort of family members in the ICU waiting room. They found that no matter the situation, waiting rooms are stressful for the patients and their families, and it is the nursing staff's job to comfort both. From this emotional distress many family members judged the waiting room furniture as "uncomfortable" and only talked about it in a negative context. From this study we have learned that there is a direct relationship between a person's emotional state and how that person perceives the physical state he or she is in, such as sitting in a chair. Is this relationship true in reverse as well? Can the way a person perceives his or her present physical state (such as sitting in a chair) affect his or her emotional state? This is the question that the present study sought to answer.

hxdbzxy/Shutterstock.com

Source: Baker, Jenna, Ashlynn Beacker, and Courtney Young. "Sitting Comfort: The Impact of Different Chairs on Anxiety." *Schemata* (2011): n. pag. Web. 15 June 2012.

Here the writers cite a previously published study that raises a question that is relevant to readers interested in psychology ("Can the way a person perceives his or her present physical state (such as sitting in a chair) affect his or her emotional state?"). The study serves as the reference point for the paper, and the question the writers pose clearly establishes the focus of the paper. One advantage of this approach is that the question sets up the expectation that the writer will answer the question. In this way, the writer gives the audience a clear sense of what will follow.

19

Telling an Anecdote

Using an anecdote to introduce a topic, which is common in many different kinds of writing, can be effective in academic writing as well. In this example, linguist Deborah Tannen shares an anecdote to illustrate the problem she will address in her article. Notice how she uses the anecdote to establish the focus of her paper and encourage the reader to continue reading:

Sex, Lies and Conversation

I was addressing a small gathering in a suburban Virginia living room—a women's group that had invited men to join them. Throughout the evening, one man had been particularly talkative, frequently offering ideas and anecdotes, while his wife sat silently beside him on the couch. Toward the end of the evening, I commented that women frequently complain that their husbands don't talk to them. This man quickly concurred. He gestured toward his wife and said, "She's the talker in our family." The room burst into laughter; the man looked puzzled and hurt. "It's true," he explained. "When I come home from work I have nothing to say. If she didn't keep the conversation going, we'd spend the whole evening in silence."

This episode crystallizes the irony that although American men tend to talk more than women in public situations, they often talk less at home. And this pattern is wreaking havoc with marriage.

Source: Tannen, Deborah. "Sex, Lies and Conversation: Why Is It So Hard for Men and Women to Talk to Each Other?" *Washington Post* 24 June 1990: C3. Print.

Using an anecdote can be very effective, but students sometimes devote too much time to the anecdote, which can make it more difficult for readers to see where the paper might be going. If you use this approach, keep the anecdote brief and follow it up with a few sentences indicating why you're sharing the anecdote and what it means—as Tannen does in her second paragraph.

Transitions

Earlier in this chapter we noted that, in effective academic writing, paragraphs must be coherent and cohesive (see page 632). The same is true for an essay or other kind of document as a whole. Your sentences can be clear and your paragraphs coherent and cohesive, but if you don't connect them to one another, your essay is likely to be more difficult for your readers to follow. The main tool for keeping your essays coherent and cohesive is the transition, which is why writing effective transitions is an essential skill in academic writing. Fortunately, it is a skill that is easy to develop.

What exactly is a *transition*? It is a device to get your reader from one paragraph—or section of your document—to the next. Transitions amount to signposts that keep your readers oriented and enable them to know where they are in your text. If you have written an effective introduction that tells your readers what to expect in your text, transitions signal when they have reached each main section.

It is important to remember that you don't need a transition between every paragraph in a document. Often, the connection between paragraphs is clear because the subject matter of one paragraph explicitly relates to the subject of the next. However, transitions are usually necessary

- when there is an important shift in the focus of discussion from one paragraph to the next
- when moving from one main section of a document to another

The section on "Achieving Cohesion" in paragraphs (page 635) describes two strategies for writing cohesive paragraphs that also can be used to write effective transitions between paragraphs to create more cohesive essays:

- using linking words or phrases (e.g., *first, second, in addition, then, therefore, that*)
- repeating key words and phrases

In addition, a third important strategy is to set up your transitions by letting a reader know what to expect in a section or in your entire document. For example, your introduction might explain that your essay will address four key questions. When making the transitions between the four main sections of your essay, you can refer back to those questions to remind your reader what will follow.

The following passage from a student literacy narrative illustrates these common strategies for transitions between paragraphs. In this slightly humorous narrative about the student's experience in a college writing class, the writer explains the first few weeks of the class. Notice how the transitions help keep the narrative coherent and enable the reader to follow the story more easily. (Key transition strategies are highlighted in yellow.)

1 Prior to college I had never had a true intensive course. My high school English classes consisted mostly of reading assigned literature, with the occasional plot summary, known as a book report, thrown in for variety. Never had a teacher of mine critiqued papers with anything more in mind than content, unless it was to point out some terrible structural flaw. That changed when I enrolled in college and found myself in a required course called Introduction to Academic Writing.

> The introductory paragraph establishes the focus of the narrative. The final sentence in particular conveys a sense of what will follow.

19

2 Introduction to Academic Writing was designed in part to eliminate from the writing of incoming students any weaknesses or idiosyncrasies that they might have brought with them from high school. Run-on sentences, incoherent paragraphs, and incorrect footnoting were given particular emphasis. To address these issues, the professor assigned a great deal of work. Weekly journal assignments and multiple formal essays kept us very busy indeed. And then there were the informal in-class essays.

This paragraph begins with a repeated phrase (*Introduction to Academic Writing*) that clearly links it to the last sentence of the preceding paragraph. Also, the final sentence of this paragraph sets up the transition to the next paragraph.

3 The first such essay took place on the second day of classes so that our professor could evaluate each student's strengths and weaknesses. Before accepting our work, however, she had us exchange papers with one another to see how well we could spot technical flaws. She then proceeded to walk around the room, interrupting our small-group discussions, and asked each of us what we thought of what we had read. It was not a comfortable situation, though the small size of the groups limited our embarrassment somewhat.

The writer uses linking words (*the first such essay*) to make the transition to this paragraph. The same strategy is used for the transition to the following two paragraphs (*This unique brand; Eventually*).

4 This unique brand of academic humiliation was a palpable threat in class, which consisted mostly of students with little confidence in their writing abilities. Most of them seemed to be enrolled in majors other than English, and they viewed this remedial writing course as a painful, albeit necessary, endeavor. Our professor sympathized, I believe, and for the most part restricted her instruction to small groups and one-on-one sessions. But the in-class writing exercises were a daily hardship for the first few weeks of the semester, and I think most of us dreaded them.

5 Eventually, we were deemed ready for the first formal essay, which was a kind of expository writing in which we were to select an academic subject of interest to us and report on that subject to the rest of the class. Most of the students seemed wary of the assignment, because it was the first one in which we were given a choice of topic. All the in-class essays were on assigned topics. So the first source of anxiety was the uncertainty about which topics would be acceptable.

Although this example is narrative writing, which is less common than other forms of academic writing, its strategies for effective transitions are the same strategies used in analytical and argumentative writing. For example, here's a passage from a psychology research report published in a professional journal. The style of this passage reflects the formal writing typical of the social sciences, yet the transition strategies the authors use are the same as those in the passage from the student narrative essay above.

1   The Action-to-Action (ATA) model of Norman and Shallice (1986) has three subcomponents: *action schemas, contention scheduling,* and a *supervisory attentional system* (SAS).

> This paragraph establishes the expectation that the authors will discuss these three key concepts in turn, thus setting up the transitions in the following paragraphs.

2   Action schemas are specialized routines for performing individual tasks that involve well-learned perceptual-motor and cognitive skills. Each action schema has a current degree of activation that may be increased by either specific perceptual "trigger" stimuli or outputs from other related schemas. When its activation exceeds a preset threshold, an action schema may direct a person's behavior immediately and stereotypically toward performing some task. Moreover, on occasion, multiple schemas may be activated simultaneously by different trigger stimuli, creating error-prone conflicts if they entail mutually exclusive responses (e.g., typing on a keyboard and answering a telephone concurrently).

3   To help resolve such conflicts, the ATA model uses contention scheduling. It functions rapidly, automatically, and unconsciously through a network of lateral inhibitory connections among action schemas whose response outputs would interfere with each other (cf. Rumelhart & Norman, 1982). Through this network, an action schema (e.g., one for keyboard typing) that has relatively high current activation may suppress the

> In the first sentence of paragraph 3 the authors use two sets of repeated words or phrases along with a linking word (*such*). The first repeated word (*conflicts*) links this paragraph to the preceding one. The second repeated phrase (*contention scheduling*) links this paragraph to the first paragraph and reminds the reader that the discussion has moved to the second of the three main concepts mentioned in that paragraph

activation of other potentially conflicting schemas (e.g., one for telephone answering). Contention scheduling allows task priorities and environmental cues to be assessed on a decentralized basis without explicit top-down executive control (Shallice, 1988). However, this may not always suffice to handle conflicts when new tasks, unusual task combinations, or complex behaviors are involved.

4. Consequently, the ATA model also has an SAS. The SAS guides behavior slowly, flexibly, and consciously in a top-down manner. It helps organize complex actions and perform novel tasks by selectively activating or inhibiting particular action schemas, superseding the cruder bottom-up influences of contention scheduling and better accommodating a person's overall capacities and goals. For example, one might expect the SAS to play a crucial role during switches between unfamiliar incompatible tasks that are not ordinarily performed together.

> Like the previous paragraph, this one demonstrates two transition strategies: linking words (*Consequently* and *also*) and a key repeated term (*SAS*).

Source: Rubinstein, Joshua S., David E. Meyer, and Jeffrey E. Evans. "Executive Control of Cognitive Processes in Task Switching." *Journal of Experimental Psychology: Human Perception and Performance* 27.4 (2001): 764. Print.

The best time to strengthen the transitions in a piece of writing is during revision (Core Concept #8). Step #8 in Chapter 3 includes advice on revising to improve your transitions. At that point in the process of revision, review your entire draft, focusing only on transitions. As you do so, keep the following **guidelines for effective transitions** in mind:

■ **Set up your transitions.** An effective introduction will convey a sense of the main parts of your text. Your transitions from one main part to the next should refer back to the key terms you use in your introduction. In addition, you can make transitions more effective by letting the reader know what will follow in each main section. In effect, write a brief introduction to each main section—as the authors did in the example above.

■ **Use linking words or phrases.** As the examples in this section demonstrate, there are many common words and phrases that writers use to signal a transition from one point or topic to the next or from one main section of a document to the next. Here's a brief list of some of the most common linking words and phrases:

next

then

also

in addition

similarly

on the other hand

therefore

consequently

first, second, third, …

finally

at the same time

sometimes

■ **Repeat key words or phrases.** The examples included in this section illustrate how writers repeat key words or phrases to link one paragraph to the next and to signal to readers that they are making a transition from one point to another. Select these words and phrases carefully so that you can keep your writing cohesive without being repetitive. Repetition in itself is not a weakness in writing, but unnecessarily repeated words or phrases can make your prose tedious and distracting for readers.

WRITING PROJECTS | PRACTICING TRANSITIONS

Add transitions to the following passage to make it more cohesive and easier for a reader to follow:

Writing developed as a visual means of communication, and a long, continuing history of close incorporation of visual elements in many different text forms has been maintained. Illustrated manuscripts, calligraphy, and tapestries are but a few of the art forms in which distinctions between word and form are blurred to the point of meaninglessness. Olson (1992) reminds us, "The calligraphic (meaning 'words written by hand') form incorporates all the elements of a painting—line, shape, texture, unity, balance, rhythm, proportion—all within its own unique form of composition" (131).

The distance between the visual and the verbal forms of information practiced in verbal-based classrooms is highly artificial. Shuman and Wolfe (1990) draw what they see as "two pertinent conclusions": (1) Early composition that was used as a means of preserving and transmitting ideas and information through the ages took the forms of singing and drawings. (2) Early alphabetic writing was an art form that may have had less to do with composing the content of what was to be communicated than with the art form itself. "Obviously, connections between language and the arts have roots deep in antiquity" (2).

Olson explores connections between writing and art. She notes that the "Greeks chose to represent each spoken sound with a symbol (or letter). Just as speech developed out of the imitation of sound, writing developed out of the imitation of forms of real objects or beings. At the beginning of all writing stands the picture" (130).

Currently educators are interested in interdisciplinary approaches at all levels, primary through postsecondary. It is a particularly opportune moment to attempt instructional approaches that bring together art and writing.

Source: Pamela B. Childers, Eric H. Hobson, and Joan A. Mullin, Eds. "ARTiculating: Teaching Writing in a Visual World." *WAC Clearinghouse Landmark Publications in Writing Studies* (1998): 3–4. Print.

19

Designing Documents 20

RECENTLY, a friend of mine who works as a regional planner was asked to review a proposal. The proposal had been submitted to her organization by a consulting company that manages commercial and residential projects, such as strip malls, parks, and housing developments. The consulting company was seeking to be hired to create a development plan for the rural county where my friend works. It was a big proposal for a big project, and my friend had to evaluate it to help the county decide whether to hire the company to develop its regional plan. So she carefully studied the proposal, assessing the company's ideas for regional development as well as its ability to complete a good plan on time. The document was nearly 100 pages, with detailed analyses of issues like water flow, population density, and infrastructure (roads, bridges, and so on). My friend liked many aspects of the proposal, but her biggest complaint was that the document itself looked unprofessional. Although its analysis was sophisticated, with many graphs and tables, its design, she said, looked amateurish. More important, she found it difficult to locate important information in the document. The proposal, she said, just didn't look professional, which influenced her evaluation of it.

This anecdote underscores the importance of design in many documents—not only in professional settings such as my friend's workplace, but in many other contexts as well:

- A campus group that trains volunteer mentors for first-year students creates a flier to announce a meeting for new volunteers.

- A community organization that runs a food pantry develops a brochure to advertise its services to local residents.

- A college rugby club compiles an annual report, complete with photos and charts, for the campus athletic department.

And of course many college instructors expect students to include graphs, tables, and other visual elements in print reports and to make presentations using tools such as Prezi. In each case, a well-designed document is more likely to achieve its rhetorical purpose.

Because widely available technologies make it easy to create professional-looking documents, readers often expect more than well-written content. They want the content to be presented with appropriate graphics, attractive color schemes, and pleasing layouts. Such features are much more than ornamentation. The design of a document is a rhetorical tool that helps writers communicate ideas and information effectively to their audiences and convince readers that a document is worth reading. Effective document design also lends credibility to the writer. Today, knowing how to design a document well is an increasingly important part of being an effective writer.

Document design includes many sophisticated elements that are beyond the scope of this textbook, but this chapter will introduce you to basic concepts to help you develop the skills you need to design documents that will achieve your rhetorical goals. (You can find related information about visual design elsewhere in this book. See "Analyzing Images" in Chapter 8, "Presenting Information Visually" in Chapter 17, and "Using Images" in Chapter 18.)

Understanding Document Design as a Rhetorical Tool

Imagine that you want to raise awareness among students on your campus about alcohol abuse. Here's a public service poster from a university health center that does just that:

Source: Freidenberg, Brian M. *Did You Know?* Digital image. *Counseling Center.* University at Albany, State University of New York, n.d. Web. 17 June 2013.

What do you notice about this document? The authors certainly intend to catch your eye with the large yellow "98%" in the center of the page that contrasts with the darker background and the smaller text below it. Using color, layout, and font size strategically, they communicate a great deal of information with relatively few words. For example, they describe six different steps students can take to drink alcohol safely (using a designated driver, avoiding drinking games, and so on), and they identify the source of the information (a survey of students at that university). The layout of this information in a horizontal line of checked items at the bottom of the page sets it apart, making it more likely that you will read that information. And notice that the question in the upper left-hand corner of the document invites you into a kind of dialogue, a provocative way to entice students to read the entire document.

The authors of this poster have designed their document, first, to attract the attention of their intended audience (students at their university), and second, to communicate specific information efficiently to that audience. A more conventional document might be less effective in achieving these rhetorical goals, especially given how much information busy college students encounter in a typical day. For example, compare the poster to an email with the same information that might be sent to students as a public service announcement:

> Do you know that 98% of UAlbany students take steps to be safer in drinking situations? A random, anonymous survey of 1,001 students conducted during spring 2010 found that students take the following steps: using a designated driver, avoiding drinking games, pacing drinks to one or fewer an hour, eating before or during drinking, alternating non-alcoholic with alcoholic beverages, and choosing not to drink alcohol.

Which document is more likely to reach students? Which is more likely to grab students' attention? Which is more likely to be memorable to students?

Document design is a powerful way to make sure you reach an audience and convey ideas and information effectively. In designing your own documents, keep these points in mind:

- **Consider your audience.** The first step in designing a document is to identify the expectations of your intended audience and the rhetorical goals for your document. Who is your audience for this document? What kind of document are they likely to expect? What design features will appeal to them? A flier announcing a campus farmer's market probably won't appeal to residents of a local retirement community if it has the flashy colors and provocative features of the public service poster on page 660, which is intended for a much younger audience with very different tastes.

- **Consider your message.** Be clear about the ideas, information, or point you want to convey to your audience. What features will best help you convey your message? How might you use those features to emphasize key ideas and help readers find important information? For example, the large font and bright color of the figure "98%" in the poster on page 660 help emphasize the key point of the poster, which is that the vast majority of students on that campus try to use alcohol safely.

- **Avoid ornamentation.** Just as you should try to eliminate unnecessary information from a piece of writing, you should avoid design features that do little more than decorate your document. The images, graphics, font styles, colors, and layout you use should help you accomplish your rhetorical goals by communicating or emphasizing important ideas or information. If a design element doesn't help you accomplish your rhetorical goals, consider eliminating or changing it.

- **Make a good impression.** First impressions can influence how an audience responds to your document. If the design is effective, your audience is more likely to take your message seriously, and you are more likely to achieve your rhetorical goals. If your design is weak, you risk undermining your credibility, as happened to the authors of the poorly designed proposal in the anecdote at the beginning of this chapter.

EXERCISE 20A   EXAMINING THE DESIGN OF DOCUMENTS

1. Visit the websites of two or three restaurants in your town or neighborhood, and review their menus. Compare the way the menus present information. How are the menus organized? How easy is it to find information about specific items that you might want to order? Which menu looks most professional? Now identify specific features that make each menu appealing or not: the colors, the layout of the pages, the use of images or graphics, and so on. Consider how these elements help you find the menu items you are looking for. What conclusions about document design might you draw from this exercise?

2. Compare the design of two or more textbooks that you are currently using for your classes (or textbooks you have used in the past). Select a representative page from each textbook and compare them. What do you notice about each page? Which pages do you find most appealing? Which are easiest to read? On the basis of this comparison, draw your own conclusions about which textbook has the most effective design.

Principles of Document Design

The public service poster on page 660 demonstrates four basic principles of document design:

- **Contrast:** a pronounced difference in color, size, or other design elements that can be used for emphasis or to help readers navigate a document

- **Repetition:** strategic repeating of text, color, patterns, or other features to emphasize information or ideas and show connections between content or sections of a document

- **Alignment:** the layout of elements of a page or document in relation to each other and to the page borders

- **Proximity:** the positioning of information or features next to one another to show connections or emphasis

These four principles can guide your decisions about how to design a document to meet the needs of your rhetorical situation.

Contrast

This light-colored text is more difficult to see against the yellow background.

These two examples illustrate the value of contrast—in this case, contrasting colors—to communicate or emphasize ideas and information. Contrast that is sufficiently strong, as in the top example, helps convey information more easily. Poor contrast can obscure information and make it difficult for readers to navigate a document.

Writers use contrast for three main reasons:

- **To emphasize ideas or information.** Notice, for example, the color, size, and font style of the phrase "to emphasize ideas or information" make it stand apart from the rest of this paragraph and give it greater emphasis. Contrasting images—say, of a crying baby and a smiling child—might be used to communicate an idea or point—for example, about the nature of childhood.

- **To organize a document.** Contrast is a common way to help readers navigate a document. For example, headings or subtitles that appear in sizes or colors that are different from the main text indicate to readers where different sections of a document begin and end. Icons can be used to indicate special information.

- **To establish a focus.** Contrast can be used to convey a sense of the focus or main idea of a document. In the poster on page 660, for example, the large contrasting type size for the figure "98%" helps focus the reader's attention on the point that most students use alcohol safely.

Contrast is commonly created with color and different font sizes or styles. For example, this 18-point font is immediately noticeable in a paragraph full of 12-point font. Similarly, you can use **a different font style like this** to set a title, subheading, or key sentence apart from surrounding text.

FOCUS   Understanding Typography

Typography refers to letters and symbols in a document. It includes features such as *italics*, underlining, and **boldface** as well as the size and style of the font. You can use typography to make documents more readable, appealing, and easy to navigate. You can also use it to emphasize important ideas or information. Understanding a few basic concepts can help you use typography effectively in your documents.

(Continued)

Serif and sans serif. Fonts appear in two basic types: *serif*, which has small horizontal lines attached to the main lines of a letter, and *sans serif*, which does not.

serif   sans serif

Although the uses of these styles can vary, serif fonts are considered more traditional and are generally used in formal writing (such as academic assignments), whereas sans serif fonts tend to be considered more contemporary. Serif fonts are generally considered easier to read and are therefore the best choice for long passages of text (as in a traditional academic paper).

Font styles. Writers can choose from hundreds of font styles, including common styles such as `Courier`, Arial, and Garamond, as well as unusual styles, such as *Lucida Calligraphy* and `Old English Text`. Although it is tempting to use uncommon font styles, the rule of thumb is to select fonts that make your document readable. For most academic assignments, a traditional font such as Times Roman, is preferable. Also keep in mind that different font styles take up different amounts of space.

Font size. Fonts sizes are measured in points. The standard font size for most extended text is 12-point. Sometimes, larger font sizes, such as this 14-point font or this 18-point font, are used for titles and headings or in tables and charts. However, varying the font size too often can be distracting to readers, so select font sizes strategically and be consistent in sizing the fonts you use. For example, use the same font size for all extended text and another font size for all subtitles.

Repetition

The careful repetition of specific features of a text—such as words, color, graphics, and font sizes or styles—can help make a document more readable and coherent. For example, the repetition of certain design features on the first page of each chapter of this textbook (such as color, the placement and style of images, the font size, and the layout of the page) enables you to identify the beginning of a chapter quickly and easily. In this same way, you already use repetition to help readers navigate your conventional print documents. For example, numbers in the same location on each page and subheadings separated from the main text are common features of essays or reports to help readers follow a document.

This use of repetition is so common that we might not even notice it, yet it can be used to communicate or emphasize important information very efficiently. For instance, the familiar repetition of the shape and color scheme of road signs tells motorists unequivocally that the signs contain relevant information, such as whether a traffic light or a pedestrian crossing lies ahead.

FIGURE 20.1 Standard Road Signs

Nelson Marques/Shutterstock.com

In the same way, a writer might use the repetition of a color or font style to indicate that certain information is important. Notice the repetition of the color blue on the web page about maintaining health in college in Figure 20.2. Blue is used to signal main ideas: the page title ("College Health: How to Stay Healthy) and the questions that represent key points ("What can I do to stay healthy?" "What should I know about nutrition and eating well?"). Blue is also used to lend a sense of cohesion to the page; notice, for example, that the bullets are blue.

FIGURE 20.2 College Health Web Page

College Health:
How to Stay Healthy

▪ Knowing About My Health	▪ Eating Disorders
▪ First Aid Supplies	▪ Alcohol and Drugs
▪ Health Services	▪ Sexual Health
▪ How to Stay Healthy	▪ Sexual Assault/Rape
▪ Common Health Problems	▪ Abusive Relationships
▪ Mental Health	▪ Survival Tips
▪ Homesickness	▪ Resources

What can I do to stay healthy?

Eat nutritious food, exercise, and get plenty of rest.

What should I know about nutrition and eating well?

Eating well will keep your body strong, and help your immune system fight off germs that cause colds and other common illnesses.

Learn to:

- Eat a variety of healthy foods. Try to eat 5-7 servings of fruits and vegetables every day.
- Choose foods that are baked, steamed, or grilled, rather than fried.
- Choose fresh foods such as steamed vegetables, fresh fruits, and grilled chicken instead of fast food or processed food.
- Limit the amount of salt that you use. Check out food labels to see if the food you choose is low in sodium.
- Cut down on junk food (candy, chips, soft drinks, etc.).
- Snack on healthy foods such as popcorn, string cheese, fruits, and vegetables.
- Drink 8-10 glasses of water or non-caffeinated fluids every day.
- Remember dairy products. Dairy products such as milk, yogurt, and cheese are high in calcium, which keeps your bones healthy. Eat or drink 3 servings a day of low-fat or fat-free dairy products.
- Take a daily multivitamin (with iron and 0.4 mg folic acid) and 600 units of vitamin D each day.
- If you're a vegetarian, get all the nutrients that you need .

What do I need to know about exercise?

Another important way to stay healthy, reduce stress, and manage your weight is to exercise. Try to include aerobic exercise, muscle strengthening, and stretching exercises into your daily routine. It is recommended that you exercise approximately 60 minutes each day.

- Aerobic exercises include biking, running, fast walking, swimming, dancing, soccer, step aerobics, etc. You can tell that you are doing aerobic exercise because your heart will speed up and you will start breathing faster. However, you should still be able to talk when you are doing aerobic exercise.
- Strengthening exercises (such as sit-ups, push-ups, leg lifts, or weight training) will build up your muscles and keep your bones healthy.
- Stretching exercises (such as yoga) will make you more flexible, so you will be less likely to strain a muscle.
- You can also get exercise by doing simple things, such as walking or riding a bike (with a helmet, of course), instead of driving or taking the bus.

Source: College Health: How to Stay Healthy. *Center for Young Women's Health*. 1 Feb. 2013. Web. 24 June 2013

Center for Young Women's Health

Alignment

Alignment is the primary means by which writers make documents easy to read and create a sense of unity on a page or screen. When you set margins for a report or essay and keep all the paragraphs justified to the left-hand margin, you are using alignment to make your document easier to follow.

Readers depend on conventions for alignment—such as justifying paragraphs to the left or centering titles—which standardize some elements of document design to avoid confusion. Because of these conventions, most readers find it annoying to read text that is aligned to the right-hand margin. And notice how the insertion of columns in the middle of this paragraph makes it harder to follow.

Writers can use alignment to present information efficiently and in visually appealing ways. Notice how the columns at the top of the web page in Figure 20.2 make it easy for a reader to find the right link to other pages on that website. Notice, too, that the bullet points are all aligned in the same way: indented from the left margin. Such an alignment helps set off the main questions and makes it easier for readers to follow the text.

In some kinds of documents, including brochures, newsletters, and web pages, alignment is an essential tool for designing a page or screen that is both visually appealing and easy for a reader to navigate. When aligning elements on a page, consider how the placement of elements will draw a reader's eye and enable the reader to move comfortably from one element to the next.

Proximity

Proximity creates cohesion and shows relationships among elements on a page or screen. Using this principle can help you create documents that are less cluttered and more efficiently organized, especially when you are combining text with visual elements.

Proximity can have a big impact on the appearance and effectiveness of a page. Let's imagine that you are part of a student organization that oversees all club sports on your campus, and you are creating a one-page flier to inform students about the different club sports available to them. You might simply list all the sports:

Join a Club Sport!

Softball	Swimming
Ski Team	Badminton
Bowling	Men's Baseball
Field Hockey	Equestrian
Fencing	Women's Ultimate Frisbee
Wrestling	Men's Ultimate Frisbee
Men's Soccer	Women's Soccer
Snowboarding	Ice Hockey
Men's Volleyball	Men's Lacrosse
Mixed Martial Arts	Women's Volleyball
Women's Rugby	Tae Kwon Do

This unorganized list is visually aligned but tedious to read. To make it easier for students to make sense of the information, you can organize the sports by categories and place similar sports together:

Join a Club Sport!

Co-Ed Sports
- Badminton
- Bowling
- Equestrian
- Fencing
- Swimming
- Tae Kwon Do
- Ultimate Frisbee

Men's Team Sports
- Baseball
- Lacrosse
- Mixed Martial Arts
- Soccer
- Wrestling

Women's Team Sports
- Field Hockey
- Rugby
- Softball
- Soccer
- Volleyball

Winter Sports
- Hockey
- Ski Team
- Snowboarding

Simply by placing similar items together and adding space between the groups, you have organized the page in a way that makes it easier for a reader to find relevant information.

In more sophisticated documents that include images and graphics as well as text, the proximity of elements can significantly improve appearance and readability. For example, notice how many different elements catch your eye on this main web page from Yahoo.com. To make it easier for viewers to find information on a screen with so many elements, similar items are grouped together:

Key links are listed vertically here.

News stories appear together in the center of the page.

Current updated information is placed together in the right-hand column.

Source: *Yahoo!* Yahoo!, n.d. Web. 1 May 2013.

Strategic use of proximity can make such a complex page even more readable. Here's the main page for the social media site Flickr:

Source: *Flickr*. Yahoo!, n.d. Web. 1 May 2013.

Careful grouping of similar items and the use of white space make this page appear clean and coherent, even though it contains a great deal of information. Notice, too, that repetition, contrast, and alignment make the page visually appealing and well organized: The main titles appear in similar font style and size (repetition) but in larger fonts than other text on the page (contrast), which makes them more noticeable; in addition, all the main items are aligned vertically and horizontally, creating a balanced, cohesive, and unified page.

The most effectively designed documents, even relatively simple print texts, use all four design principles together. **When deciding on the design of a document, follow three basic steps:**

1. **Consider your rhetorical situation.** Who is your intended audience? What are your goals in addressing that audience with this document? What expectations might this audience have when it comes to the design of a document?

2. **Be clear about your message.** What is the central point you want to make with this document? What primary information do you hope to communicate?

3. **Apply the four principles of basic design.** How can you use contrast, repetition, alignment, and proximity to communicate your message effectively to your intended audience? How can you use these principles to make your document appealing and efficient?

Use the four basic principles of document design to evaluate this flier from a public television station. The document is intended to help parents identify potential reading problems in their children. Assess how effectively the document uses design elements to convey its message to its intended audience.

Ed|Extras

Place your school name
or logo here

Helpful information about learning brought to you by Reading Rockets, Colorín Colorado, and LD OnLine

Recognizing Reading Problems

Learning to read is a challenge for many kids, but most can become good readers if they get the right help. Parents have an important job in recognizing when a child is struggling and knowing how to find help.

What to look for:
- Difficulty rhyming
- Difficulty hearing individual sounds
- Difficulty following directions
- Difficulty re-telling a story
- Struggles to sound out most words
- Avoids reading aloud

What to do:
- **Step 1: Meet with your child's teacher**
  Gather examples of your child's work that reflect your concerns. Ask the teacher for his/her observations and discuss what can be done at school and at home. Stay in touch with the teacher to monitor your child's progress.
- **Step 2: Meet with the principal and/or reading specialist**
  If your child's performance does not improve, meet with other professionals in the building to see if there are classes, services, or other interventions available.
- **Step 3: Get a referral for special education**
  If you have tried all interventions, request an evaluation. Talk to the principal to schedule this.
- **Step 4: Get an evaluation**
  A professional team—which may include a school psychologist, a speech-language pathologist, or a reading specialist—gives your child a series of tests and determines whether s/he is eligible to receive special education services.
- **Step 5: Determine eligibility**
  - If your child is found eligible for services, you and the school develop your child's Individualized Education Program (IEP), a plan that sets goals based on your child's specific learning needs and offers special services like small group instruction or assistive technology.
  - If your child is not eligible, stay involved and keep talking to the teacher about your child's progress. You can also turn to private tutoring for extra support.

Check out the *Assessment* section for more information on identifying reading problems:
www.ReadingRockets.org/article/c68

Visit our sister sites, ColorinColorado.org and LDOnLine.org, for more information about learning.

Reading Rockets, Colorín Colorado, and LD OnLine are services of public television station WETA, Washington, D.C. Reading Rockets is funded by the U.S. Department of Education, Office of Special Education Programs. Colorín Colorado, a web service to help English language learners become better readers, receives major funding from the American Federation of Teachers. Additional funding is provided by the National Institute for Literacy and the U.S. Department of Education, Office of Special Education Programs. LD OnLine is the world's leading website on learning disabilities and ADHD, with major funding from Lindamood-Bell Learning Processes.

Source: *Recognizing Reading Problems*, Reading Rockets. WETA. 2012. Web. 12 April 2013.

Working with Visual Elements

Many documents include photographs, charts, graphics, and other visual elements. Increasingly, college instructors expect students to incorporate such elements into conventional papers. However, visual elements should never be used simply as ornamentation; rather, they should be used in a way that communicates information, conveys important ideas, and enhances the effectiveness of the document.

This section provides advice on using two common kinds of visual elements:

■ tables, graphs, and charts
■ images

Working with Tables, Graphs, and Charts

Many college assignments require students to work with quantitative information. For example, an analysis of the economic impact of college loan debt for an economics course will likely include various kinds of statistical data. Often, such data are most effectively presented in a table, bar graph, line graph, or pie chart. Contemporary word processing programs make it easy to create such elements in a variety of formats. However, the key to using such elements effectively is knowing what you want your readers to understand from the information you are presenting. Consider:

■ **What is the nature of the information?** Numerical data can be easy to convert into a chart or table. Other kinds of information, such as directions for a procedure or a list of specific responses to a survey question, might not work as well in a graphical format. A chart or table should make the information easier for a reader to understand. Avoid using a graphical format if it makes the information more complicated or confusing.

■ **What is the purpose of the information?** You present information for various reasons: to explain a concept, event, or development; to support a claim or assertion; to strengthen an argument; to illustrate a key idea or principle. The purpose can shape your decision about how best to present the information. For example, if you want to emphasize a specific set of statistics to support a central claim in an argument, using a graph or pie chart to present the data can make them more persuasive.

■ **Tables, charts, and graphs have four basic elements:**

■ a title
■ a vertical axis, called the y axis
■ a horizontal axis, called the x axis
■ the main body of data

Numerical data such as survey results are commonly reported in the form of tables or graphs, but deciding how best to present that information depends on how you are using it in your report. Let's imagine you are writing a report on the benefits of a college education and want to report the results of a survey of students who graduated in the past three years from three different departments on your campus. The survey was intended to learn about average starting salaries of graduates from your school. If you are simply reporting the survey results to help your readers understand the average salaries of recent graduates, you might use a simple **table**. In this example, the *y* axis is used for the three different departments and the *x* axis for the three recent years; the main body of data is the starting salaries. The table would look like this:

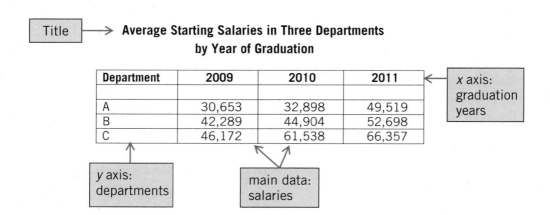

This table helps readers easily find the average salary for a specific department in a specific graduation year. Consider how much more tedious it is for readers to read an explanation of this information, which might look like this:

> The average starting salary for students who graduated from Department A in 2009 was $30,653; in 2010 it was $32,898, and in 2011 it was $49,519. For students who graduated from Department B in 2009, the average starting salary was $42,289; in 2010 it was $44,904, and in 2011 it was $52,698. Students who graduated from Department C in 2009 earned an average starting salary of $46,172; for 2010 graduates the average starting salary was $61,538, and in 2011 it was $66,357.

Although presenting numerical information visually isn't always the most effective approach, in a case like this one, it is much more efficient than a verbal explanation.

A simple table might be too limited for presenting more complicated bodies of data, especially if you want to compare information. Let's say that for the same report on the benefits of college, you wanted to emphasize differences in the potential earnings of students entering specific professions. A **bar graph** is an effective means for comparing information. This graph presents salary ranges in a way that makes it easy for a reader to compare the top, median, and bottom salaries in three different professions:

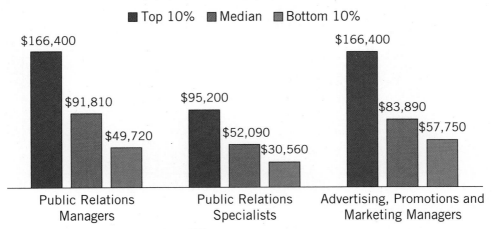

Salary Range for Advertising and Public Relations Professions

■ Top 10%   ■ Median   ■ Bottom 10%

Public Relations Managers: $166,400 / $91,810 / $49,720
Public Relations Specialists: $95,200 / $52,090 / $30,560
Advertising, Promotions and Marketing Managers: $166,400 / $83,890 / $57,750

Source: *Gradschools.com*. N.p., n.d. Web. 15 June 2013.

Here the *y* axis is used for salary ranges and the *x* axis for the type of position; the data are the salaries.

If you wanted to show a trend or trajectory reflected in statistical information over time, **a line graph** might be a better option. For example, let's say you included in your report data to show trends in the starting salaries of male and female college graduates over the past two decades. This line graph makes it very easy for readers to see those trends and compare the salaries of men and women who earned college degrees:

20

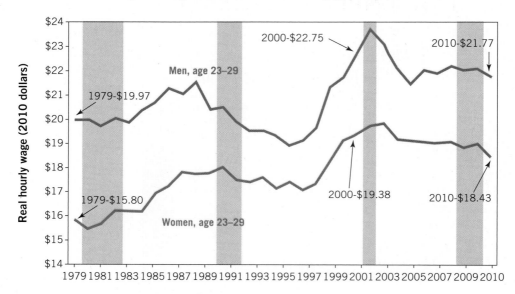

New college graduates losing ground on wages

Entry-level wages of male and female college graduates, 1979–2010

Real hourly wage (2010 dollars)

Men, age 23–29

1979-$19.97

2000-$22.75

2010-$21.77

1979-$15.80

Women, age 23–29

2000-$19.38

2010-$18.43

Source: EPI's analysis of the Current Population Survey, Outgoing Rotations Group.

Source: *New College Graduates Losing Ground on Wages.* Digital image. *Trends in Starting Salaries for College Grads.* Sociological Images, 4 Sept. 2011. Web. 17 June 2013.

In this example, the *y* axis shows hourly wages and the *x* axis shows the years from 1979 to 2010.

Tables, graphs, and charts can present information efficiently, but they also can be misleading. For example, let's say you want to show the percentage of four items in the budget of a student organization you work for: item A (11%), item B (42%), item C (5%), and item D (42%). In addition, you want to highlight item C, which is the smallest expenditure. Your pie chart might look like this:

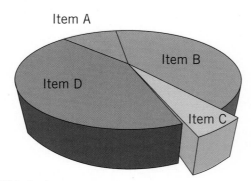

Item A

Item B

Item D

Item C

Source: "Misleading Graph." *Wikipedia.* Wikipedia Foundation. N.d. Web. 15 June 2013.

This three-dimensional chart, which makes it seem that you are looking at it from the side and slightly above it, is visually striking. Notice, however, that item C, which is only 5% of the budget, appears bigger than item A, which is 11% of the budget. Now here's the same information presented in a simpler, two-dimensional pie chart:

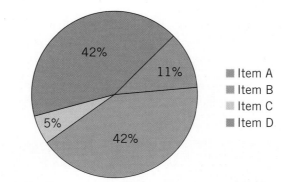

Source: "Misleading Graph." *Wikipedia*. Wikipedia Foundation. N.d. Web. 15 June 2013.

In this case, the simpler chart presents the information more accurately. Keep in mind that small changes in the design of a table, chart, or graph can dramatically affect the appearance of the information, sometimes making small differences appear much larger and thus conveying a misleading idea about that information. Although such strategies might seem effective in supporting a claim or point of view, they might also be ethically questionable. You should always use graphical elements in a way that presents information not only accurately but also ethically.

Working with Images

For many documents, effective design includes the use of images, but simply incorporating images into a document isn't necessarily enough to improve its design. Using images effectively is a matter of making sure the images are appropriate for your document and help address your rhetorical situation.

When using images, follow the same basic principles that apply to document design in general (see page 662):

- **Consider your audience.** The images you select should be relevant to your subject matter and appropriate for your rhetorical situation. For example, a photograph of a car on a brochure about campus transportation services is probably a poor choice if the majority of students live on campus, do not drive cars to campus, and use the campus bus service. Moreover, consider whether the images you select might seem confusing or offensive to your audience. A photograph that might convey relevant information dramatically could also weaken your document if the image is considered inappropriate for some reason by your readers.

- **Consider your message.** Images in your document should reinforce important ideas or information. Ideally, images should convey information rather than just supplement written text. For example, a photograph of a specific location should enable the audience to gain an understanding of that location without a lengthy verbal description to accompany the image.

- **Avoid ornamentation.** Sometimes, images are used to enhance the appearance of a document, but too many images used simply as decoration can become distracting for readers and therefore undermine the document's effectiveness.

- **Make a good impression.** Any images used in a document should contribute to the overall impression a document makes on the intended audience. A poorly selected image could weaken an otherwise effective document.

In addition to these basic principles, **consider how the content and perspective of an image fit your rhetorical situation**. For example, compare these two versions of the same photograph:

What is the difference between them? How does the potential impact of each differ? As this example demonstrates, simply "cropping" an image—that is, selecting a section of it and eliminating the rest—can dramatically change its impact and message. In this example, the version on the left might be appropriate for a report in a zoology class that includes descriptions of various kinds of raptors; the photograph could be used to show the size and color of a specific species of raptor. The cropped version on the right might be used to emphasize the extraordinary eyesight of raptors or to dramatize the fierce nature of a particular species. Your rhetorical purpose should dictate how you use an image and how you might alter it.

The **perspective** of an image can have a powerful effect on the message it communicates. Let's imagine you are writing an analysis of the social and economic impact of severe weather, such as a hurricane. The photograph on page 677 dramatically conveys the devastating effects of the storm on property as well as the lives on local residents.

FEMA/Alamy

Notice that the perspective from which the photograph was taken (above and at a distance from the subjects) highlights the sense of vulnerability of the people in the photo, who appear small in comparison to the damaged homes surrounding them. This photo would be less effective in conveying these ideas if it were taken from ground (or water) level or from closer to the subjects. This photograph dramatically highlights the extent of storm-caused devastation and its impact on residents in a way that would be challenging to explain in words alone. At the same time, such an image can provoke strong emotions in readers and therefore can be used to influence readers—for example, to convince readers of the need to prepare for future storms or to contribute to a fund to help storm victims.

Like any other design elements, images should be placed strategically so that they convey their messages without undermining the overall appearance of a document. Images that are too large, for example, might distract a reader from other important information on a page. Images that are too small might not communicate important information clearly.

1. Imagine you are writing an analysis of the impact of smartphone technology on college students for a general audience. For each of the following items, decide whether to present the information in a chart, table, graph, or written description; explain your reasons for your decision in each case:

   - The most common uses of smartphone among college students are surfing the Internet, texting, and playing games; 85% of students report using their smart phones for playing games much more often than for any other purpose.

   - In 2010, 42% of college students reported owning a smartphone. In 2013, 73% of college students reported owning a smartphone. In 2010, 27% of Americans owned smartphones. In 2013, 65% of Americans owned smartphones.

   - Since 2008, sales of smartphones have increased by an average of 15% annually.

   - In 2009, college students spent an average of $65 per month for their cell phone service. In 2012, college students spent an average of $80 per month for smartphone service.

2. Using some of the information in Question #1, create a table, graph, and chart. (You can easily create these elements using a word processing program such as Microsoft Word.) Use the same information for each graphic. Compare the table, chart, and graph. What are the differences in the way they present the same information? What advantages and disadvantages do you see to each kind of graphic?

3. Using the example from Question #1, search online to find one or two images that you might use in your analysis of smartphones. Explain how you would use each image in your analysis. Justify your selection of images in terms of how they would help you accomplish specific rhetorical goals.

Designing Documents: Three Sample Projects

This section presents three common kinds of projects that illustrate how the same basic design features can make different kinds of documents effective in meeting the needs of a rhetorical situation.

Print Documents

For most college assignments, you are likely to be asked to submit a conventional paper, whether in hard copy or in a digital form (such as a Microsoft Word file), but even conventional papers can be more effective when writers apply the principles of design. Whenever you submit a conventional paper for an assignment, be sure to follow the appropriate conventions for formatting, which include such elements as font size, the uses of underlining and boldface, and the format for citing sources. (See Chapters 24 and 25 for information about proper format for papers in MLA and APA style.) You can also use the design principles in this chapter to enhance even the most traditional kind of paper by making sure that your font sizes and styles are consistent, you use features such as underlining strategically, and you avoid ornamentation.

Sometimes, however, your rhetorical situation might call for a print document that is not a conventional paper—for example, a flier, brochure, or memo. In such cases, applying the principles of document design can enhance the document's effectiveness, even when the document is relatively simple. Here, for example, is a one-page flier with information for college students about getting proper sleep. The flier was developed by a college health and counseling center and made available in print as well as in PDF format on the center's website. It illustrates how even a basic print document can more effectively meet the needs of a rhetorical situation when design principles are carefully applied.

1. Consider the rhetorical context. ⇒	2. Be clear about your message. ⇒	3. Apply the principles of design.
• The health and counseling center helps students deal with lifestyle and health issues common to college life. One such problem is insomnia. The center's goal is to inform students on its campus about the importance of proper sleep without overwhelming busy students with information.	• The main point is to show that students can use several easy strategies to avoid insomnia and get proper rest. Also, knowing the common causes of poor sleep can help students avoid sleep problems.	• The one-page flier incorporates no images and only two small graphics, but it uses the principles of contrast, alignment, and repetition to convey a great deal of information efficiently and to reinforce the main point about getting proper sleep.

H&C | HEALTH & COUNSELING

health.geneseo.edu

Division of Student and Campus Life
State University of New York at Geneseo
1 College Circle, Geneseo, New York 14454
Phone: (585) 245-5716; Fax: (585) 245-5071

GETTING A GOOD NIGHT'S SLEEP

Insomnia Triggers to Avoid

Diet. caffeine; alcohol; nicotine; prescription and non-prescription medication, including sleeping pills
Lifestyle. irregular bedtimes; exercising just before bedtime/lack of exercise; daytime naps

Bedroom Environment. noise; light
Psychological Factors. academic and other stress; family problems; other interpersonal issues

Behavioral Strategies for Improving Sleep

Develop a Bedtime Routine. Stop doing anything stimulating (including studying!) about a half hour *before* you are ready to go to bed. Develop a wind-down ritual that includes doing something relaxing—such as reading for pleasure, listening to soft music, watching a mindless TV show, performing gentle stretches—followed by set pre-bed activities (e.g., washing up, brushing your teeth). As much as possible, you should try to go to bed at about the same time every night. Finally, try to get up at approximately the same time every day as well; don't oversleep to make up for lost sleep.

Plan the Right Time to Go To Bed. Go to bed *at the time when you usually fall asleep*—i.e., if you usually fall asleep at 2 a.m., go to bed *then*, not at 12 a.m. Once your body adjusts to this, you can gradually try pushing this time back earlier, first to 1:45 a.m., then to 1:30 a.m., etc.

Stop Intrusive Thoughts. Keep a pad and pencil handy by your bed. If you think of something you want to remember, jot it down. Then let the thought go; there will be no need to lie awake worrying about remembering it. You might also want to try this visualization technique: pretend that your mind is a chalk board. Every time a worrisome thought enters your head, visualize it as written on the chalk board and then immediately erase it. Keep erasing these thoughts as they pop up and refuse to think about them until later. Remember that sometimes it doesn't hurt to be like Scarlet O'Hara and say "I'll think about that tomorrow!"

Reduce Physical Stress. If you find that your are physically unable to relax, you might benefit from progressive muscle relaxation, a technique which involves alternately tensing and relaxing each major muscle in your body one-by-one. For example, starting with your upper body, flex your shoulders tightly towards your ears. Hold this position, making the muscles as tight as you can, for 10 seconds. Release and relax your shoulders, noticing the difference between the tense and relaxed positions and feeling the warmth associated with the relaxation of the muscle; relax and breathe for 15-20 seconds. Continue this process with the other muscles in your body, working from your shoulders, neck, and arms down to your midsection, buttocks, and legs.

Get Out of Bed! If you are lying in bed and are unable to sleep, the best thing you can do is to get *out of bed*. Most people fall asleep within 15 minutes of going to bed, so if you're not asleep after half an hour, get up and go elsewhere to engage in a quiet activity—reading, writing letters, etc. Do not eat, drink, or smoke, which could cause you to wake up for these things in the future. When you start to feel sleepy, return to bed. Repeat this routine as often as necessary, and follow these same steps if you wake up in the middle of the night and can't fall back asleep. If you awake in the early morning hours, get up to start your day. Try to avoid naps; instead, go to bed your usual time the following night.

Other Resources

NOTE: Both of the books below can be borrowed from the Counseling Services Self-Help Lending Library, Lauderdale 205.

Getting a Good Night's Sleep—This book by Moore-Ede and LeVert helps identify factors which affect sleep, find solutions to common sleep problems, develop more healthy sleep habits, and work towards stress reduction.

The Relaxation and Stress Reduction Workbook—This book by Eshelman and McKay contains in-depth descriptions of various techniques for increasing relaxation and reducing stress, both of which improve sleep.

Still having problems? Visit us on the web at go.geneseo.edu/HotTopics and select "College Students & Sleep."

because it's your health.   *Rev. 2/12*

Source: Division of Student and Campus Life. Getting a Good Night's Sleep. Geneseo, NY: State University of New York at Geneseo, 2008. Web. 15 May 2013. Available at http://www.geneseo.edu/health/sleep; see also http://www.geneseo.edu/health/sleep.

Prezi Presentation

College students today are routinely asked to make presentations as part of their assignments. Often, students turn to presentation software, especially PowerPoint, which enables a speaker to present information visually to an audience. Prezi is an online tool for making presentations that is similar to PowerPoint in that it enables a writer to convey information efficiently and in visually engaging ways on screens or "slides." (See "Using Prezi.") Like PowerPoint, Prezi also allows the writer to embed images, sound, and video in a presentation. However, there are **two important differences between Prezi and PowerPoint**:

- PowerPoint presentations usually supplement the presenter's spoken words. By contrast, Prezi presentations are generally intended to be viewed online rather than presented by the author. However, increasingly students use Prezi in place of PowerPoint to supplement their oral presentations.

- Unlike PowerPoint, which requires you to present information sequentially from one slide to the next, Prezi is a dynamic tool that enables you to arrange text and images on a single screen according to an organizing theme or metaphor; a viewer clicks arrows to move from one place on the screen to another to follow a story or access information. Each individual screen in a Prezi presentation is therefore a section of the whole presentation rather than a discrete slide, as in PowerPoint.

Despite these differences, the same principles for designing an effective PowerPoint presentation apply to Prezi. The best presentations

- are well organized
- have a coherent visual theme
- do not overwhelm the viewer with text
- take advantage of the visual capabilities of the presentation tool
- apply the principles of design

SIDEBAR   USING PREZI

Although there are differences between Prezi and PowerPoint, learning to use Prezi is no more difficult than learning to use PowerPoint. To use Prezi, you must create a Prezi account (visit prezi.com). The Prezi website includes a great deal of information and advice for using the tool and taking advantage of its multimedia capabilities.

Here's an example of a Prezi presentation that meets these criteria and uses design principles effectively. The author, Hayley Ashburner, created this presentation for an assignment in a writing class at the University of North Carolina at Wilmington. The assignment called for students to tell their own literacy histories and how their experiences fit into larger cultural and historical contexts. Hayley's narrative focused on her journey from her birthplace in South Africa to a new home in Australia and the impact of that journey on her literacy and use of technology.

1. Consider the rhetorical context.	2. Be clear about your message.	3. Apply the principles of design.
• Hayley's presentation was intended for students in her writing class, but because it would be available online at prezi.com, it might also be viewed by a much broader audience. Her primary purpose was to tell her literacy history in a way that was consistent with the expectations of her course, but she also wanted her story to resonate with viewers outside her class who might simply be interested in her unique story.	• Hayley's main idea was that her experiences growing up in two different cultures shaped her as a person and as a reader and writer. She wanted to explore how her experiences affected her sense of herself and her uses of literacy and technology in her life.	• Hayley developed her presentation so a viewer could follow her journey as a person who grew up in two different cultures. She relied on the principles of proximity and alignment to make her presentation engaging and to organize her journey into a coherent story.

Here's the main screen of Hayley's presentation, titled "African Dreams":

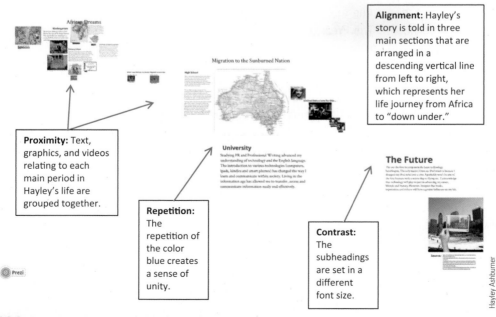

Alignment: Hayley's story is told in three main sections that are arranged in a descending vertical line from left to right, which represents her life journey from Africa to "down under."

Proximity: Text, graphics, and videos relating to each main period in Hayley's life are grouped together.

Repetition: The repetition of the color blue creates a sense of unity.

Contrast: The subheadings are set in a different font size.

Hayley Ashburner

A viewer navigates the presentation by clicking arrows that appear at the bottom of the screen. Here's what a viewer sees after the first three clicks:

1. The first click emphasizes the title, "African Dreams":

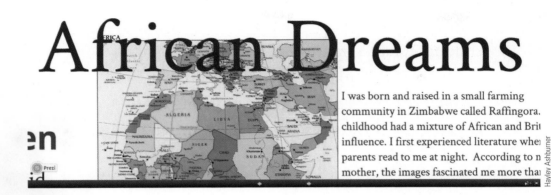

2. The next click zooms in on a map to show Hayley's birthplace:

3. The next click highlights text describing Hayley's early years:

I was born and raised in a small farming community in Zimbabwe called Raffingora. My childhood had a mixture of African and British influence. I first experienced literature when my parents read to me at night. According to my mother, the images fascinated me more than the words. My brothers and I were exposed to a variety of music by my parents and encouraged to perform in community plays.

Hayley Ashburner

Throughout her presentation, which included 35 separate screens, Hayley combined carefully written text with images and video clips to keep her audience engaged and to make her story coherent. Her selection of these elements also reflected her effort to communicate her main point about the influence of culture on her. The text in the following screen, for example, explains how various media helped her become familiar with Australian culture:

Television, phones, radio and computers helped my family adjust to life in Australia. The internet offered a cost effective way to communicate with friends and family back in Zimbabwe. Whilst, local television and radio exposed us to Australian culture, lifestyle and events. Listening to the radio, watching television and communicating with new peers changed the way I spoke. "Ya" became "yeah", "Chum" became "Mate" and "That's tight" became "hell good!" It also advanced my taste in music.

Hayley Ashburner

The next few clicks take the viewer through two embedded videos that illustrate her evolving taste in music:

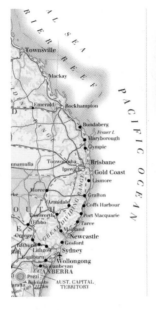

Clicking the video on the left starts a video clip with music that Hayley listened to in South Africa; clicking the right-hand video starts music that she listened to in Australia. Using sound and video in this way, she conveys to the viewer a deeper sense of her experience. The proximity of these videos and the contrast between them highlight the change in her musical tastes over time and communicate a sense of her development as a person.

(You can view Hayley's complete presentation at http://prezi.com/c1q2bitx009e/literacy-narrative/).

Designing a Website

Websites are an invaluable means by which organizations and individuals establish a presence and communicate information to various audiences. Web authoring software (e.g., Dreamweaver) can make it easy to create a sophisticated website, but the use of basic design principles is what makes a website rhetorically effective. The most effective websites are:

- **Clean and uncluttered.** Too much text and too many images can make a website messy and difficult for visitors to find information. A website should not overwhelm visitors. Use relevant graphics that bconvey important ideas or information, and keep text limited and easy to read.
- **Easy to navigate.** Websites are tools that should be easy for visitors to use. The design should enable visitors to find information easily and quickly. Even extensive websites with

many separate pages can be designed so that visitors don't get lost or confused as they seek specific information.

- **Coherent.** Appealing websites have a consistent appearance that unifies the various pages and gives the entire site a feeling of coherence. Color schemes, font styles, and graphics tend to be consistent from one page to another, which can give the site a sense of focus and make it easier for visitors to find what they are looking for.

Following these guidelines and applying the principles of design can give a website a professional appearance and enhance its ability to address its intended audience. This website was developed for the Capital District Writing Project, a non-profit organization that promotes effective writing instruction in schools and provides services to teachers, students, and communities to help improve writing. Shown here is the main page of the site. Notice how clean and uncluttered the page appears. It also has a coherent visual theme, with two main colors and consistent font styles and sizes, that is applied to all individual pages on the site. Significantly, the page is designed so that various audiences—teachers, school administrators, and parents—can get a sense of the organization's purpose and find the specific information they need.

1. Consider the rhetorical context.	⇒	2. Be clear about your message.	⇒	3. Apply the principles of design.
• The organization serves teachers, students, and schools in its region. Its website is intended to convey a sense of its mission to those audiences and to provide relevant information about its services. It must compete with many other organizations that are involved in education.		• The central point of the main page of the website is that the organization is an important resource for teachers and administrators interested in improving writing, teaching, and learning in their school districts.		• The main page of the website uses contrast, alignment, and proximity to convey its message and highlight important information contained on the website. It presents a clear and professional image through its strategic use of image, layout, and color.

Capital District Writing Project

Notice that the main elements on this page are easier to find because of the strategic use of white space between them. Also, the single image of a teacher writing reflects the organization's purpose without distracting a visitor. The navigation bar includes links for specific audiences.

Designing Documents: Three Sample Projects **687**

Finding Source Material

RECENT STUDIES INDICATE that research-based writing, which has always been a mainstay of academic writing, is becoming ever more common in the assignments students encounter in their college courses. So being able to work effectively with sources is essential for successful college writing. This chapter will guide you in learning how to locate relevant information from a variety of sources.

Understanding Research

To understand research-based writing, we have to go back to the beginning, Core Concept #1: "Writing is a process of discovery and learning" (see Chapter 2). When you write, you are engaged in a powerful form of inquiry. You are writing to learn, to explore an idea, to examine an issue or problem, to understand an experience, to solve a problem, to participate in conversations about subjects that matter to you. You are *not* writing for the purpose of using source material. Consulting sources is part of the process of inquiry that writing should be; it is not the *reason* for writing.

Let me illustrate with a story about my own writing. While I was still in college, I made a road trip with a friend that took me through the Badlands of South Dakota, a remote, sparsely populated, and starkly beautiful region of pastel-colored hills, mesas, and prairies etched with countless canyons and dry creek beds. As we drove along a desolate stretch of Interstate 90, we passed one of those large green exit signs. Under that sign someone had attached another sign: a weathered plank with hand-painted red letters that read, "Doctor wanted." The sign surprised us and made us wonder: Were the residents of that isolated area really so desperate for medical care that they resorted to posting hand-painted signs on the Interstate? Was their situation common in rural areas? Was medical care scarce for Americans who lived in such areas? I had never really thought about what it might be like to live in a remote area where things that I took for granted—like medical care—might not be available.

When I returned from my trip, I contacted a cousin who is a family doctor and told him about the sign. He explained that providing doctors for remote rural areas was a longstanding challenge in the United States that was complicated by rising health care costs and the growing use of expensive medical technology. I was intrigued and wanted to know more. I contacted a magazine editor, who expressed interest in an article on the topic. At that point, I had a topic, an interesting and relevant experience, some basic information, and a lot of additional questions. I also had a goal: to inform the readers of the magazine about a little-known problem in American health care. I was ready to learn more. I could now begin my research.

Alan Crawford/Gannet77/iStockphoto.com; xyno/iStockphoto.com

As my story suggests, research should begin with a question or problem that you want to address—one that matters not only to you but also to a potential audience. Once you have a topic and a sense of your rhetorical situation, you can begin gathering information to help you understand your topic and answer your questions. Finding sources is then a purposeful activity: the sources help you achieve your rhetorical goals.

So the most important thing to remember about working with sources is that it isn't about the sources. In other words, your focus should be, first, on the purpose of your project and how it fits your rhetorical situation. So start there:

- What are you writing about and *why*?
- What are you trying to accomplish with a particular writing project?
- What do you need to know in order to accomplish your rhetorical goals?

By the time you're ready to begin consulting sources, you should already have begun exploring your subject and have a sense of your intended audience and the purpose of your project. Your rhetorical goals should guide your research—not the other way around.

A common mistake many students make in research-based writing is moving too quickly to the process of finding sources. After receiving an assignment, the first thing they do is go online to search for information about a possible topic before they have begun to develop some idea of what they will say about that topic. As a result, what they find online (or elsewhere), rather than their rhetorical purpose, guides their project. In such cases, the resulting project is often a compilation of source material rather than a genuine inquiry into the subject.

To avoid that mistake, follow the steps in Chapter 3 and don't focus on looking for source material until you have begun exploring your topic and have a good sense of your rhetorical situation. It's certainly OK to peruse source material to get ideas about a topic, but if your research is purposeful rather than haphazard, finding sources will be part of the process of inquiry that writing should be.

Doing research today is a kind of good news/bad news proposition. The good news is that students have ready access to an astonishing amount and variety of material online so that they can quickly find information on almost any conceivable topic. The bad news is that having access to so much information can be overwhelming and make it difficult to distinguish useful information from erroneous or dubious information. Following a few simple guidelines will enable you to take advantage of the wealth of material available to you and avoid the common pitfalls of finding useful and reliable sources.

The key to finding appropriate sources is threefold:

- determining what you need
- understanding available sources
- developing a search strategy

The remainder of this chapter is devoted to examining these three aspects of finding relevant source material.

Determining What You Need

To make your research efficient and successful, it's best to identify the kinds of information you need. Otherwise, your searches are likely to be haphazard and overly time-consuming. Follow these basic steps:

1. Consider the purpose of your project and your intended audience.

2. Generate questions you will probably need to address.

3. Identify possible sources of information to address those questions.

To illustrate, let's look at three writing assignments that call for research:

- a literacy narrative requiring you to analyze your own experiences as a young reader and writer in terms of available research on literacy development

- an argument in favor of abolishing the electoral college in U.S. presidential elections

- a history of your neighborhood focusing on the period since the end of World War II

1. Consider Your Purpose and Audience

Literacy narrative	• To gain insight into your own literacy experiences • To understand literacy development in general • To share this learning with students in your writing class
Argument against electoral college	• To illuminate problems with the current election system • To propose an increasingly popular solution to an important problem • To encourage other voting citizens to consider this solution
History of your neighborhood	• To understand important developments in your neighborhood's past • To understand how the past affects the present • To share these insights with other students of history and neighborhood residents

2. Generate Questions You Might Need to Address

Literacy narrative	• What important childhood experiences shaped you as reader and writer? • What role did literacy play in your life as an adolescent? • What influence did your family have in your writing and reading habits? • What does research indicate are the key factors that affect literacy ability?
Argument against electoral college	• How exactly does the electoral college work? Why was it developed? • What are the main criticisms of the electoral college? • What problems have occurred in past elections? • What solutions have others proposed? What concerns do critics have about these solutions?
History of your neighborhood	• What key economic, political, and social developments occurred in your neighborhood since WWII? What changes have taken place in that time? • How do these developments relate to broader developments in your region or the nation? • What problems does the neighborhood face today? How are those problems related to past developments?

3. Identify Possible Sources to Answer Your Questions

Literacy narrative	• Family members; former teachers • Relevant artifacts from your childhood (school papers, books, letters) • Scholarly articles and books about literacy development • Published studies of childhood literacy
Argument against electoral college	• Reference works on political science and elections • Articles in political journals, newspapers, newsmagazines • Blog posts, public affairs websites • Materials from political watchdog groups
History of your neighborhood	• Archived newspaper articles • Documents from local historical society or state museum • Op-ed essays in local newspapers, websites, blogs • Interviews with local leaders

These examples illustrate **several important points about finding sources:**

- **The kind of information you need and the possible sources for that information depend on the nature of your project and rhetorical situation.** For example, the literacy narrative assignment requires finding specialized information about literacy development that is most likely available only in academic publications. Moreover, because of the specialized nature of the assignment and the fact that it is intended for an academic audience, the instructor will probably expect students to consult scholarly sources. By contrast, the argument about the electoral college is intended for a more general, less specialized audience. It addresses a topic that has been discussed in a variety of contexts, including academic journals as well as the popular press and digital media. Given that rhetorical situation and the more general appeal of the topic, some relevant sources will probably be less specialized than those for the literacy narrative assignment.

- **Identifying what you don't know will help you find the right sources for what you need to know.** By starting the research process with questions that you need to answer, you will quickly identify what you don't know about your topic, which will help you identify what you *need to know*. For example, for the argument against the electoral college, you might already have a sense of the problems with the current election system, but you might have little knowledge of the history of that system or what experts and others have said about it. Similarly, for the neighborhood history, you might know a lot about the present economic and political situation in your neighborhood but little about how it came to be that way. Posing questions about your topic helps you identify such gaps in your knowledge and points you to possible sources of information to fill those gaps.

- **Some projects call for original research.** Two of these three examples point to the possibility of students doing their own *primary research* (see "Primary vs. Secondary Research"). For the neighborhood history project, for example, students might interview politicians and other local leaders as well as examine archived documents in a local historical society or museum. For the literacy narrative assignment, students might interview family members and former teachers and use documents such as old school papers. These original sources will be supplemented by *secondary sources*, such as academic journals, newspapers, books, or websites.

- **Research begets research.** The more you learn about your topic, the more questions you are likely to have. That's as it should be. For example, in researching the history of your neighborhood, you might discover that the closing of a local factory after World War II left many residents out of work, which led to an exodus of young people to other towns and states. Learning about that development might lead to questions about the basis for the local economy, which in turn might lead you to look at sources (e.g., economic data) that you had not previously considered. Similarly, in reading a journal article about childhood literacy for your literacy narrative, you might encounter a reference to a study about the relationship between literacy development and social class. That study in turn might prompt you to re-examine your own literacy development in terms of your socio-economic background. As you proceed with your research, you will learn more about your topic, which will probably mean that you will begin to understand better what you need to know to complete your project.

FOCUS Primary vs. Secondary Research

Scholars usually distinguish between two kinds of research.

Primary research is first-hand investigation. It involves conducting experiments, collecting various kinds of data (such as through surveys, interviews, or observation), or examining original documents (such as manuscripts, public records, or letters) or artifacts in libraries or museums. If you interview someone, design and distribute a survey, conduct a laboratory experiment, or analyze data that have not been previously published, you are conducting primary research. Most college students do not engage in primary research, although some college assignments require such research.

Secondary research is based on the work of others. It involves investigating what other people have already published on a given subject—in other words, finding information about a topic online, in books, in magazine or journal articles, and in similar sources. Most of the research college students do is secondary research. The advice in this chapter generally assumes that you are doing secondary research.

Understanding Sources

The examples in the previous section suggest the wide variety of available sources for research-based writing. The main challenge is finding the right sources containing the material you need to meet the rhetorical goals for your project. Understanding the different kinds of available sources will help you do so.

In this section, we will examine **two main categories of sources:**

- print materials
- online resources

The distinction between print and online resources has become increasingly blurred as many traditional print sources become available online or disappear altogether. Most print newspapers and magazines now have websites where online versions of print articles are available. Similarly, scholarly journals usually make articles available in both print and online form. For our purposes, *print materials* will refer to anything that appears in conventional print form (e.g., books, newspaper articles, magazines), whether or not it appears in an online version; materials that appear only online, such as blogs and websites, will be considered *online resources*. Despite some similarities between traditional print and online materials, there are important differences between these two categories of source materials, and understanding those differences will enable you to make the best use of available resources.

Print Materials

Despite the growing importance of online resources, print materials remain essential for much academic research. The main kinds of print materials that students are likely to consult for college assignments are the following:

- books (scholarly or trade)
- scholarly journals
- magazines and newspapers

Books. In today's instant-access digital age, books can seem archaic. It can be easy to find up-to-the-minute information on media websites, quickly get facts about a topic by using a search engine like Google, or instantly access information about a subject on a reference website like Wikipedia. Getting information from a book, on the other hand, requires you to go to the library (or bookstore) and physically page through the book to find what you need (unless you are using an e-reader like a Kindle, which enables you to search the contents of the book digitally). Nevertheless, printed books tend to be stable sources of information compared to many online resources, which can change without notice or even disappear, making it difficult for readers to access or verify the information. The involved process of producing a book requires writers and editors to consider the relevance of the content over a longer term than is necessary for much online material. Unlike websites, which can be revised and updated constantly, books are likely to remain in print for years before being revised or updated. In general, that means that if you cite information contained in a book, readers who want to track it down will be able to do so.

In addition, books, notably scholarly books, often contain the best of what is known about a subject. That's partly because scholarly publishers generally do not publish with an eye toward what is trendy or popular; rather, they look for material that reflects state-of-the-art understanding in a particular field. As a result, scholarly books often reflect the knowledge that an academic field has generated over many years. This does not mean that books are always accurate or unbiased (see "Detecting Bias" in Chapter 22); sometimes a new development in a field will significantly change or even invalidate previous thinking about an important subject in that field, and like trade books, scholarly books can reflect a particular perspective or school of thought. But by and large, scholarly books and many trade books are credible, stable sources of information.

Scholarly journals. If you search your college library's periodical holdings, you will discover that there are thousands of scholarly journals devoted to every academic subject and their many sub-specialties. For example, in 2012 the library of the State University of New York at Albany listed 429 scholarly journals in the field of general biology and an additional 597 journals in subspecialties such as genetics and microbiology. Taken together, these journals (most of which appear online as well as in print form) reflect the most up-to-date knowledge in biology and its subfields. Every academic field, no matter how small or specialized, has its own scholarly journals. In addition, some prestigious journals publish articles from many related fields. The journal *Science*, for example, publishes articles from all fields of science.

As a general rule, scholarly journals are considered reputable, dependable, and accurate sources of information, ideas, and knowledge. Most scholarly journals are *peer-reviewed*, which means that each published article has been evaluated by several experts on the specific subject matter of the article. By contrast, articles in trade and popular magazines are usually reviewed by an editor (or sometimes by an editorial team); they are generally not evaluated by an outside panel of experts. Consequently, articles that appear in scholarly journals are generally considered to meet rigorous standards of scholarship in their respective fields. If your research leads you to material in a scholarly journal, you can usually be confident that it is credible.

The challenge facing most student writers, however, is that scholarly articles are written by experts for other experts in their respective fields. These articles can often be difficult for a novice (as almost all students are) to understand, and students can find it hard to assess whether the material in such articles fits the needs of their project. If you find yourself in such a situation (and you probably will at some point), use the following strategies to help you decide whether the material in a scholarly article is useful to you:

- **Read the abstract.** Most scholarly articles include an *abstract*, which is a summary of the article. Reading the abstract will generally give you a good idea about whether the article contains the kind of information you need.

- **Ask a librarian.** Librarians are trained to understand the characteristics and nuances of the many different kinds of source materials available in their libraries. If you're not sure about whether a specific scholarly article is relevant for your project, ask a librarian.

- **Search the internet.** Often a scholarly article is part of a larger body of work by the author(s) and others in a specific field. If you find an article that seems relevant but are not sure whether it contains material you need, do a quick Internet search using the subject or title of the article and/or the authors' names. Such a search might yield links to websites, such as the authors' university web pages, that are less technical and contain information that can help you decide whether the scholarly article is useful for your project.

Magazines and newspapers. For many topics, especially topics related to current events, magazines and newspapers provide rich sources of information. But there are many different kinds of magazines and newspapers, and their quality and dependability can vary widely. Here are the main categories:

- **Trade magazines.** Trade magazines and journals are specialized periodicals devoted to specific occupations or professions. Many are considered important sources for information and opinions relevant to those occupations or professions. *Automotive Design and Production*, for example, publishes articles about the latest technology and news related to the automobile industry. Other well-known trade journals include *Adweek, American Bar Association Journal, Business & Finance*, and *Publishers Weekly*. Although most trade publications do not peer-review the articles they publish, they nevertheless can provide reliable information and important perspectives on subjects related to their professions.

- **Popular magazines.** This category includes numerous publications on every conceivable topic, but the main feature that distinguishes popular publications from trade or public affairs journals is that they are intended for a general, non-specialist audience. *Sports Illustrated*, for example, a popular magazine, might publish an article about the top track and field athletes competing in the Olympic Games, whereas *Track & Field News*, a trade publication, might include technical articles about the latest training techniques used by world-class sprinters to prepare for the Olympics. Popular magazines tend to value the latest news and often cater to specific segments of the general population (for example, *Seventeen Magazine* targets teenage girls) in an effort to attract advertising revenue. Although they vary widely in quality and dependability, they can be an important source of information, depending upon the nature of your project. However, some college instructors consider many popular magazines less credible sources than either trade or scholarly publications, so check with your instructor to determine whether to use such magazines as sources for your project.

■ **Public affairs journals.** A number of periodicals focus on politics, history, and culture and publish carefully researched articles, often by well-known scholars and other experts. Many public affairs journals have developed reputations as respected sources of the most knowledgeable perspectives on important political, economic, and social issues. Some of these journals have been publishing for many decades. Among the most well-known public affairs journals are *The Atlantic, National Review, The Nation*, and *Foreign Affairs*.

■ **Newspapers and newsmagazines.** Daily and weekly newspapers and weekly or monthly newsmagazines are general sources for the most up-to-date information. Among the advantages of these publications for researchers is that they tend to be accessible, are intended for a wide audience, and publish material on a wide variety of topics. Like popular magazines, newspapers and newsmagazines can vary significantly in quality, focus, and dependability. In general, well-established newspapers, such as *The New York Times, The Washington Post*, and the *Los Angeles Times*, and newsmagazines, such as *Time*, tend to have rigorous editorial review and often employ fact-checkers to verify information they publish. However, like all sources, these publications are subject to bias, no matter how objective and thorough they might claim to be (see "Detecting Bias" in Chapter 22). They might be dependable and well respected, but they also represent various points of view. Don't assume that because something is published in a reputable newspaper or newsmagazine, it is free from bias.

Depending on the nature of your project, any of these kinds of publications can provide useful material, but it is important to be aware of the differences among them so that you can better judge the appropriateness of a specific source.

Online Resources

Because the Internet contains an almost inconceivable amount of material, it can be a boon for researchers. At the same time, the great variety of resources available online can create challenges for students looking for credible, accurate information.

As noted earlier, many print resources are now available online. If your search leads you to a journal or newspaper article, check to see whether it is available online. For example, major newspapers like *The New York Times* archive their articles, so that you can usually gain access to them through the newspapers' websites or an online database offered through your college library.

There are **three main kinds of online sources of information**.

- **Websites.** Businesses, government agencies, media outlets, individuals, and organizations of all kinds maintain websites that can be excellent sources of information for researchers. For example, if you looking for information about standardized testing in K–12 schools, you can search the website of the U.S. Department of Education; you can visit the websites of state education departments, school districts, and related government agencies; and you can consult the websites of the many not-for-profit organizations and advocacy groups devoted to education issues, many of which provide a wide variety of information on education-related issues. Similarly, for-profit organizations that provide education services maintain websites that can also be useful sources for information. In addition, the websites of media organizations devoted to education issues can be excellent resources. It's safe to say that with careful searching you can almost always find relevant websites that provide useful and reliable information, no matter what subject you are researching.

- **Reference materials.** The Internet has become the digital equivalent of the traditional reference section of a library, providing such resources as encyclopedias, statistical abstracts, dictionaries, maps, almanacs, and related reference materials. If you need statistical information about employment rates in the United States, for example, you can search the *Statistical Abstract of the United States* as well as databases maintained online by the U.S. Department of Labor and the U.S. Census Bureau, among other such resources. Venerable reference resources such as *Encyclopedia Britannica* are now available online along with more recently developed resources such as *Wikipedia*. Many organizations, agencies, and institutions (such as universities) also maintain specialized reference materials online.

- **Social media.** Increasingly, social media have become important sites for debate, discussion, and the exchange of information. Many blogs have become as important and respected as the most reputable journals as sources of ideas, opinions, and information, and even sites like Tumblr and Facebook can be useful sources for some kinds of information. Often, such sites contain the most up-to-date perspectives and information because they are constantly revised to reflect current developments.

The nature of your project and your rhetorical situation will dictate which sources are the most relevant. For many academic writing tasks, some sources will be considered inappropriate. If you're not sure whether a specific source is appropriate for your project, check with your instructor or a reference librarian.

Locating the Right Sources

Given the wealth and variety of available resources, how do you find the information you need? There are **three primary tools for finding the right source materials** for your project:

- library catalogs
- databases
- online search engines

Library Catalogs

A library lists all the materials it holds in its online catalog, which is usually easily accessible from the library's home page. In addition to listing books held by the library, the library website typically enables you to access other resources maintained by the library, including its reference collections; periodicals (scholarly journals as well as newspapers and magazines); audio, video, and digital media holdings; government documents; and special collections (such as local historical materials or manuscripts from a well-known author). If you are searching for books on your subject, the library online catalog is the best place to start. But the library website is also a good place to start your search for other materials as well. Get to know what is available on your college library's website. It will serve you well in your research.

Databases

Databases are listings of published materials that enable you to locate articles in scholarly journals, trade journals, or popular newspapers and magazines. Some databases provide only citations or abstracts of articles in the periodicals they list; some also provide direct access to the full texts of the materials they list. The most popular databases are general and interdisciplinary because they index a wide variety of materials from all subject areas. However, many databases are specialized and index only periodicals relevant to their subject. For example, MedLine indexes periodicals and related materials on medicine, nursing, dentistry, veterinary medicine, the health care system, and pre-clinical sciences.

Chances are that you will need to search several different databases for many of your college writing projects, so it makes sense to become familiar with the databases available through your college library. Among the most widely used databases are the following:

- **Academic Search Complete** is a multidisciplinary scholarly database that includes thousands of full-text periodicals in the social sciences, humanities, science, and technology.
- **Article First** is a general database that indexes the content page of journals in science, technology, medicine, social science, business, the humanities, and popular culture.
- **EBSCOhost** is one of the most widely used general databases. It includes citations and abstracts from thousands of journals in many different disciplines and provides access to full-text articles from many journals.

- **FirstSearch Online Reference** is a general reference portal that provides access to a wide variety of databases in many different subject areas.

- **Google Scholar** is an increasingly popular multidisciplinary scholarly database that lists citations for articles, papers, books, and related scholarly documents in all major academic disciplines.

- **JSTOR** is a scholarly database that provides access to full-text articles from many different journals in a variety of academic disciplines.

- **LexisNexis Academic** is an extensive database providing citations and full-text articles from newspapers, magazines, and many different periodicals in law, business, biography, medicine, and reference.

- **MasterFILE Premier** is a general database that includes access to full-text articles from periodicals in general reference, business, health, education, culture, and science.

- **Scopus** is a general database that indexes abstracts and provides access to the contents of thousands of international journal titles as well as conference proceedings, book series, and scientific web pages and patents, with a focus on science, technology, and medicine.

Keep in mind that although some databases (such as Google Scholar) are freely available on the Internet, others are available only through a subscription or license. If your library has a subscription to these databases, you can usually access them by signing in through your library's website.

Search Engines

Search engines are websites that search the Internet for available materials. Typically, search engines return a list of links to websites and other web-based resources. Google is the most popular search engine, but there are many other search engines, including specialized search engines that focus on specific subject areas, such as automobiles, business, computers, or education. Among the most commonly used general search engines are Yahoo!, Bing, Ask.com, and Answers.com.

Like databases, search engines enable you to find relevant materials very quickly; however, unlike databases, search engines typically do not screen the results of searches, which means that you often have to work harder to sort through and evaluate the references returned by a search engine. If you find a citation in a specialized database, it is likely to be related to the specific subject area and from a source that has been evaluated by the editors of the database. By contrast, search engines return links to *any* site or resource related to the search term, no matter the source of that site.

Although these three kinds of resources overlap, in general you can use them as follows:

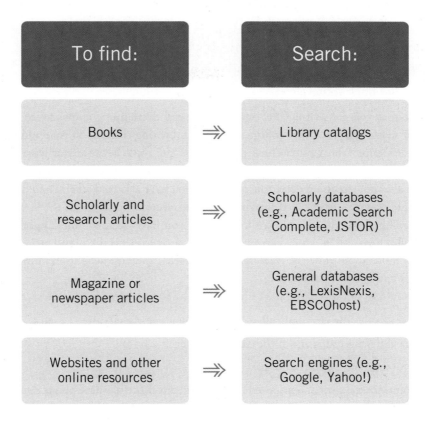

To find:		Search:
Books	⇒	Library catalogs
Scholarly and research articles	⇒	Scholarly databases (e.g., Academic Search Complete, JSTOR)
Magazine or newspaper articles	⇒	General databases (e.g., LexisNexis, EBSCOhost)
Websites and other online resources	⇒	Search engines (e.g., Google, Yahoo!)

Of course, you can use an Internet search engine such as Google to find references to books, scholarly articles, and newspaper and magazine articles, but if you limit your search tools to Internet search engines, you might miss important resources, especially if your topic is specialized and your assignment is academic in nature. It is best to use the three basic kinds of online resources in combination to be able to identify the most useful sources for your project.

Developing a Search Strategy

Understanding the many different sources available to you and knowing which search tools to use still isn't quite enough for successful research. For example, your library catalog lists thousands of book titles, but how do you even know whether searching for a book makes sense for your project? Similarly, a search engine such as Google can point you to thousands of links related to a certain topic, but what will you look for among those many links? How do you know which ones to pursue? You will more likely find what you need if you develop a general search strategy that focuses on the kinds of information you need for your project and takes advantage of all potential sources to find that information rather than limiting your search to one set of resources, such as online materials or scholarly journals.

To illustrate, let's return to one of the examples from the section titled "Determining What You Need" (page 691): an argument in favor of abolishing the electoral college in U.S. presidential elections. We identified the purpose of the project as follows:

- to illuminate problems with the current election system
- to propose an increasingly popular solution to an important problem
- to encourage other voting citizens to consider this solution

Let's imagine that you are writing this essay with several overlapping audiences in mind: classmates in your writing course, other college students, and voting citizens. So your audience is both general and academic. You have become interested in the topic because you have heard many young people of voting age express apathy about the presidential election, partly because the popular vote does not necessarily elect the president. You have also read several op-ed essays about this issue, some of which have called for abolishing the electoral college.

After reading about the electoral college online, you have decided you support the idea of replacing it with a system in which the national popular vote elects the president. However, you need to learn more about how the electoral college works, and you need to examine the various arguments for and against that system.

Here's the list of questions you have identified as a starting point for your research:

- How exactly does the electoral college work? Why was it developed?
- What are the main criticisms of the electoral college?
- What problems have occurred in past elections?
- What solutions have others proposed? What concerns do critics have about these solutions?

And here are some potential sources you have identified for addressing these questions:

- reference works on political science and elections
- articles in political journals, newspapers, and newsmagazines
- blog posts, public affairs websites
- materials from political watchdog groups

How should you proceed? When you have a general idea about what you might want to say about your topic (in this case, that the electoral college should be replaced with a national popular vote for U.S. presidential elections) but limited knowledge of the subject, a good search strategy is to start broadly and narrow your search as you learn more about your topic and refine your main point (Core Concept #4). That means beginning with general searches of the major categories of resources—library catalogs, databases, and Internet search engines—and then searching for more specific materials as you identify questions or subtopics that you need to explore, using the appropriate search tools at each stage. In our example, the process might look like this:

1. General search for materials on electoral college:
- Library catalog for books
- Search engine (e.g., Google)
- General database (e.g., LexisNexis, EBSCOhost)

2. Narrower search for critiques and studies of electoral college:
- Specialized databases (e.g., Worldwide Political Science Abstracts, Google Scholar)

3. Targeted search for alternatives to the electoral college:
- Advanced search of relevant database (e.g., LexisNexis, Google Scholar) and search engine

1. Do a General Search for Materials on the Electoral College

Recall your questions about your topic:

- How exactly does the electoral college work? Why was it developed?
- What are the main criticisms of the electoral college?
- What problems have occurred in past elections?
- What solutions have others proposed? What concerns do critics have about these solutions?

These should guide your general searches. You need basic information about the electoral college, its history, and the criticisms of the system. You also need information about proposed solutions. Search the three main kinds of resources for relevant materials:

Library catalogs. Libraries have different kinds of search mechanisms, but most allow users to do **keyword searches** of their catalogs for subjects or titles of books and related materials in their collections. In this case, you could use *electoral college* as a subject keyword. In 2012, a search using these keywords yielded 47 books in the library of the State University of New York at Albany. Here's what the first page of the results screen looked like:

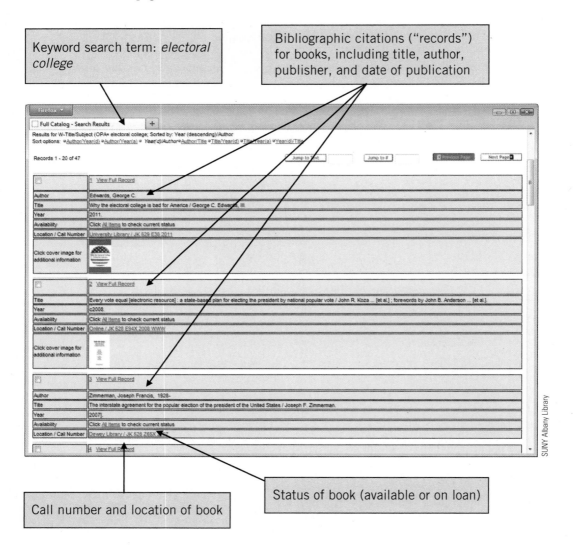

Keyword search term: *electoral college*

Bibliographic citations ("records") for books, including title, author, publisher, and date of publication

Call number and location of book

Status of book (available or on loan)

This screen shows the first three of 47 total "records," which provide bibliographic information about each book as well as its call number so that you can locate it in the library. You can also click a link to check on the status of each book (whether it is out on loan, when it is due, and so forth). Although the search screen will differ from one library to the next, each screen will have these key components, including complete bibliographic information about the book (author, publisher, date of publication) and the status of the book (whether it is available for loan, where it is located in the library).

Review the search results to see which books seem most likely to contain the information you need about the electoral college. Some of the books found in this sample search will likely provide general information about the electoral college:

> *After the People Vote: A Guide to the Electoral College* (2004), edited by John C. Fortier

> *Electoral College and Presidential Elections* (2001), edited by Alexandra Kura

Some specifically address the controversy about the electoral college and proposals to reform it:

> *Every Vote Equal: A State-Based Plan for Electing the President by National Popular Vote* (2008), by John R. Koza et al.

> *Enlightened Democracy: The Case for the Electoral College* (2004), by Tara Ross

> *Why the Electoral College Is Bad for America* (2004), by George C. Edwards

Some might be too specialized for your purposes:

> *Electoral Votes Based on the 1990 Census* (1991), by David C. Huckabee

Based on the information in the search results, select the books that seem most useful and visit the library to review them. (You might also do an online search to find additional information about each book before visiting the library. For example, a Google search of the book's title and author will often yield descriptions of the book, reviews, and related information that can help you determine whether the book is worth borrowing from the library.)

General databases. Search one or more general databases using the same or similar keywords. A good place to start is *LexisNexis Academic*, which indexes many different newspapers and magazines as well as other kinds of materials; it also indexes more specialized journals.

Like many databases, *LexisNexis Academic* has an "easy" search screen and an "advanced" search screen. Begin with an "easy" search of the news using your keywords *electoral college*. Notice that this database allows you to select categories of sources (newspapers, magazines, blogs).

In some cases, it might make sense to narrow your search to one such category; in this example, however, a broader search is appropriate:

Keywords: *electoral college*

Use this pull-down menu to select the type of source to search (e.g., Major World Publications, Newspapers, Magazines).

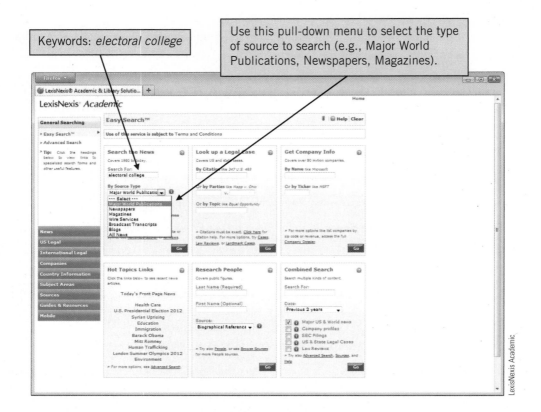

This search of "Major World Publications" returned 995 entries. Here's the first screen:

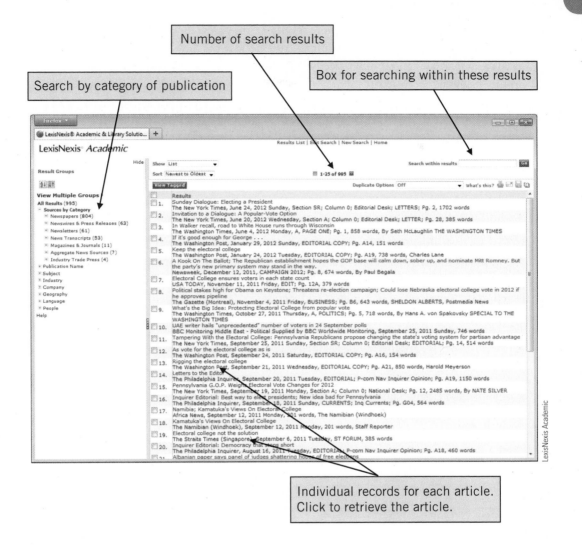

Number of search results

Box for searching within these results

Search by category of publication

Individual records for each article. Click to retrieve the article.

Databases have very different search screens, and it might take some time to become familiar with the ones you are using. However, all major databases allow you to specify the parameters of your search (e.g., by publication type, date, author, title, keywords, and so on) so that you can search broadly or be more strategic. Moreover, they all provide the same basic information about the sources that are returned in a search, which in this example are called "records." Usually, that information includes the author, title, publication, and date of the entry. Sometimes the entry will include an abstract or summary of the source. You can use this information to review the entries and decide which ones to examine more closely.

Obviously, the 995 records returned in this sample would be too many to review, but you can **narrow your search** in several ways:

- **Search within the results.** Use more specific terms to search within the results of searches that yield too many entries. For example, you can use the keywords *presidential election* to exclude any articles about other elections. Using those keywords reduced the search results in this example to 776 records.

- **Search specific publications.** Because you are interested in the American electoral college, you might search only American newspapers. You can limit your search further by searching only major newspapers (e.g., *The Washington Post, The New York Times*). You can do the same for magazines and other types of publications.

- **Specify dates.** If you want to find materials related to a specific time period, you can specify the dates of the materials you want. For example, if you want articles about the 2000 presidential election, you might search for materials published from 1998 through 2001.

Notice that you can also search by subject. Expanding the subject list reveals a number of subtopics. The numbers in parentheses after each subtopic indicate how many of the 995 records relate to that subtopic. For example, among the 995 entries in the original search in this example, 343 are related to the subtopic "U.S. Presidential Elections":

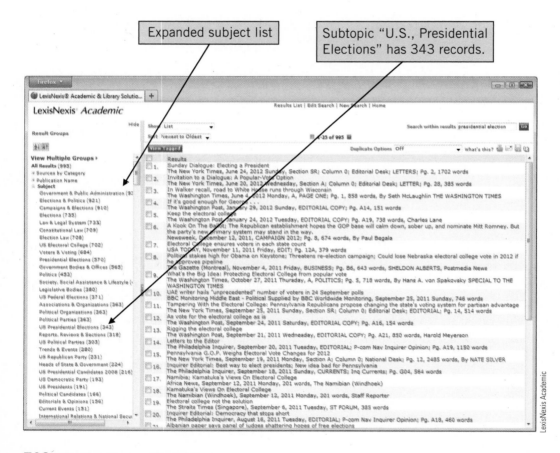

You can use the subject categories to narrow your search further. For example, you could click on the subject "U.S. Presidential Elections" and search within that category, which contains 343 sources. In this way, you can find sources that are more likely to be relevant to your specific topic.

As you gain experience in research, you will become more efficient in finding the materials you need. In the meantime, **when searching databases, follow these guidelines:**

- **Experiment with keywords.** Sometimes it takes several different combinations of search terms before you begin to see the search results you want. In our example, the search term *electoral college* returned good results, but depending upon what you are looking for, you might have to try various other search terms: *elections, popular election, presidential elections, election controversies*, and so on.

- **Use several search strategies.** Sometimes a basic keyword search gets you right to the materials you need. More often you will have to try different search strategies to narrow your search to manageable numbers and to find the most relevant materials. If various keyword searches don't yield what you need, try subject searches. Try various searches within your search results. Don't rely on a single approach.

- **Use different databases.** Different databases have different search options and will return different results. Although most databases allow for refined or advanced searching, each database has its own interface with its own peculiarities. So the same keywords are likely to yield different results in different databases. In this sample search, for example, using the same keywords (*electoral college*) with the *EBSCO* database will turn up some of the same sources but also different sources. You might also find some databases easier to use than others. Be aware that it can take some time to become familiar with the characteristics of each database, so if you have trouble finding what you need in a specific database, ask a librarian or your instructor for guidance.

Internet search engines. Having searched your library catalog and one or more databases, you can expand your search to include online materials using a general search engine such as Google or Yahoo!. Remember that search engines will return many more entries than a library catalog or database, so you might have to adjust your search terms to keep the search results manageable. In our sample search, you might begin with a general search term, such as *electoral college*, but be aware that such general searches will usually yield an enormous number of results. A search of Google using this term in 2012 yielded more than 10 million items, for instance. That kind of result isn't surprising when you remember that Google is searching the entire Internet for anything (websites, documents, and so on) that contains those two words. So try different strategies for narrowing your search. For instance, placing those terms in quotation marks (see "An Important Tip for Searching Databases and Search Engines") reduced the results by half:

Five million is still an unmanageable number, but you can review the first few pages of search results to determine whether any of the links might be useful. In this example, the very first item is a link to the website of the U.S. Electoral College itself, which probably has relevant information for your purposes.

After reviewing the first several pages of search results, narrow your search using different search terms: e.g., *electoral college presidential election, electoral college controversy, history of electoral college.* Each of these terms will yield different results. Review each set of results for materials that seem promising. Continue to narrow your search so that the results are not only relevant but manageable.

As you proceed with these three kinds of general searches, you will gather relevant information and begin to gain a better understanding of your subject, which can help you search more strategically for additional materials.

You can search databases and search engines more efficiently by using quotation marks strategically. Placing search terms in quotation marks tells the search engine to look for exactly those words in exactly that order. For example, if you search for *online privacy,* your search will turn up sites with both those words as well as sites that have either one word or the other; however, placing that term in quotation marks (*"online privacy"*) will yield only sites containing the phrase *online privacy*, which is more likely to point to relevant sources. Experiment with different combinations of search terms, with and without quotation marks, to find the most useful sources.

2. Narrow Your Search for Specific Critiques of the Electoral College

Your general search should yield enough information for you to begin to identify specific issues, questions, and subtopics that you need to explore further. The general searches in our example have yielded a lot of information about the electoral college, how it works, its history, criticisms of the system, and proposals to reform it. Although much of that information is general (e.g., books and websites explaining the electoral college), some is more specialized (e.g., analyses of specific elections in which the popular vote did not elect the president, scholarly critiques of the system). Given that your intended audience is both general and academic, you might now look more closely at what scholars and other experts have to say about the pros and cons of the electoral college.

- **Examine the references in the books you have found.** Most books contain bibliographies or works cited pages that can point you to additional sources. The references in those bibliographies often include citations of relevant scholarly articles. Make a list of citations that seem promising, and use your library catalog or a general database to track down the articles that seem most relevant.

- **Search specialized databases.** Your library website will list its available databases. Find one or more that relate specifically to your subject. In this example, you could search general scholarly databases, such as *JSTOR, Academic Search Complete*, or *Google Scholar*, as well as databases specific to political science or the social sciences, such as *Worldwide Political Science Abstracts, PAIS,* or *Social Sciences Abstracts*. Given the nature of your project (which is intended for a general academic audience rather than a more specialized audience of readers in political science), it makes sense to search a general scholarly database, such as *JSTOR*. If you were writing your argument for a political science course, it might make more sense to search the specialized databases specific to that field, such as *Worldwide Political Science*.

Boolean, or logical, operators are words that command a search engine to define a search in a specific way. The most common Boolean operators are *AND, OR*, and *NOT*. Understanding how they work can help you search the Internet and databases more efficiently:

- *AND* tells the search engine to find only sources that contain both words in your search. For example, if you entered *sports AND steroids*, your search would yield sources that deal with steroids in sports and would not necessarily return sources that deal with steroids or sports in general.

- *OR* broadens a search by telling the search engine to return sources for either term in your search. Entering *sports OR steroids*, for instance, would yield sources on either of those topics.

- *NOT* can narrow a search by telling the search engine to exclude sources containing a specific keyword. For example, entering *steroids NOT sports* would yield sources on steroids but not sources that deal with steroids in sports.

In addition, keep these tips in mind:

- You can use parentheses for complex searches: (*sports AND steroids*) NOT (*medicine OR law*); this entry would narrow the search to specific kinds of sources about sports and steroids that did not include medical or legal matters.

- With most search engines, you can use Boolean operators in combination with quotation marks to find a specific phrase. For example, "steroid use in sports" would return sources that included that exact phrase. (See "An Important Tip for Searching Databases and Search Engines.") Using this strategy allows you to narrow your search further: ("*steroid in sports*") AND ("*steroid controversies*"). Such a search would find sources that include both phrases in the parentheses.

- Generally, you should capitalize Boolean operators.

Let's imagine that after reviewing the materials you found in your general searches, you want to know what scholars say about the implications of the electoral college for modern elections. You can search *JSTOR* for relevant scholarly articles. Here's the opening screen:

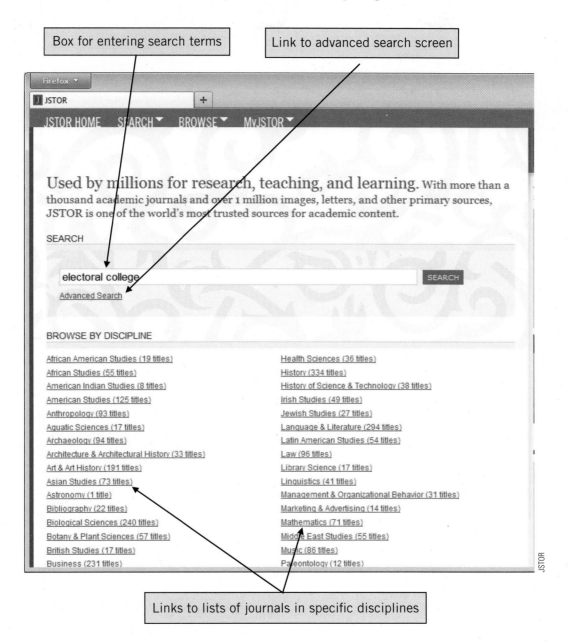

Box for entering search terms

Link to advanced search screen

Links to lists of journals in specific disciplines

Notice that, like most scholarly databases, *JSTOR* allows you to browse journals by discipline. However, doing so is very time-consuming. Also, a general search using the search term *electoral college* is likely to yield too many results (in this case, such a search returned more than 23,000 articles in 2012), so an **advanced search** would make more sense. Here's the *JSTOR* advanced search screen:

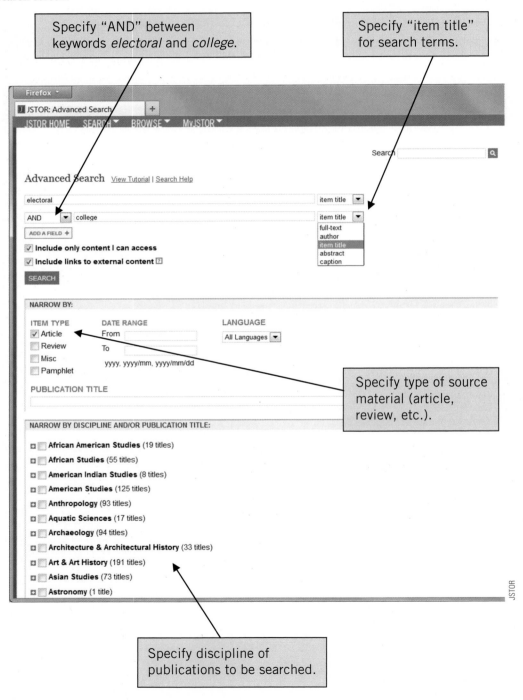

Such an advanced search screen allows you to limit your searches in various ways to increase the likelihood that the results will be useful. For example, you can specify that the search terms appear in the article titles rather than the body of the articles, making it more likely that the focus of the article will be relevant to your needs. Also, you can use the *Boolean operator* "AND" to make sure that the titles of the articles have *both* search terms (see "Using Boolean Operators with Databases and Search Engines"). In addition, you can search only journals in certain disciplines and limit your search by dates and type of publication. Doing so can dramatically narrow your search and yield much more relevant results. For example, a search of *JSTOR* in 2012 using the search term *electoral college* only in the title of political science journal articles yielded 36 results:

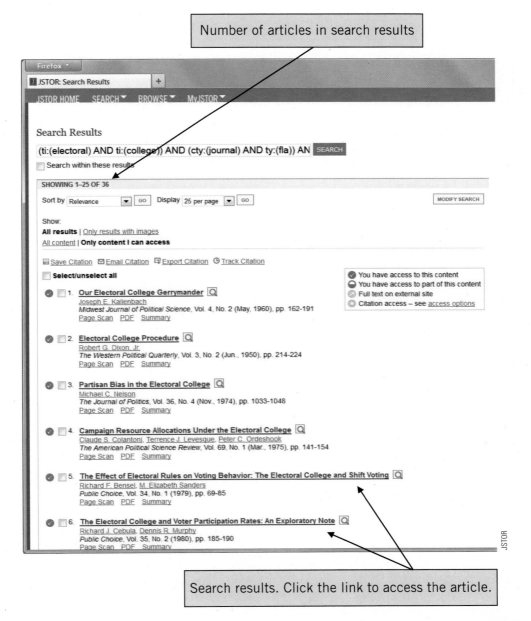

Number of articles in search results

Search results. Click the link to access the article.

These results include several older articles as well as more recent ones. For example, the first three results shown in this image were published in 1960, 1950, and 1974, respectively. If you wanted to narrow your focus to more recent elections, you could modify your search to include only articles published since 1998. Such a search returned 11 articles in 2012. Here's part of the results:

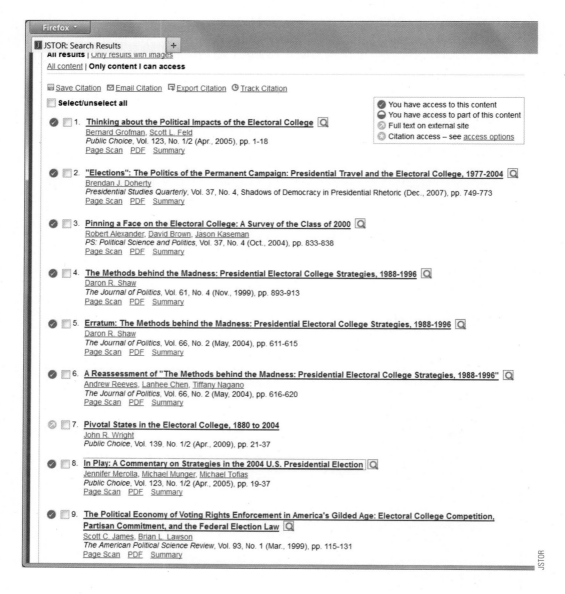

Browse these results to find articles that are most relevant for your needs. In this example, several articles promise to examine the implications of the electoral college for modern elections, including #8: "In Play: A Commentary on Strategies in the 2004 U.S. Presidential Election," by Jennifer Merolla, Michael Munger, and Michael Tofias, published in 2005 in a journal called *Public Choice*. Click the link to access the article. The first page of the article appears:

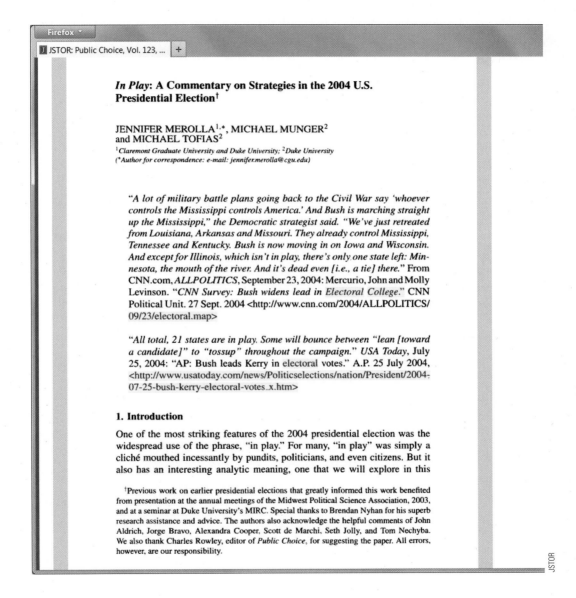

A quick review of the opening passage reveals that the article focuses on strategies employed by the campaigns in the 2004 election, which is relevant for your project.

Like general databases, specialized databases can differ noticeably, and you might have to experiment with several different databases to become familiar enough with their search screens to conduct effective searches. But all databases will have features such as those in this example that allow you to target your search by entering specific parameters (type of publication, dates, subject terms, and so on). No matter which database or search engine you are using, you can apply these same basic strategies to make your searches successful. As always, consult your librarian for help, if necessary.

3. Do a Targeted Search for Alternatives to the Electoral College

As you narrow your search further, more specific questions might arise or you might identify subtopics that you hadn't previously considered. For example, in reviewing scholarly articles about the role of the electoral collect in recent U.S. presidential elections, you might come across references to legal challenges to the electoral college, a topic that seems relevant to your project but one that you had not previously encountered. At this point, if you decide you need more information about such a specialized topic, you can return to the databases that you have already searched (such as *JSTOR*) and do an additional search focused on legal challenges to the electoral college system; you can also search specialized databases, such as *Westlaw Campus*, which provides access to legal decisions. The goal at this stage is to identify any specific issues or questions you need to explore as well as gaps in the information you have already gathered.

21

Keep in mind that a search is not necessarily a linear process. The strategy described here assumes you will be continuously reviewing the materials you find. As you do, you might need to return to a general search for information on a new topic that seems important. For example, as you examine arguments in favor of using the popular vote to elect the president, you might discover that some experts have concerns about the wide variety of voting systems used by different states. If you decide that this concern is an important topic for your project, return to your library catalog or a general database or search engine to find some basic information about the regulations governing the way states allow citizens to vote.

Remember that writing is a process of discovery (see Core Concept #1 in Chapter 2), and research is part of that process. You are learning about your subject matter to achieve your rhetorical goals. (The advice for Core Concepts #2 and #5 in Chapter 2 can also help you conduct more effective searches for useful source materials.)

Evaluating Sources 22

FINDING INFORMATION for your project is one thing. Deciding whether a source is appropriate, credible, and reliable is another. Given the enormous variety of available sources, evaluating the materials you find can be challenging, but it is an integral part of research.

When evaluating sources, you need to address two main questions:

- Is the source trustworthy?
- Is the source useful for your purposes?

Answering the first question involves understanding the nature and purpose of the source itself. For example, a newspaper article about a political campaign and a campaign flier can both be useful sources, but they are very different kinds of documents with different purposes. The purpose of a newspaper is to provide readers information about important and relevant events—in this example, a political campaign. A political campaign flier, by contrast, is intended to present a candidate in the best possible light to persuade voters to support that candidate. Both documents can provide accurate information about the candidate, but the information they present must be considered in terms of their different purposes. The campaign flier, for instance, might emphasize the candidate's record of voting against tax increases, whereas the newspaper article might explain that the candidate's vote against a specific tax increase resulted in reduced funding for a special program for disabled military veterans. Both sources are technically "true," but each presents information from a particular perspective and for a specific purpose.

As a writer evaluating sources for a project, you have to sort through these complexities to determine how trustworthy a source might be and whether it suits your own rhetorical purposes. The advice in this chapter will help you do so.

Determining Whether a Source Is Trustworthy

Evaluating source material requires understanding the different kinds of sources that are available to you. (Chapter 21 describes the characteristics of various kinds of sources.) It helps to develop a sense of the main similarities and differences in the general categories of sources you are likely to consult:

Wikipedia; iStockphoto.com/Aimintang

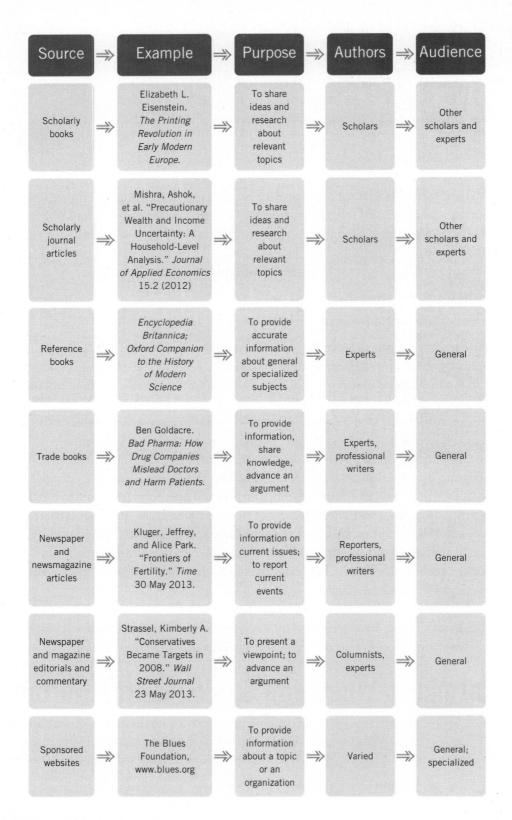

Source ⇒	Example ⇒	Purpose ⇒	Authors ⇒	Audience
Scholarly books	Elizabeth L. Eisenstein. *The Printing Revolution in Early Modern Europe.*	To share ideas and research about relevant topics	Scholars	Other scholars and experts
Scholarly journal articles	Mishra, Ashok, et al. "Precautionary Wealth and Income Uncertainty: A Household-Level Analysis." *Journal of Applied Economics* 15.2 (2012)	To share ideas and research about relevant topics	Scholars	Other scholars and experts
Reference books	*Encyclopedia Britannica; Oxford Companion to the History of Modern Science*	To provide accurate information about general or specialized subjects	Experts	General
Trade books	Ben Goldacre. *Bad Pharma: How Drug Companies Mislead Doctors and Harm Patients.*	To provide information, share knowledge, advance an argument	Experts, professional writers	General
Newspaper and newsmagazine articles	Kluger, Jeffrey, and Alice Park. "Frontiers of Fertility." *Time* 30 May 2013.	To provide information on current issues; to report current events	Reporters, professional writers	General
Newspaper and magazine editorials and commentary	Strassel, Kimberly A. "Conservatives Became Targets in 2008." *Wall Street Journal* 23 May 2013.	To present a viewpoint; to advance an argument	Columnists, experts	General
Sponsored websites	The Blues Foundation, www.blues.org	To provide information about a topic or an organization	Varied	General; specialized

A glance at this graphic reveals that different kinds of sources can be very similar in some respects (e.g., their intended audiences) but very different in others (e.g., their primary purpose). Having a general sense of the characteristics of these categories of sources can help you evaluate information from specific sources and determine its usefulness for your project.

Source materials within any of these general categories can also vary in terms of three important considerations when it comes to trustworthiness: credibility, reliability, and bias.

Credibility

Credibility is the extent to which a source is respected and can be trusted. It refers to your sense of whether a source is reputable and dependable and the information found there generally reliable. The credibility of a source can arise from a reputation built over time. Well-established newspapers, magazines, and publishers are usually considered credible sources because of their record of publishing certain kinds of reliable, accurate information and their commitment to high standards of integrity. Scholarly publications, for example, are generally considered credible because they tend to be peer-reviewed and because of their commitment to holding their authors to high standards of quality and accuracy. The fact that an article published in a scholarly journal has likely been carefully evaluated and critiqued by established scholars can give readers confidence that the article meets high standards for accuracy and integrity.

Credibility can also be a function of a writer's general approach to the subject matter: his or her tone, the level of fairness with which subject matter is treated, how carefully he or she seems to have examined the subject, how accurate or believable his or her statements are, and so on. For example, if you notice a writer making easy generalizations or drawing dubious conclusions about a complicated subject, you might be skeptical of the writer's credibility when it comes to that subject. Consider this passage from a post on Alternet, a website devoted to politics and culture; the writer, an editor for Alternet, is reporting on a newspaper survey of recent Harvard graduates regarding their career choices after college:

> Wall Street's propensity to ravage the economy, launder money, and illegally foreclose on families with no harsher punishment than a slap on the wrist seems to have irked some of the nation's brightest. Either that or the shrinkage of jobs in the finance sector is turning them off. According to a survey by the student newspaper the *Harvard Crimson*, Harvard graduates are just saying "No" to Wall Street, with some of them looking instead to put their smarts to work making America a better place.
>
> The paper reports that about a third of new graduates plan to work in finance, with 15 percent working on Wall Street and 16 percent doing consulting. In 2007, before the recession, 47 percent of Harvard grads went onto work in finance and consulting, a number that fell to 39 percent in 2008, and 20 percent in 2012.
>
> As the Huffington Post noted, it looks like the financial crisis may have triggered a change in the aspirations of the nation's brightest, prompting millennials to prefer work in industries where they can contribute to social good, like health and tech, although

many of them, no doubt, want to score big in tech. At the same time, Wall Street is laying off more employees than it hires, so grads' reasons for career shifts may be more pragmatic than idealistic.

Source: Gwynne, Kristen. "Even Harvard Grads Don't Want to Work on Wall Street Anymore." *Alternet,* 29 May 2013. Web. 1 Jun. 2013.

As the editor of an established news website, the writer might be seen as a credible professional source for information about current political, economic, and cultural issues. At the same time, Alternet is well known for having a left-leaning political slant, which can affect the kind of information it publishes and how that information is presented. (See "Understanding Bias" later in this chapter.) That does not mean that the information in this passage is inaccurate, but it does mean that the information is likely to be presented in a way that reflects a certain political perspective on the issue at hand. Notice, for example, that the first sentence of the passage makes an unsupported assertion that financial firms on Wall Street have a "propensity to ravage the economy, launder money, and illegally foreclose on families." Such a claim is debatable, but it is presented here as fact. Moreover, the writer draws a conclusion from the newspaper survey that even she acknowledges might be mistaken. She suggests that the survey conducted by the student newspaper the *Harvard Crimson* indicates that the behavior of Wall Street firms has "irked some of the nation's brightest" college graduates. Although the survey results, which are reported in the second paragraph of the passage, indicate a decline in the percentage of Harvard graduates seeking employment in finance, the reasons for that decline are unclear. In the final sentence of the passage, the writer herself acknowledges that the decline might be a result of a decline in the number of job opportunities on Wall Street. The conclusion that Harvard graduates are "irked" by Wall Street is not supported by the evidence presented here.

This example illustrates that skepticism can be healthy when evaluating source material. In this case, the writer could be considered credible as a professional journalist, but the way she presents the information about the student survey and the rhetorical situation (that is, the fact that she is writing for a left-leaning website whose readers would very likely be critical of the financial firms on Wall Street) should make you look carefully and critically at the information she presents. Moreover, her conclusions and claims about the views of Harvard graduates regarding Wall Street are questionable. So when it comes to this particular issue—the financial industry—it might make sense to be skeptical about what the writer states, even if she can be considered a credible source, and to be judicious in deciding how you use any information from this source. You might, for example, use the figures from the student survey to show that college graduates' career decisions have changed in recent years, but you might avoid using the writer's conclusions about the reasons for that change.

In determining the credibility of a source, consider the following:

- **Author.** Who is the author? Do you know anything about his or her background? Is the author an expert on the subject at hand? Does he or she have an agenda with respect to this subject?

- **Publication.** What is the source of the publication? Is it a scholarly book or journal? A trade magazine? A sponsored website? What do you know about this source? What reputation does it have? Is it known to have a particular slant? Is it associated with a group that espouses a particular point of view on the subject?

- **Purpose.** What is the purpose of the source? To what extent might the purpose influence your sense of the trustworthiness of the information in the source? For example, is the author presenting a carefully researched analysis of a controversial topic—say, gun control—as in a scholarly journal article, or is the writer vigorously arguing against an opposing perspective on that topic for an audience of people who share the writer's views, as in an op-ed essay on a sponsored website? Both sources might be credible, but having a sense of the purpose of the source and the rhetorical situation can help you determine how skeptical to be about the information contained in the source.

- **Date.** How recent is the publication? Is it current when it comes to the subject at hand? For some kinds of information, the date of publication might not matter much, but for many topics, outdated information can be problematic.

Reliability

Reliability refers to your confidence in the accuracy of the information found in a source and the reputation of a source for consistently presenting trustworthy information. In general, credible sources gain a reputation for publishing accurate information over time. For example, major newspapers and magazines, such as the *Los Angeles Times* and *The New Yorker*, usually employ fact checkers to verify information in articles they are preparing to publish; respected publishing houses usually edit manuscripts carefully to be sure they are accurate; and scholarly publishers employ expert reviewers to evaluate manuscripts. These practices usually mean that material published by these sources tends to be consistently accurate and trustworthy, so they gain a reputation for reliability. By contrast, many popular news outlets emphasize breaking news and sometimes publish information quickly before it can be carefully verified. Often, such publications are not subject to the kind of rigorous editorial review that characterizes scholarly publications, which can result in inaccuracies and weaken your confidence in their reliability.

Because you are not likely to be an expert on many of the subjects you write about in college, you often won't have a sense of the reliability of a particular source, so you will have to make judgments on the basis of the nature of the source and its credibility. **Follow these guidelines:**

- **Choose credible sources.** In general, if you have a choice of sources, use those that you know or believe to be credible. Sources with reputations for credibility are more likely to supply reliable information. In general, scholarly publications, reference works (such as encyclopedias), well-established newspapers or magazines, and respected government agencies or non-governmental organizations (such as the Centers for Disease Control and Prevention or the American Heart Association) tend to be safe bets as sources for your research.

- **Consult multiple sources.** Using multiple sources on the same topic can help you avoid using unreliable information. If you have information that is consistent across several sources, including sources you consider to be credible, that information is more likely to be reliable as well.

Determining whether a source is trustworthy is usually not an either–or proposition. Even credible and reliable sources might have information that isn't accurate or is inappropriate for your purposes. Your decisions about the trustworthiness of a source, then, should be guided by your rhetorical situation as well as by your own growing understanding of your subject. As you gain experience in reviewing unfamiliar sources, you will begin to develop a sense of what to look for and what to avoid when determining whether information from a source can be trusted. Such decisions about source material must also be made with an understanding of the potential bias of a source, which is discussed in the following section.

Understanding Bias

Bias is a tendency to think or feel a certain way. It is the inclination of a source to favor one point of view over others that might be equally valid—the privileging of one perspective at the expense of others. Bias is sometimes thought of as prejudice, though bias is not necessarily a negative quality. One might have a bias in favor of cats rather than dogs as pets, for example. In this textbook, bias generally refers to a source's perspective or slant.

It is important to understand that all sources are biased in some way. We tend to think of some kinds of source material, such as encyclopedias and other kinds of reference works, as objective or neutral. But even a venerable reference such as the *Encyclopedia Britannica* can be said to have certain biases, despite its extensive efforts to present accurate information as objectively as possible. For example, the kind of information that is considered appropriate for inclusion in *Encyclopedia Britannica* reflects a set of beliefs about what kinds of knowledge or information are relevant and important for its purposes. Although such a reference work is intended to be comprehensive, it inevitably excludes some kinds of information and privileges others. For instance, extremely technical information about the rhythms of hip hop music might be excluded from an encyclopedia, even though more general information about that musical form might be included. The decisions the editors make about what to include in and what to exclude from the encyclopedia represent a bias, no matter how open-minded the editors might be.

Bias, then, is not necessarily a negative quality in a source, but it is essential to recognize bias in any source you consult so that you can evaluate the usefulness of information from that source. Some kinds of sources are transparent about their biases. Scholarly journals, for example, tend to make their editorial focus and purpose clear. Here is a statement of the editorial policy of a journal titled *Research in the Teaching of English,* published by a professional organization called the National Council of Teachers of English (NCTE):

> *Research in the Teaching of English* publishes scholarship that explores issues in the teaching and learning of literacy at all levels. It is the policy of NCTE in its journals and other publications to provide a forum for open discussion of ideas concerning the teaching of English and language arts.

Scholarly journals often provide such descriptions of the kinds of articles they seek to publish; they might also provide explanations of the processes by which manuscripts are reviewed. These editorial policy statements help make the biases of a journal explicit.

Many sources, even credible and reliable ones, are not so transparent about their biases. For example, although many readers consider newspapers to be trusted sources of information, many newspapers have well-established points of view. *The New York Times* is generally considered to have a liberal bias, whereas *The Washington Times* is usually thought to reflect a more conservative viewpoint. However, if you did not already have a sense of such biases, you might find it difficult to determine them. Here, for example, is the description that *The New York Times* provides of its editorial board:

> The editorial board is composed of 18 journalists with wide-ranging areas of expertise. Their primary responsibility is to write *The Times's* editorials, which represent the voice of the board, its editor and the publisher. The board is part of the *Times's* editorial department, which is operated separately from the *Times* newsroom, and includes the Letters to the Editor and Op-Ed sections.

Source: "The *New York Times* Editorial Board." *The New York Times*, 2013. Web. 3 June 2013.

Although this statement explains that the editorial department is separate from the newsroom at *The New York Times*, which might give readers confidence that the newspaper's reporting is not influenced by its editorial opinions, the statement does not describe a particular political slant or perspective. You would have to examine the newspaper more carefully—and probably over time—to gain a sense of its political bias. Similarly, consider the following statement from the "About" page on the website of *The Washington Times*:

> *The Washington Times* is a full-service, general interest daily newspaper in the nation's capital. Founded in 1982, *The Washington Times* is one of the most-often-quoted newspapers in the U.S. It has gained a reputation for hard-hitting investigative reporting and thorough coverage of politics and policy. Published by The Washington Times LLC, *The Washington Times* is "America's Newspaper."

Source: "About." *Washington Times*, 2013. Web. 3 June 2013.

Nowhere in this statement is there any indication that the newspaper tends to reflect a conservative point of view.

These examples underscore the important point that even the most credible and reliable sources will have biases that might not be obvious; however, a bias does not mean that a source is untrustworthy. Rather, bias influences the kind of information a source might contain and how that information is presented, even when the information is trustworthy. For example, like major newspapers, major public affairs magazines are usually considered to have either a liberal (e.g., *The Nation*) or conservative (e.g., *National Review*) bias. Those biases mean that each magazine is likely to focus on some issues as opposed to others and to examine issues from a particular perspective. For instance, *The Nation* might publish an argument in favor of a proposal to increase the national minimum wage, reflecting a liberal perspective on the government's role in economic matters. *National Review*, by contrast, might publish a critique of the same proposal, reflecting a conservative bias in favor of less government intervention in economic matters. Both articles might contain reliable and accurate information about the proposal, but the information is presented in a way that reflects the political bias of the publication.

Often, the bias of a source is much more subtle and difficult to detect. For example, advocacy groups often try to appear objective in their treatment of certain issues when in fact they have a strong bias on those issues. For example, an environmental advocacy group might oppose the development of a large wind farm in a wilderness area. Its website might seem to be a neutral source of information about various kinds of energy, including wind power, but its opposition to large wind farms means that its treatment of wind power is likely to focus on the disadvantages of wind power and the harmful impact of wind turbines on wilderness areas. In such a case, even though the information on the website might be accurate, that information might also be incomplete or presented in a way that paints a negative picture of wind power. (See "Detecting Bias.")

When evaluating a source for bias, consider these questions:

- Does this source reflect a particular perspective or point of view?

- Does this source represent a specific group, political party, business, organization, or institution?

- Does the source seem to have an agenda regarding the subject at hand?

- To what extent is the bias of this source evident? Are there blatantly slanted statements? Do you notice questionable information? To what extent does this bias seem to affect the trustworthiness of the information it presents?

FOCUS   Detecting Bias

Many sources appear at first glance to be neutral or objective on a particular issue or subject but actually reflect a strong bias. The website shown on page 729, for example, contains information about education reform but is sponsored by an organization that advocates a particular perspective on school reform in favor of charter schools and related movements that are controversial. Notice that nothing on the web page conveys a sense of the organization's strong views about specific kinds of education reforms; instead, the language is neutral ("The leading voice for lasting, substantive and structural education reform in the U.S.") and seemingly nonpartisan ("Join us in our fight to make *all* schools better for *all* children."). The information on such a site can be useful, but it is important to understand that it is being presented from a particular point of view. In this case, you might find accurate information about charter schools, but you are unlikely to find studies whose results are not flattering to charter schools; therefore, although the information might be accurate, it might also be incomplete or present a misleading view of the impact of charter schools.

Before using information from a source, try to determine how the source's bias might affect the usefulness and reliability of the information. Identifying any bias in a source can help you determine whether to trust the information you find there and whether you might need to balance it with information from other sources.

Source: *The Center for Education Reform.*

All sources should be evaluated for trustworthiness, but different sources can present different challenges when you are trying to determine trustworthiness. **Use the following questions to guide you as you evaluate specific sources:**

Print Sources	Websites
• **Who published this article or book?** (scholarly press, trade publisher, respected newspaper or magazine, professional organization, non-profit organization, government agency, advocacy group, business) • **Who is the author?** (Is the author's name provided? Is the author an expert on the subject?) • **What is the purpose?** (to share information or knowledge, to advocate for a point of view) • **Does the source have a reputation for reliability?** (Is the source known to have a bias or slant? Is the source generally considered credible?) • **When was it published?** (Is the date of publication indicated? Is the book or article current or outdated?)	• **Who sponsors the site?** (a news organization, business, political organization, advocacy group, non-profit foundation, government agency) • **What is the purpose of the site?** (to inform, to advertise or sell a product, to promote a point of view) • **What are the contents of the site?** (Does it include relevant information? Does it have advertisements? Does it seem to contain accurate information? Are the sources of information indicated?) • **Is the site current?** (Is the site regularly updated? Are the web pages dated? Is the information current?)

Although the advice in this chapter applies to all kinds of sources, you can follow additional steps to help you determine the trustworthiness of online sources:

- **Read the "About" page.** Many websites have pages titled "About" or "About Us" that provide useful information about the authors, the purpose, and sometimes the history of the site. Sites sponsored by advocacy groups and non-profit organizations often include information about their boards of directors or administrators. Such information can help you evaluate the trustworthiness of a site and determine the extent to which it might be biased. For example, a site of an organization that seems to advocate green energy but whose board of directors includes mostly business leaders from large energy companies might have a bias in favor of large business interests. By contrast, the site of a clean energy advocacy group whose directors are members of well-known environmental organizations will be less likely to support business interests when it comes to energy issues.

- **Look for a date.** Most websites sponsored by legitimate organizations indicate the date when the website or individual web pages were updated. Many organizations, especially respected media organizations, update their websites daily. However, some websites are never adequately maintained. Such sites can be readily available on the Internet many years after they cease to be updated or revised. If you cannot find dates on a website or if the only dates you find are well in the past, be wary of the material on that site.

- **Check the links.** Many websites contain pages with various kinds of resources, including links to related websites sponsored by other organizations. Often, those links reflect a website's own biases and can help you determine whether the site is trustworthy or biased in a way that should concern you. If these links are not active, it indicates that the site is not well maintained—another reason to be skeptical about information you find there.

Evaluating Source Material for Your Rhetorical Purposes

Once you have determined that information from a source is trustworthy, you must still decide whether it is useful and appropriate for your project. It isn't enough to determine whether a source is credible and reliable or to identify its biases; you must also evaluate the information in terms of your own rhetorical situation and especially in light of the purpose of your project.

To illustrate, let's imagine two related but different kinds of writing assignments: an analysis of the debate about health care reform in the United States and an argument about the Affordable

Care Act (ACA), often called Obamacare, which was passed by the U.S. Congress and became law in 2010. The analysis is for an assignment in a writing course that requires students to examine public debates about a controversial issue; the audience includes other students in the course as well as the instructor. The argument is intended for the student newspaper on your campus. Both pieces require research.

Let's consider how these different rhetorical situations, with their different audiences and purposes, might shape your decisions about whether and how to use information from the following three sources: an article posted on the website of Fox News, a blog post from a website called California Healthline, and an article from Alternet:

22

Smoke? Overweight? New Regulations Could Raise Your Insurance Rates

by Jim Angle

Foxnews.com 31 May 2013

If you smoke or you're overweight, have high cholesterol or high blood pressure, you could be forced to pay a lot more for health insurance, according to new regulations just issued by the Obama administration.

"For smoking, for being overweight, for being obese and basically, for generally not meeting the health guidelines, the employer can charge 30 percent more—for smoking, 50 percent more," explains John Goodman, President of the National Center for Policy Analysis in Dallas.

Obamacare does prevent insurers from charging more for pre-existing conditions, or from charging as much as they currently do for older people who use more health care.

But when it comes to smoking and being overweight as well as other health problems, if employees don't participate in wellness programs, they could pay more.

Ed Haislmeier of the Heritage Foundation says "on the one hand they're trying to ban discrimination based on health status, but on the other hand they're trying to say that some discrimination based on health status is good discrimination."

Goodman adds that "it is definitely the nanny state trying to tell us what we're going to do, and unleashing the employers to be the agent of the government in telling us what we're going to do."

Smokers, of course, run up more health care bills than non-smokers. But that habit and some other unhealthy conditions are associated with lower incomes, so higher rates would hit those the administration was aiming to help.

(Continued)

"Allowing premium differentials based on these factors will push premiums higher primarily on people that will be struggling to pay the premiums in the first place," says Jim Capretta of the Ethics and Public Policy Center.

Many employers already offer wellness programs, but the new 123-page regulation tells them exactly how they must operate.

"This is just one more massive regulation on top of the thousands and thousands of pages that have already been issued that employers have to deal with," says Capretta. "I think the whole system is starting to choke on so many rules."

Ironically, on the day officials released the new regulations, a Rand Corporation study about wellness programs was released—and not with good news.

Goodman noted it was "a Rand Corporation study, which was paid for by the Obama administration, and called for in the affordable care act. And the Rand Corporation has studied wellness programs all over the country, and basically says they don't work."

In fact, the study found that those trying to lose weight in these programs lost an average of a pound a year. And although some employers offer gym memberships, those who take them are the ones using the gym already—not those who need it most.

Source: Angle, Jim. "Smoke? Overweight? New Regulations Could Raise Your Insurance Rates." *Foxnews.com*, 31 May 2013. Web 1 June 2013.

The Premium Conundrum: Do Smokers Get a Fair Break under Obamacare?

by Dan Diamond

California Healthline 23 Jan. 2013

The Affordable Care Act contains a number of provisions intended to incent "personal responsibility," or the notion that health care isn't just a right—it's an obligation. None of these measures is more prominent than the law's individual mandate, designed to ensure that every American obtains health coverage or pays a fine for choosing to go uninsured.

But one provision that's gotten much less attention—until recently—relates to smoking; specifically, the ACA allows payers to treat tobacco users very differently by opening the door to much higher premiums for this population.

That measure has some health policy analysts cheering, suggesting that higher premiums are necessary to raise revenue for the law and (hopefully) deter smokers' bad habits. But other observers have warned that the ACA takes a heavy-handed stick to smokers who may be unhappily addicted to tobacco, rather than enticing them with a carrot to quit.

Under proposed rules, the department of Health and Human Services would allow insurers to charge a smoker seeking health coverage in the individual market as much as 50% more in premiums than a non-smoker.

That difference in premiums may rapidly add up for smokers, given the expectation that Obamacare's new medical-loss ratios already will lead to major cost hikes in the individual market. "For many people, in the years after the law, premiums aren't just going to [go] up a little," Peter Suderman predicts at Reason. "They're going to rise a lot."

Meanwhile, Ann Marie Marciarille, a law professor at the University of Missouri-Kansas City, adds that insurers have "considerable flexibility" in how to set up a potential surcharge for tobacco use. For example, insurers could apply a high surcharge for tobacco use in older smokers—perhaps several hundred dollars per month—further hitting a population that tends to be poorer.

Is this cost-shifting fair? The average American tends to think so.

Nearly 60% of surveyed adults in a 2011 NPR-Thomson Reuters poll thought it was OK to charge smokers more for their health insurance than non-smokers. (That's nearly twice the number of adults who thought it would be OK to charge the obese more for their health insurance.)

And smoking does lead to health costs that tend to be borne by the broader population. Writing at the Incidental Economist in 2011, Don Taylor noted that "smoking imposes very large social costs"—essentially, about $1.50 per pack—with its increased risk of cancers and other chronic illness. CDC has found that smoking and its effects lead to more than 440,000 premature deaths in the United States per year, with more than $190 billion in annual health costs and productivity loss.

As a result, charging smokers more "makes some actuarial sense," Marciarille acknowledges. "Tobacco use has a long-term fuse for its most expensive health effects."

But Louise Norris of Colorado Health Insurance Insider takes issue with the ACA's treatment of tobacco users.

Noting that smokers represent only about 20% of Americans, Norris argues that "it's easy to point fingers and call for increased personal responsibility when we're singling out another group—one in which we are not included."

As a result, she adds, "it seems very logical to say that smokers should have to pay significantly higher premiums for their health insurance," whereas we're less inclined to treat the obese differently because so many of us are overweight.

(Continued)

This approach toward tobacco users also raises the risk that low-income smokers will find the cost of coverage too high and end up uninsured, Norris warns. She notes that tax credits for health coverage will be calculated prior to however insurers choose to set their banding rules, "which means that smokers would be responsible for [an] additional premium on their own."

Alternate Approach: Focus on Cessation

Nearly 70% of smokers want to quit, and about half attempt to kick the habit at least once per year. But more than 90% are unable to stop smoking, partly because of the lack of assistance; fewer than 5% of smokers appear able to quit without support.

That's why Norris and others say that if federal officials truly want to improve public health, the law should prioritize anti-smoking efforts like counseling and medication for tobacco users. And the ACA does require new health insurance plans to offer smoking cessation products and therapy.

But as Ankita Rao writes at Kaiser Health News, the coverage of those measures thus far is spotty. Some plans leave out nasal sprays and inhalers; others shift costs to smokers, possibly deterring them from seeking treatment.

Some anti-smoking crusaders hope that states will step into the gap and ramp up cessation opportunities, such as by including cessation therapy as an essential health benefit.

"The federal government has missed several opportunities since the enactment of the ACA to grant smokers access to more cessation treatments," the American Lung Association warned in November. "Now, as states are beginning implementation of state exchanges and Medicaid expansions, state policymakers have the opportunity to stand up for smokers in their states who want to quit."

Source: Diamond, Dan. "The Premium Conundrum: Do Smokers Get a Fair Break Under Obamacare?" *California Healthline*, 23 Jan. 2013. Web. 31 May 2013.

How's Obamacare Turning Out? Great If You Live in a Blue State, and "Screw You" If You Have a Republican Governor

by Steve Rosenfeld

Alternet 25 May 2013

Obamacare implementation is becoming the latest dividing line between blue- and red-state America, with Democrat-led states making progress to expand healthcare to the uninsured and the poor—and Republican-led states saying "screw you" to millions of their most vulnerable and needy residents.

The latest sign of the Republican Party's increasingly secessionist tendencies comes as Obamacare passed a major milestone in California, which late last week announced lower-than-expected healthcare premiums for its 5.3 million uninsured, less than many small businesses now pay in group plans.

"Covered California's Silver Plan... offers premiums that can be 29 percent lower than comparable plans provided on today's small group market," the state's new insurance exchange announced Thursday, referring to the least-expensive option of four state-administered plans and posting this price comparison chart.

In contrast, the refusal by red-state America to create these health exchanges, which would be more local control—a supposed Republican value—and to accept federal funds to expand state-run Medicaid programs for the poor, means that about half the states are turning their backs on their residents, especially millions of the poorest people.

The federal government plans to step in later this summer and offer uninsured people in recalcitrant red states the option of buying plans via federally run health care exchanges. But the poorest people can't afford that, meaning the refusal to expand Medicaid programs will leave them in the cold. They will see ads selling new federal healthcare options that will be unaffordable for them.

The *New York Times* reports that local healthcare advocates in red states are predicting a backlash once Obamacare is rolled out and the poor realize that they cannot take advantage of it because Republicans are blocking it. However, that does not change the bottom line in state-run Medicaid programs: the GOP is again penalizing the poor.

Progress in Blue States

Meanwhile, in blue states, there have been surprising developments in the cost of Obamacare for those people who currently are uninsured. There, the bottom line is insurance premiums are hundreds of dollars a month lower than what employers are now paying for their workers under existing group plans.

California, with 5.3 million uninsured adults, is the biggest state to release cost estimates for Obamacare. Its lower-than-expected estimates are in line with announcements in Washington, Oregon, Maryland and Vermont. The actual prices will be known after insurers file rate documents in coming weeks.

Source: Rosenfeld, Steven. "How's Obamacare Turning Out? Great If You Live in a Blue State, and 'Screw You' If You Have a Republican Governor." *Alternet*, 25 May 2013. Web. 31 May 2013.

All three sources are relevant to both assignments, but are they useful? To answer that question, first determine whether each source is trustworthy by addressing the three main aspects of trustworthiness described in this chapter:

- Is the source credible?
- Is the source reliable?
- What is the bias of the source?

Is the Source Credible?

As we saw earlier (see pages 723–725), the credibility of a source depends on several important factors: the author, the nature of the publication, the purpose of the publication, and the date. Review each source accordingly:

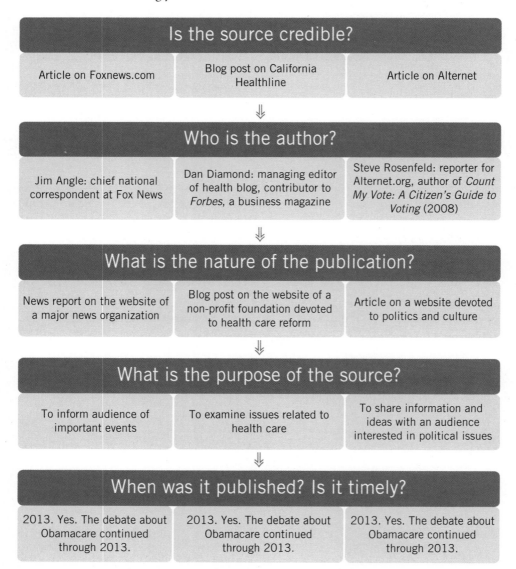

Is the source credible?

| Article on Foxnews.com | Blog post on California Healthline | Article on Alternet |

Who is the author?

| Jim Angle: chief national correspondent at Fox News | Dan Diamond: managing editor of health blog, contributor to *Forbes*, a business magazine | Steve Rosenfeld: reporter for Alternet.org, author of *Count My Vote: A Citizen's Guide to Voting* (2008) |

What is the nature of the publication?

| News report on the website of a major news organization | Blog post on the website of a non-profit foundation devoted to health care reform | Article on a website devoted to politics and culture |

What is the purpose of the source?

| To inform audience of important events | To examine issues related to health care | To share information and ideas with an audience interested in political issues |

When was it published? Is it timely?

| 2013. Yes. The debate about Obamacare continued through 2013. | 2013. Yes. The debate about Obamacare continued through 2013. | 2013. Yes. The debate about Obamacare continued through 2013. |

Addressing these questions will help you develop a better sense of the nature of each source, which will help you determine its credibility. Evaluating these sources in comparison to each other also reveals some important differences among them. For example, Fox News and Alternet cover all kinds of newsworthy topics, whereas California Healthline focuses only on health issues and can therefore be assumed to have more in-depth and expert coverage of issues like the Affordable Care Act.

If necessary, you can find more information to answer each of these questions about these sources. For example, you can look for more information about each author. Visiting a website like Amazon.com or Alibris.com might enable you to learn more about Steven Rosenfeld's book *Count My Vote*, which could give you insight into his background and his perspective on political issues. Similarly, you could find more information about the sponsor of California Healthline to determine whether the site could be considered a credible source of information.

As noted earlier in this chapter, credibility can also be a function of a writer's tone, fairness, and general approach to the subject. With those criteria in mind, you might note that the general tone of the Fox News article toward the Affordable Care Act is negative, and the language of the Alternet article is explicitly dismissive and disrespectful of a conservative viewpoint. These characteristics should make you a bit more skeptical about these two sources. Nevertheless, both sources seem to have accurate information about the topic of health care reform, even though they present that information from a decidedly partisan perspective.

Let's say that after examining each source in this example, you have determined that all three sources can be considered credible, despite your reservations about the Alternet and Fox News articles. Next, try to decide whether the source is reliable.

Is the Source Reliable?

Reliability generally has to do with your confidence that a source has established a record for accuracy and credibility. In this example, both Fox News and Alternet represent perspectives that are consistent over time. Both sources are respected by their constituencies. You are aware of their respective political leanings, and you can judge the reliability of information from each site in the context of those perspectives. For example, you expect Fox News to be skeptical about the Affordable Care Act because of Fox's generally conservative perspective on large government programs; by contrast, you expect articles on Alternet to be supportive of the ACA and critical of conservative resistance to it. Neither article is surprising in this regard. In other words, each site is reliable in terms of its political perspective and generally reliable in the kinds of information it presents.

The reliability of the blog post from California Healthline is less clear, mostly because it is a less well-known and more specialized source. To gain a better sense of its reliability, you should investigate further. For one thing, you can check the "About" page on its website. Here's what you would find:

California Healthline is a free, daily digest of health care news, policy and opinion. It is designed to meet the information needs of busy health care professionals and decision makers. *California Healthline* is part of the California HealthCare Foundation's commitment to important issues affecting health care policy, delivery, and financing.

The Advisory Board Company is a leader in national health care research and publishing. It independently publishes *California Healthline* for the California HealthCare Foundation and is responsible for the editorial content of the publication. *California Healthline* editors review more than 300 newspapers, journals, and trade publications to produce daily news summaries.

Source: "About California Healthline." *California Healthline,* 2013. Web. 3 June 2013.

This description provides the important information that California Healthline is sponsored by an organization called California Healthcare Foundation but is published independently by a national health care research and publishing organization. That information lends credibility to the site because it suggests that the publication is non-partisan and lacks a particular political or ideological agenda. The site also indicates that it has been in operation since 1998, which gives you confidence in its reliability as a source for information about health care issues. Finally, the author of the blog post seems to be an established observer of health care and business matters (he writes for *Forbes* magazine, a leading and well-respected business publication). All these facts can give you confidence that this is a reliable source for information about health care issues.

This analysis enables you to conclude that all three of these sources can be considered reliable.

What Is the Bias of the Source?

You have established your sources as credible and reliable, but their usefulness to you will also depend on the extent to which they are biased.

You have already determined that Fox News and Alternet reflect conservative and left-leaning political biases, respectively. What about California Healthline? Your review of its "About" page led you to conclude that it is credible, reliable, and probably politically non-partisan, but even if it does not reflect a political bias, it might reflect other kinds of bias. It makes sense to look more closely at this source.

The "About" page indicates California Healthline is sponsored by a non-profit organization called California Health Care Foundation. Here's how the organization describes itself on its website:

CHCF is a nonprofit grantmaking philanthropy based in Oakland, California. Founded in 1996, the staff of about 50 people issues around $40 million in grants each year from an endowment of $700 million. CHCF does not participate in lobbying or fundraising.

Source: "About CHCF." *California Health Care Foundation,* 2013. Web. 3 June 2013.

This explanation tells you that the foundation is not a political group and supports health care reform by providing grants rather than by lobbying on behalf of specific reforms or political interests. But on the same web page you also find the following statement:

The passage of the federal Affordable Care Act creates an extraordinary opportunity to provide health coverage to millions of Californians. Its success will depend on how the law is implemented by the states. This initiative focuses on elements of health reform that have the greatest potential to affect California.

From this passage you could reasonably conclude that the organization is generally supportive of the Affordable Care Act. That conclusion doesn't necessarily call into question the information on the California Healthline site, but it does suggest that the site is likely to cover the Affordable Care Act closely and is not likely to be consistently critical of it. In other words, articles and blog posts on the site are likely to reflect a bias in favor of expanded and effective health care reform, including the ACA.

You can examine the biases of your three sources in more depth by addressing the four sets of questions listed on page 728:

To what extent is the source biased?

Article on Foxnews.com	Blog post on California Healthline	Article on Alternet

Does the source reflect a particular viewpoint or perspective?

Yes, a generally conservative viewpoint	No obvious political or ideological perspective	Yes, a left-leaning political point of view

Does the source represent a specific group or organization?

Yes, website is part of the Fox News organization.	Yes, sponsored by a non-profit foundation that supports health care reform.	No, the site is an independent, non-profit news entity.

Does the source have an agenda regarding the subject?

Yes, generally opposed to federal health care reform initiative	Yes, supports health care reform	Yes, generally supportive of the presidential administration's reform efforts

To what extent is the bias of the source evident?

The critical stance toward the ACA is noticeable.	Bias in favor of health care reform is implicit.	Overt bias in favor of presidential administration and against its conservative opponents.

At this point, you should have a good sense of the biases of your three sources.

Now that you have carefully evaluated your sources, examine their usefulness for your rhetorical purposes. Recall that both your hypothetical assignments—the analysis and the argument—are about health care reform in the United States, but their purposes and intended audiences differ, which will influence your decisions about whether and how to use the sources you have evaluated.

Let's imagine that your analysis is an effort to answer this question:

Why is the debate about the Affordable Care Act in the United States so intense and confrontational?

You want to understand some of the reasons for the vitriolic nature of this debate and what it might reveal about public debates in general. You are writing your analysis primarily for your instructor and other students in your class. For your argument, let's imagine that you want to make the case that the intense debates about the Affordable Care Act are relevant to college students. For this piece, your audience is broader than for your analysis: students and faculty who read your campus newspaper. We can sum up the rhetorical situations for these two pieces of writing as follows:

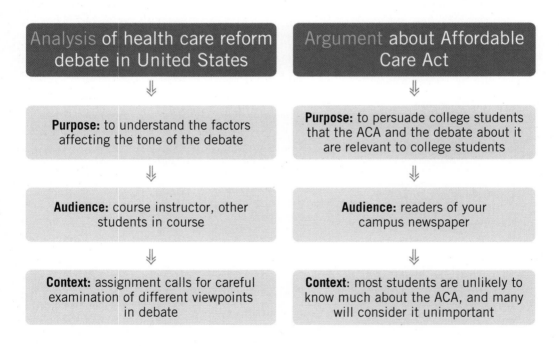

With these factors in mind, you can examine how each of the three sources you found might fit into these two assignments.

For your analysis of the debate about the Affordable Care Act, you might use the articles from Fox News and Alternet as examples of more extreme political positions in the debate. In this case, you don't need to worry much about the accuracy or reliability of the sources because you would be using them as examples of how conservative and left-leaning viewpoints emerge in the debate about health care reform. Your analysis would require you to identify clearly the political perspectives represented by each source and how those perspectives influence the way each source represents the Affordable Care Act. For example, you might examine the quotations from experts that are included in the Fox News article to show that the author cites only experts who are critical of the ACA. Similarly, you might evaluate the specific language used in the Alternet article to refer to Republican or conservative positions—for example, "secessionist" and "recalcitrant"—and the unsupported claim that "the GOP is again penalizing the poor." For your purposes, it would not be necessary to decide how accurate the information in each source is; you are simply analyzing *how* the sources present the information, not the information itself, so the overt biases of the sources is not a problem.

For your argument, by contrast, you would likely need to present accurate information about the Affordable Care Act and the problems it is intended to address, especially in terms of how it might affect college students. You want to convince your audience that the debate about health care reform is one they should pay attention to. In this case, some of the information from the California Healthline blog post is likely to be useful in arguing that the debate matters to college students. For example, the author notes that the new law is "designed to ensure that every American obtains health coverage or pays a fine for choosing to go uninsured." That fact should be important to college students, many of whom will lose their health care insurance once they graduate. If you include that quotation in your argument, you will need to be confident that it is accurate. Your evaluation of this source should give you that confidence, but you can also look for other sources that could corroborate it. At the same time, the information included in the Fox News and Alternet articles might also be useful, but given your rhetorical purpose, you would have to take into account the clear political biases of those sources as you decide whether to use specific information. For instance, the author of the Alternet article identifies differences in how individual states will enact the Affordable Care Act. Those differences could be important to college students because they could affect the kind of health insurance that is available to them in one state or another. However, you might be more skeptical of the author's claim that "Republican-led states [are] saying 'screw you' to millions of their most vulnerable and needy residents." Given the author's political perspective, which makes him more likely to be critical of Republican policies, it would be sensible to verify such a claim before using it in your own argument. Moreover, you would want to avoid undermining your argument by relying on sources whose political views might alienate some of your intended readers.

These examples illustrate how the rhetorical situation can influence your decisions about how to use the source material you find in your research. Obviously, you should evaluate *all* source material in terms of credibility, reliability, and bias. But how your evaluation will affect your decisions about using source material will ultimately depend upon the rhetorical goals you hope to achieve with your intended audience.

Using Source Material 23

STUDENT WRITERS sometimes have less trouble finding the source material they need for their projects than they do using that material effectively in their own writing. The challenge for many students is resisting the tendency to rely too heavily on source material so that it doesn't take over the student's own writing. Using source materials effectively, then, is partly a matter of keeping in mind the purpose and main point of the project. The most important guideline to follow when using any source material is to focus on your own ideas and the point *you* are making. The source material you cite should support *your* thinking and should not become the focus of your writing. (See Core Concept #4: "A writer must have something to say.") So it is important to be able to *integrate* source material into your writing rather than simply reproduce information from a source. This chapter describes some basic strategies for using your source material strategically and maintaining control of your own writing.

Quoting from Sources

In academic writing, there are three main ways to integrate source material into your own prose:

- summarizing
- paraphrasing
- quoting

Summarizing and paraphrasing are discussed in Chapter 19 (see pages 635–639). In this section, we will examine how to quote sources appropriately.

To integrate source material smoothly into your writing, **follow these basic guidelines:**

- Quote only what you need and when necessary.
- Reproduce the original text accurately.
- Be concise.
- Make it fit.

Quote Only What You Need and When Necessary

Writers quote from a source when the rhetorical situation dictates that it is important to include information or ideas *as stated in the original language of the source.* If you are consulting a source for specific information and don't need the exact language of the source, summarize or paraphrase the source passage. (See Chapter 19 for advice about summarizing and paraphrasing.) Sometimes, however, the original wording of the source is necessary to make or emphasize a point. In such cases, quoting can enhance your writing.

For example, imagine that you are writing an analysis of the debate about what should be done to address global climate change. One of your sources is *Field Notes from a Catastrophe*, in which author Elizabeth Kolbert reviews scientific data indicating that climate change is an increasingly serious problem. Here are two passages that you consider important and want to include in your analysis:

> All told, the Greenland ice sheet holds enough water to raise sea levels worldwide by twenty-three feet. Scientists at NASA have calculated that throughout the 1990s the ice sheet, despite some thickening at the center, was shrinking by twelve cubic miles per year. (52)

> As the effects of global warming become more and more difficult to ignore, will we react by finally fashioning a global response? Or will we retreat into ever narrower and more destructive forms of self-interest? It may seem impossible to imagine that a technologically advanced society could choose, in essence, to destroy itself, but that is what we are now in the process of doing. (189)

Source: Kolbert, Elizabeth. *Field Notes from a Catastrophe*. New York: Bloomsbury Press, 2006. Print.

The first passage contains important information about shrinking glaciers, which scientists consider a sign of climate change that could have a significant impact on coastal communities. The second passage is taken from Kolbert's conclusion, where she makes a plea for action to address climate change. Here's how you might use these passages in your analysis:

> Scientists have documented the decline of glaciers and arctic sea ice over the past several decades. For example, the Greenland ice sheet, which contains enough water to increase global sea levels by 23 feet, is shrinking by 12 cubic miles per year (Kolbert 52). To many scientists, the loss of glacial and sea ice is one of the most worrisome indicators that climate change is accelerating, and some argue that humans must act now to avoid potentially catastrophic impacts on human communities in the coming decades. Elizabeth Kolbert expresses the concerns of many experts: "As the effects of global warming become more and more difficult to ignore, will we react by finally fashioning a global response? Or will we retreat into ever narrower and more destructive forms of self-interest? It may seem impossible to imagine that a technologically advanced society could choose, in essence, to destroy itself, but that is what we are now in the process of doing" (189).

Notice that the first passage from the source text (p. 52) is cited but not quoted. Although the information in that passage is important, the wording of the source text is not. The second passage (p. 189), however, is quoted, because Kolbert's wording conveys her point more effectively than a summary or paraphrase would.

This example illustrates the need to be judicious in deciding whether to quote or summarize and cite your source. In making that decision, always consider the purpose of your project and the impact you wish to have on your audience.

Reproduce the Original Text Accurately

Quotation marks indicate to a reader that everything inside the quotation marks is exactly as it appears in the source text. So whenever you are using a quotation, make sure that you have reproduced the passage you are quoting accurately. Although this advice might seem obvious, misquoting is a common problem in student writing that can lead to misleading or inaccurate statements. For example, here's a statement from an article reporting the results of a study of the link between childhood obesity and cancer:

> Those whose Body Mass Index placed them in the range of obesity in adolescence had a 1.42% greater chance of developing urothelial or colorectal cancers in adulthood.

A misplaced quotation mark or incomplete quotation could significantly change the meaning of this statement:

> According to a recent study, "Those whose Body Mass Index placed them in the range of obesity in adolescence had a 1.42% greater chance of developing urothelial or colorectal cancers."

In this example, the writer failed to include the phrase "in adulthood" at the end of the quoted statement. Although everything else included in the quotation marks is accurate, the quoted statement is now misleading. The original study indicates that obese adolescents have a 1.42% greater chance of developing two specific kinds of cancer *in adulthood*. Because the quotation in this example omits that phrase, a reader could misinterpret the results of the study to mean that obese adolescents have a greater chance of developing specific cancers at any time in their lives, even before adulthood, which is not what the study found.

As this example indicates, even a minor mistake in quoting from a source could result in erroneous or misleading statements.

Be Concise

One of the most common problems students have when quoting from a source is wordiness. Often, students use unnecessary words to introduce a quotation. Here's an example:

> In the article "New Teachers" by Neil Postman and Charles Weingarten, the authors state, "One of the largest obstacles to the establishment of a sound learning environment is the desire of teachers to get something they think they know into the heads of people who don't know it" (138).

Technically, there is nothing wrong with this sentence, but the writer could introduce the quotation more smoothly with fewer words:

> In "New Teachers," Neil Postman and Charles Weingarten state, "One of the largest obstacles to the establishment of a sound learning environment is the desire of teachers to get something they think they know into the heads of people who don't know it" (138).

In their article, Neil Postman and Charles Weingarten state, "One of the largest obstacles to the establishment of a sound learning environment is the desire of teachers to get something they think they know into the heads of people who don't know it" (138).

Neil Postman and Charles Weingarten state, "One of the largest obstacles to the establishment of a sound learning environment is the desire of teachers to get something they think they know into the heads of people who don't know it" ("New Teachers" 138).

Here are a few more examples:

Wordy: Janet Emig, in her work "Writing as a Mode of Learning," argues that "writing serves learning uniquely because writing as process-and-product possesses a cluster of attributes that correspond uniquely to certain powerful learning strategies" (122).

Better: According to Janet Emig, "Writing serves learning uniquely because writing as process-and-product possesses a cluster of attributes that correspond uniquely to certain powerful learning strategies" ("Writing as a Mode of Learning" 122).

Wordy: "Nobody Mean More to Me than You and the Future Life of Willie Jordan" is an essay written by June Jordan that analyzes Black English as a language "system constructed by people constantly needing to insist that we exist, that we are present" (460).

Better: In "Nobody Mean More to Me than You and the Future Life of Willie Jordan," June Jordan analyzes Black English as a language "system constructed by people constantly needing to insist that we exist, that we are present" (460).

The rule of thumb is to be concise and include only the necessary information about the source. If you're not sure how to introduce a quotation, use one of the standard approaches to introducing a quotation. (See "Four Common Ways to Introduce Quotations in Academic Writing.") Keep in mind that if you have a bibliography or works cited page (which you should if you are using sources), you need to give your readers only enough information in your text to be able to find the citation in your bibliography or works cited page.

FOCUS   Four Common Ways to Introduce Quotations in Academic Writing

If you pay attention as you read scholarly writing in books and journals, you will notice four common patterns that writers use to introduce quotations from source materials. You can use these patterns to make your own use of source material more effective and help give your own prose a more scholarly "sound":

1. In [title of source], [name of author] states (argues, asserts, claims, suggests), "[insert quotation]."

    In *Contemporary Philosophy of Social Science*, Brian Fay argues, "Knowledge of what we are experiencing always involves an interpretation of these experiences" (19).

2. According to [name of author], "[insert quotation]."
   According to Brian Fay, "Knowledge of what we are experiencing always involves an interpretation of these experiences" (19).

3. [Name of author] states (argues, asserts, claims, suggests), "[insert quotation]."
   Brian Fay argues, "Knowledge of what we are experiencing always involves an interpretation of these experiences" (19).

4. "[Beginning of quotation]," according to [name of author], "[rest of quotation]."
   "Knowledge of what we are experiencing," according to Brian Fay, "always involves an interpretation of these experiences" (19).

You can use all four patterns to vary the way you introduce quotations and therefore avoid making your prose sound repetitive.

Make It Fit

Core Concept #9 ("There is always a voice in writing, even when there isn't an I") underscores the importance of voice in academic writing, no matter what the specific writing task might be. Many students weaken their voices by failing to integrate quotations and source material smoothly into their writing.

For example, in the following passage, the student discusses ideas for education reform proposed by the authors of a source text:

> In the article "New Teachers" by Postman and Weingartner, there are several explanations as to why change is not an option for some teachers. The biggest problem is, "Where do we get the new teachers necessary to translate the new education into action? Obviously, it will be very difficult to get many of them from the old education. Most of these have a commitment to existing metaphors, procedures, and goals that would preclude their accepting a 'new education'" (133). Older teachers have no use for the "new education." This article focuses mainly on how teachers can be trained to translate this "new education" to their students.

In this example, the student relies too heavily on the source and does not allow her own voice to emerge. Part of the problem is wordiness, but also notice that the quotations from the source text tend to overpower the student's own writing style. Compare this passage to the following one, in which a student also writes about the possibility of education reform and draws on the work of a well-known education theorist. Unlike the previous example, in this case the student effectively integrates references to and quotations from the source text while maintaining her own voice:

> One of a teacher's main objectives in the classroom should be to equip students with cognitive and metacognitive skills so that they are mindful of the world around them. This process of critical thinking is an essential practice that students must not only understand but also be able to utilize in order to become knowledgeable, empowered individuals. In "The Banking Concept of Education," a chapter from *Pedagogy of the Oppressed*, however, Paulo Freire discusses something *more* than providing students with critical thinking skills in school. He encourages teachers to raise students' awareness about themselves and society, so that they are able to work towards the broader idea of social change; this is what he calls "critical consciousness" (35). According to Freire, it is the responsibility of the teacher to instill in his/her students a sense of agency, fostering the potential and possibility for change. Without knowing that they have the capacity to transform society, Freire argues, students will become passive members of society; change, therefore, will never be possible. With this argument, Freire places great responsibility on the shoulders of those who work within the education system. But can educators really take on this role?

In this passage, the student maintains control of the material. The paragraph includes summary, paraphrase, and quotations from the source text, but the main point of the paragraph is the student's own. (See "A Strategy for Integrating Source Material into Your Writing.") Moreover, the voice of the source never takes over, and the student's voice remains strong.

As you work with source material, remember that even when your assignment calls for a review or critique of a source text, the analysis and conclusions about that text are yours. So work the source material into your own writing—not the other way around.

FOCUS | **A Strategy for Integrating Source Material into Your Writing**

Chapter 19 provides advice for writing clear, cohesive paragraphs. Sometimes paragraphs become incoherent because the student loses control of the source material. Use the advice in this chapter to avoid that problem. You can also follow a basic structure for your paragraphs when you are integrating source material into a paragraph:

1. **Topic statement.** Introduce the subject of the paragraph and provide context for the source material to follow.

2. **Source material.** Summarize, paraphrase, or quote from the source.

3. **Takeaway.** Comment on the source material to connect it to your topic statement.

Be sure to cite the source using MLA or APA format (see Chapters 24 and 25).

The sample paragraph on page 746 illustrates this structure:

One of a teacher's main objectives in the classroom should be to equip students with cognitive and metacognitive skills so that they are mindful of the world around them. This process of critical thinking is an essential practice that students must not only understand but also be able to utilize in order to become knowledgeable, empowered individuals. In "The Banking Concept of Education," a chapter from *Pedagogy of the Oppressed*, however, Paulo Freire discusses something *more* than providing students with critical thinking skills in school. He encourages teachers to raise students' awareness about themselves and society, so that they are able to work towards the broader idea of social change; this is what he calls "critical consciousness" (35). According to Freire, it is the responsibility of the teacher to instill in his/her students a sense of agency, fostering the potential and possibility for change. Without knowing that they have the capacity to transform society, Freire argues, students will become passive members of society; change, therefore, will never be possible. With this argument, Freire places great responsibility on the shoulders of those who work within the education system. But can educators really take on this role?

Topic Statement: The student establishes the focus of the paragraph and provides context for the source material.

Source Material: The student paraphrases and quotes from the source.

Citation: Using MLA format, the student properly cites the source of the quoted phrase.

Takeaway: The student connects the source material to the topic statement and poses a question about the material to provide a transition to the next paragraph.

23

Additional Guidelines

Punctuate Complete Quotations Correctly

When including a complete quotation from a source in your writing, use quotation marks and final punctuation marks as follows:

Direct Quotation:

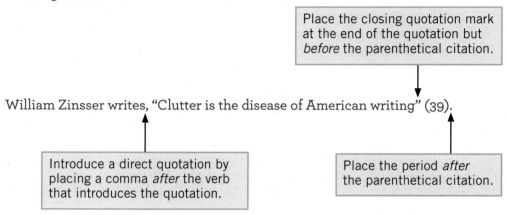

William Zinsser writes, "Clutter is the disease of American writing" (39).

Introduce a direct quotation by placing a comma *after* the verb that introduces the quotation.

Place the period *after* the parenthetical citation.

Direct Quotation Following *that*:

When the word "that" follows the verb introducing the quotation, there is *no* comma after "that."

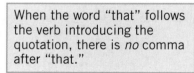

William Zinsser believes that "[c]lutter is the disease of American writing" (39).

The capital *C* is made lowercase because the quotation is a continuation of the sentence. (If the first word of the quotation is a word that is always capitalized, such as a name or proper noun, then it is capitalized here.) The brackets indicate that the letter *C* is capitalized in the original.

You can also introduce a quotation with a colon:

Zinsser makes a provocative point: "Clutter is the disease of American writing" (39).

Insert Phrases When You Don't Need an Entire Statement

Sometimes you only want to quote a word or phrase from a source rather than an entire sentence or passage. In such cases, integrate the phrase into your sentence, using quotation marks to indicate the quoted words and citing the source properly with a parenthetical citation:

> The economist E. F. Schumacher argued that "work and leisure are complementary parts of the same living process" and therefore should not be considered separate from one another (55).

> In this example, there is no need for commas around the quoted phrase because it is used as part of the sentence.

> This sentence requires a comma after the quoted phrase because of the coordinating conjunction *but*.

> The economist E. F. Schumacher argued that "work and leisure are complementary parts of the same living process," but he also acknowledged that few people in industrialized societies understand work and leisure in this way (55).

Use Ellipses to Indicate Missing Words from a Quotation

If you quote a passage from a source but omit part of that passage, you can indicate that something is missing by using ellipses—that is, three periods, each followed by a space:

Original Passage from Source:
> To my mind, voyaging through wildernesses, be they full of woods or waves, is essential to the growth and maturity of the human spirit.

Quotation with Missing Words:
> Despite his ordeal at sea, in which he survived alone in a life raft for 76 days, Steven Callahan still believed in the value of wilderness experiences. "To my mind," he writes, "voyaging through wildernesses . . . is essential to the growth and maturity of the human spirit" (234).

In this case, the writer decided that the phrase *be they full of woods or waves* was unnecessary and therefore omitted it; the ellipses indicate to a reader that words are missing at that point in the quoted passage.

Use Brackets to Indicate a Modified Quotation

If you have to modify a quotation in order to fit it into your sentence, use brackets to indicate changes you have made to the source material:

Original Passage from Source:

> I have focused on two people, one familiar, the other less so: Plymouth governor William Bradford and Benjamin Church, a carpenter turned Indian fighter whose maternal grandfather had sailed on the *Mayflower*.

Modified Passage in Quotation:

> In his provocative history of the Pilgrims, Nathaniel Philbrick "focuse[s] on two people, one familiar, the other less so: Plymouth governor William Bradford and Benjamin Church, a carpenter turned Indian fighter whose maternal grandfather had sailed on the *Mayflower*" (xvii).

In this example, the writer has changed the original verb *focused* to *focuses* so it fits into the passage. The brackets indicate to a reader that the *s* at the end of *focuses* is not in the original text.

Avoiding Plagiarism

Plagiarism is the use of others' words or ideas without giving credit or presenting someone else's words or ideas as your own. It is tantamount to intellectual theft. It goes without saying that plagiarism is unethical. It is dishonest as well as unfair to your classmates, your instructor, and the plagiarized source. It is also a squandering of an opportunity to learn or make something new and useful through your academic work.

Because plagiarism is such a serious breach of ethical standards, it can have serious consequences. In the most extreme cases, plagiarism can result in lawsuits, penalties, or fines. Most colleges and universities have strict codes of student conduct that often include severe sanctions for students caught plagiarizing, including failing an assignment, failing a course, and even expulsion from school.

Plagiarism can range from failing to cite a source to submitting someone else's work as your own (which includes purchasing a paper online from a so-called "paper mill" and submitting it to your instructor as if you wrote it yourself). But students sometimes plagiarize unintentionally—often because they misunderstand the nature of academic research or rely too heavily on source material instead of using sources to support or extend their own ideas. The best way to avoid plagiarism is to apply the Ten Core Concepts in your writing and follow the advice presented in Chapters 21, 22, and 23 for finding and using source material. If you focus on what you have to say in your writing, you are much less likely to plagiarize. Also, review the advice for summarizing and paraphrasing in Chapter 19. Sometimes students inadvertently plagiarize by borrowing too heavily from a source because they don't sufficiently understand the functions of summary and paraphrase.

To avoid plagiarizing inadvertently, follow these guidelines:

- **Use sources to support or extend your own ideas.** As noted earlier, if you focus on making and supporting your main point (Core Concepts #4 and #5), you are less likely to fall victim to unnecessarily borrowing from a source or unintentionally presenting ideas from a source as your own.

- **Integrate source material into your own writing.** Following the advice in this chapter will help you present source material appropriately. Learn to use summary and paraphrase effectively. Apply the strategies for quoting from sources described in this chapter to make it clear to your readers when the material you are presenting is taken from a source.

- **Credit your sources.** Follow the conventions for citing sources that are explained in Chapters 24 and 25. Use APA or MLA format correctly (or use another format approved by your instructor). Be sure to cite sources correctly so that there is no confusion about whether the material you are presenting is yours or taken from a source.

- **Take careful notes.** When you are researching a topic, keep accurate notes about the sources you have consulted so that you know where you found the material you are using and have the correct information for citing the sources. If you are using online sources, it is a good idea to bookmark the pages from which you have taken information.

23

Citing Sources Using MLA Style

24

THE PURPOSE OF CITING SOURCES is to be as clear as possible in showing where your information comes from. Citing your sources according to established style guides not only enables you to give credit to the source for the material you are using but also provides your readers with sufficient bibliographic information to judge or even find your sources for themselves. In general, you must document the source of

- a direct quotation
- an idea or opinion that is not your own
- visual materials, such as photographs, maps, or graphs, that you did not create
- multimedia content, such as videos or audios, that you did not create
- information (a fact or statistic) that is not general knowledge

In most academic writing today, writers use the Modern Language Association (MLA) style guide when they are writing in the humanities: literature, languages, performing and visual arts, history, classics, philosophy, and religion. This chapter explains how to cite sources using MLA style. (APA style, which tends to be used in the social sciences—psychology, sociology, education, economics, anthropology, geography, and political science—is explained in Chapter 25.) The guidelines in this chapter are based on the *MLA Handbook for Writers of Research Papers,* 7th ed., and the *MLA Style Manual and Guide to Scholarly Publishing,* 3rd ed.

Two Main Components in MLA Style

MLA style uses in-text parenthetical citations to document sources. There are **two main components to in-text parenthetical citation systems:**

1. **In-text citations.** Parenthetical citations, which appear in the body of your writing, indicate to a reader that information you are presenting is taken from another source.
2. **A Works Cited list.** The Works Cited list is a separate section at the end of your document that includes bibliographic information for every source you cited in your document.

Let's imagine you are writing an essay about the cultural significance of heavy metal music and you want to refer to a specific analysis of so-called death metal music in a book by Natalie J. Purcell titled *Death Metal Music: The Passion and Politics of a Subculture.* On page 188 of that book,

Claudio Divizia/Cutcaster; Elena Rostunova/Shutterstock.com

Purcell makes a point about the philosophical function of death metal music that you want to include in your essay. Using MLA style, you would cite your source as follows:

> Death metal music performs a genuine philosophical function by examining the dark side of human nature (Purcell 188).

If you mention the author's name in your sentence, you do not need to include it in the parenthetical citation:

> Critic Natalie Purcell considers death metal a "philosophical response, whether conscious or subconscious, to terrifying questions about nebulous human nature"(188).

The information in parentheses indicates to readers that the idea about the philosophical function of death metal is taken from page 188 of a work by Purcell. Readers can then consult your Works Cited page, where they will find the following entry:

> Purcell, Natalie J. *Death Metal Music: The Passion and Politics of a Subculture*. Jefferson: McFarland, 2003. Print.

Each in-text citation in your document must have a corresponding Works Cited entry to give your readers the means to find and read the original source themselves.

FOCUS   Footnotes, Endnotes, and Content Notes

Traditionally, footnotes or endnotes were used to document sources. Strictly speaking, a **footnote** appears at the foot of the page and an **endnote** appears at the end of the paper. However, the MLA now recommends that writers use parenthetical, or in-text, citations of the kind described in this chapter. Traditional footnotes are used not for documenting sources but for additional explanation or discussion of a point in the main text. These notes are called **content notes.**

Creating In-Text Citations in MLA Style

MLA style, which reflects the conventions of the humanities, emphasizes the author and the author's work and places less emphasis on the date of publication. When citing a work parenthetically, the author's last name is followed by a page number or range of pages. There are particular situations in which somewhat different information is given in parentheses, but *the general rule is to provide enough information to enable a reader to find the source in your Works Cited list*. You do not need to include inside the parentheses information you have already provided in the text. For instance, if you start the sentence with the author's name, you do not need to include the author's name in the parentheses.

A. Work by one author

If you were citing information taken from page 82 of a book called *The Printing Revolution in Early Modern Europe* by Elizabeth L. Eisenstein, the parenthetical citation would look like this:

> The widespread adoption of the printing press in the 16th century helped standardize the major European languages (Eisenstein 82).

If you used Eisenstein's name in your sentence, the citation would include only the page reference:

> Elizabeth Eisenstein examines how the widespread adoption of the printing press in the 16th century helped standardize the major European languages (82).

There is no punctuation between the author's name and the page number. Note that the parentheses are placed *inside* the period at the end of the sentence. Also, the abbreviation *p.* or *pp.* is not used before the page reference in MLA style.

B. Work by multiple authors

When citing a work by two or three authors, include all the authors' names in the citation (or in your sentence). For example, if you wanted to quote from page 2 of *Undead TV: Essays on Buffy the Vampire Slayer*, by Elana Levine and Lisa Parks, you could do so as follows:

> We might consider how the hit television series *Buffy the Vampire Slayer* "dramatizes the travails of its title character but uses its metaphorical representations of life and

death, good and evil, comedy and tragedy to speak about the power struggles inherent in many people's everyday lives in the Western world" (Levine and Parks 2).

or

Elana Levine and Lisa Parks assert that *"Buffy the Vampire Slayer* dramatizes the travails of its title character but uses its metaphorical representations of life and death, good and evil, comedy and tragedy to speak about the power struggles inherent in many people's everyday lives in the Western world" (2).

If you are referring to a work by more than three authors, list only the first author's name followed by the Latin phrase *et al.* (which means "and others"). For example, if you were citing information from page 79 of a journal article titled "Empirical Foundations for Writing in Prevention and Psychotherapy," by Brian A. Esterling, Luciano L'Abate, Edward J. Murray, and James W. Pennebaker, the parenthetical citation would look like this

Studies have shown that writing has therapeutic benefits for some patients (Esterling et al. 79).

Note that there is no comma after the name of the author.

C. Work by a corporate author

A "corporate author" is an organization, committee, or agency (rather than an individual or group of individually named authors). When citing a corporate author, use the same format as for a single author. For example, if you were citing a study by the Center for Research on Educational Outcomes, you would do so as follows:

According to the Center for Research on Educational Outcomes, in 37 percent of charter schools, students had math scores that were lower than their public school peers (3).

You could also include the corporate author in the parentheses; omit any initial article:

In one recent study, 37 percent of charter schools had student math scores that were lower than in public schools (Center for Research on Educational Outcomes 3.).

D. More than one work by the same author

If you cite more than one work by the same author, you need to distinguish among the works by using a shortened form of the title of each work you cite. For example, if you were quoting from two different books by Paulo Freire, *Pedagogy of Hope* and *Letters to Cristina*, your parenthetical citations might look like this:

Freire emphasizes the crucial role of hope in the struggle for change. Acknowledging that hope "seldom exists apart from the reverses of fate" (*Letters* 14), Freire argues that the "dream of humanization . . . is always a process" (*Pedagogy* 99).

The shortened titles (*Letters* and *Pedagogy*) enable a reader to find the specific references in the Works Cited list. Also note that because it is clear from the context that both works cited are by the same author, the author's name does not need to be placed inside the parentheses. If the author's name is not included in the text itself, include it inside the parenthetical citation:

> Hope is a crucial element in the struggle for change. We should acknowledge that hope "seldom exists apart from the reverses of fate" (Freire, *Letters* 14) and remember that the "dream of humanization . . . is always a process" (Freire, *Pedagogy* 99).

Note that a comma separates the author's name from the shortened title, but no comma appears between the title and the page number.

E. Work without an author listed

If you cite a work without an author listed, include a brief version of the title in parentheses. For example, if you cited information from page 27 of an article from *The Economist* titled "Carrying the Torch," you would do so as follows:

> The sports management industry in Great Britain received a significant boost in business as a result of the 2012 Olympic Games in London ("Carrying" 27).

F. Entire work

When you refer to an entire work, include only the author's name, either in your sentence or in parentheses. No page numbers are needed.

> Cheryl Sandberg discusses the reasons women are still not adequately represented in leadership positions.

G. Quotation within a cited work

When using a quotation from one source that you have found in another source, you must show that the quotation was acquired "secondhand" and was not taken directly from the original source. In such cases, use the abbreviation *qtd. in* (for "quoted in") to indicate that you are taking the quotation from a second source rather than from the original text. For example, let's say you were reading a book titled *Literary Theory* by Terry Eagleton that included a quotation by Sigmund Freud. If you wanted to use Freud's quotation in your essay, you would cite it as follows:

> Even Freud acknowledged the central importance of economics in human relations, famously stating, "The motive of human society is in the last resort an economic one" (qtd. in Eagleton 151).

In this instance, you are signaling to readers that you read Freud's statement in the book by Terry Eagleton. Your Works Cited list will contain an entry for Eagleton's book but not Freud's original text.

H. Work in an anthology

Name the author of the particular work, not the editor of the entire anthology, in your citation. For example, if you were citing a story by Nathan Englander that appears in the anthology *The*

Best American Short Stories 2012, edited by Tom Perrotta and Heidi Pitlor, you would not need to mention the editors of the anthology:

> Nathan Englander plays off Raymond Carver's famous story title in his short work "What We Talk About When We Talk About Anne Frank."

The entry in your Works Cited list would include the editors' names.

I. Electronic sources

When citing electronic sources, follow the same principles you would use when citing other sources. However, there are many different kinds of electronic sources, which might not include the same kinds of information that are available for a print book or journal article. For example, online sources, such as websites, often do not have page numbers. In such cases, if possible provide the number of the paragraph in which you found the information or quotation you are citing:

> (Martinez, par. 8)

Note that a comma is placed after the author's name.

> If page numbers are not available, include sufficient information for readers to find the source you are citing, such as the author's last name or a brief title:

> (Martinez)

J. Long quotations

In MLA style, a long prose quotation is defined as one that takes more than four lines in your paper. Quotations of more than three lines of poetry are considered long, and any amount of quoted dialogue from a play is treated as a block quotation. These quotations should be indented one inch from the left as a block quotation—*without* quotation marks. The entire block should be double-spaced, and no additional space should be used above or below the block quotation. In this example, the writer introduces a long quotation from an author named Sharon Crowley:

> Sharon Crowley offers contemporary composition a radical inspiration from ancient times:
>
>> I can see no reason why contemporary teachers cannot develop theories of composition that are fully as rich as those developed in ancient times. Much thinking remains to be done, and I do not doubt that enterprising teachers of composition will do it—because there is a place for composition in the university, and that place does not depend on Freshman English. (265)

The page number for the quotation is included in parentheses at the end of the block quotation. Notice that the parenthetical citation is placed *after* the final period of the block quotation. If the author's name does not appear in the main text, include it in the parentheses.

K. Work in more than one volume

If you use more than one volume from a multivolume work in your paper, indicate the volume and page number in each citation. The volume number is followed by a colon. In this example, page 236 in volume 3 of a work by Trieste is cited:

(Trieste 3: 236)

If you cite only one volume, however, you can provide the page number only. In your Works Cited entry, list the volume number.

Creating a Works Cited List in MLA Style

Each source you cite in your text must correspond to an entry in your Works Cited list. Your list of Works Cited should appear at the end of your project, beginning with a new page. Organize the Works Cited list alphabetically according to the authors' last names (or, if the work includes no author, the first main word of the title). In MLA style, follow these rules:

- Capitalize the first word, the last word, and every important word in titles and subtitles. Do not capitalize prepositions (such as *on* and *to*), coordinating conjunctions (such as *and* and *but*), or articles (*a, an, the*) unless they begin the title or subtitle.

- Italicize the titles of long works such as books and periodicals.

- Place the titles of shorter works, such as articles, stories, and poems, in quotation marks.

- Indicate the medium of publication for every entry (e.g. Print, Web, DVD), but do not include the URL for websites or other online sources.

- Double-space citations but do not skip spaces between entries.

- Using hanging indents for entries in the Works Cited list.

FOCUS | **Find the Works Cited Citation Model You Need**

Books (Print and Online)

1. Book with one author (page 763)

2. Book with two or more authors (page 763)

3. Two or more books by the same author (page 764)

4. Anthology with an editor (page 764)

5. Work(s) in an anthology (page 764)

6. Book with an author and an editor (page 764)

7. Book with a translator (page 764)

8. Book by a corporate author or without an author listed (page 765)

(Continued)

Note: The list of in-text citation models appears on page 757.

Books

Here is the general format for an entry for a book in the Works Cited list:

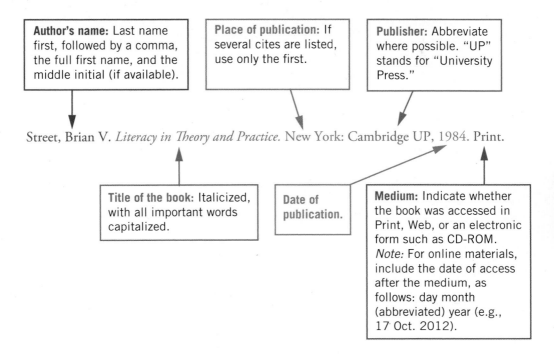

Author's name: Last name first, followed by a comma, the full first name, and the middle initial (if available).

Place of publication: If several cites are listed, use only the first.

Publisher: Abbreviate where possible. "UP" stands for "University Press."

Street, Brian V. *Literacy in Theory and Practice.* New York: Cambridge UP, 1984. Print.

Title of the book: Italicized, with all important words capitalized.

Date of publication.

Medium: Indicate whether the book was accessed in Print, Web, or an electronic form such as CD-ROM. *Note:* For online materials, include the date of access after the medium, as follows: day month (abbreviated) year (e.g., 17 Oct. 2012).

1. Book with one author

> Fineman, Howard. *The Thirteen American Arguments: Enduring Debates That Define and Inspire Our Country.* New York: Random, 2008. Print.

> Lockhart, Charles. *Gaining Ground: Tailoring Social Programs to American Values.* Berkeley: U of California P, 1989. Web. 20 Aug. 2012.

In the second example, the date of access is included at the end of the citation because the work was accessed online.

2. Book with two or more authors

> Stewart, David W., Prem N. Shamdasani, and Dennis W. Rook. *Focus Groups: Theory and Practice.* Thousand Oaks: Sage, 2007. Print.

If there are two or three authors, list all the authors' names. Notice that only the first author is listed with the last name first.

For books with four or more authors, use the abbreviation *et al.*:

> Wysocki, Anne Frances et al. *Writing New Media: Theory and Applications for Expanding the Teaching of Composition.* Logan: Utah State UP, 2004. Print.

3. Two or more books by the same author

When you are listing two or more books by the same author, you do not repeat the author's name for each entry. Instead, use three hyphens and a period in place of the author's name for the second, third, and subsequent entries by the same author. Also, list the entries in alphabetical order by the book title.

> Freire, Paulo. *Letters to Cristina: Reflections on My Life and Work*. New York: Routledge, 1996. Print.
>
> ---. *Pedagogy of Hope: Reliving Pedagogy of the Oppressed*. New York: Continuum, 2004. Print.
>
> ---. *Pedagogy of the Oppressed*. Trans. Myra Bergman Ramos. New York: Continuum, 1970. Print.

4. Anthology with an editor

> McComiskey, Bruce, ed. *English Studies: An Introduction to the Discipline(s)*. Urbana: NCTE, 2006. Print.
>
> Hill, Charles A., and Marguerite Helmers, eds. *Defining Visual Rhetorics*. Mahwah: Erlbaum, 2004. Print.

Use the abbreviation *ed.* for a single editor and *eds.* for multiple editors. Place the abbreviation after the editor's name, which is followed by a comma.

5. Work(s) in an anthology

> Dittrich, Luke. "The Brain That Changed Everything." *The Best American Science and Nature Writing*. Ed. Mary Roach. Boston: Houghton, 2011. 46–68. Print.

Notice that the page numbers for the article are provided. Also, the abbreviation *Ed.* appears *before* the editor's name (Mary Roach).

If you cite two or more articles (or other short works) from the same anthology, use a shortened form of the citation for each one, and then cite the entire anthology according to example 4 above:

> Bhattacharjee. "The Organ Dealer." Roach 1–14.
>
> Dittrich, Luke. "The Brain That Changed Everything." Roach 46–68.

6. Book with an author and an editor

> Thoreau, Henry David. *Walden*. Ed. Jeffrey S. Cramer. New Haven: Yale UP, 2004. Print.

The author's name is placed first. The editor's name is placed after the title, preceded by the abbreviation *Ed.*

7. Book with a translator

> Tsunetomo, Yamamoto. *Hagakure: The Book of the Samurai*. Trans. William Scott Wilson. Tokyo: Kadansha Intl., 1979. Print.

The abbreviation *Trans.* appears before the translator's name (William Scott Wilson).

8. Book by a corporate author or without an author listed

> ACT. *The Condition of College and Career Readiness 2011*. Iowa City: ACT, 2011. Web. 17 Sept. 2012.

If no author or organization is listed, omit the author and begin the entry with the title of the book.

9. Introduction, preface, foreword, or afterword written by someone other than the author of the work

> Zelazny, Roger. Introduction. *Do Androids Dream of Electric Sheep?* By Philip K. Dick. New York: Del Ray, 1968. vii–x. Print.

In this example, Roger Zelazny wrote the introduction to the book *Do Androids Dream of Electric Sheep?* by Philip K. Dick. Include the page numbers of the introduction after the date of publication.

10. Subsequent editions of a book

> Creswell, John W., ed. *Qualitative Research and Design: Choosing Among Five Approaches*. 2nd ed. Thousand Oaks: Sage, 2007. Print.

Use the abbreviation *ed.* for "edition."

11. Work in more than one volume

> Milton, John. *The Prose Works of John Milton*. 2 vols. Philadelphia: Moore, 1847. Print.

12. Book in a series

> Pedersen, Isabel. *Ready to Wear: A Rhetoric of Wearable Computers and Reality-Shifting Media*. Anderson: Parlor, 2013. Print. New Media Theory.

The series name ("New Media Theory") is placed after the medium of publication (which is "Print" in this example).

13. Encyclopedia article

The format for entries for encyclopedia articles is similar to articles in anthologies or edited collections.

> Sockett, Hugh. "The Moral and Epistemic Purposes of Teacher Education." *Handbook of Research on Teacher Education*. 3rd ed. Eds. Marilyn Cochran-Smith, Sharon Feiman-Nemser, and D. John McIntyre. New York: Routledge, 2008. 45–66. Print.

This example shows an article written by Hugh Sockett that appeared in the third edition of an encyclopedia called the *Handbook of Research on Teacher Education* edited by Marilyn Cochran-Smith, Sharon Feiman-Nemser, and D. John McIntyre. If no author is listed, begin with the title of the article. The rest of the citation is the same.

If you accessed the encyclopedia article through an online database, include the name of the database (in italics, placed after the date of publication) followed by the medium and date of access:

> Lacey, Alan. "The Meaning of Life." *The Oxford Companion to Philosophy.* Ed.
> Ted Honderich. New York: Oxford UP, 1995. *Oxford Reference Online.* Web.
> 19 Aug. 2012.

14. Sacred text

> *The King James Version Bible.* New York: American Bible Society. 1980. Print.

Begin the entry with the name of the version you are using. Include names of editors or translators after the title.

FOCUS   **Citing Wikipedia and Other Online References**

Many instructors have policies regarding the use of *Wikipedia* and similar online references, so check with your instructor before using such resources in your research. In MLA style, if you cite information taken from such sources, the format is similar to the format for citing a web page (see example 21):

> "Ultramarathon." *Wikipedia, The Free Encyclopedia.* Wikimedia Foundation, Inc.
> 16 Aug. 2012. Web. 21 Aug. 2012.

In this example, because there is no author, the entry begins with the title of the article, followed by the name of the website in italics (*Wikipedia, The Free Encyclopedia*), the sponsoring organization (Wikimedia Foundation, Inc.), the publication date, the medium, and the access date, all separated by periods.

Periodicals

Here is the general format for an article from a scholarly journal:

Author's name: Last name first, followed by a comma and the full first name and middle initial (if available).

Title of article: Place title in quotation marks and capitalize all important words.

Title of periodical: Italicize and capitalize the title of the journal, magazine, or newspaper.

Buck, Amber. "Examining Digital Literacy Practices on Social Network Sites." *Research in the Teaching of English* 47.1 (2012): 9–38. Print.

Volume and number of the issue: Include the volume of the publication followed by a period and then the number of the issue. This example shows issue #1 of volume 47. Note that there is no space between the volume and issue numbers; also, no other punctuation marks appear before or after the volume and issue number.

Date of publication: Year of publication is placed in parentheses followed by a colon.

Pages: The page numbers on which the article appears followed by a period. If the article does not appear on continuous pages, separate the pages with a comma.

Medium: Indicate whether the journal was accessed in Print, on the Web, or in a database. ***Note:*** If the work is accessed online, the title of the database (in italics) is placed *before* the medium; also include the date of access *after* the medium, as follows: day month (abbreviated) year (e.g., 17 Oct. 2012).

This example shows a scholarly journal. **For magazines and newspapers:**

- omit the volume and issue number
- eliminate the parentheses from the date of publication

15. Article from a scholarly journal

Mayers, Tim. "One Simple Word: From Creative Writing to Creative Writing Studies." *College English* 71.3 (2009): 217–228. Print.

If you accessed this article via the journal's website, the citation would appear like this:

Mayers, Tim. "One Simple Word: From Creative Writing to Creative Writing Studies." *College English* 71.3 (2009): 217–228. Web. 14 Jan. 2013.

Note that the date you accessed the article is placed *after* the medium.

If you accessed this article online via a database such as *JSTOR, LexisNexis, InfoTrac,* or *Academic Search Complete*, the citation would appear as follows:

> Mayers, Tim. "One Simple Word: From Creative Writing to Creative Writing Studies." *College English* 71.3 (2009): 217–228. *JSTOR*. Web. 14 Jan. 2013.

Note that the title of the database (*JSTOR* in this example) is placed in italics and appears *after* the page numbers but *before* the medium. The date of access appears last.

Be sure to place periods after the page numbers, the title of the database, and the medium.

16. Article from a weekly or monthly magazine

> Gover, Robert. "One Novel's Sojourn Through Culture Wars and Privacy." *The Writer's Chronicle* Sept. 2011: 50–57. Print.

If you accessed the article online through a database such as *Academic Search Complete*, include the italicized title of the database followed by the medium and date of access (all separated by periods):

> Gover, Robert. "One Novel's Sojourn Through Culture Wars and Privacy." *The Writer's Chronicle* Sept. 2011: 50–57. *Academic Search Complete*. Web. 8 Oct. 2012.

If you found the article through the magazine website, cite it as follows:

> Gover, Robert. "One Novel's Sojourn Through Culture Wars and Privacy." *The Writer's Chronicle* Sept. 2011: n. pag. Web. 12 Feb. 2012.

Note that the abbreviation *n. pag.* (for "no page numbers") replaces the page numbers. Also include the date you accessed the article (12 Feb. 2012, in this example).

17. Article from a daily newspaper

> Kepner, Tyler. "Grand Home of a Larger-Than-Life Team." *The New York Times* 21 Sept. 2008, natl ed.: N1. Print.

Note that the page number includes the section in which the article appeared—in this example, section N, page 1. Also, if available, include the edition (in this example, *natl. ed.* for "national edition") before the colon. (If there is no edition, place a colon after the year instead of a comma.)

If the article is accessed online through a database, include the italicized title of the database, followed by the medium and date of access—just as you would cite a magazine article:

> Kepner, Tyler. "Grand Home of a Larger-Than-Life Team." *The New York Times* 21 Sept. 2008, natl ed.: N1. *LexisNexis Academic*. Web. 3 June 2011.

If you accessed the article through the newspaper's website, cite it as follows:

> Kepner, Tyler. "Grand Home of a Larger-Than-Life Team." *The New York Times* 21 Sept. 2008, natl ed.: N1. Web. 3 June 2011.

If there is no page number, follow the date (and edition, if there is one) with a period instead of a colon.

18. Editorial

> Kayyem, Juliette. "A Rainy Day Fund Doesn't Work If It's Always Raining." Editorial. *Boston Globe* 23 May 2013. Web. 25 May 2013.

The term *Editorial* appears after the title of the article, followed by a period. In this example, there is no edition or page number.

19. Letter to the editor

> Goldberg, Anita. Letter. *New York Times* 22 May 2013. Web. 25 May 2013.

20. Review

> Uglow, Jenny. "The Saga of the Flaming Zucchini." Rev. of *Consider the Fork: A History of How We Cook and Eat,* by Bee Wilson. *New York Review of Books* 6 June 2013. Web. 24 June 2013.

Notice that the name of the author of the review is placed first. The name of the author of the work being reviewed follows the title of the work being reviewed, preceded by the word *by* (in this example, "by Bee Wilson").

If the review does not include a title, omit that part of the citation. For publication information, use the format for the kind of source you used.

For film reviews, include the name of the director of the film, placed after the title of the film and preceded by the abbreviation *dir.*:

> Sharkey, Betsy. "*Before Midnight* Finds Its Couple in a Dark Place." Rev. of *Before Midnight,* dir. Richard Linklater. *Los Angeles Times* 24 May 2013. Web. 17 June 2013.

Other Sources

21. Website

When citing an entire website, include the author, editor, or compiler of the site (if available), followed by the title of the site in italics, the name of the organization sponsoring the site, the publication date, the medium, and the date of access:

> *Swing Dance America.* Swing Dance America. N.d. Web. 15 May 2013.

In this example, there is no author, so the entry begins with the title of the website (*Swing Dance America*). Because there is no date on the website, the abbreviation *N.d.* is used.

22. Web page

For a web page, include the name of the author (if available), the title of the page in quotation marks followed by the italicized title of the website, the name of the sponsoring organization (if available), the date of publication, the medium, and the date of access:

> Pollan, Michael. "Sustainable Eating and Nutrition: FAQs and Useful Links." *Michael Pollan.* N.p. 2010. Web. 23 July 2012.

The title of the web page is placed in quotation marks. If there is no sponsoring organization, use the abbreviation *N.p.* (for "no publisher"). If you can't find a date of publication, use the abbreviation *n.d.* (for "no date").

The citation for a web page by a corporate author (such as an organization or business) is similar in format:

> People for the Ethical Treatment of Animals. "Turned Away: A Closer Look at 'No-Kill.'" *PETA.* People for the Ethical Treatment of Animals, n.d. Web. 15 May 2013.

Notice that the name of the agency or organization appears in place of an author's name.

For a web page without an author, the citation appears like this:

> "How to Anchor Securely." *West Marine West Advisor.* West Marine. N.d. Web. 23 July 2012.

In this example, the title of the web page ("How to Anchor Securely") appears first, followed by the italicized title of the website (*West Marine West Advisor*) and the name of the sponsoring organization (West Marine).

23. Blog

> Schoenkopf, Rebecca. "Breitbart's Ghost: Obama Exploited Catholics by Being Endorsed by Them." *Wonkette.* Wonkette Media, LLC. 6 Apr. 2012. Web. 9 Apr. 2012.

Note that the title of the blog (*Wonkette*) is italicized and appears *after* the title of the blog entry ("Breitbart's Ghost: Obama Exploited Catholics by Being Endorsed by Them"). Follow the title of the blog with the sponsor (Wonkette Media, LLC), the date of the blog entry, the medium, and finally the date of access—all separated by periods.

24. Podcast

> Gross, Terry. "Do Voter ID Laws Prevent Fraud, or Dampen Turnout?" *Fresh Air.* Natl. Public Radio. 15 Aug. 2012. Web. 25 Aug. 2012.

Begin with the performer's or author's name, followed by the title of the podcast, the italicized name of the program on which the podcast was broadcast, the sponsor of the program, and the date of the original broadcast. Also include the medium of publication (Web) and the date you accessed the podcast.

25. Interview

For an interview that you conduct, indicate whether the interview was conducted via email, by telephone, or in person.

> Gallehr, Don. Telephone interview. 19 Apr. 2010.

For a published or broadcast interview, include the title, if available. Add the name of the interviewer if pertinent to your use. Be sure to include the medium (as well as the date of access if you accessed the interview online).

> Pollan, Michael. "A Coffee Date with Michael Pollan." Interview by Keane Amdahl. *City Pages.* City Pages, 7 May 2013. Web. 15 May 2013.

26. CD-ROM

For a nonperiodical published on CD-ROM, start with information from the most relevant example from 1 to 8 (pages 763–769). Add the edition or release number, if there is one, and the medium. If the publication information for a printed source is provided, start with that information.

> *Flower Designs and Motifs*. New York: Dover Publications, 2005. CD-ROM.

> Reid, T. R. "The New Europe." *National Geographic* Jan. 2002: 32+. *The Complete National Geographic*. Washington: The National Geographic Society, 2010. CD-ROM. Disk 6.

For material from a periodically published database and for periodicals such as journals, magazines, and newspapers that are published in both print and on CD-ROM, provide the print information first, then the medium of publication, the title of the database, the name of the vendor, and the publication date of the database. (See the third item in example 15.)

27. Film, video, DVD

> *The Great Gatsby*. Dir. Baz Luhrmann. Perf. Leonardo DiCaprio, Joel Edgerton, Tobey Maguire, and Carey Mulligan. Warner, 2013. Film.

Begin with the name of the director or performer if you are citing that person's contribution. For videos, DVDs, and filmstrips, use the same format. Place the medium at the end of the citation, followed by a period.

28. Television or radio program

> "Second Sons." Dir. Michelle MacLaren. *Game of Thrones*. HBO. 19 May 2013. Television.

Begin with the title of the episode. If you include additional information about the episode, place it after the episode title; however, if the added information pertains to the series, place it after the series title. Insert the call letters and city of the local station and broadcast date (if any) after the name of the network. Place the medium at the end of the citation, followed by a period.

29. Sound recording

> Rollins, Sonny. *Saxophone Colossus*. Prestige, 1987. CD.

Begin with the name of the artists, followed by the title of the recording, manufacturer, and year of issue. Indicate the medium (CD, Mp3, LP, Audiocassette) after the date, followed by a period.
To cite a specific song, include the song title, in quotation marks, after the name of the artist.

> Rollins, Sonny. "You Don't Know What Love Is." *Saxophone Colossus*. Prestige, 1987. CD.

30. Advertisement

> Nike. Advertisement. *Adweek*. 27 Mar. 2013. Web. 28 May 2013.

31. Art

> Cave, Nick. *Soundsuit*. 2011. Found objects, knit head and bodysuit, and mannequin. Museum of Mod. Art, New York.

Cite the artist first and then the title of the work. Describe the medium, and then indicate where the art is housed. If you found the art in a print source, follow the appropriate format for publication details.

32. Government publication

> United States. Dept. of Transportation. *Bridge Management*. Washington: GPO, 2012.
> Print.

For government documents, the name of the nation or state appears first, followed by the agency (Department of Transportation, in this example) and the title of the publication (*Bridge Management*). Also include the place of publication (Washington), the publisher (Government Printing Office, abbreviated as GPO by MLA), date of publication (2012), and medium (Print).

If you accessed the publication online, indicate the medium and date of access:

> United States. Dept. of Transportation. *Bridge Management*. Washington: GPO, 2012.
> Web. 25 April 2012.

Sample MLA-Style Research Paper

The following essay by Matt Searle, written for the "Evolution of Expression" class he took as a freshman at Emerson College, follows MLA guidelines for formatting a research paper. Matt's essay is a causal analysis (see Chapter 6) that explores the potential impact of digital technologies on literacy and cognition. Matt addresses the question, What effects are the rapidly growing uses of digital technologies having on how we read and think? As you read, notice how Matt examines this question from various angles, taking into account what different experts think and what research has shown. Notice, too, how Matt carefully documents his sources using MLA style.

For research papers, MLA recommends placing your name, the title of your paper, and other relevant information (such as the date, the course number, and the instructor's name) on the first page, as Matt has done, rather than on a separate title page. If you are required to use a title page, center this information on the page.

When formatting a paper in MLA style, remember to

- use one-inch margins
- double-space the text throughout the document (including the title and Works Cited list)
- double-space between the heading and the title and between the title and the main text on the first page
- indent paragraphs one-half inch
- number all pages, including the first page, in the upper-right-hand corner
- place your last name before the page number on each page (if you are using a program such as Microsoft Word, you can use the header function to create a running head that includes your name and the page number on each page)
- include the Works Cited list on a separate page at the end of the document

Matt Searle

Dr. John Dennis Anderson

Evolution of Expression

20 October 2011

Anxieties Over Electracy

Over the course of the past decade, technology has shaped the way society accesses and absorbs information. In *Internet Invention: From Literacy to Electracy*, Gregory L. Ulmer argues that our culture is transitioning from traditional literacy to a type of "electracy" afforded by the digital age. However, this transition has been met with resistance by those who fear the changes it will bring. Concerns involving the superficiality of Internet reading, loss of memory, and depletion of traditional literary skills have been brought to the forefront of the debate between literacy and electracy. As the Internet continues to rewire our brains and becomes a ubiquitous presence in our world, we must take the time to fully understand its impact.

One of the primary criticisms of electracy, defined by Ulmer as being to digital media what literacy is to print, is that it causes superficial understanding (Ulmer, *Internet* xii). Just as Johann Gutenberg's invention of the printing press increased freedom of thought and public expression, the advent of the Internet has increased the availability of information. Those who welcome this influx of data subscribe to a philosophy that Adam Gopnik has coined "Never Better-ism," a belief in the Internet's potential to create a new utopia (Gopnik). However, there are others who are as skeptical as the "Never-Betters" are optimistic. In a well-known article titled "Is Google Making Us Stupid?," writer Nicholas Carr expresses the belief that digital literacy leads to a depletion of textual analysis and cognition. Citing his own inability to read lengthy articles without skimming and an increasing lack of patience with text, Carr claims that the Internet leads to ADD-like behavior. He contends that we are no longer "scuba divers" of information—that is, we no longer critically assess what we read (Carr 57). Furthermore, Internet users often feel the need to hop around to various sites rather than focus on one in particular. Though some believe this habit of "power browsing" stimulates creativity, Internet critics such as Carr worry that our culture will be permanently unable to perform in-depth analysis (59). With newspapers such as *The New York Times* attracting readers by adding abstracts for every three pages and online journalists peppering their articles with hyperlinks, the medium is gradually adjusting to our changing behavior (61).

While the criticisms lodged by Carr and others towards electracy may seem extreme, some research suggests that the Internet is shaping the way we think. Human brains are extremely malleable as neurons often break old connections and form new ones. Just as reading Chinese text from right to left is not a natural talent, electrate reading is very much a learned skill. Rather than following the typical linear progression of alphabetic literacy, numerous hyperlinks and a virtual cornucopia of information encourage a "zigzag" approach to reading (Rich A27). Thus, the question is not whether the Internet is affecting the way we think, but whether it is modifying the brain in a positive fashion. It is possible that our neurological transition to electrate thinking is a natural progression in our mental development, but anxiety still exists over electracy's permanent effects. For example, studies have shown that the Internet can have a serious impact on memory (Johnson).

Because websites such as Google easily provide the answers to our questions, some consider it no longer necessary to attempt to memorize information. In this way, we as a culture tend to "outsource" our memories to electronics rather than use our brains for retention (Johnson A7). In one study, three thousand people were asked to remember the birthdate of a relative; only forty percent of people under thirty years old were able to answer correctly as compared to eighty-seven percent of people over the age of fifty (Thompson). Even more staggering was the fact that fully a third of youths were able to recite their phone number only after checking the phone itself (Thompson).

This loss of recall seems to be directly linked to electracy, as further studies have shown that people are more likely to remember information that they believe will be deleted. According to neuroscientist Gary Small, "We're . . . [u]sing the World Wide Web as an external hard drive to augment our biological memory stores" (Johnson A7). However, as with any neurobiological development, there are some psychological benefits. With less of our brain used for memory storage, we can free up our grey matter to be used for brainstorming and daydreaming. Some experts promote the idea that intelligence is not truly about knowing information, but instead knowing where to find it. University of Pittsburgh psychology professor Richard Moreland has labeled the perceived need to retain all information "maladaptive" (Johnson A7). Thus, skeptics of electracy must consider both the positive and negative aspects of the transition.

The question of whether electracy will supersede traditional literacy has also become an issue in recent years. Children between the ages of eight and eighteen have increased their Internet usage from an average of forty-six minutes per day in 1984 to an hour and forty-one minutes per day in the present (Rich A16). At the same time, only one-fifth of seventeen-year-olds read for fun every day, a statistic that some critics argue seems to correlate with a drastic drop on critical reading test scores (Rich A16). Proponents of Internet reading claim that it is simply a new type of literacy that allows its users to create their own beginnings, middles, and ends. Reading online can also allow those who have learning disabilities such as dyslexia to read in a more comfortable environment and format (Rich A17).

Another argument against electrate skepticism is that the Internet encourages reading amongst those who would not normally read otherwise. For example, giving Internet access to low-income families who may struggle to buy books has been shown to increase overall reading time (Rich A16). With ninety percent of employers listing reading comprehension as very important (Rich A16), it is essential that future generations be able to comprehend the information they take in. This means that while electracy may have a place in our culture, where it belongs is still unclear. Groups such as the Organization for Economic Cooperation and Development plan to add electronic reading sections to aptitude tests, but these actions have been scoffed at by many (Rich A17). The experts that fear our transition from literacy to electracy are aware that only the reading of traditional literate texts has been proven to cause higher comprehension and performance levels (Rich A16). Therefore, electracy opponents do not necessarily want to dissolve the medium, but simply do not want it to replace what is currently known as reading.

Ulmer does not see the Internet as destroying our literate abilities, but rather building on them in what he calls a "society of the spectacle" (*Internet* xiii). In Ulmer's vision, imagination and visualization can be used in combination with critical thinking in order to solve problems: "What literacy is to the analytical mind, electracy is to the affective body: a prosthesis that enhances and augments a natural or organic human potential" ("Gregory Ulmer"). For Ulmer, electracy is an apparatus that is to be used for future generations, which is why he labels *Internet Invention* as a new generation textbook (*Internet* xiii). Ulmer's convictions are reflected by others who support the movement towards electracy. These thinkers point out that when literacy first began, it also caused cynicism, but it ultimately became the widely accepted norm. Indeed, it seems that the advent of new technologies has always made people uneasy and stirred fears that the capacities of the human brain may either be replaced or diminished. However, as Ulmer sees the situation, technological progression is both a natural and welcome development. We may no longer be able to think in a purely literate and literal sense, but as Michigan State University professor Rand J. Spiro puts it, "[T]he world doesn't go in a line" (Rich A16). If we as a culture can harness the potential of the Internet, perhaps Ulmer's vision can come to fruition.

The world is constantly evolving as new technologies and philosophies begin to dominate the cultural landscape. With the Internet a ubiquitous presence in the lives of almost all human beings, becoming fluent in what Greg Ulmer has dubbed electracy is integral. Fears that the Internet causes superficiality, rewires our brains, and decreases literacy have been corroborated by studies, but that does not mean that the Internet is without benefits. By understanding its effects and using electracy to build off our literate knowledge, we can determine where this skill fits within our society.

Works Cited

Carr, Nicholas. "Is Google Making Us Stupid?" *Atlantic Monthly* Jul./Aug. 2008: 56–63. Print.

Gopnik, Adam. "The Information: How the Internet Gets Inside Us." *The New Yorker* 14 Feb. 2011. Web. 16 Oct. 2011.

Johnson, Carolyn Y. "Memory Slips Caught in the Net." *Boston Globe* 15 July 2011: A1+. Print.

Rich, Motoko. "Literacy Debate: Online, R U Really Reading?" *New York Times* 27 July 2008, late ed.: A1+. Print.

Thompson, Clive. "Your Outboard Brain Knows It All." *Wired.com*. Conde Nast, 25 Sept. 2007. Web. 16 Oct. 2011.

Ulmer, Gregory L. "Gregory Ulmer–Quotes." European Graduate School Faculty. 2011. Web. 16 Oct. 2011.

---. *Internet Invention: From Literacy to Electracy*. New York: Longman, 2002. Print.

THE PURPOSE of citing sources is to be as clear as possible in showing where your information comes from. Citing your sources according to established style guides not only enables you to give credit to the source for the material you are using but also provides your readers with sufficient bibliographic information to judge or even find your sources for themselves. In general, you must document the source of the following:

- direct quotations
- ideas or opinions that are not your own
- visual materials, such as photographs, maps, or graphs, that you did not create
- multimedia content, such as videos or audios, that you did not create
- information (a fact or statistic) that is not general knowledge

In most academic writing today, writers use the American Psychological Association (APA) style guide when they are writing in the social sciences: psychology, sociology, education, economics, anthropology, geography, and political science. This chapter explains how to cite sources using APA style. (MLA style, which tends to be used in the humanities—literature, languages, performing and visual arts, history, classics, philosophy, and religion—is explained in Chapter 24.) The guidelines in this chapter are based on the *Publication Manual of the American Psychological Association*, 6th edition (2009).

Two Main Components in APA Style

APA style uses in-text parenthetical citations to document sources. There are **two main components to in-text parenthetical citation systems:**

1. **In-text citations.** Parenthetical citations, which appear in the body of your writing, indicate to a reader that information you are presenting is taken from another source.

2. **A References list.** The References list, sometimes referred to as a bibliography, is a separate section at the end of your document that includes bibliographic information for every source you cited in your document.

Let's imagine you are writing an essay about the cultural significance of heavy metal music and you want to refer to a specific analysis of so-called death metal music in a book titled *Death Metal*

Music: The Passion and Politics of a Subculture, by Natalie J. Purcell. On page 188 of that book, Purcell makes a point about the philosophical function of death metal music that you want to include in your essay. If you were using APA style, you would cite the source as follows:

> Death metal music performs a genuine philosophical function by examining the dark side of human nature (Purcell, 2003, p. 188).

or

> Critic Natalie Purcell (2003) considers death metal a "philosophical response, whether conscious or subconscious, to terrifying questions about nebulous human nature" (p. 188).

The entry in the References list would look like this:

> Purcell, N. J. (2003). *Death metal music: The passion and politics of a subculture.* Jefferson, NC: McFarland.

Each in-text citation in your paper must have a corresponding entry on the References page, which enables your readers to consult the original source themselves.

FOCUS Content Notes

The American Psychological Association recommends that writers use parenthetical, or in-text, citations of the kind described in this chapter when documenting sources (rather than traditional footnotes or endnotes). Writers can also use **content notes** for additional explanation or discussion of a point in the main text. APA discourages the use of such notes unless they are essential to the discussion. If you do use content notes, APA format requires them to be placed on a separate page titled "Footnotes" that appears at the end of the document. Indicate the presence of a content note in your main text by using a superscript number. For example, if you wanted to include a content note related to the following sentence in your main text, place the superscript number at the end of the sentence:

> Some research suggests a correlation between literacy and higher-order cognitive skills.[1]

The corresponding footnote would appear at the end of your main document on the Footnotes page:

---

[1] The correlation between literacy and cognition has been seriously questioned by many scholars, notably Sylvia Scribner and Michael Cole in their well-known study *The Psychology of Literacy*.

Creating In-Text Citations Using APA Style

APA style for citing sources reflects the conventions of empirical research. Because research tends to build on previously conducted studies and the relative currency of research is important, APA emphasizes the author's last name and year of publication in in-text citations. APA style also requires that in-text citations include page number(s) for material quoted directly from a source. However, direct quotation in APA style is not as common as paraphrase and summary.

FOCUS **Find the In-Text Citation Model You Need**

A. Work by one author (page 783)

B. Work by multiple authors (page 784)

C. Work by a corporate author (page 785)

D. More than one work by the same author (page 785)

E. Two or more works cited within one set of parentheses (page 785)

F. Authors with the same last name (page 785)

G. Work without an author listed (page 785)

H. Online source (page 786)

I. Quotation within a cited work (page 786)

J. Long quotations (page 786)

K. Work in more than one volume (page 787)

L. Personal communications (page 787)

Note: The list of References models appears on page 788.

25

A. Work by one author

If you were citing information taken from a book called *The Printing Revolution in Early Modern Europe* by Elizabeth L. Eisenstein, published in 1983, the parenthetical citation would look like this:

> The widespread adoption of the printing press in the 16th century helped standardize the major European languages (Eisenstein, 1983).

Note that there is a comma between the author's name and the year of publication. As always in APA style, you could use Eisenstein's name in your sentence and include only the year of publication in the parentheses immediately following the name:

> Eisenstein (1983) examines how the widespread adoption of the printing press in the 16th century helped standardize the major European languages.

B. Work by multiple authors

APA has several rules for citing works by multiple authors.

- **Work by two authors.** When citing a work by two authors, use both authors' names in the citation or in your sentence. If authors are named in parentheses, use an ampersand (&) to join them; however, if you name the authors in your sentence, use the word *and*. For example, if you wanted to quote from page 2 of the introduction to *Undead TV: Essays on Buffy the Vampire Slayer*, by Elana Levine and Lisa Parks, published in 2007, you could do so as follows:

  > We might consider how the hit television series *Buffy the Vampire Slayer* "uses its metaphorical representations of life and death, good and evil, comedy and tragedy to speak about the power struggles inherent in many people's everyday lives in the Western world" (Levine & Parks, 2007, p. 2).

  Note that a comma is placed after the second author's name and another comma is placed after the year of publication.

  If you use the authors' names in your sentence, cite the quotation like this:

  > Levine and Parks (2007) assert that *Buffy the Vampire Slayer* "uses its metaphorical representations of life and death, good and evil, comedy and tragedy to speak about the power struggles inherent in many people's everyday lives in the Western world" (p. 2).

  Place the date in parentheses immediately after the authors' names. The page reference should be placed in parentheses at the end of the sentence.

- **Work by three to five authors.** If you are referring to a work by three, four, or five authors, list all the authors' names the first time you cite the work. For example, if you were citing a journal article titled "Empirical Foundations for Writing in Prevention and Psychotherapy," by Brian A. Esterling, Luciano L'Abate, Edward J. Murray, and James W. Pennebaker, the parenthetical citation would look like this:

  > Studies have shown that writing has therapeutic benefits for some patients (Esterling, L'Abate, Murray, & Pennebaker, 1999).

  If you cite the same work again, list only the first author's name followed by the Latin phrase *et al.* (which means "and others"):

  > The therapeutic benefits of writing include lower blood pressure and higher self-esteem (Esterling et al., 1999).

  Note that there is no comma after the name of the author, but a comma is placed before the date of publication. Also note that there is no period after *et*, but there is a period after *al*.

- **Work by six or more authors.** When citing a work by six or more authors, use the first author's last name followed by the phrase *et al.* For example, if you cited a 2008 book co-written by Mark Smith and eight additional authors, the citation would appear as follows:

  > Researchers have found that many mammals mate for life (Smith et al., 2008).

If you included the name of the author in your sentence, the citation would look like this:

> Smith et al. (2008) found that many mammals mate for life.

C. Work by a corporate author

A "corporate author" is an organization, committee, association, or agency (rather than an individual or group of individually named authors). When citing a corporate author, use the same format as for a single author. For example, if you were citing a 2012 study by the Center for Research on Educational Outcomes, you would do so as follows:

> According to the Center for Research on Educational Outcomes (2012), 37 percent of charter schools had math scores that were lower than their public school peers.

You could also include the corporate author in the parentheses; omit any initial article:

> In one recent study, 37 percent of charter schools had math scores that were lower than their public school peers (Center for Research on Educational Outcomes, 2012).

D. More than one work by the same author

If you cite more than one work by the same author, you need to distinguish among the works by including the publication date of each work you cite. For example, if you were citing two different books by Paulo Freire—*Pedagogy of Hope*, published in 1994, and *Letters to Cristina*, published in 1996—your parenthetical citations might look like this:

> Some reformers emphasize the crucial role of hope in the struggle for change. They argue that hope is part of the process of improving human existence (Freire, 1994), but they also acknowledge that hope "seldom exists apart from the reverses of fate" (Freire, 1996, p. 14).

The dates enable a reader to find the specific works in the References list.

E. Two or more works cited within one set of parentheses

List the works alphabetically, separated by a semicolon, as they appear in your References list:

> (Harden, 2012; Raine, 2013)

F. Authors with the same last name

Include the author's first and middle initials (if given) in all in-text citations to avoid confusion.

> B. Brown (2013) and S. T. Brown (2011) found that weather patterns have changed significantly in the past decade.

G. Work without an author listed

If you cite a work without an author listed, include a brief version of the title, either in parentheses or in the signal phrase. Here the title "Carrying the Torch" is shortened to "Carrying":

> The sports management industry in Great Britain received a significant boost in business as a result of the 2012 Olympic Games in London ("Carrying," 2012).

In in-text parenthetical citations, titles of articles and web pages are placed in quotation marks; titles of books are italicized or underlined.

H. Online source

When citing online sources in in-text parenthetical citations, follow the same principles you would use when citing print sources. However, there are many different kinds of electronic sources, and they might not include the same kinds of information that are available for a print book or journal article. For example, websites don't usually have page numbers. In such cases, provide the number of the paragraph in which you found the information or quotation you are citing, using the abbreviation *para.*:

> (Martinez, 2000, para. 8)

If page numbers are not available or paragraph numbers are not feasible, include sufficient information for readers to find the source you are citing, such as the subheading or name of the section in which the source material appears:

> (Madoff, Bradley, & Rico, Results section).

If the heading is too lengthy to cite, then use a shortened title. For the long heading "Genetic Variations Link Found in Bipolar Twins Separately Adopted," you could use the first several words:

> (Bico & Marley, 2013, "Genetic Variations Link Found," para. 3).

According to APA style, if you do not have reliable page numbers or paragraph numbers, leave them out of the parenthetical citation:

> (Martinez, 2000)

I. Quotation within a cited work

When using a quotation from one source that you have found in another source, you have to show that the quotation was acquired "secondhand" and was not taken directly from the original source. In such cases, indicate the original source in your text and the secondary source in parentheses. For example, let's say you were reading a book called *Literary Theory* by Terry Eagleton that included a quotation by Sigmund Freud that you wanted to use in your essay. You would cite the Freud quotation as follows:

> Even Freud acknowledged the central important of economics in human relations, famously stating, "The motive of human society is in the last resort an economic one" (as cited in Eagleton, 1983, p. 151).

Note the phrase *as cited in* in the parenthetical citation. In this instance, you are signaling to readers that you read Freud's statement on page 151 of the book by Terry Eagleton.

J. Long quotations

In APA style, a long quotation is defined as one than contains more than 40 words. These quotations should be indented one inch from the left margin as a block quotation—*without* quotation marks.

> LeVine et al. (1994) describe the child care practices of the Gusii people of Kenya in regard to cultural assumptions:
>> Gusii mothers are devoted to the welfare and development of their infants, and their sense of what is best for them is framed in terms of indigenous cultural models that

assume high infant mortality, high fertility (but with protective birth-spacing), and a domestic age-hierarchy in which young children acquire useful skills and moral virtues through participation in household food production. (p. 2)

The page number for the quotation is included in parentheses at the end of the quotation. Include the abbreviation *p.* for "page." Notice that the parenthetical citation is placed *after* the final period of the block quotation. If the author's name does not appear in the main text, include it in the parentheses.

K. Work in more than one volume

If you use more than one volume from a multivolume work in your paper, indicate the years of publication in each citation.

> (Trieste, 1999–2002)

If you cite only one volume, provide the year of its publication only. In your References entry, you will list the volume number.

L. Personal communication

Personal emails, letters, interviews, conversations, and other private communications are not retrievable by others and so are not listed in the References list. In the in-text citation, provide initials and last name for the correspondent, provide an exact date, and use the label "personal communication":

> (L. L. Fothergill, personal communication, October 5, 2013)

Creating a References List in APA Style

Each source you cite in your text must correspond to an entry in your bibliography, which is called the References list in APA style. Your list of References should appear at the end of your document, beginning with a new page. Organize the References list alphabetically according to the authors' last names (or, if the work includes no author, the first main word of the title). In APA style, follow these rules:

- Capitalize only proper nouns and the first word in the titles and subtitles of books, chapters, and articles.
- Capitalize all important words in the names of journals, newspapers, and magazines.
- Italicize the titles of books and longer works.
- Do *not* italicize names of journals, newspapers, and magazines.
- For both print and electronic sources, provide the DOI if available. (See "What Is DOI?" on page 790) If there is no DOI for an online source, include the URL.
- Double-space entries but do not skip spaces between entries.
- Using hanging indents of one-half inch for entries in the References list.

24. Film, video, DVD (page 797)

25. Television or radio program (page 797)

26. Music recording (page 797)

27. Advertisement (page 797)

Note: The list of in-text citation models appears on page 783.

Books (Print and Online)

Here is the general format for an entry for a book in the References list:

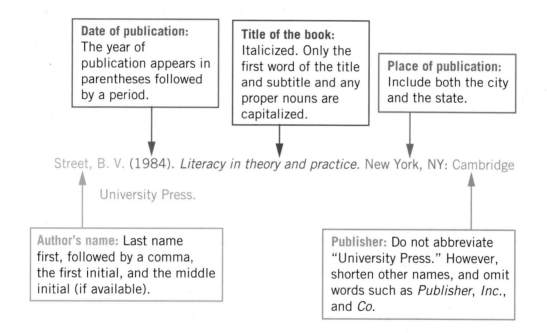

Date of publication: The year of publication appears in parentheses followed by a period.

Title of the book: Italicized. Only the first word of the title and subtitle and any proper nouns are capitalized.

Place of publication: Include both the city and the state.

Street, B. V. (1984). *Literacy in theory and practice.* New York, NY: Cambridge University Press.

Author's name: Last name first, followed by a comma, the first initial, and the middle initial (if available).

Publisher: Do not abbreviate "University Press." However, shorten other names, and omit words such as *Publisher*, *Inc.*, and *Co.*

However, for books that are accessed online, the publisher and place of publication are eliminated and replaced by the URL (web address) where the book was found:

Authors' names: Last name first, followed by a comma, the first initial, and the middle initial (if available). Note that the same form (last name followed by initials) is used for the second and subsequent authors.

Date of publication: The year of publication appears in parentheses followed by a period.

Title of the book: Italicized. The first word of the title and subtitle are capitalized; proper names (*Lord Keynes*, in this example) are also capitalized.

Buchanan, J. M., and Wagner, R. E. (1977). *Democracy in deficit: The political legacy of*

Lord Keynes. Retrieved from

http://www.econlib.org/library/Buchanan/buchCv8.html

Online Location: Indicate that the work was accessed online with the phrase *Retrieved from*. Include the URL (web address) where the book was accessed online. If the publication has a DOI (see "What is DOI?"), replace the URL with the DOI and replace the phrase *Retrieved from* with *doi* in lowercase followed by a colon. Do not place a period after the URL or DOI number.

FOCUS   What Is DOI?

DOI stands for digital object identifier. A DOI is a unique string of numbers that identifies an electronic publication. It is more stable than a URL, which can change or be deleted. APA style requires that, when available, the DOI be included in an entry in the References list. Use the DOI in place of the URL.

Many scholarly journals now include DOIs for online publications. Usually, the DOI appears on the first page of the article, as in the example of an article published in the scholarly journal *School Effectiveness and School Improvement* on page 791; the DOI appears at the very bottom of the page. The entry in the References list would look like this:

Ross, J. A., and Gray, P. (2006). Transformational leadership and teacher commitment to organizational values: The mediating effects of collective teacher efficacy. *School Effectiveness and School Improvement, 17*(2), 179–199. doi: 10.1080/09243450600565795

School Effectiveness and School Improvement
Vol. 17, No. 2, June 2006, pp. 179–199

R **Routledge**
Taylor & Francis Group

Transformational Leadership and Teacher Commitment to Organizational Values: The mediating effects of collective teacher efficacy

John A. Ross* and Peter Gray
Ontario Institute for Studies in Education, University of Toronto, Ontario, Canada

Transformational leadership researchers have given little attention to teacher expectations that mediate between goals and actions. The most important of these expectations, teacher efficacy, refers to teacher beliefs that they will be able to bring about student learning. This study examined the mediating effects of teacher efficacy by comparing two models derived from Bandura's social-cognitive theory. Model A hypothesized that transformational leadership would contribute to teacher commitment to organizational values exclusively through collective teacher efficacy. Model B hypothesized that leadership would have direct effects on teacher commitment and indirect effects through teacher efficacy. Data from 3,074 teachers in 218 elementary schools in a cross-validation sample design provided greater support for Model B than Model A. Transformational leadership had an impact on the collective teacher efficacy of the school; teacher efficacy alone predicted teacher commitment to community partnerships; and transformational leadership had direct and indirect effects on teacher commitment to school mission and commitment to professional learning community.

Introduction

Previous research has demonstrated that transformational leadership contributes to valued teacher outcomes. For example, teachers in schools characterized by transformational principal behavior are more likely than teachers in other schools to express satisfaction with their principal, report that they exert extra effort, and be more committed to the organization and to improving it (Leithwood, Jantzi, & Steinbach, 1999). Few studies of the relationship between principal behavior and teacher outcomes have examined the mechanisms through which leadership impacts

*Corresponding author. OISE/University of Toronto, Trent Valley Centre, Box 719, Peterborough, Ontario, K9J 7A1, Canada. Email: jross@oise.utoronto.ca

ISSN 0924-3453 (print)/ISSN 1744-5124 (online)/06/020179–21
© 2006 Taylor & Francis
DOI: 10.1080/09243450600565795

Routledge Taylor & Francis Group

1. Book with one author

Fineman, H. (2008). *The thirteen American arguments: Enduring debates that define and inspire our country*. New York, NY: Random House.

Cowles, J. T. (1937). *Food-tokens as incentives for learning by chimpanzees*. Baltimore, MD: The Johns Hopkins Press. doi: 10.1037/14268-000

2. Book with two or more authors

Stewart, D. W., Shamdasani, P. N., & Rook, D. W. (2007). *Focus groups: Theory and practice*. Thousand Oaks, CA: Sage.

Buchanan, J. M., & Wagner, R. E. (1977). *Democracy in deficit: The political legacy of Lord Keynes*. Retrieved from http://www.econlib.org/library/Buchanan/buchCv8.html

The second example shows a book accessed online. Eliminate the publisher and place of publication and include the URL where the work was accessed. If a DOI is available, use that instead of the URL (as shown in "What Is DOI?" on page 790).

Notice that an ampersand (&) is used in place of *and* before the name of the last author. If there are more than six authors, follow the sixth name with *et al.* (meaning "and others").

3. Two or more books by the same author

If you cite two books by the same author or by the same set of authors whose names are given in the same order in both books, arrange them by publication date in the References list. List the earlier work first.

Freire, P. (1970). *Pedagogy of the oppressed*. (M. B. Ramos, Trans.). New York, NY: Continuum.

Freire, P. (1996). *Letters to Cristina: Reflections on my life and work*. New York, NY: Routledge.

Freire, P. (2004). *Pedagogy of hope: Reliving* Pedagogy of the oppressed. New York, NY: Continuum.

If the works were both published in the same year, alphabetize the works by title, excluding *A* and *The*.

4. Anthology with an editor

Hill, C. A., & Helmers, M. (Eds.). (2004). *Defining visual rhetorics*. Mahwah, NJ: Erlbaum.

5. Work in an anthology

Olson, C. (1973). Projective verse. In D. M. Allen & W. Tallman (Eds.), *The poetics of the new American poetry* (pp. 147–158). New York, NY: Grove Press.

6. Introduction, preface, foreword, or afterword

Zelazny, R. (1968). Introduction. In P. K. Dick, *Do Androids Dream of Electric Sheep?* (pp. vii–x). New York, NY: Del Ray.

In this example, Roger Zelazny wrote the introduction to the book *Do Androids Dream of Electric Sheep?* by Philip K. Dick. Include the page numbers (in parentheses) of the introduction after the title of the book.

7. Work by a corporate author or without an author listed

> Center for Research on Education Outcomes. (2009). *Multiple choice: Charter school performance in 16 states.* Stanford, CA: Stanford University.

If no author or organization is listed, begin the entry with the title of the book. Place the year after the title.

8. Translated book

> Tsunetomo, Y. (1979). *Hagakure: The book of the samurai.* (W. S. Wilson, Trans.). Tokyo, Japan: Kadansha International.

Place the name of the translator and the abbreviation *Trans.* (for "translator") in parentheses, separated by a comma. Note that the abbreviation is capitalized. Also, the name of the translator appears with the first and middle initials first, followed by the last name.

9. Subsequent editions of a book

> Creswell, J. W. (Ed.). (2007). *Qualitative research and design: Choosing among five approaches* (Rev. ed.). Thousand Oaks, CA: Sage.

10. Work in more than one volume

> Milton, J. (1847). *The prose works of John Milton* (Vols. 1–2). Philadelphia, PA: John W. Moore. Retrieved from http://app.libraryofliberty.org/

11. Encyclopedia article

The format for entries for encyclopedia articles is similar to articles in anthologies.

> Sockett, H. (2008). The moral and epistemic purposes of teacher education. In M. Cochran-Smith, S. Feiman-Nemser, & D. J. McIntyre (Eds.), *Handbook of Research on Teacher Education* (3rd ed., pp. 309–330). New York, NY: Routledge.

If no author is listed, begin with the title of the article. The rest of the citation is the same. (See also "Citing Wikipedia and Other Online References" on page 766.)

12. Government publication

> United States Department of Transportation. (2012). *Bridge management.* Washington, DC: Government Printing Office.

For government documents, the name of the nation or state appears first combined with the agency (Department of Transportation, in this example). If you accessed the publication online, indicate the URL:

> U. S. Department of Transportation. (2011). *National evaluation of the Safe Trip-21 initiative.* Washington, DC: Government Printing Office. Retrieved from http://ntl.bts.gov/lib/38000/38500/38510/safetrip_cfr.pdf

Periodicals (Print and Online)

Here is the general format for an article from a scholarly journal:

Title of article: Only the first word of the title and subtitle (if there is one) and proper names should be capitalized. Do *not* place titles of articles in quotation marks.

Author's name: Last name, followed by a comma, the first initial, and middle initial (if available).

Title of periodical: Italicize and capitalize the title of the journal, magazine, or newspaper. Place a comma after the title.

Buck, A. (2012). Examining digital literacy practices on social network sites. *Research in the Teaching of English, 47*(1), 9–38. Retrieved from http://www.ncte.org.libproxy.albany.edu/library/NCTEFiles/Resources/Journals/RTE/0471-aug2012/RTE0471Examining.pdf

Date of publication: Year of publication appears in parentheses followed by a period. For newspapers and magazines, place a comma after the year and include the month as follows: (2012, April).

Volume and issue number: Include the volume of the publication in italics followed by the issue number in parentheses. This example shows issue #1 of volume 47. Place a comma after the closing parenthesis.

Pages: The page numbers on which the article appears followed by a period. If the article does not appear on continuous pages, separate the page numbers with a comma.

Source: If you found the article in print, end the citation with the page numbers. If you found the article on a website or through an online database, indicate that by including "Retrieved from" followed by the URL (web address). If there is a DOI, use that in place of the URL and replace the phrase "Retrieved from" with "doi" in lowercase followed by a colon. Do not place a period after the URL or the DOI.

13. Journal article with one author

> Mayers, T. (2009). One simple word: From creative writing to creative writing studies. *College English,* 71(3), 217–228.

If you accessed this article via the journal's website or from another online resource, the citation would look like this:

> Mayers, T. (2009). One simple word: From creative writing to creative writing studies. *College English,* 71(3), 217–228. Retrieved from http://www.ncte.org/journals/ce/issues/v71-3

If a DOI is available, include it in place of the URL:

> Desimone, L. M. (2009). Improving impact studies of teachers' professional development: Toward better conceptualizations and measures. *Educational Researcher, 38* (3): 181–199. doi: 10.3102/0013189X08331140

The abbreviation *doi* is in lowercase and followed by a colon. Do not place a period after the DOI number.

Note: APA style does not require that you include the name of the database if you accessed the work through an online database such as *Academic Search Complete*.

14. Journal article with multiple authors

For a work with two authors:

> Bowles, S., & Gintis, H. (2002). *Schooling in Capitalist America* revisited. *Sociology of Education, 75* (1): 1–18.

In this example, part of the article title is capitalized and italicized because it includes the title of a book (*Schooling in Capitalist America*).

For a work with three to seven authors:

> Esterling, B. A., L'Abate, L., Murray, E. J., & Pennebaker, J. W. (1999). Empirical foundations for writing in prevention and psychotherapy: Mental and physical health outcomes. *Clinical Psychology Review, 19* (1): 79–96.

Note: For a work by more than seven authors, include the first six authors' names, as in the previous example, and use an ellipsis in place of the remaining author names. Include the final author's name after the ellipsis.

15. Magazine article

> Gover, R. (2011, September). One novel's sojourn through culture wars & privacy. *The Writer's Chronicle, 44,* 50–57.

If you found the article through the magazine website or other online resource, cite it as follows:

> Gover, R. (2011, September). One novel's sojourn through culture wars & privacy. *The Writer's Chronicle, 44,* 50–57. Retrieved from https://www.awpwriter.org/library/writers_chronicle_overview

Note: If the magazine is published weekly or biweekly, include the day in the parentheses: (2011, September 15).

16. Newspaper article

> Kepner, T. (2008, September 21). Grand home of a larger-than-life team. *The New York Times,* p. N1.

Include both the day and month of publication for daily newspapers. Note that the page number includes the section in which the article appeared (in this example, section N, page 1). Also, for newspapers, include the abbreviation *p.* (for "page") before the page number.

If you accessed the article through the newspaper's website, cite it as follows:

Kepner, T. (2008, September 21). Grand home of a larger-than-life team. *The New York Times*, p. N1. Retrieved from http://www.nytimes.com

17. Editorial

Fighting "Patent Trolls." [Editorial]. (2013, June 6). *The New York Times*, p. A22.

Notice that the word *Editorial* is capitalized, placed in brackets, and followed by a period. It is *not* italicized.

18. Letter to the editor

Griffey, D. (2013, July). The price is wrong. [Letter to the editor]. *Money*, 10.

19. Review

Krugman, P. (2013, June 6). How the case for austerity has crumbled. [Review of the books *The alchemists: Three central bankers and a world on fire; Austerity: The history of a dangerous idea;* and *The great deformation: The corruption of capitalism in America*]. *The New York Review of Books*. Retrieved from http://www.nybooks.com/articles/archives/2013/jun/06/how-case-austerity-has-crumbled/

Other Sources

20. Web page

Cite a web page as you would an article from a journal, including the following information, if available: author's name, the title of the document or page, the date of publication, and the online location:

Pollan, M. (2010). Sustainable eating & nutrition: FAQs and useful links. Retrieved from http://michaelpollan.com/resources/sustainable-eating-nutrition/

If you can't find a date of publication, use the abbreviation *n.d.* (for "no date").

The citation for a web page by a corporate author (such as a government agency or business) is similar in format:

U.S. Department of the Interior. (2011, April 23). Climate change. Retrieved from http://www.doi.gov/index.cfm

Notice that the name of the agency or organization appears in place of an author's name. For a web page without an author, the citation appears like this:

How to anchor securely. (2012, July 23). Retrieved from http://www.westmarine.com/webapp/wcs/stores/servlet/TopCategories1_11151_10001_-1

21. Blog

Schoenkopf, R. (2012, April 6). Breitbart's ghost: Obama exploited Catholics by being endorsed by them [Web log comment]. Retrieved from http://wonkette.com/

22. Podcast

> Gross, T. (Executive Producer). (2012, August 15). Do voter ID laws prevent fraud, or dampen turnout? [Audio podcast]. *Fresh Air Podcast*. Retrieved from www.npr.org

Begin with the name of the most relevant contributor. The contributor's title—*director, host,* or (as in this example) *executive producer*—appears next, capitalized and in parentheses, followed by a period.

23. Interview

Personal, telephone, and email interviews are cited only within the text because they are not retrievable by other researchers.

24. Film, video, DVD

> Luhrmann, B. (Director). (2013). *The Great Gatsby* [Motion picture]. United States: Warner.

For videos, DVDs, filmstrips, and similar media, use this same format, noting the medium in brackets.

25. Television or radio program

> MacLaren, M. (Director). (2013, May 19). Second sons. *Game of Thrones* [Television broadcast]. New York, NY: HBO.

Note that the episode title ("Second Sons" in this example) precedes the name of the program (*Game of Thrones*).

26. Music recording

> Kuhn, J. (2013). *All this happiness* [CD]. New York, NY: PS Classics.

27. Advertisement

> Nike [Advertisement]. (2013, March). *Adweek*, 14.

In this example, the page number (14) appears after the title of the publication (*Adweek*).

Sample APA-Style Research Paper

In the following essay, which was written for an introductory writing class at Emerson College, Duncan Gelder follows APA guidelines for formatting a research paper. Duncan examines differences between the generations, focusing on the ways in which different generations use new technologies and how those technologies relate to the way people think. He makes an argument that the differences between generations are not caused by technology but are a function of the values of each generation. Duncan's essay is a good example of an argument to inquire (see Chapter 10). His goal is not to "win" an argument about why generations think differently; rather, he makes his argument as a way to understand this complex question and share that understanding with his audience.

Duncan adheres to the APA guidelines in formatting his paper. First, he includes a title page with the title and his name centered on the page. APA does not require information on the title page other than the title, author's name, and institutional affiliation, but if the course instructor requires his or her name, the course name, and a date, omit the institutional affiliation and replace it with the information required by the instructor, as Duncan has done. Notice that the title page is numbered and includes the same running head ("Generations") as the rest of the paper.

Second, Duncan includes an abstract, which is a summary of his paper. According to APA style, abstracts should not exceed 250 words. Notice that the word "Abstract" is centered one inch from the top of the page.

When formatting a paper in APA style, remember to

■ double-space the entire document

■ use one-inch margins

■ indent paragraphs one-half inch

■ include the title at the start of the paper (on the third page, after the abstract), centered above the main text

■ use running head with a shortened version of the title, in capital letters, on the left side of the page and the page number on the right side (include the running head on every page of the document)

Running Head: THE GENERATIONS THAT INFLUENCE TECHNOLOGY   1

The Generations That Influence Technology

Duncan Gelder

Professor Betsy Milarcik

WR 101 14 Introduction to College Writing

November 26, 2012

Abstract

Some experts believe we are witnessing a shift in cognitive styles between the Baby Boomer generation and younger generations as a result of the emergence of new technologies and the growing role of media in the lives of young people. However, in the past century, it has not been the technology and appliances that separate one generation from another; instead, the generation's needs and values at the time determine what innovations are prevalent for them.

The Generations That Influence Technology

How often does a person hear someone use the cliché phrase "back in my day…" followed by a long-winded explanation of how things used to be? Differences in generations is a common theme through much of the discussion about today's technology. According to N. Katherine Hayles (2007), "we are in the midst of a generational shift in cognitive styles" (p. 187). She believes that an "obvious explanation for the shift… is the increasing role of media in the everyday environments of young people" (189). However, in the past century, it has not been the technology and appliances that separate one generation from another; instead, the generation's needs and values at the time determine what innovations are prevalent for them.

A look back to the beginnings of the idea of "modern" technology, the Industrial Revolution in the 19th century, reveals that there are correlations between the ideas of that generation and the increase in technological innovations. The United States was going through major changes at the time. Increasing numbers of people who were willing to work quickly and for cheap were immigrating into the country. Owners of the factories and mills that dominated the era's industry wanted to ensure that this new surplus of workers were doing the work they were supposed to do. The capitalists who owned these businesses created the factory setting and the major technologies, such as the steam engine, that drove industrial growth (Backer, n.d.).

In a way, Hayles' (2007) idea of hyper attention comes into play during this era as well. Hayles (2007) describes hyper attention as being characterized partly by "switching focus rapidly between different tasks" (p. 187). The factories could take care of the steps of production from start to finish in one huge building. The technologies that were designed were, in a way, a mechanical form of hyper attention. This is really where our modern idea of capitalism began as well, with the wealthy starting businesses and buying out their competitors. Major monopolies became common during this generation because the upper class were not content with just owning one factory; they needed to own all of the factories and have the biggest hold on their sector of the industry, which is just another large-scale form of hyper attention among the wealthy. The attitudes, both of the workers being accountable for their work and the capitalists wanting to do as much as possible in a shorter amount of time, shaped what technology was prevalent and created the need for the innovations in the first place.

The way in which generational attitudes affected the technology of the era continued on as the industrial revolution began to fade. With two major world wars taking place, the country found itself in need of weapons and military technology. The unified attitude of the country forced these generations to come up with new innovations that would help protect our country. Aircraft and other forms of war transportation were made to be more

25

efficient and able to withstand harsher conditions, bombs were perfected, and boots and uniforms were mass produced; the generations that were affected by these major wars fueled the need for new innovations that would help them succeed. The women, many of whom were not able to fight overseas, turned to other ways to assist the country; they began to build and assemble all of the parts needed by the soldiers. The first World War coincided with the women's suffrage movement, a major point in generational attitudes (National Women's History Museum, 2007). These women wanted to prove that they were equals to men, but not all of them were able to operate undercover overseas or as switchboard operators. So they turned to the factories and began to find new ways of creating wartime innovations that would prove to be instrumental in winning these two major wars.

When the Second World War ended, the generation known commonly as the "Baby Boomer" generation was born as soldiers were now coming home from war and families were complete once again. The country was now focused on family life. Children were born, couples were together again; the home was the most important value during this era. Because there was need for products to be tailored to the consumer again, instead of for the military, many companies found that they needed to create products for the home life. This was the generation of appliances and at-home technology. The housewives that women were now expected to be meant that the women who had been hard at work during the war were now faced with the need to find power and freedom. Here again the idea of hyper attention comes into play. Women, who were the ones who took care of the house and were unable to work due to social inequalities, were now faced with monotonous, time-consuming household tasks. They needed new and unique innovations to make housework faster, giving them less work to do. Thus came the major changes in appliances and at-home technology, with faster washing machines and stronger vacuums being invented and updated as quickly as they were released. The Baby Boomer generation, which focused on family life more than any other idea, influenced what technology and innovations were available and invented during this era. Women were not housewives because they had washing machines available; the washing machines were available because of the strong social inequalities that required women to find ways of coping with the new work they had at home. The invention of the birth control pill during this era was another example of an innovation being influenced by the ideas of the generation. Many women were looking for freedom from the household life. The birth control pill was invented to give them a chance to live their lives without being burdened by children (Walsh, 2010).

The same correlations between values and technology are evident. We live in a time when social equality is a common theme. Women have broken away from the housewife stereotype and are now working to try and break the glass ceiling in the workplace. The racism and prejudice towards people of color is being challenged, a change best symbolized by the election and reelection of our country's first African American president. Gays and lesbians are fighting to receive equal rights. The country is in the midst of a new emphasis on uniqueness and individual rights. And because of this emphasis, technology has adapted to become more customizable for each and every person. Netflix allows us to watch the shows we want to watch. Smart phones allow us to download any app we choose. The current generation is fueled by the need for individualism and customization, and our technology reflects that. Our "hyper attention" is not so much a product of technology; the human need to be entertained and to move forward influences the technology that is a major part of our day-to-day lives. Technology, in a way, is the result of hyper attention. It isn't the technology which influences us; it's us that influences the technology.

References

Backer, P. R. (n.d.). *The cause of the industrial revolution.* Retrieved from
    http://www.engr.sjsu.edu/pabacker/causeIR.htm

Hayles, N. K. (2007). Hyper and deep attention: The generational divide in
    cognitive modes. *Profession,* 187–199.

National Women's History Museum. (2007). *Clandestine Women: Spies
    in American History.* Retrieved from http://www.nwhm.org/online-
    exhibits/spies/12.htm

Walsh, K. T. (2010, March 12). The 1960s: A decade of change for women.
    U.S. News & World Report. Retrieved from http://www.usnews.com/
    news/articles/2010/03/12/the-1960s-a-decade-of-change-for-women

25

1. COMPANY SECRETARY
(with license)
2. LEGAL ADVISOR
(expertise in Contract Law, Share Financing & Conveyancing)
3. QUANTITY SURVEYOR
(with M&E backgound)
4. TAX MANAGER
5. ACCOUNTS EXECUTIVE
6. PURCHASING EXECUTIVE
REQUIREMENTS
Bachelor Degree in related fields
At least five (5) years of related working
construction & ICT environment
Ability to work independ
Good comm
(1) Customer Service Officers
(2) Part Time Order Clerks
(3) Full Time/Part Time Cashiers
RESUME
Career Objectives:
challenging role in any engineering, information
ding my knowledge in Manufacturing and
nce:

Avoiding Common Problems In Style, Grammar, and Usage

26

CORE CONCEPT #10—"Good writing means more than good grammar"—underscores a reality about writing that eludes many people: "good" writing and "correct" writing aren't necessarily the same thing. In fact, as noted elsewhere in this textbook, the complexity of writing and the importance of rhetorical context make it impossible to define "good" writing in a way that applies to all circumstances. What counts as good writing in one situation might look like poor writing in another. The same principle applies to the rules for "correct" writing. Rules that must be followed in one situation can be ignored in others. For example, using the first person ("I") is perfectly fine in an op-ed essay for the campus newspaper but inappropriate in a chemistry lab report.

At the same time, the widespread belief that good writing is also correct writing is powerful, both in academic settings and in American culture generally. Many people equate grammar with character, and they interpret errors in writing as signs of laziness, sloppy thinking, or, worse, ignorance and even stupidity. Of course, a punctuation error doesn't mean a student is lazy or stupid, and such attitudes about "good grammar" ignore the complexity and rhetorical nature of writing. Nevertheless, these common attitudes influence how readers respond to a writer's words. What that means for you is that it is important to follow the conventions of writing so that you avoid errors that can interfere with the clarity of your prose and weaken your credibility as a writer.

As every student writer knows, rules for usage, punctuation, and spelling can be confusing and often seem capricious. One teacher might take off points for an "error" that another teacher ignores. How can student writers produce clear, effective, "correct" writing when the rules often seem so vague and relative? This chapter is intended to help answer that question.

Despite the confusing nature of many rules for grammar and usage and despite the variability with which these rules are applied by teachers and others, there are some basic principles of grammar and usage that apply to most writing situations. Moreover, in academic writing, certain conventions for style and usage are widely followed. In addition, research has identified the kinds of errors students tend to make in their writing. The advice provided in this chapter is based on prevailing conventions of academic writing as well as research on writing quality and error.

This chapter is not a comprehensive guide to grammar and usage. Instead, it explains the most important principles of grammar and usage in academic writing and offers advice for avoiding the most common errors. If you follow this advice, chances are that your writing will have fewer errors. Moreover, the strategies described in this chapter should help you grasp important rules for writing and gain a better understanding of the conventions of writing.

Strategies for Avoiding Errors

Let's start with two important points.

- **You already know most of the important rules of grammar and usage.** If you've made it to college, you are already a competent writer, and you have a working knowledge of most of the basic rules of writing, including punctuation, spelling, verb tense, and so on. This is true even if you can't actually state the rules you apply in your writing. For example, you might know that a comma belongs in a certain place in a sentence without knowing exactly why a comma belongs there. The point is that you have a good foundation for strengthening your grasp of the conventions of writing. You can build on that foundation by identifying the rules you do know and learning the ones you should know—which this chapter will help you do.

- **You can't learn all the rules of grammar and usage.** Nobody can. I've been writing professionally for three decades, I've written textbooks (like this one) for writing courses, and I've been a consultant for various kinds of writing tests, yet I still need to check handbooks and style guides to clarify a rule or learn one that I didn't know. Sometimes I even find that I was mistaken about a rule I thought I knew. If someone who does this kind of thing for a living can't know all the rules, it makes little sense for student writers to expect to learn them. The fact is that you already know most of the important rules, and the ones you still need to clarify or learn are probably relatively few in number. Focus on identifying those.

These two points should help reduce your anxiety about grammar and usage. Students often tell me that they "have bad grammar" or that they know they "need better grammar." What they really need—what most student writers need—is to build on what they already know about grammar to increase their confidence as writers and determine what they should know in order to avoid the errors that might be weakening their writing.

To accomplish these goals, follow these three steps:

1. Identify the errors you make in your writing.

2. Learn the rules related to those errors.

3. Practice.

Identify the Errors You Make in Your Writing

What kinds of errors do you routinely make in your writing? What kinds of problems do your instructors point out in your writing? Once you pinpoint the specific errors you tend to make, you can begin to work on avoiding them. Although this approach might seem daunting, especially if you have often received papers back from instructors full of red ink, the challenge is probably not as great as you think. Research suggests that most students tend to make the same errors repeatedly in their writing. If they can identify and eliminate those errors, they will significantly improve their writing.

Learn the Rules Related to Those Errors

Once you have a sense of the errors you tend to make in your writing, use this chapter (perhaps in conjunction with a comprehensive grammar handbook) to understand the rules related to those errors. If you're like most students, most of the errors you make are probably minor, such as missing or misplaced commas or incorrect apostrophes. It's quite possible that you make those errors because you either misunderstand the appropriate rule or never learned the rule in the first place. In addition, college-level academic writing is governed by conventions that you might not have learned in high school, so you might need to learn some new rules. Understanding the principles of usage and the conventions that apply to the errors you make will help you avoid those errors.

Practice

The best way to improve as a writer is to practice writing. The same is true for learning to avoid errors. If you want to eliminate errors from your writing, you have to practice identifying and correcting those errors in your writing. You can do so in two general ways:

- **First, consult handbooks or style guides** that have exercises for applying the specific rules related to the errors you tend to make. Doing such exercises will sharpen your ability to identify and correct those errors and strengthen your knowledge of specific rules of usage and grammar.

- **Second, practice editing your own drafts** in a way that focuses specifically on the kinds of errors you tend to make. If you follow the procedure in Chapter 3 when you are working on a writing project, include in Step #10 an additional step that focuses on the specific errors you have identified as common in your own writing. If you make such a step a routine part of your practice as a writer, you will eventually begin to notice that fewer and fewer errors appear in your finished projects.

This rest of this chapter focuses on the problems that research indicates college students tend to make in their writing. The errors you commonly make in your own writing are probably on this "hit parade," and the usage and syntax problems that can make your sentences unclear are very likely the ones described here.

Coordination, Subordination, and Parallelism

The structure of a sentence—what teachers often call *syntax*—is more than a function of rules for usage and grammar. It is also a means of conveying relationships and emphasizing words, phrases, and ideas. The elements of a sentence must fit together syntactically, but the syntax should also match the intended meaning so that the structure of the sentence not only is grammatically correct but also helps convey the writer's ideas.

The many complexities and nuances of syntax are well beyond the scope of this chapter, but you can improve the clarity of your prose by avoiding common problems in three areas of syntax: coordination, subordination, and parallel structure.

Coordination

Coordination refers to the use of similar or equivalent grammatical constructions to link ideas or show relationships between generally equal ideas or information in a sentence. Writers use coordinating conjunctions (*and, but, so, yet, or*) to show coordinate relationships between elements of a sentence:

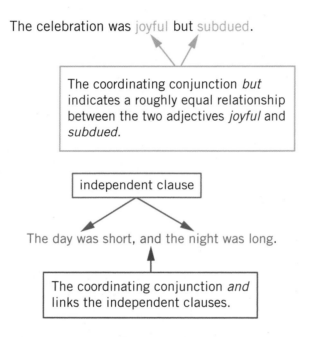

The celebration was joyful but subdued.

> The coordinating conjunction *but* indicates a roughly equal relationship between the two adjectives *joyful* and *subdued.*

> independent clause

The day was short, and the night was long.

> The coordinating conjunction *and* links the independent clauses.

It is important to note here that using different coordinating conjunctions can change the relationships between the coordinate elements:

The day was short, but the night was long.

In this example, *but* changes the relationship between the first clause ("the day was short") and the second ("the night was long"). Although this point might seem obvious, using coordinating conjunctions strategically to convey specific or precise ideas about the relationships between elements of a sentence is a hallmark of effective academic writing. For example, consider how the choice of *and* or *but* in the following example affects the relationship between the first clause ("Life can be a constant struggle") and the second ("death is final"):

Life can be a constant struggle, and death is final.

Life can be a constant struggle, but death is final.

In both sentences, the clauses are still coordinate, but replacing *and* with *but* changes both the relationship between the clauses and the emphasis of the sentence—which is turn affects the meaning conveyed by the sentence. In the first sentence, the two clauses have equal emphasis and can be seen as two equal statements of the human condition. We might interpret the sentence as follows: Let's recognize the two important realities about human existence that life is hard and death is final. In the second sentence, however, the use of *but* shifts the emphasis to the second clause, which alters the meaning of the entire sentence. We might state the meaning this way: Yes, life is hard, but death is final. The implication might be something like this: Because death is final, live life to the fullest, no matter how hard it can be.

This example illustrates how the choice of a single coordinating conjunction, even in a seemingly straightforward sentence, can significantly affect the ideas conveyed by the sentence. In this sense, coordination can be a powerful tool for writers. Notice that greater emphasis is usually attached to the final element in a coordinate relationship.

Students commonly make two mistakes in using coordination in their writing: they use the wrong coordinating conjunction (usually *and* when *but* or *so* is more appropriate), and they use too much coordination:

Shifts in climate patterns have resulted in more frequent severe weather in many regions, and local governments are struggling to develop more effective emergency services.

coordinating conjunction | independent clause

In this example, there is nothing grammatically incorrect about the sentence, but the conjunction *and* does not quite convey the correlation between the first and second clauses of the sentence. If the writer wanted to show that local governments are struggling to develop effective emergency services specifically as a result of changes in several weather patterns, *but* would be a better choice to link the two main clauses:

Shifts in climate patterns have resulted in more frequent severe weather in many regions, but local governments are struggling to develop more effective emergency services.

As you revise your drafts for style, usage, and grammar, it is a good idea to pay attention to your use of coordinating conjunctions so that you can identify sentences in which the coordination does not convey the specific ideas or relationships you intend. If you notice that you are relying on *and* to link elements of a sentence—especially main clauses, as in this example—it is often a sign that you might need to adjust some of your sentences by using a different conjunction.

Subordination

Subordination refers to the use of elements in a sentence to show hierarchical relationships or relationships among ideas that are not equal. Subordination is indicated through the use of dependent clauses and is signaled by the use of *subordinating conjunctions*. The most common subordinating conjunctions are *if, although, because, before, after, since, whether, when, whereas, while, until,* and *unless*; writers also commonly use *than* and *that* to indicate subordination. Here are some examples.

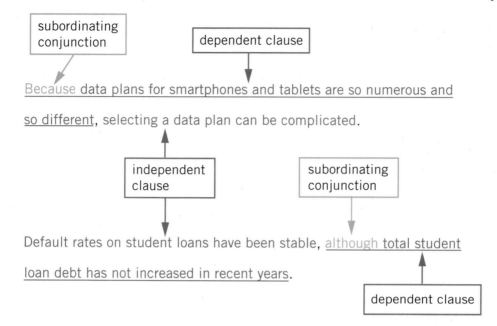

In these examples, the information in the dependent clauses is subordinated to the information in the main independent clause. Writers can use subordination to emphasize the ideas in the independent clause and to indicate the relationship between those ideas and the less important ideas in the dependent clause.

Notice that although the ideas in the independent clause receive emphasis, you can use the order of the clauses to adjust the relative emphasis of each clause. Consider how reversing the order of the clauses in the second example can change the emphasis on each clause and subtly influence the meaning of the sentence:

> Default rates on student loans have been stable, although total student loan debt has not increased in recent years.

> Although total student loan debt has not increased in recent years, default rates on student loans have been stable.

In both versions of this sentence, the main emphasis is on the independent clause; however, because the dependent clause comes last in the first version, there is slightly greater emphasis on the information in the dependent clause than in the second version. In this way, you can use subordination strategically to direct your readers' attention to specific ideas or convey a more precise sense of the relationship between the ideas in each clause.

Students often use coordination where subordination would be more effective. Consider this sentence:

> Genetically modified foods can have significant risks for farmers, but such foods can be less expensive for consumers.

The use of the coordinating conjunction (*but*) in this sentence results in equal emphasis on both independent clauses. Although the sentence is perfectly acceptable in this coordinate form, the writer can use subordination to emphasize one or the other independent clause:

> Although genetically modified foods can have significant risks for farmers, such foods can be less expensive for consumers.

> Although genetically modified foods can be less expensive for consumers, such foods can have significant risks for farmers.

In these two versions of the sentence, the emphasis is noticeably stronger on the ideas in the independent clause than in the coordinate version of the sentence, which gives more or less equal weight to the ideas in both clauses.

Parallel Structure

In general, sentences should be written so that words and phrases have the same grammatical form, especially if they are used in a series. Varying the form of words or phrases in a sentence can result in awkward prose:

> The protest movement was a failure for three reasons: lack of organization,
>
> excess ego, and having unclear ideas.

> The third item ("having unclear ideas") in this series takes a different form from the first two items ("lack of organization" and "excess ego"), making the sentence awkward.

Make the series parallel by changing the form of the third item so that it is consistent with the form of the first two:

> The protest movement was a failure for three reasons: lack of organization, excess ego, and unclear ideas.

Sometimes two verb constructions in the same sentence take different forms and upset the parallelism of the sentence:

> It is easier to get lost in the past than planning the future.

> *Than* creates a comparison between two verb phrases: *to get lost in the past* and *planning for the future*; however, the verb phrases take different forms: an infinitive (*to get*) and a participle (*planning*).

Simply make the forms of the two verb phrases consistent:

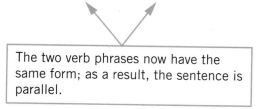

It is easier to get lost in the past than to plan the future.

The two verb phrases now have the same form; as a result, the sentence is parallel.

Common Sentence-Level Problems

Most student writers have a grasp of the basic rules of sentence structure, but sometimes writers stumble when trying to write academic prose. Usually, the sentence-level problems that result are of the three main types discussed here.

Run-on or Fused Sentences

A run-on occurs when two or more independent clauses are joined without proper punctuation or linking words:

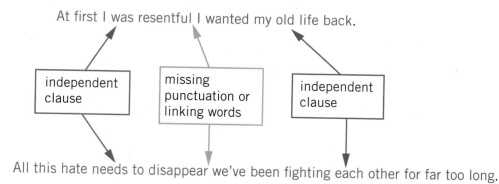

At first I was resentful I wanted my old life back.

independent clause

missing punctuation or linking words

independent clause

All this hate needs to disappear we've been fighting each other for far too long.

Often, the easiest solution is adding the proper punctuation mark (usually a period or semi-colon):

At first I was resentful. I wanted my old life back.

All this hate needs to disappear; we've been fighting each other for far too long.

Sometimes, adding linking words or rewriting the sentence is a better option:

At first I was resentful, and I wanted my old life back.

We've been fighting each other for far too long, so let's eliminate the hate.

In many cases, run-on sentences result from an effort to write a complex sentence that contains several ideas:

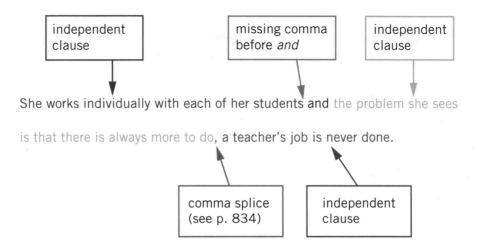

In this example, three independent clauses are fused without proper punctuation. To correct these errors, the writer has several options:

■ **Insert correct punctuation:**

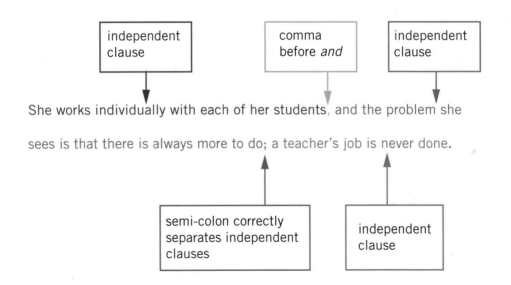

- **Break up the sentence into two or more shorter sentences:**

She works individually with each of her students, and the problem she sees is that there is always more to do. A teacher's job is never done.

- **Rewrite the sentence:**

Working individually with each of her students, she sees that there is always more to do and that a teacher's job is never done.

Working individually with each student means that she always has more to do. A teacher's job is never done.

Which option is best depends on the context within which this sentence occurs and the effect you want to have on your audience.

Fragments

A sentence fragment is an incomplete sentence, often lacking either a subject or a main verb. Sentence fragments often occur when a period is placed incorrectly between a dependent clause or phrase and the main clause of the sentence:

Her parents decided that there wouldn't be time to visit the last college on her list.

Although she was still very interested in applying to that school.

Sentence fragment: This is a dependent clause that must either be revised or appropriately attached to the independent clause.

Correct sentence: This independent clause correctly has a subject and verb to make it a complete sentence.

This error can be corrected by using the proper punctuation between the two clauses:

Her parents decided that there wouldn't be time to visit the last college on her list, although she was still very interested in applying to that school.

Replacing the period with a comma correctly attaches the dependent clause to the independent clause.

This error can be also corrected by rewriting the sentence fragment to make it an independent clause:

Her parents decided that there wouldn't be time to visit the last college on her list. Still, she remained very interested in applying to that school.

Sometimes fragments occur when a phrase, such as a prepositional phrase or an appositive, is incorrectly set off from the main clause by a period:

There was one thing he loved about that old house. The ivy-covered brick.

This period incorrectly separates the appositive phrase (*the ivy-covered brick*) from the main clause.

sentence fragment

In this case, the error can be corrected by using the proper punctuation (either a comma or a colon) or by rewriting the sentence slightly:

There was one thing he loved about that old house: the ivy-covered brick.

There was one thing he loved about that old house, the ivy-covered brick.

The one thing he loved about that old house was the ivy-covered brick.

Faulty Sentence Structure

This category of common error is large. It includes a variety of problems that make sentences unclear, difficult to follow, or grammatically incorrect. Two of the most common types of this problem are dangling modifiers and a lack of parallel structure.

- **Misplaced and dangling modifiers.** In general, phrases and clauses that modify a word should be placed as close to that word as possible. Often, a sentence is written so that a clause or phrase modifies the wrong sentence element, as in this example:

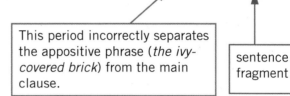

When quoting the teachers at the working-class school, the tone is

negative and seems critical of teachers' efforts.

Grammatically, this clause modifies the subject of the main clause (*tone*). But the sentence doesn't make sense, because it is not the tone that is doing the quoting but the writer.

Address the problem by rewriting the sentence:

> When quoting the teachers at the working-class school, the writer adopts a negative tone and seems critical of teachers' efforts.

In this revised sentence the modifying clause (*When quoting the teachers at the working-class school*) is placed close to the noun it modifies (*the writer*).

Sometimes, the problem is that the modifier is misplaced, which can change the meaning of the sentence:

> Tad only played tennis on Wednesday.

> With the adverb *only* placed here, the sentence means that the only thing Tad did on Wednesday was play tennis.

Simply move the modifier:

> Tad played tennis only on Wednesday.

> Moving the adverb *only* changes the meaning of the sentence. Now it means that Tad plays tennis only on Wednesdays rather than other days.

The same problem can occur when a modifying phrase is placed too far from the noun it modifies:

> Chaz spent the rest of the night playing video games, having finally turned in his assignment.

> Placed here, the phrase "having finally turned in his assignment" modifies the phrase "playing video games" rather than the subject of the sentence, "Chaz."

Clarify matters by moving the phrase closer to the word it modifies (*Chaz*):

> Having finally turned in his assignment, Chaz spent the rest of the night playing video games.

Here is another very common version of the same problem; however, in this case, the intended subject of the main clause is replaced by an indefinite pronoun (*it*), which makes the sentence more awkward and confusing:

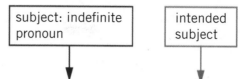

By using this research, it can help guide educators in developing

teaching strategies to help adolescents become better readers.

Grammatically, the prepositional phrase ("By using this research") modifies the subject of the main clause ("it"), but *it* isn't using the research; "educators" are using the research. As written, the sentence is nonsensical.

There are two basic ways to address this kind of dangling modifier:

- **Rewrite the sentence to make the intended subject the grammatical subject:**

    By using this research, educators can develop curriculum and teaching

    strategies to help adolescents become better readers.

    The pronoun *it* is deleted and the intended subject ("educators") is now the grammatical subject of the sentence.

- **Change the modifying phrase into the subject of the sentence:**

    The phrase "using this research" is now the subject of the sentence.

    Using this research can help educators develop curriculum and

    teaching strategies to help adolescents become better readers.

Common Pronoun Errors

There are many different kinds of pronouns, which means that there are many opportunities for incorrectly using pronouns. However, most pronoun errors are of two kinds: (1) lack of agreement between the pronoun and its antecedent (that is, the word the pronoun refers to) and (2) a missing or vague antecedent for the pronoun.

There are three basic principles governing the uses of pronouns:

- The pronoun must be in the correct *case* corresponding to its function in the sentence.
- Every pronoun (except indefinite pronouns) must have an ***antecedent***—that is, the noun to which the pronoun refers.
- The pronoun must agree with its antecedent in number and gender. (If the antecedent is singular, the pronoun must also be singular; if the antecedent is female, so must the pronoun be.)

If you apply these principles, you are unlikely to make the following common mistakes with pronouns.

Incorrect Pronoun Case

Case refers to the form of a pronoun that reflects its specific function in a sentence: subject, object, or possessive:

He is an excellent dancer. (The pronoun *He* is the subject of the sentence and is therefore correctly in the subjective case.)

Me and Jose went swimming yesterday. (*Me*, which is the objective case of the first-person pronoun *I*, is incorrect because it is being used as a subject. The correct form is *I* in this instance.)

The dance club gave **he** and **I** an award for best dancer. (The pronouns *he* and *I*, which are in the subjective case, are incorrect because they are being used as indirect objects of the verb *gave*. They should be in the objective case: *him* and *me*.)

He brought **his** dancing shoes. (The pronoun *his* is possessive and is therefore correctly in the possessive case.)

Most students are able to identify the proper case of pronouns. In academic writing, however, students sometimes lose track of the proper case when writing lengthy, complex sentences.

Lack of Pronoun-Antecedent Agreement

This error is usually easy to avoid if you identify the antecedent; however, this kind of pronoun error is common in part because the wrong pronoun often "sounds" right:

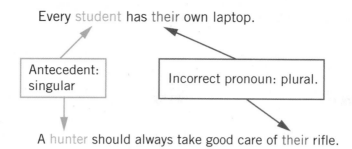

Every student has their own laptop.

Antecedent: singular

Incorrect pronoun: plural.

A hunter should always take good care of their rifle.

Correct these errors either by changing the pronoun or rewriting the sentence:

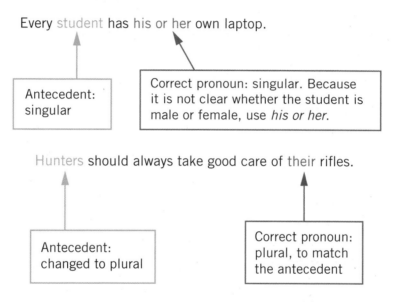

Every student has his or her own laptop.

Antecedent: singular

Correct pronoun: singular. Because it is not clear whether the student is male or female, use *his or her*.

Hunters should always take good care of their rifles.

Antecedent: changed to plural

Correct pronoun: plural, to match the antecedent

Making sure that the pronoun agrees with its antecedent can be tricky when the antecedent is an **indefinite pronoun** (e.g., everyone, anyone, anybody, someone):

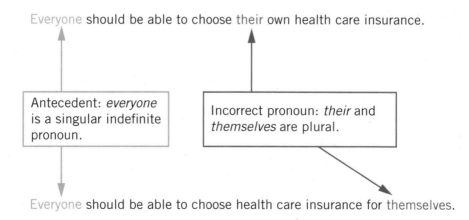

Everyone should be able to choose their own health care insurance.

Antecedent: *everyone* is a singular indefinite pronoun.

Incorrect pronoun: *their* and *themselves* are plural.

Everyone should be able to choose health care insurance for themselves.

Again, correct the errors by changing the pronoun or rewriting the sentence:

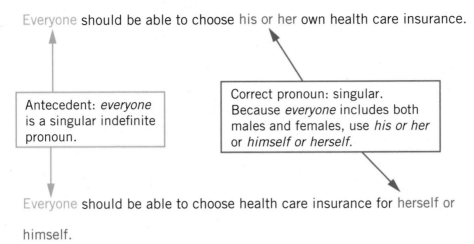

Everyone should be able to choose his or her own health care insurance.

Antecedent: *everyone* is a singular indefinite pronoun.

Correct pronoun: singular. Because *everyone* includes both males and females, use *his or her* or *himself or herself.*

Everyone should be able to choose health care insurance for herself or himself.

Vague Pronoun Reference

Usually, the antecedent is the noun closest to the pronoun. Sometimes, however, the antecedent can seem to refer to more than one noun. In this example, technically the antecedent for the pronoun *he* should be *Steve*, because *Steve* is the closest noun to the pronoun. But a reader might assume that *he* refers instead to *Bob*.

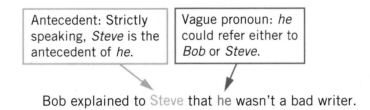

Antecedent: Strictly speaking, *Steve* is the antecedent of *he.*

Vague pronoun: *he* could refer either to *Bob* or *Steve.*

Bob explained to Steve that he wasn't a bad writer.

In such cases, rewrite the sentence to clarify the antecedent:

Bob explained to Steve that Steve wasn't a bad writer.

Bob said to Steve, "You're not a bad writer."

According to Bob, Steve wasn't a bad writer.

Word Choice and Style

An effective style in academic writing is partly a matter of careful and strategic selection of words, not only to craft clear sentences but also to meet the needs of the rhetorical situation. Sometimes that means using specialized terminology (often called "jargon") that is appropriate for the subject—say, economics or psychology. More often, though, writers must make choices among words that have slightly different shades of meaning to convey precisely what they want to say to their readers. Consider the differences in the following statements:

The audience was **interested** in the speaker's argument.

The audience was **engaged** by the speaker's argument.

The audience was **fascinated** by the speaker's argument.

The audience was **enthralled** by the speaker's argument.

Although all of these sentences generally mean that the audience listened intently to the speaker, each sentence conveys a different sense of the impact of the speaker's argument on the audience. Selecting the verb that conveys precisely what you want to convey about that impact is part of what it means to write effective prose.

Students tend to make three errors when it comes to word choice:

- making imprecise word choices
- using the wrong word
- confusing similar words

Imprecise Word Choices

The best word choice is always shaped by the rhetorical situation—especially the writer's sense of the audience's expectations and the appropriate style—as well as by the writer's own preferences. However, students sometimes rely too much on general words when more specialized or specific words would be more precise:

The mayor gave a **great** speech to the residents after their town was hit by the hurricane.

Words like *great, good, bad,* and *awesome* are overused and vague, even if their general meanings are clear. In this example, the writer conveys a positive sense of the mayor's speech but not much more than that. Consider these alternatives:

The mayor gave a **comforting** speech to the residents after their town was hit by the hurricane.

The mayor gave an **encouraging** speech to the residents after their town was hit by the hurricane.

The mayor gave an **emotional** speech to the residents after their town was hit by the hurricane.

Which of these choices is best will depend on the specific meaning you want to convey to your readers and the context of the text in which the sentence appears, but any of these choices conveys a clearer, more precise description of the mayor's speech than the original sentence. As this example shows, a single word can significantly improve a sentence.

Wrong Word

Studies show that one of the most common errors in student writing is the use of the wrong word or word form; however, those same studies do not identify specific words that students routinely misuse (other than the ones discussed in the next section). That might be because of the richness of the English language and the idiosyncrasies of each of us as writers. In other words, all writers sometimes use the wrong word, but we all make different versions of this error. You might have trouble remembering the correct form of a specific verb, while your classmate struggles with a different kind of word that you find easy to use. This variability does not allow us to make generalizations about specific errors in word choice that are common in student writing, and it underscores the need to become aware of the errors that you tend to make, as noted in the first section of this chapter.

Confusing Similar Words

Words that look and sound alike but have very different functions can sometimes confuse writers and lead to common errors. In such cases, the best approach is simply to learn the correct uses of these words and any rules related to their usage. Being aware that these words are often the source of errors is also important. You can be vigilant in using these words and focus on them when editing your drafts.

The three most commonly confused sets of words are *their, there,* and *they're; affect* and *effect;* and *then* and *than.*

- **Their/there/they're.** Each of these words has a very different function:

  Their is a plural possessive pronoun.

  The players put on **their** uniforms.

  Voters never seem to be able to make up **their** minds.

- **There** is an adverb denoting place; it can also be used as a pronoun.

  We don't want to go **there**. (adverb)

  There are three reasons to support this candidate. (pronoun)

- **They're** is a contraction for *they are.*

  They told us that **they're** not going on the field trip.

  Although the peaches are inexpensive, **they're** not very fresh.

A common mistake is using ***their*** in place of ***they're***:

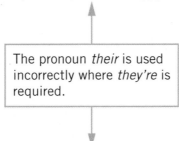

The students can't explain why their unhappy with the new class.

The pronoun *their* is used incorrectly where *they're* is required.

Although the workers are tired, their planning to finish the job.

To avoid this mistake, replace the word (*their, there,* or *they're*) with the words *they are*. If the sentence makes sense, then you must use the word *they're*.

Another common mistake is using **there** in place of **their**:

The children forgot to bring there towels to swimming class.

There can never be correctly used in place of the pronoun *their*.

When it began to rain, the workers covered up there tools with plastic tarps.

■ **Affect/effect.** Although both these words can be either nouns or verbs, *affect* is most often used as a verb meaning to act upon, whereas *effect* is most often used as a noun to mean an impact, result, or consequence:

The heavy rains will probably **affect** the harvest.

Seemingly, he was not **affected** by the long hours and lack of sleep.

The weather always **affects** our vacation plans.

Growing up in a small town had a big **effect** on me.

Historians have long debated the **effects** of the industrial revolution.

What is the **effect** of the new regulation?

The two most common errors involving these terms are using *effect* as a verb when *affect* is required and using *affect* as a noun when *effect* is required:

Hot weather doesn't effect me.

Effect is incorrectly used as a verb where *affect* should be used.

The farm was not effected by the drought.

The police returned his personal affects.

Affects is incorrectly used as a noun where *effect* should be used.

The economist could not anticipate the affects of the hurricanes.

26

Be aware that *affect* can be used as a noun and *effect* as a verb, although these uses are much less common than those explained above. As a noun, *affect* refers to an emotional state or feeling:

> The patients lacked **affect** in their expressions.

> The woman had a joyful **affect**.

> The criminal displayed a disturbing **affect**.

When used as a verb, *effect* means to cause something to happen or to bring about:

> The reformers sought to **effect** significant change in the way schools are run.

> The farmers were successful in **effecting** an increase in commodity prices.

- **Then/than.** The easiest way to distinguish between these two common words is to remember that *then* refers to time, whereas *than* is always used in comparisons:

> I'll go to the bank, and **then** I'll go to the grocery store.

> The book's influence has been much greater **than** the author could ever have imagined.

> We were much more optimistic back **then**.

> She liked the green sweatshirt better **than** the blue one.

The most common mistake with these two words occurs when *then* is used in place of *than*:

> I have always been a better athlete then my sister.

> Because a comparison is being made, *then* is incorrect and *than* must be used.

> He wanted to visit Europe more then anything.

Here are some other commonly confused words.

- **Accept/except.** *Accept* is a verb meaning to receive something. *Except* is generally used as a preposition:

> She was happy to **accept** the award.

> Everyone **except** the boss received a raise.

- **Advice/advise.** The easiest way to avoid confusing these words is to remember that *advice* is a noun meaning guidance, whereas *advise* is a verb meaning to give guidance or advice:

> My lawyer always provides me with good **advice** when I'm trying to make a decision involving legal matters.

> The lawyer will **advise** a client about the best way to handle a legal problem.

- **Complement/compliment.** *Complement* can be used as a noun or a verb; it means to complete or add to. A *compliment* can also be a noun or verb; it means to praise.

  The blue hat nicely **complemented** his tan suit.

  I paid him a **compliment** on his blue hat.

- **Lie/lie/lay.** These often-confused words have very different meanings and functions. The irregular verb *lie* means to recline or place your body in a prone position and takes three forms: *lie, lay, have lain*. The regular verb *lie* (which takes the forms *lie, lied, and have lied*) means to tell a falsehood. The regular verb *lay* (which takes the forms *lay, laid, and have laid*) means to place something or put something down. Most often students use *lay* when they should use *lie*:

  Incorrect: She likes to **lay** down on the sofa after lunch to take a nap.

  Correct: She likes to **lie** down on the sofa after lunch to take a nap.

  Incorrect: He **laid** down on the sofa to take a nap.

  Correct: He **lay** down on the sofa to take a nap.

  Incorrect: Before he finished his paper, he had **laid** down on the sofa to rest.

  Correct: Before he finished his paper, he had **lain** down on the sofa to rest.

  Incorrect: She commanded her dog to **lay** down.

  Correct: She commanded her dog to **lie** down.

  Incorrect: He **lied** the baby down in the crib. He lay the baby in the crib.

  Correct: He **laid** the baby down in the crib.

- **Past/passed.** *Past* is a preposition meaning gone by or a noun meaning a time period before the present. *Passed* is the past tense of the verb *pass*, which means to go by.

  He drove **past** the accident.

  He **passed** by the accident.

  The accident occurred in the **past**.

- **To/too/two.** These three words that sound similar have very different functions. *To* is a preposition. *Too* is an adverb. *Two* is a noun or adjective.

  She ran **to** the finish line.

  He gave his car **to** his friend.

  She wanted a new car, **too**.

  He, **too**, was interested in running the race.

There were **too** many runners in the race.

There were **two** runners who did not finish the race.

Two is better than one.

■ **Through/threw.** *Through* is used either as an adverb or preposition. *Threw* is the past tense of the verb *throw*.

He went **through** the tunnel.

She **threw** a rock into the tunnel.

Only **through** hard work can you succeed.

Common Punctuation Errors
Missing Commas

Missing commas where they are required are among the most common errors student writers make. This section reviews the rules for seven required uses of commas:

■ before a coordinating conjunction

■ after an introductory element

■ before a quotation

■ around nonessential elements

■ in a series

■ between coordinate adjectives

■ to set off nouns of direct address, *yes* and *no,* interrogative tags, and interjections

If you become familiar with the rules for these seven uses of commas, you will avoid these common errors.

■ **Before a coordinating conjunction (for, and, nor, but, or, yet, so).** In most cases a comma should be placed *before* a coordinating conjunction (such as *for, and, nor, but, or, yet, so*) that connects two independent clauses:

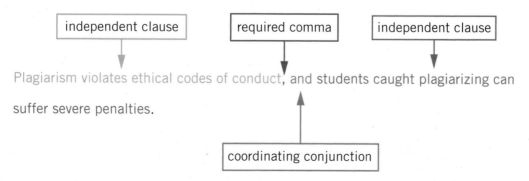

The weather promised to turn stormy later that afternoon, so we took along rain jackets.

Every student is potentially affected by tuition increases, but students who rely on loans might suffer the most because they will end up borrowing more money to pay for their educations.

One important exception to this rule: no comma is needed before a coordinating conjunction that joins two very short sentences:

I was tired but I slept well.

- **After an introductory element.** A comma should be placed after an introductory word, phrase, or clause in a sentence:

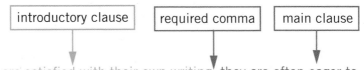

When students are satisfied with their own writing, they are often eager to

share it with classmates.

- **Introductory phrase:**

Worried about his car, Brian decided not to drive the long distance back to his apartment.

Despite her misgivings, she signed up for the backpacking trip.

- **Introductory word:**

Furthermore, I was starting school that fall.

Ultimately, they found what they were seeking.

Traditionally, conservative teachers have never questioned the principle of school governance by part-time citizens.

Notice that in this last example, the comma changes the meaning of the sentence. Without the comma, the adverb "traditionally" modifies the adjective "conservative," which modifies the subject (teachers), and the sentence means that teachers who are traditionally conservative have never questioned the principle of school governance by part-time citizens. However, with the comma, "traditionally" modifies the main verb (questioned), and the sentence means that conservative teachers have traditionally not questioned the principle of school governance by part-time citizens.

- **Before a quotation.** Direct quotations of complete sentences must be preceded by a comma:

John Lennon once said, "Life is what happens to you while you're busy making other plans."

Audre Lorde wrote, "It is not our differences that divide us. It is our inability to recognize, accept, and celebrate those differences."

Common Punctuation Errors **829**

- **Around nonessential elements.** Use commas to set off elements of a sentence that are not essential for understanding who or what is being discussed. Nonessential elements include appositives, modifying phrases or clauses, transitional words or phrases, or parenthetical words or phrases.

With appositives:

When my second brother was born, we switched rooms so that the boys could share the larger room and I, the only girl, could have the small room for myself.

In this sentence, the phrase "the only girl" is an appositive modifying the pronoun "I" and must be set off by commas.

Nonessential (non-restrictive) modifying phrases or clauses:

In the following sentences, the highlighted words are nonessential clauses or phrases that must be set off by commas. (In these cases, removing the highlighted words does not change the meaning of the main sentence, which is why they are called "nonessential.")

The car, which was brilliant red, was stuck on the side of the road.

David, who was wearing a blue rain jacket, quickly ran for shelter.

Hungry and cold, the stray cat hid under the back porch.

With transitional words or phrases:

What is interesting, though, is that they never realized what they were doing.

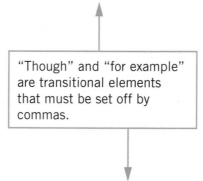

"Though" and "for example" are transitional elements that must be set off by commas.

Her most recent novel, for example, examines unconventional families.

With parenthetical words or phrases:

Parenthetical phrases or words are like "asides" or related but nonessential comments: They are not necessary, and removing them does not affect the meaning of the main sentence.

Jasmine heard the comment and, understandably, left the room.

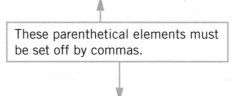

These parenthetical elements must be set off by commas.

Jerry believed that everyone, except maybe people with debilitating illnesses, should have to work.

- **In a series.** Place a comma after each item in a series, whether those items are words, phrases, or clauses. (In these examples, the different items in each series are shown in different colors.)

Students were told to bring a pencil, a paper, and an eraser.

The tired sailors found themselves struggling to stay on schedule, worried about the condition of their boat, and hoping for better weather.

The triathletes were wondering whether to emphasize swimming, running, or bicycling in their workouts.

Only a few days after the hurricane, power was restored, stores reopened, and people returned to their homes.

Note: The preceding sentences all contain **the Oxford Comma**, which is placed after the second-to-last item in a series and before the coordinating conjunction (and, or). The Oxford Comma is typically expected in academic writing; however, it is rarely used in popular writing. For college writing assignments, I recommend using the Oxford Comma unless instructed otherwise.

- **Between coordinate adjectives.** Coordinate adjectives are adjectives that are equal and reversible, so that their order does not affect the meaning of the phrase. Usually, if adjectives can be connected by "and," they are coordinate and should be separated by commas:

PJ Harvey's album *To Bring You My Love* is full of dirge-like, erotic vocals.

These two adjectives (*dirge-like* and *erotic*), which modify the noun *vocals*, could be reversed without altering the meaning of the phrase or the sentence, so they must be separated by commas.

The juicy, ripe, sweet peach is one of the best tastes of summer.

> The adjectives modifying *peach* could be reversed without altering the meaning of the phrase or the sentence, so they must be separated by commas.

Compare the previous two examples with this one:

He bought seven red apples.

In this case, no comma separates the adjectives *seven* and *red* because the two are not equal. *Seven* modifies the entire phrase *red applies*. The adjectives *seven* and *red* are cumulative. They cannot be logically reordered or be connected with *and*: For example, we would not say, "seven and red apples" or "red seven apples." Commas should not be used to separate cumulative adjectives.

- **With nouns of direct address, the words *yes* and *no*, interrogative tags, and mild interjections.** Names and other terms used in direct address must be set off by commas:

  Mike, turn it up. (direct address)

  No, I won't turn it up.

  You're not going to turn it up, are you? (The phrase "are you" is an interrogative tag.)

  Look, take it easy. (The word "Look" is an interjection.)

Unnecessary Commas

Maybe because there are so many rules governing the uses of commas, students often place commas where they are not needed. Two kinds of unnecessary commas are among the most common punctuation errors: commas that incorrectly separate sentence elements and commas placed around essential (or restrictive) elements.

- **Separating sentence elements.** Commas should not be used to separate essential elements in a sentence, such as the subject and verb, compound words or phrases, and necessary phrases or clauses unless those essential elements are separated by other elements that must be set off by commas. Here are some examples of unnecessary commas:

> This comma incorrectly separates the two parts of a compound verb (*is* and *keeps*) with the same subject (*she*) and should be deleted.

She is meticulous, and keeps her equipment stored carefully in its original boxes.

If an element that must be set off by commas were included between the essential elements, then be sure to use commas:

> She is meticulous, almost to a fault, and keeps her equipment stored carefully in its original boxes.

This comma incorrectly separates the infinitive phrase (*to increase their power*) from the main clause of the sentence (*nations are taking land*).

The European nations are taking land from weaker nations, to increase their power.

■ **With an essential (restrictive) element.** An element that is necessary for the intended meaning of a sentence should not be set off by commas. In many cases involving restrictive elements, the use of commas changes the meaning of the sentence.

Because the relative clause ("who receives the most votes") indicates a specific candidate and affects the meaning of the sentence, it should not be set off by commas. These two commas should be deleted.

The candidate, who receives the most votes, will win the election.

The Democratic Party supports quotas, which are consistent with the ideal of equality.

This comma significantly changes the meaning of the sentence. With the comma, the sentence means that *all* quotas are consistent with the ideal of equality. Without the comma, the sentence means that the Democratic Party supports *only those quotas* that are consistent with the ideal of equality.

Comma Splices

A comma splice, sometimes called a comma fault, occurs when a comma is incorrectly used to separate two independent clauses. The commas in the following sentences are incorrect:

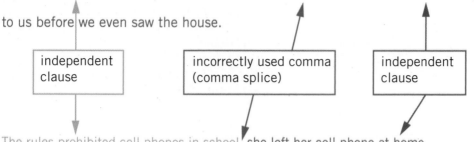

My brother and I raced up the stairs to our rooms, these rooms had been assigned to us before we even saw the house.

| independent clause | incorrectly used comma (comma splice) | independent clause |

The rules prohibited cell phones in school, she left her cell phone at home.

In many cases, there are several ways to correct a comma splice. Often, the simplest way is to replace the comma with a period or semi-colon:

> My brother and I raced up the stairs to our rooms. These rooms had been assigned to us before we even saw the house.

> The rules prohibited cell phones in school; she left her cell phone at home.

Sometimes, rewriting the sentence is a better option:

> My brother and I raced up the stairs to the rooms that had been assigned to us before we even saw the house.

> My brother and I raced up the stairs to our rooms, which had been assigned to us before we even saw the house.

> The rules prohibited cell phones in school, so she left her cell phone at home.

> Because the rules prohibited cell phones in school, she left her cell phone at home.

Incorrect Semi-colon

The semi-colon might well be the most misunderstood and misused punctuation mark. Learning a few basic rules can help you avoid misusing semi-colons and, more important, use them strategically to strengthen your writing.

The semi-colon has three main functions:

- to separate two independent clauses whose subjects are closely linked, as in the following examples:

> With writing, the audience is usually absent; with talking, the listener is usually present.

> Apples in Des Moines supermarkets can be from China, even though there are apple farmers in Iowa; potatoes in Lima's supermarkets are from the United States, even though Peru boasts more varieties of potato than any other country.

Protecting the health of the environment is a prudent investment; it can avert scarcity, perpetuate abundance, and provide a solid basis for social development.

■ to separate elements in a series when those elements include other punctuation marks, as in the following examples:

Present at the meeting were the board president, John Smith; April Jones, treasurer; Molly Harris, secretary; and Josh Jordan, who was filling in for an absent board member.

If you plan to hike in the mountains in winter, you should always carry proper clothing, especially dependable raingear; extra food and water; matches, a lighter, or a portable stove for cooking and for melting snow for water; and a tarp for shelter.

■ to separate two independent clauses that are linked by a conjunctive adverb, such as *however, therefore, moreover, nevertheless*, and *consequently*, as in the following examples:

The students planned to attend the opening night of the play at the campus theater; however, when they arrived for the show, they learned that it was sold out.

Although many colleges do not use standardized test scores when evaluating applicants for admission, most colleges still require applicants to submit SAT or ACT scores; therefore, high school students who wish to attend college should plan to take either the SAT or the ACT or both.

There are other uses for the semi-colon, but if you learn to use the semi-colon in these three main ways, you will avoid the most common mistakes that student writers make with semi-colons.

■ **Semi-colon instead of a colon.** One of the most common mistakes students make is using a semi-colon instead of a colon to introduce a sentence element, such as a series:

> The semi-colon should *never* be used to introduce a series. The correct punctuation mark here is a colon.

The mud was horrendous, and it got onto everything; our clothes, our

skin, our hair.

He argued that the U.S. is too dependent on one kind of energy source; oil.

> In this example, either a colon or a comma would be correct, but a semi-colon is incorrect.

- **Missing semi-colon.** Another very common error occurs when the writer neglects to use a semi-colon with a conjunctive adverb (e.g., *however, therefore, nevertheless, consequently*). When two independent clauses are joined by a conjunctive adverb, a semi-colon must precede the conjunctive adverb, which is followed by a comma. In such cases, a comma preceding the conjunctive adverb is incorrect:

The internal resistance of the battery was found to be lower than it was in

the other circuit, however, it still resulted in a significant difference in voltage.

| This comma is incorrect. A semi-colon must be used here. | The conjunctive adverb (*however*) should be followed by a comma. |

Incorrect Use of Apostrophe

Apostrophes can be confusing because they are used in several very different ways. The two main functions of apostrophes are

- to indicate possession
- to indicate omitted letters, especially in contractions

If you understand these functions, you will be able to avoid the most common mistakes student writers make in using apostrophes.

- **Missing or incorrect apostrophe to indicate possession.** An apostrophe followed by the letter *s* indicates possession or ownership for most **singular nouns**:

John's car

the student's book

the government's role

Thomas Jefferson's signature

the musician's instrument

the tree's shadow

The most common violation of this rule occurs when a writer neglects to use an apostrophe where it is necessary to show possession:

She remembered to bring her husbands jacket when she left the house.

> In this example, *husbands* is possessive and should have an apostrophe before the *s*: *husband's*.

In most cases, this rule also applies if the singular form of the noun ends in *s*:

New Orleans's mayor

the dress's hem

progress's risks

the witness's memory

Note that **possessive pronouns** (mine, yours, hers, his, theirs, ours, its) *do not* have an apostrophe:

If you don't have a bicycle, you can use **mine**.

The horse had a scar on **its** left foreleg.

To form **the possessive of a plural noun that already ends in *s***, use an apostrophe at the end of the word *without* an additional *s*:

the birds' nests

the ships' destinations

the cowboys' horses

However, if the plural form of a noun does not end in *s*, use an apostrophe followed by an *s* to indicate possession:

the children's scarves

women's rights

the sheep's pen

Note that in these examples, the nouns are already in their plural forms, and the apostrophe does not make the nouns plural; rather, the apostrophe designates possession.

- **Missing apostrophe in a contraction.** An apostrophe is required in a contraction, such as *isn't, can't, doesn't,* or *won't.* In contractions, the apostrophe stands for a missing letter or letters: *isn't* for *is not; can't* for *cannot; doesn't* for *does not; won't* for *will not.*

He couldnt see what was right in front of him.

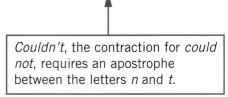

Couldn't, the contraction for *could not*, requires an apostrophe between the letters *n* and *t*.

■ **Confusing *its* and *it's*.** *Its* and *it's* are two very different kinds of words: *its* is a possessive pronoun and *it's* is a contraction meaning *it is*. Students often confuse the two and, as a result, misuse them. To avoid this very common error, you need to **remember two rules**:

■ *its* is a possessive pronoun and therefore does not have an apostrophe

■ *it's* is the contraction for *it is* and therefore must always have an apostrophe

Use this simple strategy:

1. Replace *its* or *it's* with *it is* in the sentence.

2. If the sentence makes sense with *it is*, then *it's* is the correct word.

3. If the sentence doesn't make sense with *it is*, then *its* is the correct word.

Here's how it works:

Example 1

Sentence: The dog became extremely aggressive whenever anyone approached **it's** cage.

Strategy: Replace *it's* with *it is*: The dog became extremely aggressive whenever anyone approached **it is** cage.

Result: The sentence does not make sense with *it is*, so *it's* must be replaced with *its*: The dog became extremely aggressive whenever anyone approached **its** cage.

Example 2

Sentence: He is bringing a jacket on because **it's** very cold outside.

Strategy: Replace *it's* with *it is*: He is bringing a jacket on because **it is** very cold outside.

Result: The sentence make sense with *it is*, so *it's* is correct.

Example 3

Sentence: The sailboat was distinctive because of the loud color of **its** sails.

Strategy: Replace *it's* with *it is*: The sailboat was distinctive because of the loud color of **it is** sails.

Result: The sentence does not make sense with *it is*, so *its* is correct.

Incorrect Use of Colons

The colon is a kind of "pointing" mark of punctuation; it calls attention to the words that follow it. A colon is commonly used to introduce a list or series, a quotation, or an appositive.

To introduce a list or series

By the time she was twenty, my grandmother Virginia knew how to play several musical instruments: piano, fiddle, guitar, banjo, and mandolin.

The protest movement was a failure for three reasons: lack of organization, excess ego, and unclear ideas.

To introduce a quotation

Rainer Maria Rilke has unusual advice for young poets: "Love the questions themselves."

Among Thoreau's best-known statements is a line from *Walden*: "The mass of men lead lives of quiet desperation."

With appositives

As my father once told me, there is only one way to do things: the right way.

The gymnast had only one goal: a gold medal.

Notice that when a colon precedes a complete sentence, the first word after the colon *must* be capitalized; however, if the word or phrase following the colon does not make a complete sentence, the first word following the colon is *not* capitalized.

26

Index